KOVELS'
ADVERTISING
COLLECTIBLES
PRICE LIST

RANDOM HOUSE REFERENCE
NEW YORK TORONTO LONDON SYDNEY AUCKLAND

Published in the United States by Random House Reference,
an imprint of the The Random House Information Group, a division of
Random House Inc., New York, and simultaneously in Canada
by Random House of Canada Limited, Toronto.

Random House is a registered trademark of Random House, Inc.

This book is available for special discounts for bulk purchases for
sales promotions or premiums. Special editions, including personal-
ized covers, excerpts of existing books, and corporate imprints, can be
created in large quantities for special needs. For more information,
write to Random House, Inc., Special Markets/Premium Sales,
1745 Broadway, MD 6-2, New York, NY, 10019
or e-mail *specialmarkets@randomhouse.com.*

Visit the Random House Reference Web site: *www.randomwords.com*

Library of Congress Cataloging-in-Publication Data is available.

Printed in the United States of America

ISBN 0-375-72080-4

10   9   8   7   6   5   4   3   2   1

BOOKS BY RALPH AND TERRY KOVEL

American Country Furniture, 1780–1875

A Directory of American Silver, Pewter, and Silver Plate

Kovels' Advertising Collectibles Price List

Kovels' American Antiques, 1750–1900

Kovels' American Art Pottery

Kovels' American Silver Marks, 1650 to the Present

Kovels' Antiques & Collectibles Fix-It Source Book

Kovels' Antiques & Collectibles Price List

Kovels' Bid, Buy, and Sell Online

Kovels' Book of Antique Labels

Kovels' Bottles Price List

Kovels' Collector's Guide to American Art Pottery

Kovels' Collectors' Source Book

Kovels' Depression Glass & Dinnerware Price List

Kovels' Dictionary of Marks—Pottery & Porcelain

Kovels' Guide to Selling, Buying, and Fixing
Your Antiques and Collectibles

Kovels' Illustrated Price Guide to Royal Doulton

Kovels' Know Your Antiques

Kovels' Know Your Collectibles

Kovels' New Dictionary of Marks—Pottery & Porcelain

Kovels' Price Guide for Collector Plates, Figurines,
Paperweights, and Other Limited Editions

Kovels' Quick Tips—799 Helpful Hints
on How to Care for Your Collectibles

Kovels' Yellow Pages: A Resource Guide for Collectors

The Label Made Me Buy It: From Aunt Jemima to Zonkers—
The Best-Dressed Boxes, Bottles, and Cans from the Past

INTRODUCTION

Before the 1950s, collectors concentrated on furniture, glass, ceramics, and other decorative arts. The only advertising antiques found in shops and shows were handmade store signs and cigar store Indians. A few collector-historians searched for early nineteenth-century blown glass whiskey flasks and bitters bottles or for labeled handmade boxes that held Shaker herbs. Twentieth-century advertising was available only in thrift stores and garage sales, or was set aside as unimportant relics at excavation sites.

During the 1950s we joined other serious collectors and started hunting for old advertising. We were finding Ivory soap packing crates and Diamond Dye cabinets on the curb, ready to be picked up by city trash collectors. Old labels, bottles, boxes, and signs were often stored and forgotten in warehouses or manufacturing plants—our best items were gifts from companies that thought their history unimportant. Our first purchase was the now-famous tin Grape-Nuts sign that pictures a girl and a Great Dane. It cost us $18. In this book it's listed for $3,520.

Colorful lithographed signs and packages made in the 1890s are rare and pricey today. Especially desirable are items that are considered historic "documents": they show houses, home furnishings, ethnic stereotypes, patriotic emblems like the flag or Uncle Sam, Santa Claus, planes, trains, or cars. Today a beginning collector can easily find advertising signs, packages, and figures made since the 1940s at reasonable prices. Sometimes the buyer wants to decorate a kitchen or laundry. Most times the collector has a serious interest in the graphics, the history, or the product. Collectors specialize in such things as enamel-painted soda bottles, animated counter displays, Coca-Cola, one-pound coffee cans, automotive items like gas pump globes, beer, cloth dolls, fast-food giveaways, advertising mirrors, or anything related to oysters. A small group collects enough to create a pseudo country store or drugstore in their homes.

Collecting methods, too, have changed in the twenty-first century. Internet shops and auctions are now important sources of advertising collectibles. About twenty on-land auction houses hold special sales that offer only advertising materials. These auctions are advertised online and through the mail and usually publish catalogs. Research is easier than it used to be. The Internet can be used to find company histories, stories about collectibles, prices, and other sorts of information; just remember that some Internet sources are more trustworthy than others.

THE HISTORY OF ADVERTISING

Advertising has existed for centuries, but methods and wording have changed over the years. In 1729 Benjamin Franklin's newspaper, the *Pennsylvania Gazette*, stopped copying the form of listings found in English newspapers and originated an American look for his newspaper's ads. White space and headlines were added, then illustrations. Franklin persuaded ship owners and storekeepers to write long ads describing their products. "Attack the competition" ads were used as early as 1768, and doctors often advertised with testimonials from patients. At the time of the American Revolution, in 1776, there were thirty-seven newspapers in the colonies and they all carried advertising.

Newspapers flourished in the years after the Revolution, but the style and content of their advertising did not change much until the 1820s. Before then, a shortage of paper forced newspapers to print as many ads as possible in a limited space. But new methods of papermaking developed during the 1820s led to lower paper prices and larger supplies, so newspapers could run many pages of innovative ads—and make a lot more money. During those years, magazines did not accept advertising and newspapers never offered display advertising. It was not until after the Civil War that print advertising as we know it became commonplace. Advertising agencies appeared, and magazines permitted display ads. J. Walter Thompson purchased all the available space in women's magazines and offered to sell sections to advertisers and other ad agencies. Thompson controlled the advertising space in women's magazines until after 1898. Low postal rates, high circulation, and many pages of advertising made magazines successful.

So-called "broken-record" ads were first used about 1870. Advertisers in magazines and newspapers had already discovered that many people did not like to read the same ads in every issue, but that the use of a repetitive slogan was definitely an attention-getter. Ads were written as a long message into which penny-pinching advertisers crowded as much information as possible and presented it in the tiniest of type. The ad's headline was the eye-catching attraction. But during the 1870s and 1880s, advertising went into a transitional period. Many new ads were simple announcements that were repeated as often as possible. By the late 1890s, most ads featured a slogan and a character or cartoon that could be considered a trademark. The first registered trademark in the United States was recorded October 25, 1870, for the Averill Chemical Paint Company (the trademark was an image of an eagle holding a pot of paint in its beak). However, the Federal Trade-Mark Act of 1870 was found unconstitutional in 1879, so it was not until the end of the nineteenth century that trademarks came into general use in the United States. The still-familiar Underwood Devil and the paint-covered earth of Sherwin-Williams date from that era.

Many advertisers were inspired to patriotism by the Spanish-American War in 1898. Flags and battleships appeared in many ads. The slogans of the period were often puns. The brand name Uneeda helped make the slogan, "Do You Know Uneeda Biscuit," a success. Another advertising approach was the "domestic deity," such as the Quaker Oats man or Aunt

Jemima. An Indian chief, a boy in a raincoat, and a top-hatted peanut were also designed to represent products.

Outdoor advertising, popular in England since the seventeenth century, had moved to the colonies, too. Printers produced single-page ads that could be pasted on posts, buildings, and store windows and doors. But true billboards did not come into use until the 1840s, when they were displayed in railroad stations and along railroad tracks. The first transit ad appeared in New York City's horse-drawn streetcars in 1850; it promoted Lord & Taylor, the department store. Posters became popular forms of advertising after the Civil War. The first leased space on a billboard was sold in New York City in the 1870s. The first electric sign appeared on Broadway in 1891. Sets of small signs by the side of the road were pioneered by Burma-Shave in 1925. Mail Pouch tobacco used the painted barn as a huge ad from the turn of the twentieth century until the 1990s. The first national advertising campaign, launched in 1898, was for Uneeda biscuits. The campaign, which eventually cost $1 million, used magazines, newspapers, store signs, and other outdoor ads.

Of course, problems developed. Advertising claims were so outrageous by 1914 that the industries involved started enforcing standards of truth. The government stepped up its involvement, too. The Wheeler-Lee Amendment of 1938 broadened the power of the Federal Trade Commission to police ads. In 1971 the advertising industry created the National Advertising Review Board. Today truth in advertising is enforced, and even minor questionable statements are stopped. Does the vegetable soup look thicker because there are marbles under the vegetables in the bowl pictured on TV? Does the mouthwash really prevent colds?

Advertising has taken many forms. Bookmarks were popular from 1880 to 1915. The first advertising trade cards were adapted from broken-record ads about 1870. They were introduced as giveaways to present more information, slogans, color pictures, and new products. The cards were popular in the days when color pictures were rarities. The colorful trade card was saved, admired, and frequently pasted into a scrapbook or album. Some were amusing and some educational. Some were printed with catchy rhymes or jingles. Trade cards lost favor by about 1910. Baseball and other sports cards are a special form of advertising that has been used since the 1880s. Advertising calendars became popular in the 1860s and the calendar plate about 1906. Stuffed cloth dolls representing products were introduced during the 1890s and are still being made. The tin advertising tray was first used in the 1880s and is still popular. Giveaways and point-of-sale material, such as signs, furniture, pot-scrapers, puzzles, recipe books, ashtrays, fans, bottle openers, dinnerware, kitchen wares, and even clocks with ads were first made in the late 1800s and have remained popular. Book matches became a widespread advertising form after 1892, although today they are not as available as they once were. Stickers were first used on fresh bananas in 1961 to give brand-name status to the fruit. The use of tiny stickers has expanded and many unpackaged fruits and other items are now identified with these small ads. T-shirts became walking billboards during the 1970s.

The package that holds a product is also the focus of an advertising collector's interest. Bottles, cans, labels, lithographed tins, boxes, paper bags, gas pump globes, and other wrappings are saved. Individual oranges were wrapped in special paper during the late nineteenth century, and by the 1880s many fruit crates were identified with printed paper labels. Pails, lunch boxes, and decorative tins were made so the consumer would save and reuse them.

Radio and television had a huge impact on advertising. Words and slogans were changed to appeal to the ear and eye in a new way. Print ads were altered, too, as the public became accustomed to "dancing cigarettes," cartoon characters, and celebrity endorsements. Many product premiums were directly related to radio and TV shows. From the 1930s to the 1960s, adventure shows often offered decoder rings, space guns, or other toys that were part of the program's plot. By the mid-1980s many television ads had an "MTV look" featuring obscure meanings and psychedelic colors.

One special area of collecting is movie memorabilia. This book lists only those items that were actually used as advertisements for movies, not the many memorabilia items related to the movies in other ways. Another special area of interest is fast-food collecting. Anything connected to a fast-food restaurant, from store signs to coffee stirrers and paper napkins, is collected. "One man's trash is another man's treasure" if you collect advertising.

Twenty-first-century collectors save unusual or clever advertising, including funny beer ads and medication ads that don't even explain what the medicine treats. TV commercials can be copied on tape or DVD. You can save posters and cutout pages of magazines that are part of a series like the "Got Milk?" celebrity-with-milk-mustache ads or the Absolut Vodka artist-created ads. And don't pass up the countless magnets, pens, flashlights, Post-its, backpacks, key chains, and shoelaces that advertise a product. If they're not in your collection, they'll be in someone else's.

RECORD PRICES 2001–2004

Colt "Jaguar & Lady" store poster: $18,814 for a Colt store poster, "Jaguar & Lady," with original brass hanger, picturing a woman pointing a revolver at a jaguar roped and tied with line attached to a horse, 21 x 26 in., 1921, produced by W.F. Powers Co. Sold May 26, 2004.

Remington-UMC hanging store poster: $3,517 for a Remington-UMC hanging store poster featuring three hunting dogs, 1920s, 17 x 24³/4 in. Sold May 27, 2004.

Remington-UMC hanging store die-cut poster, Boy with Rifle: $1,877 for the die-cut hanging store poster, "Remington-UMC," picturing a boy with rifle, 12 x 5 in. Sold May 26, 2004.

Trade sign: $113,525 for a double-sided wooden cobbler's trade sign, elephant form, painted in gray, red, yellow, white, and black, elephant wearing boots and carrying a banner in his trunk reading "John M. Dyckman," also wearing a blanket reading "Boots & Shoes," 19th century, 57 x 79 in. Sold October 9, 2002.

Winchester product sign: $3,413 for a framed Winchester indoor multiproduct sign behind glass, lithograph image on canvas, $63^{1}/_4$ x $24^{1}/_4$ in. One of only three known to exist. Sold May 27, 2004.

Gas globe: $20,350 for a Gilmore Red Lion Plus Tetraethyl gas globe picturing a red lion, 15-in. diam., c.1930. Sold June 28, 2003.

Beer can: $19,299 for a steel, flat-top Clipper Pale Beer can, made by Grace Bros. Brewing Co., picturing Boeing's transoceanic "flying boat," the Yankee Clipper, stamped date 6-10-41. Sold November 20, 2002.

Facchino Ice Cream Kids: $6,512 for a figural pair of Facchino Ice Cream Kids, boy and girl, each holding a large ice cream cone. Sold June 16, 2002.

Pub jug: $4,919 for a Barnsley Brewery beer jug made by Royal Doulton in 1906, 6 in. Sold November 11, 2001.

ACKNOWLEDGMENTS

Advertising collectors and dealers are a very special group of people who know each other and compare information and great buys at every opportunity. We have been collectors of advertising since our first year of marriage and are privileged to know many of these experts. They responded to our requests for photographs for this book in a manner well beyond what we could have expected or even hoped. We want to give special thanks to Jeanne and Rich Bertoia (Bertoia Auctions), Ted Hake (Hake's Americana & Collectibles), James Jackson and Scott Schmidt (Jackson's International Auctioneers & Appraisers), Gary Metz (Metz SuperlativesAuction), Dan Morphy and Tom Sage Jr. (Morphy Auctions), Steve and Donna Howard (Past Tyme Pleasures), Randy and Sue Inman (Randy Inman Auctions), Rich Penn (Rich Penn Auction Company), Richard Opfer (Richard Opfer Auctioneering), Mike Eckles (Showtime Auction Services), Andy & Becky Ourant (Village Doll & Toy Auction), and Bill Morford (William Morford Auctions). These auctioneers provided many of the pictures in this book.

To the others who knowingly or unknowingly helped us find prices and information, we say "thank you." Some of them are: Anderson Auction & Realty, Aumann Auctions, Austin T. Miller American Antiques, BBR Auctions, Big Kid Collectables, Bloomington Auction Gallery, Buffalo Bay Auction Company, Collection Liquidations Auction Services & Sales, cooltoys.com, Cowan's Historic Americana Auctions, cyberattic.com, Daniel Auction Company, Davies Auctions, Doyle New York, Early American History Auctions, Franks Antiques & Auctions, Glass-Works Auctions, Henry Peirce Auctioneers, James D. Julia, Joy Luke Auctioneers & Appraisers, Lang's Sporting Collectables, Live Free or Die Antique Tool Auction, Lynn Geyer's Advertising Auction, Manion's International Auction House, Maritime Antiques Auction, McMurray Antiques & Auctions, Mike Murphy's A+ Auctions, Miscellaneous Man, Neal Auction Company, Norman C. Heckler & Company, O.J. Club, Political Bandwagon, R.O. Schmitt Fine Arts, Rex Stark-Americana, Robert C. Eldred Co., Robert Edward Auctions, Robert S. Brunk Auction Services, S & D Classic Toys, Seeck Auctions, Serious Toyz, Smith House Toy & Auction Company, Stanton's Auctioneers & Realtors, Sweeney's Emporium, Theriault's, Woody Auctions, Yankee Peddler Antique Toys, and York Town Auction.

We also thank those at the Random House Information Group who worked through the problems of assembling a price book of this type. To Dottie Harris, our editor who always liked this project, thank you for keeping us all on track. And thank you to David Naggar, president of the Random House Information Group; Sheryl Stebbins, vice president and publisher of Random House Reference; Beth Levy, associate managing editor; Lisa Montebello, production manager; Lindsey Glass, editorial assistant; and the talented staff of the art department: Fabrizio La Rocca, creative director; Tigist Getachew, art director; and Moon Sun Kim, designer.

Merri Ann Morrell at Precision Graphics is the miracle worker who solved problems with the computer program that helped us assemble this new book. She chased data to the proper locations and even found a few of our errors.

But the hardest work was done by our staff. They recorded prices, assembled photographs, traced factory histories, and then checked and rechecked the entries for accuracy. We thank Linda Coulter, who did much of the research on companies; Grace DeFrancisco; Doris Gerbitz; Marcia Goldberg, our amazing copy editor; Katie Karrick; Karen Kneisley, our photo editor; Kim Kovel; Liz Lillis; Heidi Makela; Tina McBean; Nancy Saada; Julie Seaman; June Smith; and Cherrie Smrekar. Once again, Benjamin Margalit took many of the special photographs in this book, and we thank him. But most of all, we thank Gay Hunter, who keeps tabs on all of us and who reads the copy and solves day-to-day problems. We thank them because we know that even though our names are on the book, the work was done by many.

CLUBS & PUBLICATIONS

MAG = magazine, NL = newsletter, NP = newspaper

American Breweriana Journal (MAG)
PO Box 11157
Pueblo, CO 81001-0157
e-mail: breweriana1@earthlink.net
website: www.americanbreweriana.org

Anheuser-Busch Collectors Club
First Draft (MAG)
PO Box 503058
St. Louis, MO 63150-3058
website: www.budshop.com

**Antique Advertising Association of
America**
Past Times (NL)
PO Box 5851
Elgin, IL 60123
website: www.pastimes.org

**Antique Poison Bottle Collectors
Association**
*Antique Poison Bottle Collectors
Association Newsletter* (NL)
312 Summer Ln.
Huddleston, VA 24104
e-mail: joan@poisonbottle.com
website: antique.poisonbottle.com

**Antique Telephone Collectors
Association**
ATCA Newsletter (NL)
PO Box 1252
McPherson, KS 67460
e-mail: office@atcaonline.com
website: www.atcaonline.com

Badger State Matchcover Club
Badger State Matchcover Club (NL)
3201 S. 72nd St.
Milwaukee, WI 53219-3969

Brewery Collectibles Club of America
Beer Cans & Brewery Collectibles
(MAG)
747 Merus Ct.
Fenton, MO 63026-2092
e-mail: bcca@bcca.com
website: www.bcca.com

British Beermat Collectors' Society
*British Beermat Collectors' Society
Newsletter* (NL)
69 Dunnington Ave.
Kidderminster DY10 2YT, UK
e-mail: cosmic@tmmathews.
freeserve.co.uk
website: www.britishbeermats.org.uk

**British Matchbox Label & Booklet
Society**
Match Label News (MAG)
122 High St.
Melbourn, Cambridgeshire SG8 6AL,
UK
e-mail: secretary.bml&bs
@phillumeny.com
website: www.phillumeny.com

**Canadian Corkscrew Collectors
Club**
The Quarterly Worme (NL)
One Madison St.
East Rutherford, NJ 07073
e-mail: ccccdues@aol.com
website: www.corkscrewnet.com/
CCCC.htm

**Cigarette Pack Collectors
Association**
Brandstand (NL)
61 Searle St.
Georgetown, MA 01833
e-mail: cigpack@aol.com
website: hometown.aol.com/cigpack

Citrus Label Society
Citrus Peal (NL)
131 Miramonte Dr.
Fullerton, CA 92835
e-mail: trspellman@prodigy.net
website: www.citruslabelsociety.com

**Coca-Cola Collectors Club
International**
Coca-Cola Collectors News (NL)
4780 Ashford Dunwoody Rd., Suite A,
    PMB 609
Atlanta, GA 30338
website: www.cocacolaclub.org

**Coin Operated Collectors
Association**
C.O.C.A. Times (MAG)
C.O.C.A.
15200 Mansel Ave.
Lawndale, CA 90260
e-mail: djdavids@earthlink.net
website: www.coinopclub.org
(pre-1951 coin-operated slot machines,
trade stimulators, arcade machines,
vending machines, and related
collectibles)

Cracker Jack Collectors Association
Prize Insider (NL)
3225 Edward St. NE
Anthony, MN 55418
e-mail: raegun@comcast.com
website: www.collectoronline.com/
    CJCA

**Crown Collectors Society
International**
Crown Cappers' Exchange (NL)
9449 Ridge Rd. W.
Brockport, NY 14420-9348
e-mail: LID33@aol.com
website: www.bottlecapclub.org
(for collectors of crown caps from beer
and soda bottles)

Dr Pepper 10-2-4 Collectors Club
Lion's Roar (NL)
4040 N. Central Expressway, Suite 600
Dallas, TX 75204
website: www.dublindr
    pepper.com/club.htm

Ephemera Society of America, Inc.
Ephemera News (NL)
PO Box 95
Cazenovia, NY 13035-0095
e-mail: info@ephemerasociety.org
website: www.ephemerasociety.org

**Federation of Historical Bottle
Collectors**
Bottles and Extras (MAG)(NL)
401 Johnston Ct.
Raymore, MO 64083
e-mail: osubuckeyes71@aol.com
website: www.fohbc.com

52 Plus Joker
Clear the Decks (MAG)
670 Carlton Dr.
Elgin, IL 60120-4008
e-mail: illhawkeye@msn.com
website: www.52plusjoker.org
(playing cards)

Figural Bottle Opener Collectors
Opener (NL)
1774 N. 675 E.
Kewanna, IN 46939
e-mail: fbocclub@att.net
website: www.fbocclub.com

Hamm's Club, Inc.
Bruin's Gazette (NL)
2300 Central Ave. NE
Minneapolis, MN 55418
e-mail: hammsclub@hammsclub.com
website: www.hammsclub.com

**International Association of Jim
    Beam Bottle and Specialties Clubs**
Beam Around the World (NL)
PO Box 486
Kewanee, IL 61443
website: www.jimbeamclubs.com

International Match Safe Association
International Match Safe Association
Newsletter (NL)
PO Box 791
Malaga, NJ 08328-0791
e-mail: mrvesta1@aol.com
website: www.matchsafe.org

International Perfume Bottle Association
Perfume Bottle Quarterly (NL)
295 E. Swedesford Rd., PMB 185
Wayne, PA 19087
e-mail: susanarthur@comcast.net
website: www.perfumebottles.org

International Swizzle Stick Collectors Association
Swizzle Stick News (NL)
PO Box 1117
Bellingham, WA 98227-1117
e-mail: veray.issca@shaw.ca
website: www.swizzlesticks-issca.com

International Watch Fob Association Inc.
International Watch Fob Association
Newsletter (NL)
18458 Boston Rd.
Holmen, WI 54636
e-mail: freemansspec@hotmail.com
website: www.watchfob.com

Keychain Tag & Chauffeur's Badge Collectors Newsletter (NL)
c/o Dr. Edward Miles
888 Eighth Ave.
New York, NY 10019
e-mail: emiles33@aol.com

M&M Collectors Club
M&M Collectors Club Newletter (NL)
8325 Broadway, Suite 202, PMB 253
Pearland, TX 77584
website: mnmclub.com

McDonald's Collectors Club
McDonald's Collectors Club
Newsletter (NL)
1153 S. Lee St., PMB 200
Des Plaines, IL 60016-6503
website: mcdclub.com

Mechanical Bank Collectors of America
Banker (NL)
PO Box 13323
Pittsburgh, PA 15243
e-mail: raytoys@aol.com
website: mechanicalbanks.org

National Association Breweriana Advertising
Breweriana Collector (NL)
PO Box 64
Chapel Hill, NC 27514-0064
website: www.nababrew.org

National Association of Avon Collectors
PO Box 7006
Kansas City, MO 64113
(write for list of Avon clubs in your area)

National Association of Milk Bottle Collectors
The Milk Route (NL)
18 Pond Place
Cos Cob, CT 06807
e-mail: gottmilk@msn.com
website: www.collectoronline.com/
club-NAMBC-wp.html

National Association of Paper and Advertising Collectors
P.A.C. (NP)
PO Box 500
Mount Joy, PA 17552
e-mail: pac@engleonline.com
website: www.engleonline.com

National Association of Watch and Clock Collectors
NAWCC Bulletin (MAG)
514 Poplar St.
Columbia, PA 17512-2130
e-mail: patti@nawcc.org
website: www.nawcc.org

National Pop Can Collectors
Can-O-Gram (NL)
1330 Carriage Hills Dr.
Cambridge, MN 55008
e-mail: bruce@one-mans-junk.com
website: www.one-mans-
junk.com/npcc

New England Moxie Congress
Nerve Food News (NL)
445 Wyoming Ave.
Milburn, NJ 07041
e-mail: njmoxie1@worldnet.att.net
website: www.moxieland.com

Novelty Salt & Pepper Shakers Club
*Novelty Salt & Pepper Shakers Club
Newsletter* (NL)
PO Box 416
Gladstone, OR 97027-0416
e-mail: dmac925@yahoo.com
website: www.saltandpepperclub.com

**Old Sleepy Eye Collectors Club of
America, Inc.**
Sleepy Eye Club Newsletter (NL)
P.O. Box 5445
Rockford, IL 61125
e-mail: ose@oldsleepyeye
collectors.org
website: www.oldsleepyeye
collectors.org

**On the LIGHTER Side,
International Lighter Collectors**
OTLS: On the LIGHTER Side (NL)
PO Box 1733
Quitman, TX 75783-1733
website: otls.com

Peanut Pals
Peanut Papers (NL)
32 E. Diaz Ave.
Nesquehoning, PA 18240
e-mail: lyleaug@ptd.net
website: www.peanutpals.org
(Planters Peanuts)

Pepsi-Cola Collectors Club
Pepsi Express (NL)
PO Box 817
Claremont, CA 91711

Postcard History Society
Journal of the Postcard History Society
(NL)
1795 Kleinfeltersville Rd.
Stevens, PA 17578-9669
e-mail: midcreek@ptd.net

Rathkamp Matchcover Society
R.M.S. Bulletin (NL)
1509 S. Dugan Rd.
Urbana, OH 43078-9209
e-mail: trowerms@ctcn.net
website: www.matchcover.org

Society of Inkwell Collectors
Stained Finger (NL)
PO Box 324
Mossville, IL 61552
e-mail: inkwellsociety@aol.com
website: www.soic.com

Society of Tobacco Jar Collectors
Tobacco Jar Newsletter (NL)
1705 Chanticleer Dr.
Cherry Hill, NJ 08003
e-mail: agurst@aol.com
website: www.tobaccojarsociety.com

Still Bank Collectors Club
Penny Bank Post (NL)
4175 Millersville Rd.
Indianapolis, IN 46205
e-mail: egelhoffl@juno.com
website: stillbankclub.com

Telephone Collectors International
Singing Wires (NL)
2859 Central St., PMB 152
Evanston, IL 60203-1234
e-mail: membership@singingwires.org
website: www.singingwires.org

Watkins Collectors Club
Watkins Collectors Club Newsletter
(NL)
1623 Poplar Dr.
Red Wing, MN 55066

**Whisky Pitcher Collectors
Association of America**
Black & White (NL)
8044 Tiger Lily Dr.
Naples, FL 34113- 2636
e-mail: dcdowdall@msn.com
website: pubjug.com
(pub jugs)

OTHER PUBLICATIONS

Always Jukin' (NP)
404 E. Howell St., #100
Seattle, WA 98122
e-mail: AlwaysJuke@aol.com
website: AlwaysJukin.com

*Antique Amusements, Slot Machine &
   Jukebox Gazette* (NP)
909 26th St. NW
Washington, DC 20037
e-mail: durham@GameRoom
   Antiques.com
website: www.GameRoom
   Antiques.com

Antique Bottle & Glass Collector
   (MAG)
PO Box 180
East Greenville, PA 18041
e-mail: glswrk@enter.net
website: www.glswrk-auction.com

Avon Times (NL)
PO Box 9868
Kansas City, MO 64134
e-mail: avontimes@aol.com

Barr's Post Card News (NP)
PO Box 601
Vinton, IA 52349-0601

BBR (MAG)
Elsecar Heritage Center
Nr. Barnsley, South Yorkshire S74
   8HJ, UK
e-mail: sales@onlinebbr.com
website: www.onlinebbr.com
(British Bottle Review)

Card Collectors News (NL)
London Cigarette Card Co. Ltd.
Sutton Rd.
Somerton, Somerset TA11 6QP, UK
e-mail: cards@londoncigcard.co.uk
website: www.londoncigcard.co.uk

Card Times (MAG)
70 Winifred Ln.
Aughton, Ormskirk, Lancashire L39
   5DL, UK
e-mail: david@cardtimes.co.uk
website: www.cardtimes.co.uk
(cigarette cards, trading cards, sports
and nonsports cards, phone cards,
printed ephemera)

Clocks (MAG)
5151 Candlewood St., #1
Lakewood, CA 90712
e-mail: info@wiseowlmagazines.com
website: www.wiseowlmagazines.com

Gameroom Magazine (MAG)
PO Box 1718
Land O Lakes, FL 34639-1718
e-mail: coinop@gameroom
   magazine.com
website: www.gameroom
   magazine.com
(arcade games, carousels, Coca-Cola
collectibles, music boxes, neon, radios,
slots, etc.)

Gloria's Corner (NL)
PO Box 507
Denison, TX 75021-0507
e-mail: gmj@texoma.net
(postcards)

Just For Openers (NL)
PO Box 64
Chapel Hill, NC 27514
e-mail: jfo@mindspring.com
website: www.just-for-openers.org
(bottle openers and corkscrews, with an
emphasis on beer and soda advertising
openers and corkscrews)

Miniature Bottle Collector (MAG)
PO Box 2161
Palos Verdes Peninsula, CA 90274
e-mail: editor@bottlecollecting.com
website: www.bottlecollecting.com

Non-Sport Update (MAG)
4019 Green St.
Harrisburg, PA 17110
website: www.nonsportupdate.com

Paper Collectors' Marketplace (MAG)
PO Box 128
Scandinavia, WI 54977-0128
e-mail: pcmpaper@gglbbs.com
website: www.pcmpaper.com

Picture Postcard Monthly (MAG)
15 Debdale Ln.
Keyworth, Nottinghamshire NG12
  5HT, UK
e-mail: reflections@argonet.co.uk
website: www.postcardcollecting.co.uk

Postcard Collector (MAG)
700 E. State St.
Iola, WI 54990
e-mail: info@krause.com
website: www.krause.com

Zippo Click Magazine (MAG)
33 Barbour St.
Bradford, PA 16701
website: www.zippoclick.com

MUSEUMS

B&O Railroad Museum, 901 W. Pratt St., Baltimore, MD 21201, 410-752-2490, website: www.borail.org.

Colonel Sanders Café and Museum, Highway 25W, Corbin, KY 40701, 606-528-2163.

Curt Teich Postcard Archives, Lake County Museum, 27277 Forest Preserve Dr., Wauconda, IL 60084, e-mail: teicharc@co.lake.il.us, website: www.lcfpd.org/teich_archives.

Dr Pepper Museum, 300 S. 5th St., Waco, TX 76701, 254-757-1024, fax: 254-757-2221, e-mail: dp-info@drpeppermuseum.com, website: www.drpeppermuseum.com.

The George Eastman House International Museum of Photography and Film, 900 East Ave., Rochester, NY 14607, 585-271-3361, website: www.eastmanhouse.org.

Hulman & Co. Clabber Girl Museum, 900 Wabash Ave., Terre Haute, IN 47807, 812-232-9446, website: www.clabbergirl.com/history_museum.htm.

The Huntley & Palmers Collection, Reading Museum, Blagrave St., Reading, Berkshire, RG1 1QH, UK, 44-0-118-939-9800, website: www.readingmuseum.org.uk.

Jell-O Museum, 23 E. Main St., Le Roy, NY 14482, 585-768-7433, website: www.jellomuseum.com.

John Deere Collectors Center, 320 16th St., Moline, IL 61265, 800-240-5265, website: www.deere.com.

John Deere Historic Site, 8393 South Main St., Grand Detour, Dixon, IL 61021-9406, 815-652-4551, website: www.deere.com.

McDonald's #1 Store Museum, 400 N. Lee St., Des Plaines, IL 60016, 847-297-5022, website: www.mcdonalds.com/usa.html.

Museum of American Financial History, 26 Broadway, New York, NY 10004-1763, e-mail: krichards@financialhistory.org, website: www.financialhistory.org.

The Museum of Television & Radio, 25 West 52nd St., New York, NY 10019, 212-621-6600, and 465 North Beverly Dr., Beverly Hills, CA 90210, 310-786-1000, website: www.mtr.org.

National Bottle Museum, 76 Milton Ave., Ballston Spa, NY 12020, 518-885-7589, website: www.NationalBottleMuseum.org.

National Lighter Museum, 5715 South Sooner Rd., Guthrie, OK 73044, 405-282-3025, website: www.natlitrmus.com.

The Schmidt Museum of Coca-Cola Memorabilia, 109 Buffalo Creek Dr., Elizabethtown, KY 42701, 270-234-1100, website: www.schmidtmuseum.com.

Spam Museum, 1937 Spam Blvd., Austin, MN 55912, 800-LUV-SPAM, 800-588-7726, website: www.spam.com.

The World of Coca-Cola, 55 Martin Luther King Jr. Dr., Atlanta, GA 30303-3505, 800-676-COKE, website: www.woccatlanta.com.

BIBLIOGRAPHY

Alberts, Robert C. *The Good Provider: H.J. Heinz and His 57 Varieties* (Houghton Mifflin, Boston, MA, 1973).

Bruce, Scott, and Bill Crawford. *Cerealizing America: The Unsweetened Story of American Breakfast Cereal* (Faber and Faber, Winchester, MA, 1995).

Bull, Donald, and John R. Stanley. *Just for Openers: A Guide to Beer, Soda, & Other Openers* (Schiffer, Atglen, PA, 1999).

Bull, Donald, and John R. Stanley. *Soda Advertising Openers* (Schiffer, Atglen, PA, 2000).

Bull, Donald, Manfred Friedrich, and Robert Gottschalk. *American Breweries* (Privately printed, Bullworks, PO Box 106, Trumbull, CT 06611, 1984).

Chen, Aric. *Campbell Kids: A Souper Century* (Harry N. Abrams, New York, 2004).

Dantzic, Cynthia Maris. *Antique Pocket Mirrors: Pictorial and Advertising Miniatures* (Schiffer, Atglen, PA, 2002).

Darden, Robert. *Secret Recipe: Why KFC is Still Cookin' After 50 Years* (Tapestry Press, Irving, TX, 2002).

Davidson, Joe. *The Art of the Cigar Label* (Wellfleet Press, Edison, NJ, 1989).

Ellis, Harry E. *Dr Pepper: King of Beverages* (Dr Pepper Company, Dallas, TX, 1979).

Friedrich, Manfred, and Donald Bull. *The Register of United States Breweries, 1876–1976*, 2 vols. (Privately printed, Donald Bull, 21 Frelma Dr., Trumbull, CT 06611, 1976).

Hoy, Anne. *Coca-Cola: The First Hundred Years* (The Coca-Cola Company, Atlanta, GA, 1986).

Institute for Brewing Studies. *2003–2004 North American Brewer's Resource Directory* (Brewers Publications, Boulder, Colorado, 2003).

Kovel, Ralph and Terry. *The Label Made Me Buy It: From Aunt Jemima to Zonkers—The Best-Dressed Boxes, Bottles, and Cans from the Past* (Crown, New York, 1998).

Lewis, Russell E. *Zippo Lighters: An Identification and Price Guide* (Krause, Iola, WI, 2004).

Losonsky, Terry and Joyce. *McDonald's Happy Meal Toys Around the World* (Schiffer, Atglen, PA, 1995).

Love, John F. *McDonald's: Behind the Arches* (Bantam Books, New York, 1986).

Marcot, Roy. *Remington: America's Oldest Gunmaker* (Primedia, Remington Arms Company, 1999).

Petretti, Allan. *Petretti's Soda Pop Collectibles Price Guide: The Encyclopedia of Soda Pop Collectibles,* 3rd ed. (Krause, Iola, WI, 2003).

Poore, David. *Zippo: The Great American Lighter* (Schiffer, Atglen, PA, 1997).

Rickards, Maurice. *Encyclopedia of Ephemera* (Routledge, New York, 2000).

Robinson, Joleen A., and Kay F. Sellers. *Advertising Dolls* (Collector Books, Paducah, KY, 1980).

Sim, Jack. *An Illustrated Guide to Gas Pumps: Identification and Price Guide* (Krause, Iola, WI, 2002).

Stoddard, Bob. *The Encyclopedia of Pepsi-Cola Collectibles* (Krause, Iola, WI, 2002).

Summers, B.J. *Antique & Contemporary Advertising Memorabilia: Identification and Value Guide* (Collector Books, Paducah, KY, 2002).

Summers, B.J. *B.J. Summers' Guide to Coca-Cola,* 4th ed. (Collector Books, Paducah, KY, 2003).

Summers, B.J. *Collectible Soda Pop Memorabilia Identification and Value Guide* (Collector Books, Paducah, KY, 2004).

Veilleux, Joseph A. *Moxie Since 1884 ... An Acquired Taste* (Authorhouse, Bloomington, IN, 2003).

Yates, Donald and Elizabeth. *Ginger Beer & Root Beer Heritage, 1790 to 1930* (Privately printed, 8300 Rivers Corners Rd., Homerville, OH 44235, 2003).

A&P Tea and spice merchants George Huntington Hartford and George Gilman founded the Great American Tea Company in 1859. Their first store opened in New York City in 1861. When the first transcontinental railroad was completed in 1869, the company was renamed The Great Atlantic & Pacific Tea Company. In 1919 the company's bulk coffee was trademarked "Eight O'Clock Coffee." A&P, the first chain of general food stores in America, is now headquartered in Montvale, New Jersey, and operates hundreds of supermarkets with various names throughout the United States and Canada.

Bank, Glass, Vial, Dimes, 100th Anniversary, 1959, 3 3/4 In.	20.00
Bin, Slant Lid, Red, White, Black, Wood, 1910-1920, 30 x 19 x 18 In.	248.00
Can, Bokar Coffee, 1 Lb., 5 3/4 x 4 1/4 In.	10.00
Needle Book, 6 Needle Packets, Threader, Western Germany, 5 3/4 x 4 In.	11.00
Pail, Sultana Peanut Butter, Tin Lithograph, Atlantic & Pacific Tea Co., 1 Lb., 4 x 4 In.	83.00
Sign, Cup Of Tea Nectar Is Refreshing, Woman, Cup, New Frame, 1888, 13 x 15 In.	89.00
Sign, Woman Riding Elephant, Die Cut Cardboard, 1884, 10 1/2 In.	60.00
Tin, Bokar Coffee, 3 3/4 x 2 x 1 1/2 In.	10.00
Tin, Ginger, 2 Oz.	12.00
Tin, Spanish Peanuts, Key Wind Lid, 7 Oz., 3 x 3 1/2 In.	24.00

A&W Roy Allen started selling root beer in Lodi, California, in 1919. The nickel-a-mug drink was made from roots, herbs, barks, and berries. Soon he opened another concession stand in Sacramento, California, which may have been the country's first drive-in. Allen was joined by Frank Wright in 1922. They combined their initials to form the name A&W, first used in Houston, Texas, later that year. Between 1950 and 1970, the company was sold or acquired four times, becoming part of a new corporation, United Brands, in 1970. The following year, United Brands formed two subsidiaries, A&W Beverages, Inc., to make canned and bottled drinks for grocery stores, and A&W Restaurants, Inc. In 1983 A&W Beverages, Inc., which owns the trademark, was purchased by an investment group and became A&W Brands, Inc. In 1993 A&W Brands became part of Cadbury Beverages, Inc. Cadbury-Schweppes acquired Dr Pepper/Seven-Up Companies Inc. in 1995 and A&W became part of that division. Since 1982, the restaurant chain has changed hands a few times. In 2002 Tricon Global Restaurants, now named Yum! Brands, acquired the A&W chain. Sugar Free A&W, introduced in 1974, was reformulated as Diet A&W in 1987. Regular and Diet A&W Cream Soda was introduced in 1986. The Great Root Bear has been the brand's mascot since 1974.

Clock, A&W Root Beer, Bubble, Light-Up, 1940-1950	1210.00
Sign, A&W Root Beer, Ice Cold, Round, 1940s-1950s, 36 In.	495.00
Sign, Root Beer Mug, Orange Band, White Ground, Embossed, Metal, 47 In.	77.00
Tumbler, Bear, Outstretched Arms Around, 5 3/4 In.	6.00

ALKA-SELTZER Dr. Franklin L. Miles set up a medical practice in Elkhart, Indiana, in 1875. He found that the best treatment for many chronic illnesses was calming the nerves. He began bottling Dr. Miles' Restorative Nervine in 1882. By 1884 he had formed Miles Medical Company to sell his home remedies. Miles made many well-known products, including Dr. Miles' Restorative Nervine (1882–1979); Dr. Miles' Restorative Nerve and Liver Pills, later known as Little Pills (1884–1949); Dr. Miles' Restorative Blood Purifier, later called Alterative Compound (1885–1937); and Dr. Miles' Pain Pills, also called Anti-Pain Pills (1893–1973). Miles published and gave away almanacs, calendars, and Little Books (1902–1942) to help advertise its products. Alka-Seltzer was first marketed in October 1931. It was advertised in Little Books, motion pictures, newspaper ads, and drugstore displays. The radio show *Saturday Night Barn Dance* was sponsored by Alka-Seltzer from 1933 to 1946. *The Quiz Kids,* which debuted in 1949, was the first Alka-Seltzer TV show. Speedy Alka-Seltzer was a cartoon character who appeared in commercials from

Alka-Seltzer, Sign, Be Wise, Alkalize, Reverse Glass,
Metallic Letters, Frame, 9 1/8 x 21 In.

Fray Check, a product found in sewing supply stores, is useful for repairing tears in cardboard signs.

1954 to 1964. The company name became Miles Laboratories, Inc., in 1935. In 1969 Alka-Seltzer Plus Cold Medicine was introduced. About 1978 the company was acquired by Germany's Bayer AG. In 1992 all of Bayer's U.S. holdings were merged under the name Miles, Inc., and in 1995 Miles, Inc., became Bayer Corp. Today a line of Alka-Seltzer products is available, including Alka-Seltzer Heartburn Relief, Alka-Seltzer Gold, and Alka-Mints. Bayer Corp. is headquartered in Pittsburgh, Pennsylvania.

Bottle, Dr. Miles' Blood Purifier, Embossed, Contents, Booklet, Box, $1.00, 8 1/4 In.	187.00
Bottle, Dr. Miles' Little Pills, Unopened	15.00
Bottle, Dr. Miles' Medical Co., Contents, Label, Box, Aqua, ABM, 8 1/4 In.	187.00
Caluclator, Dr. Miles' Pain Pills For Headache, Postal, Celluloid, c.1930, 2 1/2 In.	43.00
Compact, Dr. Miles' Anti-Pain Pills, Tin Slider, Mirror, 2 1/4-In. Diam.	303.00
Dispenser, Be Wise Alkalize, Dr. Miles Laboratories, Tin, 14 1/2 In.	385.00
Dispenser, Dr. Miles' Anti-Pain Pills, Blue, Red, White, Tin, Hanger, 17 x 3 In.	303.00
Dispenser, Speedy, Metal, 16 1/2 x 4 1/2 In.	138.00
Dispenser, Tin Lithograph, Countertop, 14 In.	264.00
Dispenser, Tumbler, Chrome Base, Tin Lithograph, Countertop, 14 5/8 x 5 In.	440.00
Sign, Be Wise, Alkalize, Reverse Glass, Metallic Letters, Frame, 9 1/8 x 21 In. . . . . . *Illus*	275.00
Sign, Dr. Miles', Dolly Quincy, 3 Costumes, Die Cut, Easel Back, c.1902, 22 x 9 In.	176.00
Sign, I Talk For Dr. Miles' Anti-Pain Pills, Girl, Pink Dress, Cardboard, Easel, 16 x 7 In. .	330.00
Sign, I Talk For Dr. Miles' Laxative Tablets, Girl, Sailor Dress, Cardboard, Easel, 16 x 7 In.	1540.00
Sign, Speedy Holds Glass, Die Cut Cardboard, Easel Back, 21 3/4 x 39 3/4 In.	132.00

ANHEUSER-BUSCH In 1860 Eberhard Anheuser bought a failing brewery in St. Louis, Missouri. His son-in-law, Adolphus Busch, became a salesman for the company and eventually its president. He was one of the first to make pasteurized beer and to refrigerate the beer when it was shipped. Pasteurized beer was packed in bottles in 1873. The company's advertising often pictured attractive women, but the most famous ad, introduced in 1896, reproduced *Custer's Last Stand,* a painting by F. Otto Becker. This bloody battle scene was copied on cardboard, paper, and tin, and over nine million copies were given to bars and patrons. The Anheuser-Busch symbol, the A & Eagle, was first used on products in 1872. The symbol was trademarked in 1877 and redesigned in 1939. The logo picturing an eight-horse Clydesdale hitch was first used in 1933, the year Prohibition ended. The company sold many different products and brands, including Malt-Nutrine (1895), Michelob (1896), Busch (1955), ginger ale (1921), and Bud Light (1982). Its famous Budweiser brand was introduced in 1876. The Budweiser trademark was registered in 1878 by Carl Conrad, but the beer was brewed by Anheuser-Busch, which gained rights to the name in 1891. The Budweiser brand name was also used by the Budweiser Brewing Company of Brooklyn, New York (c.1885–1898) and the DuBois Brewing Company of Dubois, Pennsylvania (1905–1970). A federal court order in 1970 prohibited DuBois from continuing to use the brand name. Among the many Anheuser-Busch promotional items made over the years was an unusual pocketknife marked Budweiser. It has a peephole at one end, and a picture of Adolphus Busch at the other. At least forty-seven different versions of the knife were made before 1910. In 1950 Budweiser became the first beer to sponsor a television show, the *Ken Murray Variety Show*. The trademarked Budweiser label is often seen on towels, place mats, and even decorative pictures. Advertising slogans include "Old Time Flavor" (1935), "Where There's Life, There's Bud" (1957), "Pick a Pair" (1957), "This Calls for Budweiser" (1962), and "It's Worth It... It's Budweiser" (1965). Bud Light was introduced in 1982. Over the years, snack foods, yeast, and refrigerated products have been among Anheuser-Busch offerings. Today the company focuses on beer and theme parks.

Advertisement, Budweiser, 2 Couples Sailing, Bottle, Can, Glass, 1949, 11 x 14 In. 12.00
Advertisement, Budweiser, Man, Cards, Know What's The Difference, 1964, 10 x 13 In. . 13.00
Ashtray, Budweiser, Bucket, Clip, Metal, Cheinco, 4 1/4 In. 18.00
Bar Light, Michelob Light Beer, Clamp, 5 x 4 In. 18.00
Bell, Brass, A & Eagle, Wood Mounted, Liakos Nameplate, 1979, 9 In. 72.00
Bic Lighter Holder, Budweiser, Mini Beer Can, Foam Insulation, 3 x 1 3/4 In. 5.00
Calendar, 1892, Budweiser, Knapp Co., New York, Paper Lithograph, Frame, 15 x 18 In. . 1650.00
Can, Natural Light, Pull Tab, 12 Oz. 10.00
Cigar Box Nail Tag, Adolphus Busch, Oval 75.00
Clock, Mantel, Bulova, Wood, Battery Operated, 14 1/2 x 11 1/2 x 6 In. 143.00
Clock, Rotating, 20 In. 44.00
Clock, Wall, Round, Battery Operated, Wisconsin Clock, Box, 16 In. 72.00
Display, Busch Bavarian Beer, Plastic, Light-Up, 12 x 6 1/2 x 5 In. 38.00
Etching, 100th Anniversary, Limited Edition, Simulated Marble, Frame, 24 x 29 In. 275.00
Figure, Bud Man, Instructions, Lakeside Industries, Minneapolis, 18 In. 110.00
Figure, Bud Man, Molded Rubber, Plastic Cape, Paperwork, 18 In. 116.00
Figure, Budweiser, Spuds MacKenzie, Bud Light, Plastic, Hollow, 15 x 16 In. 75.00
Figure, Budweiser, Spuds MacKenzie, Light-Up, Plastic, 15 x 10 x 18 In. 275.00
Golf Bag, Budweiser, Olympics, Official Sponsor, Leather, Los Angeles, Box, 1972 . .55.00 to 72.00
Ice Bucket, Oak, 10 x 10 In. 44.00
Lamp, Budweiser, Hand Holding Beer Can, Gooseneck, Box, 1990, 14 1/2 In. 32.00
Match Safe, Eagle, 2-Sided, Silver Plate, 3 x 1 1/2 In. 303.00
Mirror, Buschtee, Horse Jumps Fence, Celluloid, Pocket, 1920s, 2 3/4 x 1 1/4 In. 227.00
Mirror, Clydesdales, 50th Anniversary, Reverse On Glass, Frame, 20 x 27 In. 171.00
Mug, Budweiser, Grant's Farm, Champion Clydesdales, Ceramarte, Brazil, 1976 .... 675.00
Mug, Budweiser, Holiday, Champion Clydesdales, St. Louis, Mo., 1980 .... 155.00
Mug, Dimensions Of Excellence, Stoneware, Wick-Werke, 1/2 Liter, 5 In. ....39.00 to 50.00
Paperweight, Clydesdale, Caithness, Sulphide, Numbered, Box 171.00
Paperweight, Eagle, Caithness, Sulphide, Numbered, Box 171.00
Picture, Budweiser, Clydesdale, Oak Frame, 12 x 27 3/4 In. 250.00
Pitcher, Pewter, Applied A & Eagle, Reed & Barton, 7 1/2 In. 110.00
Plaque, Trumpeter On Horse, Bronze, Round, Henry Bonnard, N.Y., 1892, 12 In. 352.00
Plate, Malt Nutrine, Risque Victorian Woman, Tin Lithograph, Vienna Art, 10 In. 239.00
Plate, Malt Nutrine, Tin Lithograph, Gilt Gesso Frame, 9 1/2 In. 147.00
Print, Budweiser Girl, Red Dress, Lithograph, Signed, Frame, 23 x 39 In. ....1650.00 to 1815.00
Print, Budweiser, Clydesdale Wagon, Paper Lithograph, Frame, 10 x 25 In. 170.00
Print, Custer's Last Fight, Lithograph, Gilt Frame, 1896, 38 x 48 1/2 In. 1035.00
Print, Levee Scene, Robert E. Lee Boat, 17 1/2 x 41 In. 202.00
Print, Train In Early West, 19 x 41 In. 202.00
Saltshaker, Bud Man, Ceramarte, 3 1/2 In. 83.00
Sign, 2 Bismarcks, Augustus Busch, c.1918, 19 1/4 x 14 1/4 In. 633.00
Sign, Bud Light Beer, Welcome To The Kemper Open, 112 x 36 In. 39.00
Sign, Bud Light, White Letters, Blue Ground, Light-Up, Star Wars, 1986, 66 In. 94.00
Sign, Budweiser Girl, Holding Beer Bottle, Tin, Self-Framed, 37 1/2 x 25 1/2 In. 3300.00
Sign, Budweiser Girl, Victorian Lady, Red Dress, Frame, 24 x 38 In. 1430.00
Sign, Budweiser On Tap, Embossed, Celluloid, Frame, 20 x 32 In. 11550.00
Sign, Budweiser Rocks, Hanging, Neon, Light-Up 110.00
Sign, Budweiser, 25 Cents 12 Oz. Bottle, Preferred Everywhere, Tin Over Cardboard 105.00
Sign, Budweiser, 3 Girls Water Skiing, Glass, Light-Up, Plastic Frame, 14 x 20 In. 118.00
Sign, Budweiser, Attack On The Overland Stage, Cardboard, Self-Framed, 1952, 28 x 42 In. 23.00
Sign, Budweiser, Barley Malt Syrup, Hop Flavored, Cardboard, Hanger, 6 1/2 x 12 In. ... 127.00
Sign, Budweiser, Bottle, Foil & Wire Top, Tin, c.1910, 41 1/2 x 14 In. 825.00
Sign, Budweiser, Clydesdales & Wagon, Cardboard, Die Cut, Frame, 17 1/2 x 45 In. 303.00

Sign, Budweiser, Custer's Last Stand, Cardboard, Self-Framed, 1940s, 41 x 28 In. 143.00
Sign, Budweiser, King Of Beers, Bottle, Glass, Tin, Cardboard, Self-Framed, 15 x 18 In. . 94.00
Sign, Budweiser, King Of Beers, Light-Up, 24 x 14 In. 39.00
Sign, Budweiser, King Of Beers, Neon, Modern, 29 x 14 In. 165.00
Sign, Budweiser, King Of Bottled Beer, Tin, Embossed, Wood Frame, 20 x 72 In. 575.00
Sign, Budweiser, Lady, Pink Dress, Bottle, Tin Lithograph, Self-Framed, 22 x 28 In. 3850.00
Sign, Budweiser, Overland Stage, Cardboard, Self-Framed, 30 x 20 In. 88.00
Sign, Budweiser, Revolving Clydesdale Team, Light-Up, Hanging, 24 In. Diameter 523.00
Sign, Budweiser, Son, Father Carves Duck Decoy, Metal, Light-Up, 1950s, 12 x 9 In. 55.00
Sign, Dr. Stork, 1915, 7 5/8 x 12 5/8 In. 150.00
Sign, Drink Busch Pale Dry Ginger Ale, Cardboard, 6 x 11 In. 149.00
Sign, Extra Dry Ginger Ale, Cardboard, Frame, Prohibition Period, 18 x 43 In. 176.00
Sign, Ginger Ale, Logo In Center, Tin, 4 1/2 x 6 In. 83.00
Sign, Michelob Beer, A & Eagle, Plastic, 18 x 11 1/2 In. 17.00
Sign, Michelob Light, Neon, 25 x 25 In. 132.00
Sign, Victory For Liberty, Cardboard, U.S. Presidents, 1942, 13 1/2 x 24 1/2 In. 193.00
Slot Machine, 5 Cents, Budweiser, Michelob Labels, Mills Sahara Tahoe, 1960s 968.00
Stein, Budweiser, Budman, Figural, Ceramarte, 1989, 8 x 4 1/4 In. 55.00
Stein, Budweiser, Girls, Historical Reflections, Box, 1997 .... 130.00
Stein, Budweiser, Holiday, Clydesdales, 50th Anniversary, 1983 .... 65.00
Stein, Budweiser, Old World Heritage, Collectors Club, No. 33907, Box, 1998 .... 100.00
Stein, Thewalt, No. 1256, Engraved A Lid, Paperwork, Western Germany, 6 In. 254.00
Telephone, Budweiser, Beer Can, 6 1/4 In. 28.00
Toy, Budweiser, Horse Drawn Delivery Van, White, 2 Brown Horses, Yellow Letters, Box 16.00
Tray, Bevo, All Year Round Soft Drink, Horse Drawn Wagon, 6 3/4 x 4 1/2 In. 132.00
Tray, Brewery Complex, Tin Lithograph, Oval, 15 5/8 x 18 5/8 In. 853.00
Tray, Budweiser, Bottle, Glass, Red Rim, 1960s, 13 In. 50.00
Tray, Budweiser, Pub Scene, Fox Hunters Enjoying Brew, 10 1/2 x 13 1/4 In. 61.00
Tray, Cherubs, Holding Bottles, Woman, Tin Lithograph, 13 5/8 x 16 5/8 In. 1320.00
Tray, Factory Scene, Tin Lithograph, Oval, 18 3/4 x 15 1/2 In. 385.00
Tray, Malt Nutrine, Woman With Flowing Hair, Round, 1905, 10 In. 110.00
Wagon, Ceramic, Metlox Poppytrail, Box, 12 x 9 In. 121.00

ARBUCKLE McDonald and Arbuckle Wholesale Grocers was founded in Pittsburgh, Pennsylvania, in 1859 by Charles Arbuckle and Duncan McDonald. John Arbuckle, Charles's brother, joined the firm in 1863. After McDonald's retirement, the firm became Arbuckle & Company. By 1865 Arbuckle's coffee was sold roasted, polished, and packaged. It was so successful that the company opened headquarters in New York City. The major brands sold by Arbuckle were Ariosa (introduced in 1873) and Yuban (introduced in 1905). Handbills, premiums, and trade cards were offered to the public. The company may be best known for its slogan, "You get what you pay for." After John Arbuckle's death in 1912, Arbuckle & Company was managed by the two Arbuckle sisters. The company remained in business until 1945. The Yuban brand was sold to General Foods in 1944 and is marketed today by Kraft Foods. Arbuckle's Ariosa coffee has been resurrected and is now available over the Internet.

ARBUCKLE BROS.
NEW YORK CITY.

Bag, Arbuckles' Cane Sugar, 100 Lbs. Net Weight, Cloth, 18 x 33 In. 20.00
Box, Wood, Shipping, Stenciled, Impressed, 36 x 12 x 12 In. 110.00
Sign, Pure, Wholesome Coffee, Tin Lithograph, Embossed, 19 1/2 x 5 1/2 In. .....219.00 to 385.00
Thermometer, Arbuckles' Coffee, Summer, Winter, Tin Lithograph Over Wood, 19 x 4 In. 198.00
Tin, Anona Coffee, Arbuckle Brothers, Contents, 1 Lb., 6 x 4 x 2 3/4 In. 55.00
Tin, Arbuckles' Tea, Russian Blend, Landscape Scene, 1/4 Lb., 4 x 2 1/2 x 2 1/2 In. 253.00
Tray, Enjoy Our Finest Coffee & Teas, 3 Women In Bonnets, Oval, 13 3/4 x 16 1/2 In. ... 1540.00

ARM & HAMMER Vulcan, the Roman god of war, made weapons for other ancient gods and heroes. In the early 1860s, James Austin Church chose the arm of Vulcan striking an anvil with a hammer as the trademark for his spice and mustard company, Vulcan Spice Mills. In 1867 Church joined his father, Dr. Austin Church, at Church & Company, a baking soda manufacturer founded in 1846 in Rochester, New York. Church & Company packaged baking soda under several labels, but the Arm & Hammer brand became the company's best-seller—so the other brands were discontinued. Meanwhile, Austin Church's brother-in-law, John Dwight, had founded a company that sold a competing brand of baking soda called Cow Brand. The two companies merged in 1896 and became Church & Dwight Company. For many years, Church & Dwight sold both Arm & Hammer and Cow Brand products, identical products with different names. Today the company's products also include toothpaste, cat litter, and laundry detergent.

Box, Bicarbonate Of Soda, Free Sample, 2 3/8 x 1 3/4 x 1 In. 95.00
Box, Refined Crystals, Washing Soda, Contents, Cardboard, 3 1/2 x 2 1/2 In. 85.00
Poster, Baking Soda, Birds, Nature's Protectors, 1940s, 20 x 41 In. 66.00
Poster, Woodcocks, c.1910, 25 x 16 5/8 In. 348.00
Print, Hunting Scene, Wal-Ef I Ain't Put Them Shot In First, Frame, 22 x 31 In. 220.00
Sign, Birds, Paper, 16 x 22 In. 132.00

ARMOUR   Philip Danforth Armour and John Plankinton were running a provision business in Milwaukee, Wisconsin, by the mid-1800s. They established a meat-processing plant in Chicago in 1863, and in 1867 they started using the name Armour & Company. Armour processed pork, then lamb. In 1872 the company moved again to a new plant at the Union Stock Yards. Meat was salt-cured until 1872, when refrigeration was introduced, and Armour Star ham and bacon marked with an oval label was first sold in 1877. Armour started to can meat in 1879. The Veribest trademark for canned food was first used at the turn of the twentieth century. Pork and beans date from 1897, sliced bacon in jars from 1902, and condensed milk from 1912. The line eventually included soups, peanut butter, fruits, vegetables, jellies, and soda fountain supplies. The brands all used oval labels. In 1931 the company's packaging was redesigned and the trademarks Armour and Armour's Star were on every label. Packages were again redesigned in 1943 and in 1960. The trademark was modified into a star and rectangle in 1963. Armour began making Armour Family Soap, a laundry bar, in 1888. In 1901 it began making toilet soaps; early brands were Fine Art, Stork, and Flotilla. Dial soap was introduced in 1948. Greyhound Corp. acquired Armour & Company in 1970, but sold the meat-packing operations to ConAgra, Inc., of Omaha, Nebraska, in 1983. But Greyhound Corp., renamed Dial Corp. in 1991, still produces and markets canned Armour Star products, as well as Dial soaps, Purex laundry detergents, and other household products. ConAgra, however, makes Armour Star refrigerated and frozen meats. So today two different companies make Armour products: ConAgra (refrigerated/frozen) and Dial Corp. (canned).

Fan, Pork & Beans, 19 Characters, Paper, Fold-Out, 12 In. 44.00
Pail, Armour's Veribest Peanut Butter, Armour & Co., Chicago, 3 3/4 x 3 3/8 In. 390.00
Pail, Peanut Butter, Nursery Rhyme Characters, Tin Lithograph, 1 Lb., 3 7/8 x 3 5/8 In. .. 260.00
Sign, Armour's Star Cooked Ham, Easter Bunny, Die Cut, Cardboard, Easel Back, 1940s . 50.00
Sign, Armour's Star Ham For Easter, Rabbit, Ham, Die Cut, Stand-Up, c.1920, 25 x 58 In. 600.00
Sign, Cloverbloom Butter, Girl Eating Bread, Cow, Die Cut, Easel Back, 39 x 28 In. 288.00

ASHTRAY   The ashtray became a necessity in the nineteenth century when cigarette smoking became a widespread habit. In 1857 an English dictionary referred to an "ash-pan." By 1887 the word had become "ash-tray." Some ashtrays have special indentations on the rim for use as cigarette rests, but many are plain dishlike pieces. Many were specially made for restaurants, hotels, and bars. These often have the name of the establishment or other advertising as part of the design.

Abdulla Cigarettes, 2 Egyptian Soldiers, 4 3/4 x 4 In. 24.00
Aladdin Alacite, 1930-1940, 3 1/2 In. 115.00
Alligators, Chrome, Cigarette In Mouth, Round, Pincherette, 4 1/2 x 1 1/2 In. 29.00
Black & White Scotch Whiskey, 2 Scottie Dogs, Square, Arklow, England, 5 1/2 In. .28.00 to 55.00
Bridgestone Tyre, Japan, 6 3/4 In. 51.00
Cleveland Memorial, Amethyst, Carnival Glass 7000.00

Comella Cacao-Drink, Grinning Cannibal, Red, White, Black, Bakelite, 5 1/2 In. 771.00
Corning Glass Works, Smoky Glass, 1960-1970, 6 3/4 x 4 3/4 In. 22.00
Crown Of Crowns, German Wines, Porcelain 51.00
Dinah's Shack, Palo Alto, California, Black, Gold Accents, Japan, 5 1/4 In. 89.00
Diplomats Resorts & Country Clubs, Hollywood By The Sea, Royal China, 5 3/8 In. . . . 15.00
Doral Hotels, Miami Beach, Harkerware, East Liverpool, Ohio, 5 1/2 In. 15.00
Ellis's, Ruthin Waters, Goat, Oval, 4 1/2 In. 121.00
Fireman, Metal, Advance Products, 7 x 4 1/2 In. . . . . *Illus* 85.00
Fisher's, Ye Monks Whisky, Round, 5 1/2 In. 20.00
Flowers Keg, Shakespeare Bust, Cartlonware, 3 1/4 x 9 In. . . . . .41.00 to 51.00
Gallagher & Burton Whiskey, Tin Lithograph, Round, 4 1/2 In. 33.00
Gonzalez Bypass Tio Pepe Dry Sherry, Spanish Bullring, Ironstone, 1950s 69.00
Greenberg Hydrants, Figural, Hydrant, Cast Iron, Plated, 4 x 4 In. 66.00
Greenfield Recorder, Glass, August 1, 1968, 8 3/4 x 6 3/4 In. 12.00
Greers O.V.H. Scotch Whisky, Round, 4 1/4 In. 24.00
Harolds Club Casino, Play Longer, Win More, Black Amethyst Glass, Gold Letter, 4 In. . . 12.00
Holiday Inn, Dixie Highway, Coral Gables, 6 In. 16.00
Holiday Inn Motel, World's Innkeeper, Octagonal, Glass, 4 3/4 In. 10.00
Jim Brown, Aluminum, 75th Birthday, 50th Anniversary, 1939 . . . . 25.00
Jimmy Wilson Jr. Van Lines, Storage Warehouses, Glass, 4 1/4 x 3 x 7/8 In. 18.00
Johnnie Walker, Born 1820, Still Going Strong, Square, 4 In. 41.00
Key City Diner, Phillipsburg, New Jersey, 4 1/4 In. 29.00
Kinkers Pharmacy, Your Headache Is Our Business, Glass, 5 1/2 In. 6.00
Lang Bros Ltd., Distillers, Dumgoyne & Glasgow, Round, 5 1/2 In. 55.00
Macbeth-Evans, Green, Square, 3 1/4 In. 50.00
Marston Thompson & Evershed, 4 Compartments, Cut Corner Square, England, 4 3/4 In. 19.00
Mitchell's Prize Crop Cigarettes, Scotland, 4 1/4 In. 55.00
N. Brezner & Company, Composition Wood Tray, Elfin Cobbler, 1940s, 5 1/2 x 7 In. 48.00
North State Cigarettes, Superfine, Ready Rolled, 6 x 3 1/4 In. 31.00
Old Elk, Always's Pure Whisky, Elk Head, Horseshoe, Tin Lithograph, Round, 3 5/8 In. . . 99.00
Old Judge Coffee, Owl, Tin Lithograph, Coffee Can Shape, 2 7/8 x 2 3/4 In. 63.00
Patterson's Tuxedo Tobacco, Green, Gold, 4 1/2 x 2 3/4 In. 248.00
Pendleton, Figural, Cowboy, Bucking Horse, Iron, Painted, Sept. 1932, 7 1/2 x 4 In. 633.00
Pirelli, Miniature Rubber Tire, Glass Insert, 6 In. 15.00
Player's, Country Life, Tobacco, Cigarettes, 4 1/4 x 3 1/2 In. 31.00
Pollits Motel, Air Cooled, Steam Heat, Glass, Oval, Palmyra, Mo., 4 1/4 x 3 In. 16.00
Premium Promotions, White Ground, Homer Laughlin, Newell, W. Va., 5 1/2 In. 10.00
R. Bell & Co., Safety Match, Match Holder, Square, England, 2 x 5 In. 173.00
Richmond Gem Cigarettes, Man, Black Hat, Clothes, Glass, 5 1/2 x 3 5/8 In. 121.00
S&H Green Stamps, Glass, 6 x 4 x 1 1/2 In. 15.00
Sanka Coffee, 3-Sided, Black Glass, 4 1/2 In. 18.00
Seiberling Tire, S Inside Shield, All Tread, Canada, 6 3/4 x 1 1/2 In. 12.00
Shenango China, Restaurant Ware, Indian Logo, New Castle, Pa., c.1915, 3 3/4 In. 52.00
Shenango China, Restaurant Ware, New Castle, Pa., 1952, 4 In. 42.00
Shirley Havana Cigars, Match Holder, Colorado Cigar Co., 1890s 350.00
Slim Jims, 10 Cents, Make Your Next Drink Taste Better, Phila., Pa. 12.00
Smokey The Bear, Aluminum, Embossed, 4 Different Colors, 4 In., 4 Piece 20.00
Standard Plumbing, Bulldog, 4 1/2 x 5 x 6 1/2 In. 125.00

Ashtray, Fireman, Metal,
Advance Products,
7 x 4 1/2 In.

Ashtray, TWA Jet,
Aluminum, Riffe
Models, Shawnee
Mission, Kans., 7 In.

Suntory Whisky, 1 1/4 x 4 In. 20.00
Swiss Air, DC8, Chrome, Switzerland, c.1950 .... 275.00
TWA Jet, Aluminum, Riffe Models, Shawnee Mission, Kans., 7 In. .... *Illus* 30.00
Unisphere, New York World's Fair, 1964-1965, Pink, Melmac 18.00
United States Tires, Tire Shape, Raised Treads, Metal Glass, 1920s, 6 In. 253.00
Warwicks' Ales & Stouts, Newark On Trent, Associated Potteries, 4 3/4 In. 91.00
Wetter Stoves & Ranges, Lion In 3-Sided Logo, Porcelain, 6 In. 55.00
Whitbread's, Ale & Stout, Royal Doulton, 4 1/4 In. 31.00
White Horse Cellar, Good Luck, Horseshoe Shape, Match Holder, Shelley, 2 x 5 In. 70.00 to 100.00
White Horse Whisky, Hoof Shape, Matchbox Holder, 5 1/4 x 4 In. 172.00
Winton Auto, Sabina Line, Antique Car, Gold Rim, 1898, 6 In. 8.00
Wrekin, Famous Ales, Man In Top Hat, Round, Old Foley, 6 In. 24.00
Wright Co., Atlanta Georgia, Syracuse China, 1938, 5 1/4 In. 24.00
Wyandotte Products, Pressed Copper, Arrowhead Shape, 5 In. 33.00
Young Victory Ales, Sailing Ship, Blue Print On White Ground, Round, England, 5 1/4 In. 95.00

AUNT JEMIMA   The Aunt Jemima symbol was used by the Pearl Milling Company in 1889, the R.T. Davis Milling Company in 1890, the Aunt Jemima Mills Co. in 1914, and the Quaker Oats Company in 1926. Her appearance has changed through the years. A live Aunt Jemima appeared at the 1893 Chicago World's Fair. She was first played by a former slave, Nancy Green, a thin woman who didn't resemble the Aunt Jemima drawing of a heavy woman wearing a bandanna. Anna Robinson became the second live Aunt Jemima in the 1930s. She was the basis for the next brand logo. In 1968 Aunt Jemima became slimmer and younger. In 1989 she was modernized with a new hairstyle, pearl earrings, and a lace collar. Aunt Jemima cloth dolls were introduced in 1896. Another version was made of oilcloth. In 1931 an 18 1/2-inch composition doll was available. Ceramic salt and pepper shakers were made in the 1920s and 1930s, and again in the 1980s. Plastic salt and peppers date from the 1950s. Many other Aunt Jemima premiums have been made, but collectors should be very careful. Many, including the iron doorstop, have been reproduced. Aunt Jemima syrups and mixes are still made by Quaker, a division of PepsiCo since 2001. Since 1996, Aurora Foods has had a license for frozen Aunt Jemima products.

Bank, Cast Iron, Red & White Dress, Apron, Red & Gold Dotted Bandanna 35.00
Banner, Aunt Jemima Pancakes, Cloth, 1953, 34 x 57 1/2 In. 385.00
Banner, Aunt Jemima's Face, White, Oilcloth, 2-Sided, 17 In. 60.00
Banner, Aunt Jemima's Face, Yellow, Oilcloth, 2-Sided, 17 In. 65.00
Banner, Pancake Jamboree, Yellow, Oilcloth, 2-Sided, 29 In. 60.00
Box, Cardboard Lithograph, Shipping, 13 1/2 In. 181.00
Button, I'se In Town Honey, Black Woman, Bandanna On Head, 1 In. 40.00
Cookie Jar, Painted Plastic, 10 In. 237.00
Cookie Jar, Plastic, Black Face, F & F, 11 1/4 In. ....316.00 to 367.00
Cookie Jar, Red Dress, Apron, Plastic, c.1935, 11 1/2 In. 425.00
Display Box, Cardboard Lithograph, 4-Sided, Stand-Up, 27 1/2 In. 311.00
Doorstop, Cast Iron, 9 x 5 1/4 x 3 1/2 In. 400.00
Doorstop, Littco Products, 13 1/4 x 8 In. 715.00
Kitchen Set, Aunt Jemima & Uncle Mose, Syrup, Salts, Peppers, F & F, 5 Piece 99.00
Mask, Pancake Flour, I'se In Town Honey, Ask Your Grocer 700.00
Paper Doll, Family, Clothing Before & After Recipe Was Sold, 12 In. 1495.00
Place Mat, Story Of Aunt Jemima, Scalloped Edge, 1950, 10 x 14 In. 25.00
Recipe Box, Plastic, Green, 5 1/4 In. ....192.00 to 215.00
Recipe Box, Plastic, Red, 5 1/4 In. ....79.00 to 147.00
Recipe Box, Plastic, Yellow, 5 1/4 In. ....79.00 to 113.00
Salt & Pepper, Uncle Mose, F & F, 5 x 2 1/2 In., Pair 65.00
Shaker, Spice, Nutmeg, F & F Mold & Die, Dayton, Ohio, 1950s 45.00
Sheet Music, Squeeze Me, Picture Of Aunt Jemima, Leff, 1926 .... 15.00
Sign, Pancake Flour, On Swing, Hanger, Cardboard, Die Cut, 2-Sided, 17 In. 3540.00
Sign, Pancake Flour, Paper Lithograph, 2-Sided, String Hanger, 17 1/2 In. 5311.00
Sign, Ready Mix Buckwheat, Corn & Wheat Flour, 22 x 12 1/4 In. ....1210.00 to 1375.00
Spice Set, Painted Plastic, F & F, Box, 12 In. 735.00

Sugar & Creamer, Aunt Jemima & Butler, Plastic, F & F, 4 In. . . . . .102.00 to 283.00
Syrup, F & F Mold & Die Co., Dayton, Ohio, 1950s, 5 1/2 In. . . . . .70.00 to 85.00
Tea Bell, Cloth Dress, Holladner Novelty, Box, 5 In. 79.00
Tin, Pancake, Quaker Limited Edition, 1983, 6 In. 10.00

AUTO   In 1901 the Curved Dash Oldsmobile became the first mass-produced automobile in the United States. About 1913, Henry Ford installed the first conveyor-belt-based assembly line. Soon he was the largest car manufacturer in the world. Automobile parts, ads, and accessories are collectors' items today. Gas pump globes and license plates are part of this specialty. Prices are determined by age, rarity, and condition.

Badge, Delco, Freedom V, Battery, Camel, Metal, Blue, Flasher, 1960s, 2 1/2 In. . . . . *Illus*   23.00
Badge, Esso Service, Cap, Metal, Cloisonne Enamel, 1 1/2 x 2 3/8 In. 132.00
Badge, Tydol Veedol Serviceman, Inlaid Cloisonne Enameled Letters, 2 7/8 x 2 1/4 In. . . . 743.00
Banner, Atlantic Motor Oil, Wolf, Don't Be Afraid Of Big Bad Wolf, Cloth, 58 x 36 In. . . 232.00
Banner, Studebaker, Centennial, Red, White, Blue, Cloth, 9 x 36 In. 295.00
Booklet, Oldsmobile, Color Illustrations, 1954, 8 1/2 x 11 In. 65.00
Box, Majestic Spark Plugs, Unused Spark Plug, 1940s, 1 1/4 x 1 1/4 x 3 In. . . . . *Illus*   25.00
Button, Champion Spark Plugs, Charlie Orbit Time, Rocket, Green, Yellow, c.1960, 3 In.   15.00
Button, Valvoline, It's In The Ring, Valvoline Wins Or Else, Red, Blue, c.1940, 3 In. 20.00
Calendar, Chevrolet, 1926, Frame, 31 1/4 x 22 In. 193.00
Calendar, Esso, Oil Cans, Gasoline Globes, 1941, 8 3/4 x 15 In. 32.00
Calendar, Fisk Motor Sales, Roll Down, Bear & Cubs, 1948, 16 1/2 x 11 In. 44.00
Calendar, Frary's Ford Garage, Goodwin, 1927, 14 1/2 x 11 1/2 In. 176.00
Calendar, Nash Motor Cars, Fight To The Finish, Moose, G.A. Fulton, 1930, 42 x 29 In. . 232.00
Calendar, Peppy Gas, Berry's Atlantic Station, Notebook, 1933, Pocket 9.00
Calendar, Pitrolo Pontiac Co., Embossed, Foiled Cardboard, Box, 1950, 32 x 20 In. 1430.00
Calendar, Standard Automotive Brushes, Pinup Girl, Card, 1938, 10 x 4 3/4 In. 18.00
Calendar, U.S. Tires, Perfect Target, 1931, 17 x 10 In. 55.00
Can, Boston Coach Axle Oil, Standard Oil Company, 6 In. 28.00
Can, Capitan Parlube Motor Oil, 2 Gal., 11 x 9 In. 154.00
Can, Cities Service Blue Club Motor Oil, Contents, Qt., 4 x 5 1/2 In. 43.00
Can, Cities Service Koolmotor Motor Oil, Contents, Qt., 4 x 5 1/2 In. 17.60
Can, Cities Service Trojan Motor Oil, Contents, Qt., 4 x 5 1/2 In. 23.00
Can, D-X Sunray Oil Company, Wooden Bail Handle, 5 Gal., 16 In. 25.00
Can, Defender Motor Oil, 100% Pure, Paraffin Base, Tin, 2 Gal., 12 x 8 1/2 In. 39.00
Can, Duplex Motor Oil, No. 1, Enterprise Oil Co., 15 x 7 1/2 x 2 1/2 In. 2750.00
Can, Eastlube Motor Oil, 100% Paraffin Base, Tin, 2 Gal., 11 x 8 1/2 In. 28.00
Can, Eveready Prestone, Prefect Anti-Freeze, Tin Lithograph, 10 In. 66.00
Can, Falcon, Motor Oil, Oscar Bryant, Hollis, Oklahoma, Qt., 5 1/2 x 4 In. 17.00
Can, Gulflube Motor Oil, 11 x 8 In. . . . . *Illus*   33.00
Can, Hudson Motor Oil, Oil Tanker, Tin Lithograph, Crimped Seam, Unopened, 5 x 4 In. . 303.00
Can, Kendall, Hypoid Lube, 90 Weight, 1 Lb., 5 1/2 In. 27.00
Can, Mother Penn Motor Oil, Unopened, Qt., 5 1/2 x 4 In. 17.00
Can, Pennsylvania Motor Oil, Industrial Oil Corp., Warren, Pennsylvania, 13 3/8 x 12 In. . 245.00
Can, Pep Boys Pure As Gold Grease, Multicolored, Manny, Moe & Jack, 1 Lb. 45.00
Can, Pep Boys Water Pump Grease, Manny, Moe, Jack, Tin Lithograph, 1 Lb. 66.00

Auto, Badge, Delco,
Freedom V, Battery,
Camel, Metal, Blue,
Flasher, 1960s,
2 1/2 In.

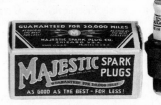

Auto, Box, Majestic Spark Plugs, Unused
Spark Plug, 1940s, 1 1/4 x 1 1/4 x 3 In.

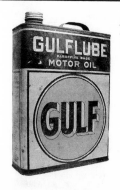

Auto, Can,
Gulflube Motor Oil,
11 x 8 In.

Auto, Can, Red Bell
Motor Oil, Sico Co.,
Mt. Joy, Pa., 2 Gal., 11 In.

Can, Quaker City Bonded Motor Oil, Pennsylvania Petroleum Products, Qt., 5 1/2 x 4 In. . . 125.00
Can, Red Bell Motor Oil, Sico Co., Mt. Joy, Pa., 2 Gal., 11 In. . . . . *Illus*   50.00
Can, Richmond Motor Oil, Biplane, Horizontal, 6 x 8 In. 55.00
Can, RPM Outboard, Contents, Qt. 40.00
Can, Shamrock Oil, 1960-1970, 5 In. 15.00
Can, StaCool Oil, Keeps The Motor Cool, Red, Green, 2 Gal. 11.00
Can, Streamline Motor Oil, Charles New, High Speed, Tin, 2 Gal., 10 1/2 x 8 1/2 In. 220.00
Can, Sunoco, Motor Oil, Mercury Made, 2 Gal., 12 x 8 1/2 In. 17.00
Can, Ward's Sea King Motor Oil, Contents, Pt. 88.00
Card, Esso Gasoline, Scottish Terrier In Basket, Merry Christmas, 1940s, 9 1/2 In. 15.00
Catalog, Spyker Automobile, Heavy Board, Holland, England, 12 1/2 x 19 In., 10 Pages . . 374.00
Clock, Atlantic Refining Co., Gilbert Clock, Oak Case, Cleveland, Ohio, 36 In. 452.00
Clock, Atlas Tires, Batteries, Accessories, Neon, Metal, Reverse Glass, 8-Sided, 18 3/8 In. 440.00
Clock, Auto-Lite Sta-Ful Battery, Lighted, 18 1/2 In. 248.00
Clock, Cadillac Service, Neon, c.1940 . . . . 990.00
Clock, Ford, Ford Parts, Light-Up, Pam 323.00
Clock, GMC Truck, Sales, Service, Neon, Octagonal 1485.00
Clock, Gulf, Diamond Shape, 1963, 15 In. 600.00
Clock, Kendall Motor Oil, Light-Up, 15 In. 165.00
Clock, Kendall Oil, Neon, Spinner, 20 1/2 In. 1100.00
Clock, McCord Motor Gaskets, Time To Buy, 14 1/2 In. 110.00
Clock, Mobil Oil, Red Centaur At Center, Convex Glass Front, Light-Up, c.1945, 15 In. . . 414.00
Clock, Mohawk Tires, Octagonal, Neon, 18 1/2 In. 990.00
Clock, Monroe, All You Need To Know About Shock Absorbers, Light-Up, Square, Pam . 20.00
Clock, Packard, Neon 1100.00
Clock, Shell Gasoline, Neon, Steel, Pull Chain, 20 In. 400.00
Dispenser, Oil, Esso, Figural, Oil Drop Character 60.00
Display Box, U-Auto Varnish, 24 Cans 1760.00
Display Box, Union Auto Fuses, Tin, Glass, Contents, 20 Tins 1210.00
Display Box, Whiz Stop Leak, Radiator Compound, 6 Cans 3080.00
Display Rack, Gulf Batteries, Metal, White, Sign On Top, 35 x 24 1/2 x 12 In. 165.00
Display Rack, Gulf, Tourguide Service, Maps, 11 x 9 x 5 In. 165.00
Display Rack, Michelin Tires, Michelin Man, Drum, Tin Lithograph, Die Cut, 19 x 22 In. . . 2360.00
Display Rack, STP, Gasoline & Oil Treatments, Quiets Motors, 32 x 17 x 11 In. 55.00
Figure, BP Oil Man, Arm Upraised, Yellow Shirt, White Hat, Vinyl, c.1950, 3 1/2 In. 55.00
Figure, Michelin Man, Horsehair Plaster, Painted, c.1915, 32 In. 3630.00
Figure, Michelin Man, Jiggle Cord, Soft Rubber, 3 1/4 In. 18.00
Figure, Michelin Man, Plastic, Black Letters On Sash, Metal Bracket, England, 19 In. . . . 95.00
First Aid Kit, Phillips 66, Plastic 18.00
Flask, Shell Oil, Sheffield Pewter, 5 1/4 x 3 1/4 In. 175.00
Gas Pump, Flying A, Art Deco Design, 2-Sided, 92 x 29 x 16 In. . . . . *Illus* 2090.00
Gas Pump Globe, Capitol, Atlantic Gasoline, Reverse Painted, 2-Sided, 20 In. . . . . . *Illus* 467.00
Gas Pump Globe, Diamond D-X Lubricating Motor Fuel, White, Red, Black 396.00
Gas Pump Globe, Genuine Ethyl, Ethyl Logo, Glass Body, 13 1/2-In. Lens 413.00
Gas Pump Globe, Gulf, Glass Casing & Lenses, 17 In. 413.00
Gas Pump Globe, Red Crown, Standard Oil, c.1940 . . . . 531.00
Gas Pump Globe, Sico Gas, Porcelain Lens, Steel Body 550.00

Auto, Gas Pump Globe, Capitol, Atlantic Gasoline, Reverse Painted, 2-Sided, 20 In.

Auto, Gas Pump, Flying A, Art Deco Design, 2-Sided, 92 x 29 x 16 In.

Gas Pump Globe, Sinclair Ethyl, Red, White, Black, Yellow	83.00
Gas Pump Globe, Skelly, Fortified Gasoline, Red, White, Blue ....220.00 to	253.00
Gas Pump Globe, Sky Chief, Glass, Black T, Hull Body, 13 1/2 In.	400.00
Gas Pump Globe, Standard Oil, Figural, Crown, Opaque White, Red Details, c.1940, 16 In.	374.00
Gas Pump Globe, Standard Oil, White, Gold, Crown, 17 In.	495.00
Gas Pump Globe, Victoria, Ethyl Logo, Glass, Oval, 3 Piece	385.00
Key Ring, Michelin Man, White, Plastic, c.1960, 1 1/4 In.	15.00
Knife, Gulf Oil Co., Inlaid Enamel, Airplane, Airship, Refineries, Derricks, 3 1/4 x 3/4 In.	605.00
Knife, Sandri, Sunoco, Paring & Grapefruit, Wooden Handles, Box	10.00
Letters, Gulf, Die Cut, Black, 10 In., 65 1/2 x 10 In., 4 Piece	330.00
License Plate Holder, Harold's Club, Covered Wagon, Die Cut, Reno, 1950s, 14 x 8 In.	55.00
License Tag, Bausch & Lomb, Drive Safely, Reflective Eye, Tin Lithograph, 4 x 4 5/8 In.	142.00
Map, American Oil, Amoco, Space Mysteries, New Window Of Universe, 1958, 18 x 25 In.	25.00
Pail, Whiz Transmission Grease, Tin, Bail Handle, Camden, N.J.	385.00
Paperweight, Arco Motor Oil Club, Cast Metal, 5 In.	110.00
Paperweight, Exide Battery, Batteries On Top, Factory On Bottom, Glass, 4 x 3 x 3/4 In.	84.00
Pegasus, Riding, Ride The Flying Red Horse, Coin-Operated	30800.00
Pencil, Chevron Gas Not A Substitute, Truck, Mechanical, Logan, N.M.	25.00
Pencil, Dixel Gas, Drive Safely, C.A. Norman, Tank Wagon, Warrensburg, Mo., Mechanical	25.00
Pencil, Marathon Oil & Gas, Rogers Marathon Service, Carmi, Ill., Mechanical	22.00
Pencil, Shell Oil Gas, Red, Yellow, Gold Clip	22.00
Postcard, 1959 Ford Custom 300 Tudor Sedan, Red, White	18.00
Postcard, Ambassador, Nash, 1958	8.00
Postcard, Ford, 1954	12.00
Postcard, Free Miniature Edsel For Test Driving Real One, 5 x 8 In.	35.00
Poster, Golden Shell Motor Oil, Change Now, 55 x 40 In.	55.00
Poster, Haynes 55 Auto, Paper, Mounted On Linen, 1922, 35 1/2 x 23 1/2 In.	220.00
Poster, Model A Ford, Frame, 12 x 18 In.	39.00
Poster, Monaco, Grand Prix Automobile, Paper, Frame, 1966, 30 In.	220.00
Poster, Shellubrication, After Vacation, 1940s, 55 x 40 In.	88.00
Poster, Shellubrication, Man By Car With Wheel Off, Paper, c.1940, 55 x 40 In. ..... *Illus*	92.00
Pump Plate, Amlico, Regular Gasoline, Porcelain, Round, 10 In.	523.00
Pump Plate, DX Marine Gasoline, Porcelain, 26 x 15 In.	385.00
Pump Plate, Ethyl, Porcelain, Round, 8 In.	77.00
Pump Plate, Gloco, Hi'R Octane, Porcelain, 9 x 15 In.	605.00
Pump Plate, Gloco, Super Ethyl, Porcelain, 9 x 15 In.	605.00
Pump Plate, Humble, Porcelain, 7 x 14 In.	523.00
Pump Plate, Mobil Premium, Porcelain, 14 x 12 In.	61.00
Pump Plate, Mobilfuel, Diesel, Porcelain, 13 x 12 In.	358.00
Pump Plate, Royal, Porcelain, 8 1/2 x 9 1/2 In.	138.00
Pump Plate, Shamrock, Cloud Master Premium, Porcelain, 12 1/2 x 10 1/2 In.	248.00
Pump Plate, Sinclair, Diesel, Porcelain, 13 1/2 x 12 In.	248.00
Pump Plate, Standard Heating Oils, Porcelain, 12 1/2 x 10 In.	330.00
Rack, Atlantic Lubrication Service, Metal, Wall Mount, Gas Station, 16 x 9 1/2 x 8 1/2 In.	39.00
Salt & Pepper, Gas Pump, Conoco, R.R. Sublette's Station, Mo., Plastic, Box, 2 3/4 In.	95.00
Salt & Pepper, Pure Oil Company Gas Pump, Mower County Oil, Minn., Plastic, 2 3/4 In.	135.00

Sign, AAA Approved, Red, White, Blue, Oval, Porcelain, 23 x 30 In. 165.00
Sign, AAA, Georgia State, Official Service Station, Die Cut, Porcelain, 2-Sided, 22 In. . . . 176.00
Sign, AC Spark Plug, Cleaning Station, Donkey In Tub, Die Cut, Flange, 2-Sided, 20 x 9 In. 413.00
Sign, Aladdin Gasoline, Lake Co. Farm Supply, Tin, Embossed, Reliance, 19 1/2 x 7 In. . . 231.00
Sign, Albaine Oil, Standard Oil Co., Paper, Metal Bands, 16 x 11 In. 880.00
Sign, Amoco, Courtesy Cards Honored Here, Porcelain, 2-Sided, 16 x 24 In. 165.00
Sign, Armould Oil Products, Porcelain, 2-Sided, Round, 32 In. 605.00
Sign, Atlantic Gasoline, Porcelain, 52 In. 300.00
Sign, Atlantic Motor Oil, Porcelain, White, Red, Blue, 52 x 35 1/2 In. . . . . .247.00 to 325.00
Sign, B-A Peerless Motor Oil, Service Man Pours Oil Into Car, Die Cut, Cardboard 3350.00
Sign, Bachelder, Piston Ring Size Chart, Sexy Women, Mat, Frame, 28 x 39 In. 220.00
Sign, Baudou Tires, Bandage Increvable, Brevele S.G.D.G., Tin Lithograph, 27 x 19 In. . . 1440.00
Sign, Beacon Oil, Porcelain, 2-Sided, Round, 30 In. 2310.00
Sign, Boston Coach Axle Oil, Standard Oil Co., Contents, Tin, 3 x 5 1/2 x 2 In. 33.00
Sign, Buick, Authorized Service, Porcelain, 2-Sided, Round, Walker Company, 42 In. 4180.00
Sign, Buick, Goetsch Bros., Franklin, Wis., Tin, Embossed, 13 1/2 x 19 1/2 In. 495.00
Sign, Cadillac Service, Black, White, Porcelain, Round, c.1950, 48 In. 2310.00
Sign, Cadillac Service, Porcelain, 2-Sided, Hanging Ring, Round, 60 In. 5500.00
Sign, Champion Spark Plugs, Dependable, Tin, Flange, c.1960, 23 3/4 x 35 1/2 In. 149.00
Sign, Champion Spark Plugs, Tin, Flange, 2-Sided, 12 x 18 In. 770.00
Sign, Champion Spark Plugs, Woman On Globe, Tin Lithograph, Oval, 6 1/2 x 4 3/4 In. . . 468.00
Sign, Champion, Dependable Spark Plugs, Metal, 12 x 26 In. . . . . *Illus* 44.00
Sign, Champlin Hi-Vi Motor Oil, Porcelain, 2-Sided, 20 x 32 In. 495.00
Sign, Chevrolet Service, Neon, Porcelain, Walker & Co., 42 In. 3850.00
Sign, Chevrolet, Economical Transportation, Tin, Embossed, 12 x 23 In. 385.00
Sign, Chevrolet, Sales & Service, Blue Ground, 2-Sided, Porcelain, 28 x 40 In. 4620.00
Sign, Chevron, Porcelain, 24 x 21 In. 66.00
Sign, Chevy OK, Porcelain, Round, 1936, 36 In. 2200.00
Sign, Chevy, OK Quality Used Cars, Tin, 28 x 16 In. 1100.00
Sign, Chicago Motor Club, Porcelain, Die Cut, 2-Sided, 43 x 36 In. 385.00
Sign, Chore Boy Gasoline Engines, Paper, Waterloo, Iowa, 28 x 41 In. 308.00
Sign, Chrysler Plymouth Approved Service, 2-Sided, 1930s-1940s, 30 In. 1980.00
Sign, Chrysler Service, Black, Yellow, Porcelain, 2-Sided, 26 3/4 x 21 In. 440.00
Sign, Citgo, Light-Up, Plastic, Metal Frame, 25 x 25 In. 110.00
Sign, Colonial Minuteman Regular Gasoline, Porcelain, 15 x 12 In. 770.00
Sign, Conoco, Bronze Gasoline, Greasing Charts, Tin, 2-Sided, 24 1/2 x 37 1/2 In. 2420.00
Sign, Conoco, Credit Cards, Porcelain, 2-Sided, Round, 30 In. 1100.00
Sign, Conoco, Gasoline, Yellow, Red, Blue, Porcelain, 2-Sided, 25 In. Diam. 2640.00
Sign, Conoco, Motor Oil, Porcelain, 30 x 27 In. 468.00
Sign, Conoco, Red, White, Tin, Metal Frame, 16 1/2 x 50 In. 165.00
Sign, Conoco, Super Motor Oil, Curb, Porcelain, 2-Sided, Stand, 30 x 27 In. 825.00
Sign, Conoco, Tin Lithograph, Wood Frame, 1940s, 36 x 120 In. 600.00
Sign, Conoco, Travel Bureau, Tin, 2-Sided, 1936, 18 x 24 In. 440.00
Sign, Crown Gasoline, Standard Oil Company, Porcelain, Flange, 2-Sided, 26 x 26 In. . . . 1870.00
Sign, Crown Premium, Tin, Embossed, 2-Sided, 15 x 20 In. 275.00
Sign, D-X Motor Oil, Porcelain, 2-Sided, 24 x 40 In. 303.00
Sign, D-X, Diamond Shape, Enamel, 84 x 48 In. 99.00

Auto, Poster,
Shellubrication,
Man By Car With
Wheel Off, Paper,
c.1940, 55 x 40 In.

Auto, Sign, Champion, Dependable Spark Plugs,
Metal, 12 x 26 In.

Sign, Daimler 15, Comfortable Car, Front End Of Bentley, Enamel, England, 24 x 15 In. . 265.00
Sign, De Soto, Approved Service, Red, White, Blue, Porcelain, Round, 30 In. 413.00
Sign, Delta Tires, Tin, 1969, 15 1/2 x 60 In. 198.00
Sign, Devoe Motor Car Finish, Herbert Mayer, Paper, Frame, 26 x 38 In. 2145.00
Sign, Dodge Trucks, Job Rated, Sales & Service, Blue, White, Yellow, 42 x 42 In. 2700.00
Sign, Duplex Motor Oil, Outboard Special, Tin, 12 x 24 In. 800.00
Sign, Durant Motor Cars, Authorized Maintenance, Porcelain, 2-Sided, 28 x 42 In. 4400.00
Sign, En-Ar-Co Motor Oil, Boy Holding Sign, 2-Sided, Tin, Round, 40 In. 633.00
Sign, En-Ar-Co Motor Oils, Tin, Self-Framed, 1930, 41 x 26 In. 319.00
Sign, Energee True Gasoline, Pure Oil Co., Tin, Flange, Round, 17 1/2 x 20 In. 330.00
Sign, Esso, Ethyl, Porcelain, 2-Sided, Octagonal, Red, White, Blue, 25 1/2 x 30 In. 660.00
Sign, Esso, Porcelain, 2-Sided, 21 x 30 In. 1210.00
Sign, Esso, Standard Dealer, Porcelain, Oval, 40 x 60 In. 358.00
Sign, Federal Tires, Authorized Sales Agency, Service, Porcelain, 2-Sided, 36 x 18 In. . . . 330.00
Sign, Firestone Tires & Auto Supplies, Porcelain, Die Cut, 24 x 30 In. 2750.00
Sign, Firestone, Red Inner Tubes, Paper, Frame, 14 x 42 In. 5500.00
Sign, Fisk Tires, Gasoline, Auto Supplies, Porcelain, Flange, 18 x 24 1/4 In. 1018.00
Sign, Flying A Service, Porcelain, 2-Sided, Hanger, Round, 42 In. 2860.00
Sign, Flying A, Super Extra, Winged A, Red Ground, Porcelain, 10 In. 231.00
Sign, Ford & Fordson, Sales & Service, Porcelain, Blue Ground, 27 x 50 In. 5775.00
Sign, Ford Genuine Parts, Tin, 2-Sided, Hanger, 16 1/2 x 24 In. 1210.00
Sign, Ford Tractor, Neon, Porcelain, Mulholland Sign Co., 48 x 72 In. 2970.00
Sign, Ford, Lightning Emblem, Cast Aluminum, 1953-1956, 21 In. 303.00
Sign, Ford, Neon, Porcelain, White Script Name, Oval, 72 In. 1600.00
Sign, Ford, Neon, Red Offset Letters, Decorative Molding, Oval, 72 In. 2200.00
Sign, Ford, Porcelain, Veribrite, 25 x 39 In. 660.00
Sign, Fordson Tractors, Oliver Tractor Implements, Tin, Ellis Tiger Co., 13 x 19 1/2 In. . . 770.00
Sign, Francisco Auto Heater, Car, House, Tin, Self-Framed, c.1920, 18 x 40 In. 1370.00
Sign, Francisco Auto Heater, Summer, Automobile, Self-Framed, 18 x 40 In. . . .1100.00 to 1325.00
Sign, Francisco Auto Heater, Winter, Cut-Away Car, Tin, 18 x 40 In. . . . . .1595.00 to 2475.00
Sign, Fred'k Gamash Automobiles, Ford Parts, Tin, Embossed, Newport, 13 x 20 In. 660.00
Sign, Galena Motor Oil, Tin, Embossed, 12 x 60 In. 220.00
Sign, Gargoyle Lube Chart, Mobiloil, Yellow, Red, Black, Tin, 38 x 19 In. 358.00
Sign, Gargoyle Mobiloil, Ask For, Authorized Service, Porcelain, Metal, 24 x 19 1/2 In. . . 468.00
Sign, Gargoyle Mobiloil, Make The Chart Your Guide, Porcelain, Flange, 15 1/2 x 24 In. . 187.00
Sign, Gas Dealer, Porcelain, 2-Sided, 48 x 32 In. 55.00
Sign, Gas Pump, Atlantic Premium, 11 x 13 In. 275.00
Sign, Gas Pump, Atlantic, Porcelain, Red, White Letters & Stripes, 9 x 13 In. 88.00
Sign, Gas Pump, Pure Premium, Be Sure With Pure, Porcelain, 10 x 12 In. 49.00
Sign, Gas Pump, Veltex, Porcelain, 12 x 16 In. 990.00
Sign, Gasoline, Oil, White, Black Letters, Wood, Picture Frame Molding, 14 x 19 In. 413.00
Sign, Genuine Ford Parts, Porcelain, 2-Sided, 16 1/2 x 24 In. 715.00
Sign, Getty Oil Company, Porcelain, 9 x 25 In. 22.00
Sign, Gillette Tires, A Bear For Wear, White, Red, Black, Tin, Metal, 48 x 29 In. 88.00
Sign, GMC Trucks, Sales, Service, Porcelain, 2-Sided, Hanger, Round, 42 In. . . .2035.00 to 4675.00
Sign, Good Gulf Gasoline, White, Orange, Blue, Porcelain, Round, 10 1/2 In. 138.00
Sign, Goodrich Safety Tires, Canadian Mountie, Porcelain, 56 x 20 In. 10200.00
Sign, Goodrich Tires, Black, White, Red, Porcelain, 78 x 18 In. 1050.00
Sign, Goodrich, Batteries, Tires, Accessories, Porcelain, 23 x 63 In. 413.00
Sign, Gulf Authorized Dealer, Porcelain, 9 x 40 In. 413.00
Sign, Gulf Dealer, 2-Sided, Orange, Black, Round, 66 In. 209.00
Sign, Gulf Dealer, Red, White, Black, 2-Sided, Porcelain, 65-In. Diam. 330.00
Sign, Gulf Supreme Motor Oil, At The Sign Of The Orange Disc, 60 x 27 1/2 In. 1320.00
Sign, Gulf, Porcelain, Orange Ground, Blue & White Letters, Round, 28 In. 275.00
Sign, Hudson Essex Service, Porcelain, 16 x 30 In. 385.00
Sign, Hudson Sales & Service, Enameled, 2-Sided, 72 x 48 In. 50.00
Sign, I-H Farmall Cub Tractor, Paper Lithograph, Frame, 32 x 42 In. 385.00
Sign, Invincible Motor Insurance Co., Car, Ship, Tin, 9 x 20 In. 358.00
Sign, Jaguar, Sales & Service, Porcelain, 2-Sided, Original Hanger, 41 x 39 In. 3025.00
Sign, Kanotex, Ethyl Logo, Porcelain, 2-Sided, Hanging Ring, Round, 42 In. 3850.00
Sign, Kasier-Frazier Parts & Service, Porcelain, 2-Sided, Hanging Ring, Round, 60 In. . . . 4675.00
Sign, Kendall Motor Oil, Red & White, Porcelain, Round, 24 1/4 In. . . . . .77.00 to 143.00
Sign, Kendall Motor Oil, Red & White, Tin, 2-Sided, Round, 23 1/4 In. 83.00

Sign, Kendall Motor Oil, Red, White, Tin, 2-Sided, Round, 22 In. 55.00
Sign, Kendall Oil, Tin, Embossed, Red, White, 71 x 12 In. 242.00
Sign, Little Scotchman Oiler, We Use, Tin, Black, Yellow, 4 x 28 In. 28.00
Sign, Lubri-Gas, Lubricated Gasoline, Camel, Tin, Embossed, 32 x 56 In. 1600.00
Sign, Mack Trucks, Parts Dealer, Tin, 2-Sided, 36 x 30 In. 523.00
Sign, Macmillan Motor Oils, Tin, 28 x 30 In. 88.00
Sign, Magnolia Petroleum Co., Porcelain, 2-Sided, Round, 30 In.   523.00
Sign, Marathon, Ohio Oil Co., Porcelain, 16 x 30 In. 143.00
Sign, Marigold Coach Lines, Coaches Stop Here, Porcelain, c.1920, 10 x 42 In. 5170.00
Sign, Mercedes-Benz Service, 2-Sided, Round, 42 In. 523.00
Sign, Michelin Pneus Tracteurs, Michelin Man, Tractor, Porcelain, 26 x 31 In. 440.00
Sign, Michelin Pneus Tracteurs, Michelin Man, Tractor, Porcelain, France, 24 1/4 x 18 In.   88.00
Sign, Michelin, Porcelain, 2-Sided, 31 x 27 In. 330.00
Sign, Miller Tires, Geared To The Road, Tin, 2-Sided, Trapezoidal Shape, 28 1/2 x 44 In. .   468.00
Sign, Miller Tires, Geared To The Road, Waltman Brothers, Porcelain, 2-Sided, 60 x 30 In.   1100.00
Sign, Mobil Gas Co., Pegasus, Porcelain, Die Cut, 3 Dimensional, 96 x 72 In. 2200.00
Sign, Mobil Gas, Fill Up, Porcelain, 2-Sided, Round, 36 In. 2145.00
Sign, Mobil Oil Gargoyle, Porcelain, For Oil Cabinet, 24 x 15 1/2 In. 468.00
Sign, Mobil Oil, Let Us Mobiloil Your Car, Engine, Chassis, Gears, Porcelain, 36 x 60 In.   193.00
Sign, Mobil Oil, Motor Oil Is Made Not Found, Tin, Red, White, 27 3/4 x 19 1/2 In. 550.00
Sign, Mobil Oil, Pegasus, Neon, Porcelain Finish, 74 x 96 In. 8800.00
Sign, Mobil Regular, Porcelain, 12 x 13 3/4 In. 95.00
Sign, Mobil, Pegasus, Die Cut, Porcelain, 36 x 48 In. 5500.00
Sign, Mona Motor Oil, Best Because Purest, Porcelain, 2-Sided, 24 x 40 In. 1320.00
Sign, Nash Authorized Service, Shield Shape, Porcelain, 2-Sided, 22 x 36 In. . . .2640.00 to 6270.00
Sign, National Motor Service Club Inc., Orange, Metal, Embossed, 3-Sided, 5 x 4 In., Pair   358.00
Sign, Oilzum Motor Oil, Quart Can Form, Tin Lithograph, 48 x 33 In. 440.00
Sign, Oilzum Motor Oil, Tin, Wood Frame, 1975, 36 x 72 In. 495.00
Sign, Oldsmobile Service, Porcelain, 2-Sided, Hanging Ring, Round, 60 In. . . . .3025.00 to 6875.00
Sign, Packard, Approved Service, Neon, Porcelain, Round, 42 In. 4125.00
Sign, Packard, Cable, Girl On Post In Lake, Paper, Wood Frame, c.1900, 18 x 25 1/2 In. . .   350.00
Sign, Packard, Car, Plane, Boat, Dirigible, Paper, Mat, Frame, 26 x 38 1/2 In. 1650.00
Sign, Packard, Service, Approved, Porcelain, 60 In. 3300.00
Sign, Pegasus, Neon, Porcelain, 48 x 60 In. 3850.00
Sign, Pennfield Motor Oils, Tin, Donaldson Art Company, 13 1/2 x 19 1/2 In. 495.00
Sign, Pennzoil, 100% Pure Pennsylvania, Safe Lubrication, Metal, 2-Sided, 18 x 31 In. . . .   121.00
Sign, Pennzoil, Motor Oil, With Z-7, Tin, Can Shape, 48 x 32 1/2 In. 275.00
Sign, Pennzoil, Motor Oils, Metal, Wood Frame, 14 x 42 In. 198.00
Sign, Pennzoil, Safe Lubrication, Liberty Bell, Tin Lithograph, Self-Framed 303.00
Sign, Pennzoil, Sound Your Z, 100% Pure Pennsylvania, Safe Lubrication, Tin, 22 x 31 In.   275.00
Sign, Pennzoil, Sound Your Z, 100% Pure Pennsylvania, Tin, Flange, Oval, 22 x 17 In. . . .   303.00
Sign, Pennzoil, Sound Your Z, Safe Lubrication, Metal, 2-Sided, 12 x 16 In. . . . . . .165.00 to 220.00
Sign, Pennzoil, Sound Your Z, Tin, 1961, 60 x 11 3/4 In. 550.00
Sign, Phillips 66 Motor Oils, Wood Frame, Tin, 34 x 22 In. 330.00
Sign, Phillips 66, Porcelain, 2-Sided, 30 x 30 In. 605.00
Sign, Phillips 66, Porcelain, Orange, Blue, Shield Shape, 2-Sided, 47 x 47 In. 413.00
Sign, Phillips, World's Finest Oil, Porcelain, 11 x 21 1/2 In. 880.00
Sign, Plymouth Service, Ship, Porcelain, 18 x 24 In. 1650.00
Sign, Polarine Motor Oil, Consult Chart, Porcelain, Round, 42 In.   468.00
Sign, Polarine, Oil & Greases, Best Motor Lubricants, Porcelain, 12 x 36 In. 1870.00
Sign, Pontiac, Authorized Service, Porcelain, Walker Co., 2-Sided, Round, 48 In. 5775.00
Sign, Pontiac, Embossed Tin Frame, 8-In. Glass Center, 24 x 24 In. 165.00
Sign, Pontiac, Goodwill, Porcelain, 36 x 36 In. 825.00
Sign, Power-Lube Motor Oils, Smooth As The Tread Of A Tiger, 28 x 20 In. 1800.00
Sign, Pure Tiolene Motor Oil, Tin, Die Cut, Flange, 2-Sided, 17 1/2 x 20 In. 660.00
Sign, Quaker State Cold Test Oil, Use, For Winter Driving, Porcelain, 2-Sided, 6 x 26 In. .   275.00
Sign, Quaker State Winter Oil, It's A Lucky Day, Horseshoe, Paper, 34 x 57 1/2 In. 880.00
Sign, Quaker State, Motor Oil, Green Ground, Bowed Front, Metal, Round, 24 In. 88.00
Sign, Quality OK Used Cars, Enamel, 16 x 28 In. 198.00
Sign, Reading Battery Service, Tin, Embossed, 14 1/2 x 14 In. 523.00
Sign, Red Crown Gasoline, Porcelain, Round, 42 In. 660.00
Sign, Red Crown, Gasoline & Polarine, Tin, Embossed, 27 1/2 x 19 In. . . . . *Illus*   7425.00
Sign, Reo Motor Cars, Tin, Embossed, Bartlesvill, Okla., 10 x 28 In. 220.00

Sign, Restrooms, Sonoco Gas Station, Porcelain, 2-Sided, Iron Bracket, 14 x 22 In. 853.00
Sign, Riley Bros., That's Oil, Yellow, Red, Black, 13 x 5 1/2 In. 88.00
Sign, Royal Triton Motor Oil, Porcelain, Die Cut, 2-Sided, Dark Blue, White, 30 x 25 In. . 220.00
Sign, Scholl's Axle Grease, Independent Oil Co., Red, Tin, 6 1/2 x 6 In. 66.00
Sign, Shell, Bulk Service, Yellow, Red, Porcelain, 18 x 24 In. 385.00
Sign, Shell, Gasoline, World Experience In Every Gallon, Stamps, Paper, 33 x 58 In. 144.00
Sign, Shell, Motor Oil, Can Shape, Red, Yellow Letters, Enamel, 20 x 15 3/4 In. 984.00
Sign, Shell, No Admittance & No Smoking, Porcelain, 6 x 15 In. 440.00
Sign, Shell, Porcelain, 2-Sided, 1936, 12 x 36 In. 550.00
Sign, Shell, Porcelain, 5 1/2 x 33 1/2 In. 1100.00
Sign, Shell-Penn Motor Oil, Scallop Shell, Die Cut, Yellow, Red, Porcelain, 30 x 29 In. . 173.00
Sign, Short Line, Nation Wide Bus Service, Ticket Office, Porcelain, Flange, 20 x 30 In. . . 209.00
Sign, Sico Straight Gas, White, Blue, Porcelain, Round, 36 In. 50.00
Sign, Sinclair, Gasoline, Dinosaur, Enamel, 13 1/2 x 12 In. 150.00
Sign, Sinclair, H-C Gasoline, Porcelain, Round, 2-Sided, 48 In. 44.00
Sign, Sinclair, Oil & Gas Company, Porcelain, 24 x 58 In. 358.00
Sign, Sinclair, Opaline Motor Oil, Porcelain, 2-Sided, Round, 26 In. 4070.00
Sign, Socony Air-Craft Oils, Porcelain, 20 x 30 In. 3080.00
Sign, Sonic Tires, The Tire Of The Future Today, 16 x 60 In. 66.00
Sign, Standard Oil Products, Porcelain, Self-Framed, 12 x 120 In. 770.00
Sign, Standard Polarine Motor Oil, Porcelain, Round, 2-Sided, 30 In. 275.00
Sign, Standard Red Crown, Porcelain, 12 x 15 In. 49.00
Sign, Star Cars, Low-Cost Transportation, Porcelain, 2-Sided, 28 x 42 In. 2475.00
Sign, Sterling Motor Oil, Tin, Embossed, 14 x 28 In. 770.00
Sign, Studebaker, Authorized Service, Porcelain, 2-Sided, Round, 42 In. 2750.00
Sign, Studebaker, Authorized Service, Red, Yellow, White, Porcelain, Round, 42 In. 190.00
Sign, Studebaker, Service Station, Blue Ground, Porcelain, 14 x 30 In. 550.00
Sign, Sunoco Winter Oil, Grease, Donald Duck, Walt Disney Enterprises, 1938, 58 x 36 In. 330.00
Sign, Sunray D-X Petroleum Products, Orange, Porcelain, Octagonal, 9 x 9 In. 1320.00
Sign, Supreme Motor Oil, Gulf Refining, Orange Dot, Porcelain, Flange, 18 x 22 In. 275.00
Sign, The Trucker's Friend, Tin, Mounting Brackets, 14 x 20 In. 165.00
Sign, Tydol Gasoline, Porcelain, Round, 42 In. 468.00
Sign, U.S. Tires, Porcelain, 24 x 72 In. 165.00
Sign, Union 76, Orange, Blue, White, 14 x 74 In. 50.00
Sign, Union 76, Stop Your Motor, No Smoking, Porcelain, 6 x 30 In. 358.00
Sign, Union Brake Service, Porcelain, 6 x 22 In. 83.00
Sign, Union Wheel Alignment, Porcelain, 6 x 22 In. 330.00
Sign, United Motors, Authorized Service, Hyatt, Porcelain, Die Cut, 2-Sided, 17 x 18 In. . 4400.00
Sign, United States Tires, Tin, 3 Panels, 2-Sided, Window Display, 33 x 54 In. 4510.00
Sign, Unoco Motor Oils, Union Oil Company, Cleveland, Oh., Tin, Embossed, 13 x 19 In. 550.00
Sign, U.S. Tires, Porcelain, 18 x 71 In. 248.00
Sign, Used Cars, Safety Tested, Porcelain, Round, Black, Red, Yellow, 42 In. 2310.00
Sign, Valiant Authorized Service Dealer, Porcelain, 2-Sided, Round, 40 In. 1650.00
Sign, Valvoline, Pennsylvania Oil, Tin Lithograph, Embossed, Self-Framed, 13 x 29 In. . . 550.00
Sign, Vesta Battery Service, Tin, Reflective, 17 1/2 x 11 1/2 In. 55.00
Sign, We Drive A Buick, Tin, Embossed, 12 x 17 In. 440.00
Sign, We Use An Overland Motor Car, Tin, Chalkboard Form, 9 3/4 x 13 3/4 In. 220.00
Sign, Weed Chains, As Necessary As Gasoline, Rotating Price Disc, 23 1/2 x 17 In. 4675.00
Sign, Weed Chains, For Safe Driving, Rotating Price Disc, Tin, Wood Frame, 23 x 17 In. . 1705.00
Sign, White Star Gasoline, Staroleum, Blue, White, Porcelain, Round, 28 In. 633.00
Sign, White Trucks Autocar, Porcelain, 2-Sided, 36 x 36 In. 660.00
Sign, Willys Approved Service, Red, White, Blue, 2-Sided, Porcelain, 42 In. 2400.00
Sign, Willys Knight Service, Genuine Parts, Die Cut, Porcelain, 2-Sided, 30 x 40 In. 2320.00
Sign, Willys Overland, Grand Canyon, Cardboard, 1914, Countertop, 9 x 6 In. 66.00
Sign, Willys Service, Overland, Arrow, Red, White, 2-Sided, Porcelain, 60 In. Diam. 1900.00
Sign, Woco Pep, King Of Motor Fuel, What Gasoline Can't Do, Porcelain, 32 x 108 In. . . . 1050.00
Sign, Wolf's Head Motor Oil, Curb, Tin, 2-Sided, 1971, 30 x 23 In. 523.00
Sign, Wolf's Head Motor Oil, Tin, Flange, 22 x 17 In. 193.00
Songbook, Esso, Allen's Service Center, Salisbury, N.C., 9 x 6 In., 23 Pages 22.00
Thermometer, Fleet Wing, Kennedy Bros. Oil, Corsica, Pa., Tin Lithograph, Box, 6 x 2 In. 176.00
Thermometer, Marathon Gasoline, J.B. Hollerman, Turners Station, Ky., Box, 7 In. 35.00
Thermometer, Prestone Anti-Freeze, You're Safe, You Know It, Porcelain, 36 In. .110.00 to 144.00
Thermometer, Red Crown Gasoline, Polarine, Porcelain, Wood Frame, 72 x 19 In. 4400.00

Auto, Tumbler, Sunoco, Go Wild
With American Wildlife
Glasses, 3 1/2 In., 1980s, 4 Piece

Auto, Sign, Red Crown,
Gasoline & Polarine,
Tin, Embossed,
27 1/2 x 19 In.

Thermometer, Red Crown Gasoline, Power Mileage, Porcelain, 72 x 20 In.	1700.00
Thermometer, Standard Oil, Round Bubble Glass Lens, Red Pointer, Logo, Metal, 19 In.	201.00
Thermometer, Stanolux Fuel Oils, Standard Oil Co., Live Heat, Metal, Sticker, 11 In.	28.00
Thermometer, Thermo Denatured Alcohol, Non Rusting Radiator Anti Freeze, 72 x 16 In.	550.00
Thermometer, Universal Batteries, Heart Of Your Car, 39 x 8 In.	132.00
Thermos, Esso, Happy Motoring, Metal	65.00
Tin, Axle Oil, Sample, Detailed Buggy, Contents, Lithograph, 2 7/8 x 2 In.	232.00
Tin, Boston Coach & Axle Oil, Standard Oil Co.	46.00
Tin, Cascade Motor Oil, Cataract Refining Co., MacDonald Mfg. Co., Toronto, Gal.	550.00
Tin, Cities Service Blue Club Motor Oil, Gal.	17.00
Tin, Hartford Tire Repair Kit, Hartford Rubber Works Co., 1/2 x 3 x 1 7/8 In.	28.00
Tin, Mohawk Motor Oil, 2 Gal.	95.00
Tin, Pep Boys, Handy Bulb Kit, Cadet Batteries, Cornell Tires, 4 x 2 3/4 In.	65.00
Tin, Purity Oil Co., Transmission Grease, 5 Lb.	61.00
Tin, Red Indian Auto Oil, McColl Bros. & Co., Gal.	2900.00
Tin, Scholl's Axle Grease, Runaway Horse & Buggy, Red, Black, 7 In.	490.00
Tin, Schrader Valve Caps, 1950s, 1 In.	10.00
Tin, Sunoco Mercury Oil, 2 Gal.	50.00
Tire Chart, Michelin Tire, Foreign, Heavy Plastic, 13 x 33 In.	11.00
Tire Clip, Braender Tires, Tire, Bulldog, Tin Lithograph, Spring Loaded, 2 3/4 x 2 1/4 In.	110.00
Tire Cover, Drink Sparkling Pepsol, Red, White, 1920s, 30 In.	500.00
Tumbler, Sunoco, Go Wild With American Wildlife Glasses, 3 1/2 In., 1980s, 4 Piece *Illus*	15.00

AVON In 1886 bookseller David H. McConnell gave away rose oil
perfume as a premium to people who bought his books. When he discovered that the perfume was the reason people where buying his
books, he started a new company. Even though the firm was located in
New York City, the company was named the California Perfume Company. McConnell recruited independent sales representatives to sell his
perfume. Mrs. P.F.E. Albee, one of the first representatives, pioneered
the company's direct-selling methods. Avon's first product was a set of
five perfumes called Little Dot. The Avon brand was first used in 1928
on talcum powder, a toothbrush, and a vanity set. The name Avon was a
tribute to William Shakespeare and his hometown, Stratford-on-Avon.
By 1936 the name on all of the company's products, including perfumes,
toothbrushes, and baking items, was Avon. The company's name was
officially changed to Avon Products, Inc., in 1939. Avon became a public company in 1946. Collectors want the bottles, jewelry, and sales
awards, but there is also interest in early advertising and pamphlets.

Award, Bowl, Sales Excellence, Paul Revere, Jostens Pewter, 1977	20.00
Award, Figurine, Albee, 1981	65.00
Award, Figurine, Albee, 1982	50.00
Award, Figurine, Albee, 1983	60.00
Award, Figurine, Albee, 1987	60.00
Award, Pitcher, Silver, 35th Anniversary, 1980s	100.00
Award, Plate, 15 Year Anniversary, Avon Rose, Porcelain, Box, 8 1/2 In.	30.00

Award, Plate, 20 Year, First Avon Rep, Porcelain, Box, 8 1/2 In. 40.00
Award, Silver Server, 1963 . . . . 50.00
Bottle, Barber Pole, Wild Country After Shave, c.1974, 3 Oz., 6 3/4 x 2 In. 7.00
Bottle, Cable Car, Leather After Shave, Contents, Box, c.1974, 4 Oz. 11.00
Bottle, Catch-A-Fish, Sonnett Cologne, c.1977, 9 In. 9.00
Bottle, Charlie Brown, Shampoo, Plastic, c.1950, 5 1/2 In. 3.00
Bottle, Christmas Ornament, Glass, Bubble Bath, Red, c.1967, 4 Oz., 4 In. 5.00
Bottle, Christmas Ornament, Glass, Bubble Bath, Silver Color, c.1967, 4 Oz., 4 In. 5.00
Bottle, Cotillion Sachet, Pink Glass, Sprinkle Top, 2 1/2 In. 5.00
Bottle, Elizabethan Fashion Figurine, Moonwind Perfume, Pink, 1972, 4 Oz. 18.00
Bottle, Garden Girl, Charisma Cologne, c.1978, 4 Oz., 6 1/2 In. 6.00
Bottle, Gold Cadillac, Leather After Shave, Contents, Box, 7 1/4 In. 125.00
Bottle, Little Bo Peep, Sweet Honesty Cologne, Contents, Box, 1976, 2 Oz., 5 1/2 In. . . . 5.00
Bottle, Little Bo Peep, Unforgettable Perfume, Contents, Box, 1976, 2 Oz., 5 1/2 In. 12.00
Bottle, Mary Mary, Sweet Honesty Cologne, Contents, Box, 2 Oz., 5 1/2 In. 5.00
Bottle, Occur Cologne, Crystal, Gold Trim, 4 Oz., 5 1/2 x 2 In. 5.00
Bottle, Paid Stamp, Windjammer After Shave, c.1970, 4 Oz., 5 1/4 x 3 1/4 In. 5.00
Bottle, Pheasant, Leather After Shave, Contents, Box 15.00
Bottle, Roll-A-Hoop, Field Flowers Cologne, Contents, Box, c.1977, 3 3/4 Oz., 8 In. 5.00
Bottle, Silver Swirls Saltshaker, Topaz Cologne, Box, c.1978, 3 Oz. 5.00
Bottle, Skin-So-Soft, Contents, Box, 1971, 2 Oz. 5.00
Bottle, Skip-A-Rope, Bird Of Paradise, 1977, 4 Oz., 4 x 7 In. 9.00
Bottle, Snoopy, Bubble Bath, Plastic, c.1969, 5 1/2 In. 3.00
Bottle, Stage Coach, Oland After Shave, 1970-1977, 3 1/2 x 5 1/2 In. . . . . .5.00 to 8.50
Bottle, Stanley Steamer, Windjammer After Shave, c.1971, 5 Oz., 3 x 6 In. 5.00
Chess Set, Board, Full, Box 175.00
Cup & Saucer, Honor Society, Mrs. Albee, Box 25.00
Doll, Cinderella, 1984, 9 1/4 In. 25.00
Doll, Fairy Princess, 1989, 8 1/2 In. 30.00
Doll, Little Red Riding Hood, 1985, 8 1/4 In. 25.00
Doll, Roaring Twenties, 1989, 8 In. 30.00
Organizer, Bureau, American Eagle, Box, 1972 . . . . 35.00
Organizer, Collectors, Duck Shape, Box, 1971 . . . . 35.00
Organizer, Whale, Box, 1973 . . . . 35.00
Plate, Christmas, 1974, Box 35.00
Plate, Christmas, 1975, Box 20.00
Plate, Tenderness, 1974, Box 10.00
Stein, Blacksmith, Ceramic, Pewter Top, Box, 1985, 8 1/2 In. 45.00
Stein, Casey At The Bat, Opaque Glass, 1980, 6 In. 10.00
Stein, Flying Classic, Ceramic, 1981, 9 1/2 In. 10.00
Stein, Iron Horse, Box, 1976-1984 . . . . 25.00
Stein, Racing Car, Box, 1989, 9 1/4 In. 30.00
Stein, Shipbuilder, Ceramic, Pewter Top, Box, 1985, 8 1/2 In. 45.00
Stein, Tall Ships, Box, 1976-1984 . . . . 25.00
Tin, Talcum Powder, Victorian Skating Scene, 25th Anniversary, 5 In. 17.00
Treasure Chest Set, Skin-So-Soft, Cologne, Soap, Contents, Full, Box, 1973 . . . . 35.00

AYER James Cook Ayer received a degree in medicine in 1841. While working in Jacob Robbin's Drug Store in Lowell, Massachusetts, he developed a product called Ayer's Cherry Pectoral. In 1841 the drink, a mixture of morphine, ipecac, assorted herbs, and wild cherry syrup, was advertised as a cure for pulmonary ills. Ayer bought out Robbins and continued developing medicines for drugstores. He marketed Ayer's Sarsaparilla in 1848 and then Cathartic Pills (1854), Ague Cure (1857), and others. He was successful in advertising and selling his products nationally. In 1857 he moved to new headquarters in Lowell. In 1871 the town of Groton Junction, Massachusetts, was renamed Ayer in his honor. Ayer branched out into other ventures, including managing a paper mill that made his wrappers and labels. He also chartered his own railroad line and purchased an interest in sawmills, iron mines, textile mills, and other money-making ventures. Ayer died in 1878, but his family continued to make Ayer's Cherry Pectoral, Ayer's Pills, and other Ayer's products into the 1940s.

Bottle, Ayer's Ague Cure, Aqua, Partial Contents, 7 In. 33.00
Bottle, Ayer's Cathartic Pills, Contents, Package, Unopened, c.1865 .... 339.00
Bottle, Cherry Pectoral, Open Pontil, Aqua 70.00
Bottle, Hair Vigor, Peacock, Stopper 90.00
Sign, Ayer's Cherry Pectoral, Santa Claus, Best Gift To A Friend, Cardboard, 13 x 7 In. .. 413.00
Sign, Ayer's Cherry Pectoral, Santa, Green Coat, Sleigh, Die Cut, Cardboard, 13 x 7 In. .. 770.00
Sign, Ayer's Sarsaparilla, Old Folks At Home, Cardboard, Die Cut, Easel Back, 13 x 7 In. 176.00
Sign, Ayer's Sarsaparilla, The Deacon, Cardboard, Die Cut, Easel Back, 13 x 7 In. 330.00

BAG   Before the Civil War, grocery purchases were wrapped in paper or a poke, a paper cornucopia folded by the clerk. Cotton bags were used for shipping flour, grain, and a few other bulk products. Francis Walle of Bethlehem, Pennsylvania, patented a machine in 1852 that could cut, fold, and paste paper to form a bag. Few stores seemed to care about the paper bag until 1869, when Union Company of Pennsylvania bought all of the U.S. paper bag patents and manufactured a bag-making machine. In 1870 ads for paper bags were appearing in the *American Grocer.* The shopping bag with handles was perfected in 1936, but the "designer" bag was an innovation of the 1960s. Collectors search for these attractive bags and the Smithsonian's Cooper-Hewitt Museum has mounted a traveling exhibition that displays the best of this form of advertising.

Bambino Pinto Bean, Babe Ruth Graphic, Burlap, Mingo, Kansas, 100 Lb. 14.00
Big Jo Flour, Elephant Holding Sack, Cloth, Frame, 23 1/2 x 19 1/2 In. 176.00
Blue Boy, Medium White Beans, Paper, 2 Lb. 6.00
Duluth Flour, Black Chef, Paper, Frame, 16 x 1/2 In. 61.00
Jack Sprat Flour, Color Logo On Both Sides, 98 Lb. 66.00
Pure Food Flour, Paper, 25 Lb., 13 x 22 In. 15.00
Red Star Milling Co. Flour, Sample, 3 x 1 3/4 x 1 1/4 In. 75.00
Texas Pioneer Flour, Sample, Miniature, 3 x 1 3/4 x 1 1/4 In. 75.00

BAKER   John Hannon, a chocolate maker from Ireland, convinced Dr. James Baker to finance a chocolate mill in Dorchester, Massachusetts, in 1765. Dr. Baker began making a chocolate blend named Baker's in 1780. His son, Edmund, joined the company in 1791 and Edmund's son, Walter, started working there in 1818. The business was named the Walter Baker Company in 1824. Its trademark, adopted after 1824, is a copy of *La Belle Chocolatiere,* a 1745 painting of a waitress who married a prince. The painting, one of the first United States trademarks, hangs in a museum in Dresden, Germany. It gained international fame once it was pictured on millions of boxes of chocolate. The Walter Baker Company became part of General Foods Corp. in 1927. After several management changes, the Baker's brand name and trademark are still used by Altria's Kraft Foods Company.

Bookends, Figural, Cocoa Girl, Cast Iron, 5 3/4 x 3 3/4 x 3 1/4 In. 198.00
Box, Breakfast Cocoa, Cardboard, Metal, Pry Lid, 1/2 Lb., 5 x 3 1/8 x 2 1/8 In. 165.00
Box, Deluxe Cocoa, Cardboard, Metal, Pry Lid, 3 1/4 x 2 3/8 x 1 1/4 In. 175.00
Display Jar, Baker's Chocolate, 8 3/4 x 7 In. 150.00
Painting, Oil On Canvas, Woman, Tray, Cup, Glass, Composition Frame, 50 x 38 In. 800.00
Saucer, Instant Cocoa, Restaurant Ware, Roman Numerals Around Edge 15.00
Sign, La Belle Chocolatiere, Tin Lithograph, Self-Framed, 19 x 15 In. 424.00
Tip Tray, Baker's Breakfast Cocoa, Le Chocolatier, Round, Dorchester, Mass., 6 In. 96.00
Tray, Walter Baker & Co. Chocolate, Tin, Oval, 16 x 14 In. 22.00
Tray, Woman Holding Tray, Tin Lithograph, Round, Walter Baker Co., 10 1/4 In. 358.00

BAKING POWDER   The practice of combining acid and alkali to leaven baked goods was common by the time it was first recorded in a 1796 gingerbread recipe. In the 1850s, premixed baking powders became available. Brands such as Rumford, Calumet, and Clabber Girl were developed in an effort to have a more reliable product. Tins and advertising items for these brands and others are available. Related items may be found in the Arm & Hammer, Calumet, and spice categories.

Basket, Sno King, Wire, 17 1/2 x 16 x 25 In. 275.00

Biscuit Cutter, Rumford, Early 1900s 26.00
Biscuit Cutter, Rumford, Metal, 3 x 7/8 x 2 1/2 In. 32.00
Bottle, Sea Gull Baking Powder, Embossed, Label, Cork Sealed, 4 1/2 x 2 1/2 In. 154.00
Box, Elkay, Cardboard, Paper Label, Pour Spout, 5 5/8 x 3 In. 85.00
Box, Keever Starch Co., Contents, Cardboard, 4 1/8 x 3 1/4 x 1 5/8 In. . . 175.00
Box, Rawleigh's Economy Baking Powder, Cardboard, Pry Lid, Sample, 2 3/4 x 1 1/4 In. . 110.00
Calendar, Horsford Baking Powder, 1893, Child On Toboggan, Die Cut, 10 x 8 In. 300.00
Display Rack, Snow King Baking Powder, Tin, Embossed, Collapses, 30 x 18 x 15 In. . . . 440.00
Door Push, Magic Baking Powder, Porcelain, 1920s, 12 In. 468.00
Jar, KC Baking Powder, Metal Lid, Glass Insert, Paper Label 21.00
Rack, Snow King Baking Powder, Tin, Wire, Paper Sack Dispenser 1320.00
Sign, Clabber Girl, Healthy, Baking Powder, Cardboard, 34 x 12 In. 44.00
Sign, Grape-Cream, Boy, Girl, Celluloid Over Cardboard, 10 x 14 In. . . . . *Illus* 1760.00
Sign, Horsford Baking Powder, Self Raising, Cardboard, 12 1/2 x 9 1/2 In. 165.00
Sign, KC Baking Powder, For Better Baking, Red, White, Black, 2-Sided, 26 1/2 x 11 In. . 385.00
Sign, Snow King Baking Powder, Santa, Sleigh, Reindeer, Die Cut, Cardboard, 17 x 27 In. 495.00
Tin, Barbour's Acadia Baking Powder, G.E. Barbour, Saint John, N.H., 5 1/8 x 3 1/4 In. . 80.00
Tin, Blue Ribbon Baking Powder, 5 1/8 x 3 In. 90.00
Tin, Clabber Girl, Paper Label, 1931, 4 x 2 3/4 In. 10.00
Tin, Common Sense Baking Powder, 2 1/2 x 1 5/8 In. 120.00
Tin, Davis Baking Powder, R.B. Davis, Hoboken, N.J., Pry Lid, 1 3/4 x 2 In. 65.00
Tin, Eggo Baking Powder, 5 1/8 x 3 1/8 In. 95.00
Tin, Heekins Pure Baking Powder, Lithograph, No Lid, 27 x 15 In. 88.00
Tin, Jewel Tea Baking Powder, Pry Lid, Contents, 3 x 4 1/2 In. 60.00
Tin, Napolean Baking Powder, Emperor, Paper Label, 5 1/2 x 3 In. 80.00
Tin, Our Baking Powder, Paper Label, Bischoff Bros., 1917, 4 1/2 x 2 1/2 In. 176.00
Tin, Richelieu Brand Baking Powder, Sprague, Warner & Co. 80.00
Tin, Royal Baking Powder, Paper Label, 1/8 Lb., 2 3/4 x 1 1/2 In. 44.00
Tin, Royal Baking Powder, Paper Label, 8 1/4 x 5 1/4 In. 25.00
Tin, Schilling Baking Powder, Paper Label, Push-On Top, 5 x 3 In. 10.00
Tin, Success Baking Powder, Cardboard, Tin Lid, 4 Oz., 3 1/4 x 2 1/4 In. 40.00
Tin, Vision Baking Powder, Paper Label, 25 Oz., 7 x 3 In. . . . . .160.00 to 170.00

BALTIMORE & OHIO, see Railroad

BANK   All types of banks have been used as advertising premiums.
Iron banks from the late nineteenth century, lithographed tin banks from
the early twentieth century, and plastic banks from the mid-twentieth
century are the most popular with collectors.

Amherst Stoves, Bank, Buffalo, Embossed, Cast Iron, 8 In. 550.00
Amoskeag Savings Bank, Manchester, N.H., Tin, Mechanical, 1942, 4 1/4 In. 73.00
Ancostia Federal Savings & Loan, Indian Chief, Bronzed Metal, Washington, D.C., 5 In. . 54.00
Arbide Employees Federal Credit Union, Pig, Bowtie, Jacket, Hat, Plastic, 5 In. 10.00
Arctic Circle Drive In, Figural, Acey, Arctic Circle Chicken, Chalkware, c.1940s, 6 1/2 In. 71.00
B.B. Rice Sausage Co., Pig Shape, Plastic, 9 In. 28.00
Boscul Coffee, Sesquicentennial Celebration, Key Wind, Unopened, 1926, 2 x 2 7/8 In. . . 140.00

Baking Powder,
Sign, Grape-
Cream, Boy, Girl,
Celluloid Over
Cardboard,
10 x 14 In.

Bank, Pizza
Hut, Pizza
Pete, Figural,
Blue Apron, Slot
In Hat, Plastic,
1969, 7 1/2 In.

Bank, Thompson Products,
Indian & Teepee, Pottery, Painted,
TP Logo, c.1950, 6 3/4 In.

C.C. Harvey & Co. Pianos, Clock, 6 In. 132.00
Chase National Bank, Baseball, Tin Lithograph, Box, 3 In. 55.00
Cheesasaurus, Vinyl, 1992, 7 In. 16.00
Chevrolet, Globe Shape, Map Of The World, Tin, 4 3/8 In. 65.00
Chicken Delight Figure, Vinyl, c.1960s, 6 In. 45.00
Chittenden Bank, Pig, Rubber Stopper, Porcelain, Made In USA, 3 1/2 x 6 1/4 In. 9.00
Cities Service, Koolmotor 5D Oil, Tin, 1950-1960, 2 3/4 x 2 In. 15.00
Citizens Savings & Loan, Umbrella, Plastic, Metal, 1950s, 5 In. 13.00
Commerce Bank, C-Shaped Logo, Plastic, Metal, New Jersey, 6 x 6 In. 6.00
Community First, Pig, White, Plastic Stopper, 3 1/2 x 5 1/2 In. 6.00
Compliments Of Economy Foundry & Machine, Pig, Syracuse, Cast Iron, 7 1/4 In. 99.00
Curtis Candy, Plastic, Metal, 5 Cents, Marx Toy Co., 3 3/8 x 2 1/8 x 7 3/8 In. 40.00
Dodge, Switch To Dodge & Save Money, Oil Drum Shape, Red, Tin, 1930s, 3 1/4 In. 76.00
Ever-Ready Blades, Tin, 1 3/4 x 2 x 1 In. 25.00
Eveready Batteries, Black Cat, Union Carbide, 5 1/2 x 8 1/3 In. 29.00
Farmers & Merchants State Bank, New Ulm, Minn., House, Plastic, Metal, 4 x 3 x 3 In. .. 60.00
First Federal Savings & Loan, Rocket, Metal, Astro Mfg., c.1957, 11 In. 374.00
First Federal Savings & Loan, Salt Lake City, Calendar, 2 Coin Slots, 4 x 4 1/4 In. 56.00
Frears, Save Your Money By Shopping At Frears, Santa, Tin, Oval, 3 x 4 1/4 x 1 3/4 In. ... 265.00
Frigidaire, Refrigerator, Metal, 4 x 2 x 1 1/2 In. 84.00
Galaxy Syrup, Space Scout, 8 1/2 x 3 3/8 x 1 7/8 In. 35.00
Harris Trust & Savings Bank, Lion, Spelter, 5 x 6 In. 75.00
HLK Savings, Glass, Leather Lid, Watch Money, Climb Ladder, Montreal, 4 x 3 In. 30.00
Independent Bank, California, Mercury Space Capsule, Plastic, Gold, c.1965, 5 In. 104.00
Indian Head National Bank, Grandfather Clock, White Metal Cast, 7 1/2 In. 77.00
Knicker Bocker Hound, Head Pulls Up, 9 3/4 In. 65.00
Light Reading Premium Beer, 12 Oz., 5 In. 17.00
Monarch Paints, 2 1/4 x 2 1/8 In. 95.00
MoorMans, Pig, 4 1/4 x 4 In. 45.00
Mutual Federal Savings & Loan Association, Penny, Cardboard, Metal Caps, 3 1/2 In. 13.50
Nash-Underwood Prepared Mustard, Lucky Joe, Figural, Tin, Screw Lid, 4 1/2 In. ..30.00 to 67.00
National City Bank, Umbrella, Paper Label, Tin, 3 13/16 x 2 7/16 In. 20.00
National City Bank Of Cleveland, Tin, Paper Label, Stopper, 4 x 3 In. 20.00
Nestle, Hot Cocoa Mix, White Plains, N.Y., 5 1/2 x 3 1/2 x 2 1/4 In. 12.00
Nestle, Treasure Chest, 6 x 5 1/4 x 3 In. 8.00
New Revised Encyclopedia, 10 Cents A Day, Bookcase, Tin Lithograph, 5 In. 187.00
New York Life Insurance Company, Calendar, Bank Building, Celluloid, Metal, 1940s ... 34.00
Norco Foundry, Buy At Norco & Save, Pottstown, Pa., Pig, Cast Iron, 6 x 3 In. 150.00
Peoples Drug Stores, See Your Savings Daily, Glass Clock, 4 3/4 x 4 3/4 x 3 1/4 In. 62.00
Peoples National Bank, Satellite, Rocket On Globe, Metal, Duro Mold, 1950s, 10 In. 322.00
Pilot Life Insurance Co., Ship Captain At Wheel, Mechanical, Pot Metal, Bronzed, 6 In. . 73.00
Pizza Hut, Pizza Pete, Figural, Blue Apron, Slot In Hat, Plastic, 1969, 7 1/2 In. .... *Illus* 42.00
Planter's Bank, Sikeston, Mo., Strato Bank, Rocket, Moon, Duro Mold, 1950s, 7 x 3 In. . 207.00
Prepared Battleship Mustard, Glass Jar, Screw-On Lid, Wm. S. Scull Co., Dayton, Ohio 36.00
Reliance Savings & Loan, Treasure Chest, Tin, 3 1/2 In. 11.00
Rex, Cleveland Heater Co., Water Heater Shape, Tin Lithograph, 7 3/4 In. 77.00
Security Safe Deposit, Cast Iron, Keyser & Rex, 3 3/4 x 2 3/4 x 2 1/2 In. 99.00
Service Savings & Loan Assn., Detroit, Mich., Banthrico, Umbrella, Box 27.00
Shell Motor Oil, Die Cast Metal, Red, Yellow, Gold Trim, Gearbox Toy, Box 34.00
Shenandoah Caverns, Virginia, Donkey, White Metal Cast, 5 1/2 In. 154.00
State Mutual Savings, Los Angeles, Freedom 7 Space Capsule, Plastic, Silver, 1961, 5 In. 104.00
Stoney Haven Hotel, Pig, Cast Iron, Red Eyes, Embossed, New Paint, 3 In. 33.00
Thompson Products, Indian & Teepee, Pottery, Painted, TP Logo, c.1950, 6 3/4 In. . *Illus* 101.00
Thurmont Bank, Mrs. Claus, Felt Apron, Plastic, Frederick, Md., Late 1960, 9 x 4 1/4 In. 10.00
Twinkie, Shoes, Paper Label, Cardboard, Tin Top & Bottom, 2 1/8 x 2 1/4 x 1 3/8 In. 185.00
Unity Building & Loan, Slots For Each Coin, Chrome Plated Steel, Oval, Box, 4 In. 28.00
Universal Stoves & Ranges, Globe, 4 x 3 1/2 In. 715.00
Wonder Bread, Plastic Wrapped Bread Loaf, Colored Dots, Slogan, 1 3/4 x 1 3/4 x 4 In. . 35.00
Woods Syrup, Tin, 2 1/4 x 2 3/8 In. 85.00

BANNER All types of products and companies have been advertised
with this specialized type of cloth sign. See related items under Sign.

Atlantic Motor Oil, Aviation, 100% Pennsylvania Oil, Canvas, 36 x 26 In. 88.00

Don't open a collectible beer can from the top. Leave the pull tab intact and open the can from the bottom using a standard punch-type opener.

Banner, Pure Gold
Lemons, Mutual
Orange Distributors,
Cal., 10 1/2 In.

Cletrac Tank-Type Tractor, Cleveland Tractor Co., Canvas, 33 x 92 In. 3300.00
Crystal White Soap, The Perfect Family, Canvas, 41 x 118 In. 154.00
Dee-Cee, Western Wear, Denim, Blue, Red, Yellow, 36 x 46 In. 110.00
Interwoven Socks For Christmas, Lithograph, Cloth, Mat, Frame, 17 x 42 In. 136.00
Leg Liberty Makes For Better Sports, Helen Wills, Tennis, Cotton, 33 1/2 x 45 1/4 In. . . 1955.00
Maverick Denim Jeans, Bell Bottoms, Unconditionally Guaranteed, 40 x 72 In. 110.00
Pierce Cycles, Geo. N. Pierce Co., Woman On Bike, Bull, Roll Down, 87 1/2 x 41 1/2 In. 4400.00
Pure Gold Lemons, Mutual Orange Distributors, Cal., 10 1/2 In. . . . . *Illus* 10.00
Walter A. Wood Binder, Frame, c.1880, 12 x 14 3/4 In. 330.00
Who's Your Druggist?, Hang On For Pure Drugs, Silk Screened, Ithaca, N.Y., 49 x 37 In. . 489.00
Will Rogers, Irvin S. Cobb, Gulf, N.B.C., Columbia Network, Cloth, 30 x 66 In. 413.00

BARREL   Barrels were used by the Romans as early as A.D. 300. Since then wooden barrels have been used to store and ship all types of consumer goods, as well as to age wine and other alcoholic beverages. Those with applied brand names and logos are listed here.

Bull Meat Brand Flour, Paper Ads, Oak, 32 1/2 x 22 1/2 In. 230.00
Columbian Hog & Cattle Powder, Wood, 25 In. 28.00
Fresh Fish, Lay Bros., Sandusky, Ohio, 36 In. 165.00
Knight's Sweet Pickles, Wood, 24 In. 118.00
Old Doc Brox Horehound Drops, Cardboard, Round, 1936, 25 Lb. 44.00
Tones Bro's. Coffee, No. 3, Lid, Des Moines, Iowa, Shipping, 25 x 15 1/2 In. 55.00
Wood's Mince Meat Barrel, Paper Label, Painted Wood, Wood Bail Handle, 12 In. 121.00

BEECH-NUT TOBACCO, see Lorillard

BEER   Everything connected with beer is collected, including cans and bottles, which are listed in their own categories. Signs are listed here or by brand name. Trays are listed under Tray or by brand, tip trays under Tip Tray or by brand, and openers with Bottles. Breweriana publications and shows may have the collectible you seek. Even if a show is listed as a bottle show, you will find dealers there selling other small beer advertising collectibles.

Ashtray, Aristocrat Brewery, Tin Lithograph, Round, 4 1/2 In. 33.00
Ashtray, Figural, Labatt's Schmiley Figure, White, Ceramic, c.1960s, 3 x 4 x 3/4 In. 24.00
Ashtray, Huntsman Ale, A Good Square Drink, Yellow Ground, 4 x 5 1/4 In. 91.00
Bag, Charrington, Plus Four, 4 Beer Can Size, Paper, 14 In. 4.00
Booklet, Stroh Brewing Co., Products, Testimonials, c.1893, 6 3/4 x 7 3/4 In. 98.00
Bottle Holder, Elf, Piels Beer, Spelter, 9 x 9 In. 99.00
Box, Dick Bros. Beer, Hinged Lid, Wood, Metal Corners, Quincy, Ill., 11 1/2 x 20 1/2 In. . 49.00
Box, Heilman Brewing Co., LaCrosse, Wisc., Hinged Lid, Wood, Metal, 11 x 21 In. 24.00
Button & Clicker, Lyon's Beer, I Chirp For, Lion, Bug Shaped Clicker, Celluloid, 1 In. . . 149.00
Case, Jacob Schmidt, Wood, St. Paul, Minn. 50.00
Charger, Bartels Brewing Co., Woman, Bonnet, Flowers, Tin Lithograph, Round, 17 1/2 In. 413.00
Charger, Bartels Brewing Co., Woman, Yellow Hair, Scarf, Tin Lithograph, 17 1/2 In. . . . 226.00
Charger, Champagne Velvet Beer, Terre Haute Brewing, Tin Lithograph, Round, 24 In. . . 248.00
Clicker, Fort Pitt, 1 7/8 x 7/8 In. 55.00
Clock, Iroquois, Beer, Ale, Light-Up, Double Bubble, Round, 16 In. 578.00

Clock, Pearl Beer, Octagonal, Neon, 18 1/2 In. . . . . .358.00 to 468.00
Clock, Reading Premium, Friendly Beer For Modern People, Glass Lens, Round, 15 In. 154.00
Cuff Links & Tie Tack, Miss Reingold Beer, Gold Color, Enamel Skirt, Figural, Case 40.00
Cup, Fehr's, Metal, Handle, Cone Top, Frank Fehr Brewing, Louisville, Ky., 4 1/4 In. 95.00
Display, Grolsch Holland Beer, Dutch Girl & Boy, Vinyl, 1970s, 9 1/2 x 5 x 11 In. 60.00
Display, Heineken Holland Beer, Shoe, Wood, 3 3/4 x 9 x 4 In. 16.00
Figure, Boxer Ales, Sid, Boxing Trainer, Rubberoid, Black Base, England, 7 1/2 In. 303.00
Figure, Courage, Brewers Since 1787, Rooster, Heavy Metal, Oblong Base, 12 1/2 In. . . . 222.00
Figure, Drewrys Beer, Mounty, Beer Bottle, Chalkware, 7 In. 50.00
Figure, Frankenmuth Beer, Ale, Dog, Dachshund, Plaster, c.1930s, 4 x 7 x 6 In. 50.00
Figure, Fremlin's Beers, Elephant, Plastic, Gray, Red Sash, England, 5 1/2 In. . . . . .75.00 to 132.00
Figure, Heineken, Dutch Man Smoking Pipe, Heineken Bottle, Ceramic, 19 x 14 In. 44.00
Figure, Horse, Cart, Couple, Old Shay Beer & Ale, Fort Pitt Brewing, 13 1/4 x 11 1/2 In. . . 110.00
Figure, Huntsman Ales, Fox Hunter, Monocle, Holding Glass, England, 7 1/4 In. 95.00
Figure, Johnny Fifer, Plaster, Plasto Manufacturing, c.1950s, 7 1/4 x 4 In. 60.00
Figure, Labatt's Pilsener, Hollow Barrel, 1960s, 3 1/4 x 5 1/2 x 9 1/2 In. 24.00
Figure, Lowenbrau, Lion, Holding Bottle Of Beer, Gold, Composition, 17 In. 55.00
Figure, Lowenbrau, Wagon, Rubber Horses & Figures, Wood Wagon & Barrels, 48 In. . . . 193.00
Figure, M&B Marvellous Beer, Stag, Leaping, 9 1/2 In. 91.00
Figure, McEwans, Cavalier, Best Buy In Beer, Rubberoid, Black Base, 10 In. 91.00
Figure, Oertel's, Owl Holding Bottle, 14 1/2 x 8 In. 250.00
Figure, Oertel's, Snowman Holding Bottle, Louisville, Kentucky 295.00
Figure, Pfeiffer's Beer, Johnny Fifer, Chalkware, 7 In. 77.00
Figure, Pfeiffer's Beer, Man Playing Flute, Red Coat, Ceramic, Countertop, 8 In. 22.00
Figure, Schmidt's Beer, Waiter Holding 2 Beer Mugs, Ceramic, Countertop, 12 1/2 In. . . . 39.00
Figure, Schmidt's Beer, Waiter Holding 2 Beer Mugs, Pot Metal, Countertop, 8 1/2 In. . . . 118.00
Figure, Truman's, Brewers Of Good Beer For Over 300 Years, Pirate, Rubberoid, 7 In. . . . 101.00
Figure, William Younger, Man, Pint, Get Younger Every Day, Rubberoid, 9 In. . . . . . .65.00 to 91.00
Figure, Worthington E, Large E As Bar, 2 Men Drinking, Ceramic, England, 9 In. 303.00 to 359.00
Figure, Worthington E, Large E, Man & Woman, Ceramic, Beswick, England, 9 In. 162.00
Foam Scraper, Fort Pitt Beer, That's It, Red, White 45.00
Foam Scraper, Golden Glow Beer, Black, White 60.00
Keg, Storz Beer, Oak, Wood Spigot, Omaha, Nebraska, 20 In. 132.00
Label, Amberlite, Temperance Beer, Serve Ice Cold, Fresno Brewing Co., Calif., Paper . . 18.00
Label, La Boheme Beverage, Eilert Products Co., Fresno, Calif., Paper 26.00
Map, Crocker's Guide To San Francisco, 1896, 28 x 23 In. 110.00
Mug, Fred Sehring Brewing Co., Joliet, Ill., 1904, 2 1/4 In. 174.00
Mug, Gesundheit Beer, Yellowware, Altes Rathaus Muenchen, 1930s, 5 x 3 1/4 In. 12.00
Mug, Gluek's Beer, Minnesota, 4 3/4 In. 35.00
Mug, South Bend Brewing Association, Factory Scene, Mettlach, 4 1/2 In. 139.00
Poster, Bock Beer, Indianapolis Brewing Co., Lady With Goats, 29 x 10 1/2 In. 495.00
Poster, Capitol Beer, Be Modern In The Beer You Drink, Lithograph, 22 3/4 x 17 In. 150.00
Sign, A-1 Pilsner, Cowboy Dreams, Clouds, Cardboard, Wood Frame, 26 x 38 In. 50.00
Sign, Alpen Brau, Light-Up, 16 1/2 x 6 3/4 In. 275.00
Sign, Altes Lager, Beer In The Green Bottle, Woman Hugging Dog, 28 x 22 In. 220.00
Sign, Banks's Traditional Draught Beers, White, Green, Yellow, England, 25 x 20 1/2 In. . 19.00
Sign, Barley Mow Ales & Stout, Taylor Walker Crate, Tin, Wood Frame, 29 x 21 1/2 In. . . 738.00
Sign, Bartels Beer, Blue, White, Tin Lithograph, Round, Self-Framed, 18 1/4 In. 286.00
Sign, Becker Brewing Co., Bismarck Beer, Reverse On Glass, Convex, Oval, 20 x 16 In. . 1438.00
Sign, Beverwyck Wuerzburger Brand, King Holding Beer Mug, Tin, Cardboard, 14 x 9 In. 440.00
Sign, Blue Ribbon Malt Co., Chicago Cubs' Photographs, Frame, 1930, 11 1/2 x 38 In. . . . 275.00
Sign, Buckeye Beer, On Draught Here, Tin, Embossed, Self-Framed, 2 3/4 x 13 1/2 In. . . . 99.00
Sign, Buffalo Brewing Co., Bottles, Tankard, Table, Tin, Self-Framed, 22 x 28 In. 495.00 to 523.00
Sign, Bull's Eye Beer, Golden West Brewing Co., Red, White, Blue, Porcelain, 18 x 18 In. 575.00
Sign, Bunker Hill Breweries, Owl Musty, PB Ale, Cardboard, 1906, 14 In. 250.00
Sign, Burger Bohemian, Men Fishing, Bucket Of Beer, Tin, Self-Framed, 20 1/2 In. 104.00
Sign, Burger Brewing, Vas You Efer In Zinzinnati, Light-Up, Frame, Glass Front, 8 x 25 In. 55.00
Sign, Burgermeister, Premium Beer, Embossed Tin, 14 1/2 x 28 In. 231.00
Sign, Burtonwood Ales, Man In Top Hat, Wood, England, Frame, 23 x 18 In. 104.00
Sign, Carlsberg Pilsner, Hof, Tin Over Cardboard, Embossed, 13 x 9 In. 135.00
Sign, Centlivre Beer, Black Porter, Couple On Train, Nickel Plate, 24 x 20 In. . . . . . .358.00 to 605.00
Sign, Centlivre Brewing Co., Factory, Paper Lithograph, Mat, Frame, 29 x 40 In. 468.00
Sign, Centlivre Brewing Co., Lithograph, Ft. Wayne, Ind., Factory, Frame, 23 x 36 In. . . . 440.00

Sign, Champagne Velvet, 2 Men In Boat, Tin Over Cardboard, 14 x 19 In. . . . . . . .220.00 to 330.00
Sign, Champagne Velvet, Man With Box, Skunks, Million Dollar Flavor, Tin, 14 x 19 In. . .   330.00
Sign, Champagne Velvet, Man With Fishing Net, Tin Over Cardboard, 14 x 19 In. 358.00
Sign, Champagne Velvet, Men Sitting At Table, Tin, Hy Hintermeister, 14 x 19 In. 248.00
Sign, Cincinnati Burger Brau Beer, Tin, Embossed, 9 1/2 x 13 1/2 In. 220.00
Sign, Columbian Extra Pale Bottled Beer, Tin Lithograph, Embossed, 14 x 10 In. . .250.00 to 385.00
Sign, Cook's Beer & Ale, 7 Bottles, Tin, Oval, 17 1/2 x 13 3/4 In. 138.00
Sign, Cook's Beer, Paperboard, F.W. Cook Co., Evansville, In., c.1915, 11 x 28 In. 55.00
Sign, Cook's Beer, Quality Cargo, Tin Lithograph, Frame, 30 x 23 In. 143.00
Sign, Cook's Goldblume Beer & Ale, 2 Bottles, Tin Over Cardboard, 8 1/2 x 19 In. 138.00
Sign, Cook's Goldblume Beer, Best Beer On Earth, Tin, Die Cut Bottle, 40 x 11 1/4 In. . .   440.00
Sign, Cook's, De Boss Sho' Likes His Cook's, Tin Over Cardboard, 13 x 21 In. 605.00
Sign, Cook's, Preferred Since The Old Days, Policeman In Traffic, Tin, 13 x 21 In. 121.00
Sign, Country Club, Famous Since Days Of The Pony Express, Copper, 11 x 13 1/2 In. . .   61.00
Sign, Country Club, Flavor Blended, Painted Glass, Die Cut Bottle, 33 x 13 In. 220.00
Sign, Drewrys, Ale, Beer, Horseshoe, Mountie, Horse, Die Cut, Composition, 15 x 10 In. .   110.00
Sign, Drewrys, Ale, Beer, Thrill Of A Lifetime, 2 Men, Canoe, Tin Lithograph, 23 x 17 In.   146.00
Sign, E & O Pilsener, Pittsburgh Brewing Co., Tin Over Cardboard, 9 x 11 In. 55.00
Sign, Eberhardt & Ober Brewing Co., Buildings, Print, Frame, 36 x 50 In. 1155.00
Sign, Eigenbrot Brewery, Baltimore, Md., Tin Lithograph, 20 1/2 x 14 1/2 x 2 5/8 In. 440.00
Sign, Emmerling Brewing Co., Grossvader German Beer, Tin Lithograph, 14 3/4 x 12 In. .   303.00
Sign, English Fullers Beer, Independent Family Brewers, Porcelain, 21 x 25 In. 165.00
Sign, Esquire Beer, 2-Color Neon, Late 1940s, 13 x 26 In. 170.00
Sign, Esslinger's, Ale, Beer, Little Man Holding Tray, Tin, 58 x 34 In. 480.00
Sign, Excelsior Beer, Bottle, Celluloid Over Cardboard, 13 x 9 1/2 In. 72.00
Sign, Falls City Brewery, Woman, Gloves, Frame, 44 x 33 In. 275.00
Sign, Famous Beer, On Tap, Black, Red, White, Porcelain, 42 1/2 x 30 In. 550.00
Sign, Fell Beer, Superior Quality, Tin, Round, c.1930, 14 In. 776.00
Sign, Fred Koch Brewery, Wood, Old Couple Eating & Drinking, 15 x 21 In. 495.00
Sign, Genesee Beer, Horse Team, Wagon, Lithograph, Frame, 22 x 13 In. 55.00
Sign, Geo. Walter's Appleton Beer, Waiter, Tin Over Cardboard, 9 x 12 3/4 In. 110.00
Sign, Gettelman, 2 Bears, Fiberboard, Embossed, Metal Frame, 10 1/2 x 16 1/2 In. 165.00
Sign, Gibbons, Tin Lithograph, Cardboard, Easel Back, String Hanger, 11 1/4 x 7 3/8 In. . .   138.00
Sign, Goebel Bantam, In The Original Bantam Bottle, Tin Over Cardboard, 14 x 10 In. 138.00
Sign, Goetz Country Club, Beer Glass, Tin, Embossed, 39 1/2 x 13 1/2 In. 330.00
Sign, Grossvater Beer, 5 Men, Drinking, Around Table, Tin Lithograph, 12 x 14 1/2 In. . . .   113.00
Sign, Harvard Brewery, Chromolithograph, Mat, Frame, 35 x 27 In. 440.00
Sign, Hoffman Brewing, Roses, Cigar, Paper Lithograph, c.1900, 26 x 23 In. . . . . .219.00 to 385.00
Sign, Hunt's Prize Medal Ales, 3 Servicemen, England, Frame, 33 x 23 1/2 In. 870.00
Sign, Ind Coope's, Double Diamond, Beer Label, Green Ground, Frame, 32 x 17 In. 95.00
Sign, Jax, Drink Jax Bottled Beer, General Jax On Rearing Horse, Composition, 8 x 18 In.   143.00
Sign, John Gund Brewing Co., Wisconsin Deer Hunt, Tin Lithograph, Frame, 21 x 26 In. . 1045.00
Sign, John Smith's Tadcaster Brewery, Green, Magnet, Enamel, England, 41 x 31 In. 47.00
Sign, Kamm & Schellinger Brewing Co., Lithograph, Frame, 26 x 27 In. 578.00
Sign, Koch's Deer Run Ale, Tin, Cardboard, 13 x 9 In. 105.00
Sign, Krueger Beer Sales, Celluloid, Tin, Cardboard, Chain Hung, 5 1/2 x 13 In. 123.00
Sign, Krueger Cream Ale, Tin Lithograph Over Cardboard, 5 3/4 x 13 In. 140.00
Sign, L. Hoster Brewery, Monk, Man, On Keg, Tin Lithograph, 1880-1900, 20 x 17 In. 88.00
Sign, Lowenbrau Beer, Gold Stylized Lion, Border, Light-Up, Plastic Cover, 18 x 15 1/2 In.   30.00
Sign, Lowenbrau, Munich, Standing Lion, Shield Shape, Die Cut, Porcelain, 14 x 11 In. . . .   77.00
Sign, Marathon Beer, Fisherman, Signed, J.F. Kernan Artwork, Frame, 15 1/2 x 24 In. . . .   50.00
Sign, Muehlebach's Pilsener, 3 Gentlemen, Cardboard, 20 x 24 In. 55.00
Sign, National Bohemian, Oh Boy What A Beer, Reverse Glass, Light-Up, 14 In. Diam. . . .   578.00
Sign, National Brewing Co., 2 Women, Lute, Tin Lithograph, Self-Framed, 23 x 17 In. 2530.00
Sign, New England Brewing Co., Superior Ales, Lager, Hunting Scene, Hartford, 33 x 23 In. 2750.00
Sign, Northern Beer, Tin Over Cardboard, Superior, Wisconsin, 6 x 13 In. 61.00
Sign, Old Export Beer, Cumberland Brewery, 3 Fishermen, Self-Framed, 15 3/4 x 20 In. . .   880.00
Sign, Old Export Beer, Cumberland Brewing Co., Tin Lithograph, 42 In. 121.00
Sign, Openshaw Brewery House, Glass, Recessed Letters, Yellow, England, 18 x 12 In. . .   76.00
Sign, Pearl Lager Beer Distributor, Plastic, 2-Sided, Light-Up, 40 x 49 In. 165.00
Sign, Peter Schoenhofen Brewing, Chicago, Paper Lithograph, Frame, c.1890, 20 x 25 In. .   413.00
Sign, Pfeiffer Beer, Derby, Race Horse, Jockey, Tin, Self-Framed, 18 x 14 In. 242.00

Sign, Pickwick Ale, Ale That Is Ale, Horses, Beer Barrels, Tin, 6 1/2 x 23 In. 94.00
Sign, Prince Pilsen, America's Finest Beer, Glass, Reverse Painted, 12 x 10 In. 110.00
Sign, Red Dog, Neon, 33 x 12 In. 83.00
Sign, Rheingold Extra Dry Lager Beer, Porcelain, 23 x 19 In. 83.00
Sign, Russells' Ales, From The Country, 2 Brewers, Barrels, Tin, Self-Framed, 29 x 21 In. 110.00
Sign, Russells' Ales, Men Unloading Kegs, Tin, Self-Framed, 21 x 29 In. 413.00
Sign, Schell's Beer, Die Cut, Cardboard, Menu Board, 12 x 9 In. 25.00
Sign, Schmidt's City Club, Celluloid, Round, 9 In. 138.00
Sign, Schmidt's City Club, Served Cold In Bottles, Bottle, Tin, Embossed, 54 x 18 In. . . . 1100.00
Sign, Silver Spring Brewery, Fireman, Life Saver, Victoria, B.C., Paper, Round, 19 In. . . . 132.00
Sign, Stag Beer, Sportsman Scene, Light-Up, Plastic Cover, Frame, 17 x 25 In. 65.00
Sign, Sterling Ale, Clock Shape, Movable Hands, Tin, Cast Iron, 1914, 18 In. Diam. 880.00
Sign, Sterling Super-Bru, Leisurely Aged, Always, Trapezoid Shape, 17 1/2 x 9 In. .330.00 to 495.00
Sign, Sunshine Beer, 3 Triple Crown Winners, Paper, Frame, 27 x 34 In. 275.00
Sign, Tech Beer, Tin Lithograph, c.1950, 35 x 54 In. 140.00
Sign, Tennent's Lager, Beer At The Best, Man Pouring Bottle, Tin, 12 x 8 In. 121.00
Sign, Tivoli Select Pale Beer, Horse, Horseman, Tin, Self-Framed, 28 x 22 In. 220.00
Sign, Toby Ale, Tin Over Cardboard, Self-Framed, 14 3/4 x 21 In. 99.00
Sign, Walter Beer, Curved Glass, Enamel, Frame, Eau Claire, Wis., 22 1/2 x 16 x 4 1/4 In. 1210.00
Sign, West End Brewery Co., 2 Children, On Bench, Lithograph, 17 1/2 x 13 3/4 In. 300.00
Sign, West End Utica Beer, Reverse Glass, Crimped Metal Frame, 18 x 4 1/2 In. 1661.00
Sign, Whitbread's London Stout, Beer Bottle, Deer Head, Frame, 21 1/2 x 15 1/2 In. 95.00
Sign, White Ribbon Beer, 2 Seated Men, Dog, Meek & Co., Tin, Self-Framed, 20 x 24 In. 633.00
Sign, Wiedmann's Beer, Man Reading Newspaper, Children, Tin, Die Cut, 14 x 9 3/4 In. . . 605.00
Sign, Wieland's Pale Lager, Indian Girl, Tin Lithograph, Self-Framed, 1901, 17 In. Diam. . 4840.00
Sign, William Gerst Brewing Co., Nashville, Tenn., Paper Lithograph, Frame, 40 x 27 In. . 4300.00
Sign, Yuengling's Beer, Reverse Glass, Round, 24 In. 2200.00
Tap Knob, Ranier Brewing Co., Inc., San Francisco, Cal. 175.00
Tray, see Tray category or brand name
Tumbler, Christian Moerlein Brewing, Standard Of Purity, Etched, Cincinnati, 4 In. 83.00
Tumbler, Detroit Brewing Co.'s Bohemian, Raised Letters, 4 In. 55.00
Tumbler, F.W. Cook Brewing, Goldblume, Factory Scene, Etched, Evansville, Ind., 4 In. . . 139.00
Tumbler, Home Brewing & Ice Co., Meddle West, That's The Beer, Joplin, Mo., 3 1/2 In. 55.00
Tumbler, Lion Brewery Export, Raised Letters, Cincinnati, 1890-1910, 5 1/2 In. 45.00
Tumbler, Siebert Prst. Salvator, Lebanon Brewing, Enamel, 1893-1920, 6 5/8 In. 280.00
Tumbler, W.J. Lemp, Brewing Co., Man, Top Hat, Etched Shell, St. Louis, Mo., 3 1/2 In. . 110.00
Tumbler, Walter's Beer, 5 Cents, 6 1/2 In. 66.00
Tumbler, Wiedmann's Fine Beer, Enamel, GAR Souvenir, c.1898, 3 3/4 In. 448.00

BEER BOTTLE   Beer was sold almost exclusively in kegs until the late nineteenth century. Bottling beer became more safe and practical after 1876, when Louis Pasteur of France discovered how to control the fermentation and spoilage of beer using heat, a process known as pasteurization. But in the United States, brewed beverages were taxed by the barrel and bottling was not allowed in brewery buildings. Many breweries could not afford to build a second structure, so bottling was done mostly by private bottlers. In 1890 U.S. tax law changed; beer could be bottled in breweries, and bottled beer became widely available. Collectors search for blob tops, the bottles made before the crown stopper. They want unusual colors and embossed city or brewery names. Condition is important, but many collectors literally dig bottles out of old dumps, so discoloration is not a major concern. Bottle caps, paper labels, and other features add to the value of later bottles. There are many beer and brewery collectibles. They can be found at advertising shows, bottle shows, swap meets, flea markets, and antiques shops.

Acme Brewing, Glass, Oversize, 31 In. 83.00
Cornbrook Brewery, Manchester, Relief Logo, Amber, Early 1900s, 8 1/4 In. 30.00
Dr. Cronk Gibbons & Co., Superior Ale, Buffalo, N.Y., Green, Pontil, 1840-1860, 6 1/2 In. 728.00
H. Ingermann's, XXX Ale, Cambridge City, Ind., Amber, 1880-1890, 9 1/4 In. 168.00
John Lyon, Manchester, Fluted Neck, Dark Green, Early 1900s, 9 1/4 In. 30.00
Lucky Lager, Cap, 1936, Qt. 12.00

Nude Beer Golden Beverage Co., Wilkes-Barre, Brunette In Bikini, Unopened, 12 Oz. 15.00
P.E. Cumaer Trademark, Port Jervis, N.Y., Blob, Aqua, Qt. 19.00
Peerless Beer, Gnome, 12 Oz., 9 5/8 In. 15.00
Phipps Brewers, Northampton, Moss Green, Screw Cap, Early 1900s, 9 In. 30.00
R.W. & S. White Ltd., Screw Top, Riley's Patent W, Dark Green, 9 x 2 1/2 In. 30.00
Red Top Beer, Ferd. Westheimer & Sons, Cincinnati, Ohio, St. Joseph, Mo., 4 1/4 In. 83.00
Saltzmann Palace Hill Brewery, Oil City, Pa., Blob, Amber 8.00
Schmulback Brewing Co., Bird Type Monogram, Amber, Tall 5.00
Texas Three Rivers Glass Company, Clear, Cap, 1922-1937 . . . .   40.00
W. Simpson Ltd, Newcastle-On-Tyne, Embossed Logo, Stopper, Moss Green, 9 1/2 In. . .   30.00

BEER CAN   The first successful can to hold beer without affecting its flavor was made in 1935. The G. Krueger Brewing Company of Newark, New Jersey, began selling beer early that year in flat-top cans made by the American Can Company. By July 1935 Pabst was selling beer in a can, and later the same year Schlitz was using a cone-top can. The cone-top can looked like a bottle and could be opened without an opener. It remained popular until the late 1950s, when the aluminum can was introduced. The lift-top aluminum can was first made in the late 1950s and the tab top in 1962. Tin-free steel cans were made after 1965. The two-piece can—a seamless cylinder with a concave bottom to which the top was attached after filling—was introduced in the 1970s. Because of the variety of cans available, old and new United States, Canadian, and foreign cans are desired. Collectors should open beer cans from the bottom, leaving the top tab in place. Cans should be in good condition with no rust or dents. See also Anheuser-Busch, Blatz, Carling, Coors, Falstaff, Miller, Pabst, and Schlitz.

Alpine Lager, Pull Tab, England, 15 1/2 Oz. 10.00
Asahi, Pull Tab, Tokyo, Japan, 12 Oz. 3.50
Boddingtons Pub Ale Draught, Aluminum, Manchester, England, 16 Oz. 5.00
Bohemian, Pull Tab, Huber Breweries, Monroe, Wisc., 12 Oz. 5.00
Brador Molson Malt Liquor, Pull Tab, 12 Oz. 10.00
Braumeister, Aluminum, Pull Tab, 12 Oz. 2.50
Brown Derby, Aluminum, Pull Tab, Pearl Brewing Co., 12 Oz. 5.00
Carlsberg, Pull Tab, La Brasserie O'Keefe Limitee, Montreal, Quebec, 12 Oz. 10.00
Cerveza Tecate, Pull Tab, Mexico, 12 Oz. 11.00
Champagne Velvet, Aluminum, Pull Tab, 12 Oz. 2.50
Champale Malt Liquor, Aluminum, Pull Tab, 12 Oz. 5.00
Cold Spring, Minnesota, 12 Oz. 5.00
Colt 45 Malt Liquor, Pull Tab, 12 Oz. 9.00
Columbia, Aluminum, Pull Tab, 12 Oz. 3.00
Corona, Puerto Rico, Aluminum, Pull Tab, 10 Oz. 2.50
Duquesne Bavarian, Pull Tab, 12 Oz. 2.50
Esquire, Aluminum, Pull Tab, 12 Oz. 3.50
Fehr's, Beer Can Mug, 1940, 12 Oz., 4 1/2 In. 94.00
Fehr's, Cone Top, Frank Fehr Brewing Co., Louisville, Kentucky, 5 In. 55.00
Foster's Lager, Pull Tab, Carlton & United Breweries, Australia, Qt. . . . . .13.00 to 16.00
Fox Deluxe, Aluminum, Pull Tab, Cold Spring Breweries, Minn., 12 Oz. 5.00
Gambrinus Gold, Aluminum, 12 Oz. 4.00
Genessee Cream Ale, Aluminum, Pull Tab, Rochester, N.Y., 12 Oz. 2.50
Heiliman's Old Style Lager, LaCrosse, Wis., Shield, Cone Top 943.00
Heineken Lager, Aluminum, Pull Tab, 10 Oz. 2.50
Hudepohl Pure Grain Beer, Commemorative, Reds, 76 World Champions 3.85
Iron City Beer, 1979 Pirates Champions, Pull Tab, 12 Oz. 14.95
Iron City Beer, Steeler Defense, Football Players Signatures, Aluminum, 12 Oz. 9.95
Iron City Beer, Steelers Super Bowl, Aluminum, Pull Tab, 1975, 12 Oz. 14.95
John Courage Ale, Pull Tab, England, 12 Oz. 9.90
John Labbatt's Extra Stock, Tin, 1978 . . . .   2.69
JR Ewing's Private Stock, Pull Tab, Pearl Brewing Co., San Antonio, 11.6 Oz. 9.00
Karjala Finnish, Pull Tab, Finland, 15.2 Oz. 10.00
Kirin, Aluminum, New Tab, Japan, 12 Oz. 2.50
Koehler, Pull Tab, Erie Brewing, Pa., 12 Oz. 5.00

Labatt Pilsner, Aluminum, Pull Tab, 12 Oz. 9.00
Light Reading Premium Beer, Blue Mountain Water, Pop Top 4.00
Lion Lager African, Pull Tab, Ohlsson's Cape Breweries, South Africa, 340 Ml 22.00
Lord Chesterfield Ale, Tin, 1970s 4.29
Lucky Salutes U.S.A. Bicentennial, Aluminum, 1976 .... 1.79
Mark V, Aluminum, Pull Tab, Pittsburgh Brewing Company, 12 Oz. 5.00
Medalia Premium, Aluminum, Pull Tab, Puerto Rico, 10 Oz. 2.50
Mickey's, Pull Tab, 12 Oz. 2.50
Mickey's Malt Liquor, Pull Tab, Heileman Brewing, 16 Oz. 2.50
Miss Olde Frothingslosh, Fatima Yechburgh, Pittsburgh Brewing, 1969 .... .4.00 to 9.95
Modelo, Aluminum, Pull Tab, Mexico, 340 Ml. 5.00
Molson Canadian Lager, Tin, 1970s 2.29
New Castle Brown Ale, Tin, 1970s, 15 1/2 Oz. 3.00
Oertel's '92, Aluminum, Pull Tab, 12 Oz. 5.00
Old Chicago Dark, Pull Tab, 12 Oz. 3.00
Old Crown, Aluminum, Pull Tab, Peter Hand Breweries, 12 Oz. 5.00
Old Dutch Brand Beer, Tin, 1970s 2.49
Old Milwaukee, Pull Tab, Puerto Rico 3.00
Old Style, Heileman's, Pull Tab, Pt. 6.00
Old Style Light, Modern Tab, 12 Oz. 3.00
Olde English 800, Aluminum, Pull Tab, Blitz Weinhard, Evansville, In., 12 Oz. 10.00
Olympia Gold Light, Pull Tab, 12 Oz. .... .3.00 to 9.00
Olympia Pale Export, Pull Tab, 12 Oz. 3.00
Oranjeboom Pilsener, Pull Tab, Holland, 11 2/3 Oz. 10.00
Ortlieb's Beer, Liberty Bell, George Washington, Aluminum, Pull Tab, 12 Oz. 5.00
Pearl Light, Pull Tab, Indented Bottom, 12 Oz. 3.00
Pearl Premium Light, Pull Tab, 12 Oz. 3.00
Peter Hand Extra Light, Aluminum, Pull Tab, 12 Oz. 5.00
Pfeiffer, Aluminum, Pull Tab, 12 Oz. 3.00
Piel's Real Draft, Pull Tab, 12 Oz. 3.00
Pig's Eye Pilsner, Contents, Minnesota Brewing Co. 4.95
Pilsener Club, Pull Tab, Pearl Breweries, 12 Oz. 2.54
Reading Premium Light, Star Spangled Banner, Bicentennial, Aluminum, Pull Tab, 12 Oz. 5.00
Rheingold Extra Light, Pull Tab, 12 Oz. 3.00
Rheingold Premium, Pull Tab, 12 Oz. 3.00
Rolling Rock, Aluminum, Pull Tab, 12 Oz. 2.54
Royal Amber, Aluminum, Pull Tab, Heileman, La Crosse, Wisc., 12 Oz. 3.00
Schmidt's, Aluminum, Pull Tab, Kick-Up Bottom, 12 Oz. 5.00
Schmidt's, Buffalo, Pull Tab, Tin, 12 Oz. 10.00
Schmidt's, Elk, Pull Tab, Tin, 12 Oz. 10.00
Schmidt's, Musical, How Dry I Am, Windup 10.00
Sierra, Aluminum, Pull Tab, Pittsburgh, Pa., 12 Oz. 3.00
Sparkling Stite Malt Liquor, Pull Tab, 12 Oz. 5.00
Steinlager, Aluminum, Pull Tab, New Zealand Breweries, 12 Oz. 5.00
Suntory, Golfers, Stay Tab, Japan, 12 Oz. 5.00
Swan Lager, Aluminum, Pull Tab, Australia, 370 Ml. 5.00
Swan Lager Export, Pull Tab, Australia, 12 1/2 Oz. 8.00
Texas Pride Lite, Pull Tab, 12 Oz. 3.00
Tuborg Gold, Pull Tab, Denmark, 12 Oz. 5.00
Valley Brew Pale Beer, Premium, Cone Top, Bottle Cap, 5 x 2 3/4 In. 105.00
Van Merritt, Pull Tab, Peter Hand Breweries, 12 Oz. 2.50
Victoria Bitter, Aluminum, Pull Tab, Australia, 370 Ml. 5.00
WFBG Radios Keystone Country, Pittsburgh Brewing Co., 11.6 Oz. 10.00
Windhoek Lagerbier, Pull Tab, South Africa, 340 Ml. .... .12.00 to 20.00
Windhoek Lagerbier, Pull Tab, South Africa, 450 Ml. 10.00

BIG BOY   Bob Wian bought a ten-seat diner in Glendale, California, in 1936. He introduced a double-deck cheeseburger and named it the Big Boy. His company grew and franchised restaurants around the country. They all used the Big Boy logo of a chubby boy with a pom-padour hairdo and checkered overalls, but some used different names, including Azar's, Bob's, Elias', Feisch's, Frisch's, J.B.'s, Manner's,

T.J.'s, and Kip's. In 1967 the chain was acquired by Marriott Corp., which sold it to Elias Brothers in 1987. It was spun off in 2000 to form Big Boy Restaurants International based in Warren, Michigan. Frisch's, a Cincinnati-based chain, also has rights to call its restaurants Big Boy. Following a 1985 contest to decide if the Big Boy logo should be redesigned or discarded, the symbol was kept in its original form. Today Big Boy and Frisch's each has its own updated version of the icon.

Bank, Big Boy, Marriott Corp., Copyright 1973, 8 3/4 x 4 1/4 In.	20.00
Bank, Soft Vinyl, Red Checker Overalls, Head Slot, 1973, 9 In.	21.00 to 45.00
Cookbook, Big Boy Barbecues, Kingsford Charcoal	10.00
Doll, Pillow, 15 In.	35.00
Frisbee, Plastic, Blue Ground, Humphrey Flyers, 9 In.	15.00
Lunch Box, Red Plastic, Gold Paper Sticker Label, c.1970s, 5 x 7 x 11 In.	100.00
Matchbook, 20 Matches, Location List, California, 1 1/2 x 2 In.	12.00
Mug, Frosted, Evolution Of Big Boy, c.1988, 4 1/2 In.	27.00
Night-Light, Big Boy's Face, Plastic, Plug In, Brass Prongs, 1960s, 2 x 3/4 In.	18.00
Patch, Employee's, Fabric, Double Burger, c.1960, 2 3/4 x 4 1/4 In.	15.00
Patch, Frisch's, Boy, Title Bar, c.1960, 1 1/2 x 4 In.	15.00
Puzzle, Envelope, 2-Sided, Big Boy & Double Cheeseburger, c.1960s, 6 1/4 x 9 1/4 In.	45.00
Tumbler, Weighted Bottom, 1936 Logo, 50th Anniversary, 1986, 6 1/2 In.	18.00

BIN Large bins were used to store many types of food in an old country store. Bins could be tin or wood. They often had lift-up lids. Many bins were decorated with the name of the store or brand. Bins lost favor when supermarkets replaced smaller grocery stores. In the early 1980s, the idea of selling bulk candy, dried fruit, crackers, and other products again became feasible and bins started to reappear.

Cream City Flour, Sifter, Metal, 1893, 27 1/2 x 12 1/2 In.	770.00
Drink Chapman's Teas, Wood, Slanted & Hinged Lift Lid, Brass Handle, 17 x 18 In.	150.00
E.C.H. English Breakfast Tea, Stenciled, Countertop, 10 In.	116.00
High Grade Brand Teas, Steinwender Stoffgren Coffee Co., Tin, 17 x 18 1/2 x 13 In.	330.00
Mays Seed, Tin Lithograph, Wood Base, Tripod, Patent 1902, Display, 45 In.	1430.00
Reid, Murdoch & Co., Wood, Round, Lift Top, 33 In.	22.00

BLATZ Valentine Blatz was born in Bavaria in 1826. He apprenticed at his father's brewery, then worked for a larger brewer in other German cities. In 1849 he moved to Milwaukee, Wisconsin, to work at John Braun's brewery, but in 1851 he opened his own brewery. When Braun died, Blatz married his widow and the Braun brewery was renamed Blatz. The Blatz brand was one of the first to be "exported," which then meant it was sold in another city. The brand became well-known nationally, and in 1891 the brewery was sold to a syndicate of London financiers. In the early 1940s, Val Blatz Brewing Company was purchased by Schenley Distillery. Pabst bought the label in 1958 and the brewery closed the following year. The United States government filed an anti-monopoly suit against Pabst in 1959. After a decade of litigation, it was decided that Pabst had to sell the Blatz brand. The G. Heileman Brewing Company purchased it in 1969. Heileman was purchased by Stroh's in 1996. Stroh's quit the beer industry in 1999, and Blatz was sold to Pabst. Blatz beer remains a nationally recognized brand.

Clock, Bartender, Gray Hair, Mustache, Animated, Light-Up, Plastic, 12 In. .... *Illus*	110.00
Figure, Blatz Man, Serving Beer, Bottle Body, 20 In.	55.00
Figure, Waiter, Beer Bottle Body, Thumbs Up, Countertop, 16 In.	33.00
Group, Baseball, Catcher, Umpire, Base Runner, Metal, 16 In.	132.00
Salt & Pepper, Pilsener, Bottle Shape, Amber Glass, Metal Lids, 3 In.	26.00
Sign, Milwaukee's Finest Bottled Beer, Glass, Frame, 6 1/2 x 12 1/2 In.	28.00
Sign, Old Heidelberg, Hand Painted, Chalk, 1933	231.00
Sign, Old Heidelberg, Men In Hats Sit Around Table, Plaster Relief, 1933, 42 x 24 In.	385.00
Sign, Old Heidelberg, Milwaukee, Wis., Tin, 24 x 17 In.	600.00
Sign, Philadelphia's First Bottled Beer, 4 3/4 x 8 3/4 In.	61.00

Blatz, Clock, Bartender, Gray
Hair, Mustache, Animated,
Light-Up, Plastic, 12 In.

**Commercial false teeth cleaners are
good to use to remove scum from
the inside of old glass bottles.**

BLOTTER   Blotters were important during the days of the dip pen. The
advertising blotter was a giveaway from 1890 to 1920. A blotter showing the 1876 Centennial Exposition was made in 1888. Several firms
made blotters each year and a complete series is important to a collector. Blotters may also be listed in this book by brand name.

Brown's Iron Bitters, Victorian House & Family, 3 7/8 x 6 7/8 In.	49.00
Lawson-Cavette Sporting Goods Co., It Pays To Play, May, 1951	9.00
Lindale Dairy, Ms. Liberty, Spirit Of Liberty, Highpoint, North Carolina, 1940s, 9 x 4 In.	20.00
Miami Powder Co., Coil Of Fuse, Carload Of Powder, 3 7/8 x 9 1/4 In.	110.00
Montague City Rod Co., Woman, Holding Fishing Pole, c.1905, 3 3/8 x 6 1/8 In.	70.00
Sheer Nonsense, Hulbert's Smash-Proof Creepers, Ashtabula, Ohio, 1940, 6 1/8 x 3 3/8 In.	7.50
Texto Alley Dust Cloth, Red, Black, White Ground, 3 7/8 x 9 In., 5 Piece	18.00

BOOKLET   Many types of booklets belong to the world of advertising
collectibles. A few children's books have been written featuring characters that are product trademarks. Booklets that are advertisements for
products were made as giveaways by many companies from 1880 to
1920. These booklets included product information, games, pictures,
jokes, advice, or other helpful information. Patent medicine makers
were especially fond of this form of advertising. Booklets with paper
covers and a few pages, books with hard covers, pamphlets, and flyers
are listed. Many books are listed by brand name in this guide. Catalogs
are in their own category.

Brown's Iron Bitters, Scenes Of Sports & Bitters In Use, 13 1/2 x 5 1/2 In., 4 Pages	72.00
Coupon Book, Octagon Soap, 1930	24.00
Crocker Fertilizer & Chemical Company, 1891, 3 1/2 x 6 1/2 In., 62 Pages	2.00
Evinrude, Detachable Rowboat Motor, Boating Scenes, Flyer, 1930s, 7 x 11 1/2 In.	28.00
G-Man Manual Of Instructions, Codes, Signals, Post Toasties, 1930s, 7 x 5 In.	22.00
Harley-Davidson, Payment Pass Book, c.1950, 5 x 3 In. .... *Illus*	45.00
Harley-Davidson, Service, Repair, Soft Bound, Fourth Edition, 1977, 183 Pages	9.10

Booklet, Harley-
Davidson,
Payment Pass
Book, c.1950,
5 x 3 In.

Booklet, Radio Orphan Annie's Secret Society, Envelope,
1936, 8 3/4 x 6 In., 12 Pages

Humphrey's Witch Hazel Oil, c.1894, 3 3/4 x 5 1/2 In., 12 Pages 28.00
Ideal Sight Restorer, Ideal Eye Masseur, 1904, 8 x 5 1/4 In., 72 Pages 440.00
Lester Lightbulb Safety, Decals, Coloring, Mass. Electric Co., 1977, 8 x 11 In., 15 Pages   15.00
Marble's Game Getter, Moose, 3 Colors, Bifold, Brochure, c.1938, 6 1/4 x 3 1/4 In. 29.00
Marble's Outing Equipment, Moose, Geese, 1937, 6 x 3 1/4 In., 32 Pages 61.00
Natural Eye Normalizer, Quack, Flyer, 1928, 11 x 16 In., 4 Pages 50.00
Oak Stove, Girl By Oak Tree, Estate Of P.D. Beckwith, Frame, 9 x 12 In. 35.00
Octagon Soap, Premium Coupon, Premium List, 1930 .... 24.00
Penny Flame, Northern Illinois Gas Co., Travel Time Games, 1966, 61 Pages 15.00
Phenoid Cleaner & Polish, Some Shine, Black Boy Holds Melon, 1915, 12 1/2 In. 132.00
Radio Orphan Annie's Secret Society, Envelope, 1936, 8 3/4 x 6 In., 12 Pages ..... *Illus* 75.00
Red Rose & Blue Ribbon Tea, Space Age, Brooke Bond Album, No. 12, 1969 .... 12.00
Regal Shoes, Regal Rhymes, Cartoons, Die Cut, Early 1900s, 3 1/2 x 6 1/2 In., 12 Pages . 12.00
Sterns, Pocket Calendar & Facts, Leather Cover, c.1910, 2 3/4 x 5 3/4 In., 100 Pages 22.00
Tri City Dairy, Coupon, 35 Coupons, $1.00 Value, Cow Head Cover, Durand, Wis., c.1950   22.00
Tri City Dairy, Coupon, 60 Coupons, $2.00 Value, Cow Head Cover, Durand, Wis., c.1950   22.00
Western Field, Four Aces & A King, Brochure, 6 1/8 x 3 1/2 In. 341.00

BOOKMARK   Bookmarks have been used for centuries, but those made before 1850 are rare. The period of Victorian advertising bookmarks, stiff paper bookmarks printed with ads for all kinds of products, ran from 1880 to 1901. From 1901 to 1914, many insurance companies and publishers gave away promotional bookmarks. Ads still appear on modern bookmarks, but most have been designed as gifts with verses or clever pictures.

American Brake Company, Locomotive, Coal Car, Silk, 3 x 9 5/8 In. 110.00
Crown Pianos & Organs, Child, Violets, Masonic Fair, 1906, Boonville, 6 x 1 7/8 In. 12.00
Donald Duck Bread, Embossed, Tin Lithograph, 10 x 2 1/2 In. 95.00
Elastica Floor Finish, Boy On Rocking Horse, Celluloid, 5 3/4 x 2 In. 66.00
First Love Chocolates, Pacific Coast Biscuit Co., Embossed Cardboard, 6 x 2 In. 55.00
Hoyt's German Cologne, Rubifoam, Girl With Bottle, Die Cut, 4 5/8 x 2 In. 10.00
Libby, McNeil & Libby, Rose, 1901 Pan American Exposition, Celluloid, 5 In. 77.00
Libby's Canned Meats, Red Rose, Green Flowers, Die Cut, Celluloid, Early 1900s, 5 In. . 25.00
Maltine, Owl, Celluloid, 3 1/2 x 1 3/8 In. 85.00
Stollwerk Gold Brand Chocolate & Cocoa, Celluloid, Bastian Bros., 5 5/8 x 1 5/8 In. ... 65.00
T. Eaton Co., Birthstones, 6 Year Calendar, Toronto, Winnipeg, Celluloid, 1913-1918 .... 25.00

BORDEN   Gail Borden was given a medal at the 1851 Great Exhibition in London, England, for his dried biscuit of wheat flour and beef. It kept indefinitely and could be reconstituted with water to provide food at any time. Borden developed another product when he noticed that children aboard a ship had no fresh milk. His method of condensing milk by boiling off its water content was patented by 1856. In 1857 Jeremiah Milbank became a partner in Gail Borden, Jr., and Company, which was renamed the New York Condensed Milk Company in 1858. Borden also patented and sold Borden's Extract of Coffee (1856–1920s), a condensed cream, sugar, and coffee drink. He patented a process for preserving fruit juice by reducing its water content (1862), and made Borden's Extract of Beef (c.1866–1874) and Borden's Roast Beef (c.1873). The company became the Borden Condensed Milk Company in 1899 and The Borden Company in 1919. Elsie the Cow, the famous Borden trademark, was introduced in ads in 1936. A live Elsie was exhibited at the 1939 New York World's Fair. Later she traveled the country, appearing on stage, screen, and television. Elsie had a husband named Elmer; a son, Beauregard; and a daughter, Beulah. Elmer's Glue was named for Elsie's husband. About 1941 it was decided that if Elsie could talk in her ads, she and her family could also stand on two feet. In 1957 Elsie gave birth to twin calves named Larabee and Lobelia. In 1995 Borden Inc., under new ownership, sold the dairy and food businesses. Borden Chemical, based in Columbus, Ohio, now focuses on resin and adhesive technology. Dairy Farmers of America acquired the Elsie and Borden brand license for cheese in 1998. Dean Foods, Milk Products, and other companies use the brand

for other dairy products sold around the country. Elsie items are the most popular of the many Borden collectibles.

Advertisement, Elsie & Elmer, Borden's Skim To Keep You Slim, 1958, 10 x 12 In. 16.00
Advertisement, Elsie The Cow Cartoon, Color, 1942, 10 x 14 In. 20.00
Badge, Elsie The Cow, Brass, World's Fair, New York, 1939, 2 1/4 In. 38.00
Ball, Elsie's West Texas State Buffaloes, Plastic, 4 In. 29.00
Bank, Van, Elsie The Cow, Borden Ice Cream, Grumman Olson Route Star, Key, Ertl 11.00
Belt Buckle, Elsie, Brass, 50th Anniversary, 1986 .... 50.00
Bottle, Milk, Elsie Logo, Red ACL, 1/2 Gal. 18.00
Bottle, Milk, Property Of Borden's Farm Products, Quality Service, Qt., 9 3/4 In. 20.00
Button, Elsie The Cow, Metal, 1 1/2 In. 12.00
Button, Elsie, In Yellow Plastic Flower, 1950s, 1 5/8 In. 48.00
Can, Malted Milk, 6 x 6 1/4 In. 88.00
Canister, Nickel, Script Letters, Embossed, 1920s, 9 x 5 3/8 In. 675.00
Charm, Elsie The Cow, Molded Loop, Yellow, Plastic, 3/4 In. 18.00
Clock, Ice Cream, Elsie The Cow, Light-Up, Glass, Metal, 15 In. ....220.00 to 385.00
Container, Ice Cream, Elsie The Cow, 1957, Pt. 10.00
Container, Ice Cream, White House Flavor, 1957, 1/2 Gal. 16.00
Container, Malted Milk, Aluminum, 8 In. 100.00
Cookbook, Borden's Eagle Brand Magic Recipes, 1946, 27 Pages ....3.00 to 9.00
Dish, Sundae, Elsie, 4 x 4 In. 20.00
Display, Milk Wagon, Horse, Borden's Farm Products, Milk & Cream, 60 In. 10450.00
Greeting Card, Elsie, Wreath, Milkman's Name, Die Cut Paper, 5 x 5 1/2 In. 14.00
Jar, Malted Milk, Glass, Lid, Label, 9 In. ....*Illus* 330.00
Jug, Elsie The Cow, Red, 1954, 1/2 Gal. 20.00
Lamp, Elsie The Cow, Head, Daisy Necklace, Figural, c.1960, 9 x 8 In. 395.00
Mug, Elsie The Cow, Flowers, Gold Trim, Child's, 3 x 4 In. ....95.00 to 110.00
Napkin, Elsie, Borden Cow, Multicolored Design, 1960s, 6 1/2 x 6 3/4 In. 3.00
Pail, Elsie Dairy, Wooden Handle, Ohio Art, 5 x 6 In. 65.00
Postcard, Borden Condensary Factory, Norwich, N.Y. 15.00
Postcard, Borden's Plant, Norwich, N.Y., Stamp, June 24, 1911 .... 12.00
Postcard, Home Scene, Elsie, Elmer, Beauregard 6.00
Salt & Pepper, Elsie's Babies, Buelah, Beauregard, Japan, 3 1/2 In. 75.00
Sherbet, Elsie, 4 x 3 In. 25.00
Sign, Big Boy Borden's Ice Cream, 10 Cents, Cone, Elsie, Porcelain, 61 x 23 In. .....*Illus* 633.00
Sign, Borden's Ice Cream, Elsie, Tin, 15 x 24 In. 800.00
Sign, Eagle Brand Condensed Milk, 2 Ladies, Girl, Cardboard, Frame, 10 1/2 x 14 3/4 In. . 468.00
Sign, Eagle Brand Condensed Milk, Girl, Blue Ribbon, Cardboard, c.1910, 10 x 14 In. ... 375.00
Sign, Eagle Brand Condensed Milk, Girl, Cardboard, 13 1/2 x 10 In. 275.00
Sign, Eagle Brand, Partners Since 1857, Trolley Card, 11 x 21 In. 39.00
Sign, Elsie The Cow, Sunflower, Embossed Tin, 18 x 18 In. ....39.00 to 55.00
Sign, Flower Basket, 3-Dimensional, Die Cut, Cardboard, 19 x 13 In. 44.00
Sign, Fountain, Borden's Ice Cream, Elsie, 3-Dimensional, Cardboard, Frame, 46 x 24 In. . 187.00

Borden, Jar, Malted Milk,
Glass, Lid, Label,
9 In.

Borden, Sign, Big Boy Borden's
Ice Cream, 10 Cent, Cone, Elsie,
Porcelain, 61 x 23 In.

Bottle, Solon Palmer Perfume
Co., Painted Label Under
Glass, 9 x 3 In.

Sign, Ice Cream, Elsie The Cow, Yellow, Red, Blue, White, Tin, c.1954, 28 x 54 In. 150.00
Sign, Lady Borden Ice Cream, Neon, Porcelain, 1952, 42 x 60 In. 1210.00
Sign, Welcome Home Elsie, 1980s, 11 x 18 In. 30.00
Spoon, Elsie Ice Cream, Wax Wrapper, Ritwrap-O.W.D. Corp., 2 Piece 5.00
Tin, Borden's Malted Milk, Full Pry Lid, 1950s, 5 1/4 x 2 3/8 In. 115.00
Toy, Van, Kingsbury 395.00
Toy, Wagon, Borden's Milk, Horse Drawn, Tin Lithograph, Wood, Paint, 20 In. 136.00
Trade Card, Eagle Brand Condensed Milk, Big Girl Trying To Get Bite Of Baby's Food ..   14.00
Tumbler, Elsie, Federal Glass Co., 4 7/8 In. 20.00
Tumbler, Elsie, Federal Glass Co., 6 1/8 In., 6 Piece 72.00

BOTTLE   Almost every bottle that held a commercial product is collected by someone. There are milk bottles, liquor bottles, soft drink
bottles, medicine bottles, and many more. Some collectors prefer bottles with raised lettering; others want figurals. Some prefer bottles with
their original paper labels. Collectors also search for go-withs, small
items that might picture a bottle or be used with a bottle. Bottle collecting is a special hobby with shows, publications, and clubs.

3 In 1 Lubricant, 15 Cents, Cork Stopper, Box, c.1927, 1 Oz. 30.00
A.J. White Ltd., Aqua, Label, Contents, Cork, Box, c.1918, 4 3/4 In. 88.00
Abbey's Effervescent Salt, Shakespeare, Square, Contents, 3 1/2 In. ....248.00 to 468.00
Absolutely Pure Dr. Jones Sangvin, Blood & Nerve Remedy, Aqua, Albany, N.Y., 9 In. ...   45.00
Acme Hair Vigor, Label Under Glass, Phil Eismann, Cork, Metal Stopper, 8 In. 231.00
Ambercrude For Hair And Scalp, Phila., U.S.A., Bimal, Contents, Labels, 8 1/4 In. 45.00
Angelo Myers, Rye Whiskey, Philadelphia, Backbar, 1885-1910, 11 1/8 In. 280.00
Anthracite Brand California Brandy, L. Lewith & Sons, Pa., Flask, ABM, c.1910, Qt. 39.00
Arliss, Robinson, Lindum Works, Sutton, Blue Top, Pottery, England, 6 3/4 In. 204.00
Ascatco, Gnu Image On Front, Wrapper, Unopened, 4 In. 28.00
Baker's Orange Grove Bitters, Amber, 1865-1875, 9 5/8 In. 336.00
Balsam Copiaba, Standard Drug, Elizabeth City, N.C., Box, 1910-1930 ....   25.00
Barry's Tricopherous For Skin & Hair, Aqua, Open Pontil, N.Y., 6 In. 35.00
Bed-Bug Poison, H.T. Waldner, Apothecary, Cylinder, Cobalt Blue, c.1885, 8 3/4 In. 39.00
Beer, see Beer Bottle
Beggs Liver Pills, Jar, Etched, Dakota Globe, Ground Glass Stopper, 11 1/2 In. 220.00
Ben Franklin, Bitters, Figural, Medium Blue Green, c.1850, 10 In. 8960.00
Bennett's Hyssop Cure Stockport, Cornflower Blue, 4 7/8 In. 27.00
Big Bill Best Bitters, Amber, 1890-1910, 12 1/4 In. 308.00
Billie Taylor Whiskey, Embossed, Flask, Paper Label, Box, c.1910, 1/2 Pt. 115.00
Bishop's Reliable Cough Cure, Label, Aqua, Contents, Front & Rear Labels, 5 3/4 In. ...   88.00
Blood Ball, Flask, Paper Label, Box, 3 In. 248.00
Boerhaves, Holland Bitters, B. Page Jr. & Co, Pittsburgh, Pa, Aqua, 1855-1865, 7 5/8 In. .   420.00
Borgfeldt Propfe Co. Whiskey, Embossed, Flask, c.1910, 1/2 Pt. 230.00
Bonplands, Fever & Ague Remedy, New York, Aqua, Open Pontil, Square, 5 1/4 In. 165.00
Bouvier Buchu Gin, For Kidneys & Bladder, ABM Label, Square, c.1906, Pt., 12 In. 69.00
Bracer, Backbar, White Enamel, 2-Piece Mold, 4 x 8 1/2 x 5 In. 121.00
Brandons Diarrhoea Remedy, Box, 5 In. 165.00
Breinig, Fronefield & Co., Cattle Liniment, Aqua, Open Pontil, Whittle, 6 1/2 In. 413.00
British Oil, Steelman & Archer Wholesale Druggists, Phila., ABM, 5 1/2 In. 12.00
Brown's Celebrated Indian Herb Bitters, Indian Queen, Amber, 1867-1875, 12 1/4 In. ..   504.00
Burlingame Whiskey, Backbar, White Enamel, San Francisco, 3 1/2 x 10 1/2 In. 385.00
C.&R. Canandaigua, Ringbone & Spavin, Liniment, Label, Aqua, Pontil, 6 In. 1705.00
Cafi-Aspirin, Glass, Tubular, 20 Tablets, Box, Insert, 4 1/8 x 7/8 In. 35.00
Caldwell's, Great Tonic, Herb Bitters, Amber, Iron Pontil, 1865-1875, 12 5/8 In. 283.00
Centaur Liniment, Aqua, Dried-Up Contents, Wraparound Label, c.1891, 3 1/2 In. 154.00
Cereal Extract Of Oats And Barley, F.R. Gross & Co., Amber, 7 1/2 In. 69.00
Chamberlain's Diarrhoea Remedy, Aqua, Dry Contents, Wrapper, Canada, 4 1/2 In. 33.00
Cherry Smash, Fowlers, 5 Cents, Metal Cover, Label Under Glass, 1910-1920, 12 In. 336.00
Cherry Smash, Hot Soda, Metal Cap, 12 In. 187.00
Circassian Hair Restorer, Cincinnati, Amber, Applied Mouth, 1875-1890, 7 1/2 In. 420.00
Clayton's Cough Syrup, Clayton's Dog Remedies, Screw Cap, Box, 5 In. 121.00
Co-Re-Ga Denture Adhesive, Insert, Box, Sample Size 38.00
Compound Extract Of Roots, Aqua, Wraparound Label, Pontil, 4 7/8 In. 61.00
Crane's Penetrating Liniment, Label, Contents, Instructions, Box, 1906, 5 In. 19.00

Crisp's Hot Shot Treatment For Running Fits, Clear, ABM, Contents, Label, Box, 7 In. . 154.00
Dam-I-Ana Invigorator, 2 Nymphs, Man, Forest, Amber, Label, 8 3/4 In. 187.00
David Andrews, Vegetable Jaundice Bitters, Providence, R.I., Aqua, 1840-1860, 8 1/8 In. . 2016.00
Davis Vegetable Pain Killer, ABM, Labels, Partial Contents, Pamphlet, Box, 6 1/2 In. . . . 209.00
Davis Vegetable Pain Killer, Aqua, Open Pontil, Label, 4 7/8 In. 440.00
Decanter, Bells, Charles & Diana Wedding, Commemoration, Box, 1981, 9 3/4 In. 222.00
Decanter, Bells, Prince William's Birth, Commemoration, Contents, Box, 1982, 8 In. 44.00
Dewitt's Stomach Bitters, Contents, Amber, 7 1/2 In. 358.00
Dickey Pioneer, Creme De Lis, Embossed, Amber, 1850, 5 1/2 In. 143.00
Doct. Motts Magic Cough Balsam, Aqua, Contents, Label, Tax Stamp, 6 1/2 In. 275.00
Dr. A.B. Simpson's Vegetable Compound, Reliable Remedy, Label, Box, 7 1/2 In. 550.00
Dr. A.P. Sawyers Sunrise Cough Balsam, Embossed, Aqua, Contents, Box, 8 In. 275.00
Dr. Baker's Pain Panacea, Aqua, Open Pontil, Applied Mouth, 1840-1860, 7 5/8 In. 336.00
Dr. Balle's Hustena, Coughs Asthma & All Throat Troubles, Aqua, Triangular, Label, 5 In. 39.00
Dr. C.N. Barber's Inflammation Remedy, 3 Labels, Unopened, Dry Contents, 3 1/2 In. . . . 187.00
Dr. C.W. Roback's Stomach Bitters, Cincinnati, Amber, Barrel, 1865-1875, 10 In. 420.00
Dr. D. Jayne's Carminative Balsam, Aqua, Flared Lip, Open Pontil, Cork, 4 3/4 In. 143.00
Dr. D. Jayne's Tonic Vermifuge, Aqua, Open Pontil, Cork, 5 In. 132.00
Dr. E.L. Robertson's Eclectic Balsam, Front & Rear Labels, Contents, Box, 6 3/4 In. 385.00
Dr. H. Austin's Genuine Ague Balsam, Plymouth, Aqua, Iron Pontil, 1840-1860, 7 3/8 In. . 476.00
Dr. H.M. Purinton's Tiko, Square, Label, Contents, Box, 5 In. 132.00
Dr. H.S. Flint's Quaker Bitters, Man With Can, Bottle, Contents, Aqua, 1872, 9 1/2 In. . . 121.00
Dr. Harris' Summer Cordial, Contents, Label, Box, 6 In. 33.00
Dr. Hobson's Wire Fence Liniment, Pfeiffer Chemical Co., Label, Contents, Box, 10 In. . 297.00
Dr. J. Hostetter's Stomach Bitters, Olive Amber, 1870-1880, 9 In. 448.00
Dr. James Cannabis Indica, Craddock Co., Proprietors No. 225, Embossed, Aqua, 8 In. . . 248.00
Dr. Kay's Renovator, Square, Contents, Cork, Flyer, Box, Saratoga Springs, N.Y., 9 3/4 In. 176.00
Dr. Kline's Great Nerve Restorer, Aqua, Embossed, $2.00, 8 1/2 In. 154.00
Dr. Legear's Colic Remedy, Label Only, Amber, AMB, Box, 7 In. 61.00
Dr. Lew Arntz Eye Remedy, Greatest Known, Partial Contents, Iowa, 3 1/2 In. 154.00
Dr. Mclean's Strengthening Cordial & Blood Purifier, Aqua, Label, Contents, Box, 8 In. . 688.00
Dr. P. Hall's Celebrated Catarrh Remedy, Wrapped, Unopened, Erie, Pa., 2 3/4 In. 165.00
Dr. Pierce's Anuric Tablets For Kidneys & Backache, Blue, Cylinder, 3 1/8 In. 20.00
Dr. Samuel H.P. Lee's Lithontriptic, Cork, Wrapper, c.1940, 2 1/2 x 2 In. 39.00
Dr. Shoop's Restorative, Great Nerve Tonic, Contents, Wrapper, Box, 8 In. 275.00
Dr. Simmons Squaw Vine Compound, Strictly Vegetable, Indian, 9 In. 121.00
Dr. Smith's Dentrifice, James J. Ottinger, Metal Cap, Contents, 4 In. 440.00
Dr. Smith's Tissue Remedy Eye Tablets, Round, Cylinder, Contents, Box, 3 1/4 In. 132.00
Dr. Thatcher's Liver & Blood Syrup, Rectangular, Chattanooga, Tenn., Sample, 3 1/2 In. . 75.00
Dr. Townsend's Sarsaparilla, Albany, N.Y., Olive Green, 1840-1860, 9 1/4 In. 364.00
Dr. Van Dyke's Holland Bitters, Headless Man Running, Embossed Base, 9 3/4 In. 330.00
Dr. Warren's Tonic Cordial, Aqua, Square, Contents, 9 In. 220.00
Dr. Yates Asparagus Wine, For The Kidneys, 3-Sided, Light Aqua, Embossed, Box, 7 In. . 165.00
Drake's Palmetto Compound, Palm Tree, Duck, Label, Contents, Box, 9 1/4 In. 77.00
Drake's Plantation Bitters, 5-Log, Amber, 1862-1870, 10 1/8 In. 728.00
E.M. Parmelee Sarsaparilla & Iodide Of Potassa Compound, Aqua, Rear Label, 8 1/4 In. 88.00
Empire Quinine Hair Tonic, Gal., 12 x 6 1/2 In. 25.00
Fellows Syrup Of Hypophosphites, Aqua, Contents, Label, Canada, 5 1/4 In. 50.00
Fleming's Veterinary Eye Lotion, Paper Label, Round, Dry Contents, c.1914, 3 In. 66.00
Fleming's Veterinary Healing Oil, Wraparound Label, Contents, 3 3/4 In. 99.00
Fly Dope, Paper Label, Minot, Maine, 4 1/2 In. 12.10
G.O. Blake's Rye & Bourbon Whiskey, Adams Taylor & Co., Qt., 12 1/2 In. 29.00
G.S. Emerson's American Hair Restorative, Cleveland, Aqua, Oval, Iron Pontil, 6 1/2 In. . 504.00
G.W. Laird's Perfumers New York, Milk Glass, Labels, Battleship Tax Stamp, 5 In. 275.00
Gargling Oil Liniment, Cobalt Blue, Paper Label, 5 1/4 In. 330.00
Geo. R. Lamb & Co., Red Bank, N.J., Yellow Green, Squat, Crown Top, c.1880, 7 In. 45.00
George Foster's Jim Dandy, Oil Of 100 Uses For Home, Farm, Factory, 8 Oz., 8 1/3 In. . . 10.00
Glover's Imperial Tonic, Dogs & Horses, 65 Cents, Unopened, Box, 2 1/4 x 6 In. 154.00
Glycozone, Ch. Marchand, Contents, Label, Wrapper, 5 1/4 In. 72.00
Gold Metal Celery Seed, Shaker Cover, 5 In. 7.50
Goodall's Culinary Herbs, Glass, England, 1930s, 6 In. 10.00
Granular Citrate Of Magnesia, Cobalt Blue, Rectangular, 6 1/8 In. 29.00
Granuline, Milk Glass, Eye Dropper, Murine Eye Remedy Co., Chicago, Box, 3 1/2 In. . . 187.00

Grape Smash, Label Under Glass, Metal Cover, 1910-1920, 11 7/8 In. . . . . .605.00 to 1064.00
Great Northern, I.L. Lamm Co., White Enamel, Backbar, Qt., 5 x 12 In. 259.00
Greeley's Bourbon, Bitters, Barrel, Cherry Puce, 1860-1870, 9 1/4 In. 258.00
Griffith Hyatt & Co., Whiskey, Baltimore, Bulbous, Yellow Amber, 7 In. 952.00
Gypsy Dy-Kleen, Screw Top, Label, Gypsy Dyes, Inc., Chicago, 3 3/8 x 1 1/2 x 5/8 In. . . . 32.00
H. Clay Glover Co., Distemper Medicine, New York, Amber, Paper Label, 5 In. 55.00
H.P. Herb Wild Cherry Bitters, Tree, Cabin Shape, Green, 1890-1900, 8 3/4 In. 7280.00
Hall's Balsam For The Lungs, Aqua, Rear Label, Sunken Panels, Long Neck, 7 In. 16.50
Hall's Bitters, Barrel, Amber, Label, c.1842, 9 1/4 In. 358.00
Hamilton & Church Excelsior Mineral Water, 8-Sided, Pontil, Blue, 1840-1860, 7 3/4 In. 840.00
Harter's Iron Tonic, Contents, Label, Box, Amber, April 1, 1895, 9 In. 209.00
Hazen's Vermont Maple Syrup, Embossed, 8 1/4 x 3 1/2 In. 176.00
Healy & Bigelow, Indian Sagwa, Embossed Indian, Aqua, Contents, Label, 8 1/2 In. 1375.00
Helmbold's Sarsaparilla, Aqua, Label, Open Pontil Base, 6 1/4 In. 154.00
Hepatone, Cobalt Blue, Label, Contents, Aluminum Cap, 7 In. 55.00
Hirsts Pain Exterminator, Indian, Barrel, Aqua, Label, Contents, Box, 5 3/4 In. 110.00
Hollywood Whiskey, Embossed, Amber, Qt., 11 1/2 In. 19.00
Holtzermann's Patent Stomach Bitters, 4-Sided, Log Cabin, Amber, 1890-1900, 9 7/8 In. 308.00
Holtzermann's Stomach Bitters, Swirl Ribs, Backbar, Stopper, 1885-1910, 11 3/8 In. . . . 476.00
Hopkins Chalybeate, Baltimore, Green, Iron Pontil, Double Collar, 1850-1860, Pt. 672.00
Hoyt's Rubifoam, Liquid Dentrifice For The Teeth, Embossed, Contents, 2 Oz., 4 1/2 In. . 88.00
Hughes Colic Remedy, Cow On Back, Contents, Unopened Box, 7 5/8 x 3 x 1 5/8 In. 143.00
Ideal Tooth Powder, Eye On Neck, 25 Cents, Vail Bros, Philadelphia, c.1885, 4 1/4 In. . . 550.00
J. Schweppe & Co. Genuine Superior Aerated Waters, Aqua, Embossed, 8 1/4 In. 123.00
J. Steel Premium Mineral Water, 8-Sided, Green, 1840-1860, 7 3/4 In. 308.00
J.B. Marchisi, M.D., Uterine Catholicon, Aqua, Contents, Rear Label, 8 In. 44.00
Jacobs Cholera & Dysentery Cordial, Aqua, Square, Open Pontil, Cork, Box, 6 1/2 In. . . 132.00
Jay-Gee Syrup, Label Under Glass, 11 3/4 x 3 3/8 In. 261.00
John C. Hurst, Bitters, Philada, Rising Sun, Yellow Amber, 1875-1885, 9 1/2 In. 336.00
Johnson's Anodyne Liniment, Aqua, Round, Label, Partial Contents, 4 1/2 In. 44.00
Johnson's Calisaya Bitters, Amber, Label, Square, Burlington, Vt., 10 In. 220.00
Keough's N-F Foul Remedy For Fouls Or Hoof Rot, Rear Of Cow, Aqua, 7 In. 154.00
Kickapoo Oil, Aqua, Contents, Label, Pamphlet, Box, 7 In. 88.00
Kickapoo Oil, Indian At Top, Contents, Label, 7 In. 143.00
Kickapoo Oil, Indian On Front, Label, Contents, Cork, Box, 5 1/4 In. 88.00
L. Lyons, Pure Ohio, Catawba Brandy, Tobacco Amber, 1875-1885, 13 1/4 In. 392.00
Lash's Bitters, Natural Tonic Laxative, Label, Amber, Contents, Square, 1913, 9 1/2 In. . . 132.00
Lash's Bitters, Natural Tonic Laxative, Paper Label, Amber, Contents, Square, 4 3/4 In. . . 440.00
Leak's Kidney & Liver Bitters, Best Blood Purifier, Red Amber, 1890-1900, 8 7/8 In. . . . 146.00
Lemon Life Syrup, Best What Gives, Glass Label, Reverse Painted, John Graf Co., 12 In. 173.00
Lemon Life Syrup, Label Under Glass, John Graf Co., 11 3/4 x 3 3/8 In. 227.00
Liggett's Cherriade Syrup, Enamel Over Glass, 12 In. 303.00
Linden Cough Balsam, A.G. Groblewski, Aqua, Contents, Box, 6 1/4 In. 187.00
Lippincott's One Night Roup Remedy, 25 Cents, Chickens, Embossed, Box, 2 Oz., 5 In. . 99.00
Litthauer Stomach Bitters, Milk Glass Case, Gin Form, 1880-1895, 9 1/2 In. 179.00
Loeffler Drug Store, Dr. Hanna, Formaldehyde For Shoes, Label, Stevensville, Mi., 6 In. . 10.00
Lucky Tiger Remedy Co., Kansas City, Mo., Dispensing Top, 1890-1930, 8 5/8 In. 308.00
Marble's Nitro Solvent, Glass, Embossed, c.1907, 2 Oz., 4 3/4 x 1 1/2 In. 115.00
Mexican Mustang Liniment, Embossed, Aqua, Cylinder, Rolled Lip, 5 1/2 In. 121.00
Michelson's Brandy, Cork, 15 Cents, Backbar, 14 In. 121.00
Milk, see Milk, Bottle
Minnequa Mineral Water, Bradford Co., Pa., Blue Aqua, Double Collar Top, Pint 89.00
Mixer's Cancer & Scrofula Syrup, Label, 24 Page Booklet, Box, c.1921, 7 3/4 In. 523.00
Monopole Rye, Black Bar, Cut Glass, Zipper Neck, Gilt, 3 3/4 x 9 1/2 In. 110.00
Moore's Liver-Ax, Label, Contents, Box, 7 In. 105.00
Moses Dames, Wine Of The Woods, Aqua, Front & Rear Labels, 8 In. 220.00
Mother Seigel's Curative Syrup, A.J. White, Aqua, Label, Box, Pamphlet, 4 1/2 In. 440.00
Mrs. Winslow's Soothing Syrup, Curtis & Perkins, Aqua, Rolled Lip, OP, 5 In. 39.00
Mullins & Crigler Distillers, Embossed, Covington, Ky., 10 1/2 In. 14.00
Munyon's Inhaler Cures Colds, Green, Cylinder, Cork, Dropper, Tablets, Box, 4 In. 413.00
Nome Brewing & Bottle Co., Soda, 4-Piece Mold, Aqua, c.1900, 7 13/16 In. 1265.00
Norwich Children's Aspirin, Box, 30 Tablets 25.00
Norwood's Tinct. V. Viride, Partial Contents, Label, Shakers, Mt. Lebanon, 5 1/2 In. 176.00

Nyal's Corn Remover, Vial, Wraparound Label, 52 Gr. Cannabis Per Oz., Glass, 3 In. 66.00
O-Sa-To Tonic, Indian, Superior Laxative Tonic, Embossed Graduations, Label, 8 In. 88.00
Occuline, Brilliant Eye, Front, Rear & Neck Label, Label Only, 3 1/4 In. 132.00
Old Hickory, Backbar, White Enameled, Ground Pontil, 3 1/2 x 10 3/4 In. 231.00
Old Jug Whiskey, Stoneware, Freiberg Bros., Cincinnati, 1879, 10 3/4 In. 112.00
Old Kitchen Klatter Cherry Flavoring, Label, 3 Oz. 12.00
Old Prentice Whisky, Inside Fluted Panels, Ground Pontil, 3 1/2 x 11 In. 209.00
Old Rosebud Whiskey, Jockey On Horse, Backbar, 1885-1910, 9 In. 1344.00
Old Sachem Bitters & Wigwam Tonic, Barrel, Amber, 1860-1870, 9 1/2 In. 476.00
Old Sachem Bitters & Wigwam Tonic, Straw Yellow, 9 1/2 In. 9520.00
Old Underwood, Pure Rye, Baltimore, Enamel Letters, Backbar, 1890-1915, 11 1/4 In. 123.00
One Night Cough Cure, Wrapper, Sealed, Contents, Embossed, 6 In. 286.00
Otto's Cure, German Remedy, Throat & Lung Diseases, Box, 6 1/2 In. 286.00
Owen Casey, Eagle Soda Works, Sac City, Blue, Blob Mouth, 1865-1875, 7 3/8 In. 179.00
Perrins Pile Specific, Rocky Mountain Pile Remedy, Label, Contents, Box, 6 1/4 In. 154.00
Pflueger, Speede, Reel Oil, No. 379, Plastic Screw Cap, Applicator, 1 1/2 x 2 3/4 x 3/4 In. 11.00
Planters Cuban Relief, For Internal & External Pains, 1 Oz., 6 1/4 In. 154.00
Podophyllin, Teal Green, Cork, 3 1/2 In. 99.00
Pond's Extract, Aqua, Wraparound Label, Wrapper, 5 1/4 In. 66.00
Porter's, Cure Of Pain, Bundysburg, O., Aqua, Open Pontil, 1840-1860, 5 In. 308.00
Prentice, Hand Made Sour Mash, J.T.S. Brown & Sons, Backbar, 1875-1910, 9 3/4 In. ... 1008.00
Professor Horsford's Acid Phosphate, 8-Sided, Contents, Wrapped, Unopened, 6 In. 132.00
Quaker Oil Of Balm, Front & Rear Paper Labels, Box, 5 1/2 In. 28.00
Radium Leather Dye, For Shoes, Other Leather, Nigger Brown, England, 1920s, 3 1/2 In. 88.00
Rawleigh's Trade Mark Colic & Bloat Compound, Aqua, ABM, 7 3/4 In. ....105.00 to 187.00
Red Cap Cleaner, Wind-O-Wash, Black Man, Winking, Paper Label, 5 1/2 In. 314.00
Reel Man After Shave Lotion, Paper Label, 4 3/4 x 2 3/4 In. 35.00
Rexall Ammoniated Tooth Powder, Paper Labels, Contents, 4 3/8 x 2 1/2 x 1 5/8 In. 46.00
Richardson's Fruited Orangeade, Syrup, Label Under Glass, 11 x 3 3/8 In. 1870.00
Rohrer's Expectoral, Wild Cherry, Tonic, Lancaster, Pa., 1865-1875, 10 1/2 In. 1568.00
Roy Rogers Molasses Barbecue Sauce, Montana Beef Council, Amber, Label, 8 1/2 In. .. 150.00
Royal Cough Cure, Cold Expeller, Dill Medicine Co., Contents, Label, Box, 6 1/2 In. 220.00
Royal Pepsin, Stomach Bitters, L&A Scharff, Lion, Unicorn, Amber, 1890-1910, 9 In. 202.00
Rush's Bitters, Amber, Square, A.H. Flanders, M.D., New York, 8 3/4 In. 231.00
S.B. Goff's Oil Liniment, Aqua, Label, Box, 5 3/4 In. 55.00
Salvation Oil Trade Mark, A.C. Meyer, Aqua, Label, Contents, Baltimore, 6 1/2 In. 39.00
Samaritan Nervine, Embossed Bearded Man, S.A. Richmond, Md., St. Joseph, Mo., 8 In. 132.00
Sanford's Radical Cure, Cobalt Blue, Applied Mouth, 1873-1880, 7 5/8 In. 504.00
Schenck's Seaweed Tonic, Aqua, Square, Box, 8 1/2 In. 154.00
Schenck's Syrup, Aqua, 8-Sided, Label, Contents, Cork, Sealed, 5 1/4 In. 61.00
Sherbet-Tade Syrup, Foil & Enamel Label, 12 In. 247.00
Smile, Contents, Box, Gal., 18 In. 550.00
Smoker's Tooth Powder, Contents, Pour Top, Label Only, 6 In. 385.00
Smyrna Stomach Bitters, Prolongs Life, Paper Labels, Amber, 1890-1910, 9 In. 1064.00
Sniteman's X Ray Liniment, Label, Contents, Box, Wisconsin, 12 In. 330.00
Soda, see Soda Bottle
Solon Palmer Perfume Co., Painted Label Under Glass, 9 x 3 In. .... *Illus* 303.00
Soule's Eradicator, Contents, Labels, Box, 5 In. 231.00
St. Antonius Liniment, Aqua, Contents, Labels, 1875, 6 In. 132.00
St. Drake's Plantation X Bitters, 6-Log, Apricot, 1862-1870, 10 In. 392.00
Star Kidney & Liver Bitters, Amber, 1885-1895, 8 3/4 In. 123.00
Strickland's Wine Of Life, Amber, Cylinder, Whiskey Shape, Label, 11 In. 242.00
Stromeyer's Grape Punch Syrup, Reverse Label On Glass, 12 1/2 In. 577.00
Sunny Brook Whiskey, Inspector Holding Bottle, Backbar, 1890-1910, 10 7/8 In. 560.00
Syrup Heroin Co., Label Only, Thorn & Co., 5 In. 253.00
Tangin, Amber, Labels, Gin Shape, 8 1/2 In. 66.00
Telegram Rye, David Netter & Co., Embossed, c.1900, 11 In. 19.00
True Peppermint Extract Bottle, Sample, 5 1/4 In. 12.00
U.F.M. & PK, 6-Sided, Aqua, Open Pontil, Contents, Label, Philadelphia, 2 In. 330.00
Udolpho Wolfe's, Schiedam, Aromatic Schnappe, Olive, 1855-1870, 9 3/4 In. 157.00
United Drug Co., Sodium Phosphate, Cork, Aluminum Screw Top, 4 Oz. 30.00
University N.Y. Medical, Cobalt Blue, Embossed Lines, Applied Top, Box, $2.00, 7 In. 242.00
Vanderhoof's Sexual Disease/Nerve Pills, ABM, Contents, Box, 3 1/2 In. 22.00

Velvetina Skin Beautifier, Milk Glass, Contents, Label, 5 1/4 In. 154.00
Vernal Female Tonic For Women, Label, Contents, Pamphlet, Box, 9 In. 66.00
Vetters Dyspepsia Remedy, Contents, Labels, Pamphlet, Tax Stamp, Box, 6 1/2 In. 176.00
W. Brinker & Son Co., Druggist, New York & Brooklyn, Blob, 8 In. 8.00
W.K. Lewis & Co., Ext. Lemon, Aqua, 3-Sided Label, Open Pontil, 4 3/4 In. 286.00
Wharton's Whiskey, 1850 Chestnut Grove, Golden Amber, Bubbles, Flask, 5 1/2 In. 229.00
Wharton's Whiskey, Yellow Amber, Handle, Whitney Glass, c.1865, 10 1/8 In. 784.00
Wheeler's Nerve Vitalixer, ABM, Label, Pamphlet, Box, 7 1/2 In. 88.00
White House Vinegar, 2 Handles, Cabbage Rose, Cork Stopper, 9 1/2 In. 30.00
White Pine & Tar Compound Cough Syrup, Contents, Label, Wrapper, 7 In. 187.00
Wilbur's Spavin Cure, Man, Horse, Paper Label, Contents, Cork, 7 1/8 In. 77.00
William Jameson & Co., Whiskey Distillers Dublin, Kennedy Stamp, Diamond, Jug 139.00
Winter's Stomach Bitters, Amber, 1885-1895, 9 5/8 In. 157.00
Wishart's Pine Tree Tar Cordial, Pine Tree, Paper Label, Amber, 1875-1890, 9 7/8 In. ... 336.00
Worners Rattler Oil, $2.50, F.M. Worner, Label, Box, 4 3/4 In. 154.00
Yorkshire Relish, 1950s, 7 In. 12.00
Yucca For The Hair, Indian, Headdress, Aqua, Label, Box, Vermont, 7 1/2 In. 33.00

BOTTLE OPENER   Many types of bottle openers can be found, most dating from the twentieth century. Collectors prize advertising and figural openers.

Anchor Beer, 3 1/2 In. 3.00
Ballantine Ale & Beer, Metal, Handy Walden, 3 1/2 In. 5.05
Banner Dairy, Chas. T. Markwort Prop., Metal, Triangular & Rounded Ends 22.00
Benson & Hedges 100's, Cigarette Pack Shape, Key Chain, 1 1/2 x 2 3/4 In. 6.00
Beverwyck Beer, Wire Type 6.00
Compliments Of Your Marathon Dealer, Spoon, 1960s 6.00
Fehr's Beer, Bottle Shape, 4 3/8 x 1 In. 10.00
First State Bank, Your Full Service Bank, Plastic, Metal, White, Blue Letters, 12 In. 2.00
Genesee Beer & 12 Horse Ale, Rochester, N.Y., 5 In. 5.00
Gunther Premium Dry Beer, Copper, 3 In. 10.00
Krueger Beer, Krueger's Finest Beer, Ambassador Beer, Wire Type, Newark, N.J. 5.00
Old German Beer, 3 In. 14.95
Pearl Beer, Folding, Bead Chain, Vaughn 17.95
Piels Light Beer, Metal, 3 1/2 In. 5.05
Rheingold Beer, Metal, 3 3/4 In. 5.05
Sunshine Extra Light, Premium, Wire Type 6.00
Warsteiner Beer, Crown, Metal, Gold Finish, German Text 5.00

BOX   Commercial boxes of cardboard, wood, or metal have been used to hold products since the eighteenth century. Many have advertising stenciled, lithographed, painted, or otherwise labeled on the sides. Advertising can sometimes be found on the inside of the box lid. All types of boxes are collected. Most boxes are rectangular, but many other types were used. An oval-shaped wooden box was favored in the 1850–1870 period. Elaborate figural boxes were used for British biscuits and are listed under Tin.

Ackers Dyspepsia Tablets, Girl, Fancy Hat, Cardboard, 6 x 5 1/2 In. 187.00
Acme Brand Confectionery, Wood, Cedar Rapids, Iowa, 22 x 9 In. 39.00
Acme Chocolates, Bucket Shape, Cedar Rapids, Iowa, Cardboard, 13 In. Diam. 99.00
Acme Chocolates, Paper, Cedar Rapids, Iowa, 7 1/2 x 10 1/2 In. 55.00
Adams Sweet Fern Chewing Gum, Victorian Woman, Cardboard, 9 x 5 x 2 3/8 In., 2 Piece 66.00
Albers Instant Tapioca, Gold Miner, Round, Cardboard, 1920s, 1 Lb., 5 x 3 1/2 In. 385.00
Alma Boot Polish, Wood, Paper Labels On Top & Sides, Hinged Lid, 16 x 7 In. 115.00
Assorted Hair Pins, Peacock, Gold Ink, 2 3/4 In. ....*Illus* 10.00
Atwood's LF Bitters, Wood, Dovetailed, Paper Label, Crate, 10 1/2 x 8 x 7 1/2 In. 66.00
Babe Ruth Underwear, Babe Ruth In No. 9, Green Ground, 1920s, 2 3/4 x 10 x 13 In. 920.00
Bambina Toupee Plasters, Slide Tray, Lynn, Mass., 4 1/4 x 1 5/8 In. 242.00
Barkers Powder, Vegetable, Horse, Cattle, Poultry, Girl Milking Cow, Contents, 4 x 6 In. . 209.00
Baum's Horse & Stock Food, Castorine, Wood, Syracuse, N.Y., 50 Lb., 12 x 21 x 10 In. . 48.00
Bear Brand Hosiery, Cardboard, 7 x 9 x 3 In. 149.00
Beech-Nut Gum, Peppermint Flavor, Green, Cardboard, 4 x 15 x 2 1/2 In. 110.00
Big Chief Fruit Jar Rings, Indian, R.E. Tongue Bros., 1 Doz., 3 1/4 In. 264.00

Biscuit, Oak, Carved-Out Handles, Austin Young & Co., 1880s, 21 1/2 x 14 x 11 3/8 In. . . .   100.00
Bixby's Satinola, 6 Paper Labeled Bottles, 8 1/2 x 7 x 11 In. 17.00
Bola-A Tonic, For The Nerves & Blood, Wood, 12 x 17 In. 50.00
Candy, Bouquet Of Flowers, Mirror, Red Velvet Bottom, 12 x 10 x 3 In. 58.00
Cellu Sugarless Sweetener, Cardboard, Metal Top & Bottom, 4 1/4 x 1 3/4 In. 85.00
Certified Aspirin, 100 Tablets, Cardboard, Metal Top & Bottom, 1 7/8 x 2 3/8 In. 49.00
Choice Flower Seeds, D.M. Ferry & Co., Oak, 11 x 7 x 4 In. 165.00
Clark & Morgan Crackers, Candies, Flip Top Lid, Factory, Horse, Buggy, 20 x 11 x 8 In. .   75.00
Clean-BE-Tween, Tooth Brush Refills, 3/4 x 2 1/8 x 1 1/8 In. 28.00
Colgan's, Taffee Tolu Gum, Wood, Handle, 17 x 9 x 8 In. 550.00
Compound Oxygen Treatment, Wood, Dovetailed, Crate, Starkey & Palen, 14 x 8 x 5 In.   61.00
Cool Candy Cigarettes, World Candies Inc., Brooklyn, N.Y., 1960s, 2 3/4 x 1 In. 9.00
Cottage Cheese, Portland, Ind., Waxed Cardboard, 12 Oz., 3 1/4 In. . . . . *Illus*   6.00
Cottolene Cottonseed Oil, Cardboard, Tin Top & Bottom, Sample, 2 x 1 3/4 In. 120.00
Crane's Candy, Gessoed Wood, Parrish Rubaiyat, 1920s, 6 x 12 1/4 x 2 7/8 In. 798.00
Creek Chub Bait Co., Jointed Pikie Minnow, No. 2600, 4 1/2 In. 121.00
Cretors Pop Corn, Happy Child Eating Popcorn, 1929, 5 x 2 1/4 x 7 In. . . . . .7.00 to 30.00
Curlox Oversize Hairnets, Wood, Decals, Countertop, 15 In. 220.00
Cuticura Resolvent, New Blood Purifier, Potter Drum, Wood, Boston, 10 x 8 x 8 1/2 In. .   79.00
D.M. Ferry & Co. Flower Seeds, Wood, 14 x 9 In. 44.00
Dana's Sarsaparilla, Crate, Wood, Belfast, Maine, 11 1/4 x 10 1/4 x 9 In. 121.00
Davy Crockett Candy & Toy, Cardboard, Novel Package Co., Brooklyn, 3 3/4 x 2 x 7/8 In.   20.00
Dean's Mentholated Cough Drops, 5 Cents, Cardboard, 10 x 7 x 3 In. 99.00
Diamond Matches, Pine, Hinged Lid, 25 x 13 In. 58.00
Diamond Matches, Wood, Dovetailed, 12 x 24 In. 88.00
Doctor Daughter Blood Builder Nerve Tonic, Contents, Flyer, c.1914, 2 3/4 x 2 1/8 In. .   72.00
Dr. Charles Face Powder, Cardboard, Insert, Contents, 1 1/2 x 1 7/8 x 1 7/8 In. 95.00
Dr. Claris Veterinary Hospital, Diuretic Powders, Contents, 4 1/4 x 3 1/8 In. 66.00
Dr. Green's Nervura Nerve Tonic, Crate, Wood, 1 Dozen, 10 1/2 x 8 1/2 x 11 1/4 In. 88.00
Dr. Grosvenor's Bellcapsic Porous Plaster, Boston, Mass., 6 1/2 x 9 1/4 In. . . . . *Illus*   40.00
Dr. Harter's Wild Cherry Bitters, Wood, 21 x 9 x 12 In. 61.00
Dr. Herrick's Sugar Coated Pills, Wood, Oval, Sealed, 2 In. 154.00
Dr. Hess Stock Tonic, Scientific Compound, Free Sample, 5 1/4 x 3 7/8 In. 187.00
Dr. John Bull's Round Worm Lozenges, 2 Women, Children, 50 Cents A Box, 3 x 2 In. . .   220.00
Dr. LeGear's Guaranteed Stock Powders, Horse, Cardboard, 4 3/4 x 2 3/4 In. 209.00
Dr. LeGear's Nerve Sedative Tablets, Red Ground, Canister Inside, Contents, 2 3/8 In. . .   39.00
Dr. LeGear's Poultry Ascarid Worm Powder, 6 7/8 x 4 1/2 x 2 1/4 In. 65.00
Dr. LeGear's Poultry Powder Guaranteed, Contents, 4 3/4 x 2 3/4 In. . . . . .110.00 to 198.00
Dr. Rand's Family Remedy, Cardboard, Battleship Tax Stamp, Unopened, 4 x 2 1/2 In. . . .   77.00
Dr. Raymond's Pills, For Female Menstrual Irregularities, Multicolored, 3 x 2 In. 39.00
Dr. Shores Catarrh Cure, Salt Lake City, Utah, $2.00 A Box, 1 5/8 x 2 1/2 In. 330.00
Dr. Strong's Vegetable Stomach Pills, Wood, Oval, Paper Wrapper, 2 1/4 In. 61.00
Dr. Thacher's Liver Medicine, 5 Boxes, 25 Cents Each, 7 5/8 x 3 x 2 1/4 In. 99.00
Drummer Dyes, Nigger Brown, Contents, 2 In. 84.00
Dutch Hand Soap, Free Sample, Cudahy, Omaha, 2 3/8 x 1 1/2 x 5/8 In. 95.00

Box, Assorted Hair Pins,
Peacock, Gold Ink, 2 3/4 In.

Box, Cottage Cheese,
Portland, Ind., Waxed
Cardboard, 12 Oz., 3 1/4 In.

Box, Dr. Grosvenor's Bellcapsic
Porous Plaster, Boston, Mass.,
6 1/2 x 9 1/4 In.

Box, Fairy Soap, Wood,
Hinged Lift Lid, Fairy In
Roses, Lithograph,
8 x 17 In.

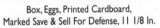

Box, Eggs, Printed Cardboard,
Marked Save & Sell For Defense, 11 1/8 In.

Eggs, Printed Cardboard, Marked Save & Sell For Defense, 11 1/8 In. . . . . *Illus*	15.00
Electric Bitters, 2 Dozen, World's Greatest Cure, Wood, 20 x 10 x 13 In.	121.00
Elkay Snow Flake Fresh Buttered Popcorn, 5 x 2 1/4 x 7 In.	19.80
Fairy Soap, Wood, Hinged Lift Lid, Fairy In Roses, Lithograph, 8 x 17 In. . . . . *Illus*	489.00
Federal Poultry Food, Tonic, Girl Feeding Chickens, 25 Cents, Contents, 7 3/4 x 5 In. . . .	220.00
Federal Stock Food, Only 1 Cent Per Day, 50 Cents, Farm Scene, Contents, 9 1/2 x 5 In. .	176.00
Ferry Seeds, Girl, Basket Of Flowers, Wood, Paper Label, 12 3/8 x 16 1/2 x 9 In.	495.00
Flecks Conditioning Powders, Horse, 4 1/4 Lb., 8 5/8 x 6 x 3 1/4 In.	495.00
Foley Kidney Pills, Backache, Rheumatism, Kidneys, Wood, Crate, 24 x 11 x 13 In.	121.00
Fountain Of Youth Crystals, Woman Playing Tennis, Cardboard, 5 x 3 x 2 In.	28.00
Franklin Biscuit Co. Steam Bakers, Philadelphia, Wood, Hinged Lid, Paper Labels, 9 In. .	66.00
Fun To Wash, Washing Powder, Mammy, 25 Cents, Unopened, 7 x 5 x 2 1/2 In. . . . .45.00 to	154.00
Gibbs Hollow Suppositories, Wood, Dovetailed, Slide Lid, Directions, 1/2 Gross, 6 x 4 In.	220.00
Glycerine Tablets, Cardboard, Slide Tray, 2 1/2 x 1 1/2 In.	39.00
Gold Dandruff Cure, Wood, Dovetailed, Crate, 9 x 8 x 10 In.	39.00
Golden Rule Dairy, Cumberland Case Co., Wooden Slat, Metal, 12 x 16 In.	75.00
Gooch's Mexican Root Capsules Or Pills, Unopened, Cincinnati, Ohio, 2 1/4 In.	154.00
Gordon & Clark's Remedy For Piles, Lynn, Mass., 3/4 x 2 1/2 In. . . . . *Illus*	55.00
Grandpa's Wonder Pine Tar Soap, Cardboard, Contents, Guest Size, 2 5/8 In.	35.00
Grants Hygienic Cracker, Daily Regulator, Mock-Up Display, 8 3/4 x 6 In.	55.00
Guardian Service Cleaner, Cardboard, Metal Top & Bottom, 5 1/8 x 2 5/8 In.	25.00
H&H Tender & Tasty Popped Corn, Red Ground, Cardboard, 4 1/4 x 2 1/2 x 6 1/2 In. . . .	5.50
Hamilton's Sugar Coated Root & Plant Pills, Wood, Oval, Contents, Paper Label, 2 In. .	154.00
Hargrave Biscuit Co., Fine Cakes & Crackers, Wood, Paper Label, Hinged Lid, 11 In. . . .	33.00
Hickmans Chewing Gum, Silver Birch, 5 Cents, Contents, 20 Piece, 5 x 6 3/8 x 4 In.	2530.00
Hildreth's Original & Only, Velvet Molasses Candy, Girl, Monkeys, Early 1900s, 4 x 7 In.	66.00
Hill's Cascara Quinine Compound, 5 Boxes, Contents, Cardboard, 10 1/2 x 5 In.	83.00
Hit For The Horse, Safe & Sure Liniment, Dr. Carey Medical Corp., Elmira, N.Y., 10 In. .	720.00
Holleb's Corn Flakes, Cardboard, 10 x 13 In.	22.00
Holmes & Coutt's Biscuits, Wood, 19 x 9 In.	33.00
Improved Foot Soap, American Druggists, Contents, 4 1/4 In. . . . . *Illus*	5.00
Independent Baking Co., Davenport, Ia., Lady, Winter Dress, Pine, Hinged Lid, 21 x 14 In.	69.00
J.S. Ivins' Son Steam Bakery, Philadelphia, Pa., Wood, 2 Paper Labels, Hinged Lid, 9 In. .	99.00
Jack Sprat Tea, Cardboard, Consolidated Food Corp., 4 1/4 x 3 x 2 1/4 In.	85.00
Jergens, Rachel, 3 Ladies, 1 Oz., 2 1/2 x 2 1/2 x 1 In.	38.00
Jiffy Toothache Drops, Cardboard, Contents, Hamilton Drug Company, 4 x 1 In.	40.00
Jocka Biscuit Chocolat, Black Bellhop, Lithograph Cardboard, France, 1918, 8 In.	167.00
Johnson's Belladonna Plaster, Cardboard, 9 x 6 In.	61.00
Jolly Time Pop Corn, World's Choicest, American Pop Corn, 1930, 7 x 3 x 10 1/4 In.	30.00
Kerr Blue Inlay Casting Wax, Partial Contents, Detroit, Michigan, 3/4 Oz.	12.00
Keystone Biscuit, Tin, Glass Front, Stencil, 12 In.	154.00
Kibbe Bros., Molasses Candy, Springfield, Mass., Wood, 17 x 5 1/2 x 13 In.	61.00
Kilgore Perforated Caps, 250 Shots, American Toys, Westerville, Ohio, 2 x 1 In.	5.50
Kingsford Corn Starch, Paper, Cardboard, National Starch Co., Sample, 2 5/8 x 1 3/8 In. .	140.00
Kirk & Company, Spanish Tablets, Wood, Pin Hinged Lid, 13 x 7 In.	44.00
Lambert's Death To Lice, Contents, Pamphlet, 7 In. . . . . *Illus*	125.00
Land-O-Lakes Butter, Recipe, Tin, 5 1/2 x 3 x 3 In.	45.00
Landesfreund, Razor Blades, Extra Dunn, 2 In. . . . . *Illus*	10.00

Box, Gordon & Clark's Remedy For Piles,
Lynn, Mass., 3/4 x 2 1/2 In.

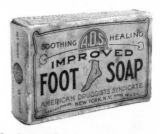

Box, Improved Foot Soap, American Druggists,
Contents, 4 1/4 In.

Lapidar, Order At Once, Large Box Of Lapidar, 1000 Tablets, Contents, Square, 3 1/2 In. .   143.00
Lash's Bitters, Tonic Laxative, Wood, Dovetailed, 13 x 10 1/2 x 10 In. . . . . .44.00 to 83.00
Lava Chemical Resolvent Soap, Cardboard, Contents, Trial Size, 2 1/4 x 1 5/8 In. 75.00
Libby, McNeill & Libby Condensed Mince Meat, Cardboard, 2 5/8 x 3 3/4 x 2 In. 135.00
Ligget's United Chocolate Candy, Little Bits From The East, St. Louis, Mo., 3 1/2 x 2 In.   42.00
Lincoln Seyms & Co., Spices, Pepper, Wood, 8 1/2 x 16 In. 39.00
London Cocoa, Wood, 15 1/2 x 3 1/2 x 15 In. 39.00
Mammoth Barkers Toilet Soap, Wood, Dovetailed, Glass Lid, 16 x 5 1/4 x 11 In. 33.00
Mann's Best White Birch Clothespins, Cardboard, 3 Pins, 5 x 2 x 3/4 In. 25.00
Mason's Blacking, 3 Doz., No. 4, Wood, Dovetailed, Paper Labels, 8 x 11 1/2 x 5 In. 44.00
Mason's Blacking, Wood, Paper Label, Crate, 2 1/2 x 11 3/4 x 9 In. 121.00
Mason's Blacking Shoe Dressing, Wood, Paper Labels, Hinged Lid, 3 x 12 In. 138.00
Mason's Challenge Blacking Shoe Polish, Wood, 11 x 3 x 8 In.   55.00
Mason's Challenge Blacking Shoe Polish, Wood, 12 x 9 x 3 In.   110.00
Medlar Co.'s Biscuits, Wood, Dovetailed, Hinged Lid, 2 Paper Labels, 8 In. 55.00
Mel'o All Purpose Cleaner, Sample, Cardboard, Hygienic Products, Canton, 3 x 2 x 1 In. .   28.00
Merlins Cleaning Powder, Cleans Like Magic, Paper Label, Contents, 1929, 6 x 3 x 1 In. .   94.00
Min Rock Cow Licks, Gardner Products, Wood, Albany, N.Y., 54 Lb., 17 x 8 1/2 x 8 In. . .   25.00
Mitchell's Original Kidney Plasters, Wood, Paper Labels, 13 1/2 x 9 1/2 x 2 3/4 In. 176.00
Mohican Mince Meat, Cardboard, Sample, 9 Oz., 2 1/2 x 3 3/4 x 2 In. . . . . .44.00 to 66.00
Mother Goose Child's Shoes, 7 5/8 x 4 5/8 x 3 In. 50.00
Mother Hubbard Cake Flour, Cardboard, Tin Top, Bottom, 9 1/4 x 6 1/8 x 4 1/8 In. 145.00
National Remedy Co., Dr. Swan's Remedy, Wood, Dovetailed, Crate, 8 x 10 x 7 1/2 In. . .   44.00
New York Knife Co., Fine Pocket Knives, No. 2439, 3 5/8 x 2 1/4 In. 29.00
Ney's Hay Rack Clamps, Hinged Lid, Contents, Instructions, Wood, 4 1/2 x 18 In. 44.00
Niagara Baking Co., Crackers & Biscuits, c.1900, 19 x 11 In. 144.00
None Such Mince Meat, Stenciled, Wood, 16 x 6 x 8 1/2 In. 33.00
Oakite Cleans A Million Things, Cardboard, Sample, 4 x 2 3/8 x 7/8 In. 26.00
Old Gold Tip Gum, Lift Top, Pre 1965, 2 1/4 x 3 1/4 In. 10.00
Old Mother Hubbard Popcorn, Cardboard, Metal Top, Bottom, Unopened, 5 x 1 7/8 In. . .   73.00
Paine's Celery Compound, Wood, Crate, 10 x 10 1/2 x 13 1/2 In.   39.00
Parachute Powder, Dry Lubricant For Plastic Chutes, 3 1/4 In. . . . . *Illus*   15.00
Paramount Brand Cream Cheese, Scallions, Rosedale Dairy, 2 Lb., 7 1/2 x 3 1/2 x 3 In. .   22.00

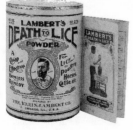

Box, Lambert's Death To Lice, Contents,
Pamphlet, 7 In.

Box, Landesfreund, Razor
Blades, Extra Dunn, 2 In.

Box, Parachute Powder, Dry
Lubricant For Plastic
Chutes, 3 1/4 In.

Box, Poli-Grip Denture
Adhesive, Tube, Block Drug
Company, 6 In.

Box, Red Top Sportsmen's
Socks, Seneca, Arrowhead,
Indian, Pair Of Socks, 15 In.

Philips Seeds, Wood, Dovetailed, Lithograph Label, 28 1/2 In. 413.00
Pixie, Strained Carrots, Infant Food, Letters, Poems, 5 Oz., 2 1/2 x 2 1/2 x 2 5/8 In. 11.00
Pixie, Strained Spinach, Infant Food, Letters, Poems, 5 Oz., 2 1/2 x 2 1/2 x 2 5/8 In. 12.00
Pocahontas Pills, 2 Indians & Other Man Near Tree, Cylinder, Unopened, 1 3/4 In. 209.00
Poli-Grip Denture Adhesive, Tube, Block Drug Company, 6 In. . . . . *Illus* 20.00
Popeye Bubble 'n Clean, Paper Lithograph, Red, Woolfoam Corp., 8 1/2 x 6 In. 17.00
Pratts Poultry Regulator, A Tonic & Appetizer, Rooster Pulling Cart, 11 7/8 x 8 1/2 In. . . 121.00
Pratts Poultry Regulator, It Helps To Make Hens Lay, Rooster Pulling Cart, 8 1/2 x 6 In. 176.00
Pratts Poultry Regulator, Unopened, 2 1/2 x 4 1/2 In. 83.00
Red Top Sportsmen's Socks, Seneca, Arrowhead, Indian, Pair Of Socks, 15 In. . . . . . *Illus* 66.00
Rex Bitters, Mixed Case, Wood, Dovetailed, Crate, Chicago, 14 1/2 x 12 1/4 x 11 In. 72.00
Rice's Barreled Sunlight Paint, Pine, Hinged Lid, 23 x 15 In. 69.00
Rice's Flower Seeds, Paper Label, Wood, Hinged Lid, 4 x 6 x 5 In. 193.00
Rice's Seed Packets, Cambridge Valley Seed Gardens, N.Y., Wood, 4 x 5 x 6 In. 275.00
Rice's Seeds, Wood, Display, 11 3/4 x 11 x 8 1/2 In. 174.00
Robertson's Plum Pudding, Golliwog, Lithograph Cardboard, 2 Lb., 5 1/2 In. 96.00
Roderic Compound, Wild Cherry Cough Balsam, Wood, Dovetailed, 6 x 10 x 5 In. 154.00
Rogers & Baldwin Hardware Co., Buckeye Cutlery, Box, 1880s, 4 1/4 x 3 1/4 In. 68.00
Root's Underwear, Polar Bear In Long Underwear, 18 In. 66.00
Rush Park Seed, Unrivaled Garden Seeds, Wood, Dovetailed, 6 x 31 In. 288.00
Rush Park Seed, Unrivaled, Try Them, Oak, Tongue & Groove, 5 x 9 1/2 In. 110.00
Scott's Emulsions, 1 Doz. Bottles, Cardboard, Unopened, 8 x 8 x 7 In. 132.00
Security Stock Food, Glutenized, Farm Scene, Man At Fence, 50 Cents, 9 x 6 In. 1210.00
Simmons' Liver Regulator, 4 Individual Boxes, 2 1/8 x 7 3/4 In. 61.00
Simpson's Cigars, Sit Down & Smoke, Little Chair, Joke, 1 In. . . . . *Illus* 100.00
Skipper Pop Corn, Boy In Sailor Suit Feeding Dog, 4 1/2 x 2 1/4 x 6 3/4 In. 6.60
St. Jacobs Oil, Great German Remedy, 1 Dozen, Wood, Dovetailed, 7 x 7 x 5 1/2 In. 55.00
St. Johnsbury Cookies, Homemade, Wood, 21 x 11 x 15 In. 165.00
Steam Bakery, J S Ivins' Son, Original Labels, Wood 550.00
Steele's Bilious Ball, 1 Empty Package, Cardboard, New York, 8 1/2 x 4 1/2 In. 605.00

Box, Simpson's Cigars, Sit Down & Smoke,
Little Chair, Joke, 1 In.

Box, Tintex, All-Fabric Tints & Dyes,
Tube, Park & Tilford, 4 In.

Sturtevant Roup Powder, Wood, Cylindrical, Wraparound Label, Contents, 3 x 1 1/2 In. . . 61.00
Sunlight Soap, 13 1/2 x 16 x 4 1/2 In. 715.00
Superior Condition Powders, Hagerty Bros., Horse, Contents, 6 1/2 x 3 In. 198.00
Sweet Clover Dairy Box, Wood, Metal On Edges, 16 x 9 x 12 In. 28.00
Tar-Oid, 12 Lithographed Tins In Boxes, 5 1/4 x 7 In. 743.00
Tasti-Spred Oleomargarine, Baltimore Butterine Co., Baltimore, Md., 1 Lb., c.1920s 18.00
Tea, Thos. C. Fluke, Wood, Paper Lithograph, 9 x 9 x 9 In. 11.00
Tennessee Biscuit Co., Glass Front, 10 1/2 x 6 In. 22.00
Tintex, All-Fabric Tints & Dyes, Tube, Park & Tilford, 4 In. *Illus* 5.00
Tree Tea Orange Pekoe, Cardboard, M.J.B. Co., San Francisco, 2 5/8 x 2 In. 118.00
Tru-Aspingum, Cardboard, Unopened, 5/8 x 2 3/4 x 2 1/4 In. 32.00
True's Elixir, Old Standard Family Medicine, Wood, Dovetailed, Crate, 5 x 6 1/2 x 6 1/2 In. 50.00
Ulster Knife Co., Superior Pocket Knives, No. 24610, 3 7/8 x 5 3/8 In. 30.00
Uncle William Jar Rubbers, Contents, 12 Piece, 3 1/4 x 3 1/4 x 1 1/4 In. 130.00
United Pure Cocoa Hancock Nelson Mercantile, Cardboard, Tin, 4 3/4 x 3 x 9 1/4 In. . . . 75.00
Vitaline & Nerve Tone, Hall Medicine Co., Toledo, Ohio, 5 x 1 1/4 In. 50.00
Warner & Co., Granular Effervescent Salts, Sodium Phosphates, Dovetailed, 9 x 11 x 8 In. 248.00
Washington Crisps, Corn Flakes, Bust Of Washington, Stripes, c.1900, 31 x 19 In. 1870.00
Watling Shipping, Wood, For 3-Reel Slot Machine, Crate, 28 x 18 1/2 In. 165.00
Wertz Bakery Crackers, Reading, Pa., Wood, Dovetailed, Paper Label, 13 In. 59.00
Western Reserve Mince Meat, Cardboard, William Edwards & Co., 2 1/2 x 3 1/2 x 2 In. . . 44.00
White House Biscuit, Crackers, Wood, Paper Label, Dubuque, Iowa 99.00
Wilbur's Sure Heave Cure, Pure Vegetable Remedy, 3 3/8 x 5 In. 110.00
Williams' Root Beer Extract, Wood, Paper Labels 715.00
Wilson Cheese, Wood, 5 Lb., 4 x 3 3/4 x 12 In. 9.00
Wm. Radam's Microbe Killer, Man Beating Skeleton, Wood, Crate, 8 x 12 x 18 In. 165.00 to 176.00
Worcester's Ivory Salt Co., Cardboard, New York, N.Y., 2 1/8 x 1 1/4 In. 70.00
Zoagraine, Asthma Conqueror, New York, 3 1/4 x 2 x 9 1/4 In. 22.00

BROMO SELTZER Bromo Seltzer was first made in a Baltimore drug-store in 1888 by Captain Isaac Emerson. He built a plant in 1891 to make the product. The first famous blue bottles, manufactured by Hazel Atlas Glass Company, were partly machine-made. In 1907 the Maryland Glass Corp. began making the bottles by a completely auto-mated system. These bottles are marked on the bottom with the letter "M." Corks were used until 1920, when metal seals were introduced for large bottles. The small bottles had seals by 1928. The metal screw cap was introduced in 1954. Emerson Drug Company and the Bromo Seltzer brand were bought by Warner Lambert in 1967. A plastic bot-tle with a seal over the metal cap was used by 1981. The brand had faded into obscurity by the 1990s but was purchased and reintroduced to the market in 2000 by Numark Laboratories of Edison, New Jersey. The blue bottle has been retired and Bromo Seltzer is now sold in boxes containing premeasured foil packs.

Bottle, Unopened, Square, Box, 2 3/4 x 1 1/4 In. 90.00
Calendar, 1904, Emerson Drug Co., Mechanical Trade Card, 5 x 2 1/2 In. 165.00
Dispenser, Cobalt Blue Glass, Glass With Bottle, 1930, 15 In. . . . . 176.00 to 220.00
Matchbook, Diamond Match Company, N.Y., 2 x 1 1/2 In. 5.00
Mirror, Cures All Headaches, Woman, Oval, Pocket, 2 1/2 In. 102.00
Sign, Emerson's, King & Queen, Frame, 26 x 43 In. 688.00
Tip Tray, Cures All Headaches, Bottle, Tin Lithograph, Round 79.00

BUDWEISER, see Anheuser-Busch

BURGER KING Burger King Corp. was founded by James W. McLamore and David Edgerton, who opened their first Burger King restaurant in Miami, Florida, in 1954. It grew to a chain of 274 restau-rants by 1967, when it became a wholly owned subsidiary of the Pills-bury Company. After several changes in ownership, it was sold to an investment group in 2002. Burger King has advertised on radio and television and in newspapers and magazines with slogans like "The Bigger the Burger the Better the Burger" (1968), "It Takes Two Hands to Handle a Whopper" (1970), "Have It Your Way" (1974, reintroduced in 2004), "Make It Special, Make It Burger King" (1980), "Aren't You Hungry for Burger King Now" (1982), "This Is a Burger King Town" (1986), "Best Food for Fast Times" (1987), "We Do It Like You Do It" (1988), "Sometimes You Gotta Break the Rules" (1989), "Your Way, Right Away" (1991), "BK Tee Vee" (1992), "Back to Basics" (1994), "Get Your Burger's Worth" (1994), "It Just Tastes Better" (1996), "When You Have It Your Way It Just Tastes Better" (1999), "Got the Urge" (2000), "The Whopper Says" (2001), "At BK, You Got It!" (2002), and "The Fire's Ready" (2003). The company has issued many premiums. Most popular are the stuffed dolls made in 1972, 1973, and 1977.

Booklet, Draw & Color, c.1972, 5 1/2 x 8 1/2 In., 8 Pages	10.00
Decorated Tumbler Set, Disney Collectors Series, Plastic, Box	90.00
Figure, Cape, Crown, Hamburger, Ring, Bag, Yellow Boots, Stand, 1980, 19 1/2 In.	42.00
Milkshake Lid, Home Of The Whopper, Cardboard, 3 1/8 In.	12.00
Toy, Catapult Ball Into Basket, Red Plastic, 1980, 2 x 4 x 1 In.	1.00
Toy, Saucer Launcher, Blue Plastic, 1979, 2 x 5 In.	2.00

BUSCH BAVARIAN BEER, see Anheuser-Busch

BUSTER BROWN Buster Brown and his dog, Tige, first appeared in Richard Felton Outcault's cartoon strip in 1902. The comic characters were licensed to merchants at the 1904 St. Louis World's Fair for use as trademarks. Over fifty different products used the Buster Brown name and figures. Touring midgets with dogs portrayed Buster Brown and Tige at promotional shows in theaters and fairs from 1904 to 1915. The Buster Brown Gang was featured on radio in 1943 and on television from 1951 to 1954. Three companies, Brown Shoe Company, Buster Brown Apparel Inc., and Gateway Hosiery (makers of Buster Brown socks) still use Buster Brown logos. There are many old and new Buster Brown collectibles available. Brown Shoe's logo is a line-drawn profile of Buster & Tige. The clothing company uses a silhouette of Buster & Tige playing tug-of-war.

Bank, Buster & Tige, Cast Iron, A.C. Williams, 6 In.	165.00
Bank, Good Luck, Horse, Horseshoe, Tige, Cast Iron, Arcade, 5 In.	303.00
Button, Bread, Detroit Baseball Player, Celluloid, Pinback, 1 1/4 In.	303.00
Button, Buster Brown Bread, Type, Multicolored, Celluloid, 1 1/4 In.	17.00
Button, Pinback, 1901-1910, 1 1/2 In.	88.00
Clicker, Boy & Dog, Celluloid, 1 1/4 In.	275.00
Clock, Shoes, Light-Up, 14 1/2 In.	578.00
Cloth, Printed, Buster Brown & Tige, Frame, c.1900, 20 x 24 In.	105.00
Dish, Cap Shape, Tige Balancing Teakettle On Nose, 4 5/8 In.	81.00
Display, Stand-Up, Quality Children's Clothing, Buster & Tige Pulling Sock, 8 In.	83.00
Display, Tige Pulling Buster In Shoe, Tin Lithograph, Die Cut, 24 In., 2 Piece	9400.00
Doll, Buster & Tige, Knickerbocker Specialty, Cloth, Uncut, 17 x 36 In. *Illus*	275.00
Key Chain Fob, Blue Ribbon Shoes, Silver, Oval	28.00
Knife, Woodcraft Pattern, Leather Handle & Sheath, Marble's, 4 1/4-In. Blade	173.00
Match Holder, Buster Brown Bread, 6 3/4 x 2 1/8 x 3/4 In.	2150.00
Mirror, Buster, Blue Bowtie & Collar, Whitehead & Hoag, c.1905, 2 In.	176.00
Mirror, Full-Length Buster & Tige, E.G. Adams & Co., c.1900, 2 1/4 In.	242.00
Mirror, Shoes For Boys & Girls, Buster, Tige, Celluloid, c.1910, 1 1/2 In.	66.00 to 94.00
Plaque, Chalkware, Dimensional, Winking Buster, Tige, 17 x 18 In.	201.00
Playing Cards, U.S. Playing Card Co., c.1906, 2 1/2 In.	55.00
Pocketknife, Brown Shoe Co., Lady's Leg Shape, St. Louis, Early 1900s	39.00
Pocketknife, Buster Standing Over Tige, Blue On White Pearl, 4 In.	104.00
Pocketknife, For Boys, For Girls, 1940s, 3 1/2 In.	81.00
Puzzle, Put Your Feet In Brown Bilt Shoes, Metal Ball, Tin, 2 In. Diam.	55.00
Rug, Buster & Tige, Yellow Ground, Blue Edge, Stars, Mohawk, Round, 53 In.	141.00 to 330.00
Sign, Buster Brown Shoes, Buster, Tige, Plaster, Relief, Square, 18 x 17 3/4 In.	173.00
Sign, Golden Sheaf Bakery, Buster Brown Bread, Embossed, 1920s, 20 x 28 In.	1165.00 to 1375.00
Tray, Shoe Advertising, Brown Grain Painting, Gold Letters, 13 3/8 In.	55.00
Waffle Iron, Cast Iron	138.00

BUTTON   The buttons listed here are sometimes called pinbacks or celluloids in other books. Most collectors refer to them as buttons. They can be made of celluloid, tin, or some other metal. Some have a sharp pin on the back to push through a shirt; others have a small metal attachment that's bent to hold the button on a lapel. Round buttons with a picture and a slogan were popular as giveaways from about 1896 to 1920. Whitehead & Hoag Company of Newark, New Jersey, started making buttons in 1896 and continued to be the major producer for years. Most of these buttons ranged from 7/8 to 1 3/4 inches in diameter. The craze for buttons, especially large ones, returned after World War II.

Acme Queen Farm Machinery, 4 Jacks & A Queen, 1 1/4 In.	264.00
Amoco, Join The American Party, Tin Lithograph, Pinback	15.00
Atlantic City, Steel Pier, Black, White, Celluloid, c.1930, 1 1/4 In.	22.00
Baker, Tractor, A.D. Baker Co., Swanton, Ohio, Round, Celluloid, 1 3/4 In.	133.00
Black Cat Stove & Shoe Polish, Black Cat, Pinback	155.00
Bond Bread, Amelia Earhart, No. 5, Pinback, Round, 1 1/4 In.	70.00
Bond Bread, Commander Byrd's Floyd Bennett, No. 3, Pinback, Round, 1 1/4 In.	55.00
Bond Bread, First Flight Paris To New York, Celluloid, No. 4	38.00
Buitoni, Joe DiMaggio Club, Lithograph, 1949, 1 1/2 In.	805.00
Bush & Bull, Santa's Good Behavior Award, Santa Claus, Winking, Lithograph, 1 3/4 In.	20.00
Buy Right In Richmond Hill, Ask For Coupons, Santa, Multicolored, Celluloid, 1 1/4 In.	83.00
Crescent Flour Mills, Pride Of Colorado, Red, Green, Gold, Cream, Celluloid, 1 1/4 In.	49.00
Cub Shoe Polish, Tin Lithograph, Bear Cub Polishes Shoes, Red Ground, Round, 1 1/2 In.	234.00
Deering Harvester Co., Farmer, Harvesting Crop, Celluloid, Pinback, 1896, 1 1/4 In.	44.00
Diamond C Hamms, Pinback, Celluloid, Round, 1 1/2 In.	95.00
Dodge Bicycle, Our Defender, Sailboat, 1890-1900, 7/8 In.	28.00
Ducks Unlimited, Celluloid, Round, 1 1/4 In.	77.00
Eatons, Greeting From Santa Claus, Multicolored, Celluloid, 1 1/4 In.	120.00
Every Year I Am Here In Rudges Toyland, Santa, Multicolored, Celluloid, 1 1/4 In.	54.00
Ford, I'm Fired Up, Flasher Badge, Orange, Yellow, Vari-Vue, Pinback, c.1960, 3 In.	31.00
Frog In Your Throat?, 10 Cents For Coughs & Colds, Green Frog, Celluloid, 3/4 In.	99.00
Give Something Electrical, Santa Claus, Multicolored, Celluloid, 1 1/4 In.	85.00
Glenville Banking & Trust, Santa On Phone, Multicolored, Celluloid, 1 1/4 In. 40.00 to	75.00
Globe, Just Kids Safety Club, Pinback, Marjory, 1930s	18.00
Golden Guernsey, America's Table Milk, Peterboro, N.H., Celluloid, Pinback	36.00
Golden Guernsey, Celluloid, Paper, American Cattle Clug, Peterboro, N.H.	36.00
Golden Sheaf Bread, Bungalow Given Away, Celluloid, 1 1/2 In.	248.00
Gourlay, Winter & Leeming Pianos, Celluloid, Pinback, Oval, 1 3/8 x 1 In.	85.00
H.H. Barber, Big Store, Teddy Bear, Multicolored, Celluloid, 1 In.	64.00
Hall's, Santa Claus, Holly Wreath, Around Head, Multicolored, Celluloid, 1 1/4 In.	66.00
Headquarters At Hunter, Tuppens, Santa, In Chimney, Multicolored, Celluloid, 1 1/4 In.	97.00
Holden's, For Shoes, Santa Claus, Short Beard, Multicolored, Celluloid, Round, 1 1/4 In.	67.00
Hoosier Drill Co., Richmond, Ind., Celluloid Over Metal, Oval, 1 x 5/8 In.	125.00
Hoppy's Favorite, Polk Dairy	29.00
Hunter Bicycles, Hunter Arms Co., Dog, Bird In Mouth, Whitehead & Hoag, 7/8 In.	266.00
Hush Puppies, The People's Choice, Red, White, Blue, c.1968, 1 3/8 In.	48.00
International Shirt & Collar, Camel In Shirt, 2 1/8 In.	285.00
Iszard's, My Headquarters, Santa Claus, Going Down Chimney, Celluloid, 1 1/4 In.	109.00
J.N. Adam & Co., Santa Claus, Multicolored, Celluloid, Round, 1 1/4 In.	73.00
Kresge Department Store, Newark, Santa Claus, Building, Celluloid, 1 1/2 In.	334.00
Land O' Lakes Creameries, Indian Maiden, Celluloid, 1928, 1 1/2 In.	89.00
Liquozone, Oxygen Method, Gives Life, 2 Children, Celluloid, 1 1/4 In.	92.00
Muskogee Arkansas On The River, Gas Coal And Gas, Celluloid, Pinback	175.00
National Wool Growers Convention, Salt Lake, January 19, 1901, Celluloid, 1 3/4 In.	25.00
Oh Boy Gum, Booster, Chew To Your Heart's Content, Celluloid, 1 1/4 In.	308.00
Orange Crush, Philadelphia Badge Co., Celluloid, Cardboard, 9 In.	165.00
Otis Company, What Is Home Without A Good Bed, Duck, House, c.1915, 1 1/4 In.	45.00
Pearline Soap, Baltimore Badge, Celluloid, Pinback, 1901 Patent	18.00
Pearline Soap, Bell, Hello Give Me Pearline, Celluloid, Pinback	18.00
Pure As Butterine, 2 Girls, Swift Jersey, Celluloid, 1 1/4 In.	182.00
Sanders Candies, Merry Xmas, Santa Claus, Multicolored, Celluloid, 1 1/4 In.	99.00

Sanders Candies, Santa Claus, Candle, Multicolored, Celluloid, 1 1/4 In. 121.00
Shoot Blue Rocks, Celluloid, 7/8 In. 381.00
Sibley, Lindsay & Curr, Santa Holding Building Picture, Multicolored, Celluloid, 1 1/4 In. 133.00
Simmons Keen Kutter, Ax Head Shape, 10K Gold, Hinged, 1 1/4 In. 340.00
Southwestern Iowa Firemens Assoc., July 4-5, 1906, Multicolored, Celluloid, 1 1/4 In. . . 36.00
Special Patent Flour, Ask Your Mother, Celluloid, 1 1/2 In. 198.00
Sportsmans League, 2 Men, In Canoe, Fishing, Celluloid, Pinback, 1 1/4 In. 99.00
Sportsmans League, Bradshaw Fancy, Wet Fly For Trout, Celluloid, Pinback, 1 1/4 In. . . 77.00
Sportsmans League, Johnson, Wet Fly For Trout, Celluloid, Pinback, 1 1/2 In. 88.00
Thrifty, Has Krona Chrome, Think Bug, Blue, White, c.1960, 3 1/2 In. 20.00
Tiffin Wagon Co., Green Wagon, Celluloid, Ohio, 1 1/4 In. 194.00
Wellsville Driving Park, Home Of Direct Hal, Celluloid, 2 1/8 In. 117.00
Why Yes, I Am Staying With D.P. & S., Santa, Phone, Multicolored, Celluloid, 1 1/4 In. . . 85.00
Winkelman's Quaker Bread, Baerwald, Turtle, Memphis, Round, c.1909, 1 1/4 In. 1150.00
Ye Olde Mill, Amusement Ride, Celluloid, Pinback, 1 1/4 In. 95.00
Yetter's Wallpaper, Dutch Girl, Tulip, Celluloid, Omaha, Neb., 1 1/4 In. 165.00

C.D. KENNY In the early 1900s, Baltimore-based C.D. Kenny Company was a wholesale distributor of tea, coffee, and sugar. The company gave away tip and serving trays with patriotic, holiday, and other themes. It also offered paper dolls and other toys as premiums. In 1939 Nathan Cummings purchased C.D. Kenny, expanding the company and purchasing others, including Sprague Warner & Company and Reid Murdoch & Company (see Monarch), eventually forming Consolidated Grocers Corp. in 1945. In 1985 the company became the Sara Lee Corp.

Ashtray, BPOE, Grand Lodge, Elk, Tin Lithograph, Baltimore, 1916, 4 1/2 In. 28.00
Bank, Papoose, Painted, Porcelain, 4 In. 71.00
Calendar, 1903, 4 Pages, Frame, 26 x 30 In. 440.00
Can, Mammy's Favorite Brand, Tin Lithograph, 11 In. 424.00
Nodder, Bisque, Painted, 3 In. 60.00
Plaque, Easter, Girls, Animals, Table, Tin Lithograph, Oval, 12 In. . . . . .170.00 to 203.00
Plate, Santa, Tin Lithograph, Round, 9 1/2 In. 237.00
Rolling Pin, Milk Glass, Wooden Handles, 18 In. 791.00
Tin, Kenny's Maid Coffee, Dutch Girl, Tin Lithograph, Baltimore, 4 Lb., 8 In. . . . .220.00 to 275.00
Tin, Mammy's Favorite Brand Coffee, Bail Handle, Lid, Baltimore, 4 Lb. . . . . .215.00 to 695.00
Tip Tray, America's Pride, Soldier, Sailor, Tin Lithograph, Round, 4 3/8 In. . . . . . .124.00 to 303.00
Tip Tray, C.D. Kenny Coffee & Tea, Drink & Enjoy, Girl, Rose Bouquet, 1899, 6 In. 303.00
Tip Tray, Democratic Convention, 5th Regiment, Tin Lithograph, 1912, 6 In. . . . . . .80.00 to 154.00
Tip Tray, Drink & Enjoy, Tin Lithograph, Oval, 6 In. 28.00
Tip Tray, Drink & Enjoy, Woman, Flowers In Hair, Round, 4 1/4 In. 124.00
Tip Tray, For Iced Tea, Use Cheon, Asian Woman, Tin Lithograph, Round, 4 3/8 In. .57.00 to 110.00
Tip Tray, Raising Flag At Valley Forge, Tin Lithograph, c.1911, 5 1/4 In. . . . . .113.00 to 253.00
Tip Tray, Thanksgiving Greetings, Girl Praying, Tin Lithograph, Round, 4 3/8 In. . . .90.00 to 170.00
Toy, Alligator, Squeeze, Tin Lithograph, 7 In. 143.00
Toy, Clown In Barrel, Penny, Tin Lithograph, Articulated, 3 In. 220.00
Toy, Top, Circus Images, Tin Lithograph, 3 In. 330.00
Tray, Boy & Small Dog, Tin Lithograph, Round, 9 1/2 In. 385.00
Tray, Francis Scott Key, Star Spangled Banner, c.1914, 9 3/4 In. . . . . .66.00 to 225.00

Buster Brown, Doll, Buster & Tige, Knickerbocker Specialty, Cloth, Uncut, 17 x 36 In.

C.D. Kenny, Tray, Santa Claus, Sleeping Child, Tin Lithograph, Round, 9 1/2 In.

Tray, Girl, Holding Doll, Tin Lithograph, Round, 10 In. .158.00 to 220.00
Tray, Girl, Muff, Tin Lithograph, Round, 9 In. . . . . .79.00 to 113.00
Tray, Patriotic, Tin Lithograph, Round, 9 1/2 In. 28.00
Tray, Santa Claus, Sleeping Child, Tin Lithograph, Round, 9 1/2 In. . . . . *Illus* 220.00
Wall Hanging, George Washington, Stamped, Tin Lithograph, 6 7/8 x 5 In. 165.00

CABINET   A cabinet is a special type of container used in a store. It
usually held a selection of small packages made by one manufacturer.
Dye cabinets and spool cabinets are the best-known. Value is determined by rarity, condition, and decorative appeal. Cabinets with lithographed tin fronts are especially popular.

Ace Comb, 3 Glass Sides, Wood, Revolving, Back Door, 14 In. 33.00
Adams Express Co., Wall, Oak, Paneled Door, Pigeonhole Interior, 30 x 24 In. 230.00
Angel Dainty Dye, Paneled Front, Hinged Back Door, 24 Pigeonholes, 15 x 15 In. 86.00
Belding Bros. & Co., Spool, Walnut, 13 Drawers, Mirrored Sides, 36 x 19 1/2 In. 900.00
Belding's Silk, Spool, Wood, 13 Drawers, 35 x 18 x 18 In. 1540.00
Blyda, Spool, Single Cylinder, Revolving, Silk 2970.00
Boye Sewing Needles, Best Quality, Partial Contents 605.00
Brooks Glace, Spool Cotton, Oak, 2 Drawers, Blue Glass Inserts, 7 x 22 1/2 x 14 1/2 In. . 288.00
Cadbury's Chocolate, Makers To The Queen, Glass Front & Sides, 20 x 24 x 9 In. 1419.00
Carr & Co. Biscuits, 3 Compartments, Reverse Gold Leaf Glass, 41 x 53 In. 1375.00
Corticelli, Spool Silk, Oak, 2 Drawers, Stenciled Drawer Fronts, 4 x 14 3/4 x 9 1/2 In. . . . 86.00
Corticelli, Spool, Oak, 22 Glass Front Drawers, 41 1/2 x 44 1/2 x 18 In. 1045.00
Corticelli, Spool, Poll Brand, Wood, 5 Shelves, Drawer, 23 x 12 In. 201.00
Corticelli, Spool, Walnut, Slant Front, 3 Glass Drawers, 1 Wood Drawer, 23 x 11 In. 121.00
Corticelli, Spool, Wood, 4 Turned Legs, 3 Drawers, 21 3/4 x 21 1/2 x 15 1/4 In. 165.00
Corticelli, Spool, Wood, 9 Drawers, 25 x 21 x 16 In. 825.00
Crowley's Needles, 2 Drawers, Ruby Glass, c.1890, 9 x 5 In. . . . . .440.00 to 523.00
Crowley's Needles, 2 Drawers, Ruby Glass, 16 x 6 In. 358.00
Crowley's Needles, 2 Tiers, 14 Drawers, 18 x 18 1/2 In. 1485.00
Dewhurst's Sylko 3 Shells Machine Twist, 3 Drawers, England, 5 1/2 x 13 1/2 x 8 1/2 In. 19.00
Display, Curtiss Fresh Candies, Red Metal, White Letters, 4 Shelves, 27 x 14 1/2 In. 236.00
Display, Schaefer Fineline Pencils, Semicircular, 14 x 27 In. 251.00
Display, Yale Flashlight, Tin Lithograph, 30 In. 649.00
Dr. Calvin Crane's Quaker Remedies, Wood, Glass, 10 x 14 x 10 In. 3960.00
Dr. E.S. Sloane's Medicines, Hanging, Wood, Glass Paned Door, 26 x 16 x 6 In. 299.00
Dr. Lesure's Famous Remedies, Veterinary, Embossed Tin Front, 28 1/4 x 19 1/4 In. 3575.00
Dr. Lesure's Veterinary Medicine, Horse Head, Tin Lithograph, c.1910, 21 x 27 In. 5610.00
Dr. Lesure's Warranted Veterinary Medicines, Wood, Glass, 27 1/2 x 20 3/4 In. 1485.00
Dy-O-La, Tin Door, Packets, Booklets, Burlington, Vermont, 16 1/2 x 12 1/2 x 8 1/4 In. . . 275.00
German Household Dyes, Ash, Paul Oppeman Mfg., Milw., c.1890, 23 x 30 In. 440.00
Goff's Braid, Spool, Oak, 2 Glass Front Drawers, Gold Letters, 7 1/2 x 17 1/4 In. . .121.00 to 220.00
Goff's Braid, Spool, Walnut, Ash, 2 Drawers, 8 In. 198.00
H. Pauk & Sons, Ribbon, Glass, Wood, St. Louis, 37 In. 2420.00
Hardware, Nut & Bolt, 72 Drawers, 6-Sided, Spins, 33 In. 1100.00
Hickory 6-Spool, Cotton, Oak, 2 Drawers, 9 1/2 x 21 1/2 In. 173.00
Humphreys' Remedies, Tin Lithograph, Wood Base, 6 Shelves, Doors, 17 x 19 x 5 1/2 In. 605.00
Humphreys' Remedies, Tin, 2-Color Lithograph, 28 In. 963.00
Humphreys' Specifics, Medicines, Cures, On Tin, Drawers, c.1900, 22 x 27 In. . . . .550.00 to 605.00
Humphreys' Veterinary, Horse, Embossed Composition, Wood, 27 1/2 x 21 x 10 In. 5390.00
Humphreys' Veterinary Remedies, Tin Lithograph, Oak Case, 29 x 21 In. 4510.00
McVitie & Price, Glass Front & Sides, 2 Glass Shelves, Plumes, 34 3/4 x 22 x 14 3/4 In. . 1060.00
Merrick's, Spool Cotton, 6 Cord, Curved Glass Panels, Turntable, c.1890, 18 In. 1925.00
Merrick's, Spool Cotton, Mirror, Oak, Countertop, c.1890, 36 x 31 In. . . . . .1980.00 to 2365.00
Merrick's, Spool Cotton, Oak, Curved Glass, Oval, 23 1/2 x 31 x 17 In. 3120.00
Merrick's, Spool Cotton, Oak, Tambour Door, Curved Glass, Round, 20 x 18 In. 3163.00
Merrick's, Spool, Wood, Round, Vertical Slots, Drawer, Knob On Top, 20 x 17 3/4 In. 2310.00
Milward's Helix Needles, Oak, 2 Drawers, 5 1/4 x 13 In. 173.00
Milward's Needle, 2 Drawers, Ruby Glass Inserts, c.1890, 16 x 6 In. . . . . .413.00 to 523.00
Munyon's Homeopathic Remedies, Doctor Yourself, Wood, Tin Panel, 1905, 18 x 24 In. . 660.00
Peerless Dye, Roll-Up Front Panel, 36 In. 440.00
Potter's Silk, Spool, 4-Sided, 3 Drawers, Turntable Center, c.1910, 18 x 18 x 33 In. 1870.00
Potter's Silk Thread, Oak, Glass, Turned Legs, 60 In. 2200.00

Pratt Food Co., Wood, Broken Pediment Top, Glass Front, 32 1/2 x 17 In. 275.00
Pratts Veterinary Remedies, Oak, Tin Lithograph, Horses, Medicines, 17 x 30 In. 1760.00
Pratts Veterinary Remedies, Tin Lithograph Insert, 32 1/2 x 17 In. 3300.00
Richardson's Silk, Spool, Wood, 3 Drawers, Glass Fronts, 8 x 16 In. 413.00
Richardson's Spool Silks, 4-Sided, 2 Turntables, Drawer, c.1900, 25 x 25 x 30 In. 3080.00
Sergeant's Vet Medicine, 2 Puppies, Tin Lithograph, Countertop 165.00
Sherwin-Williams, Paint, Salamander Logo, c.1900 . . . . 495.00
Snows Veterinary Remedies, No Cure, No Pay, Wood, 36 3/4 x 22 1/2 x 10 In. 605.00
Spencerian Steel Pens, Oak, Glass Top, 2 Drawers, 6 1/2 x 16 In. 288.00
Standard Paper Co., File, Wood, Milwaukee, 14 x 8 In. 77.00
Stick & Ball, Oak, Curved Glass Corners, Mirrored Back, 27 x 32 In. 578.00
Stollwerck's Chocolates, Cocoa, None Nicer, Wood Frame, Glass Front, 23 x 15 In. 468.00
Willimantic, Spool, 4 Drawers, 23 x 17 In. 187.00

CALENDAR

CALENDAR By the 1750s, almanacs in the American Colonies included calendars. But the oldest advertising calendar we have seen is an 1863 calendar for Hummewells Universal Cough Remedy and Eclectic Pills. Insurance companies, patent medicine firms, gunpowder makers, and others used calendars as giveaway ads in the nineteenth century. The tradition continues today.

A. Hirschauer, Embossed, Die Cut, Cardboard, Chicago, 1908, 12 x 14 In. 220.00
A.E. Anderson & Co., Art In Dress, 1901, 14 x 11 In. 66.00
A.F. Bullion, 2 Men In Canoe, August, Goodwin, 1926, 5 1/4 x 10 1/2 In. . . . . .88.00 to 253.00
A.F. Bullion, Sporting Goods, Goodwin, July, 1926, 5 1/4 x 10 1/2 In. . . . . .66.00 to 105.00
A.W. McGee Garage, Bayard, Iowa, Feathers, Red Felt, Cardboard, 1951, 7 x 12 In. 25.00
Antikamnia, 1903, 11 x 8 In. 17.00
Arlington National Bank, Moose, Tower Of Strength, Goodwin, 1918, 9 x 14 In. 110.00
Arthur L. Potter Insurance Co., Log Rollers, April, 1924, 3 3/4 x 10 1/4 In. . . . . *Illus* 143.00
B & B Plumbing, Girl In Hat, Horse, 1951, Frame, 13 x 20 In. 55.00
Baby Rice Popcorn, Parents Rocking Baby In Cradle, 1915, 13 x 7 1/2 In. 33.00
Betsy Ross Bread, Ty Cobb, 1954, Frame, 23 x 11 In. 154.00
Boufford & Turcot, Victorian Lady, Die Cut, Embossed, Cardboard, 1911, 12 x 8 In. 198.00
Boy Scouts Of America, A Scout Is Helpful, Norman Rockwell, 1941, 14 x 8 In. 65.00
Boy Scouts Of America, America Builds For Tomorrow, Rockwell, 1938, 14 x 8 In. 44.00
Bradley Fertilizer Co., Boston, Ocean Liner Scene, Full Pad, 1899, 17 x 11 In. 266.00
Bristol Fishing Rods, Honeymoon Campers, 1912, 17 1/4 x 30 3/4 In. 413.00
Broadmoor Hotel, Celluloid, Parrish, 1938, Pocket, 2 1/4 x 3 3/4 In. 330.00
Brown & Bigelow, Evening Shadows, Parrish, 1940, 33 3/8 x 16 In. 330.00
Brown & Bigelow, Old Glen Mill, Parrish, 1954, 33 1/2 x 16 In. 385.00
Brown & Bigelow, Peaceful Valley, House, Mountains, Landscape, 1955, 22 1/4 x 16 In. . . 132.00
Brown & Bigelow, Sunlit Valley, Parrish, 1950, 33 1/4 x 16 In. 209.00
Brown & Bigelow, The Glen, Deep Woods, Parrish, 1938, 18 1/4 x 13 1/2 In. 330.00

Calendar, Arthur L. Potter
Insurance Co., Log Rollers, April,
1924, 3 3/4 x 10 1/4 In.

Calendar, Clicquot Club,
Eskimo Boy, Lady, In Swimsuit,
1951, 14 x 22 1/2 In.

Calendar, F. Marquardsen,
Cowgirl, Sitting On Rock,
1908, 11 1/4 x 21 In.

Brown & Bigelow, Twilight, White House, Attached Barn, 1937, 16 x 11 1/4 In. 165.00
Brown & Bigelow, Village Church, Steeple & Belfry, 1949, 16 1/2 x 11 1/2 In. 176.00
Buckeye Harvest Machine, 1894, 8 x 7 1/2 In. 61.00
Buckwalter Supply Co., Lancaster, Pa., Embossed, Cardboard, 1907, 14 x 7 In. 110.00
Butcher Shop, Die Cut, Cardboard, Sanford, Maine, 1910, 15 1/2 x 8 1/2 In. 121.00
Campbell, Monkey, On Swing, Die Cut, Hanging, Full Pad, 1909, 15 1/2 x 8 In. 605.00
Campbell Electrical Supply Contractor, 1940, Mat, Frame, 21 1/4 x 15 1/4 In. 55.00
Campbell Electrical Supply Contractor, 1941, Mat, Frame, 15 1/2 x 10 3/4 In. 44.00
Clicquot Club, Eskimo Boy, Lady In Swimsuit, 1951, 14 x 22 1/2 In. . . . . *Illus* 72.00
Coes Fertilizer, Lady By Fence, 1901, Frame, 13 x 8 1/4 In. 154.00
Conradi's Pharmacy, Goodwin, 1936, 7 3/4 x 15 3/4 In. 110.00
Corn Belt Laboratories, Baby With Pig, 1944, Frame, 17 x 23 In. 99.00
Corn Belt Serum Company, Baby, 2 Pigs On Bike, 1937, Frame, 17 x 23 In. 110.00
Curlee Men's Clothing, Die Cut, Stand-Up, Tin Lithograph, 1922, 5 1/2 x 3 1/2 In. 358.00
D. Diersson Co. Groceries, Girl On Swing, Sacramento, Cal., 1911, 21 x 14 In. 413.00
Davis Bread, Die Cut, Embossed, 1906, Frame, 11 x 7 In. 143.00
Dawson Supply Co., Woman At Beach, 1905, Mat, Frame, 21 1/2 x 18 1/2 In. 44.00
Doe-Wah-Jack, Indian, Pipe, Geese, 1926, 10 x 21 In. 253.00
Doe-Wah-Jack, Round Oak Stoves, Gilbert General Merchandise, 1926, 21 x 10 In. 154.00
Drifted Snow, 3 Baby Girls, Die Cut, Embossed, Cardboard, 1908, 9 x 7 In. 330.00
Dutch Boy Painter, 1931, Frame, 40 x 21 In. 440.00
Dutch Boy Painter, Armstrong & McKelvey, 1917, Frame, 20 x 44 In. 558.00
Dutch Boy Painter, Dutch Boy White Lead, 1930, Frame, 20 x 40 In. 550.00
Dutch Boy Painter, Full Pad, Lithograph, 1913, Frame, 18 x 42 In. 275.00
Dwight & Lawler Grocery Store, Hunting Scene, 1959, 14 x 11 In. 55.00
E.J. Wade Groceries, Milltown, Maine, Hunting Scene, 1938, 16 x 8 In. 44.00
Economy Feed Store, New Castle, Va., Boy, Dog, 1942, 13 x 8 In. 66.00
Ed V. Price & Co., Merchant Tailors, 2 Children At Pump, 1908, 20 x 15 In. 2420.00
Eilers & Bolton, Die Cut, Embossed Cardboard, 1900, 18 x 10 In. 132.00
Emil Cermak Apothecary, Indian Maiden, 1915, Frame, 25 x 13 In. 358.00
F. Marquardsen, Cowgirl, Sitting On Rock, 1908, 11 1/4 x 21 In. . . . . *Illus* 1210.00
Farmers Lumber & Supply Co., An Interrupted Duel, 2 Men In Canoe, 1926, 15 x 11 In. . 204.00
Florette, Feed & Grain Store, Valley, Nebraska, Stock Yards, 1911, 20 x 12 In. 77.00
Frank Fountain General Merchandise, 1914, 10 x 5 In. 77.00
Frank Svoboda Monuments, Die Cut, Cardboard, Embossed, 1937, 8 x 14 In. 104.00
Fred L. Anderson, Ladies Fine Boots & Shoes, 1886, 9 1/4 x 5 1/2 In. 44.00
Gay Products Company, If It's Gay, It's Okay, Woman, 1952, 10 1/2 x 5 1/2 In. 49.00
Geo. B. Gehring Grocery Store, Submarine, Mat, Frame, 1918, 24 1/2 x 21 In. 110.00
George Newsome Miners & Loggers Clothing, Big Horn Sheep, 1929, 16 x 11 In. 66.00
Goetz Country Club Pilsener Beer, 1946, 20 x 27 In. 88.00
Gold Label, Empire Brewery, Chromolithograph, Mat, Frame, 1898, 33 x 27 In. 523.00
Grand Union Tea Co., Girl In Swing, Die Cut, 1906, 10 x 29 In. 413.00
Griffith & Boyd Co. Fertilizers, Roll Down, 1919, 38 x 23 In. 88.00
H. Levinson Wines, Liquors & Cigars, Black Boy & Goose, 1908, 13 1/2 x 10 1/2 In. 24.00
H.A. Smalley & Co., Fisherman, Full Pad, 1936, Frame, 35 x 25 In. 132.00
Hanover Stream Bakery, Baby On Swing, Cardboard, Die Cut, 1908, 16 x 7 1/2 In. 259.00
Harley-Davidson, Tin Lithograph Back, So. Dakota Dealer, 1940, 3 x 5 3/4 In. 578.00
Harry's Place, Artist Lynn Bogue Hunt, Full Pad, 1948, 16 x 9 In. . . . . *Illus* 94.00
Harrys Place, Dog, Wild Turkey, 1948, 9 x 16 In. 94.00
Hartzler's Cash Store, Girl, Deer, Die Cut, 1901, Frame, 15 x 27 In. 187.00
Hercules Powder Co., Boy, Dog, Norman Rockwell, 1941, 30 x 13 In. 232.00
Hercules Powder Co., The Alchemist, N.C. Wyeth, 1938, 13 x 30 In. 99.00
Hudson's Bay Company, Envelope, 1928, 6 1/2 x 11 1/2 In. 303.00
J.C. Driscoll Merchandise, Bear In Mind, Goodwin, 1928, 20 x 15 In. 303.00
J.D. Newcomer, Child, 2 Dogs, Embossed, Die Cut, Cardboard, 1909, 11 1/4 x 10 1/2 In. . 165.00
J.F. Stiefvater, Car, Filled With Flowers, Die Cut, Cardboard, 1908, 11 3/4 x 17 In. 99.00
John Mignola & Bro., Die Cut, Cardboard, 1905, 10 3/4 x 7 1/4 In. 55.00
Joint Hardware Co., Savona, N.Y., 2 Men, Canoe, 1928, 17 x 10 In. 176.00
Kaufman Ladies & Misses Wearing Apparel, Princeton, Ky., 1922 . . . . 45.00
Kerr Thread Co., Children Picking Flowers, Field, House, 1896, 10 In. 99.00
L.C. Chase & Co., Moose, Answering The Call, 1913, 37 x 18 In. 715.00
L.L. Croner, Butcher & Grocer, Boy, Girl, Die Cut, Embossed, 1910, 14 x 20 In. 248.00
Libby, McNeil & Libby, Corned Beef, Girl, In Straw Hat, 1906, Frame 187.00

Calendar, Harry's Place,
Artist Lynn Bogue Hunt,
Full Pad, 1948, 16 x 9 In.

Calendar, Osborne Harvesting
Machines, Cowboy, Shooting
Antelope, 1909, 14 x 20 In.

Libby, McNeil & Libby, Girl, Blue Dress, Glass Back, 1916, Frame, 12 x 18 In. 276.00
Listers Animal Bone Fertilizer, Mounted On Fabric, 1898, 13 x 23 In. 121.00
Lowell Fertilizer, Boston, Mass., Girl, Dog, Cat, 1917, 23 x 15 In. 77.00
Lowell Fertilizer, Girl In Hat, 1913, 25 x 15 In. 495.00
Lucerne Market, Loggers, Recipe Fold-Out, 1935, 8 1/2 x 5 3/4 In. 165.00
Maas & Steffen, Wandering Herd, R.L. McCollister, 1948, 13 1/2 x 26 In. 413.00
Maawattee Tea, Old Woman, Girl, Tin, Perpetual, England, 8 x 5 1/4 In. 1211.00
Mankato Minnesota Shoe Merchant, Indian Maiden, Louis Janda, 1929, 16 x 10 In. 303.00
Marble's Outing Equipment, December Page, 1922, 21 x 16 3/4 In. 4200.00
Marble's Outing Equipment, Men, Boat, Bear, 1922, Frame, 28 x 33 In. 4851.00
McCormick Deering Co., Lady, With Basket, 1926, Frame, 18 x 30 In. 198.00
McCrady Grain Co., Girl Sleeping Next To Dog, 1945, 16 x 12 In. 176.00
McCrady Grain Co., Girl, Dog, Stream, 1940, 16 x 12 In. 198.00
McGee's Baby Elixir, Girl, Cat, Dog, Be Sociable, 1942, 10 1/2 x 6 In. 45.00
Melchior Schmit, Die Cut, Embossed Cardboard, 1909, 12 1/4 x 8 1/4 In. 104.00
Metropolitan Life Insurance, 4 Girls, Lithograph, 1905, Frame, 8 x 25 In. .... .99.00 to 176.00
Miles City Saddlery Co., Wagon Train, 1948, 17 1/2 x 27 1/2 In. 743.00
Mott's Department Store, Girl, Bonnet, Embossed, Die Cut, 1906, Frame, 15 x 23 In. .. 330.00
Mrs. Winslow's Soothing Syrup, Lady, Baby, 1891, Frame, 12 1/2 x 15 1/2 In. 154.00
Myers Pumps, Hay Tools, Door Hangers, 1929, 48 x 16 1/2 In. 495.00
Myers Truck Lines, Knox City, Mo., Cowgirl, Horse, 1952, 12 x 20 3/4 In. 23.00
Nehi Soda, Chero-Cola, 1927, 20 x 6 In. 220.00
Nevin's Candy, 2-Ply Cardboard, 1917, 3 1/4 x 6 1/4 In. 15.00
O.H. Woodward-Gen. Hardware, Lady, Die Cut, Embossed, 1913, Frame, 14 x 20 In. 198.00
Osborne Harvesting Machines, Cowboy, Shooting Antelope, 1909, 14 x 20 In. ...... *Illus* 935.00
P. Squillanti-Wholesale Grocer, Lady, White Dress, Linen, 1916, Frame, 22 x 27 In. 264.00
Pacific International Express, Tin On Cardboard, c.1930, 19 x 12 1/2 In. 550.00
Palace Club, Buffalo Hunt, C.M. Russell, Reno, Nevada, 1953, 19 x 14 1/2 In. 176.00
Peoples Outfitting, Children, Horse Drawn Carriage, Embossed, Die Cut, 1895 .... 99.00
Peoples State Bank Of Lisbon, Ohio, Sept., 1923, Mat, Frame, 17 1/4 x 15 1/4 In. 176.00
Pratts, Woman, Apple, Horse, 1911, 8 x 12 1/2 In. 468.00
Princeton University Store, Tiger, Full Pad, 1939, Mat, Frame, 30 x 20 1/2 In. 132.00
Rainbow Court & Gift Shop, Embossed, 1949, 15 1/2 x 9 1/2 In. 99.00
Redrick Co., Girl, In Winter Coat, Chambersburg, Pa., 1900, Frame, 15 x 11 In. 77.00
Reiger & Gretz Brewers, Waving Woman, Philadelphia, 1908, Frame, 16 x 24 In. 220.00
Roberts Supply Co., Waterlox Products, 1948, 14 1/4 x 8 1/2 In. 67.00
Round Oak Stove, Chas. A. Walker, Renwick, Ia., Paper, Full Pad, 1926, 21 x 10 In. 276.00
Round Oak Stove, Doe-Wah-Jack, 4 Seasons, 1907-1908, 12 x 17 In., 4 Piece 2938.00
Sacramento Rubber Co., Evening, Parrish, 1947, Frame, 13 x 17 In. 66.00
San Francisco Life Insurance, Celluloid, 10 Years, 1910, 3 1/4 x 5 In. 66.00
Sentinel Fire Insurance Co., Tin Lithograph, c.1920, 13 x 19 In. 276.00
Sharp Bros. Milk, Lady, Red Roses, 1929, Frame, 22 x 48 In. 330.00
Sharples Separator, Children, Woman, 1920, 22 x 11 1/2 In. 1045.00
Sharples Separator, Paper On Cardboard, 1910, 14 x 7 In. 316.00
Shaw Barton, Man, Woman, Beach, 1957, Frame, 24 x 35 In. 39.00
Shaw Barton, Maryland Louise Pointer, Ray Hayden, 1945, 20 x 27 In. 28.00

South Haven, Michigan Granite & Marble, Die Cut, Embossed, 11 x 7 In. 154.00
Southern Select Beer, Frame, 1940, 15 x 29 1/2 In. 231.00
Spears Ship By Truck, Mat, Frame, December, 1932, 48 x 33 1/2 In. 121.00
Steffens Dairy Products, Pointing The Way, Boy Scouts Of America, 1962, 23 x 11 In. . .   44.00
Swift's Lowell Fertilizer Co., Mother & Daughter, Wheat, 1908, 25 x 17 1/2 In. 154.00
Thomas Murphy Co., Murphy Sunrise, Sample, Parrish, 1937, 13 3/4 x 7 1/2 In. 330.00
Thomas Murphy Co., Murphy Sunrise, Sample, Parrish, 1937, 18 1/2 x 10 3/4 In. 242.00
Thomas Pinder, Chicago Coffee, Teas & Spices, Boy, Die Cut, 1908, 11 1/2 x 8 In. 121.00
Trail Blazer, Cowboy, On Horse, 1923, Salesman's Sample, 10 x 16 1/2 In. 198.00
Trans-Canada Hotel, Breathless Moment, Goodwin, 1932, 19 x 29 In. 440.00
V.J. Plewa, Up To Date Shoe Store, 2 Girls, Roses, Die Cut, 1926, Frame, 15 x 22 In. 330.00
Walker Hardware, Stagecoach Being Held Up, 1918, 20 x 16 In. 176.00
Walkover Shoes, 4 Day Scenes, Fold-Out, 1908, 10 x 24 In. 121.00
Wells Fargo, Nevada National Bank, Chinese Characters, 1912, 9 x 18 In. 385.00
White House Shoes, Lady, Red Dress, 1912, Frame, 18 x 36 In. 605.00
Whitehead & Hoag, Celluloid, Sepia Tone, Perpetual, c.1899, 7 1/2 x 6 In. 88.00
Wm. Volkland, Kansas, Girls, In Old Car, 1913, Frame, 14 x 20 In. 330.00

CALIFORNIA RAISINS   In 1986 the California Raisin Advisory Board (CALRAB) was searching for a way to increase raisin sales. The Claymation California Raisins were created and advertising spots were produced. In no time, wrinkly raisins became cool. A national contest named the original singing trio Ben Indasun, Tiny Goodbite, and Justin X. Grape, and they were soon joined by others. The Raisins, who eventually starred in a television special and a cartoon series, appeared as rubber figurines and were featured on mugs, T-shirts, sheets, lunch boxes, and other items.

Bank, Plastic, 12 In. 15.00
Bank, Raisin, Standing Near Snack, Calrab, Applause, China, 1987, 6 1/2 In. 35.00
Can, Paper, Original Lid, Champion Company, 1988, 4 7/8 In. 4.50
Candy Dish, Indiana Glass, 4 1/2 x 3 3/4 In. 14.50
Car Sun Shield, Unopened, 1988 . . . .   12.50
Coffee Mug, 1988, 3 1/2 In. 8.50
Comforter, Raisins, Palm Trees, Singing, Playing Instruments, 60 x 86 In. 20.00
Curtains, 62 In., Pair 12.00
Figure, Butch, Skateboard, Hardee's, 1991, 2 In. 7.50
Figure, Drummer, Hat, Feather, 3 Drums, Applause, 1988, 3 1/2 x 3 x 1 3/4 In. 15.00
Figure, Eyes Closed, Playing Saxophone, 2 1/2 In. 6.00
Figure, F.F. Strings, Playing Guitar, Hardee's, 1988, 2 In. 4.00
Figure, Female, Holding Heart, Be Mine, Calrab, 1988, 2 1/2 In. 14.00
Figure, Female, Pink Shoes, 6 In. 14.99
Figure, Flat, Bendable, Blue Sneakers, 1987, 6 In. 15.00
Figure, Flat, Bendable, Microphone, 1987, 6 In. 15.00
Figure, Flat, Bendable, Orange Glasses, 1987, 6 In. 15.00
Figure, Holding Microphone, 1987, 2 In. 5.00
Figure, Hula Dancer, 2 1/2 In. 13.00
Figure, Male, Microphone, Polyvinyl, Flexible, Calrab, c.1987, 5 1/2 In. 8.00
Figure, Orange Glasses & Sneakers, Finger Pointing Up, 1987, 2 1/2 In. 6.00
Figure, Orange Glasses & Sneakers, Hardee's, 1988, 2 In. . . . . .2.50 to 6.00
Figure, Piano Player 50.00
Figure, Posable, Fabric Arms, Saxophone, 3 In. 10.00
Figure, Roller Skates, H On Hat, Gloves, Applause, 1988, 2 1/4 x 2 3/4 In. 6.00
Figure, Rollin' Rollo, Roller Skating, Calrab, Applause, 1988, 2 1/2 In. 7.00
Figure, Santa Hat, Calrab, 1988, 2 1/2 In. 14.00
Figure, Skateboarding, Calrab, Applause, China, 1988, 2 1/4 In. 2.50
Figure, Waves Weaver, Carrying Surfboard, Hardee's, 1988, 2 In. 4.00
Figure, Winking, Holding Heart, I'm Yours, Calrab, 1988, 2 1/2 In. 14.00
Game, Computer, IBM, Box, 1988 . . . .   15.00
Game, California Raisins Board Game, 1987 . . . .   12.99
Key Chain, Microphone, On Card, Calrab, Applause, China, 1988, 2 1/4 In. 6.00
Lunch Box, Thermos, Plastic, Thermos Co., Calrab, Applause, c.1988, 8 x 9 In. 11.00
Lunch Box, Yellow, Plastic, 8 x 9 x 4 In. 7.00

Toy, Blue Sneakers, Windup, 3 In. 12.50
Toy, Holding Microphone, Windup, 3 In. 12.50
Toy, Orange Glasses & Sneakers, Windup, 3 In. 12.50
Toy, Plastic, Rubber Arms, Windup, Applause, 1988, 3 x 5 x 3 1/4 In. 7.00
Toy, Plush, Female, Acme, 1988, 19 In. 30.00
Toy, Plush, Female, Acme, 1988, 32 In. 40.00
Toy, Plush, Posable, Blue Sneakers, Hardee's, 1988, 5 In. 7.50
Toy, Plush, Posable, Female, Yellow Shoes, Hardee's, 1988, 5 In. 7.50
Toy, Plush, Posable, Microphone, Hardee's, 1988, 5 In. 7.50
Toy, Plush, Posable, Orange Glasses, Hardee's, 1988, 5 In. 7.50
Toy, Walker, Microphone, Windup, Nasta Inc., 1988 . . . . 3.00
Wristwatch, Official Fan Club, 5 Function, LCD, Quartz, Nelsonic, 1987 . . . . 14.99

CALUMET In 1889 William M. Wright, a food salesman in Chicago, wanted to develop a new and better baking powder. In 1890 George C. Rew became his associate and they experimented and made a new product. It was named Calumet, the French name for the Indian peace pipe. In 1928 the Calumet Baking Powder Company was purchased by General Foods, which used the trademarks and packages of the original company. After several changes in ownership Calumet is now part of Altria's Kraft Foods Company. Collectibles include advertising cards, cookbooks, clocks, and packaging.

Bank, Baking Powder Can, Baby On Top, Thank-You, Red & Black Label 220.00
Bank, Bobbing Boy, c.1928, 5 1/2 In. 154.00
Bank, Paper Lithograph On Tin, Nodding Face, 6 In. . . . . 104.00 to 187.00
Bank, Tin & Paper Lithograph, 5 1/2 In. 88.00
Bin, Calumet Baking Powder, Double Acting, Wood, No Lid, 25 1/2 x 17 In. 33.00
Cake Pan, Calumet Baking Powder, 9 1/2 In. 15.00
Clock, Baking Powder, Oak, 16 x 38 x 4 1/2 In. 605.00
Clock, Baking Powder, Time To Buy, Wood Case, Pendulum, 39 x 17 In. 660.00
Clock, Time To Buy, Best By Test, Oak, Reverse Glass Lettering, 39 x 18 x 5 1/2 In. 2860.00
Recipe Book, 1931, 7 1/2 x 5 In., 31 Pages 5.00
Table, Porcelain Top, Child's 94.00
Thermometer, Best By Test, Trade Here, Wood, 27 In. 150.00
Thermometer, Call For Calumet, Wood, 27 x 7 1/4 In. 1210.00
Tin, Baking Powder, 5 Lb., 7 1/2 x 4 1/4 In. 75.00
Tin, Baking Powder, Indian Chief, Red, 1/2 Lb. 22.00

CAMPBELL Abraham Anderson and Joseph Campbell opened a canning plant in Camden, New Jersey, in 1869. Campbell bought Anderson's share in 1876. Soups were not made until 1897. The red and white Campbell label was introduced a year later. The gold medallion that is still part of the label was awarded to the company in 1900. Streetcar ads were first used in 1899 and magazine ads in 1905. The Campbell Kids were introduced in 1904. The Kids are now pictured as slightly thinner and more athletic than the originals. The first Campbell Kids dolls were made in 1910. Over one million souvenir postcards of the Campbell Kids were printed in 1910. Today a multinational company, Campbell owns numerous brands, including Prego, Pace, Franco-American, and V8. Did you ever notice that the Campbell Kids have no necks, no ears, no profiles, and no names?

Bank, Campbell Kids, Cast Iron, Williams, c.1915 . . . . 345.00
Bank, Truck, Die Cast Metal, Red, White, Gold Trim, Gearbox Toy, Box 34.00
Bookmark, Campbell Soup, Just Add Hot Water, Multicolored, Celluloid 49.00
Bowl, Buffalo Pottery, 7 1/2 x 1 1/4 In. 30.00
Bowl, Campbell's On Both Sides, Made In U.S.A., 4 1/8 x 2 3/4 In. 12.00
Can, Warhol Design, Tomato Soup, Yellow 2.00
Cookie Jar, Campbell Kid, Chef Hat, Soup Bowl, M'm! M'm! Good, Pottery, 9 x 6 In. . . . 11.00
Cup, Andy Warhol Design, Signature 10.00
Dish, Baby On Side, Kids, Alphabet On Rim, Gold Paint, Green Band, 7 1/2 In. 130.00
Display, Tin Marquee, Metal Rack, Cooking Unit, 28 In. 330.00
Doll, Boy & Girl, Soft Vinyl, Accessories, Order Form, 2 Soup Labels, 1972, 10 In., Pair . 150.00

Doll, Campbell Soup Kid, Boy, Composition, Jointed, Unmarked, 12 In. 400.00
Doll, Campbell Soup Kid, Rag Doll, Original Tag, c.1970, 16 In., Pair 49.00
Doll, Paul Revere & Betsy Ross, 1976, 10 1/2 In., Pair 85.00
Fan, Die Cut Cardboard, Tomato, Soup Can, Wooden Handle, 1930s, 6 1/2 x 9 In. 24.00
Figure, Wizard Of O's, Soft Vinyl, Movable Head, Late 1970s, 7 In. 20.00
Lunch Box, Campbell Kids, School Scenes, M'm! M'm! Good, 7 3/4 x 6 x 3 In. 12.50
Mirror, Campbell's Soup, 2 3/4 In. 325.00
Sign, Campbell's Soups, M'm! M'm! Good, Tin, 11 1/2 x 17 1/2 In. 165.00
Sign, Tomato Soup, Porcelain, Curved, Can Shape, 1920s, 22 1/2 x 13 In. . . . . . .2290.00 to 4950.00
Sign, Vegetable Soup, Curved, Porcelain, 1920s, 22 x 12 1/2 In. . . . . *Illus* 3630.00
Spoon, Stainless, Campbell Girl Handle, Oneida, Canada 5.00
Spoon Rest, Campbell Kid Chef, White, Red Trim 22.00
Thermometer, Tomato Soup, Porcelain, Glass, Chrome, c.1920, 7 x 12 x 1 In. 2200.00
Toy, Farm Truck, Wood, Fisher-Price, c.1955, 9 x 5 3/4 In. 169.00

CAN A can in this book is a metal container that is soldered shut. The first cans were made in France in 1810. Collectors search for cans with attractive labels. It is not uncommon to find a new can with an old label that has been added. Tins, or containers that are not soldered shut, are listed in their own category.

American Outboard, Qt. 35.00
Atlantic Oil, ODNOL, Russian Extra Heavy Mineral Oil, Gal., 10 In. 104.00
Caromel Twist, Cardboard, Round, Unopened, Tax Stamp, R.J. Reynolds, 7 x 4 3/8 In. . . . 400.00
Cities Service Outboard, Qt. 35.00
Cream O'Sea Brand, R.F. Brown Sea Food, Co., Lansing, Mich., Gal. 65.00
Esso Marvellube Outboard, Qt. 35.00
Gerber Baby Food Orange Juice, Baby's Are Our Business, Topless, 2 3/4 x 2 1/8 In. . . . 10.00
Harley-Davidson Motorcycles, Oil, Milwaukee, Gal. 2860.00
Kitchen Klenzer, Paper Label, Cardboard, Metal Top & Bottom, 5 1/4 x 2 7/8 In. 48.00
Kroger's Grapefruit Juice, Paper Label, Patent 1938, 14 Oz. 10.00
Marathon Outboard, Contents, Qt. 55.00
Maytag Oil, Tin Lithograph, Pour Spout, 8 In. 88.00
Mobiloil Outboard, Contents, Qt. 20.00
Shell Outboard Motor Oil, Contents, Qt. 220.00
Simmons House Paint, Guaranteed, No. 2016, Multicolored Label, Pt. 33.00
Venus Oil, Tin, Paper Label, 1929, 14 In. 55.00

CANADA DRY J.J. McLaughlin of Toronto, Canada, began manufacturing soda water in 1890. He introduced Canada Dry Pale Ginger Ale in 1904, then designed the trademark that included a crown and the map of Canada. Early advertising shows the mark with outlined provinces and a beaver, which are no longer included. Canada Dry was one of the first soft drink companies to use cans (1953) and to offer a sugar-free version (1964). The company was purchased several times and is now part of the Cadbury-Schweppes Dr Pepper/Seven-Up subsidiary.

Case, 6-Pack, Wood, 6 Bottles 95.00
Door Push, Best Of Them All, Porcelain, Hand Holding Bottle, 12 x 3 3/4 In. 138.00
Door Push, Ginger Ale, Beverage, Mixer, Chaser, Tin Lithograph, Embossed, 9 x 3 In. . . . 231.00
Sign, Choose Your Favorite Flavor, Welcome Change Of Pace, 5 Flavors, 47 In. 220.00
Sign, Drink Canada Dry Beverages, Porcelain, 1941, 7 x 24 In. 121.00
Sign, Green, White, Red, Yellow, Porcelain, Oval, 19 x 16 In. 88.00
Sign, Pale Ginger Ale, 5 Cents, Tin, Die Cut Bottle, 40 x 11 In. 550.00
Sign, Porcelain, Enamel, 10 x 30 In. 99.00
Sign, Spur, Big 12 Oz. Bottle, 5 Cents, Zip In Every Sip, Tin, Embossed, 12 x 3 1/2 In. . . 77.00
Sign, Spur, Zip In Every Sip, 5 Cents, Delicious, Refreshing, 8 x 6 In. 143.00

CARD Playing cards have been used for at least six hundred years. They have been popular advertising giveaways since the nineteenth century. Bicycle Brand, made by the United States Playing Card Company, has been made since 1885. The Ace of Spades includes a design that can help date the cards.

Hard A Port Tobacco, Scantilly Clad Women, Box, c.1890, 53 Cards 1323.00

Campbell, Sign, Vegetable Soup, Curved, Porcelain, 1920s, 22 x 12 1/2 In.

Carter's Ink, Salesman's Sample, Carter Inx Products, 12 Jars, 12 1/4 x 8 1/2 In.

Hiram Walker & Sons, London Dry Gin & Canadian Club, Box, 2 Decks	60.00
Hotpoint Automatic Home Laundry, Red Slip Finish, 1950s	18.00
Piedmont Airlines, Hoyle, Unopened	22.00
Westinghouse Mazda Lamps, Brown & Bigelow, Box, 3 5/8 x 2 3/8 In., 54 Cards	68.00

CARD, TRADE, see Trade Card

CARLING   Thomas Carling was a farmer in London, Ontario. His home-brewed ale was so popular with friends, he established a brewery in 1840. The Black Label brand name was being sold nationally in Canada by 1878. It was introduced in Ohio in 1933, and was available across the United States by 1962. The brand has been owned by many companies, including G. Heileman, Stroh's, and now Pabst. Its availability is limited in the United States today. In the United Kingdom, where the brand is owned by Coors, the name Black Label has been dropped and the brand is known as Carling.

Advertisement, Red Cap Ale, Red Cap, Tackle Box, Fishing Lures, 1949, Full Page	9.00
Can, Black Label Light, Pull Tab, Canada, 12 Oz.	2.50
Salt & Pepper, Black Label, Bottle Shape, Amber Glass, Metal Lids, Box, 4 In.	28.00
Sign, 9 Policemen Drinking, Tin Over Cardboard, Self-Framed, 14 3/4 x 21 1/2 In.	50.00
Sign, Carling's Ale Beer, Tin Over Cardboard, Self-Framed, 20 x 13 In.	77.00
Sign, Red Cap Ale, Red Cap Under Glass, 14 x 11 In.	55.00

CARTER'S INK   Carter, Dinsmore and Company was founded in Cambridge, Massachusetts, in 1858. It was named Carter's Ink by 1898. The company made many different types of bottles and labels that appeal to collectors. The tall RYTO brand cathedral-shaped bottles of cobalt blue glass were made during the 1920s. Ma and Pa Carter, a pair of ceramic figural inkwells, were patented in 1914. They were made in Germany and Japan. Carter's Ink Company was purchased by Dennison Manufacturing Company of Framingham, Massachusetts, in 1976. Dennison merged with Avery in 1991. Carter's ink and stamp pads are part of the Avery Dennison product line.

Bottle, Cathedral Shape, Cobalt Blue, 9 3/4 In.	358.00
Bottle, Cathedral Shape, Cobalt Blue, Original Cap, 3 In.	275.00
Bottle, Cathedral Shape, Cobalt Blue, Original Cap, 6 1/4 In.	550.00
Bottle, Cathedral Shape, Cobalt Blue, Original Cap, 8 In.	523.00
Bottle, Cathedral Shape, RYTO Ink, Labels, Lid, Cobalt Blue, 1920-1935, 7 1/4 In.	224.00
Bottle, Clear, Original Top, 7 1/2 In.	358.00
Bottle, Cobalt Blue, 1/2 Pt.	89.00
Bottle, Igloo, Aqua, Door & Window Designs, 1875-1890, 1 3/4 In.	605.00
Bottle, Koal Black Ink, Paper Labels, 8 3/8 x 3 In.	385.00
Bottle, Kongo Black Ink, Silhouette, Exaggerated Black Native, 2 3/4 In.	73.00
Bottle, Woman, Rolling Pin, Embossed Carter's Inx, Germany, 2 x 3 3/4 In.	60.00
Salesman's Sample, Carter Inx Products, 12 Jars, 12 1/4 x 8 1/2 In. .... *Illus*	250.00
Sign, Carter's Gossamer Carbon Paper, Judge, Tin Lithograph, Frame, 17 x 11 1/4 In.	880.00
Sign, Man At Desk, Embossed Tin, Self-Framed, Wood Frame, 32 x 25 1/2 In.	1430.00

Sign, Man, Writing In Book, Ink Bottle, Tin, Self-Framed, c.1900, 25 x 19 In. 1320.00
Thermometer, Carter Inx, Enamel On Metal, c.1915, 27 1/4 x 7 In. 275.00
Tin, Typewriter Ribbon, Carter's Dragon, Woman's Silhouette, Red, White, Black, 2 1/2 In. . 7.00
Tin, Typewriter Ribbon, Carter's Five O'Clock, Secretary, Powders Nose, 2 1/2 In. 28.00
Tin, Typewriter Ribbon, Carter's Midnight, Boston, 2 1/2 In. 16.00
Tin, Typewriter Ribbon, Ideal Typewriter Ribbon, Orchid, 2 1/2 In. 25.00

CASCARETS   Cascarets was a well-known laxative in the United States
during the early 1900s. The advertising was suggestive, with such say-
ings as "They Work While You Sleep" over the picture of a voluptuous
seminude woman; or it was corny with puns, such as a child seated on
a potty and the slogan "All Going Out, Nothing Coming In."

Display Box, Laxative Tablets, Lift Top, 25 Cents, 5 Tins, Cardboard, 5 x 5 In. 143.00
Mirror, Candy Cathartic, Celluloid, Round, Sterling Remedy Co., Wheeling, W. Va., 2 In. . 275.00
Mirror, Cascarets, They Work While You Sleep, Cupid On Chamber Pot, Celluloid, 2 In. . 44.00
Tin, Chocolate Flavor, Hinged Lid, Sterling Remedy Co., R.L. Watkins Co., 2 x 1 1/2 In. . 15.00
Token, Heads I Win, Tails You Lose, Metal, 1 1/4 In. 1.30

CATALOG   Catalogs for almost every product are in demand today by
collectors. Especially popular are catalogs for furniture and other decorative arts, tools, trains, automobiles, and mail order stores. They are
collected for the look of the illustrations and the information gained
from the contents.

Abercrombie & Fitch, Fishing & Camping, 1941, 9 1/2 x 6 1/2 In., 112 Pages 143.00
Abercrombie & Fitch, Fishing & Camping, 1942, 9 1/2 x 6 1/2 In., 128 Pages 77.00
Abercrombie & Fitch, Hunting & Fishing Scene, 1910, 7 x 5 1/4 In., 456 Pages 55.00
Abercrombie & Fitch, Red Gods Call, 1913, 6 3/4 x 9 3/4 In., 540 Pages 605.00
Bristol Steel Fishing Rods, 1929, 7 1/4 x 10 In., 40 Pages 101.00
Case Threshing Machine, Liberty Holding Eagle On Globe, 1905, 9 1/2 x 12 In., 72 Pages 270.00
Chicago Mail Order Co., 1938, 7 3/4 x 10 1/4 In., 76 Pages 25.00
Dent Toys, No. 10, Dent Hardware, Fullerton, Pa., 1910 . . . . 29.00
Down Bros. Medical Instruments, Hard Cover, 1929, 7 x 9 1/2 In., 2000 Pages 385.00
Edwards Miller & Co., Lamps & Cigar Lighters, 1881 . . . . 15.00
Exanthematic Method Of Cure, Hardcover, John Linden, 1892, 382 Pages, 8 x 5 3/4 In. . . 209.00
Funsten Trapping Supplies, 1920s 117.00
H.H Kiffe Co., Fishing Tackle & Hunting Outfits, c.1925, 5 1/2 x 9 In., 73 Pages 64.00
Heddon Fishing Tackle, 1955, 5 x 6 3/4 In., 30 Pages 82.00
Henry Fields Pet, Fish & Bird Supplies, 1936, 7 1/2 x 10 1/2 In., 31 Pages 15.00
Henry N. Hooper & Co., Chandeliers, Girandoles, Candelabra & Lamps, 1858 . . . . 10.00
Huck Manufacturing, Drug & Jewlery Store Fixtures, 1905, 10 1/4 x 6 1/2 In., 32 Pages . 44.00
Inter-State Nurseries, 1937, 7 1/2 x 10 3/4 In., 66 Pages 28.00
Inter-State Nurseries, Spring 1948, 7 1/2 x 10 1/4 In., 83 Pages 25.00
Iver Johnson Sporting Goods Co., 9 x 11 3/4 In., 72 Pages 73.00
J.B. Shannon & Sons Hardware, Cutlery & Guns, c.1900, 9 x 6 In., 64 Pages 28.00
Jim Brown's Farm & Home Supply, Fall & Winter, 1939 . . . . 55.00
Kingsbury, Airplane Inserts, 1927, 12 Pages 605.00
Kingsbury Toys, Motor Driven, c.1920, 24 Pages 275.00
Kirk, Geary & Co., Soda Fountain & Supplies, 1915, 9 x 6 In. 220.00
Maas & Steffen Furbearers, Man, Dogs, Polar Bear, 9 x 7 1/2 In., 26 Pages 99.00
Maher & Grosh, Quality Goods, No. 48, 10 x 7 In., 96 Pages 44.00
Marble's, Brittany Spaniel Dog On Front, No. 30, c.1918, 6 x 3 1/2 In., 12 Pages 144.00
Marble's, Specialties For Sportsmen, 1904, 6 3/4 x 5 In., 32 Pages 412.00
Marble's Outing Equipment, Moose, 1937-1938, 4 1/8 x 7 In., 32 Pages 83.00
Matchbook, Salesman's, Spiral Bound, 1940s, 9 1/4 x 7 In., 250 Pages 385.00
Meyer Brothers Druggist, Hardcover, 1889-1890, 9 x 6 1/2 In., 816 Pages 99.00
Meyer Brothers Druggist, Jan. 1893, 10 1/4 x 7 5/8 In., 63 Pages 209.00
Meyer Brothers Druggist, Vol. XXVI, No. 3, March 1905, 7 3/8 x 10 5/8 In. 121.00
Old Town Canoes & Boats, Full Color Cover, 1930, 6 x 8 In., 37 Pages 83.00
Old Town Canoes & Boats, Full Color Cover, 1932, 6 x 8 In., 37 Pages 83.00
Old Town Canoes & Boats, Full Color Cover, 1933, 6 x 8 In., 37 Pages 83.00
Old Town Canoes & Boats, Full Color Cover, 1935, 6 x 8 In., 37 Pages 83.00
Park, Davis & Co., Factory Image, 1889, 4 x 9 1/4 In., 124 Pages 50.00

Pflueger Fishing Tackle, No. 151, 1931, 5 1/4 x 8 In., 136 Pages 53.00
Pflueger Fishing Tackle, No. 156, 1936, Pocket, 5 1/4 x 8 In., 130 Pages .... .81.00 to 96.00
Pflueger Fishing Tackle, No. 157, 1937, 5 1/4 x 8 In., 130 Pages 58.00
Pflueger Fishing Tackle, No. 161, 5 1/4 x 8 In., 118 Pages 51.00
Pilling Cattle Instruments, 5 3/4 x 3 1/4 In., 48 Pages 50.00
Real Texan Outfit, Betty Leach, Smart Style, Ridgefield, N.J., 12 Pages ....13.75 to 16.50
S. Maw, Son & Thompson's Quarterly, April 1877, 7 1/2 x 10 1/2 In., 122 Pages 77.00
Shakespeare, Fine Fishing Tackle, 1949, 8 1/2 x 11 In. 25.00
Shakespeare Fishing Tackle, No. 31D, 1930-1931, 10 1/2 x 7 3/4 In., 82 Pages 58.00
Snyder Harris Basset Co., Men's Clothing, Winter 1900-1901, 17 In. 83.00
South Bend, 1924, 6 1/4 x 5 1/4 In., 68 Pages 185.00
South Bend, Boy Holding Big Fish, 1933, 5 1/4 x 6 1/4 In., 100 Pages 173.00
South Bend, What Tackle & When, 1931, 5 1/4 x 6 1/4 In., 80 Pages 28.00
South Bend, What Tackle & When, 1941, 6 1/4 x 5 1/4 In., 136 Pages ....28.00 to 30.00
South Bend, What Tackle & When, Full Color, 1950, 6 1/4 x 5 1/4 In. 30.00
South Bend Fishing Tackle, 1932, 5 1/4 x 6 1/4 In., 84 Pages 87.00
Spiros Sporting Goods, Greatest Store In The West, 1927, 9 x 6 In., 160 Pages 55.00
Superior Stoves & Range, Price List, 1913, 7 1/2 x 10 1/2 In., 168 Pages 66.00
Van Schaack, 1872, 4 3/4 x 7 1/4 In., 160 Pages 605.00
W.W. Greemers Sporting Guns & Accessories, 1922, 10 x 7 In., 24 Pages 121.00
Walrus Soda Fountains, Decatur, Illinois, 15 x 9 In. 187.00
Weber, Fishing Tackle, 1940, 6 x 9 In., 112 Pages 28.00
Weber, Fly Fishing, Stevens Point Wisc., 1941, 9 x 6 In., 112 Pages 77.00
Weber, Fly Tackle For Fresh Water Fish, Wisconsin, 1938, 6 x 9 In., 96 Pages 29.00
William Mills & Son, Fishing Tackle, Spring, 1932, 5 1/8 x 7 1/8 In., 80 Pages 46.00
William Mills & Son, Spring Booklet, Fishing Tackle, N.Y., 1932, 5 x 7 In., 80 Pages 40.00
William Mills & Son, Spring Fishing Tackle, 1930, 5 x 7 In., 80 Pages 28.00
Williams Saddlery, Deming New Mexico, Envelope, 1939, 6 1/2 x 9 In., 36 Pages 55.00

CERESOTA FLOUR   Northwestern Consolidated Mill Company made Ceresota Flour in 1891. The trademark of a boy slicing a loaf of bread has been used since at least 1912 and has also appeared on Heckers Unbleached Flour products. Both brands have changed ownership several times over the past few decades.

Bill File, Boy Slicing Bread, Cardboard Lithograph, Metal Hook 165.00
Button, Gold Color Metal Border, Celluloid, Pinback, 1 3/4 In. 115.00
Button, Pinback, Round, 1 1/4 In. 75.00
Calendar, 1913, Cardboard Lithograph, Full Pad, Frame, 14 x 19 In. 99.00
Doll, Boy, Cloth, Uncut, With Cookbook, c.1912, 17 x 18 In. .... *Illus* 275.00
Match Holder, Boy Slicing Bread, Die Cut, 5 1/2 x 2 3/8 In. .... *Illus* 303.00
Match Holder, Boy Slicing Bread, Standard Bottom Tray 66.00
Match Holder, Ceresota Prize Bread Flour, Tin, Die Cut Boy & Barrel, 5 1/2 In. 77.00
Match Holder, Child Sitting On Stool, Die Cut, Embossed, 5 1/2 x 2 3/8 In. 358.00
Mirror, Boy Sits On Bench, Multicolored, 2 1/8 In. 75.00
Mirror, Boy Slicing Bread, Brown Border, 2 In. 135.00
Mirror, Boy Slicing Bread, Celluloid, Round, 2 1/8 In. 45.00

Ceresota Flour, Doll, Boy, Cloth, Uncut, With Cookbook, c.1912, 17 x 18 In.

Ceresota Flour, Match Holder, Boy Slicing Bread, Die Cut, 5 1/2 x 2 3/8 In.

Mirror, Boy Slicing Bread, White Border, 2 1/8 In. 185.00
Sign, Boy Slicing Bread, Tin, Embossed, Sentenne & Green, 26 x 21 In. 960.00

CHANGE TRAY, see Miscellaneous, Change Receiver

CHARLIE THE TUNA   Charlie the Tuna, the tuna with good taste,
became the spokesfish for StarKist Tuna in 1961. Heinz acquired
StarKist and its mascot in 1963. Charlie was on vacation during the
1990s, but reappeared in 2001. After nearly forty years with Heinz,
Charlie became part of Del Monte when it acquired StarKist in 2002.

Necklace, Charm, Gold Luster Metal, c.1970s, 1 1/4 x 12 In. 8.00
Radio, Transistor, StarKist, Box, 1970, 5 In. 75.00
Tape Dispenser, StarKist, Plastic, Battery Operated, 1974, 6 x 4 x 3 In. 55.00
Tie Tack, Gold Tone Metal, 3/4 In. 8.00
Toy, Bean Bag, Mail-Away Premium, StarKist Tuna, Unopened Bag, 5 1/2 In. 20.00
Watch, Mailer, Certificate, 25th Anniversary, 1986, 1 x 2 1/2 x 6 1/2 In. 35.00

CHASE & SANBORN   James S. Sanborn sold coffee beans and spices
in Lewiston, Maine, in the 1850s. He met Caleb Chase in Boston and
the pair formed Chase & Sanborn in 1878. It was the first company to
sell roasted coffee in a sealed container. The coffee, Seal Brand, was
heavily advertised and became nationally known. By the late 1880s,
Seal Brand and Crusade coffee ads were placed in national magazines.
Chase & Sanborn became part of Standard Brands in 1929 and in 1999
part of Sara Lee. It has been advertised in print ads and on radio and
television. The cans are sought by collectors.

Advertisement, Ladies Home Journal, Tom Ewell Opening Tin, 1957 .... 6.00
Blotter, Granny, Hat, Rose, Coffee Or Tea, C.D. Williams, 3 3/8 x 6 1/4 In. 5.00
Blotter, Seal Brand Coffee & Tea 7.00
Catalog, Interior Photographs Of Stores, c.1900, 72 Pages 248.00
Dummy, Charlie McCarthy, Cardboard, Mechanical, 1938, 18 In. 75.00
Sign, Chase & Sanborn's Teas & Coffees, Porcelain, Flange, 8 x 16 In. 825.00
Sign, Country Store, Paper Lithograph, Frame, 1897, 15 x 7 1/2 In. 210.00
Sign, Country Store, Paper, Frame, 32 x 26 In. 110.00
Sign, Country Store, Paper, Frame, c.1897, 22 1/2 x 24 1/2 In. ....550.00 to 700.00
Thermometer, 5 In. 1.75
Tin, High Grade Coffee, Presentation Box, Sample, 2 1/8 x 2 1/4 In. 80.00
Tin, High Grade Coffee, Sample, 2 5/8 x 2 1/2 In. 145.00
Tin, Tea, c.1930, 1/2 Lb., 5 x 3 3/4 x 3 3/4 In. 125.00

CHESAPEAKE & OHIO, see Railroad

CIGAR, see Tobacco

CIGAR BOX, see Tobacco, Box

CIGAR BOX, LABEL, see Label

CIGAR LIGHTER, see Lighter

CIGARETTE, see Tobacco

CIGARETTE LIGHTER, see Lighter

CLABBER GIRL, see Baking Powder

CLARK   David L. Clark started his candy business, the D.L. Clark Company, in Pittsburgh in 1886. In 1917 the demands of World War I led
the company to change its packaging from thirty-pound cases of
chocolate drops to individually wrapped candy bars. The five-cent bar
became known as the Clark Bar. The firm was making over 150 types of
candy by 1920. It also made chewing gum, including Teaberry and Ten-
dermint. In 1921 a separate company, Clark Brothers Chewing Gum,
was incorporated. That company, now called Clark Gum Company,
was owned for a time by Philip Morris. It is now headquartered in Buffalo, New York, and still manufactures Clark's Teaberry gum. The D.L.
Clark Company was purchased by Chicago's Beatrice Foods Company
in 1955. The Clark Bar was acquired by Leaf, Inc., in 1983, then by

Clark, Tool, All-In-One,
Clark Bars Are Great,
Black Cast Iron, 7 In.

Clark, Display, Clark's
Teaberry Gum, Embossed,
Pedestal, Green Glass,
5 x 7 x 4 3/4 In.

Pittsburgh Food and Beverage Company. In 1995, under new ownership, the company became Clark Bar America. That company was purchased by New England Confectionery Company (NECCO) in 1999.

Box, Orchard Caramels Candy, Boy In Orchard, D.L. Clark, Pittsburgh, 7 x 13 x 2 1/2 In. .	56.00
Change Receiver, Teaberry Chewing Gum, Green, Glass	138.00
Display, Clark's Teaberry Gum, Embossed, Pedestal, Green Glass, 5 x 7 x 4 3/4 In. . . . *Illus*	209.00
Display, Clark's Teaberry Gum, Embossed, Pedestal, Vaseline Glass, 5 x 7 x 4 3/4 In.	50.00
Ink Blotter, Clark Twins, Pepsin Gum, Zigzag Confections, Cardboard, 4 x 9 1/4 In.	110.00
Pail, Clark's Chocolate Frozen Sweets, Cardboard, Pitts., Pa., 12 In.	28.00
Sign, Clark's Teaberry Gum, Happy Thought, Mountain Tea Flavor, Tin, 8 3/4 x 11 3/4 In.	468.00
Tool, All-In-One, Clark Bars Are Great, Black Cast Iron, 7 In. . . . . *Illus*	50.00

CLARK THREAD, see Coats & Clark

CLICKER   Given out as premiums, clickers came in a variety of shapes
and were printed with company logos. See more clickers under brand
names, such as Red Goose Shoes.

Bonnie Laddie, A Sundial Shoe	55.00
Columbus Buggy Co., Celluloid, 1 1/4 In.	185.00
New & True Coffee	65.00
Quaker State, 1 7/8 x 7/8 In.	68.00
Sohio Oil Company, 2 3/8 x 1 1/4 In.	80.00

CLOCK   Advertising clocks have been made since the nineteenth century. A manufacturer often gave a clock to a drugstore, grocery store,
bar, or barbershop. A brand name is clearly indicated on the clock.

Abbott's Ice Cream, Fountain Service Marquee, 22 1/2 x 26 In.	264.00
Beecham Pills, Baird, Worth A Guinea A Box, Pine, Papier-Mache, 1890s, 30 x 18 x 4 In.	2695.00
Bell Of Bourbon, Cast Iron, Pot Metal, Bell Shape, 12 x 13 In.	330.00
Capital Bread, Freshness, Flavor, Light-Up, Yellow, Red, Black, Plastic	77.00
Carnation Milk, Fiber Case, Round, 1950s	121.00
Cat's Paw Double Bubble, Lighted, 14 In.	440.00
Cat's Paw Heels & Soles, We Rebuild Shoes Like New, Backlit Dial, 1950s, 14 In.	413.00
Cities Service, Lighted, Pam, 14 1/2 In.	330.00
Colonial Bread Is Good, Neon, Glo Dial, 21 In.	2600.00
Curtis Hardware, Time For Quality Products & Professional Services, Plastic, 13 1/2 In. .	45.00
Dickeys Indian Blood & Liver Pills, Walnut, Waterbury Clock Co., 21 In.	660.00
Dyola Dyes, Regulator, Oak Case, 34 x 19 In.	495.00
Eavenson & Sons Soaps, Wood, Reverse Glass, Gold Leafed Pendulum, 22 x 14 In.	825.00
Ever-Ready Safety Razor, Man Shaving, Roman Numerals, 22 x 18 In. . . . . *Illus*	6400.00
Fairacres Superior Ice Cream, Grand Island, Neb., Late 1940s, 16 1/2 In. . . . . . . .200.00 to 275.00
Ferguson System Tractors, Implements, Duralite, 15 In.	650.00
Four Roses, Light-Up, Green Ground, Countertop, 12 x 18 In.	77.00
Gem Damaskeene Razor, Man, Baby, Pendulum, Wood, c.1910, 23 x 28 In. . . . .2420.00 to 4070.00
Gem Safety Razor, Wall, Wood Grained Tin Lithograph, Embossed, Calendar, 28 1/2 In. .	935.00
Grant Batteries, Red Center, Yellow Edge, Square, Pam	220.00
Grocery & Meat Market, Round, Electric Clock Co., Chicago, 22 1/2 In.	357.00
H.F. Mentley Jeweler, Middleton, N.Y., Regulator	220.00
Hester Batteries, Start & Go With, 15 In.	1000.00
Hostetter's Stomach Bitters, Reverse On Glass, Ingraham, Conn., 1880-1900, 33 5/8 In.	3250.00
Hudson Sales & Service, Neon, 20 In.	1980.00
Irodent Tooth Paste, Electric, Square Wood Frame, 15 In.	77.00

Clock, Ever-Ready Safety
Razor, Man Shaving, Roman
Numerals, 22 x 18 In.

Clock, Nestle, Cookie Mix,
Metal, Windup, Alarm, Late
1940s, 5 1/2 In.

Jolly Tar Pastime, Old Honesty, Plank Road, Boot Jack, John Finzer & Bros, Baird 3960.00
Jolly Tar Pastime, Old Honesty, Plank Road, Tobacco Manfrs., Round, c.1880, 30 In. 1650.00
Makomb Chicken, Metal Case, Square, Middlebury Elec. Co., Macomb, Il. 94.00
Mapl-Flake, It's Wheat Bran, Tin Lithograph, Battle Creek, Mich., 1902, 9 x 6 1/2 In. 2970.00
Marigold Dairy Products, Blue Numbers, Double Bubble, Round 253.00
Mark Twain Flour, Regulator 385.00
Milkmaid Milk, Now's The Time To Buy It, Metal Over Wood, 18 In. 770.00
Mother Seigels' Curative Syrup Cures Dyspepsia, Metal, London, 7 1/2 x 3 1/4 In. 495.00
National Union Radio Tubes, Light-Up, Plastic, 19 In. 743.00
Nesbitt's, Delicious Drink, Tilted Bottle, Orange, 1956 . . . . 1155.00
Nestle, Cookie Mix, Metal, Windup, Alarm, Late 1940s, 5 1/2 In. . . . . *Illus* 35.00
None Such Mincemeat, Pumpkin, Lithograph, Tin, Cardboard, 9 1/2 In. . . . . . . .1265.00 to 1808.00
NuGrape Soda, Metal, Glass, Electric, Light-Up, 16 x 13 x 3 1/2 In. 231.00
Old Drum Blended Whiskey, Drum Case, Tin Face, Letters For Numerals, Round, 12 In. . 143.00
Old Guardian Coal, Wood Case, Saint Bernard Dog, Baby, c.1940 . . . . 198.00
Old Mr. Boston, Fine Liquors, White, Blue, Bottle Form, Metal, c.1920, 22 In. 385.00
Old Mr. Boston, Fine Liquors, Wood, Flask Form, 11 x 6 In. 236.00
Orange Crush, Telechron, Light-Up, Round, 1940s 413.00
Orange Crush, Wall, Electric, Pocket Watch Shape 110.00
OshKosh, Neon 990.00
Penn Mutual Insurance, Banjo, Regulator, Mass., c.1860, 49 1/2 In. 3360.00
Picadilly Ginger Ale, R.J. Holmes Carbonating Co., Kansas City, Mo., Brass, 15 3/4 In. . . 1375.00
Reed's Tonic, Malaria, Indigestion, Gilt Edge, 24 x 10 In. 3025.00
Rival Dog Food, Red, Black, Blue, White, Metal, Wood Case, 15 1/2 In. 106.00
Sauers Extract, Regulator, Wood Case, Painted, Reverse Glass, 36 In. 1469.00
Sauers Flavoring Extracts, Reverse Glass, New Haven Clock Co., 42 1/2 x 17 x 5 3/4 In. 825.00
Sealtest Ice Cream, Southern Dairies, Neon, 8-Sided, 18 In. 468.00
Simmons Liver Regulator, Horseshoe Surrounds Dial, Ansonia, c.1900, 6 In. 224.00
St. Joseph's Aspirin, Round, 15 In. 149.00
Star Brand Shoes, Metal, Brass Wash, Gilbert-Winstead, Conn., 5 In. 72.00
Sugardale Fine Meats, Clown King, Double Bubble, Round, 15 In. 578.00
Swihart Suncrest, Bottle, Electric, Light-Up, Round, 1940-1950 . . . . 358.00
Tetley Tea Time, Tin, Embossed, Waterbury Electric Co., 20 1/4 x 14 1/2 In. 468.00
The Times, Twice As Many Pictures, Chicago's Picture Newspaper, 15 1/2 In. 88.00
Tiffany Shoes, Pam, 14 In. 55.00
Vanner & Prests Molliscorium, Embossed, Wood, Metal, 1890s, 32 x 19 x 4 In. .853.00 to 1618.00
Ward's Orange Crush, Regulator, Oak Case, Ingraham Co., 32 In. 550.00
Wasmuth's Corn-Ring, Foot, Metal, Round, Paper Face, 11 In. 358.00
West Point Hair Tonic, Bulova, Light-Up, 14 1/2 In. 121.00
Westinghouse Radio, Listen & You'll Buy, Red Center, Light-Up, Round, Pam 143.00
WocoPep Additive, Neon, Steel, Pull Chain, 20 In. 400.00
Wolf's Head, Neon, Steel, Pull Chain, 20 In. 400.00

CLOTHING Companies advertise their brands on hats, shirts, and other
clothing items. Sometimes these are given away as premiums, and
sometimes customers pay for the privilege to be a walking billboard.
Uniforms with company logos may also be found in this category.

Hat, Butternut Bread, Peanuts Gang, Paper, 1974 . . . . 15.00

Hat, Mr. Bubble, Fabric, Elastic, Cardboard, Ad-King, N.Y., 1970s, 10 x 10 In. 15.00
Hat, Soda Jerk, Dairylea Ice Cream, Miss Dairylea, Paper, 1967 . . . .   12.00
Necktie, Famous Pioneer Club, Vic Dealer, Cards, Dice, Cowboy, 1950s, 4 x 50 In. 77.00

COATS & CLARK   The Clark family of Paisley, Scotland, began making cotton thread in 1813. The Coats family started a competing thread
business in the same town in 1826. The Coats sons, James and Peter,
were running the family business by 1830 as J. & P. Coats. Coats and
Clark continued competing with each other in Scotland and other
countries. By the 1840s, members of both families lived in the United
States. George and William Clark of Newark, New Jersey, developed
a twisted cotton thread in 1866 that could be used with sewing
machines. It was named O.N.T., or Our New Thread. J. & P. Coats was
making thread in Pawtucket, Rhode Island, by 1871 and used a circled
chain as a trademark. A worldwide distribution network that sold
thread manufactured by Clark, Coats, and other companies was set up
in 1888. Though the companies retained separate identities, their interests were consolidated over the next few years and the Spool Cotton
Company became their sole selling agent in 1896. In 1952 the American companies, J. & P. Coats and the Clark Thread Company, merged
to become Coats & Clark, Inc. That company is now part of the multinational Coats Viyella Group, based in London. The company still
owns the linked-chain logo. It is the world's largest supplier of sewing
thread and craft products, which are sold under a variety of brand
names. In this book, advertising materials promoting all of these companies are listed here. Collectors search especially hard for spool cabinets and advertising cards.

Cabinet, Clark's Colors, 6 Drawers, Ruby Glass, c.1890, 26 x 23 In. . . . . .935.00 to 1100.00
Cabinet, Clark's Mile End, 2 Drawers, Oak 440.00
Cabinet, Clark's Mile End, Spool Cotton, 6 Drawers, Spool Pulls . . . . .1100.00 to 1650.00
Cabinet, Clark's O.N.T., 2 Drawers, Reverse Label, Mixed Wood Case, 22 In. 303.00
Cabinet, Clark's O.N.T., 2 Drawers, Walnut, Reverse On Glass, 7 1/2 x 22 x 15 1/2 In. . . .   345.00
Cabinet, Clark's O.N.T., 2 Tambour Doors, Oak, Turntable Base, 23 x 20 x 16 In. 805.00
Cabinet, Clark's O.N.T., 4 Drawers, Decals, 19 1/4 x 14 1/4 In. 180.00
Cabinet, Clark's O.N.T., 4 Drawers, Oak, Reverse On Glass, 17 x 23 x 17 In. 604.00
Cabinet, Clark's O.N.T., 4 Drawers, Ruby Glass Inserts, 22 x 17 In. 880.00
Cabinet, Clark's O.N.T., Embroidery, 5 Drawers, 18 1/2 x 19 x 13 1/2 In. 55.00
Cabinet, Clark's O.N.T., Roll Top Door, Oak, Wall Mount, c.1890, 21 x 23 In. 468.00
Cabinet, Clark's O.N.T., Spool Cotton, 2 Drawers, Walnut, Ruby Glass, 15 x 26 In. 204.00
Cabinet, Clark's O.N.T., Spool Cotton, 3 Drawers, Walnut, Ruby Glass, 23 x 10 In. 330.00
Cabinet, Clark's O.N.T., Spool, Square, Swivels, Tambour Panels 1650.00
Cabinet, Clark's O.N.T., Tambour Roll Top Doors, Oak, 23 In. 1870.00
Cabinet, Clark's O.N.T., Vertical Slots, 23 x 16 x 17 In. 1540.00
Cabinet, Clark's, Anchor, 3 Drawers, Walnut, Ruby Flashed Glass, 9 1/2 x 22 x 15 In. . . .   288.00
Cabinet, Clark's, Slant Front, Chalkboard, 6 Drawers, 16 x 35 x 24 In. 385.00
Cabinet, George A. Clark, 6 Drawers, Glass Inserts, 25 In. 650.00
Cabinet, George A. Clark, Spool, 5 Over 2 Drawers, Ruby Glass Inserts 2750.00
Cabinet, George A. Clark, Spool, 6 Drawers, Teardrop Pulls, Walnut, 22 x 26 In. .908.00 to 1430.00
Cabinet, J. & P. Coats, 2 Drawers, Walnut, 21 1/2 x 9 x 17 In. 215.00

Coats & Clark, Sign, Cat Congress, Paper,
Marked, Frame, c.1900, 18 x 25 In.

Coca-Cola, Blotter, Coca-Cola Gum, Chew
This, Peppermint, Pepsin, 3 3/4 x 6 In.

Cabinet, J. & P. Coats, 2 Glass Sides, Revolving, 23 x 15 In. 2395.00
Cabinet, J. & P. Coats, Spool, 6 Drawers, Column Front, Walnut, 21 x 24 In. 518.00
Cabinet, J. & P. Coats, Spool Cotton, Tambour Doors, Turntable, Oak, 23 x 20 In. 863.00
Cabinet, J. & P. Coats, Spool, Oak, Doors, Roll Top, Turntable Base, c.1890, 21 x 33 In. . 1540.00
Cabinet, John Clark, Spool Cotton, 6 Cord, Mahogany, 6 Drawers, Ruby Glass Inserts ... 1705.00
Cabinet Desk, Clark's, O.N.T., Oak, Lift Lid, 4 Drawers, Vinyl Surface, 30 In. 480.00
Display Case, J. & P. Coats Spool Cotton Thread, Wood, Glass, Lift Top, 3 x 12 x 12 In. . 283.00
Sign, Cat Congress, Paper, Marked, Frame, c.1900, 18 x 25 In. .... *Illus* 743.00
Sign, Clark's Mile End Spool Cotton, Black Man, Cotton Field, Lithograph, 22 x 17 In. ... 1017.00
Sign, Clark's O.N.T., Pup On Spool, Die Cut, Cardboard, 9 x 7 1/2 In. 39.00
Sign, Clark's Spool Cotton, O.N.T., Spool, Tin, 24 x 20 In. 275.00
Thread Card Book, 4 1/2 x 9 1/2-In. Card, 50 Piece 77.00
Trade Card, Clark's O.N.T. Spool Cotton, Boy & Girl In Woods, 4 3/8 x 2 3/4 In. 22.40
Trade Card, J. & P. Coats' Thread, Champion, Child, Rifle, Cup, 3 x 4 1/2 In. 18.00
Trade Card, J. &.P. Coats', Donaldson Brothers, Calendar, N.Y., 1887, 2 1/2 x 4 In. 10.00

COCA-COLA   Coca-Cola was first served in 1886 in Atlanta, Georgia. John S. Pemberton, a pharmacist, developed the syrup. He was trying to make a patent medicine to aid those who had nervousness, headaches, or stomach problems. The syrup was mixed with water at first; but in 1887 Willis E. Venable mixed it with carbonated water and present-day Coca-Cola was born. Pemberton sold his interests in the company to Venable and a local businessman, George S. Lowndes, in 1888. Later that year, Asa Griggs Candler, owner of a pharmaceutical company, and some of his business friends joined the partnership. A short time later, Venable and Lowndes sold their interests to Candler and his group, but Candler eventually paid a grand total of $2,300 to become the sole owner of Coca-Cola. The first ad for Coca-Cola appeared on May 29, 1886, in the *Atlanta Journal.* The company advertised heavily, and bottles, trays, calendars, signs, toys, and lamps, as well as thousands of other items, can be found. Coca-Cola written in script was trademarked in 1893. The nickname Coke, first used in 1941, was registered in 1945. It is possible to date original Coca-Cola items from the slogans used in the advertising campaigns. Over the past century the company has used these slogans: "Drink Coca-Cola," then "Deliciously Refreshing" (1904), "Thirst Knows No Season" (1922), "Stop at the Red Sign" (1926), "The Pause That Refreshes" (1929), "It's the Real Thing" (1942), "That Extra Something" (1943), "Things Go Better with Coke" (1954), "America's Family Fun Drink" (1957), "Relax with Coke" (1960), "Only Coca-Cola Refreshes You Best" (1962), "Things Go Better with Coke" again (1963), "Enjoy Coca-Cola" (1965), "It's the Real Thing" again (1969). "Coke Adds Life" (1976), "Coke Is It" (1982), "You Can't Beat the Real Thing" (1990), "Always Coca-Cola" (1993), "Coca-Cola Enjoy" (2000), "Life Tastes Good" (2001), and "Coca-Cola...Real" (2003). Many Coca-Cola items have been reproduced, including trays, glasses, lamps, mirrors, and signs.

Advertisement, Magazine, Raquel Welch, 1970, 14 x 10 1/2 In. 25.00
Advertisement, Ozzie & Harriet Ice Skating, Full Color, 1961, 10 x 13 In. 20.00
Advertisement, Patrons In Soda Shop, Massengale Magazine, c.1905, 10 3/4 x 15 In. ... 60.00
Advertisement, Sunday Newspaper Magazine, Santa, 1952 .... 20.00
Ashtray, Coke Bottle Under Lampshade Top, Match Pull, Bakelite, c.1930, 7 1/2 In. 850.00
Ashtray, Cup Holders, During The Game Enjoy Coca-Cola, Metal, 8 1/2 x 8 1/2 In. 149.00
Bank, Musical, Die Cast Metal, 2 Songs, Certificate, Instructions, 6 x 6 In. 50.00
Bank, Santa Claus, At Fireplace, Plastic, Mechanical 10.00
Bank, Santa Claus, In Chair, Plastic, Mechanical 15.00
Bank, Santa Claus, With Train, Plastic, Mechanical 15.00
Bank, Vending Machine, Die Cast Metal, Musical, Instructions, 1994, 7 1/4 x 3 1/2 In. ... 50.00
Banner, Soda Fountain, 5 Cent Coca-Cola, Canvas, 48 In. 1400.00
Baseball Scorekeeper, Red, White, Green, c.1910 .... 77.00
Bicycle, Boy's, Huffy, 26 x 70 In. 193.00
Blotter, Coca-Cola Gum, Chew This, Peppermint, Pepsin, 3 3/4 x 6 In. .... *Illus* 2320.00
Book Cover, 2 Bottles, Pause-Refreshed, No. 617, 22 x 16 In. 10.00
Booklet, Bottler, 1959 .... 33.00

| Coca-Cola, Bookmark, Drink Coca-Cola, Girl, Heart Shape, Celluloid, c.1899, 2 1/4 x 2 In. | Coca-Cola, Bottle, Syrup, Delicious & Refreshing, 5 Cents, Cap, Enameled, c.1900 | Coca-Cola, Calendar, 1902, Girl With Feathered Hat, Drink Coca-Cola, 5 Cents, Frame | Coca-Cola, Calendar, 1916, Elaine, Girl With Basket Of Flowers |

Booklet, Bottler, January, 1960 .... 39.00
Booklet, Bottler, Mar.-Sept. 1946 .... 28.00
Bookmark, Drink Coca-Cola, Girl, Heart Shape, Celluloid, c.1899, 2 1/4 x 2 In. ..... *Illus* 440.00
Bookmark, Woman, At Soda Fountains, 5 Cents, Frame, 1905, 6 x 2 In. 550.00
Bookmark, Woman, Drink Coca-Cola, Embossed, Cardboard, Frame, 1903, 6 x 2 In. 413.00
Bookmark, Woman, Mug Of Coca-Cola, Frame, 1904, 6 x 2 In. 253.00
Bottle, 1983 World Champions Orioles, Contents, 10 Oz. 17.85
Bottle, 23rd Olympiad, Los Angeles, 1984, Bird Carrying Torch, 10 x 2 1/4 In. 12.00
Bottle, Aqua, Orangeburg, S.C. 39.00
Bottle, Blue Ridge Bottling Works, Staunton, Va., c.1910, 7 3/4 In. 65.00
Bottle, c.1960, 3 In. 16.00
Bottle, Christmas, 1923, 20 In. 770.00
Bottle, Cowboy On Bucking Bronco, Flathead Bottling Co., Kalispell, Mont. 150.00
Bottle, Enameled Script, Embossed, Hot Soda, Metal Cap, 1910-1920, 12 In. 358.00
Bottle, Grand Opening Of World Of Coca-Cola, Atlanta, 1990 .... 65.00
Bottle, Hobble Skirt, Aqua, Embossed, December 25, 1923, 20 1/4 x 6 In. 385.00
Bottle, In Lucite, 75th Anniversary 75.00
Bottle, Jelly Belly, 75th Anniversary, Clear, Full Of Jelly Bellies, 1978, 10 Oz. 95.00
Bottle, Seltzer, Acid Etched, Berlin, Pa. 330.00
Bottle, Seltzer, Green, Fluted, Logansport, In. 330.00
Bottle, Seltzer, Hoover Dam, Red Pyro Glaze, Broken Stem, Las Vegas, Nev., Qt., 1936 . 1208.00
Bottle, Seltzer, Red Pyro Glaze, Billings, Montana, 26 Oz. 288.00
Bottle, Syrup, Delicious & Refreshing, 5 Cents, Cap, Enameled, c.1900 .... *Illus* 2310.00
Bottle, Syrup, Drink Coca-Cola, Foil Label, 1920s, 12 In. 523.00
Bottle, Syrup, Green, Lid, 1940s, Gal. 25.00
Bottle Holder, Shopping Cart, Wire, Red Plaque, Enjoy Coke While You Shop 65.00
Bottle Opener, Brass, Patent 2335000, Starr X, 4 x 1 1/2 In. 50.00
Bottle Opener, Metal, Embossed Letters, Starr 48.00
Bottle Topper, We Let You See The Bottle, Plastic, Metal, 1950s 1365.00
Bottle Topper, Winter Girl, Die Cut, Cardboard, 1927, 9 1/2 x 6 3/4 In. 4300.00
Box, Pepsin Gum, Wood, Dovetailed, 6 1/2 x 2 x 12 3/4 In. 440.00
Button, Bottle, Painted, Tin, 1949, 2 In. ....800.00 to 844.00
Button, Coca-Cola, Red, Aluminum, 12 In. 138.00
Button, Drink Coca-Cola, Ice Cold, Blue, Porcelain, 14 In. 523.00
Button, Drink Coca-Cola, Red, White, Metal, 12 In. 248.00
Button, Drink Coca-Cola, Red, White, Porcelain, 36 In. 330.00
Calendar, 1896, Lady With Birds 7150.00
Calendar, 1902, Girl With Feathered Hat, Drink Coca-Cola, 5 Cents, Frame .... *Illus* 11000.00
Calendar, 1907, Girl With Green Dress, Holding Glass, Drink Coca-Cola 11000.00
Calendar, 1916, Elaine, Girl With Basket Of Flowers .... *Illus* 2640.00

Calendar, 1919, Girl With Knitting Bag, Pink Dress, Hat, Frame, 21 x 40 In. 1540.00
Calendar, 1920, Golfer Girl, Golf Course, 27 1/2 x 12 In. 3400.00
Calendar, 1921, Autumn Girl .... *Illus* 2090.00
Calendar, 1924, Smiling Girl, Pad, Frame, 24 x 11 3/4 In. 990.00
Calendar, 1926, Girl With Tennis Racket, 10 x 18 1/2 In. .... .901.00 to 1013.00
Calendar, 1931, Barefoot Boy, Dog, Rockwell .... .523.00 to 904.00
Calendar, 1936, 50th Anniversary, N.C. Wyeth, Frame, 11 3/4 x 24 1/4 In. 647.00
Calendar, 1940, Girl In Red Dress, Holding Glass & Bottle, Pad, Frame 633.00
Calendar, 1947, Girl With Skis 132.00
Calendar, 1951, Party Girl, Entertain Your Thirst, Woman Holding Book, Confetti 165.00
Calendar, 1952, Square Dance, Coke Adds Zest, 22 x 12 1/2 In. 303.00
Calendar, 1954, Santa, 3 Months Per Page, Flowers, 14 x 8 In. 74.00
Calendar, 1958, Santa Claus, Sign Of Good Taste, Starts December 1957, 12 x 22 In. 225.00
Calendar, 1980, Olympics, 17 1/2 x 11 In. 160.00
Calendar Holder, Button Top, Tin, 19 1/2 x 8 In. 825.00
Can, Syrup, Delicious & Refreshing, Tin Lithograph, 1930s, 9 1/2 In. 523.00
Can, Syrup, Paper Label, c.1939, Gal. 385.00
Carrier, 6-Bottle, Bentwood, Handle 230.00
Carrier, 6-Pack, Aluminum, 6 For 25 Cents, c.1949, 8 1/2 In. 66.00
Carrier, 6-Pack, Aluminum, Separate Compartments, 1940s-1950s 85.00
Carrier, 6-Pack, Aluminum, Wire Handle, 6 Glass Bottles 39.00
Carrier, 6-Pack, Yellow, Red, Hanging Separators, Handle, Wood, 1941, 9 1/2 x 5 3/8 In. .. 495.00
Carrier, 8-Pack, Metal, 12 x 4 x 4 In. 193.00
Carrier, 12-Bottle, Aluminum, Reynolds Aluminum, 16 1/2 x 5 1/4 x 9 In. ....150.00 to 193.00
Carrier, Bottle & Wings On Sides, Handle, Wood, 1940s 220.00
Carrier, Grocery Cart, 2-Bottle Holder, Enjoy Coca-Cola While You Shop, 1950s 58.00
Carrier, Handy To Carry Home, Christmas Bottles On Ends, Wood, 1940s 275.00
Carrier, Metal, 6 6-Oz. Bottles, Different Bottlers, 1950s 150.00
Carrier, Seasons Greetings, Red, White, Green, Cardboard, Metal, Wood, 1930s 440.00
Case Holder, Wire, Drink Coca-Cola, Fishtail Sign, Hooks 225.00
Chalkboard, Fishtail, Tin, 1959, 28 x 20 In. 154.00
Cigarette Case, Frosted Glass, Embossed, 2 Piece, 1936 ....425.00 to 450.00
Clock, 8-Sided, Mahogany, Drink Coca-Cola, Key, Paperwork, 20 x 12 In. 385.00
Clock, Bottle, Sun Highlight, Electric, 1940-1950 .... 1045.00
Clock, Brown & Red, Round .... *Illus* 50.00
Clock, Cola Clan Convention Award, 17 x 41 In. 83.00
Clock, Delicious, Refreshing, Round Dial, Red Letters, Wood Frame, 24 3/4 x 17 In. 83.00
Clock, Drink Coca-Cola In Bottles, Black Wood Frame, 16 x 16 In. 220.00
Clock, Drink Coca-Cola In Bottles, Red Center Circle, Wood Frame, Square, 1939 ...... 303.00
Clock, Drink Coca-Cola In Bottles, Red, White, Duralite, 15 In. Diam. 1200.00
Clock, Drink Coca-Cola In Bottles, Shaped Metal Frame, 63 x 25 In. 220.00
Clock, Drink Coca-Cola In Bottles, Square, Selecto, Selected Devices, Chicago, 16 In. ... 240.00

Coca-Cola, Calendar,
1921, Autumn Girl

Coca-Cola, Clock,
Brown & Red, Round

Coca-Cola, Cooler, Salesman's Sample,
Open Bottom, Books, Metal, 1939

Clock, Drink Coca-Cola, Metal, Glass, Electric, 15 1/4 x 15 1/4 In. 154.00
Clock, Drink Coca-Cola, Red, White, Green, Swihart, 15 In. 1600.00
Clock, Drink Coca-Cola, Silhouette Girl, Red Center, Wood Frame, Square, 1941 . . . . 275.00
Clock, Drink Coca-Cola, Square, 36 x 36 In. 165.00
Clock, Drink Coca-Cola, Square, Pam, 1950s 121.00
Clock, Drink Coke In Bottles, Plastic Face, Wire Frame, Light-Up, 1950s, 64 In. 137.00
Clock, Green Numbers & Number Marks, Swihart, Electric, 15 In. 660.00
Clock, Ice Cold Coca-Cola, Silhouette Girl, Light-Up, Pam, Round 220.00
Clock, Ice Cold, In Bottles, Fluorescent, Black Face, Red, White 990.00
Clock, Ideal Brain Tonic, Delicious, Refreshing, Baird, 1893-1896, 30 1/2 x 18 1/2 In. . . . 2160.00
Clock, Most Refreshing Drink In The World, Battery Operated, Frame, 25 x 13 In. 299.00
Clock, Neon, Neon Clock Company, Tag, 31 x 36 In. 1760.00
Clock, Please Pay When Served, Light-Up, 9 x 19 1/2 In. 715.00
Clock, Red Numbers, Fishtail Design, Electric, 11 x 12 In. 209.00
Clock, Regulator, Delicious, Refreshing, 5 Cents, Oak Case, Ingraham, 40 In. 577.00
Clock, Revolving Wheel, West Germany, 3 In. 28.00
Clock, Silhouette Girl, Drink Coca-Cola, Square, 15 1/2 In. 550.00
Clock, Silhouette Girl, Neon, c.1941, 18 In. 2090.00
Clock, Sold Everywhere, 5 Cents, Oak Case, 31 Day, Gilbert, 38 x 16 1/2 In. 374.00
Clock, Sprite Boy Billboard, Plastic, Battery, Wall Mounted, 1990, 21 3/4 x 11 1/2 In. . . . 48.00
Clock, Sprite, Light-Up, Neon Products, 16 In. 523.00
Clock, Wall, Telechron, Metal, 1950s, 18 In. 220.00
Clock, Welch Schoolhouse, 1901 . . . . 10670.00
Clock, Wood Frame, Selected Devices, c.1940, 16 x 16 x 3 3/4 In. 330.00
Coaster, Sprite Boy, 1950s, 4 Piece 20.00
Coin Changer, Have A Coke, Get Your Nickels Here, Metal, Vendo, 1950s, 16 In. 935.00
Cooler, 1/2 Size, 1950s, 16 1/4 x 18 3/4 In. 200.00
Cooler, Airline, Bottle Opener, Red, Steel, 12 x 17 x 6 In. . . . . 248.00 to 418.00
Cooler, Airline, Stainless Steel, 1950s, 10 x 15 x 6 In. 1210.00
Cooler, Bottle Opener, Original Tray, Drain Spigot, 18 In. 220.00
Cooler, Coca-Cola Loveseat, Red, White, Embossed Lettering 495.00
Cooler, Drink Coca-Cola In Bottles, Red, Handle, Embossed, 18 In. 209.00
Cooler, Drink Coca-Cola, Metal Handle, 16 x 11 x 9 1/4 In. 325.00
Cooler, Drink Coca-Cola, Wood, Metal Lined, Yellow Paint, Stencil, 14 x 26 In. 1840.00
Cooler, Junior, 34 x 25 x 18 In. 550.00
Cooler, Metal, Red, 18 1/2 x 18 x 12 1/2 In. 180.00
Cooler, Model 240T, Westinghouse, 91 In. 110.00
Cooler, Opener, Drain, Handle, 1950s, 17 x 17 x 11 In. 285.00
Cooler, Picnic, 6-Pack, Stainless Steel, Acton, 1950s 275.00
Cooler, Picnic, Bottle Opener, Drain, Plug, Acton Mfg., 17 1/2 x 12 x 16 1/2 In. 185.00
Cooler, Picnic, Red, White, 14 x 18 In. 193.00
Cooler, Red, 11 1/2 x 11 1/2 x 9 In. 110.00
Cooler, Red, White Letters, Top Door, Bottle Opener, Westinghouse 385.00
Cooler, Salesman's Sample, Advertising Cards, 1939, 10 x 12 In. 1980.00
Cooler, Salesman's Sample, Booklets, Case, Insulation Samples, Cap Catcher, 1939 . . . . . 6050.00
Cooler, Salesman's Sample, Embossed Metal, 12 In. 1375.00
Cooler, Salesman's Sample, Open Bottom, Books, Metal, 1939 . . . . *Illus* 2860.00
Cooler, Tray, Opener, Red, Vinyl, 17 x 14 x 11 1/2 In. 248.00
Cooler, Westinghouse, Embossed Metal, Restored, 34 In. . . . . *Illus* 523.00
Cooler, Wood, Metal Liner, Yellow Paint, Red Stenciling, c.1939, 10 x 12 In. 384.00
Crate, 24-Bottle, Drink Coca-Cola, Spanish, Plastic, Wood, 1950s, 6 x 4 In. 49.00
Crate, Yellow, Red Insignia, Wood, 18 x 12 x 4 In. 65.00
Cup, Diamonds, Red, White, 10 Oz., Sweetheart, Box, 1960s, 100 Piece 61.00
Cup, Things Go Better, 10 Oz., Sweetheart, Box, 1963, 100 Piece 39.00
Cutouts, Circus, Frame, 1927, 12 1/2 x 15 1/2 In. 100.00
Dish, Pretzel, 3 Bottles Around Bowl 248.00
Dish, World, Fluted, Coke In Different Languages, 7 1/2 In. 99.00
Dispenser, Barrel, Oak, Coca-Cola, Seven-Up, Rootbeer, Countertop, 26 In. 275.00
Dispenser, Barrel, Wood, 2 Tin Signs, Multiplex Faucet Co., 29 In. 247.00
Dispenser, Fountain, White Letters, Red Ground, 1950s 248.00
Dispenser, Frosted Glass Body, Porcelain Base, c.1930, 17 In. . . . . .4620.00 to 6500.00
Dispenser, Painted Metal, Embossed Letters, Countertop, 20 In. 242.00
Display Bottle, Glass, Original Cap, 1923, 20 In. 248.00

Coca-Cola, Kickplate, Porcelain, Late 1920s

Coca-Cola, Cooler,
Westinghouse, Embossed
Metal, Restored, 34 In.

Display Bottle, Metal Cap, Trade Mark Registered, ABM Lip, 1925-1940, 20 In. 364.00
Display Bottle, Original Cap, 20 In. 605.00
Display Bottle, Patent D, Cap, 20 In. 425.00
Display Bottle, Plastic, Figural, c.1953, 20 In. 413.00
Doll, Santa Claus, Holding Coke Bottle, Black Boots 143.00
Doll, Santa, Dakin, Rich's Atlanta, 1988, 16 In. 89.00
Doll, Santa, Ruskin, Electric, Mechanical, 39 In. 145.00
Door Plate, Delicious, Refreshing, Metal, c.1939, 3 1/2 x 33 In. 633.00
Door Pull, Bottle Shape, Cast Metal, Plastic, Screws, Box, 8 In. 249.00
Door Pull, Refresh Yourself, Green, Red, White, Porcelain, 1940-1950 . . . . 880.00
Door Push, Come In!, Have A Coca-Cola, Porcelain, 11 1/2 x 4 In. 330.00
Door Push, Drink Coca-Cola, Blue, White, Aluminum, c.1905, 3 x 8 In. . . . . . . .1013.00 to 1195.00
Door Push, Drink Coca-Cola, Delicious, Refreshing, 5 Cent, Aluminum, c.1905, 3 x 8 In. 955.00
Door Push, Entrex Et Buvez Un Coca-Cola, Porcelain, 11 1/2 x 4 In. 127.00
Door Push, Have A Coke, Bottle Shape, c.1950, 7 3/4 x 2 3/4 In. 198.00
Door Push, Refresh Yourself, 6 x 3 In. 468.00
Door Push, Thanks, Call Again For A Coca-Cola, Elongated Oval, Porcelain, 11 In. 193.00
Doorknob, Incised, Porcelain, Cast Metal Stem 525.00
Doorknob, Porcelain, Drink Coca-Cola, Metal Stem 525.00
Festoon, Bathing Girls, 1946, 5 Piece 1430.00
Festoon, Howdy Partner, Horns, Rope, Horseshoes, 10 x 106 In. 2310.00
Festoon, Nautical Island Theme, Die Cut, Metal, Wood, 1930s, 22 Piece 4070.00
Festoon, State Tree, Cardboard Lithograph, 5 Part, 42 In. 90.00
Festoon, Verbena, Cardboard, Die Cut, 5 Sections, Satin Ribbon, 33 x 21 1/2-In. Center . . 1610.00
Glass Holder, Logo, Silver, c.1900, 2 1/2 In. 1400.00
Globe, Frosted Glass, Tassel, c.1930 . . . . 3200.00
Globe, Green Pinstripe, Milk, Frosted Glass, c.1930, 12 In. 800.00
Globe, Have A Coke Here, Light-Up, Metal, Plastic, Rotating Base, Neon Products 990.00
Golf Bag, Vinyl, 36 In. 17.00
Ice Bowl, Green, Vernonware, 1930s, 4 x 10 In. 468.00
Insert, Return Bottles For Free Lube Job, 1963, 5 3/4 x 4 3/4 In. 5.00
Jar, Chewing Gum, Glass, Embossed, Faceted Ball Handle 83.00
Jar, Pepsin Gum, Franklin Caro Co., Paper Label, 1912-1914, 12 x 5 In. 649.00
Kickplate, Drink Coca-Cola, Fountain Service, Porcelain, c.1950, 12 x 28 In. 550.00
Kickplate, Drink Coca-Cola, Tin, Embossed, 1933, 11 x 34 In. . . . . .625.00 to 647.00
Kickplate, Fountain Service, Porcelain, c.1950, 12 x 28 In. 563.00
Kickplate, Girl & Bottle, Tin, 1940 . . . . 605.00
Kickplate, Porcelain, Late 1920s . . . .*Illus* 1430.00
Lamp, Frosted Globe, Metal Tassel, Chain, c.1930 . . . . 3600.00
Lampshade, Ball Shape, Leaded Glass, c.1917 . . . . 28600.00
Lantern, Take Some Home, Light-Up, 12 In. 165.00
Light, Plastic, Red Ground, White Letters, Light-Up, 2-Sided, Round, 16 In. 495.00
Light Fixture, Hanging, Tin, Glass Globe, 13 In. 1320.00
Lunch Box, Coke Bottle Handle, 10 x 7 x 5 In. 50.00
Lunch Box, Silver, Bottle Shape Handle, Thermos Holder, 8 1/2 x 10 x 4 1/2 In. 48.00
Match Holder, Tin, 20 Matchbooks, 1950-1960 . . . . 440.00
Match Striker, Drink Coca-Cola, Strike Matches Here, Canada, 1939, 4 1/2 In. 770.00
Menu Board, Drink Coca-Cola, Masonite, Tin Card Holders, 29 x 17 In. 147.00

Coca-Cola, Plate, Bottle,
Glass, c.1930, 8 1/4 In.

Coca-Cola, Meter,
Mileage, Red, White,
Winston-Salem, N.C., 1950s

Menu Board, Drink Coca-Cola, Wood, Masonite, 1939, 26 In.	413.00
Menu Board, Fishtail, Robertson Co., 1963, 27 1/2 x 19 1/2 In.	303.00
Menu Board, Good With Food, Fishtail, 1945, 19 x 96 In.	770.00
Meter, Mileage, Red, White, Winston-Salem, N.C., 1950s .... *Illus*	2750.00
Mirror, Cat Outside, Slogan Inside, Germany, 1925, Pocket	450.00
Mirror, Drink Coca-Cola, Woman, Red Dress & Hat, Bastian Bros., 1908, Pocket	1137.00
Name Badge, 50th Anniversary Bottlers Conference, Celluloid, 1936, 2 x 2 3/4 In.	361.00
Name Badge, Bottlers Conference, Celluloid, Metal, c.1930s, 2 1/4 x 2 3/4 In. ..... 77.00 to 150.00	
Napkin Dispenser, Cooler Shape, Tome Coca-Cola, Bien Fria, c.1940	1100.00
Opener & Ice Pick, Wood, Red Drink Coca-Cola Bottles, 10 In.	55.00
Payroll Check, Coca-Cola Bottling Works, Lebanon, Tennessee, 1957	25.00
Pencil, Drink Coca-Cola, Mechanical, Eversharp, U.S.A., 1950s	25.00
Pencil, Mechanical, Slogan, Red Barrel, Bottle Shaped Clip, 5 1/4 In.	24.00
Pencil Box, 3 Pencils, Pen, Ruler, Eraser, 2 Blotters, 1930s	57.00
Picture, Airplane, Cardboard, 1943, 15 x 13 In.	44.00
Picture, Helicopter, Dropping Coke Bottle, 1943, 15 x 13 In.	55.00
Plaque, Dalton Coca-Cola Bottling Co., 1946 & 1956, 18 x 7 1/2 In.	220.00
Plate, Bottle, Glass Of Coke, Knowles China, 1931, 7 1/4 In. .... 500.00 to 534.00	
Plate, Bottle, Glass, c.1930, 8 1/4 In. .... *Illus*	1650.00
Plate, Coca-Cola, Good With Food, Scalloped Edge, Sample, Wellsville, 1940s, 7 1/4 In. .	1485.00
Plate, Drink Coca-Cola, Bottle, Cup, Knowles, 1931, 7 1/4 In.	534.00
Plate, Topless Woman, Vienna Art, Tin Lithograph, 9 1/2 In. .... 819.00 to 1610.00	
Playing Cards, Airplane Spotter, Blue Ground, 54 Cards, Box, 1943	125.00
Pole Light, Drink Coca-Cola, Take Some Home, 27 1/2 x 11 1/4 x 11 In.	303.00
Postcard, Motor Girl, 1911	578.00
Postcard, Soda Fountain, Welch's Grape Juice Bottles, 3 1/2 x 5 1/2 In.	275.00
Rack, Carton, 25 Cents, Red Metal, 46 1/2 In.	275.00
Radio, Bottle Shape, 1930s, 24 In.	4620.00
Radio, Bottle Shape, AM, Plastic, 1970s	45.00
Radio, Bottle Shape, Bakelite, 1933, 23 1/2 In.	5750.00
Radio, Bottle Shape, Red Bakelite, Knobs On Front, 1951	1903.00
Radio, Cooler Shape, Drink Coca-Cola, Ice Cold, 1950s, 9 1/2 x 11 1/2 x 7 In. .... 550.00 to 944.00	
Radio, Cooler Shape, Plastic, Red, 10 In.	367.00
Radio, Maharlika, Airline Cooler Shape, c.1950	1590.00
Radio, Transistor, Vending Machine Shape, Westinghouse, Box, c.1963	99.00
Ruler, Compliments The Coca-Cola Bottling Co., Wood, 12 In.	12.00
Scooter, Brakes, 47 In.	33.00
Sewing Kit, Girl, Large Brim Hat, 1981, 2 3/4 x 1 3/4 In.	20.00
Shirt, Tan, Short Sleeves, Poly-Cotton, Medium To Large, 33 x 42 x 50 In. .... 35.00 to 38.00	
Sign, 2 Bottles, Button, Sprite Boys, Fluted, 2 Panels, c.1950, 16 x 30 1/2 In.	330.00
Sign, 6-Pack, 27 Cents, 18 x 32 In.	33.00
Sign, 6-Pack, Big King Size, 1961, 20 x 28 In.	2813.00
Sign, 6-Pack, King Size, Tin, Die Cut, Embossed, 1960, 38 x 31 In. .... *Illus*	1980.00
Sign, 6-Pack, Red, 6 For 25 Cents, Tin, Die Cut, September 1950, 11 x 14 In.	1375.00
Sign, 6-Pack, Red, Die Cut, Cardboard, 1951, 11 x 14 In.	1045.00
Sign, 6-Pack, Take Home A Carton, Red, Yellow, Tin, Embossed, c.1940, 54 x 18 In.	495.00
Sign, 6-Pack, Take Home A Carton, Tin, 1939, 27 1/2 x 19 1/2 In.	920.00

Sign, 6-Pack, Tin, Die Cut, 1952, 12 x 11 In. 2200.00
Sign, 6-Pack, Top Button, Tin, 1954, 54 x 16 In. 1430.00
Sign, 12-Pack, Die Cut, 14 x 20 In. 70.00
Sign, Accepted Home Refreshment, Fireplace, Lithograph Cardboard, 1942, 27 x 56 In. . . 132.00
Sign, Arrow, Tin Lithograph, Self-Framed, c.1950, 18 x 54 In. 385.00
Sign, Be Refreshed, Cardboard, Frame, 1952, 34 In. 99.00
Sign, Betty, New, Drink Coca-Cola, Tin, Self-Framed, 1941, 11 x 35 In. 908.00
Sign, Betty, Tin Lithograph, Self-Framed, 1914, 41 x 31 In. . . . . .1100.00 to 2860.00
Sign, Black & White, Script, Die Cut, Porcelain, 5 1/2 x 18 In. 633.00
Sign, Blue Bonnet Cafe, Tin, Self-Framed, 1947, 16 x 48 In. 193.00
Sign, Bottle Shape, Bottle Pat'd Dec. 25, 1923, 38 x 12 In. 990.00
Sign, Bottle Shape, Sheet Steel Lithograph, 2-Dimensional, 108 In. 220.00
Sign, Bottle, Big King Size, Ice Cold, 1950s, 28 x 20 In. 440.00
Sign, Bottle, Convex, Cardboard, Die Cut, 1951, 108 In. 4070.00
Sign, Bottle, Die Cut, Porcelain, 1940-1950, 16 1/2 x 5 In. 366.00
Sign, Bottle, Ice Cold, 2-Sided, Tin, Die Cut, Flange, 1951, 18 x 22 In. 619.00
Sign, Bottle, Nov. 16, 1915, Metal Over Cardboard, 13 x 5 3/4 In. 590.00
Sign, Bottle, Tin, Die Cut, 3 In. 330.00
Sign, Bottle, Tin, Round, 1936, 46 In. 1045.00
Sign, Bottle, Tin, Self-Framed, Vertical, 50 x 16 In. 495.00
Sign, Bottle, Tin, Silver Wood Frame, 1947, 36 x 18 In. 248.00
Sign, Bottle, Top Button, Tin, 1948, 54 x 16 In. 715.00
Sign, Boy Eating Hotdog, Mat, Frame, 18 x 27 In. 303.00
Sign, Button With Banner, Tin Lithograph, 36 In. 220.00
Sign, Button, Bottle, Celluloid, 9 In. 138.00
Sign, Button, Bottle, Coca-Cola, Red, White, Brown, Porcelain, 1950s, 24 In. 468.00
Sign, Button, Bottle, Coca-Cola, Red, White, Brown, Tin, Painted, 1955, 24 In. 523.00
Sign, Button, Bottle, Flange, Tin Lithograph, c.1950, 22 1/2 x 18 1/4 In. 440.00
Sign, Button, Bottle, Porcelain, 24 In. 770.00
Sign, Button, Celluloid Over Cardboard, Easel Stand, c.1950, 9 In. 232.00
Sign, Button, Coca-Cola Over Bottle, Porcelain, Round, 24 In. 303.00
Sign, Button, Coca-Cola Over Bottle, Tin, Round, 48 In. 358.00
Sign, Button, Coca-Cola, Metal, 12 In. 220.00
Sign, Button, Drink Coca-Cola In Bottles, Red, White, Tin, Jan. 1957, 12 In. 385.00
Sign, Button, Drink Coca-Cola In Bottles, Tin, Red Ground, 1955, 12 In. 479.00
Sign, Button, Drink Coca-Cola, Porcelain, 44 In. 275.00
Sign, Button, Porcelain, 36 In. 374.00
Sign, Button, Red, Enamel On Tin, 15 In. 385.00
Sign, Button, Red, Steel, 1950s, 36 In. 255.00
Sign, Chewing Gum, Dutch Boy & Girl, Die Cut, Cardboard, c.1914, Pair 40370.00
Sign, Circus, Cardboard, Sundblom, 1936, 50 x 29 In. 7000.00
Sign, Clown, Ice Skater, Pause, Frame, 1950, 16 x 27 In. 1650.00
Sign, Coca-Cola Across Bottle, Red Ground, Celluloid, Round, 9 In. 220.00
Sign, Coca-Cola Belongs, Man & Woman, Picnic, Cardboard, 1942, 28 x 57 In. 440.00
Sign, Coca-Cola Delicious, Refreshing, Tin, 1963, 24 x 24 In. 193.00
Sign, Coca-Cola In Bottles, Neon, Countertop, c.1939, 12 x 24 In. 6820.00
Sign, Coca-Cola Over Bottle, Tin, Round, 46 In. 275.00
Sign, Coca-Cola, Girl Holding Out Glass, Tin, Oval, Self-Framed, c.1926, 13 x 19 In. 3520.00
Sign, Coca-Cola, Please Pay When Served, Plastic, Wood, Price Bros., 17 1/2 In. 880.00
Sign, Coca-Cola, Red, White, Porcelain, 16 x 44 In. 230.00
Sign, Coca-Cola, Sign Of Good Taste, 2-Sided, 1960s, 15 x 17 3/4 In. 468.00
Sign, Coke Adds Life To Everything Nice, Metal, 18 x 36 In. 110.00
Sign, Coke Belongs, Soldier & Woman, Logo, 1946, 27 1/2 x 57 1/2 In. 110.00
Sign, Coke Time, Join The Friendly Circle, Cardboard, Frame, c.1954, 36 x 20 In. 468.00
Sign, Coke, Bottle Shape, Porcelain, Die Cut, 1940-1950, 16 1/2 x 5 In. 328.00
Sign, Cool Contrast To Summer Sun, Frame, 1941, 64 x 34 In. 495.00
Sign, Cool Contrast To Summer Tan, Woman, Swimsuit, Cardboard, 1941, 56 x 27 In. . . . 385.00
Sign, Cooling Lift, Girl In Pool Holding Bottle, Gold Wood Frame, 1940s, 24 x 39 In. . . . 206.00
Sign, Counter Dispenser, Porcelain, 2-Sided, c.1941, 25 1/4 x 26 1/4 In. 1100.00
Sign, Cowboy, Wiping Forehead, Cardboard, 1941, 7 x 16 In. 1595.00
Sign, Delicious & Refreshing, 6-Pack, Tin, Die Cut, 1951, 11 x 13 In. 1125.00
Sign, Delicious & Refreshing, Man, Woman, Tin, 20 x 28 In. 220.00
Sign, Delicious & Refreshing, Porcelain, 2-Sided, Enamel, Frame, Tenn., 36 x 60 In. 3300.00

Coca-Cola, Sign, Drink Coca-Cola, Refreshing
New Feeling, Fishtail, Horizontal, 1960s, 53 In.

Coca-Cola, Sign, Drink
Coca-Cola, Sign Of Good
Taste, Fishtail, Vertical,
1963, 53 In.

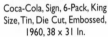

Coca-Cola, Sign, 6-Pack, King
Size, Tin, Die Cut, Embossed,
1960, 38 x 31 In.

Sign, Delicious Coca-Cola, Refreshing, Celluloid, Tin, Cardboard, Red, c.1940, 9 In. Diam.	350.00
Sign, Dimensional Aluminum Letters, 29-In. C, Mounted, 48 x 72 In.	440.00
Sign, Display, 3-Bottle, Golfing Couple, 1926	4658.00
Sign, Drink Coca-Cola Here, Porcelain, Die Cut, Flange, Canada, 1940, 20 x 17 In.	688.00
Sign, Drink Coca-Cola Ice Cold, Porcelain, Truck Cab, 1950s, 50 x 10 In.	1238.00
Sign, Drink Coca-Cola Ice Cold, Tin, Flange, 1957, 18 x 22 In.	1125.00
Sign, Drink Coca-Cola In Bottles, 5 Cents, Tin, Embossed, 1908, 12 x 36 In.	550.00 to 660.00
Sign, Drink Coca-Cola In Bottles, Metal, Plastic, Light-Up, Round, Neon Products, 16 In.	880.00
Sign, Drink Coca-Cola In Bottles, Porcelain, Die Cut, Vinyl Decals, 2-Sided, 55 x 47 In.	1760.00
Sign, Drink Coca-Cola, 2 Glasses Of Coke, Shield Shape, Wood, Metal, 9 x 11 1/2 In.	853.00
Sign, Drink Coca-Cola, A.A. Ardinger, Tin, Painted, Frame, 27 x 69 In.	440.00
Sign, Drink Coca-Cola, Betty, Holds Bottle, Cardboard, 32 x 56 In.	132.00
Sign, Drink Coca-Cola, Bottle Beneath, Tin, 1947, 54 x 15 1/2 In.	853.00
Sign, Drink Coca-Cola, Bottle In Sun, 2-Sided, Die Cut, Filigree, 1940, 24 x 20 In.	528.00
Sign, Drink Coca-Cola, Bottle, Tin Lithograph, Embossed, c.1931, 12 1/4 x 4 1/2 In.	688.00
Sign, Drink Coca-Cola, Bottle, Tin, Embossed, Robertson, 1934, 11 3/4 x 34 3/4 In.	770.00
Sign, Drink Coca-Cola, Bottle, Tin, Self-Framed, 12 x 32 In.	127.00
Sign, Drink Coca-Cola, Delicious & Refreshing, Confectionery, Porcelain, 47 x 46 In.	1760.00
Sign, Drink Coca-Cola, Delicious & Refreshing, Fountain Service, Porcelain, 42 x 60 In.	715.00
Sign, Drink Coca-Cola, Delicious & Refreshing, Porcelain, 1932, 36 x 60 In.	4125.00
Sign, Drink Coca-Cola, Delicious, Refreshing, Tin, Self-Framed, c.1937, 32 3/4 x 57 In.	385.00
Sign, Drink Coca-Cola, Die Cut, Flange, Tin, 2-Sided, 1952, 22 1/2 x 18 In.	935.00
Sign, Drink Coca-Cola, Die Cut, Porcelain, 60 x 38 In.	303.00
Sign, Drink Coca-Cola, Die Cut, Porcelain, Fountain Service Decal, 2-Sided, 39 x 60 In.	880.00
Sign, Drink Coca-Cola, Distributor, Porcelain, Tennessee Enamel Co., 72 x 96 In.	1155.00
Sign, Drink Coca-Cola, Fountain Service, Die Cut, Porcelain, 14 x 27 In.	1210.00
Sign, Drink Coca-Cola, Fountain Service, Porcelain, 1950s, 28 x 11 3/4 In.	1125.00
Sign, Drink Coca-Cola, Green Margin, Red, White, 1930s, 5 3/4 x 17 7/8 In.	306.00
Sign, Drink Coca-Cola, Hobbleskirt Bottle, Tin On Cardboard, c.1915, 13 x 6 In.	1980.00
Sign, Drink Coca-Cola, Ice Cold, Flange, Tin, 22 In.	275.00 to 440.00
Sign, Drink Coca-Cola, Ice Cold, Sidewalk, Porcelain, 2-Sided, 1935, 37 x 34 In.	11000.00
Sign, Drink Coca-Cola, Ice Cold, Tin, Fishtail, Green Edge, 54 x 18 In.	330.00
Sign, Drink Coca-Cola, Ingram Richardson, Porcelain, Frame, c.1920, 12 x 30 In.	3825.00
Sign, Drink Coca-Cola, Neon Border, Plastic, Button Type, Round, 1960s, 16 In.	550.00
Sign, Drink Coca-Cola, Porcelain, 1927, 10 x 30 In.	350.00
Sign, Drink Coca-Cola, Porcelain, Die Cut, Green Ground, 1930s, 18 x 5 1/2 In.	788.00
Sign, Drink Coca-Cola, Porcelain, Green Border, Red Ground, 10 x 30 In.	220.00
Sign, Drink Coca-Cola, Red, Embossed, Tin Lithograph, 1920s, 5 3/4 x 17 3/4 In.	330.00
Sign, Drink Coca-Cola, Refreshing New Feeling, Fishtail, Horizontal, 1960s, 53 In. *Illus*	303.00
Sign, Drink Coca-Cola, Shield, Die Cut, Flange, 1934, 13 x 20 In.	688.00
Sign, Drink Coca-Cola, Sign Of Good Taste, Fishtail, Vertical, 1963, 53 In. *Illus*	357.00
Sign, Drink Coca-Cola, Sign Of Good Taste, Lollipop, Porcelain, Iron Base, 1950s, 63 In.	990.00
Sign, Drink Coca-Cola, Sign Of Good Taste, Tin Lithograph, c.1960, 53 1/2 x 17 1/2 In.	468.00
Sign, Drink Coca-Cola, Sold Everywhere, Cardboard, Trolley Card, 11 x 21 In.	3025.00
Sign, Drink Coca-Cola, Tin, Embossed Letters, 1940s, 19 x 54 In.	83.00
Sign, Drink Coca-Cola, Tin, Embossed, 11 1/4 x 34 3/4 In.	220.00

Sign, Drink Coca-Cola, Tin, Embossed, Dasco, 1930s, 18 x 6 In. 220.00
Sign, Drink Coca-Cola, Tin, Self-Framed, Robertson, 1952, 32 x 56 In. 550.00
Sign, Drink Coca-Cola, Waitress, Car, White, Red, Black, Porcelain, 36 x 54 In. 2420.00
Sign, Drink Coca-Cola, Wood, Aluminum Bottle, c.1939, 17 In. Diam. 358.00
Sign, Drink Coca-Cola, Wood, Metal Filigree, Kay Display, 1930s, 11 3/8 x 9 In. 853.00
Sign, Drink For Busy People, 4 Scenes, Die Cut, Cardboard, Frame, 1930s, 43 x 22 In. . . . 660.00
Sign, Drink Veep, Fresh 'n' Fizzy Lemon-Light, 12 x 31 1/2 In. 138.00
Sign, Drink, In Bottles, Red Ground, White Letters, Curved Ends, Porcelain, 68 x 24 In. . . . 165.00
Sign, Edgar Bergen, Charlie McCarthy, CBS Sunday Evening, Paper, 1949, 11 x 24 In. 248.00
Sign, Enjoy A Float With Coke, Favor Any Flavor, Cardboard, 1962, 16 x 27 In. 220.00
Sign, Enjoy Big King Size, Ice Cold Here, Tin, 1960s, 20 x 28 In. 176.00
Sign, Enjoy Coca-Cola, 24 x 10 In. 55.00
Sign, Enjoy That Refreshing New Feeling, 2-Sided, Flange, October, 1961, 15 x 18 In. 422.00
Sign, Enjoy That Refreshing New Feeling, Robertson, 1950, 17 1/2 x 55 1/2 In. 440.00
Sign, Face Your Job Refreshed, Canada, 1943, 27 x 56 In. 1870.00
Sign, Fountain Dispenser, Porcelain, 2-Sided, c.1950, 28 x 28 In. 2145.00
Sign, Fountain Service, Delicious & Refreshing, Porcelain, 2-Sided, 1934, 60 x 42 In. . . . 907.00
Sign, Fountain Service, Die Cut, 2-Sided, 1930s, 22 x 26 In. 385.00
Sign, Fountain Service, Drink Coca-Cola, Enamel, Tin, 1933, 25 1/2 x 23 In. 1725.00
Sign, Fountain Service, Porcelain, 12 x 28 In. 1045.00
Sign, Fountain Service, Porcelain, 12 x 29 In. 468.00
Sign, Fountain Service, Porcelain, Die Cut, 1941, 58 x 66 In. 11000.00
Sign, Fountain Service, Shield, Red, Green, Yellow, 2-Sided, 1936, 23 x 25 1/2 In. 2320.00
Sign, Fountain, 2 Glasses Of Coke, Wood, c.1930s, 11 x 9 In. 523.00
Sign, French Canadian, Buvez, Self-Framed, Tin, c.1930, 17 1/4 x 53 In. 165.00
Sign, Friendly Pause, Cardboard, Vertical, Under Glass, Frame, 1948, 27 x 16 In. 3080.00
Sign, Gas Today, Drink Coca-Cola While You Wait, Embossed Tin, 1930s, 20 x 28 In. . . . 907.00
Sign, Gas Today, Tin, 1932, 54 x 18 In. 2600.00
Sign, Girl At Fountain, Cardboard, 3-D, 1929, 24 x 35 In. 10969.00
Sign, Girl Drinking Bottle Of Coke, Die Cut, Cardboard, 22 In. 220.00
Sign, Girl, Groceries, Cardboard, 1946, 16 x 27 In. 1463.00
Sign, Girl, Slow School Zone, Metal, Die Cut, 2-Sided, c.1940, 53 x 16 In. . . . . *Illus* 4950.00
Sign, Good Company, Man & Woman, Trolley Card, Frame, 1927, 11 x 21 In. . . . . . *Illus* 2860.00
Sign, Good With Food, c.1960s, 1 1/2 x 8 In. 309.00
Sign, Good With Food, Paper, 1951, 11 x 24 1/2 In. 440.00
Sign, Have A Coke Now, Bottle, Cardboard, 2-Sided, 1951, 16 x 27 In. 375.00
Sign, Have A Coke, Neon, Spinner, Rounded Octagonal, Countertop, c.1950, 18 In. 8470.00
Sign, Hilda Clark, Tin, 1903, 16 x 19 In. . . . . *Illus* 7150.00
Sign, Home Hospitality, 3 People Singing, 1951, 30 x 50 In. 700.00
Sign, Home Refreshment, Cardboard, 2-Sided, 1950, 16 x 27 In. . . . . .950.00 to 1013.00
Sign, Home Refreshment, Woman Holding Flowers & Bottle, 1949, 20 x 36 In. 105.00
Sign, Hospitality Coca-Cola, Girl & Candle, Paperboard, Frame, c.1950, 27 x 56 In. 660.00
Sign, Hospitality, Girl, Woman, Bonnets, Cardboard, Frame, 56 x 28 In. 523.00
Sign, Ice Cold Coca-Cola Sold Here, Tin, Embossed, 1933, 19 1/2 In. . . . . .651.00 to 675.00
Sign, Ice Cold, Coke Bottle, Die Cut, Flange, 2-Sided, 1951, 18 x 22 In. 600.00
Sign, Ice Cold, Sold Here, Tin, 1934, 28 x 20 In. 413.00

Coca-Cola, Sign, Good Company, Man &
Woman, Trolley Card, Frame, 1927, 11 x 21 In.

Coca-Cola, Sign, Girl, Slow
School Zone, Metal, Die Cut,
2-Sided, c.1940, 53 x 16 In.

Coca-Cola, Sign, Hilda Clark, Tin,
1903, 16 x 19 In.

Sign, Iced Coca-Cola Here, Porcelain, Flange, Canada, 19 x 18 In. 495.00
Sign, King Size, 6-Pack, Tin, Die Cut, Embossed, Gold Highlights, 1962, 32 x 36 In. 1969.00
Sign, Light-Up, Rotates, Plastic, Metal, 2-Sided, c.1950 . . . . 1600.00
Sign, Light-Up, Rotating Halo, Metal, Plastic, 2-Sided, Neon Products, c.1950s 1800.00
Sign, Lunch & Soda, Porcelain, c.1950, 18 x 30 In. . . . . .1126.00 to 1267.00
Sign, Lunch Refreshed, Girl, Coke & Sandwiches, Cardboard, 1949, 16 x 27 In. 138.00
Sign, Lunch Refreshed, Waitress Serving Hamburgers & Coke, 1948, 36 x 20 In. 275.00
Sign, Mind Reader, Woman In Lounge Chair, Cardboard, Frame, 1944, 27 x 56 In. 3300.00
Sign, New Feeling, Couple Dancing, Cardboard, Late 1950s, 37 x 24 In. 209.00
Sign, Pause & Refresh, Girl & Soda Fountain, Cardboard, 1948, 23 1/2 x 41 In. 770.00
Sign, Pause That Refreshes, Girl Holding Glass & Bottle, Cardboard, 1939, 30 x 50 In. . . . 358.00
Sign, Pause, Delicious & Refreshing, Reverse Painted, Foil Back, c.1937, 10 x 12 In. 13200.00
Sign, Pick Up 6 For Home Refreshment, Tin, 6-Pack, White Ground, 1954, 50 x 16 In. . . . 1688.00
Sign, Please Pay When Served, Light-Up, Plastic, Metal, 1948, 20 In. 1485.00
Sign, Policeman, Slow, School Zone, Tin, Die Cut, 2-Sided, 1950s, 60 x 30 In. . .1375.00 to 4400.00
Sign, Refresh At Our Fountain, Woman, Daughter, Die Cut, Cardboard, 1935, 44 x 41 In. . . 4400.00
Sign, Refresh Yourself, Coca-Cola Sold Here, Shield, Porcelain, 1930s, 20 x 17 In. 935.00
Sign, Refresh Yourself, Tin, Wood Frame, St. Thomas Metal Signs, 56 x 20 In. 1450.00
Sign, Refreshing New Feeling, 2-Sided, Tin, Flange, October 1961, 15 x 18 In. 423.00
Sign, Refreshment Area, White Ground, Gold Border, Tin, Self-Framed, 17 3/4 x 24 In. . . . 242.00
Sign, Refreshment Center, Metal, 46 x 10 In. 125.00
Sign, Santa Claus, Dog, Die Cut, Cardboard, 32 x 48 In. 99.00
Sign, Santa On Ladder, Tree, Free Decorations, Cardboard, Easel Back, 14 x 30 In. 61.00
Sign, Santa Standing On House, Die Cut, Cardboard, 27 x 71 In. 154.00
Sign, Santa, Helicopter, Train Set, Season's Greetings, Die Cut, Cardboard, 46 x 31 In. . . . 248.00
Sign, Serve Ice Cold, Ice King, Die Cut, Cardboard, Easel Back, 1953, 13 1/2 x 21 In. 501.00
Sign, Serve Yourself A Fresh Drink, Silk-Screened Glass, 1930-1940, 5 x 15 1/2 In. 990.00
Sign, Sidewalk, Porcelain, Red Dispenser, Red Ground, 2-Sided, 1950s, 27 x 28 In. 1125.00
Sign, Sidewalk, Take Home A Carton, Big King Size, Frame, 1961, 20 x 28 In. 2813.00
Sign, Sign Of Good Taste, 2-Sided, Tin, Flange, February 1959, 15 x 18 In. . . . . . .400.00 to 422.00
Sign, Sign Of Good Taste, Button On Arrow, Tin, 1960, 12 x 24 In. 1650.00
Sign, Sign Of Good Taste, Embossed Silver Arrow Through Button, 1948, 16 In. 2250.00
Sign, Sign Of Good Taste, Embossed Silver Arrow Through Button, 1951, 12 In. 1125.00
Sign, Sign Of Good Taste, Fishtail, Bottle, Tin, Robertson, 1950, 31 1/2 x 55 1/2 In. 550.00
Sign, Sign Of Good Taste, Take Home A Carton, Tin, c.1959, 30 x 20 In. 1200.00
Sign, Sign Of Good Taste, Tin, Self-Framed, 1959, 53 x 5 x 17 1/2 In. 413.00
Sign, So Refreshing, Cardboard, Wood Frame, 1940s, 27 x 57 In. 424.00
Sign, Sprite Boy Pointing To Bottle, Quality You Trust, Porcelain, 1933, 30 x 10 In. 523.00
Sign, Sprite Boy Pointing To Bottle, Quality You Trust, Tin, Australia, 37 x 72 In. 523.00
Sign, Sprite Boy, Coca-Cola Cap, Die Cut, Cardboard, Frame, 1970-1980, 38 x 30 In. 110.00
Sign, Sprite Boy, Coke Bottle, Export, Tin, Yellow Ground, Round, 1947, 12 3/4 In. 1040.00
Sign, Sprite Boy, Cooler & Arrow, Wood & Masonite, 30 x 11 In. 2200.00
Sign, Stock Up For The Holidays, Santa Claus, Cardboard, 1952, 27 3/4 x 19 7/8 In. 715.00
Sign, Stock Up For The Holidays, Santa Claus, Cardboard, 66 x 32 In. 176.00
Sign, Take A Case Home Today, Tin, 1950s, 19 x 28 In. 357.00

Coca-Cola, Stringholder, Take
Home In Cartons, Tin
Lithograph, 1930s, 16 In.

Coca-Cola,
Thermometer,
Bottle Shape,
Tin, Die Cut,
17 x 5 1/2 In.

Coca-Cola, Tip Tray, 1906,
Juanita, 4 In.

Coca-Cola, Tip Tray, 1907,
Relieves Fatigue, 5 Cents,
6 1/8 x 4 1/4 In.

Coca-Cola, Toy, Truck, Smitty,
Wood, Rubber Wheels, Smith
Miller, c.1940, 13 3/4 In.

Sign, Take Home A Carton, 18 x 53 1/2 In. 440.00
Sign, Take Home A Carton, Big King Size, Frame, 1961, 20 x 28 In. 2700.00
Sign, Take Home A Carton, Tin, Self-Framed, 1937, 18 x 54 In. 1320.00
Sign, The Drink They All Expect, Couple At Party, Frame, 1942, 27 x 56 In. 678.00
Sign, Things Go Better With Coke, Ice Cold, Coke In Cup, Tin, c.1963, 20 x 28 In. 1210.00
Sign, Tin, Die Cut, 2-Sided, 1934, 22 1/2 x 22 1/2 In. 3080.00
Sign, Triangle, Tin, Die Cut, 2-Sided, Iron Bracket, 1936, 28 x 36 In. ....1365.00 to 1412.00
Sign, Waterfall, Pause & Refresh, Serve Yourself, Light-Up, 20 In. 1243.00
Sign, We Serve Coca-Cola In Bottles, Reverse Painted Glass, Foil Back, 10 x 12 In. 15950.00
Sign, When Friends Drop In, Santa Claus, Dog, Cardboard, 66 x 32 In. 132.00
Sign, Woman, Groceries, 2-Sided, Cardboard, 1950, 16 x 27 In. 950.00
Sign, Woman, Hat, Coke Bottle With Straw, Mat, Frame, 18 x 27 In. 330.00
Stadium Carrier, Drink Coca-Cola, Red, Arched Handle, 12 x 10 x 12 In. 275.00
Stand, 6 Bottles, 25 Cents A Carton, Metal, Red, 60 x 28 In. 182.00
Straws, Box, 500 Straws, 1930s, 8 1/2 In. 193.00
Stringholder, Take Home In Cartons, Tin Lithograph, 1930s, 16 In. .... *Illus* 467.00
Syrup Jugs, Case, Atlanta, Gal., 12 In., 4 Piece 27.00
Thermometer, 1930s, 16 x 7 In. 229.00
Thermometer, 2 Bottles, Die Cut, 16 x 7 In. 70.00
Thermometer, Bottle Shape, 17 In. ....77.00 to 150.00
Thermometer, Bottle Shape, Christmas, 16 3/4 x 4 7/8 In. 245.00
Thermometer, Bottle Shape, Tin, Die Cut, 17 x 5 1/2 In. .... *Illus* 88.00
Thermometer, Bottle Shape, Tin, Embossed, Die Cut, 1923, 16 1/2 x 5 In. 303.00
Thermometer, Bottle, 1950s, 30 In. 132.00
Thermometer, Bottle, c.1936, 16 In. 193.00
Thermometer, Bottle, c.1950, 17 In. 88.00
Thermometer, Bottle, Christmas, Red Ground, 1923, 16 In. ....193.00 to 215.00
Thermometer, Bottle, Tin Lithograph, 1958, 30 In. 104.00
Thermometer, Dial Type, Glass Front, Metal Sides, 1950s, 12 x 2 In. 198.00
Thermometer, Double Bottle, Tin, Embossed, 1941, 16 In. 275.00
Thermometer, Drink Coca-Cola In Bottles, Dial, Red, Metal, Glass, 1950s, 12 In. Diam. . 143.00
Thermometer, Drink Coca-Cola In Bottles, Quality Refreshment, Tin, 9 x 3 In. 253.00
Thermometer, Drink Coca-Cola In Bottles, Red Ground, Tin, Round, 12 In. 88.00
Thermometer, Drink Coca-Cola, 5 Cents, Wood, c.1910, 21 x 4 3/4 In. 578.00
Thermometer, Drink Coca-Cola, Glass, Aluminum, Glass, Round, 1950s, 12 In. 385.00
Thermometer, Drink Coca-Cola, Gold Bottle, Green, Red, Pam, Box, 1950s, 12 In. 1463.00
Thermometer, Drink Coca-Cola, Sign Of Good Taste, Red, c.1950, 8 x 30 In. .....575.00 to 633.00
Thermometer, Drink, In Bottles, Dial Style, Round, Red, White Hand & Letters, 12 In. ... 110.00
Thermometer, Glass Front, Red Ground, Round, 1950s, 12 In. 110.00
Thermometer, Gold Bottle, Red Ground, Oval, 16 x 6 3/4 In. 248.00
Thermometer, On Gold Bottle, Tin, 7 x 2 1/2 In. 28.00
Thermometer, Sign Of Good Taste, Round, 9 1/2 In. 275.00
Thermometer, Things Go Better With Coke, Round, 18 In. 440.00
Tin, Polar Bears Playing Winter Sports, 1994, 6 x 5 In. 10.00
Tin, Skiing Bear, Polar Bears On Skis, 1995, 7 1/4 x 5 3/4 In. 16.00
Tip Tray, 1900, Hilda With Glass, Drink Coca-Cola, 5 1/2 In. 523.00
Tip Tray, 1906, Juanita, 4 In. ....*Illus* 1045.00

Tip Tray, 1907, Relieves Fatigue, 5 Cents, 6 1/8 x 4 1/4 In. *Illus* 715.00
Tip Tray, 1913, Hamilton King Girl, Green Edge, Oval, 6 x 4 1/4 In. . . . . .230.00 to 780.00
Tip Tray, 1914, Betty, Bonnet, Pink Ribbon, 6 x 4 1/4 In. . . . . .158.00 to 300.00
Tip Tray, 1916, Elaine, Yellow Dress, Hat, Oval, 6 x 4 1/4 In. 200.00
Tip Tray, 1920, Golfer Girl, 6 x 4 1/2 In. . . . . .248.00 to 430.00
Toy, Airplane, Curtis, Masonite, World War II, 9 x 27 In. 440.00
Toy, Airplane, Pedal, Die Cast Metal, Box, 1995, 11 1/2 x 3 1/2 x 4 In. 74.00
Toy, Car, 1957 Chevrolet, No. H862, Ertl 25.00
Toy, Car, Prop Rod, Thimble Drome Racer, Plastic, Aluminum, 12 In. 149.00
Toy, Car, Refresh With Zest, Red, White, 10 1/2 In. 94.00
Toy, Cars, Corgi Turbo Racing Team, Die Cast, Box, 3 1/2 In., 3 Piece 75.00
Toy, Fire Engine, Holiday, Die Cast Metal, Certificate, Box, Matchbox, 9 In. 85.00
Toy, Truck, 6 Cases Of Coke, Marx, 1954-1956, 12 1/2 In. 475.00
Toy, Truck, Bottles, Metal, Goodrich Tires, 1934 . . . . 595.00
Toy, Truck, Buddy L, 1961 . . . . 250.00
Toy, Truck, Buddy L, No. 4959, Brute Super Steel, Box, 1970 . . . . 85.00
Toy, Truck, Buddy L, Trailer, Box, Japan, 1979 . . . . 100.00
Toy, Truck, Coke Soda Pop Stop, Steel, Buddy L, No. 4990 . . . . 75.00
Toy, Truck, Decals, Bottles, Metalcraft 1200.00
Toy, Truck, Delivery, Buddy L, 1960s, 15 In. 200.00
Toy, Truck, Delivery, Buddy L, No. 420G, Steel, Box, 1978, 5 In. 45.00
Toy, Truck, Delivery, Buddy L, No. 4942, Steel, Box, 1970, 5 In. 60.00
Toy, Truck, Die Cast, Box, England, 1967 . . . . 60.00
Toy, Truck, Die Cast, Corgi Jr. Box Van, 3 1/2 In. 120.00
Toy, Truck, Die Cast, Keg Delivery, Box, 1967, 4 In. 12.00
Toy, Truck, Enjoy Coca-Cola, Hand Truck, Cases Of Bottles, Buddy L 65.00
Toy, Truck, Every Bottle Sterilized, Glass Bottles, Metalcraft, 5 3/4 x 11 x 3 3/4 In. 523.00
Toy, Truck, GMC, Bottles, Smith Miller, Box 1980.00
Toy, Truck, Karrier Bantam, 2 Ton, Metal, Plastic Tires, Lesney, England, 2 x 1 In. . .80.00 to 100.00
Toy, Truck, Mack Trailer, Buddy L, No. 5262, Box, 14 In. 95.00
Toy, Truck, Metalcraft, Metal Wheels, Bottles, 1931 . . . . 578.00
Toy, Truck, Pressed Steel, 10 Bottles, Metalcraft, 11 1/2 In. 550.00
Toy, Truck, Route, Yellow, White, Battery Operated, Sanyo, Box, c.1950, 12 1/2 In. 478.00
Toy, Truck, Smitty, Wood, Rubber Wheels, Smith Miller, c.1940, 13 3/4 In. . . . . *Illus* 1100.00
Toy, Truck, Stake, Pressed Steel, Marx, 2 1in. 825.00
Toy, Truck, Tin, Japan, Box, 1957 . . . . 495.00
Toy, Wagon, Horse Drawn, 8 Coke Cases, Umbrella, Cast Iron, 15 x 5 1/2 In. 48.00
Train, Pewter, Limited Edition, Engine, Coke Bottle, Bear, Caboose, 2 In., 4 Piece 275.00
Tray, 1900, Hilda Clark, At Table, Coke Glass, 9 1/4 In. 7000.00
Tray, 1903, Hilda Clark, 9 3/4 In. Diam. 2320.00
Tray, 1904, Lillian Nordica, With Bottle, 12 7/8 x 10 7/8 In. 3575.00
Tray, 1904, Lillian Nordica, With Glass, 12 7/8 x 10 7/8 In. 3050.00
Tray, 1905, Drink Coca-Cola, Woman, Drinking From Glass, 5 Cents, 13 1/8 x 10 7/8 In. . . 3300.00

Coca-Cola, Tray, 1909,
Exhibition Girl, St. Louis Fair, Oval,
16 5/8 x 13 5/8 In.

Coca-Cola, Tray, 1926, Golfers,
American Art Works,
Coshocton, 13 1/4 x 10 1/2 In.

Coca-Cola, Tray, 1938, Girl In
Yellow Hat, American Art
Works, 13 1/4 x 10 1/2 In.

Tray, 1908, Topless Woman, Coca-Cola Is Better, Tin, 12 1/4 In. . . . . .2475.00 to 7150.00
Tray, 1909, Exhibition Girl, Oval, 10 3/4 x 13 In. . . . . .467.00 to 1073.00
Tray, 1909, Exhibition Girl, St. Louis Fair, Oval, 16 5/8 x 13 5/8 In. . . . . *Illus* 1650.00
Tray, 1912, Drink Coca-Cola, Delicious & Refreshing, Woman, Hat, 12 x 10 1/2 In. 1760.00
Tray, 1913, Hamilton King Girl, 15 1/4 x 12 1/4 In. 1100.00
Tray, 1914, Betty, Oval, 16 x 13 In. . . . . .468.00 to 575.00
Tray, 1916, Elaine, Yellow Dress, 19 x 8 1/2 In. 220.00
Tray, 1922, Autumn Girl, 13 1/4 x 10 1/2 In. . . . . .165.00 to 286.00
Tray, 1923, Flapper Girl, 13 1/4 x 10 1/2 In. . . . . .102.00 to 248.00
Tray, 1924, Smiling Girl, Holding Glass, Brown Rim, 13 1/4 x 10 1/2 In. 226.00
Tray, 1925, Party Girl, 13 1/4 x 10 1/2 In. . . . . .120.00 to 385.00
Tray, 1926, Golfers, American Art Works, Coshocton, 13 1/4 x 10 1/2 In. . . . . *Illus* 187.00
Tray, 1927, Curb Service, 10 1/2 x 13 1/4 In. 480.00
Tray, 1927, Soda Jerk, 13 1/4 x 10 1/2 In. . . . . .220.00 to 283.00
Tray, 1928, Girl With Bobbed Hair, 13 1/4 x 10 1/2 In. 537.00
Tray, 1929, Girl In Yellow Bathing Suit, 13 1/4 x 10 1/2 In. . . . . .286.00 to 523.00
Tray, 1930, Bather Girl, 13 1/4 x 10 1/2 In. . . . . .220.00 to 396.00
Tray, 1930, Telephone Girl, American Art Works, 13 1/4 x 10 1/2 In. . . . . .198.00 to 242.00
Tray, 1931, Barefoot Boy, Dog, Rockwell, 13 1/4 x 10 1/2 In. 1595.00
Tray, 1932, Girl In Bathing Suit, 13 1/4 x 10 1/2 In. 275.00
Tray, 1933, Frances Dee, 13 1/4 x 10 1/2 In. . . . . .138.00 to 575.00
Tray, 1934, Johnny Weismuller, Maureen O' Sullivan, 10 1/2 x 13 1/4 In. . . . . . . .225.00 to 853.00
Tray, 1935, Madge Evans, American Art Works, 13 1/4 x 10 1/2 In. . . . . .182.00 to 214.00
Tray, 1936, Hostess, 13 1/4 x 10 1/2 In. 220.00
Tray, 1937, Running Girl, Cape, 13 1/4 x 10 1/2 In. . . . . .132.00 to 369.00
Tray, 1938, Girl In Yellow Hat, American Art Works, 13 1/4 x 10 1/2 In. . . . . *Illus* 143.00
Tray, 1939, Springboard Girl, Sundblom, American Art Works, 13 1/4 x 10 1/2 In. .165.00 to 358.00
Tray, 1940, Sailor Girl, 10 1/2 x 13 1/4 In. . . . . .154.00 to 343.00
Tray, 1941, Skater Girl, 13 1/4 x 10 1/2 In. . . . . .162.00 to 440.00
Tray, 1942, 2 Girls At Car, 13 1/4 x 10 1/2 In. . . . . .165.00 to 209.00
Tray, 1953, Menu Girl, 13 1/4 x 10 1/2 In. . . . . .83.00 to 145.00
Tray, 1955, Tin Lithograph, Central Portrait, 10 1/2 x 13 1/2 x 1 1/4 In. 60.00
Tray, 1957, Girl With Umbrella, Coke Bottle, Tin Lithograph, France, 13 In. 192.00
Tray, 1958, Picnic Cart, 10 3/4 x 13 1/4 In. 45.00
Tray, 1980, Georgia Bulldogs, Champs, Dawgs Undefeated Season, 13 x 18 In. 50.00
Tray, 1982, Sprite Boy, Bottle, 8th Annual Coke Clan Convention, 13 1/4 x 10 1/2 In. 85.00
Tray, 1985, Coca-Cola International Collectors Club, Anaheim, Ca., 13 1/4 x 10 1/2 In. . . 60.00
Tray, 1992, Space Shuttle Challenger, 18th Convention, Orlando, 10 1/2 x 13 1/4 In. 60.00
Tray, Romance Of Coca-Cola, 30th Anniversary, Tin, England, 16 1/2 x 12 3/4 In. 250.00
Tray, Tip, see Coca-Cola, Tip Tray
Truck Radiator Grill, Drink, In Bottles, Aluminum, Die Cut, c.1930, 17 1/2 x 7 1/4 In. . . . 731.00
Tumbler, Diamond, Coke Trademark, 1960s, 12 Fl. Oz. 85.00
Tumbler, Flare, Syrup Line, c.1910, 3 3/4 In. 375.00
Tumbler, Olympics, Gold, Clear, 4 Languages, Box, 12 Oz., 4 Piece 50.00
Tumbler, Wizard Of Oz, 50th Anniversary, Scarecrow, 1989, 6 In. 10.00
Uniform, Coverall Style, Metal Buttons, Patch, 1950s, 6 3/4-In. Hat, Size 40 L 149.00
Vending Machine, 10 Cent, Cavalier, Restored, 57 In. 1265.00
Vending Machine, 10 Cent, Model No. 23, 38 x 24 In. 1430.00
Vending Machine, Cooler, Beverageair, No. 8416291, Glass Top, 34 x 25 x 24 1/2 In. 1200.00
Vending Machine, Vendo 39, Red Metal, 1950s, 27 1/2 x 58 x 16 In. 6500.00
Vending Machine, Vendo 81, 10 Cent, White Top, Red Bottom, 27 x 59 In. 3905.00
Watch, Springtime Express, Box, 1992, Pocket 65.00
Window Decal, This Is The Genuine Coca-Cola, 7 x 12 In. 495.00
Writing Tablet, Flag Of The United Nations, Eisenhower Quote, 1950-1960 . . . . 12.00

COFFEE The process of roasting coffee and making a liquid beverage
was probably an accidental discovery. The first coffeehouse opened in
1475 in Constantinople. Since then, consumers have been wide awake
while they watched coffee's history: the espresso machine (1833), the
percolator (1865), vacuum packed and roasted coffee (1900), instant
coffee (1901), decaffeinated coffee (1903), coffee filters (1908), and
freeze-dried coffee (1938). Today collectors seek all types of memorabilia related to the most popular beverage in the world. See also

Arbuckle, Chase & Sanborn, Hills Brothers, and Lion Coffee for other coffee collectibles.

Bin, Blaul's B.B.B.B. Coffee, Bulk, Original Stenciling, 30 In.	385.00
Bin, Boston Coffees, Wood, Lid, c.1900, 15 x 20 In.	316.00
Bin, Full Value Coffee, Wood, 33 x 21 x 15 3/4 In.	165.00
Bin, Jersey Coffee, Stencil, Wood, Dayton Spice Mills, Dayton, O., 100 Lb., 32 x 22 In.	825.00
Bin, Jersey Coffee, Stencil, Wood, Red Paint, Slant Top, Des Moines, Iowa, 36 In. .450.00 to	578.00
Bin, Johnson's Peacemaker Coffee, Tin Lithograph, 25 In.	1265.00
Bin, Luxury Coffee, Wood, Mustard Surface, 100 Lbs., 32 x 21 1/2 x 16 In.	2970.00
Bin, Polar Bear Allspice, Coffee, Griffen Grocers, 2 7/8 x 2 1/4 In.	110.00
Bin, Washburn Halligan Coffee Co., Davenport, Iowa, Mustard Paint, 32 x 22 In.	187.00
Book, Folger's, Play & Grow, Red Apple Trees, Turn Wheel, Find Colors	6.00
Box, Glendora Coffee, Cardboard, Metal Top & Bottom, Label, Sample, 3 1/4 x 2 1/8 In.	125.00
Box, Old Judge Coffee, Owl, Red, Cardboard, Label, Unopened, Sample, 4 2 3/8 In.	223.00
Box, Red Fox Coffee, Cardboard, Ft. Smith Coffee Co., 1 Lb., 5 5/8 x 4 1/2 x 3 1/4 In.	470.00
Box, Washburn Halligan Coffee Co., Davenport, Ia., Stencil, Wood, Label, Hinge, 26 In.	138.00
Box, Web-Foot Coffee, Frog, Cardboard, 1 Lb., 6 3/4 x 4 1/4 x 2 5/8 In.	688.00
Can, Folger's, Lid, 1 Lb., 1950s	15.00
Can, Golden Harvest Coffee, Key Wind, Tin Lithograph, 1 Lb., 5 1/4 x 4 In.	88.00
Can, Luzianne Coffee, Red, 2-Color Image, Tin Lithograph, Handle, 7 1/2 In.	90.00
Can, Luzianne Coffee, Red, 6-Color Image, Tin Lithograph, Handle, 7 1/2 In.	124.00
Can, Luzianne Coffee, White, Tin Lithograph, Handle, 7 1/2 In.	85.00
Can, Millar's Magnet Brand Coffee, Key Wind, 3 7/8 x 5 In.	85.00
Can, Opeko Coffee, Paris Cafe, Key Wind Cover, 1 Lb., 4 x 5 1/8 In.	77.00
Can, Peacock Coffee, Paper Over Cardboard, Multicolored, 1/2 Lb., 5 3/8 x 3 1/8 In.	523.00
Can, Pickwick Coffee, Tin Lithograph, Key Wind, 1 Lb., 4 x 5 In.	71.00
Can, Sally Lee Coffee, Tin Lithograph, Key Wind, 1 Lb., 5 x 4 In.	99.00
Can, Steamboat Coffee, Paddleboat, Key Wind, Titus & Martin, 1 Lb., 3 5/8 x 5 1/8 In.	385.00
Canister, Severs Blend Roasted Coffee, Cardboard, 4 x 5 1/2 In., 1 Lb.	66.00
Coffeepot, Sanka Instant Coffee, Minners & Co., Hall China, 4 3/4 In.	20.00
Door Push, Ridgways Coffee, Yellow, Red, Metal, 3 1/4 x 9 In.	44.00
Poster, Golden West Coffee, Famous Coffee With A Famous Name, 1927, 39 x 26 In.	3630.00
Poster, Morning Sip Coffee, The Better Coffee, 1923, 11 x 21 In.	66.00
Puzzle, Folger's Coffee, In Can, Unopened, Cardboard, Tin Top & Bottom, 3 1/2 x 2 3/4 In.	38.00
Salt & Pepper, Luzianne Coffee Mammy, Green, 5 1/8 x 2 1/2 In.	165.00
Sign, Blue Plate Coffee, We Serve, Means Fine Flavor, Celluloid Over Tin, 7 x 12 In.	94.00
Sign, Butter-Nut Coffee, Paper, Frame, 21 x 11 In.	286.00
Sign, Colonial Dame Coffee, Tin Lithograph, Embossed, 10 x 28 In.	121.00
Sign, Dauntless Coffee, Paperboard, Massillon, Ohio, Frame, 7 3/4 x 15 1/2 In.	55.00
Sign, Dutch Java Blend Coffee, Dayton Spice Mills, Cloth Lithograph, 36 x 24 In.	472.00
Sign, Dwinell, Wright & Co. Roasted Coffees, Cans, Boxes, Bins, Tin, Frame, 22 x 16 In.	1320.00
Sign, Glendora Coffee, Can Shape, Tin Lithograph, 13 3/4 x 8 1/2 In. .94.00 to	276.00
Sign, Golden Light Coffee, Tin Over Cardboard, 15 1/2 x 8 1/4 In.	135.00
Sign, Here's To Gold Bond, Best Coffee Ever Tasted, Waiter, Diners, Cardboard, 16 x 10 In.	50.00
Sign, Mack's Coffees, Button, Metal Over Cardboard, Lancaster, Pa., 9 In.	28.00
Sign, Old Reliable Coffee, Always Good, Yellow, Black, Tin, c.1920, 6 1/2 x 14 In.	138.00
Sign, Old Reliable Coffee, Blond Woman, Cardboard, String Hanger, 9 1/2 x 15 In.	66.00
Sign, Old Reliable Coffee, Man Sitting, Tin Lithograph, Frame, 8 1/2 x 6 1/4 In.	170.00
Sign, Old Reliable Coffee, Serious Man, Coat, Fur Hat, Smoking, Tin, 6 x 9 In.	220.00
Sign, Premier, Mill Behind A Good Cup Of Coffee, Grinder, Cup Of Coffee, 18 x 12 In.	66.00
Sign, Red Gate Coffee, Oriental Arch, Mocha Java, Cardboard, Easel Back, 14 x 10 In.	83.00
Sign, Symington's Coffee Essences, Sold Everywhere, Edinburgh, Enamel, 24 x 12 In.	341.00
Sign, White House Coffee, Hand Holding Coffee Can, Die Cut, Flange, 1910-1915, 14 In.	2310.00
Sign, White House Coffee, Tin Lithograph, Embossed, Dwinell, Wright, Boston, 14 x 10 In.	2970.00
Thermometer, Arco Coffee, Pam, Bubble Glass, 12 In.	95.00
Thermometer, Mo-Ko Coffee Alternative, Wood, J. Bauer, Elmira, N.Y., Box, 3 x 12 In.	44.00
Thimble, Luzianne Coffee, Aluminum	12.00
Tin, 3/F Coffee, Paper Label, Free Sample, 3 3/4 x 2 In.	95.00
Tin, AG Coffee, Key Wind, 1 Lb.	25.00
Tin, Alpine Coffee, Nestle Product, 1 Lb., 5 1/4 x 4 1/4 In.	44.00
Tin, America's Cup Coffee, Key Wind, 1 Lb.	25.00
Tin, American Lady Coffee, Haas-Lieber Grocery, 1 Lb., 4 1/4 x 6 In.	1815.00
Tin, Ariel Club Coffee, Embossed, Paper Label, Country Club Image, 1 Lb., 6 x 4 In.	264.00

Tin, Bailey's Supreme Coffee, Key Wind, 3 1/2 x 5 In. 110.00
Tin, Black Boy Pure Coffee, Tin Lithograph, 1/2 Lb., 3 x 4 In. 116.00
Tin, Blend 150 Coffee, Key Wind, 1 Lb. 25.00
Tin, Blended Coffee, Paper Label, 5 Lb. 35.00
Tin, Blue Flame Coffee, 3 Lb. 55.00
Tin, Blue Flame Coffee, There's A Witchery In The Flavor, Paper Label, Key Wind, 1 Lb.   88.00
Tin, Blue Plate Coffee, Blue Willow Pattern On Cup & Saucer, Key Wind, 1 Lb. .... 30.00 to 45.00
Tin, Bluehill Coffee, Cup That Cheers, Turquoise, Swing Handle, 5 Lb., 7 x 10 In. 330.00
Tin, Boardman's Putnam Coffee, Boy Soldier, Horse, Lithograph, Key Wind, 1 Lb., 4 x 5 In.   72.00
Tin, Bouquet Roasted Coffee, Steaming Cup, c.1900, 1 Lb., 5 1/2 x 4 1/4 In. .... 45.00 to 66.00
Tin, Brown Gold Coffee, Key Wind, 1 Lb. 40.00
Tin, Buell's Brighton Blend Coffee, Merit-That's All, 1 Lb., 6 x 4 1/4 In. 440.00
Tin, Bumble Bee Coffee, Bees On Clover, 1 Lb. 132.00
Tin, Butter-Nut Coffee, 1 Lb., 5 x 3 In. 12.00
Tin, Butter-Nut Coffee, 10 Cent Coupon Inside, Unopened, 6 Cups, 2 1/4 In. 55.00
Tin, C.F. Blanke & Co. Roasted Coffee, Our Winner, Tin, Paper Label, 13 1/2 x 20 In. ... 138.00
Tin, Campbell & Woods Coffee, 21 In. 66.00
Tin, Campbell Brand Coffee, No. 4, Camels, Lithograph, Bail Handle, 5 Lb. 110.00
Tin, Campbell Brand Coffee, Bloomington, Ill., Camels, Tin, Cover, Handle, 4 Lb. .. 88.00 to 110.00
Tin, CAP, Drip Grind Coffee, Key Wind, Bunn Capitol Grocery, 1 Lb., 4 x 5 In. 225.00
Tin, Capitol Mills, Pure Coffee, Lincoln, Seyms & Co., Lithograph, 5 1/2 x 5 In. 132.00
Tin, Caswell's Coffee, 3 Lb., 9 In. 11.00
Tin, Chase Family Coffee, Lithograph, 2 Lb., 9 x 5 In. 55.00
Tin, Chuck Wagon Coffee, Key Wind, Urm Stores, Spokane, Wash., 1 Lb., 3 1/2 x 5 In. .. 187.00
Tin, Colombian Coffee, Key Wind, Free Sample, National Federation, 2 1/4 x 2 3/4 In. 233.00
Tin, Colombian Coffee, The Land Of Coffee, Contents, Key Wind, 2 Oz., 2 x 3 In. 143.00
Tin, Council Cup Coffee, A.W. Fey, Lithograph, 4 Lb., 8 1/2 x 7 1/2 In. 55.00
Tin, Daisy Fresh Coffee, Tin Lithograph, Key Wind, Euclid Coffee Co., 1 Lb., 4 x 5 In. .. 165.00
Tin, Denison's Colonial Inn Brand Coffee, Paper Label, 3 Lb., 8 x 5 1/4 In. 88.00
Tin, Dilworth's Golden Urn Coffee, Tin Lithograph, Sample, 2 1/2 x 2 In. 165.00
Tin, Donald Duck Coffee, Lithograph, Bank Cut Lid, Sample, Goyer Coffee Co., 2 x 3 In. . 551.00
Tin, Dot Coffee, Screw Top, 2-Sided Graphic, Sample, 2 x 2 1/2 In. 210.00
Tin, Drako Brand Coffee, Duck Image On 2 Sides, Lithograph, 1 Lb., 6 x 4 In. 1210.00
Tin, Drinket Instead Of Coffee, 2 1/4 x 1 1/2 x 3/4 In. 125.00
Tin, Duncan's Admiration Coffee, Duncan Coffee Co., Houston, Texas, 3 1/2 x 5 In. 75.00
Tin, Epicure Coffee, Waiter, Tray, Tin Lithograph, John Sills & Sons, 1 Lb., 6 x 4 In. 798.00
Tin, F.B.G. Coffee, Slip Lid, Paper Label, 1 Lb. 66.00
Tin, Fairway Brand Coffee, Children In Field, Cup Of Coffee, Key Wind, 4 x 5 In. 275.00
Tin, First Prize Coffee, Key Wind, Jefferson Grocery Co., Punxsutawney, Pa., 1 Lb. 45.00
Tin, Folger's Coffee, Golden Gate, Steel Cut, Ships, Roses, 5 Lb., 8 1/2 x 7 In. .... 110.00 to 125.00
Tin, G. Washington Instant Coffee, Flat, 3 x 2 x 1/2 In. 30.00
Tin, G. Washington Instant Coffee, Twist Lid, 4 Oz., 3 1/2 In. 35.00
Tin, Gillies Coffee, Girl At Beach, Boys Play Football, Tin Lithograph, 1 Lb., 4 3/4 x 5 In.   550.00

Coffee, Tin, Kenny's Maid
Coffee, Handle,
4 Lb., 8 In.

Coffee, Tin, Luzianne
Coffee, Tin Lithograph,
3 Lb., 7 In.

Coffee, Tin, Old Judge Coffee,
Settles The Question, Owl,
Lithograph, 10 In.

Tin, Golden Days Coffee, Roasted, Steel Cut, Ground, Early 1900s, 2 Lb., 6 x 4 In. 523.00
Tin, Golden Rule Blend Coffee, Citizen's Wholesale, Columbus, Ohio, 10 Lb., 10 x 10 In. 245.00
Tin, Golden West Coffee, Cowgirl Drinking Coffee, Red, Yellow, 1937, 3 Lb. . . . . .385.00 to 495.00
Tin, Golden West Coffee, Cowgirl Drinking Coffee, Key Wind, 2 Lb., 6 1/2 x 5 In. 330.00
Tin, Golden West Coffee, Cowgirl, Key Wind, 1 Lb., 3 1/2 x 5 In. 330.00
Tin, Governor Coffee, W.W. Harper Co., 1 Lb., 6 x 4 In. 160.00
Tin, HGF Coffee, Key Wind, H.D. Lee Mercantile Co., Kansas City, Mo., 3 7/8 x 5 In. . . . 145.00
Tin, Hoffman's Old Time Coffee, Old Lady, 9 In. 143.00
Tin, Holland House Coffee, Key Wind, 1 Lb., 5 x 3 3/4 In. 66.00
Tin, Home Brand Coffee, Mansion, Slip Lid, 1 Lb. 55.00
Tin, Honeymoon Breakfast Coffee, 3 Lb. 160.00
Tin, Hoosier Boy Coffee, Paper Label, 6 x 4 1/8 In. 715.00
Tin, Jam-Boy Coffee, Jameson Boyce Co., Binghamton, New York, 1 Lb., 6 3/8 x 4 In. . . 625.00
Tin, Kaffee Hag, Coffee That Lets You Sleep, 1 Lb., 6 x 4 1/4 In. 28.00
Tin, Kenny's Maid Coffee, Handle, 4 Lb., 8 In. . . . . *Illus* 523.00
Tin, King Cole Coffee, Jovial King, Servant, Lithograph, Canada, 1 Lb., 5 3/4 x 4 1/4 In. . 198.00
Tin, King Othon Coffee, Unopened, Key Wind, 1 Lb. 150.00
Tin, Kleeko Coffee, Cup, Red, Yellow, Green, Cloverdale Co., 1 Lb., c.1920, 6 x 4 1/2 In. 45.00
Tin, Klipp's Kaffee Bremen, 8-Sided, Paisley, Oriental Tree, Germany, 1953, 5 1/2 x 5 In. 10.00
Tin, Ko-We-Ba Coffee, Key Wind, 1 Lb. 25.00
Tin, LaKreem Coffee, Lithograph, Sample, 2 1/2 x 2 1/8 In. 166.00
Tin, Leslie Coffee, Service Set, Key Wind, 1 Lb., 4 x 5 In. 303.00
Tin, Liberty Coffee Additive, Cardboard, Paper Label, Sample, 1 5/8 x 1 1/8 In. 215.00
Tin, Lily Of The Valley Coffee, Lithograph, 1 Lb., 6 x 4 1/2 In. 99.00
Tin, Loyl Coffee, Eagle, Tin Lithograph, Rochester Seed & Supply Co., 1 Lb., 6 x 4 In. . . 132.00
Tin, Luzianne Coffee & Chicory, Tin Lithograph, Free Sample, c.1930, 2 1/2 x 3 In. 119.00
Tin, Luzianne Coffee & Chicory, W.B. Reilly & Co., Red, 6 In. 110.00
Tin, Luzianne Coffee, Tin Lithograph, 3 Lb., 7 In. . . . . *Illus* 83.00
Tin, Lyons Pure Ground Coffee, Unopened, 2 Oz., 2 1/4 In. 110.00
Tin, Machwitz Coffee, 3 Big-Eyed Black Boys, Germany, Prewar, 3 1/2 In. 119.00
Tin, Machwitz Coffee, 3 Big-Eyed Black Boys, Germany, Prewar, 5 1/2 In. 137.00
Tin, Maimone Coffee, Key Wind, Contents, 1 Lb. 45.00
Tin, Mammy's Favorite Coffee, 4 Lb., 8 x 7 1/2 In. 160.00
Tin, Manru Coffee, Yellow, Red, Black, 5 Cup, c.1920, 2 1/2 x 2 In. 35.00
Tin, Matchless Coffee, Key Wind, 1 Lb. 35.00
Tin, Mayday Coffee Millar's, 1 Lb., 5 x 4 1/2 In. 50.00
Tin, Mayfresh Coffee, Key Wind, 1 Lb. 25.00
Tin, MB Fancy Coffee, Key Wind, 1 Lb. 50.00
Tin, Medaglia D'Oro Caffe, Key Wind, Contents, 1 Lb. 35.00
Tin, Medaglia D'Oro Espresso Coffee, Key Wind, S.A. Schonbrunn, 4 Oz., 3 x 3 3/8 In. . . 145.00
Tin, Millar's Magnet Brand Coffee, Key Wind, 4 x 5 In. 80.00
Tin, Mother Joy Coffee, Pleasing Cup For All Occasions, Screw Lid, 1 Lb., 5 3/4 x 4 In. . 30.00
Tin, Nash Coffee, Milk Can Shape, Wire Handle, 14 1/2 x 8 3/4 In. 45.00
Tin, Nustad's Pointer Coffee, Key Wind 50.00
Tin, Old Dutch Coffee, Windmill, Tin Lithograph, Key Wind, 1 Lb., 5 x 5 3/4 In. 44.00
Tin, Old Judge Coffee, Settles The Question, Lithograph, 1 Lb., 6 x 4 1/4 In. 121.00
Tin, Old Judge Coffee, Settles The Question, Owl, Lithograph, 10 In. . . . . *Illus* 523.00
Tin, Old Judge Irradiated Coffee, Owl, Ashtray Top, Sample, 2 3/4 x 2 3/4 In. 88.00
Tin, Old Reliable Coffee & Tea, 6 In. 12.00
Tin, OPB Coffee, Key Wind 60.00
Tin, Parkview Coffee, Key Wind 45.00
Tin, Paul Bunyan Coffee, Tin Lithograph, Lumberjack, Red Ground, 1 Lb., 3 5/8 x 5 In. . . 413.00
Tin, Penco Coffee, Pennsylvania Coffee Co., Horses, Eagle, Ships, 1 Lb., 6 x 4 5/8 x 3 In. 44.00
Tin, Pilot-Knob Coffee, Bail Handle, 5 Lb., 9 In. . . . . *Illus* 770.00
Tin, Plee-Zing Coffee, Key Wind 25.00
Tin, Red Cow Coffee, Paper Lithograph Over Tin, 1 Lb., 6 1/4 x 4 1/8 In. 385.00
Tin, Red Turkey Coffee, 1 Lb. . . . . *Illus* 77.00
Tin, Red Wolf Coffee, Yellow, Red, Black, 6 Lb., 8 x 9 1/2 In. 550.00
Tin, Royal Blend Coffee, Pry Lid, Granger & Co., Buffalo, 1 Lb., 5 7/8 x 4 3/8 In. 110.00
Tin, Royal Blend Roasted Coffee, Granger & Co., Cardboard, Stamped Tin, 5 1/2 In. *Illus* 45.00
Tin, Royal Jewel Coffee, Key Wind, 2 Lb., 6 5/8 x 5 In. 110.00
Tin, Royal Quality Coffee, Lithograph, Fitch, Thomas Co., Youngstown, Ohio, 6 x 4 In. . . 70.00
Tin, S & W Colombian Coffee, Key Wind 40.00

Coffee, Tin, Pilot-Knob Coffee, Bail Handle, 5 Lb., 9 In.

Coffee, Tin, Red Turkey Coffee, 1 Lb.

Coffee, Tin, Royal Blend Roasted Coffee, Granger & Co., Cardboard, Stamped Tin, 5 1/2 In.

Tin, Schreiber's Manru Coffee, Screw On Lid, 1 Lb., 6 1/4 x 4 In. 35.00
Tin, Seal Of Minnesota Coffee, Knob Top, 1 Lb. 143.00
Tin, Senate Coffee, Capitol Building, Newell & Truesdell Co., 1 Lb., 6 x 4 1/4 In. 209.00
Tin, Serv-Us Coffee, Red & White Corp., Chicago, Screw Top, 1 Lb., 6 x 4 1/4 In. 77.00
Tin, Shurfine Coffee, Key Wind, 1 Lb. 70.00
Tin, Sids Coffee, Key Wind, 1 Lb. 65.00
Tin, Springfield TWA Coffee, Key Wind, 1 Lb. 75.00
Tin, Stewarts Private Blend, Key Wind, 3 7/8 x 5 In. 95.00
Tin, Super Valu Coffee, Key Wind, 1 Lb. 25.00
Tin, Sure Value Coffee, Key Wind, Contents, 1 Lb. 50.00
Tin, Tac Cut Coffee, Boy On Eagle, 3 Lb., c.1916 .... 468.00
Tin, Tastbest Coffee, Lithograph, Key Wind, 1 Lb., 3 1/8 x 5 1/8 In. 94.00
Tin, Taxico Dandelion Coffee, Screw Top Lid, England, 1920s, 1 Lb. 25.00
Tin, Turkey Coffee, Kasper Co., Tin Lithograph, 1 Lb., 5 3/4 x 4 1/4 In. 413.00
Tin, Turkey Coffee, Turkey Image On Both Sides, A.J. Kasper Co., 3 Lb., 10 x 5 1/2 In. .. 825.00
Tin, TVF Coffee, Charles & Co., New York City, 5 3/4 x 4 1/4 In. 275.00
Tin, Wishbone Combination Coffee, Bail Handle, 3 Lb., 7 1/2 In. 170.00
Tin, Wood's Canadian Souvenir Coffee, City Scenes, 1 Lb., 1904, 4 x 6 In. .... 22.00 to 77.00
Tin, Yellow Bonnet Coffee, Springfield Grocer, Tin Lithograph, Key Wind, 1 Lb., 3 x 5 In. 110.00
Trade Card, Mail Pouch Coffee, Revolving Wheel, Ship, Train, Wagon, St. Louis 65.00

COIN-OPERATED MACHINE The vending machine is an ancient invention that dates back to 200 B.C., when holy water was dispensed in a coin-operated vase. Smokers in seventeenth-century England could buy tobacco from a coin-operated box. It was not until after the Civil War that technology allowed the development of modern coin-operated games and vending machines. The coin-operated machines listed here include trade stimulators and vending machines used in stores since the nineteenth century.

Ad-Lee, E-Z Gumball 605.00
Adams Gum, 1 Cent, Yellow Enamel Paint, 22 1/2 x 10 In. 420.00
Adams Pepsin Tutti Frutti Gum, Wood, Porcelain, c.1898, 29 1/2 x 11 1/2 In. 6038.00
Candyette, Delicious Confections, 5 Cent, Venco, St. Louis, Mo. 66.00
Cent-A-Pak, Cigarette Packs On Wheels, Trade Stimulator, 12 In. 523.00
Dentyne, L-Shaped Gum, Porcelain Sign, 21 x 9 In. 550.00
Diamond Matches, 1 Cent, Arched Opening, Round Top, 13 1/2 In. 767.00
Diamond Matches, 1 Cent, Metal Case, 14 In. .... 413.00 to 523.00
Double Nugget, Gum, Double Vendor, Salesman's Sample 485.00
Dr. King's Peppermint Fruitlets Pepsin Gum, Porcelain, 1 Cent 2500.00
Ginger Line-Up, Cigarette, 15 Cent, Trade Stimulator, Key 440.00
Griswald Cigar, 5 Cent, Trade Stimulator, Original Decal, c.1910 .... 825.00
Hawkeye Peanut Machine, Free Portion 77.00
Kleenex, 5 Cent Dispenser, Metal, 7 x 37 In. 220.00

Kuertz Potato Chip Co., Glass Cylinder, 21 In. 440.00
Lindy Striker, Gumball, Skill Game, 1 Cent, c.1930 . . . . 1815.00
Makaroff Brand Cigarettes, 1 Cent, Chrome, Metal, Shipman, 12 1/2 In. 294.00
Mansfield, Pepsin Gum, 5 Cent, Reverse On Glass Marquee 935.00
Moderne, Gum, Spearmint, 1 Cent, 18 In. 220.00
National Hunter Ball Gum, Duck Shooting Gallery, 19 In. 357.00
Nestle's Chocolate, Red, White Letters, England, 28 x 9 In. 946.00
Pascall Ambrosia Milk Chocolate, Repainted, England, 29 x 6 In. 341.00
Perk Up Chlorophyll Vender, 5 Cent, Unused, 1940s 132.00
Pulver, Gum, 1 Cent, Porcelain Case, Green, Clockwork, 20 x 9 In. 1320.00
Pulver, Gum, 1 Cent, Porcelain Case, White, Clockwork, 20 x 9 In. 1320.00
Pulver, Gum, Porcelain Case, Red, Clockwork, Kid, 20 x 9 In. 1045.00
Pulver, Gum, Yellow Clown, 1 Cent 770.00
Pulver, Kola Pepsin Gum, Foxy Grandpa, 1899 Patent, 24 In. 7425.00
Pulver, Peppermint, 1 Cent, 27 In. 165.00
Smilin' Sam From Alabam', Salted Peanuts, Floor Stand . . . . .3740.00 to 6600.00
Surete Condoms, Bakelite Knob, Skyscraper Shape, 20 x 6 1/2 x 5 1/2 In. 825.00
Tempters Gum, Mills, c.1930 . . . . 99.00
Uwanta Cigar, Cigar Cutter, Indian, 5 Cent, 9 In. 495.00
Zeno, Collar Button, 10 Cent, Glass 770.00
Zeno, Gum, 1 Cent, Oak Case, Clockwork Mechanism, c.1910 . . . . .853.00 to 1210.00

COLGATE   William Colgate went into the soap and candle business in Baltimore, Maryland, in 1802. He moved to New York City in 1806 and started William Colgate & Company. The factory was moved to Jersey City, New Jersey, in 1847. After William's death in 1857, the company became Colgate & Company. Colgate toothpaste was first sold in 1877 in jars. The tube was introduced in 1890. The family-owned business, run by five brothers, went public in 1908. Colgate & Company merged with Palmolive-Peet Company in 1908, becoming Colgate-Palmolive-Peet Company. In 1910 the company moved its headquarters to Jersey City. Since 1953 the company has been called Colgate-Palmolive Company, and company headquarters have returned to New York City. Colgate-Palmolive still sells many of its longtime products, including Colgate toothpaste and Palmolive soap, plus many new and acquired items.

Box, Colgate's Ribbon Dental Cream, Display, c.1930, 22 In. 33.00
Box, Florient Face Powder, Flowers, Contents, c.1920, 1 1/2 x 3 x 3 In. 49.00
Can, Ajax Cleanser, Cardboard, Metal, Colgate Palmolive Peet, Sample, 2 1/2 x 1 3/4 In. . . 75.00
Can, Toothpowder, New 15 Cent Size, 1950s 18.00

Colgate, Soaky,
Bullwinkle, Cardboard
Neck Label & Base,
Swimsuit, 10 1/2 In.

Colgate, Soap, Palmolive,
Guest Room Size, 2 1/8 In.

Colgate, Tube,
Palmolive Lather
Shaving Cream,
Box, 6 1/4 In.

Colgate, Tube,
Wildroot Hair Dressing,
Colgate-Palmolive Co.,
Box, 6 In.

Sign, Colgate Eclat Talc Powder, Die Cut, Cardboard, Can Shape, c.1930, 22 In. 61.00
Sign, Colgate's Shaving Soap, His First Shave, Boy Shaving, Die Cut, 14 1/2 x 11 1/2 In. . . 115.00
Soaky, Bullwinkle, Cardboard Neck Label & Base, Swimsuit, 10 1/2 In. . . . . *Illus* 103.00
Soap, Palmolive, Guest Room Size, 2 1/8 In. . . . . *Illus* 5.00
Tin, Baby Talc, Baby Holding Tin, Gold Shoulders & Cap 195.00
Tin, Cashmere Bouquet, New York, 4 3/8 x 2 1/4 x 1 1/8 In. 45.00
Tin, Colgate Talc, Baby Holds Talc Tin, Box, Sample, 2 x 1 1/4 In. 166.00
Tin, Dactylis Talc Powder, Girl, Art Nouveau, Cream, Green, Gold, 4 1/2 x 2 1/2 In. 225.00
Tin, Florient, Oval Base, Trial Size, 2 14 x 1 1/4 x 3/4 In. 45.00
Trade Card, Colgate's Ribbon Dental Cream, Mechanical, Girl's Arm Moves, 5 1/2 x 3 In. 85.00
Tube, Palmolive Lather Shaving Cream, Box, 6 1/4 In. *Illus* 20.00
Tube, Wildroot Hair Dressing, Colgate-Palmolive Co., Box, 6 In. . . . . *Illus* 20.00

COOKBOOK   Cookbooks are collected for many reasons. Some are
wanted for their recipes, some for investment, and some (listed here)
because they're advertising premiums. Cookbooks and recipe pamphlets are included in this category. Others may be found in brand-specific categories.

Betty Crocker, 20th Printing, 1973 . . . . 36.00
Betty Crocker's Picture Cook Book, First Edition, 1950 . . . . 32.00
Cottolene, 600 Selected Recipes, N.K. Fairbank & Co., 1893 . . . . 13.00
Gold Medal Cook Book, Compliments Gold Medal Flour 15.00
Illuminating Company New Cooks Cookbook, 1953, 53 Pages 7.00
Metropolitan Life Insurance Co., c.1930, 64 Pages 10.00
Pyrex Prize Recipes, Greystone Press, New York, 1953, 5 1/2 x 8 1/2 In., 125 Pages 35.00
Snowdrift Secrets, Cover, Mammy, Snowdrift Shortening, Southern Cotton Oil Co., 1912 46.00
Spry, 20th Anniversary Of Old & New Favorites, 1955 . . . . 8.50
Swans Down Flour, New Cake Secrets, 1931, 5 x 7 In., 48 Pages 6.00

COOKIE JAR   Cookie jars with bright colored designs and amusing
figural shapes became popular in the mid-1930s. Many companies
made them and collectors search for cookie jars either by design or
by maker's name. Other cookie jars may be listed in brand-specific
categories.

Dreyer's Grand Ice Cream, Treasure Craft, 10 x 8 1/2 In. 150.00
Entenmann's, Ceramic, Baker Hat Lid, Brazil Made, 1992, 11 x 9 In. 20.00
Famous Amos, Clear Glass, Decal, Box, Anchor Hocking, 13 1/4 x 8 1/2 In. 55.00
Harry & David, Apple Truck, Green, Ceramic, 12 x 8 In. 59.00
Harry & David, Pear Truck, Red, Ceramic, 12 x 8 In. 59.00
Keebler, Ernie The Keebler Elf, Red Hat, 12 In. 79.00
Keebler, Treehouse, Elf At Door, Box, McCoy, 9 In. 65.00
Moon Pie, Limited Edition, 8 x 6 In. 46.00
Pepperidge Farm, Milano, No. 1 In Series, 400-P 75.00
Polar Bear, Baby Bear, Coke Bottle, Santa Cap, Teleflora, 1998, 11 In. 43.00
Volkswagen, Blue, 10 1/2 In. 38.00
Volkswagen, Lady Bug, 10 1/2 In. 38.00

COON CHICKEN   Coon Chicken Inn was a chain of restaurants in
Washington, Oregon, and Utah founded by Maxon Lester Graham and
his wife, Adelaide. The logo was a caricature of a black man's head
with the restaurant name on his teeth. The inns were in business from
1924 to 1957. The dishes, ashtrays, postcards, matchbooks, place mats,
menus, and other items with the logo are sought by collectors. Some
items picture the restaurant, which used a huge cutout of a black man's
head as its entrance. Collectors should beware. Glass tumblers, money
clips, finger rings, and a fan menu are not from the original inn. Many
other reproductions have also been made.

Ashtray, Black Bellhop's Face, Glass, Etched, Round 75.00
Cup & Saucer, Demitasse, Incaware, Shenango Pottery, 3 In. 395.00
Platter, Incaware, Shenango Pottery, 11 1/2 In. 450.00
Ring, Character's Face, Novelty, Metal, 5/8 In. 13.00
Tumbler, Juice Glass, 4 1/4 x 2 1/2 In. 59.00

COORS Adolph Coors arrived in America from Germany in 1868. He had been apprenticed to a brewery in Germany and soon found work in Illinois. In 1872 he went to Denver, Colorado, and purchased a partnership in a company that bottled beer, ale, cider, wine, and seltzer water. With the assistance of an investor, Jacob Schueler, Coors started making beer in Golden, Colorado. Adolph Coors Company has made several products, including a near-beer called Mannah, malted milk, and Coors pottery. The company made the first beer to be sold in aluminum cans (1959) and eventually operated its own bottle and aluminum can manufacturing facilities. Collectors search for bottles, cans, signs, and the 1930s dinnerware. The company's subsidiaries include Coors Brewing Company in the United States and Coors Brewers Limited in England.

Bic Lighter Holder, Beer Can Shape, 2 3/4 x 2 In.	7.99
Can, Banquet Waterfall, Push Tab, 12 Oz.	10.00
Can, Pull Top, Gold Color, Tigers, Waterfall, Red Ribbon, 12 Oz.	3.00
Display, Coors Light, Beer Wolf, White Cap, Red Bandanna, Plastic, 3-D, 13 1/2 In.	66.00
Jar, Malted Milk, Pottery, Metal Lid, Coors Thermo Porcelain, 8 x 5 3/4 In.	305.00
Knife, Cream, Red Script, 2 Blades, Riveted To Sides, Folding, Plastic, 3 1/2 In.	15.00
Tin, Malted Milk, Cow, Billboard, Tin Lithograph, 8 Oz., 4 1/4 x 2 1/2 In.	250.00

CRACKER JACK Frederick William Rueckheim started selling popcorn in Chicago in 1872. Molasses was added to the popcorn in 1896 and the mixture was named Cracker Jack. In 1910 a coupon that could be redeemed for a prize was placed in each box. An actual prize was put in each box beginning in 1912. Since then, over 23 billion toys have been given out. The Cracker Jack sailor boy and his dog Bingo were used in advertisements in 1916. They became part of the box design in 1919 and were a registered trademark by 1925. Collectors want advertising materials, boxes, and the small Cracker Jack toys, especially those made of paper, wood, ceramics, or lead. Plastic toys date from after 1948. Cracker Jack was part of the Borden Company from 1964 until 1997, when Frito-Lay purchased the brand.

Banner, Box Of Cracker Jack, Oilcloth Painted, White, Red, Blue, 25 3/4 x 42 3/4 In.	660.00
Book, Riddles, 2 3/4 x 5 In., 40 Pages	35.00
Button, Truck, Angelus Marshmallows, c.1930, 1 5/8 In.	60.00
Fork & Spoon, Tin, 1930s, 2 In.	10.00
Mug & Bowl, Sailor, Dog, Breakfast Cereal, Plastic, Stamped, Deka, Elizabeth, N.J.	42.00
Puzzle, 2 Birds In Flight, Cardboard, 1 1/4 In. Diam.	10.00
Puzzle, Cowboy, 2 Guns, Cardboard, 1 1/4 In. Diam.	10.00
Puzzle, Daisy, Cardboard, 1 3/4 x 1 1/4 In.	10.00
Puzzle, Donkey, Cardboard, 1 1/2 In. Diam.	10.00
Puzzle, Fish In Bowl, Cardboard, 1 1/2 In. Diam.	10.00
Puzzle, Man Shooting Basketball Hoops, Cardboard, 2 Metal Balls, 1 1/4 In. Diam.	10.00
Puzzle, Mouse & Cheese, Cardboard, 1 3/4 x 1 1/4 In.	10.00
Puzzle, Panda Bear, Cardboard, 1 1/4 In. Diam.	10.00
Puzzle, Parrot, Stiff Paper, Perforated, C. Carey Cloud, 1946, 2 1/4 x 3 1/4 In.	15.00
Sign, Mother, Child, Cardboard Lithograph, 1900, 14 1/2 x 10 3/4 In.	5500.00
Tin, Angelus Marshmallows, Pry Lid, Tin Lithograph, 12 Oz., 3 1/2 x 5 5/8 In.	113.00
Toy, Delivery Truck, 1 1/2 x 7/8 In.	78.00
Toy, Fortune Wheel, Sailor Boy Says To Spell Your Name, Tin, Early 1930s, 3/4 In.	65.00
Toy, Horse Drawn Wagon, More You Eat, More You Want, 2 1/4 x 1 In.	125.00
Toy, Spinner, Always On Top, White, Blue	95.00
Toy, Spinner, World's Famous Confections, Red, Blue	95.00
Toy, Train Car, Cast Metal, 1920s, 1 In.	30.00
Toy, Trumpet, Metal, 1950s, 1 1/4 In.	18.00
Toy, Watch, Tin, c.1930s, Pocket, 1 1/2 x 1/4 In.	40.00
Toy, Whistle, Flat, 1 x 2 5/8 In.	110.00
Toy, Whistle, Large Mouthed Man, Tin, Gold Color, 2 1/4 In.	34.00

CREAM OF WHEAT The Diamond Mill in Grand Forks, Iowa, started grinding flour in 1890. In 1894 Tom Amidon, the head miller, persuaded the owners, Emery Mapes and George Bull, to make a new product, a porridge developed by Amidon's wife. The product was named Cream of Wheat. The mill made cardboard boxes by hand and labeled them with an old woodcut of a black chef. Ten cases were sent to New York City. Before long the product was selling by the carload. The company moved to Minneapolis, Minnesota, in 1900. While eating in a Chicago restaurant, Mapes noticed a black waiter. He paid him five dollars to pose for one picture as Rastus, the Cream of Wheat chef. The company wanted more pictures later but never found the waiter again, so only one view has ever been used. Cream of Wheat became part of Nabisco in 1961. After several changes in ownership, it now is owned by Kraft, part of the Altria Group.

Advertisement, 2 Brothers Eating, Edward Brewer, 1923, 10 1/2 x 13 1/2 In.	22.00
Advertisement, Cartoon Li'l Abner, 1950, 10 3/4 x 6 1/4 In.	7.00
Advertisement, Cream Of Wheat Preferred, Youth's Companion, 1921, 13 x 10 In.	14.00
Advertisement, Frame, 1906, 11 x 15 In.	176.00
Advertisement, Jack The Giant Killer, Fee! Fi! Fo! Fum!, 1909, 14 x 10 In.	11.00
Box, National Biscuit Co., Sample, Unopened, 2 3/4 Oz., 3 1/4 x 2 In.	86.00
Doll, Stuffed, 16 x 7 In.	46.00
Sign, Grandma, Baby, Rastus, 1975, 25 x 18 In.	20.00
Sign, Health Authorities Urge A Hot Cereal Breakfast, 1920s, 34 x 23 In. .... *Illus*	880.00
Sign, Jack The Giant Killer, Paper, Frame, 1909, 14 x 10 In.	11.00
Sign, Man, Holding Sign, Frame, 1913, 14 x 10 In.	11.00
Sign, Uncle Sam Reading Cream Of Wheat Poster, Frame, 20 x 16 In. ....11.00 to 17.00	

CROCK, see Pottery

DECORATED TUMBLER   Decorated tumblers have been made by the Anchor Hocking Glass Company, Federal Glass Company, Hazel Atlas Glass Company, Libbey Glass Inc., and other companies since the 1930s, when the pyroglaze process of printing was introduced. Many companies gave away decorated glasses as premiums. The decoration was often based on comics or TV shows. Decorated tumblers may also be listed in Coca-Cola, McDonald's, Pepsi-Cola, and other brand-specific categories.

Allen's Red Tame Cherry, Flared, Etched, 5 x 3 In.	50.00
Big Top Peanut Butter, Pressed Glass, Tin Lid, Premium	14.00
Blakely Oil, Iced Tea Set, Pitcher, Frosted Tumblers, Wood Tray, 1957	280.00
Frigidaire, Division Of General Motors, c.1940, 4 3/4 In.	20.00
Gravee-Mixer, Rochow Swirls, 4 7/8 In.	18.00
Grimmets Sure Cure, White Enamel, Shot Glass, 2 1/4 In.	88.00
Klee-Ko Soda, 5 In.	15.00
Magic Milk Shake, Flowers, Carriage, House, Label, Hocking, 5 1/8 In.	30.00
Magnolia Straight Blend Old Bourbon, 1890-1915, Shot Glass, 1 3/4 In.	99.00
Miss Dairylea, Drive Slow Message, c.1960, 3 1/4 x 3 1/2 In.	8.00
Old Ironsides Rye Whiskey, Famous For 100 Years, 1885-1915, 2 5/8 In.	99.00
Old Mos Whiskey, Acid Etched, 1890-1910, 3 1/4 In.	56.00
Welch's Grape Juice, Howdy Doody, 4 Characters, 1953, 4 In.	20.00

Smoking is bad for the health of your antiques! Smoke causes discoloration and weakens textiles. Another reason to stop smoking!

Cream Of Wheat, Sign, Health Authorities Urge A Hot Cereal Breakfast, 1920s, 34 x 23 In.

DEL MONTE The Del Monte name was first used in 1892 as a brand for peaches. Early products included ketchup, pickles, and canned fruits and vegetables. The Oakland Preserving Company, which originated the brand name, became part of the California Fruit Packers Association (1899), which became part of the California Packing Corp. (1916). In 1967 it became Del Monte Corp. R.J. Reynolds Industries owned the company from 1979 until 1989, when it sold the fresh fruit and canning businesses. A Merrill Lynch investor group purchased the canned fruit and vegetable company, Del Monte Foods. Since 1997 the Texas Pacific Group, headquartered in San Francisco, has owned the name and trademark. Fresh Del Monte Produce, Inc., had five different owners until it was purchased in 1996 by the Abu-Ghazaleh family. Its executive offices are in Coral Gables, Florida.

Advertisement, Can Of Apricots, Country Scene, Color, 1918, 16 x 10 In.	18.00
Advertisement, Pineapple Juice, Socialite, Black Maid, 1937	16.00
Bank, Big Top Bonanza, Clown, 1985, 7 1/2 In.	22.00 to 38.00
Can, Sweet Peas, 2 3/4 x 2 In.	7.00
Christmas Ornament Set, Yumkins, Plush, Fruit & Vegetable Shapes, 3 To 5 In., 5 Piece	15.00

DELAVAL In 1878 Dr. Carl Gustaf de Laval, a Swedish engineer, developed a machine that could separate cream from milk as fast as a cow was milked. The DeLaval Separator Company was established in the United States in 1885 as part of de Laval's Swedish company, AB Separator. The company's advertising included tin and paper signs, tin tip trays, small tin cutout cows, catalogs, match safes, and more. The American company was renamed Alfa-Laval in 1980. In 1991 Tetra Pak acquired the company, then in 2000 sold part of the business, which became Alfa Laval, Inc. At the same time, Tetra Laval became the parent of both Tetra Pak and a new company named DeLaval. DeLaval's U.S. operations are based in Kansas City, Missouri. Both Alfa Laval and DeLaval still make machinery for the dairy industry. Dr. de Laval, who held ninety-two Swedish patents and started thirty-seven companies, died in poverty in 1913.

Broom Holder, Cream Separators, Tin Lithograph, Round, Envelope, 3 1/2 In.	495.00
Cabinet, Cream Separator, Parts, Oak, 18 x 25 In.	1210.00
Cabinet, Cream Separator, World's Standard, Wood, Tin Lithograph, 17 x 23 In.	990.00
Calendar, 1916, DeLaval Cream Separators, Boy, Girl On Counter, Frame, 16 x 28 In.	374.00
Change Receiver, Cream Separators, 4 1/4 In.	176.00
Match Holder, Cream Separator Shape, Tin, Die Cut Lithograph, 6 1/4 x 3 3/4 In.	209.00 to 230.00
Match Holder, Separator Co., Die Cut Cow, Tin Lithograph, 6 1/2 In.	165.00
Match Holder, Separator, 1,000,000 In Use	121.00
Match Holder, Silver Highlights, Dual Compartments, Die Cut, 6 1/2 In.	66.00

DeLaval, Sign, Cream Separators, Tin, Red Ground, Gesso Frame, 40 x 30 In.

DeLaval, Tin, DeLaval Oil, 6 x 6 1/2 In.

DeLaval, Tip Tray, Cream Separators, World's Standard, Tin Lithograph, 4 3/8 In.

Mirror, Cream Separators, Celluloid, Round, Pocket, 1 3/4 In. 385.00
Oil Can, Centrifugally Clarified & Filtered, Horizontal, 6 x 6 1/2 In. 55.00
Separator, Junior, Cast Metal Base, Tin Receptacle, Instructions, 14 In. 209.00
Sign, Authorized Agency, Milking Machine, Flange, 2-Sided, Porcelain, 27 x 18 In. 1265.00
Sign, Cream Separator, Die Cut Machine, Flange, 2-Sided, c.1900, 28 x 18 In. 4130.00
Sign, Cream Separators, 5 Scenes, Green Ground, Tin Lithograph, Frame, 31 x 20 In. 1921.00
Sign, Cream Separators, 5 Scenes, Red Ground, Tin Lithograph, Frame, 41 x 30 In. 2530.00
Sign, Cream Separators, Cow, 2-Sided, Metal, 5 In. 50.00
Sign, Cream Separators, Tin Lithograph, Embossed, Round, 1905, 26 In. 7205.00
Sign, Cream Separators, Tin, Red Ground, Gesso Frame, 40 x 30 In. .... *Illus* 4675.00
Sign, Cream Separators, Yellow, Black, White, Tin, Flange, 18 x 26 In. 880.00
Sign, Enameled, Authorized Agency, Separator Graphic, 2-Sided, Flange, 18 x 27 In. 231.00
Sign, Local Agency, Porcelain, 2-Sided, 18 x 27 In. 1980.00
Sign, Separator, Yellow, Porcelain, 26 1/2 x 18 In. 1210.00
Sign, Sooner Or Later You Will Buy A DeLaval, A.M. Kimball & Sons, 41 x 29 In. 1650.00
Sign, We Use DeLaval Cream Separator, Black, Gold Letters, Porcelain, 12 x 16 In. 204.00
Sign, Woman Uses Cream Separator, Embossed, Tin Lithograph, Round, 1905, 26 In. 7205.00
Sign, Woman, Cow, 4 Corner Scenes, Tin Lithograph, Gold Frame, 41 In. 1980.00
Tin, DeLaval Oil, 6 x 6 1/2 In. .... *Illus* 55.00
Tip Tray, Cream Separators, Over 750,000 In Use, Tin Lithograph, Round, 4 1/4 In. 99.00
Tip Tray, Cream Separators, Woman In Kitchen, Round, 4 1/4 In. 180.00
Tip Tray, Cream Separators, Woman Using Separator, Tin Lithograph, Round, 4 3/8 In. 154.00
Tip Tray, Cream Separators, World's Standard, Tin Lithograph, 4 3/8 In. .... *Illus* 242.00
Tip Tray, Separator, Gold Color Rim, Tin Lithograph, Round 90.00

DIAMOND DYES   Edward Wells, A.E. Richardson, and W.J. Van Patten began as wholesale druggists and manufacturing pharmacists in Burlington, Vermont, in 1872. In 1873 Henry Wells became a partner. F.H. Wells joined in 1881. Wells, Richardson & Company believed in advertising its products, which included butter color (1877), Kidney-Wort, a remedy (1879), and Diamond Dyes, Lactated Food, and Paine's Celery Compound. By 1881 the company was spending $150,000 a year on advertising. Diamond Dyes, introduced in 1881 and sold worldwide, were made in thirty-six different colors and were useful for all types of fabrics and feathers. Diamond Dye advertising, especially the oak cabinets with lithographed tin fronts, is popular with collectors today. The company was in business until about 1943.

Cabinet, Children Skipping Rope, Oak, Tin Lithograph, 1910-1914, 24 x 15 In. ...715.00 to 825.00
Cabinet, Children, Balloon, Tin, Embossed, 1908, 24 1/4 x 15 In. ....1045.00 to 2970.00
Cabinet, Court Jester, 27 x 21 In. 853.00
Cabinet, Evolution Of Woman, Tin Lithograph Panel, c.1890, 29 x 22 In. ....660.00 to 935.00
Cabinet, Governess, Children Playing Outdoors, 1906, 30 x 22 1/4 In. .... *Illus* 2530.00

Diamond Dyes, Cabinet,
Governess, Children Playing
Outdoors, 1906, 30 x 22 1/4 In.

Diamond Dyes, Cabinet,
Mansion, Children, 1908,
15 x 24 x 8 In.

Diamond Dyes, Cabinet, Washer
Woman, Tin Lithograph, Blue
Ground, 30 x 22 1/2 In.

Cabinet, Mansion, Children, 1908, 15 x 24 x 8 In. . . . . *Illus* 1150.00
Cabinet, Maypole, Wood, Tin Lithograph, 1904, 30 x 22 1/4 In. . . . . .1018.00 to 2640.00
Cabinet, Red-Headed Fairy, 30 1/2 x 24 x 10 In. . . . . .3410.00 to 4070.00
Cabinet, Washer Woman, Tin Lithograph, Blue Ground, 30 x 22 1/2 In. . . . . *Illus* 1320.00
Cabinet, Washer Woman, Tin Lithograph, Green Ground, 30 x 22 1/2 In. . . . . . .1320.00 to 2915.00
Cabinet, Washer Woman, Unused, Shipping Crate, 30 x 22 1/2 In. 3250.00
Sign, A Busy Day In Dollville, Tin Lithograph, Frame, 1911 . . . . 3850.00
Sign, Washer Woman, Color Wheel, Diamond, Chrome Stand, Countertop, 10 In. 2600.00
Trade Card, Victorian Women Dyeing Material, 5 x 3 1/4 In. 10.00

DISPENSER Dispensers were used in soda fountains and bars beginning at the turn of the twentieth century. They were made in ceramic
or glass and were often shaped to represent the orange or lemon used
in the drink. It is best if the original pump is in the dispenser, but value
is not lowered much if the pump is a replacement.

Banquet Tea, A Wonderful Flavor, Red, Embossed, Stoneware, Iron Base, 10 x 14 In. . . . 495.00
Birchola, Round, Leaves, c.1918 . . . . 2750.00
Buckeye Root Beer, 5 Cent, Satyrs Around Bottom 1650.00
Buckeye Root Beer, Black Body, Cleveland Fruit Juice Co. Mfg., c.1918 . . . . . . .440.00 to 743.00
Buckeye Root Beer, New Ball Style Pump, c.1918 . . . . 1870.00
Buckeye Root Beer, Tree Stump Shape, Horseshoe Ball Pump, c.1920 . . . . 495.00
Buckeye Root Beer, Tree Stump Shape, Pump, 1920, 16 x 7 In. 468.00
Buckeye Root Beer, White, Red Letters, Cleveland Fruit Juice Co., c.1918 . . . . 1430.00
Cherry Smash, Always Drink, Your Nation's Beverage, Ceramic, 14 x 9 In. 2700.00
Cherryallen, Allens Red Tame Syrup, White Globe 1760.00
Chum, Queen Dairy, Chilled, Churned Buttermilk, 5 Cent, Porcelain, 35 x 20 In. 3190.00
Crawford's Cherry-Fizz, It's A Jake-A Loo, Ceramic, 1918, 11 In. . . . . .4600.00 to 10450.00
Dewar's Perth Whisky, Barrel Shape, Glass, Gold Letters, England, 12 1/2 In. 341.00
Double Kay Salted Nuts, 3 Glass Jars On Single Porcelain Base, 9 x 21 In. 330.00
Drink Nesbitt's Fruit Drinks, Pink Depression Glass, Paper & Embossed Labels, 9 1/2 In. . 68.00
E-Z Way Canned Milk, Plastic, Flip Top Lid, Handle, Leominster, Mass., 5 In. 20.00
Fowler's Cherry Mash, Ruby Glass, Nickel Plated Top & Clamp, 13 In. 303.00
Fowler's Root Beer, 5 Cent, The Best, Ceramic, No Pump, 11 x 10 In. 1870.00
Fresh Hot Nuts, 3 Glass Jars, Single Metal Base, 16 1/2 x 22 x 6 In. 605.00
Ginger Mint Julep, Shape, Horseshoe Pump, Porcelain Knob, c.1920 . . . . 468.00
Grape Crush, Embossed Grapes, Translucent Glass, Ball Pump, c.1920 . . . . 4620.00
Grape Crush, Purple Glass, Embossed, Ball Style Pump, c.1920, 14 In. 2006.00
Grapeine Syrup, Brass Base & Top, Engraved, Glass Globe, 39 x 14 1/2 In. 770.00
Green's Muscadine Syrup, White, Red Letters, Gold Bands, Barrel Shape . . . . . . .121.00 to 242.00
Howel's Cherry-Julep, 5 Cents, Pump, Red, White Letters, c.1920 . . . . *Illus* 4400.00
Howel's Orange-Julep, 5 Cents, Horsehoe Pump, Porcelain Knob, c.1918 . . . . 1540.00
Hunters Root Beer, Syrup, Cordley & Hayes, 14 In. 708.00
Jersey Creme, Horseshoe Pump, Porcelain Knob, c.1918 . . . . 1650.00
Julep, Crock Base, Spigot, Julep Gallon Jug, 1900-1910, 18 In. 88.00
Julep, Crock Base, Spigot, Nesbitt Gallon Jug, 1900-1910, 18 In. 121.00
Kenny's Iced Tea, Glazed Ceramic, 2 Parts, 18 In. 198.00
Kenny's Iced Tea, Silver Bands, New Lid, 13 In. 66.00
Kirsch's, Ice Cream Cone, Clear Glass, Embossed Lid, 8 x 12 In. 440.00
Lash's Dixie Dew, Glass, Pedestal Base, Spigot, c.1900, 16 In. 743.00
Liberty Root Beer, Oak, Barrel Shape, Spigot, Lid, Insert, 25 In. 920.00
Mansfield 's Choice Pepsin Gum, 5 Cents, Etched Glass, Automatic Clerk, 16 In. 2300.00
Maxwell House Coffee, Iced Tea, Stoneware, Blue, White, Embossed, 12 x 9 In. . . . . *Illus* 358.00
Middleby Root Beer, Mug, Glass, Brown, Spigot, 12 In. 121.00
Milkose Malted Milk, Enamel, Glass, Tin Lid, 9 x 6 In. 120.00
Miner's Fruit Nectar, 5 Cents, Glass 2640.00
Mission Grapefruit, Black Base, Lid, Spigot, c.1900, 14 In. 330.00
Mission Grapefruit, Vaseline Glass, Metal Cone Base, Embossed, Mixer, 12 5/8 x 7 In. . . 688.00
Mission Orange, Pink Glass, Metal Cone Base, Embossed, Mixer, 12 5/8 x 7 In. 743.00
Mission Orange, Yellow, Black, c.1920-1930, 28 In. 330.00
Old Highland Whisky, John Walker & Sons Kilmarnock, Glass, 14 1/4 In. 323.00
Orange Crush, Black Glass Base, Frosted Globe, Metal Lid, c.1910, 17 In. 495.00
Orange Crush, Ceramic Base, Frosted Glass Globe, 15 1/2 x 8 In. 605.00
Orange Crush, Gravity, Cast Iron Base, Green Porcelain, Cardboard Box, 1920s-1930s . . . 2090.00

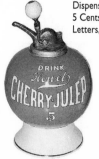

Dispenser, Howel's Cherry-Julep,
5 Cents, Pump, Red, White
Letters, c.1920

Dispenser, Maxwell
House Coffee, Iced Tea,
Stoneware, Blue, White,
Embossed, 12 x 9 In.

Orange-Julep, 5 Cents, Ceramic, Ball Pump, c.1920 .... 6820.00
Phenix, Tin Lithograph, Lift Top, Pump, Whitall Tatum Co., 10 x 12 1/2 x 6 1/2 In. 413.00
Powder, Ideal Manufacturing, No. 5, Tabletop, 1892 Patent 58.00
Richardson's Maid Of Honor, Glass Globe, Cast Metal Pedestal, 26 1/2 x 14 x 14 In. 230.00
Rochester Root Beer, 5 Cents, Red, Multiplex Faucet Co., St. Louis, Mo., 20 x 11 1/2 In. 1345.00
Safe-T-Cones, Metal, Plastic, 38 In. 50.00
Special Irish Whiskey, Hanging, Clear, Cut Glass, Stopper, Chains 1320.00
Valdespino Sherry, Amontillado, Ceramic, Spain, 12 1/2 In. 202.00
Ver-Ba, Drink Ver-Ba 5 Cents, c.1918 .... 1210.00
Ward's Grape Crush, Green, Glass, c.1918 .... 880.00
Ward's Lemon Crush, Horseshoe Pump 1320.00
Ward's Lemon Crush, Lemon Shape, Flowers Around Base, Original Pump 1430.00
Ward's Lemon Crush, Lemon Shape, Green Base 880.00
Ward's Orange Crush, Orange Shape, Flowers Around Base, Pump, 13 x 9 In. . .1100.00 to 1320.00
White King, Embossed, Green Glass, 5 3/4 x 3 In. 66.00
Zeno 1 Cent Chewing Gum, Wood, Clockwork Mechanism, Embossed Tin Panel, 17 In. . 1534.00
Zeno Chewing Gum, Drop 1 Cent Here, Porcelain, Yellow 2006.00

DISPLAY   Display boxes, boards, cases, racks, and figures were used
in stores. Cases and racks, usually marked with a company name, held
products to be sold. Boxes also contained products; they were either
oversize versions of retail boxes or were specially made and labeled
with a product name. Displays were light-up, three-dimensional, or
figural. Display jars are listed in the Jar category.

Animated, Baranger Jewelry, 7 Dwarfs Making Gold Rings, c.1950, 18 x 24 In. 3660.00
Animated, Baranger Jewelry, Couple On Tugboat, Wood Base, c.1950, 20x 16 In. 2635.00
Animated, Hillbilly, Bucking Bronco, Mechanical Window Attraction Co., 17 x 17 In. .. 1840.00
Animated, Hohner Harmonica, Revolving, Windup, Cardboard Signs, 32 x 10 3/4 In. 440.00
Board, Breing's Paints, Oak Frame, Allentown, Pa., 23 x 9 In. 35.00
Board, Diamond Tools, 9 Horseshoes, 24 In. 165.00
Board, Wilson Sun Styles Sunglasses, 6 Pairs, Cardboard, Easel Back, 18 x 9 1/2 In. 77.00
Bottle, Big Tree Burgundy, Flagon, No. 3, Wood, Grierson Oldham, England, 24 x 17 In. . 114.00
Bottle, Little Boy Blue, Bluing, Self-Serving, Tin, Wall Mount, 19 x 4 In. 88.00
Bottle, Old Mr. Boston Gin, Glass, 22 In. 77.00
Box, Adams Chiclets, Exchange Your Pennies, Glass, Tin, Countertop, 3 3/4 x 7 x 4 1/2 In. 225.00
Box, Adams Dentyne Chewing Gum, Tin, Die Cut, American Chickle Co., 7 x 4 x 3 In. .. 358.00
Box, Atlantic Faucet Washers, Be Your Own Plumber For 10 Cents, Contents 495.00
Box, B&B Corn & Bunion Plasters, 4 Drawers, Brass Pulls, Wood, Paper, 11 1/2 x 11 In. . 55.00
Box, Barton's Paste Shoe Polish, 10 Cents, 12 Tins, 9 In. 47.00
Box, Bauer & Black Adhesives, Cardboard Lithograph, Counter, 10 x 10 In. 55.00
Box, Beeman's Gum, Tin Lithograph, Die Cut, 20 Packs, 7 5/8 x 10 1/4 x 3 1/8 In. 3740.00
Box, Blatz Chewing Gum, Original, Cardboard, 10 Gum Packs, 5 1/8 x 6 1/8 x 4 1/4 In. .. 990.00
Box, Camel Friction Tape, 16 Boxes, Countertop, 1950s, 10 1/2 x 5 x 2 In. 55.00
Box, Curtiss Baby Ruth, Peppermint Gum, 18 Packages, 6 1/4 x 4 1/2 x 1 In. 660.00
Box, Dentyne, Tin, Die Cut Lithograph, Cardboard, Gum Packs, 7 1/8 x 2 7/8 x 3 7/8 In. . 3410.00
Box, Detmer Woolens, Outdoor Scene, Men, Women, Wood, c.1900, 9 x 30 In. 105.00
Box, Dr. E.L. Welbourn's Anti-Bilious Pills, Cardboard, 12 Tins, 4 1/2 x 5 x 4 3/8 In. 276.00

Box, Eveready Flash-O-Scope, Family, Batteries, Cardboard, 32 x 31 In. 303.00
Box, Exelloid Tooth Brushes, Coronet Brush Co., 6 Brushes, 6 3/4 x 4 1/4 In. 154.00
Box, Francis H. Leggett Standard Spices, Wood, 4 1/4 x 19 1/4 x 12 In. . . . . *Illus* 198.00
Box, Garcia Grande, Tin Lithograph, Electric Lighter, 9 1/2 x 8 In. 28.00
Box, Gessler's Magic Headache Wafers, 12 Packages, c.1906, 6 x 5 1/2 In. 495.00
Box, Gilt Edge Dressing Ladies Shoes, Never Injures, Lift Lid, Wood, 18 x 11 3/4 In. 81.00
Box, Kis-Me Gum, Grape Flavor, 20 Packs, 5 1/8 x 6 1/2 x 2 3/4 In. 825.00
Box, Noxaboil, Internal Remedy, Cardboard, Flip-Top Lid, 3 1/2 x 6 In. 1980.00
Box, Pal Hollow Ground Double Edge Razor Blades, 6 Boxes, 1 3/8 x 5 3/4 x 6 1/2 In. . . . 80.00
Box, Panama Gum, Cardboard, Helmet Co., 4 3/4 x 7 1/4 In. 198.00
Box, Pon-Tam-Pon, Local Medication For Women, Contents, 4 x 7 3/8 In. 1100.00
Box, Professors Laxative Tablets, 12 Tins, Contents, Cardboard, 4 3/4 x 4 In. 83.00
Box, Scotch Cellophane Tape, 12 Dispensers, Lithograph, 5 1/4 x 9 3/8 x 2 1/8 In. 171.00
Box, Sen-Sen Chewing Gum, 5 Cents, 6 x 7 In. 25.00
Box, Smart Gum, Peppermint, 20 Gum Packs, True Blue Co., 3 3/8 x 6 x 4 1/4 In. 231.00
Box, Vaseline Preparations, Metal, Countertop, 7 Boxes Of Product, 16 x 7 x 6 1/2 In. . . . 468.00
Box, Whitmore's Shoe Polish, Oil Paste Shoe Polish, Round Tins, 2 x 9 1/2 x 6 1/4 In. . . . 17.00
Box, Yanks Chewing Gum, 20 Gum Packages, 5 Cent, 1 x 3 1/4 x 6 1/2 In. 209.00
Box, Zerbst's Capsules, 25 Cents, Contents, 12 Count 330.00
Canister, Weyman's Cutty Pipe, Tin Lithograph, 13 1/2 x 10 1/4 x 9 3/8 In. 1540.00
Case, Ace Comb, Pivoting Base, 13 1/2 x 10 1/2 x 10 1/2 In. 88.00
Case, Acme White Lead & Color Works, Oak Case, Paper Roll, Detroit, 15 x 19 In. 1600.00
Case, Adams Pepsin, Tutti Fruiti Gum, Marquee, Oak, Mirror, c.1900, 12 x 18 In. 963.00
Case, Arrow Collars, 9 x 18 In. 578.00
Case, Arrow Collars, c.1910, 50 In. 1320.00
Case, Arrow Collars, Metal Frame, Curved Glass, Collars, 54 In. 1770.00
Case, Auto Strop Safety Razor, Countertop, 6 1/2 x 5 x 11 1/4 In. 198.00
Case, Beech-Nut, Tin Lithograph, 6 Slots, 11 In. 113.00
Case, Black Diamond, Instrument Strings, Tin Lithograph, Glass, 8 Shelves, 20 x 19 In. . . 210.00
Case, Blue Bird, Man's Handkerchief, Tin, 4 Boxes On Lid, 8 x 12 x 7 In. . . . . . . .165.00 to 495.00
Case, Boston Garter, Country Store, Mahogany, Glass, Lift Lid, 14 x 6 In. 214.00
Case, Boston Garter, Wood, Glass, 7 1/2 x 13 1/2 x 10 In. 275.00
Case, Calox Tooth Powder, Your 32 Teeth Are 32 Reasons, Mirror, 12 1/2 x 7 1/2 In. 440.00
Case, Colgan's Gum, Taffee Tolu, 6 Flavors, Glass, Oak, 17 x 8 x 9 In. . . . . .1320.00 to 2090.00
Case, Eveready Battery, 10 Cents Each, Tin Lithograph, Counter, 16 In. . . . . .357.00 to 550.00
Case, Eveready Flashlight, Santa, Wreath, Tin Lithograph, Countertop, 15 x 10 1/2 In. . . . 130.00
Case, Farnam's Kalamazoo Celery & Pepsin Gum, Wood, Glass, 7 1/2 x 17 x 10 In. 6160.00
Case, Golden Burst Popcorn, Edgewater Farms, Sterling, Ill., Wire, Metal, 17 x 16 x 7 In. 33.00
Case, Hanford's Balsam, Oak, 13 x 24 In. 220.00
Case, Hickory Elastic, Wood, Glass Front, Metal Dividers, Ruler, 8 x 13 1/2 In. 132.00
Case, Ide Collar, Corner, Brass Frame, Collars, 47 In. 2420.00
Case, Ingersoll Watches & Clocks, Glass, Wood Frame, Square, 31 x 18 x 17 1/2 In. 265.00
Case, Ingersoll Watches, Wood, Glass, 9 x 9 1/2 In. 523.00
Case, J.P. Primley's California Fruit & Pepsin Chewing Gum, Oak, Mirror, 9 1/2 x 18 In. . . 1155.00
Case, Johnson & Johnson, Corn, Bunion Plasters, Tin Lithograph, Drawers, 13 x 13 x 7 In. 358.00
Case, Johnson & Johnson, Medicated & Adhesive Plasters, Tin Lithograph, 13 x 15 In. . . . 687.00
Case, Jones & Hill, Jones Columbian Fruit, Pepsin, Phosphate, Oak, Glass, 8 x 17 1/2 In. . 550.00
Case, Jones & Hill, Tuxedo Pepsin Phosphate, Curved Glass, 9 1/2 x 17 1/2 x 7 In. 1870.00
Case, Jones Gum, Curved Front Glass, Countertop, 9 1/2 x 17 1/2 x 7 1/2 In. 1045.00
Case, Kaywoodie Pipes, 5 Pipes, Wood Sides, Side Hinged Front Door, 10 x 11 In. 176.00
Case, Keen Kutter, Walnut, Glass, Metal Tag, 19 x 41 In. 708.00
Case, King Collar Buttons, Oak, Slant Top, Insert Card, 9 In. 330.00
Case, La Cosca Guitar Strings, Strings For The Artist, Wood, Glass Front, 18 x 22 In. 110.00
Case, La Palina Cigars, Die Cut, Cardboard, Stair Step, Counter, 9 x 23 In. 44.00
Case, M. Hohner's Harmonica, Wood, 9 x 11 In. 220.00
Case, Mackintosh's, Best Money Can Buy, Glass Front, Tin, Countertop, 17 3/4 x 13 In. . . 151.00
Case, Marble's Outer's Knives, Bull Moose, 12 3/4 x 15 1/8 x 6 1/2 In. 606.00
Case, Marble's Outer's Knives, Metal, Glass, 12 3/4 x 15 1/4 x 6 1/2 In. 1271.00
Case, Minters Candies, Metal, Glass, 13 x 10 x 13 1/2 In. 22.00
Case, Montague's Biscuit, Santa Claus Inside, Oak, 32 In. 374.00
Case, Moody Baked Goods, Wood, Countertop 176.00
Case, Moore's Ice Cream, Oak, Glass, 14 1/2 x 15 3/4 x 10 1/4 In. 385.00
Case, Nestle Hazel Nut Milk Chocolate, 5 Cents, 4 3/4 x 10 1/8 x 7 1/5 In. 550.00

Display, Box, Francis H. Leggett Standard Spices,
Wood, 4 1/4 x 19 1/4 x 12 In.

Display, Figure, Hightop Athletic Shoe, Bel-Mar
By Bata, Cast Plaster, 12 x 8 x 24 In.

Case, Nestle's Chocolate, Metal Frame, Glass, Countertop, 8 x 10 x 6 In. 330.00
Case, Palmer Perfumes, Metal, Glass, Early 1900s, 7 1/2 x 9 1/4 In. 33.00
Case, Paterson, Good Candy, Slant Front, Wood, Glass, 26 x 21 x 12 In. 40.00
Case, Pirika Dolla A Pound Chocolates, Wood Grain Tin Lithograph, Countertop 330.00
Case, Ray-O-Vac Batteries & Bulbs, Tin Lithograph, Countertop, 9 1/2 x 7 1/2 x 11 In. 330.00
Case, Realist Webbing, Oak, Dividers, Countertop, 14 In. 154.00
Case, Schrader Tire Valve Stem, Complete Contents, Pressed Steel, 1920-1930, 16 In. ... 523.00
Case, Slidewell Collars, Oak, Glass, Stenciled Letters, 14 Collars, 25 x 14 x 8 In. 2530.00
Case, Stanley Works, Oak, Hinged Back, Shelves, Sweetheart Trademark, 1920s, 17 In. .. 770.00
Case, Tootsie Roll, Metal Frame, Glass, Etched, 4 Packages, 8 1/2 x 7 In. 440.00
Case, Victoria Helix Eyed Needles, 3 Drawers, Hardwood, 7 1/2 x 16 3/4 x 7 In. 495.00
Case, W.B. Jones Spring Co., Oak, 9 Drawers, Porcelain Fronts, 24 1/2 x 21 x 11 1/2 In. .. 209.00
Case, Woodfield & Sons, Redditch, Prize & Needles, Walnut, 3 Drawers, 13 x 8 x 9 In. .. 220.00
Case, Yuenglings Pilsner Beer, Blond Lady, Holding Beer, Die Cut, Cardboard, 24 x 36 In. 90.00
Case, Zeno Chewing Gum, Oak, Glass Shelves, Mirror Back, c.1890, 18 In. ...... .633.00 to 825.00
Figure, Hightop Athletic Shoe, Bel-Mar By Bata, Cast Plaster, 12 x 8 x 24 In. ...... *Illus* 100.00
Figure, Icee Plastic Cup, Light-Up, 14 x 28 In. 61.00
Figure, Munsing Union Suits, Man In Union Suit, Arms Crossed, Tin, 2-Sided, 42 In. 4125.00
Figure, Nut House, Tin Lithograph, 24 In. 192.00
Figure, Ohio Matches, Indian, Chalkware, c.1920, 11 1/2 x 23 In. 248.00
Figure, Ray-O-Vac Battery, Wood Metal, Cardboard Battery, 24 In. 138.00
Figure, Tavern, White Horse Whiskey, Metal, Wood Base, c.1960, 6 3/4 In. 24.00
Holder, National Mazda Lamps, Lightbulb Sockets, Tin, 2-Sided, c.1920, 28 x 13 In. 633.00
Rack, Bear Brand, Fine Gauge Stockings, Cast Metal, 25 x 11 In. 345.00
Rack, Beech-Nut Gum, Tin Lithograph, Countertop, 14 1/2 x 6 3/8 x 6 5/8 In. 2200.00
Rack, Blackman's Medicated Salt Brick, Tin Lithograph, Wood, Stencils, 30 In. 220.00
Rack, Brown's Tested Seeds, Grand Rapids, Michigan, Wood, 2 Tiers, 50 x 42 In. 385.00
Rack, Burnets Town Talk, Shoelaces, Revolving, Tin Lithograph, Countertop, 13 In. 275.00
Rack, Conforma Collars, Rokeby, 5 Collars, Wood, England, 26 1/4 In. 114.00
Rack, Curtiss Candy & Gum, Red, Plastic, Countertop, 1950s 50.00
Rack, Delta Paint Brushes, Metal, Countertop 22.00
Rack, Dentyne & Beeman's Pepsin Chewing Gum, Women On Each Side, 1920s 4200.00
Rack, Eat Magic Yeast For Health, Red & Yellow, 3 Packages, 27 In. 110.00
Rack, Edgwater Farms Golden Burst Popcorn, Wire, Multi-Tier, Tin, 15 1/2 x 17 1/2 In. .. 11.50
Rack, Hohner Harmonica, Clockwork Base, Side Crank, Pyramid Top, Wood, 32 In. 1815.00
Rack, Ivanhoe Mayonnaise, Rich & Creamy, 3 Shelves, Tin, 23 x 21 1/2 In. 55.00
Rack, Lance, Just Right, Right Now, Cracker Pack, Metal, 4 Glass Jars, Metal Covers 440.00
Rack, Martin Ware, Chicken Feeders, Metal, Wood, 1930s, 60 In. 55.00
Rack, Merkle's Blu-J Brooms, Tin Lithograph Signs, Metal Stand, 35 x 10 x 23 In. 468.00
Rack, Minnesota Line, Red, Yellow, Metal, Easel Back, 19 x 18 1/2 In. 22.00
Rack, Rice's Seeds, Fold-Out, Seed Packs, Embossed, Tin Front Sign 3740.00
Rack, Sioux Tools, Metal, 24 x 31 In. 44.00
Rack, Sunshine Biscuits, Always Ask For, Lithographed Metal 330.00
Rack, Super Zinc-Ed Wire Fences, Tin Lithograph, Pump, American Artworks, c.1910 ... 110.00
Rack, Tootsie Rolls, 5 Cents, Better Than Ever, Blue, White, Tin Lithograph, 14 x 8 x 5 In. 1210.00
Rack, Towels By Callaway, Nickel Plated, Cast Iron, Countertop, 26 In. 203.00
Rack, Triangle Collars, Wood Grain Tin, Stand-Up, 24 In. 357.00
Rack, Tydol & Veedol Oil, Lithograph, Each Leads Its Class, 2-Sided, Metal, 43 In. 275.00
Rack, Use Day's Soap, Requires No Boiling Clothes, Wood, 35 In. 590.00
Rack, West Hair Nets, Tin Lithograph, Revolves, 1922, 19 In. 1430.00
Rack, Wise Potato Chips, Boy & Girl At Counter, Cardboard, Easel Back, 17 x 20 In. 49.00

Doll, Blue Ribbon Malt Extract,
Cloth, Uncut, 18 x 19 In.

Doll, Chiquita Banana, Cloth, Uncut, Original
Mailing Envelope, 1944, 5 1/4 x 6 1/2 In.

Rack, Wrangler Jeans, Wood, 1960s, 17 x 2 3/4 In.		61.00
Shadowbox, Dr. Scholl's Products, Mounted On Stenciled Cardboard, 35 x 15 In.		1808.00
Shoe Stand, Brown Bilt, Die Cut, Metal, Shoes, 12 In.		165.00

DOLL   Advertising dolls can be found made from plastic, composition, and cloth. Rag dolls that represented products have been made since the 1890s. Some dolls are listed here; others are listed by brand name. Information about advertising dolls can be found in general doll books or in the many publications devoted to dolls.

Blue Bonnet Margarine, Betsy Ross, Mail In Premium, Box, 1969, 8 In.		50.00
Blue Ribbon Malt Extract, Cloth, Uncut, 18 x 19 In.	*Illus*	83.00
Burger Chef, Flannel Felt, Vinyl Head, Hand Puppet, Early 1970s, 10 In.		35.00
Chiquita Banana, Cloth, Uncut, Original Mailing Envelope, 1944, 5 1/4 x 6 1/2 In. .	*Illus*	40.00
Cox Gelatin, Boy, Cloth, Uncut, c.1910	*Illus*	286.00
Ediswan Radios, Wood, Jointed, Composition, 15 x 9 In.		963.00
Fels Naptha, Anty Drudge, Cloth, Cut, Sides Sewn Together, 11 1/4 x 6 1/2 In.	*Illus*	50.00
Grapette Soda, Buddy Lee		200.00
Green Giant Little Sprout, Vinyl, Mailing Bag, 1970s, 6 1/4 In.	*Illus*	25.00
Hostess Munchies, Orange, Plush, Tags, Best Made Toys, 6 x 9 x 14 In.		10.00
Jewel Skippy, Vinyl, c.1970s, 6 In.		24.00
Lennox, Lenny, Fabric, Cut & Sew, 18 x 12 In.		11.00
Nestle, Little Hans, Red Hair & Beard, Brown Pants, Yellow Hat, c.1969, 12 1/2 In. .	*Illus*	60.00
Phillips 66 Gas Station Attendant, Buddy Lee	242.00 to	413.00
Regent Baby Products, Rubber, Squeeze, Squeak, Made In Korea, 1973, 7 1/2 In.		24.00
Roman Meal Co., Dolly Dimples, Cloth, Uncut, 21 1/2 x 32 In.	*Illus*	83.00

Doll, Cox Gelatin, Boy, Cloth,
Uncut, c.1910

Doll, Roman Meal Co., Dolly Dimples, Cloth,
Uncut, 21 1/2 x 32 In.

Doll, Green Giant Little Sprout, Vinyl, Mailing Bag, 1970s, 6 1/4 In.

Doll, Fels Naptha, Anty Drudge, Cloth, Cut, Sides Sewn Together, 11 1/4 x 6 1/2 In.

Doll, Nestle, Little Hans, Red Hair & Beard, Brown Pants, Yellow Hat, c.1969, 12 1/2 In.

Tastykake Bakery, Orange Shirt, Pants, Apron, Bakers Hat, Cloth, Stuffed, 1974, 13 In.	14.00
Willie Wirehand, Bobbing Head, Hand Painted, Box, 8 In.	30.00

DOOR The first and last thing the customer sees is the door, so advertisers are always trying to find a way to put a brand name on it. Door pushes, door pulls, door handles, door decals, and door screens can be found.

DOOR PULL, Orange Crush, Tin, 9 x 4 3/4 In.	500.00
DOOR PUSH, 2 Way Soda, Bottle, Tin, Embossed, 6 3/4 x 3 1/4 In.	55.00
5 Roses Flour, Red Ground, White Letters, Bar, Porcelain, 2 1/2 x 32 In.	495.00
Ask For Kleen Maid Bread, Metal, Embossed, Brass Handle, 18 1/2 In.	207.00
Bireley's, The Natural Thing To Drink, Tin, 9 1/2 x 4 In.	165.00
Bireley's Soda, Bottle, Embossed, Tin Lithograph, 12 x 3 In.	187.00
Blue Boy Brand, Pare's Drops, Tin, England, 9 1/2 x 3 1/2 In.	170.00
Braun's Town Talk Bread, Metal, Bronze, 18 1/2 x 3 1/4 In.	88.00
Bunny, Fresher Cakes, Fresher Bread, Tin, 1 1/2 x 19 In.	83.00
Butter Krust Bread, We Recommend, It's Fresh, Tin, 2 x 20 In.	138.00
Buy Lyon's Tea, Blue Ground, Enamel, England, 10 x 3 In.	832.00
Clicquot Club, Eskimo Boy, Bottle, Yellow, Black, Embossed, Tin Lithograph, 3 x 9 In.	105.00
Columbia Ice Cream, Nonebetter Brand, Blue, White, Red, Porcelain, 7 1/2 x 4 In.	1018.00
Crescent Flour, Try A Sack, Embossed Tin Lithograph, 9 5/8 x 3 3/4 In.	330.00
Delaware Punch, Tin, Drink, Delicious, 11 x 4 In.	77.00
Dr. Caldwell's Syrup Pepsin, Porcelain, 6 1/2 x 3 3/4 In.	92.00
Dr. King's New Discovery, Porcelain, 7 x 3 In.	1815.00
Dr. Sanger's Capsules, Tin Lithograph, Match Scratcher, 7 x 3 1/2 In.	413.00
Drink Kramer's, All Flavors, Bottle, Tin, 12 x 3 1/2 In.	61.00
Drink Orange Crush, Come In, Bottle, Metal, Embossed, 1926, 12 1/4 x 3 1/4 In.	330.00 to 523.00
Drink Pal Soda, Bottle, Real Orangeade, Tin, 1949, 12 x 3 In.	165.00
Enjoy Tastee Bread, Red Letters, Porcelain, 12 x 16 In.	220.00
Ex-Lax, Get Your Box Now, Porcelain, Multicolored, 8 x 4 In.	413.00
Freihofer's Sonny Boy Bread, Protruding Handle, Tin Lithograph, 3 x 12 x 2 In.	150.00
Henkels Flour, Please Shut The Door, Cobalt Blue, Porcelain, 8 x 3 In.	88.00
J. Fenwick & Son, Dyers & Cleaners, Enamel, England, 8 x 2 1/2 In.	359.00
Ken-L Ration, Tin, 1950s	358.00
King Cole Tea, You'll Love The Flavor, Black, White, Yellow, Porcelain, c.1940, 11 In.	220.00
Kirk's Flake Soap, Come In, Red, White, Porcelain, 8 1/2 x 3 1/4 In.	385.00
Mission Orange Beverages, Bottle & Cap, Naturally Good, Tin, 11 1/2 x 3 1/2 In.	198.00
Nelsons Ice Cream, Ask For, Richer, Tastier, White, Red, Black, c.1940, 9 1/2 x 3 1/2 In.	56.00
NuGrape Soft Drink, Bottle, 10 1/4 x 4 1/4 In.	165.00
Ox-Heart Peanut Butter, Green, White, Red, Porcelain, 6 1/2 x 4 In.	1375.00
Pal, Real Orangeade, Bottle, 1949, 12 x 3 In.	138.00
Perry's Quality Beverages, Bottle, Red Ground	149.00
Salada Tea, Thank You On Back, Porcelain Over Steel, 32 x 3 1/2 In.	66.00
Schmidt's Blue Ribbon Bread, Stenciled Sheet Metal, 19 In.	176.00
Senate Beer, Bottle, Thank You, Call Again, 11 x 3 1/2 In.	220.00
Slipknot Rubber Heels, Tin, Lithograph, Blue, Green, White, 6 7/8 x 3 In.	358.00

Check the metal strips holding any heavy wall-hung shelves. After a few years, the shelf holder may develop "creep" and gradually bend away from the wall.

Door Push, Sunbeam Blue Ribbon Bread,
Stenciled, Sheet Metal, 19 In.

Star Naphtha Washing Powder, Porcelain, 6 1/4 x 3 1/2 In. 495.00
Sunbeam Blue Ribbon Bread, Stenciled, Sheet Metal, 19 In. . . . . *Illus* 297.00
Sweet Heart Products, Heart Shape, Red, Die Cut, Porcelain, 5 x 5 In. . . . . .358.00 to 495.00
Texas Punch, Hello, You'll Love It, Bottle, 10 x 4 In. 165.00
Thomas Bread, Don't Forget, Loaf Of Bread, Porcelain, 8 x 4 In. 303.00
Tip Top Bread, Tin Lithograph, 13 1/2 x 2 1/2 x 1 In. 143.00
Velvet Ice Cream, Take Home A Brick, The Velvet Kind, Embossed, Porcelain, 8 x 3 In. . 543.00
Vicks, Vatro Nol, Vaporub, Multicolored, Porcelain, 7 7/8 x 3 7/8 In. 578.00
Vimto, Drink, Delicious & Refreshing, Enamel, England, 11 x 3 In. 832.00
Walgreens, Aluminum, Embossed, 3 x 15 In. 110.00
DOOR SCREEN, Colonial Bread, Blue Push, Painted Screen, 39 x 80 In. 330.00

DR PEPPER In 1885 a pharmacist named Charles Courtice Alderton invented a new drink. It was named Dr. Pepper by W.B. Morrison and perfected by R.S. Lazenby, a Waco, Texas, chemist. It has been sold ever since. The early logo included a period after the "Dr," but the period was dropped by 1950. The company has used many advertising signs, trays, premiums, clocks, thermometers, and bottles. In 1986 Dr Pepper merged with the Seven-Up Company, forming Dr Pepper/ Seven-Up Companies Inc. In 1995 it was acquired by Cadbury-Schweppes and is part of its Dr Pepper/Seven-Up Inc. division.

Bottle, ACL Label, Cap, 10 Oz. 45.00
Bottle, Commemorative, Texas vs. Oklahoma Football Game, 1973, 16 Oz. 16.00
Bottle, Seltzer, Pink Glass, Etched, 12 In. 385.00
Clock, Light-Up, 15 x 9 In. 110.00
Cookbook, Cookin' With Dr Pepper, Recipes, 5 x 8 In. 20.00
Door Push, Drink A Bite To Eat, In Case Of Emergency, Tin, 8 1/4 x 4 In. . . . . . . .325.00 to 495.00
Door Push, Emergency Notification Insert, Metal, c.1940, 4 x 8 In. 366.00
Match Holder, 10-2-4 Logo, Green, Tin, 1940s, 6 x 3 1/4 In. 185.00
Match Holder, Wall, For Good Life, Drink A Bite Today, Green, Tin, 1940s, 6 x 3 1/4 In. . 185.00
Pin Tray, At All Soda Fountains, Boy Eating Watermelon, Oval, 3 3/8 x 2 1/4 In. 1320.00
Pin Tray, At All Soda Fountains, Kittens, Drinking Milk, Round, 2 5/8 In. 660.00
Sign, 10-2-4, Tin, 4 x 18 3/4 In. 165.00
Sign, Corral Scene, Dr Pepper Picks Your Energy Up, Cardboard, 30 x 49 In. 2000.00
Sign, Devil, Jointed Body, A Devilish Good Drink, Cardboard, Die Cut, 27 In. 1035.00
Sign, Dr Pepper Bottling Co., Inverse Triangle, Porcelain, 23 x 18 In. 990.00
Sign, Drink A Bite To Eat, Paper Lithograph, Easel, c.1940, 9 x 11 1/2 In. 281.00
Sign, Drink Dr Pepper, Good For Life, Porcelain, 10 1/2 x 26 1/2 In. . . . . .121.00 to 390.00
Sign, Drink Dr Pepper, Porcelain, 8 x 21 In. 138.00
Sign, Drink Dr Pepper, Porcelain, Raised Logo, c.1940, 10 1/2 x 26 1/2 In. 383.00
Sign, Drink Dr Pepper, Tin, Embossed, 17 1/2 x 39 In. 193.00
Sign, Enameled, Porcelain, White Letters, Red Ground, 7 3/4 x 20 In. 110.00
Sign, Fireside Fun, Cardboard, 1940s, 15 x 25 In. 187.00
Sign, Lady Popping Popcorn, Fireside Fun, Frame, 1940-1950, 33 x 52 In. 261.00
Sign, Thank You Call Again, Paper Lithograph, c.1940, 8 3/4 x 11 1/2 In. . . . . .275.00 to 281.00
Sign, Try Dr Pepper Hot, Devilishly Different, Animated, 1950s-1960s, 13 x 24 In. 2420.00
Straws, Drink Dr Pepper, Paper, 10 In., 10 Piece 25.00
Thermometer, Drink Dr Pepper, At 10, 2 & 4, Embossed, Tin Lithograph, 17 In. 203.00
Thermometer, Hot Or Cold, Tin Lithograph, 12 x 7 1/2 In. 55.00

Tray, Brinton Brosius, Woman In Center, Tin Lithograph, Round, 10 In. . . . . .339.00 to 480.00
Tray, Drink Dr Pepper At All Soda Fountains, Black & White Dog, 3 3/8 x 2 1/4 In. 605.00
Tray, Woman, Blue Dress, 2 Bottles, Tin Lithograph, Rectangular, 1939, 13 In. 147.00
Tumbler, Good For Life!, 1940s, 3 3/4 x 2 1/4 In. 55.00
Tumbler, King Of Beverages, Red Center, White Diamond, 5 5/8 In. 8.00
Watch Fob, Billiken, Holds Paper, King Of Beverages, Silver, 1935, 2 x 1 1/4 In. 48.00

DR. DANIELS   Dr. A.C. Daniels used his picture on advertising for his
veterinary medicines starting in 1878. The Boston-based company was
incorporated in 1899. At the turn of the twentieth century, Dr. Daniels
became the first to market catnip-laced cat toys. Charles C. Rogers and
Nellie Kidder purchased the business in 1914. It was sold several times
before 1959, when Dr. Donald W. Hey purchased the product line and
moved the business to Webster, Massachusetts. Today the company's
main products are pet toys and novelties. Collectors are interested in
advertising cards and the oak cabinets with lithographed tin fronts that
were used as store displays.

Bottle, Cough, Cold, Fever, Distemper Remedy, 50 Cents, Label, Cork, Box, 4 1/2 In. . . .   12.00
Bottle, Eye Wash, For Animals, Eye Dropper, 50 Cents, Amber, Label, Cork, Box, 5 In. . .   15.00
Bottle, Family Liniment, Label Only, Contents, Box, Literature, 6 In. 77.00
Bottle, Family Liniment, Sore Cord, Muscle, 35 Cents, Embossed, Label, Box, 6 In. 46.00
Bottle, Wonder Worker Lotion, Label, Contents, Box, Literature, 6 1/2 In. 121.00
Box, Catnip Ball, Toy For Cats, Cat Scenes, 3 1/2 x 1 3/4 In. 330.00
Button, Dr. A.C. Daniels Horse Medicines, Horse, Pinback, Celluloid, 7/8 In. 440.00
Cabinet, Veterinary Medicines, Ash, 27 x 21 In. . . . . .2860.00 to 5280.00
Cabinet, Veterinary Medicines, Embossed Tin Front, Oak Case, 27 x 21 In. . . . .2310.00 to 3850.00
Display, Horse & Dog Remedies, 2-Sided, Die Cut, Hanging, 1906, 7 x 31 In. 6270.00
Mirror, Horse, Cattle & Dog Medicines, Celluloid, Round, 2 In.   121.00
Sign, Horse & Dog Medicines, For Home Treatment, Tin, Embossed, 17 x 28 In. . .248.00 to 413.00
Thermometer, Dr. A.C. Daniels, Quimby Druggist, White, Black, Wood, 21 x 5 In. 385.00
Thermometer, Veterinary Medicines, Wood, 14 In. 403.00
Tin, Dr. A.C. Daniels' Absorbent, Doctor's Image, Yellow, Contents, Round, 1 7/8 In. 72.00
Umbrella, Dr. Daniels' Gall Cure, Cloth, Tractor, 61 x 63 In. 209.00

DR. KILMER   S. Andral Kilmer, M.D., of Cobleskill, New York, was
one of eleven children. He was born in 1840 and received medical
training, eventually starting a practice in Binghamton, New York. His
practice included the preparation and sale of his own remedies, including Dr. Kilmer's Swamp Root Kidney Liver & Bladder Cure, Ocean
Weed Heart Remedy, Female Remedy, and Indian Cough & Consumption Cure. His brother Jonas, who had run the Kilmer proprietary
medicine business since 1878, bought out his brother's share of the
company in 1892. Jonas credited his son, Willis Sharpe Kilmer, with
the success of the business. It was Willis who was responsible for the
heavy advertising of Dr. Kilmer's preparations in newspapers and
almanacs. Even after Dr. Kilmer left the company, customers were
invited to write to him for advice, prompting a lawsuit by Dr. Kilmer
against his brother and nephew. In the late 1940s, the manufacturing
rights for Swamp Root were sold to MedTeck Laboratories of Cody,
Wyoming. Swamp Root is still available and Dr. Kilmer's mustachioed
likeness is still on the package.

Almanac, Swamp Root, 1906, 6 x 9 In., 32 Pages 88.00
Almanac, Swamp Root, Factory, Black & White, 1919, 8 1/2 x 6 In., 16 Pages 187.00
Blotter, Swamp Root, Dr. F.S. Gray, Druggist, 4 x 9 In. 137.00
Booklet, Like A Thief In The Night, Swamp Root, 1900, 8 3/4 x 6 In., 24 Pages 99.00
Booklet, Swamp Root Makes Friends, 2 Girls In Boat, 1904, 8 3/4 x 6 In., 24 Pages 121.00
Booklet, Well Informed Know Virtues Of Swamp Root, 1900, 8 3/4 x 6 In., 24 Pages 99.00
Booklet, What People Want To Know, M.D., 1890, 11 x 8 1/2 In., 16 Pages 154.00
Bottle, Autumn Leaf, Uterine Injection, Aqua, Paper Label, Box, 4 1/2 In. 176.00
Bottle, Complete Female Remedy, Binghamton, N.Y., Aqua, 8 3/4 In. 99.00
Bottle, Cough Medicine, Aqua, Indian On Paper Label, 30 Cents, 5 1/2 In. 110.00
Bottle, Cough-Cure Consumption Oil Specific, Dark Aqua, Embossed Lungs, 8 3/4 In. . .   99.00

Bottle, Dyspeptics Delight For Stomach, Liver & Kidneys, South Bend, Ind., 7 3/4 In. ... 132.00
Bottle, Female Remedy, Aqua, Contents, Label, $1.00, 8 3/4 In. 385.00
Bottle, Herbal Extract For Uterine Injection, Aqua, Paper Label, Cork, 4 1/2 In. 99.00
Bottle, Indian Cough Cure Consumption Oil, Indian On Paper Label, Aqua, 5 3/4 In. 99.00
Bottle, Swamp Root Kidney Cure, Embossed, Cylindrical, 4 1/4 In. 165.00
Bottle, Swamp Root Kidney Cure, London, Sample 15.00
Bottle, Swamp Root Kidney Liver & Bladder Cure Specific, Aqua, Embossed, 8 1/2 In. ... 121.00
Bottle, Swamp Root Kidney Liver & Bladder Cure, Aqua, Embossed, 5 3/4 In. 77.00
Bottle, Swamp Root, Diuretic To The Kidneys, Cylindrical, Paper Label, Cork, 4 1/4 In. . 110.00
Bottle, Threaded Top, Metal Cap, U & O Binghamton, N.Y., Embossed Base, 2 3/4 In. .. 154.00
Box, Dr. Kilmer's Headache Cure, Cardboard, Slide Tray, Contents, 2 1/2 In. 358.00
Box, Swamp Root Kidney, Liver & Bladder Cure, 1 Doz., Wood, 10 x 11 x 10 In. 209.00
Display, S. Andral Kilmer, M.D., Swamp Root, Cardboard, 9 1/2 x 6 x 3 3/4 In. 132.00
Jar, Dr. Kilmer's U & O Anointment, Shield Label, Metal Top, 50 Cents, 2 7/8 In. 154.00
Letterhead, Dr. Kilmer & Co., Manufacturing Chemists, Building, c.1910, 8 x 5 1/4 In. .. 303.00
Tin, U & O Anointment, For Piles, Catarrh, Sores, Cuts, Burns, Pins, Yellow, 1 In. Diam. . 275.00
Trade Card, Dr. Kilmer & Co., Standard Herbal Remedies, Man In Bottle, 5 x 3 In. 121.00
Trade Card, Dr. Kilmer Remedies, 3 x 5 In., 12 Piece 66.00
Vial, Dr. Kilmer's Prompt Purilla Pills, Paper Label, Contents, 3 In. 187.00

DR. MILES, see Alka-Seltzer

DUPONT Eleuthere Irenee du Pont moved to America from France in
1800. He built a gunpowder mill at Brandywine, Delaware, in 1802.
The first DuPont gunpowder was sold in cans in 1804. Two hundred
years later, E.I. DuPont de Nemours and Company remains in business
making chemicals and innovative materials. Teflon, Lycra, and Stain-
master are some of its brands. Collectors are interested in the gun-
powder-related advertising items.

Award, Trap Shooting, Lead, Bronze Finish, Quail, Shield Shape, 1907, 11 x 7 1/2 In. ... 550.00
Barrel, Smokeless Powder, Dogs, Wilmington, Del., 3 1/4 x 4 In. 77.00
Blotter, Lends A Helping Hand, Westminster Champion Dog, 1938, 3 3/4 x 8 3/4 In. 32.00
Box Insert, Shoot Standard Loads, Hunter In Kayak, 1922, 3 3/4 x 3 3/4 In. 132.00
Box Insert, Trap Shooting Scenes, 2-Sided, 1917, 3 3/4 x 3 3/4 In. 44.00
Button, Established 1802, Oval, Multicolored, Whitehead & Hoag, 1 In. 21.00
Button, Gunpowder, Oval, Celluloid, 7/8 In. 27.00
Button, Infallible, Shotgun, Smokeless, Pinback, 1 In. 66.00
Button, Prosperity Follows Dynamite, Exploding Stump, Brown & Bigelow, 1 In. ...43.00 to 67.00
Button, Smokeless Powder, Quail, Multicolored, Whitehead & Hoag, 1 1/4 In. .....61.00 to 91.00
Button, Smokeless, Champions Powder, Celluloid, Pinback, 1896, 1 1/4 In. 121.00
Buttonhook, Ivory Pyralin, 3-In. Handle, 7 1/4 x 1 In. 8.00
Calendar, 1902, Quail, Wood Cock, May To December, Frame, 14 x 28 1/2 In. 5778.00
Calendar, 1903, Geneva, Winner Of Field Champions, Paper, 30 x 20 In. 743.00
Calendar, 1974, Plovers, Golden, Black Bellied, Greater Yellow Legs, 31 x 14 In. 77.00
Calendar, DuPont & T. Jefferson, Perpetual, Tin Over Cardboard, 19 x 29 In. .....165.00 to 330.00
Calendar, Tin, Revolving, 4 Men Around Desk, 28 3/4 x 18 3/4 In. .... *Illus* 385.00
Catalog, Farmers Catalogue, How To Remove Stumps, 1910, 48 Pages 165.00
Counter Felt, Shoot DuPont Powders, Yellow, Red, Black, 11 x 8 1/4 In. 127.00
Cover, Dog Carrying Duck, E. H. Osthaus, Postmark, Stamp, 1904, 6 1/2 x 3 1/2 In. 880.00
Cover, Explosives, McIntosh Hardware, Albuquerque, New Mexico, 3 1/2 x 6 1/4 In. 55.00
Cover, Generations Have Used DuPont Powder, Man, Boy, 1903, 6 1/2 x 3 1/2 In. 231.00
Cover, Man, Canoe, Moose, Goodwin, Unused, 6 1/2 x 3 1/2 In. 380.00
Cover, Miner's Choice, Man, Train Tracks, Postmark, Stamp, 1908, 6 1/4 x 3 1/2 In. 297.00
Cover, Powders, Trap Shooting Front, Quail Back, 6 1/2 x 3 1/2 In. 88.00
Cover, Smokeless Powder, Worthington Hardware, Canceled 1901, 3 1/2 x 6 1/4 In. 319.00
Display, Select Your Loads Here, Cardboard, Stand-Up, Easel Back, 16 x 21 In. 577.00
Insert, Smokeless Shotgun Powder, Quail, Multicolored, 3 5/8 x 3 4/8 In. 31.00
Letter Opener, DuPont Explosives, Giant Powder, Pewter, 9 In. 41.00
Letter Opener, Shoot Dupont Standard Loads, Faux Ivory, 1930s, 7 1/2 In. 89.00
Pocketknife, Double Bladed, Agrichemicals, Barlow, Imperial, 3 1/2 x 1 In. 18.00
Score Card, Trap Shooting, Infallible Smokeless, Jack Panning, 4 7/16 x 3 1/8 In. 110.00
Sign, 2 Dogs, Tin, Self-Framed, 1903, 22 1/2 x 28 1/2 In. 866.00
Sign, Anti-Freeze Methanol, 30 Cent Qt., Cardboard, Frame, 30 x 21 In. 94.00

DuPont, Calendar, Tin,
Revolving, 4 Men
Around Desk,
28 3/4 x 18 3/4 In.

DuPont, Tin, Indian
Rifle Gunpowder,
Reproduction,
3 5/8 x 4 In.

Sign, Ballistite, Green Wing Teal, G. Ryder Art, Frame, 1913, 25 x 35 In.	5106.00
Sign, DuPont No. 7 Polish, Boy, Shiny Car, Die Cut, Cardboard Lithograph, Easel, 22 In.	452.00
Sign, DuPont Powders, Man, Boy, Dogs, Tin Lithograph, Self-Framed	633.00
Sign, Generations, Man, Boy, Dogs, Tin, Osthaus, Self-Framed, 1903, 33 x 23 In.	1210.00
Sign, Infallible, Broadbills, Here They Come, Lynn Bogue Hunt, 27 x 17 3/4 In.	4158.00
Sign, Shoot DuPont Powders, 3 Panels, Game Birds, Hunting Dogs, 40 1/2 x 17 1/2 In.	1155.00
Sign, Smokeless Gunpowder, Dogs, Soldiers, Buffalo, Paper, Lithograph, 14 x 33 In.	578.00
Sign, Smokeless Powder, Double With DuPont Smokeless, c.1900, 13 1/2 x 8 1/2 In.	924.00
Sign, Smokeless Shotgun Powders, Trap Shooting Event, 17 1/2 x 20 3/4 In.	3545.00
Spoon, Souvenir, Trap Shooting, Tiffany & Co., 5 3/4 x 1 1/2 In.	88.00
Stickpin, Hunting Dog, Silver Plated, 2 1/4 In.	121.00
Stickpin, Powders, Dog, Figural, Gold Plated, 3/4 x 5/16 x 2 In.	523.00
Stickpin, Quail, Gold Wash, Whitehead & Hoag, 5/8 x 2 1/4 In.	495.00
Tin, Blasting Caps, Orange, White, 2 5/8 x 2 1/4 x 1 5/8 In.	40.00
Tin, DuPont Superfine HFg Gunpowder, Brown Ground, c.1880, 4 x 3 3/4 x 1 1/4 In.	390.00
Tin, DuPont Superfine HFg Gunpowder, c.1920, 6 x 4 x 1 1/2 In.	180.00
Tin, DuPont Superfine HFg Gunpowder, Red Ground, c.1880, 5 1/2 x 4 x 1 1/2 In. .300.00 to	360.00
Tin, E.I. DuPont Nemours & Co. Powder, Wilmington, Delaware, 6 1/4 Lb., 7 3/8 x 6 In.	350.00
Tin, Indian Rifle Gunpowder, FFg, Red Ground, 1908, 4 x 3 3/4 x 1 1/2 In.	575.00
Tin, Indian Rifle Gunpowder, Paper Label, 1908, 6 x 4 x 1 1/2 In., 1 Lb.	253.00
Tin, Indian Rifle Gunpowder, Reproduction, 3 5/8 x 4 In. *Illus*	25.00
Tin, Indian Rifle Gunpowder, Screw Cap, Oval, 1859 Patent, 6 x 4 In.	105.00
Tin, Schuetzen Smokeless Powder, Hunter Graphic, 1800s, 6 1/4 x 4 In.	232.00
Tin, Smokeless Gunpowder, Label, Green, Corrugated Metal, Round, c.1893, 3 3/4 x 3 In.	75.00
Tin, Superfine FFFg Gunpowder, Oval, c.1924	144.00
Tin, Superfine Gunpowder, Oval, Wilmington, Del., 1924, 1 Lb., 6 1/2 In.	45.00
Tin, Superfine HFg, Red Paint, Screw Cap, Oval, 3/4 Size Label, c.1924, 6 x 4 In.	111.00
Toy, Train Car, Oil Carrier, 5 1/4 x 3/4 In.	10.00

DURKEE   Eugene R. Durkee began grinding and selling spices door to door in 1850 in Brooklyn, New York. He had been making ground mustard and other products for druggists, but expanded his line to include spices, extracts, and related products. He was one of the men chosen to help the U.S. government write specifications for the 1906 Pure Food and Drug Act. Eugene W. Durkee, the son of the founder, was a collector of arms and armaments and chose the firm's early trademarks—"Gauntlet" for top-quality products and "Helmet" for those of lesser quality. Neither mark is in use today. The Glidden Company acquired E.R. Durkee & Company in 1929. It was sold several times and is now part of Tone Brothers, Inc., a division of Burns Philp.

Cookie Cutter & Holiday Recipe Book Set, In Package, 6 Cutters, 1970	20.00
Display Box, Food Products, Pearl Tapioca, Wood, Hinged Lid, Paper Label, 7 x 20 In.	110.00
Jar, Famous Dressing & Meat Sauce, Label, 2 Oz., 4 In.	9.00
Tin, Durkee's Mustard, Slide Lid, Durkee Famous Foods, Elmhurst, New York	12.00
Tin, Durkee's Savory, Celery Salt, Back Advertisement, 3 1/4 x 2 3/8 x 1 1/2 In.	95.00
Tin, Pumpkin Pie Spice, 1 7/8 Oz., 2 3/4 In.	11.00

EASTMAN KODAK George Eastman invented a camera in Rochester, New York, and was selling it by 1888. He knew that the public considered cameras fearful things and that his advertising had to stress workability. He also had to create demand for pictures taken at home. He named his invention the Brownie camera after a popular comic character. He dreamed up the brand name Kodak because he wanted a word that sounded incisive and distinctive. The company has been called Eastman Kodak since 1892.

Ashtray, Kodak Park Athletic Assoc., Smoky Glass, 1910-1960, 5 3/4 x 3 3/4 In.	16.00
Camera, Brownie, No. 2, Box, 6 In.	88.00
Camera, Target Six-20, Black Metal Box, 1946-1952, 2 1/4 x 3 1/4 In.	30.00
Display Case, Film, Ed Sullivan, Yellow, Blue, Red, 15 x 8 In.	22.00
Sign, Developing, Printing, Enlarging, 2-Sided, Metal, Hanging, Bracket, 17 x 17 In.	3300.00
Sign, Kodak Film, Verichrome Safety Film, Die Cut, Metal, 2-Sided, 18 x 14 In.	99.00
Sign, Kodaks, Yellow Ground, 2-Sided, Porcelain, 12 x 30 In.	248.00
Tin, Kodak Developer, Key Wind, 3 1/2 x 2 1/8 In.	38.00
Toy, Projector, Kodatoy, Hand Crank, Electric Light, 2 Film Rolls, 16 mm, c.1931	125.00

EDISON MAZDA, see General Electric

FALSTAFF The Falstaff shield was introduced in 1896 and registered in 1903 by the William J. Lemp Brewing Company of St. Louis, Missouri. The Lemp family, in the brewing business since 1840, went out of business during Prohibition. The German Griesedieck family was living in St. Louis by the 1870s and several members of the family worked in the brewery business. In 1917 Joseph Griesedieck purchased a small existing plant and named it Griesedieck Beverage Company. The Griesedieck Beverage Company bought the Falstaff trademark in 1920 and became the Falstaff Corp. It survived Prohibition by making soft drinks, near-beer, and smoked hams. In 1933, when Prohibition came to an end, the company became Falstaff Brewing Corp. Another branch of the family started Griesedieck Brothers during the early 1900s. It became part of Falstaff in 1957. Falstaff's brands included Falstaff, Narragansett, Ballantine Ale, Ballantine Beer, and Hattenietter Malt Liquor. Falstaff's last brewery closed in 1990. The brand is now owned by Pabst and has limited distribution. Sir John Falstaff was a comic character in Shakespeare's plays who is best known for the saying, "Eat, drink, and be merry."

Beer Can, Lucky Lager, Aluminum, Pull Tab, 12 Oz.	5.00
Calendar Holder, Metal, 10 x 24 In.	160.00
Can, Aluminum, Pull Tab, 12 Oz.	2.50
Can, Falstaff 96 Extra Light, Pull Tab, 12 Oz.	2.50
Can, Generic Light Beer, Pull Tab, 12 Oz.	2.50
Figure, Man Holding Sign, Bottle, Chalkware, 16 1/4 x 9 1/2 x 7 1/2 In.	125.00
Plate, Jack Falstaff, Tin, No. 206, Dresden Art Plate Co., Meek Co., 9 3/4 In.	110.00
Salt & Pepper, Amber Glass, Metal Lids, Box, 3 7/8 In.	27.50
Score Pad, Gin Rummy, Old Falstaff Beer, 8 Sheets, 8 3/4 x 7 5/8 In.	13.00

FAN Advertising fans were popular giveaways in the days before air conditioning. Many list the names of funeral parlors or casket makers because the fans were distributed at church services and funerals. Collectors seek the unusually shaped fan and those with early dates or company associations. The stiff circle of paper with a single handle is most common. Only a few are the ribbed, folding type.

666 Laxative Tonic, Die Cut Cardboard, Balsa Wood Handle, 1936, 7 x 7 1/2 In.	15.00
Bradley Knit Wear, Swimsuits, Cardboard, Wooden Handle, c.1930, 7 x 8 In.	20.00
Burke Drug Co., Come To Us For It, Morganton, N.C., 14 3/4 In.	16.00
Endicott Johnson Shoes, Valley Of Fair Play, Die Cut Thumb Hole, 9 1/2 x 10 1/2 In.	18.00
Excelsior Flour, Indian Chief Black Hawk, Wooden Handle, Round, 8 1/2 In.	121.00
Independent Insurance Co., Addresses, Office Pictures, 1920-1975	5.00
Independent Life Insurance, Jacksonville, Fla., Building, Paper, Hand Colored, 1930s, Pair	10.00
Keen Kutter, Headquarters, Simmons Hardware, Ax, Paper, 1904, 12 1/2 x 8 In.	220.00
Kiss-Me, Chewing Gum, Paper, 9 1/2 x 15 In.	66.00

Lamb's Music House, Pottstown, Pa., Flapper Bathing Beauty, 1920s, 10 1/2 x 9 3/4 In. . .   22.00
Sorin Cognac, Green Cloaked Figure In White, Holding Glass, 7 1/2 In. 25.00

FIGURE   Many companies made large figures for display on the floor or counter of a store. These could be made of ceramic, plaster, wood, or metal. The full-size cigar-store Indian is probably the best-known early figure and is classed as folk art, not advertising. Small figurines of glass, ceramic, plaster, or plastic have been used as advertising promotion pieces since the nineteenth century. Most have the company or product name clearly molded or printed on the base. A few have just a well-known company trademark, such as the Pillsbury Doughboy or Elsie the Borden cow.

Abbot's Choice Scotch Whisky, Abbot, Extended Hand, Rubberoid, England, 7 In.	104.00
Black & White Scotch Whisky, 2 Scottie Dogs, 10 1/2 x 3 x 8 In.	65.00
Black & White Scotch Whisky, 2 Scottie Dogs, Black Base, Plastic, 6 1/4 In.	20.00
Black & White Scotch Whisky, 2 Scottie Dogs, Cast Iron, England, 5 In.	136.00
Black & White Scotch Whisky, 2 Scottie Dogs, White Base, Ceramic, 6 1/4 In.	156.00
Blue Jay Corn Plasters, Don't Whittle Corns, Rocking Base, Tin, Die Cut, 13 x 6 In.	1210.00
Booth's Gin, Lion, Plaster, 9 1/4 In.	81.00
Brickwoods, Brewer Holding Mug Of Beer Aloft, Rubberoid, 6 In.	121.00
Captain Morgan, Rum, Rubberoid, 4 3/4 In.	55.00
Captain Morgan, Rum, Rubberoid, Square Base, 12 1/2 In.	243.00
Chivas Regal, Knight On Horseback, Scotland's Prince Of Whiskies, Rubberoid, 11 1/4 In.	142.00
Cognac Hine, Stag, Lying Down, Rubberoid, 10 1/4 In.	31.00
Crescent Tool, Cardboard, Stand-Up, 4 1/2 x 5 1/2 In.	28.00
Davison Chemical, Glazed Ceramic, White Face, Green Hat, Black Accents, 5 1/4 In.	38.00
Dewar's Scotch Whisky, Pipe Major, Rocky Base, Rubberoid, England, 9 3/4 In. . . .51.00 to 123.00
Double Diamond, Works Wonders, Man, Suit, Long Stride, Bottle, Briefcase, England, 8 In.	246.00
Eskimo Pie, Animated Eskimo, Arm Goes Up & Down, Electric, 32 In.	468.00
Fisk, Automaton, Boy With Candle & Tire, Time To Re-Tire, Get A Fisk, c.1920, 45 In. . .	4715.00
Florsheim, Shoe, Painted, 3 1/2 In.	40.00
Flowers Keg Bitter, Shakespeare's Bust, Rubberoid, Gold Letters, 10 In. . . . . .145.00 to 152.00
Free-Flex By Freeman, Shoe On Wooden Box, Shoe Flexes, 16 x 5 1/2 x 10 5/8 In.	439.00
Haig Whisky, Eagle, Great Scot!, Sarreguemines, France, 11 1/4 In.	1053.00
Hennessey Cognac, Richard Hennessy, Bottle, Man, Tricornered Hat, Plastic, 14 In.	132.00
Hoff's Malt, Dwarf, Long Beard, Composition, Embossed Letters, Countertop, 19 In.	385.00
Hunter Beverage, Man & Horse Leaping Fence, Pot Metal, 14 x 14 In.	77.00
Hush Puppies, Dog, Styrofoam, 17 In.	22.00
Inter-Woven Line, Wood, Trolley, Driver, Passengers, Suitcases, 17 1/2 x 12 In.	1100.00
Jacquins Cordials, Black Man, Holding Bottle Of Apricot Liqueur, Chalkware, 14 3/4 In. .	258.00
Kessler Whiskey, Man In Top Hat, Bowling Ball, Chalkware, 14 In.	132.00
King George IV's Bust, Old Scotch Whisky, Rubberoid, England, 14 1/2 In. . . . . . . .85.00 to 172.00
Lamb Knit Sweaters, 100% Pure Wool, Lamb, Papier-Mache, 14 1/2 x 16 1/2 In.	440.00
Lionstone Whiskey, Man, Bowtie, Black Hat & Coat, Red Vest, Ceramic, 14 In.	28.00
Long John, Scotch They Drink In Scotland, Scotsman Holding Glass, Rubberoid, 8 1/4 In.	114.00
Long John Scotch Whisky, Pirate, Parrot On Shoulder, Barrel, Plaster, England, 11 In. . . .	189.00
Lord Calvert, Cavalier, America's Whiskey Of Distinction, Ceramic, 16 x 5 In.	22.00
Lord Calvert Whiskey, Cavalier, Black, Wide Brim Hat, Sword, Chalkware, 24 In.	44.00
Martell Cognac, Man, Monocle, Holding Glass, Make Friends, Plastic, 7 3/4 In. . . . .34.00 to 61.00
Mazda, Lightbulb, Papier-Mache, 31 In.	176.00
Miss Dairylea, Red Dress, Vinyl, 1960s, 6 In.	65.00
National Tailoring Co., Man In Tuxedo, Oak Base, 32 In.	1045.00
Old Grand Dad, Head Of Bourbon Family, Rubberoid, White, England, 11 1/2 In.	38.00
Old Smuggler Scotch, Man In Scottish Uniform, 27 In.	44.00
Punch & Judy Kiddies Socks, Metal Top, Wood Base, 16 1/2 x 20 In.	757.00
Queen Anne Scotch Whisky, Woman, Burgundy Dress, Plastic, England, 9 1/2 In.	85.00
R.B. Rice's Country Sausage, Pig, Sold Here, Plaster, 4 1/2 x 9 In.	105.00
Remy Martin, Centaur, Throwing Spear, Plastic, Gold Color, England, 9 1/2 In.	38.00
Robin Hood Shoes, Robin Hood, Chalkware, c.1910, 15 In.	77.00
Seaforth Cologne, Scotsman Holds Bottle, Chalkware, 10 In.	83.00
Tagamet, Stomach, Arms, Legs, Vinyl, Flexible, Smith, Kline & French, 1988, 5 In. .10.00 to 14.00
Teacher's Highland Cream Scotch Whisky, Teacher, Scroll, Rubberoid, England, 14 In. . .	681.00
Walrath & Sherwood Lumber Co., Lion, Omaha, Nebraska, Brass, 4 1/2 x 2 In.	95.00

Watta Pop, Lollipop, Bulldog Shape, Chalkware, 7 x 5 1/4 x 6 3/4 In. 172.00
White Horse Scotch Whisky, Horse, Old King Cole, c.1940s 44.00
White Horse Scotch Whisky, Horse, Plastic, Blue Base, 8 1/2 In. 31.00
Williams & Humbert, Sherry Girl Holding Tray, Ceramic, England, 5 3/4 In. 38.00
Wilson Packing Co., Sow, Wood, Carved, Multicolored, Applied Letters, 25 In. 719.00

FLEISCHMANN'S YEAST   Charles and Maximilian Fleischmann and
James Gaff formed Gaff, Fleischmann & Company in Cincinnati,
Ohio, in 1868. The company made the first commercial compressed
yeast in the United States. Before this, bakers had to use their own
homemade, and sometimes inferior, yeast. The idea of manufactured
yeast was slow to gain popularity; but in 1876 the company sponsored
a bakery at the Philadelphia Centennial Exposition to promote its product. The company's name changed to The Fleischmann Company in
1905. It became part of Standard Brands in 1929 and merged with
Nabisco in 1981. Today Fleischmann's Yeast is a division of Burns
Philp Food, Inc. Fleischmann advertising includes cookbooks, pamphlets, and other materials promoting yeast. Tin store display containers for yeast cakes, to be eaten daily as a health aid, can also be found.

Booklet, Good Things To Eat Made With Bread, 1912, 6 x 4 3/4 In., 15 Pages 18.00
Calendar, 1888, 12 Cards, Paper Lithograph, Frame, 6 1/2 x 5-In. Cards 170.00
Cookbook, Fleischmann's Treasury Of Yeast Baking, 1962, 51 Pages 8.00
Trade Card, Moonlit Water, Pansies, 1890s, 3 1/2 x 5 1/2 In. 12.00
Tray, Compressed Yeast, Woman, Child, Making Dough, Round, 10 1/4 In. 1045.00

FRY'S   In 1729 Walter Churchman received a Letters Patent for
chocolate from King George II. Twenty years later, Dr. Joseph Fry
began teaching himself chocolate recipes at his Bristol, England,
apothecary. In 1761 Dr. Fry purchased the Churchman patent and
recipes. After Dr. Fry's death in 1787, his wife, Anna, and son, Joseph
Storrs Fry, changed the firm's name to J.S. Fry & Sons. The business
remained in the family for until 1919, when it merged financial interests with Cadbury. In 1935 Fry's became a wholly owned subsidiary of
Cadbury. Cadbury merged with Schweppes in 1969. The Fry's brand
name is still found on two of the company's original products, Fry's
Chocolate Cream and Fry's Turkish Delight. Fry's advertising memorabilia can be found in abundance. One of the most famous, the "Fry's
5 Boys" advertisement ("Desperation, pacification, expectation, accla-
mation, realisation…It's Fry") was first used in 1885.

Advertisement, Illustrated London News, Woman Holds Cup Of Cocoa, 1890, 16 x 11 In.   32.00
Cabinet, Fry's Chocolate, Bowed Glass, Mirrored Door, England, 26 1/2 x 17 3/4 x 10 In.   757.00
Cabinet, Fry's Chocolate, Glass Front, Sides, Shelves, Mirror, 32 3/4 x 19 1/2 x 14 1/2 In.   1135.00
Display Case, Choice Chocolate, 4 Glass Shelves, Mirrored, England, 37 x 21 x 7 In. 1987.00
Display Case, J.S. Fry & Sons, Chocolate, Cocoa, Sloping Glass Front, 36 x 11 x 12 In. . .   322.00
Mug, Fry's Hot Chocolate, Duraline Super Vitrified Grindley Hotelware, England 20.00
Sign, Fry's Chocolate, 5 Boys, Blue, Enamel, Wood Frame, England, 37 1/2 x 31 1/2 In. .   1041.00
Sign, Fry's Chocolate, Red Ground, Brown Circle, Man's Profile, England, 20 x 20 In. . . .   303.00
Sign, Fry's High Class Chocolate, Blue Shield, White Ground, Enamel, England, 19 x 15 In.   341.00

GAS PUMP GLOBE, see Auto, Gas Pump Globe

GENERAL ELECTRIC   Thomas A. Edison established the Edison Light
Company in 1878 and the Edison General Electric Company in 1889.
In 1892 General Electric Company was formed through the merger of
Edison General Electric and the Thomson-Houston Electric Company.
Advertising campaigns have included "We Bring Good Things to
Life," "Progress Is Our Most Important Product," "Live Better Elec-
trically," and "Imagination at Work." Many types of advertising mate-
rials have been issued by the company, which is still in business. GE's
oldest advertising collectibles are the most in demand.

Ashtray, GE Logo, Metal, 1950s, 4 In. 18.00
Bank, Stack Of U.S. Dollars, Silver, Plastic, 1970, 4 1/2 x 3 In. 18.00
Calendar, 1921, Edison Mazda, Primitive Man, Parrish, Frame, 22 5/8 x 12 3/8 In. 2310.00

Calendar, 1925, Edison Mazda, Small Dream Light, Parrish, Frame, 20 3/4 x 10 7/8 In. . .	468.00
Calendar, 1928, Edison Mazda, Contentment, Parrish, Frame, 20 x 9 3/8 In.	523.00
Calendar, 1930, Edison Mazda, Ecstasy, Parrish, Envelope, 19 1/8 x 8 1/2 In.	688.00
Calendar, 1931, Edison Mazda, Waterfall, Parrish, No Pad, Frame, 41 1/4 x 22 1/2 In. . . .	1485.00
Calendar, 1932, Edison Mazda, Solitude, Woman, Sunlit Canyon, Parrish, 20 x 9 1/2 In. . .	550.00
Calendar, 1933, Edison Mazda, Sunrise, 2 Women On Balcony, 22 1/2 x 12 In.	220.00
Calendar, 1933, Edison Mazda, Sunrise, 2 Women, Sunlit Canyon, Parrish, 20 x 9 1/4 In. .	770.00
Calendar, 1938, Edison Mazda, Egyptian Priestess, Parrish, 19 1/8 x 8 1/2 In. . . . .468.00 to 798.00
Display, Edison Mazda Lamps, Father, Daughter On Doorstep, Folding, Cardboard, c.1930	1073.00
Display, Edison Mazda Lamps, Suns Only Rival, Cardboard, Stand-Up, Pair	495.00
Display, Edison Mazda Lamps, Trifold Shadowbox, Light Bulb, Cardboard, 30 x 26 In. . .	605.00
Display Rack, Mazda Light Bulbs, How Are You Fixed For Lamps, Half Moon Shape . . .	1650.00
Figure, Radio Man, Bandy, Wood Ball Joint, Composition, 18 In.	1160.00
Glass, Appliances Around Garland, R. Cooper Jr., Inc., 1940, 3 3/4 x 2 1/2 In.	22.00
Pin, GE Logo, Figural Motor, Silver Metal, 2 1/3 x 1 1/2 In.	29.00
Sign, Edison Mazda Lamps, Lady, Box, Die Cut, Cardboard, c.1930, 28 x 15 In.	3960.00
Sign, GE Fans, Buy Them Here, Porcelain, Flange, 11 3/4 x 16 In.	1760.00
Sign, Good-Bye To Bulb Snatching, GE Lamps, Mazda, Cardboard, Easel, 21 x 12 5/8 In. .	121.00
Sign, TV & Radio Tubes, Tin, Flange, 2-Sided, 12 x 16 1/2 In.	248.00
Tape Measure, Edison Mazda Lamps, Get Together, Parrish, Celluloid, 1 1/2 x 1/2 In. . . .	303.00
Tape Measure, Mazda Bulbs, Paper Envelope, 48 In.	13.00
Tape Measure, Refrigerators, Blue, Black, White, Green, 1 1/4 In.	67.00
Tumbler, GE Greetings, R. Cooper Jr., Garland, Gold Decoration, 1940, 3 3/4 x 2 1/2 In. .	22.00

GILLETTE   King Camp Gillette was a salesman who thought that a perfect product would be one that was used once or twice and then thrown away. He decided on a disposable razor blade while shaving, but he needed help and six years of trials before the Gillette razor was introduced in 1903. He put his own face and signature on the package. The company, acuired by Proctor & Gamble in 2005 makes a number of products, including Gillette razors, Right Guard deodorant, Duracell batteries, and Oral-B toothbrushes.

Box, Blue Blades In Dispenser, King C. Gillette, Cardboard, 9 1/2 x 5 x 2 3/4 In.	33.00
Display, 10 Blade Dispenser, 5 Packages, Countertop, Easel Back, 12 1/2 x 9 In.	88.00
Display Case, Blue Letters, Plastic, Countertop	50.00
Display Case, Razors, Blades, Wood, 3 Compartments, Glass, Hinged Lift Top, 3 x 18 In. .	72.00
Display Case, White Letters, Plastic, Countertop	28.00
Mirror, Safety Razor, Shave Yourself, No Stropping, No Honing, Yellow, Black, 2 In.	43.00
Mirror, Safety Razors, Baby Shaving, Calendar, Celluloid, Round, 1909, 2 1/8 In.	120.00
Trade Card, Baby Shaving, Frame, 5 x 3 1/4 In.	44.00

GINGER BEER   Ginger beer was originally made from fermented ginger root, cream of tartar, sugar, yeast, and water. It was a popular drink from the 1850s to the 1920s. Today it is an alcohol-free carbonated drink similar to soda. Pottery ginger beer bottles have been made since the mid-1700s. A few products are still bottled in stoneware containers today. Ginger beer, vinegar, and cider were usually put in stoneware holders until the 1930s. The ginger beer bottle usually held 10 ounces. Blob tops, tapered collars, and crown tops were used. Some were closed with a cork, others with a lightning stopper or inside screw topper. The bottles were shades of brown and white. Some were saltglazed for a slightly rough, glossy finish. Bottles were stamped or printed with names and usually the words *ginger beer*.

Bottle, F.E. Coverdale & Son, Kirby Moorside, Pottery, England, 8 In.	31.00
Bottle, Firth's Darlington Brewed, Locomotive, Blue Print, Pottery, England, 7 1/4 In. . . .	61.00
Bottle, Gilbert Rae, Dunfermline, Green Top, Black Transfer, Pottery, England, 7 In.	41.00
Bottle, Hay & Sons, Brown Print, Pottery, England, 8 1/2 In.	45.00
Bottle, Hay & Sons, Large Logo, Trade Mark, Registered, Elgin, c.1900, 11 In.	35.00
Bottle, James Alexander, Stone Ginger Beer, Aberdeen, Pottery, Blue Print, 8 3/4 In.	41.00
Bottle, John Milne Brewed, Stonehaven, Brown Print, Pottery, England, 9 1/4 In.	20.00
Bottle, North & Randall, Aylesbury, Pottery, England, 6 3/4 In.	123.00
Bottle, Pink's, None Nicer, Stoneware, Chichester, 6 3/4 In.	35.00
Bottle, Prime, London Super Aeration, Green Top, Black Transfer, Pottery, London, 7 In. .	55.00

Bottle, R. Stothert & Sons, Ginger Beer, Atherton, Bearded Man, Pottery, England, 8 In. . . 409.00
Bottle, T. Wright, Stockton On Tees, Red Print, Pottery, England, 8 In. 286.00
Bottle, W&J Jenkinson, Leith, Seahorse, Pottery, England, 9 In. 72.00
Match Striker, Taylor's, Hop Bitters, Stone Ginger Beer, Round, 2 x 4 1/2 In. 41.00

GOLD DUST   Gold Dust products were made by the N.K. Fairbank
Soap Company of Chicago, Illinois, from the 1880s until the 1930s,
when the company was purchased by Lever Brothers. Fairbank made
many brands of soap: Fairy, Santa Claus, Lakeside, and Gold Dust
(introduced in 1880). The Gold Dust Twins trademark, two black chil-
dren sitting in a tub of water, was registered in 1884. The advertising
suggested that Gold Dust could clean the kitchen, brass, and wood, and
could keep sink pipes unclogged. The black twins were used with the
slogan, "Fast Colors Warranted to Wash Clean and Not Fade." Another
slogan was "Let the Gold Dust Twins Do Your Work." The original
Gold Dust characters were drawn by E.W. Kemble, an important illus-
trator of the time. Live twins were hired to hand out booklets at the
1904 St. Louis World's Fair. There was a Gold Dust Twins radio show
in 1925, but the brand disappeared in the 1930s. The idea of the twins
lived on with the Silver Dust twins, two blond girls who promoted
Lever Brothers Silver Dust soap.

Box, 5 Cents Size, Unopened, 6 1/2 x 4 1/2 x 2 In. 64.00
Box, Let The Gold Dust Twins Do Your Work, Hinged Lid, 27 x 12 In. 66.00
Box, Soap Chiplets, Color, Twins, Contents, c.1920s, 12 Oz. . . . . *Illus* 688.00
Box, Unopened, 8 3/4 x 6 x 3 In. 51.00
Box, Washing Powder, Orange Ground, 5 In. 77.00
Case, Sample Boxes, 60 Boxes 990.00
Display, Let The Twins Do Your Work, 60 In. 18000.00
Mirror, Fairbank's Gold Dust Washing Powder, 2 x 3 In. 40.00
Sign, Fairbank's Gold Dust Washing Powder, Cardboard, Hanger, 10 1/2 x 7 1/2 In. 110.00
Sign, Trolley Card, 14 1/2 x 25 In. 1208.00
Soap Dish, Black Baby Looking At Mouse, 2 x 4 In. 59.00

GOODYEAR   The Goodyear blimp is one of the most famous advertising items in America. There are other Goodyear advertising pieces,
including rubber-tire ashtrays, pictures of the blimp, banks, toys, and
the usual key chain or tie tack souvenirs. In 1930 the company issued
a line of souvenirs made from Duralumin, the actual metal left over
from making the skeleton of a blimp. Charles Goodyear (1800–1860),
a Connecticut inventor, had accidentally discovered how to vulcanize
rubber in 1839 when he spilled some India rubber and sulfur on a hot
stove. He obtained patents in the United States, and after many legal
battles and an attempt to start a factory in France, he was put in a Paris
debtors prison for not paying his bills. He died in poverty in New York
City. Frank and Charles Seiberling of Akron, Ohio, started a bicycle
and carriage tire manufacturing plant in 1898 and called it Goodyear
Tire & Rubber Company in honor of Charles Goodyear. Frank had a
statue of Mercury in his home and decided to use the winged foot of
Mercury as part of the company's trademark. Mercury is the ancient
Roman god of trade and the herald of good news.

Calendar, 1949, Boy Scout, Dad, Looking At Planes & Eagle, 37 1/2 x 20 1/2 In. 175.00
Container, French Talc, Cardboard, Cylindrical, 6 3/4 In. 154.00
Plaque, Cast Iron, Embossed, Friendly Relations, Elm Cycle & Auto, 17 1/2 x 12 In. 154.00
Radiator Cover, Goodyear Tires, Ned Lambert, Model T, Stenciled, Cardboard, 18 1/2 In. 110.00
Sign, Balloon Tire, Die Cut, Black, White, Yellow, 34 x 22 In. 1600.00
Sign, Goodyear Service Station, Tire Around World, Porcelain, 84 x 48 In. 990.00
Sign, Goodyear Tires, Craig's Repair Shop, Tin, Embossed, 12 x 22 In. 880.00
Sign, Goodyear Tires, Porcelain, 39 x 60 In. 330.00
Sign, Goodyear Tires, Porcelain, 94 x 16 In. 715.00
Sign, Goodyear Tires, Porcelain, 96 x 18 In. 220.00
Sign, Pay Weekly, No Interest, 55 x 40 In. 55.00
Sign, Service Station, Porcelain, 24 x 72 In. 770.00
Sign, Tires, 2-Sided, Diamond Shape, Porcelain, Brackets, 48 x 27 In. . . . . .242.00 to 385.00

Gold Dust, Box, Soap Chiplets,
Color, Twins, Contents,
c.1920s, 12 Oz.

Grape-Nuts, Sign, Girl, St.
Bernard, Tin Lithograph,
Self-Framed, c.1916, 20 x 31 In.

Greyhound, Sign, Ticket Office,
Porcelain, Die Cut, 2-Sided,
1920s, 25 x 30 In.

GRAPE-NUTS   C.W. Post went into business in Battle Creek, Michigan, in 1895. He spent $68.76 for a secondhand stove, a peanut roaster, coffee grinder, packages, two bushels of wheat, two hundred pounds of bran, and ten jugs of molasses. He used these ingredients to make his coffee substitute, Postum. The beverage sold well, and in 1897 he started to make a cereal he called Grape-Nuts. The company prospered, and between 1925 and 1929 it acquired ten other firms, including others listed in this book: Jell-O, Log Cabin Syrup, Maxwell House coffee, and Walter Baker chocolate (listed under Baker). In 1929 Post added Birdseye Frozen Foods and a small company named General Foods. Post took the name General Foods as its corporate name in 1929. Grape-Nuts brands are now part of Altria's Kraft Foods Company. One of the great advertisements of all time is the Grape-Nuts ad showing a girl, her St. Bernard dog, and the slogan "To School Well Fed on Grape-Nuts, There's a Reason." The tin sign has become so popular it has been reproduced in a slightly smaller size.

Button, Dale Evan's Horse Buttermilk, Pinback, Made In U.S.A., 1953	15.00
Button, Post Grape-Nuts Flakes, R.B., Roys Brand, Tin Lithograph, 1953	23.00
Creamer, Scottie Dog, Cereal Premium, 5 1/4 In.	20.00 to 22.50
Jar, Malted Grape-Nuts, Made Of Wheat & Barley, Glass, Chrome Lid, Label, 8 x 6 In.	440.00
Sign, Girl, St. Bernard, Tin Lithograph, Self-Framed, c.1916, 20 x 31 In. .... *Illus*	3520.00
Stringholder, Every Table Should Have Its Daily Ration, 1900-1910, 11 1/2 In.	743.00

GREEN RIVER WHISKEY   J.W. McCulloch arrived in Owensboro, Kentucky, between 1880 and 1890. He worked in a distillery and soon started his own Green River distillery. The Green River brand was the best known in the area because of the number of advertising premiums it gave away. Watch fobs, mirrors, and signs were popular. Green River's slogan was "The Whiskey without a Headache." The company was bought by a New York firm just before the distillery burned down in 1918. Green River is also the name of a soft drink.

Dispenser, Glass Center, Metal Base, Original Jug, c.1910, 17 In.	286.00
Dispenser, Porcelain, Embossed Logo, Nickel Plated Spigot, 16 x 10 In.	825.00
Figure, Black Man, Horse, Whiskey Without Regrets, Spelter, 1900s, 5 1/2 In.	393.00
Figure, Black Man, Horse, Without Regrets Jug, Hard Rubber, 10 x 13 In.	230.00
Sign, Black Man, Horse, Cardboard Lithograph, Frame, 14 x 19 In.	181.00
Sign, Black Man, Horse, Tin, Self-Framed, 23 x 32 In.	880.00
Sign, Black Man, Mule, Paper, Frame, c.1930, 6 1/2 x 8 1/2 In.	165.00
Sign, Drink Green River, Served Here, Moon, River, Tin Over Cardboard, 4 1/4 x 12 In.	440.00
Sign, Oak Frame, McCrary & Branson, Knoxville, Tenn., c.1899, 22 1/2 In.	176.00
Sign, She Was Bred In Old Kentucky, Tin Lithograph, Gilt Frame, 23 x 32 In.	593.00
Tray, Black Man & Horse, Charles W. Schaump Tin Lithograph, Round, 12 In.	303.00
Tray, Without A Headache, She Was Bred In Old Kentucky, 9 In. Diam.	314.00

GREYHOUND The origin of the name Greyhound for a bus line is unclear. Some sources say it was a bus line between Los Angeles and Bakersfield, California, in 1912. Whether or not that's true, the name was used by an intercity bus line, based in Muskegon, Michigan, in 1921. Frank Fageol, owner of the Muskegon line, had painted his buses gray and used the slogan "Ride the Greyhounds." Carl Eric Wickman, who had started a bus line from Hibbing to Alice, Minnesota, in 1914, bought, merged, and maneuvered various bus lines, including Fageol's greyhounds, to form the Motor Transit Corp. in 1926. In 1929 the company became the Greyhound Corp. and it began using the running dog symbol. For years starting in 1957, a real dog named Lady Greyhound was used on promotional tours. Greyhound Corp. divested its U.S. bus lines in 1987. The new bus company, Greyhound Lines, Inc., established its headquarters in Dallas, Texas.

Clock, Go Greyhound & Leave The Driving To Us, Light-Up, c.1950	396.00
Display Rack, Depot Map, c.1940s	330.00
Display Rack, Depot Timetable, c.1940s	688.00
Model, Bus, Cast Aluminum, Yellow, Blue, Gray Bus Co., Display, 6 x 24 In.	4675.00
Sign, Bus Flag Stop, Blue, White, Porcelain, Oval	440.00
Sign, Greyhound Lines, Blue, White, Orange, Porcelain, Oval	1265.00
Sign, Ticket Office, Porcelain On Steel, 2-Sided, c.1930, 25 x 31 In.	2800.00
Sign, Ticket Office, Porcelain, Die Cut, 2-Sided, 1920s, 25 x 30 In. .... *Illus*	9900.00
Toy, Bus, Aluminum, Dubuque Toy Co., Box, 3 x 9 1/4 x 2 1/4 In.	275.00
Toy, Bus, No. 755, Pressed Steel, Windup, Buddy L, Box, 16 In.	715.00

GUINNESS It was New Year's Eve, 1759, when Arthur Guinness signed a 9,000-year lease on a rundown Dublin brewery. Despite the nearly seventy breweries in the city, Irish ale was of poor quality, beer was almost unknown in rural parts of the country, and English products dominated the market. Arthur Guinness changed all that, brewing ales and a dark beer that became known as "porter." Eventually, Guinness porter, later called Guinness Stout, sold so well that English imports to Ireland disappeared and Guinness captured a share of the English market as well. Print advertisements for Guinness didn't appear until 1929. Slogans have included "Guinness is good for you," and "Guinness for strength." The toucan and a menagerie of other animals and their zookeeper started representing the brew in 1935 and appeared in Guinness ads through the 1950s. At one time the Guinness brewery was the largest brewery in the world. Guinness is now brewed in thirty-five countries. Guinness merged with GrandMet in 1997, forming Diageo.

Advertisement, Bottle, Wood Frame, England, 35 1/2 x 17 1/2 In.	66.00
Advertisement, Extra Stout, Laminated Card, 9 3/4 x 7 1/2 In.	265.00
Ashtray, Good For You, White, Red, Beer Glass, England, 5 3/4 x 4 1/2 In. .... .41.00 to 79.00
Ashtray, Guinness & Bass Beer, M.B. Fisher & Sons, Brass	55.00
Ashtray, Stout, Round, Brown Ground, White Letters, Ceramic, 5 In.	19.00
Ashtray & Matchbox Holder, Good For You, Center Barrel, Mintons, 3 3/4 x 5 1/2 In. ...	75.00
Badge, Mug Shape, Metal	51.00
Banner, For Strength, Zookeeper, Animals, Tug Of War, Canvas, England, 33 x 170 In. ..	284.00
Barometer, Lovely Day For A Guinness, Gold Letters, Wood, Round, England, 8 In.	38.00
Bottle, Extra Stout, Celebrated, Dunfermline, Green Top, Pottery, England, 7 In.	76.00
Bottle, Extra Stout, Matthew Knott, Blue Top, Pottery, England, 8 In.	76.00
Bottle, Stout, Miniature, 3 1/2 In.	5.00
Bowl, Pudding, Zookeeper, Animals, T.G. Green & Co., Church Gresley, 3 3/4 x 6 In.	61.00
Button, Waistcoat Set, Zookeeper, Animals, Orange Ground, Box, England, 6 Piece	79.00
Button, Waistcoat Set, Zookeeper, Animals, White Ground, Box, England, 6 Piece	79.00
Button, Waistcoat, Zookeeper, Animals, Box, Compliments Of Guinness, 6 Piece	65.00
Button, Zookeeper, Animals, 4 Piece	20.00
Cigarette Lighter, Indian Brave In Canoe, Guinness Him Strong, England	132.00
Clock, Guinness Time, Light-Up, Red, White, 11 3/4 x 5 1/2 In.	60.00
Dish, Cheese, Cover, Verse, Carltonware, 4 1/4 In.	20.00
Dish, Cover, Fireside Scene, 2 Men, Woman, Carltonware, England, 4 1/4 In.	19.00

Dish, Cover, Harp, Hops, Barley, Carltonware, 4 1/4 In. 20.00
Dish, Cover, Toucans, White Glaze, Carltonware, England, 4 1/4 In. . . . . 41.00 to 51.00
Dish, Cover, Verse, No Cheese In All The World, Carltonware, England, 4 1/4 In. 19.00
Dish, Cover, Zookeeper & Animals, Toucan, T.G. Green, Church Gresley, 4 3/4 In. . . 65.00 to 85.00
Display, Stout, Kangaroo Brand, Tin On Card, Stand-Up, 14 x 11 1/2 In. 681.00
Figure, Guinness Toucan, Wall Hanging, 2 Glasses Of Beer On Beak, England, 10 1/4 In. . 85.00
Figure, Man Pulling Horse In Cart, For Strength, Carltonware, England, 4 In. 832.00
Figure, Penguin, Blue Plaque, Draught, Sold Here, Rubberoid, England, 7 In. 132.00
Figure, Penguin, Draught Guinness Sold Here, Rubberoid, 7 In. 162.00
Figure, Sam Weller, 3 In. 61.00
Figure, Toucan, My Goodness, My Guinness, Rubberoid, 7 1/4 In. 486.00
Figure, Tweedle Dee & Tweedle Dum, 3 In. 111.00
Figure, Wellington In Boot, 3 1/2 In. 152.00
Ice Container, Guinness Draught, White Raised Letters, Round, England, 7 1/2 x 14 In. . . 19.00
Jar, Toucans, Cover, White Glaze, Carltonware, England, 5 1/4 In. 19.00
Jug, Harp, Blue Glaze, White Interior & Handle, Carltonware, England, 4 1/2 In. 85.00
Jug, My Goodness, Beer Glass Shape, Toucan Handle, Carltonware, 7 In. 1324.00
Lamp, Guinness Harp, Orange Shade, Ceramic Base, 11 1/2 In. 81.00
Lamp, Toucans, Cream Ground, Ceramic Base, 10 In. 152.00
Lampshade, We Sell Draught, Gold Letters, Blue Ground, 7 1/2 In. 624.00
Matchbox Holder, Good For You, Barrel, White Base, Mintons, 3 3/4 x 5 1/2 In. 61.00
Mirror, Rounded Top, Stand-Up, Toucan Picture, Red Letters, England, 14 x 9 1/2 In. 76.00
Plaque, Arthur Guinness Portrait, Wedgwood, 225th Anniversary, 1984, 6 1/2 In. 31.00
Plate, My Goodness, My Guinness, 2 Chinese Men, Willow Pattern, 7 In. . . . . 85.00 to 95.00
Plate, Sam Weller, White Glaze, Black Print, 8 In. 57.00
Presentation Pack, Toucan Inn Visitor, 2 Bottles Of Beer, Beer Glass, England 76.00
Shaving Mug, Black Glaze, Gold Harp, 3 3/4 In. 23.00
Sign, For Strength, Sailor Lifting Boat, Gilroy, 12 x 8 In. 445.00
Sign, Good For You, Bottle, 2 Glasses, 7 In. 405.00
Sign, Good For You, Empty Glass In Front Of Bottle, 9 x 6 In. 526.00
Sign, Guinness, Ideal Summer Resort, Animals Playing, Gilroy, 12 x 8 In. 445.00
Sign, Toucan In Headdress, See What Big Chief Toucan Do, Him Strong, 12 x 8 In. 648.00
Sugar Bowl, Harp, Black, White Rim, Carltonware, England, 3 In. 57.00
Thermometer, Treat Yourself, Good Stout Drink, Round, Tin On Card, England, 8 3/4 In. . 142.00
Tray, Game For A Guinness, Duck, Tin, Rounded Edges, Red Letters, England, 16 x 12 In. . 51.00
Tray, Lovely Day For A Guinness, Zookeeper & Seal, Tin, Round, England, 12 1/2 In. 76.00
Tray, Thirst Prize, Glass Of Beers, Round, England, 10 1/2 In. 51.00
Tray, Toucan, 2 Glasses, Verse, Tin, Round, England, 12 1/2 In. 61.00
Tray, White Label Guinness Stout, Thomas McMullen, Tin Lithograph, 13 x 10 1/2 In. . . . 220.00
Watch, Guinness Time, Happy Beer Glass, Toucan Second Hand, Plated, Pocket 984.00

GUN Boxes, buttons, calendars, signs, and other items displaying the name of any gun and ammunition manufacturer are sought by sportsmen and collectors. Calendars and posters often have illustrations by famous artists, such as Maxfield Parrish or Philip Goodwin. "Counter felts" are also collectible. These are pieces of felt on which a storekeeper placed guns and bullets while a customer examined them. Related items can be found in the DuPont, Peters, Remington, and Winchester categories.

Booklet, American E.C. & Schultze Gun Powder, Bifold, Hunters, Dogs, 3 1/2 x 5 1/2 In. . 358.00
Booklet, Chicago Air Rifle Co., 4 Sections, Flyer, 6 x 3 1/4 In. 340.00
Booklet, Colt Automatic Pistol, The Woodsman, Caliber 22, 6 1/2 x 3 1/2 In. 88.00
Booklet, Daisy Air Rifle, 24 Pages, 1925, 6 x 3 In. 215.00
Booklet, Hamilton Rifles, Models 39, 27 & 027, 3 Sections, Flyer, 3 1/4 x 6 1/8 In. 110.00
Booklet, Marlin Fire Arms Co., Rifles, New Haven, Conn., Model 1893, 10 x 7 In. 55.00
Booklet, Western Lubaloy Cartridges, Lubricating Alloy, Fold-Out, 6 x 3 1/4 In. 44.00
Booklet, Western Metallic Ammunition, The World's Best, 6 x 2 1/2 In., 2 Pages 358.00
Booklet, Western Shotgun Shells, Form No. 40, Paper, Flyer, 8-Fold 18.44
Booklet, Western, 40 Pounds, 1920 American Trapshooting, 6 x 3 1/2 In., 14 Pages 405.00
Box, A.F. Weiss & Bro., 12 Gauge, Shot Gun, 2-Piece Box, Illinois, 4 x 4 x 2 1/2 In. 220.00
Box, Browning, Special Dove & Quail, 12 Gauge Plastic Shells, Contents, 4 x 4 x 2 In. . . 59.00
Box, California Perfection, Shotgun Cartridges, 10 Gauge, 4 x 4 x 2 1/2 In. 693.00

Box, Canadian Industries, 22 Long Rifle, 100 Cartridges, Unopened, c.1940, 1 1/4 x 2 In. . 52.00
Box, Clinton Cartridge Co., Pointer, 12 Gauge, Smokeless Powder, 2 Piece, 4 x 4 x 2 In. . 393.00
Box, Federal, Hi-Power Shot Shells, 12 Gauge, Flying Duck, Contents, 4 x 4 x 2 1/2 In. . 26.00
Box, Federal, Hi-Power Shot Shells, 16 Gauge, Flying Duck, Contents, 4 x 4 x 2 1/2 In. . . 35.00
Box, National Cartridge Co., Nublend Powder, Eagle, Contents, 2 1/2 x 2 1/4 x 3/4 In. . . . 253.00
Box, Red Head Shot Shells, Flying Canada Goose, 12 Gauge, 2 Piece, 4 x 4 x 2 1/2 In. . . . 292.00
Box, Robin Hood Ammunition Co., Red, 50 Size, .32 Cal., 3 1/2 x 2 x 1 In. 88.00
Box, Rod & Gun Smoking Mixture, Fishing Scene, Ducks, Dog's Head, 3 x 4 1/2 x 1 In. . 5.50
Box, Savage Cartridges, .300 Smokeless, Top Notch, Contents, 2 1/2 x 5 In. 44.00
Box, Selby Standard Shotgun Cartridge, 12 Gauge, 2 Piece, 4 x 4 x 2 1/2 In. 143.00
Box, US Ammo Copperheads, 50, .22 Rim Fire, Self-Cleaning Short, 2 1/2 x 1 x 3/4 In. . . 688.00
Box, Vulcan Shot Shells, 2-Piece, Unopened, Dominion Cartridge, 4 x 4 x 2 1/2 In. 526.00
Box, Western Cartridge Co., Rim Fire, .22 Cal. Short, Gallery Special, Sealed, 1 1/4 x 2 In. 132.00
Box, Western Cartridge Co., Sure Shot, Waterproof, 12 Gauge, 2 Piece, 4 x 4 x 2 1/2 In. . . 462.00
Box, Western Rim Fire Cartridges, Unopened, 2 1/2 x 1 1/4 x 1 3/4 In. 176.00
Box, Xpert Western Shotgun Shells, Hunting Dog, 2 Piece, 4 x 4 x 2 3/4 In. 303.00
Brochure, Marble's Game Getter Gun, Dog, Bifold, 3-Color Print, 1920s, 6 1/8 x 8 1/2 In. 256.00
Button, Austin Ammunition, 3 Dogs, Multicolored, 7/8 In. 146.00
Button, Ballistite & Empire, Best Smokeless Powders, Red, White, Blue, Bastian Bros. . . 127.00
Button, Ballistite & Empire, Best Smokeless Powders, Whitehead & Hoag, 3/4 In. 65.00
Button, Colt Automatic Caliber 45, Sterling Silver, Handgun Shape, 1 In. 41.00
Button, Daisy Air Rifles, Shoot Safe Buddy, White, Blue, Red, Pinback, 7/8 In. 17.00
Button, Daisy Boy Air Rifle, Honorable Mention, Celluloid, Pinback, 1914, 1 1/2 In. 575.00
Button, Daisy Cadet, Captain, Shield, Star, Multicolored, Whitehead & Hoag, 1 1/4 In. . . 809.00
Button, Dead Shot Smokeless Powder, Falling Duck, Celluloid, 3/4 In. 67.00
Button, Happy Daisy Boy, Air Rifle, Celluloid, 1914, 1 1/2 In. 2168.00
Button, Infallible Shotgun Smokeless, Multicolored, Celluloid, 1 1/4 In. 61.00
Button, Laflin & Rand, Infallible, Smokeless, Wreath, 3-Stripe Flag, Round, 1 1/4 In. . . . 28.00
Calendar, Harrington & Richardson Arms, G. Muss-Arnolt, 1910, Frame, 27 x 14 In. 4422.00
Calendar, Harrington & Richardson, Hunter Near Water, 1908, 26 5/8 x 14 In. 2310.00
Calendar, Harrington & Richardson, Woman, Dog, 1905, Frame, 13 5/8 x 26 In. . . . . *Illus* 4180.00
Calendar, Laflin & Rand Powder Co., Man, Hiding Behind Canoe, 1906, 15 x 29 In. *Illus* 2475.00
Calendar, Laflin & Rand Powder, American Warrior, Flip, Cardboard, 1901, 6 2/3 x 5 In. . 55.00
Calendar, Laflin & Rand, Orange Extra, 1893, Mat, Frame, 28 1/4 x 42 1/2 In. 1733.00
Calendar, Marble's Arms, A Successful Call, Goodwin, Dec., 1918, 18 x 27 1/4 In. 4100.00
Calendar, Savage & Stevens Firearms, Hunters, Raft, Bear, Goodwin, 1927, 28 x 16 In. . . 3812.00
Calendar, Union Metallic Cartridge Co., Dog, Puppies, Dec., 1894, 13 1/2 x 27 3/4 In. 3095.00
Calendar, Union Metallic Cartridge Co., Girl, Dogs, 1891, 26 3/4 x 13 3/4 In. 1100.00
Calendar, Union Metallic Cartridge, Boy, Bird, Rifle, Nov., Dec., 1901, Frame, 22 x 35 In. 2677.00
Calendar, US Cartridge Co., Come On, What Ails Yer, W.K. Foster, 1929, 16 x 35 In. 825.00
Calendar, US Shot Shells, Cartridges, Man, Puppies, 1928, 32 7/8 x 16 1/8 In. 1071.00
Calendar, Western Ammunition, Snow Geese, 1928, 15 x 28 In. . . . . *Illus* 523.00
Calendar, Western, Future Sports, Dog, Puppies, 1926, 23 x 15 In. 1758.00
Can, Outers Gun Oil, Red, Yellow, Black, No Cap, 3 Oz. 5.50
Can, Outers 445 Gun Oil, Yellow, Red, Black, Red Cap, 3 Fl. Oz., 2 1/4 x 4 1/4 x 3/4 In. . 11.00
Can, Outers 445A, Gun Oil, 2 Flying Ducks, 3 Oz., 2 1/2 x 3 3/4 x 1 In. 11.00
Can, Superior Pressure Gun Grease, 7 5/8 x 5 1/2 In. 75.00
Can, U.B. Bray Co., Gun Oil, Los Angeles, 4 Oz., 2 1/4 x 4 1/2 x 1 In. 12.10
Catalog, Hercules Sporting Powder, 1914, 3 1/2 x 6 1/4 In., 28 Pages 177.00
Catalog, Ithaca Guns, Red Fox, Grouse, Lynn Bogue Hunt Art, 8 x 12 In., 24 Pages 269.00
Catalog, L.C. Smith Guns, Frank Wheeler, Dog, 1935, 26 Pages 132.00
Catalog, Marble's Monthly Message, Dog, Christmas Wreath, 1916, 6 x 9 In., 14 Pages . . 319.00
Catalog, Marble's Outing Equipment, Catalog D, Moose, 1924, 8 1/2 x 11 In., 24 Pages . . 83.00
Catalog, Marble's Outing Equipment, Moose, Color Covers, 1933, 4 1/4 x 7 In., 32 Pages 41.00
Catalog, Marble's Outing Equipment, No. 19, Bear, 1921, 4 x 6 7/8 In., 48 Pages 145.00
Catalog, Marlin Firearms Co., Repeating Rifles & Shotguns, 1913, 8 x 5 In., 128 Pages . . 77.00
Catalog, My First Rifle, Hopkins & Allen Arms Co., 6 x 3 1/2 In., 12 Pages 44.00
Catalog, New Ithaca Gun, Canada Geese, 1932, 13 1/2 x 8 1/2 In., 20 Pages 88.00
Catalog, New Ithaca Gun, Rifle, Ducks, 6 x 3 1/2 In., 20 Pages 44.00
Catalog, Oriental Powder Mills, Green, Embossed Logo, Me., c.1900, 10 x 8 In., 16 Pages 110.00
Catalog, Parker Guns, 1926, 9 x 6 In., 32 Pages 121.00
Catalog, Parker Guns, Geese, Red, White, Black, 3 1/2 x 6 In., 16 Pages 88.00
Catalog, Savage Arms & Ammunition, No. 65, 1928, 7 1/2 x 9 In. 44.00

Gun, Calendar, Harrington &
Richardson, Woman, Dog, 1905,
Frame, 13 5/8 x 26 In.

Gun, Calendar, Laflin & Rand
Powder Co., Man, Hiding Behind
Canoe, 1906, 15 x 29 In.

Gun, Calendar, Western
Ammunition, Snow Geese,
1928, 15 x 28 In.

Catalog, Smith & Wesson, 3 Men, 1902, 10 x 7 In., 30 Pages 253.00
Catalog, Smith & Wesson, Pirates, String Binding, 10 x 7 1/8 In. 144.00
Catalog, Stevens Arms, Reduction In Price, 1897, 6 3/4 x 3 3/4 In., 12 Pages 138.00
Catalog, Stevens Firearms, Price List, 1922, 3 1/2 x 6 In., 32 Pages 16.50
Catalog, Stevens Rifle Telescopes, c.1904, 7 3/4 x 5 In., 32 Pages 179.00
Catalog, Stevens Shot Guns, 1912, 9 x 7 1/2 In., 48 Pages 44.00
Catalog, US Cartridge Co. Ammunition, 1930s, 9 x 12 In., 10 Pages 209.00
Catalog, Western Ammunition, 1920s, 9 x 6 In., 84 Pages 121.00
Counter Felt, Dead Shot Powder, Dead Duck, Kill Your Bird, Frame, 11 1/2 x 12 1/4 In. . 275.00
Counter Felt, Dead Shot Smokeless, Dead Duck, Mat, Frame, 7 1/2 x 10 1/2 In. 307.00
Counter Felt, H&R Arms Co., Shotguns, Revolvers, Maroon, Pink, 11 x 17 In. 159.00
Counter Felt, Shoot Western Ammunition, Man Pointing Gun, 8 1/2 x 11 In. 382.00
Counter Felt, UMC Cartridges, For Every Make Rifle, Grizzly Bear, 13 3/8 x 11 1/2 In. . 318.00
Counter Felt, UMC, Steel Line Shot Shells, Quail, Mat, Frame, 10 1/2 x 12 In. 412.00
Counter Felt, Union Metallic Cartridge Co., Ask For, 22 Smokeless, 12 1/4 x 13 1/4 In. ... 231.00
Display, Buy Hubley Guns, Metal, 4 Hooks, For Cap Guns, 6 3/4 x 17 x 23 In. 61.00
Display, Marble's Gun Sights, Tester, Folding Arm, 10 1/2 x 4 In. 866.00
Display Box, Marble's Gun Sights, Cardboard, Metal Corners, 2 1/4 x 7 3/4 x 12 3/4 In. ... 55.00
Display Case, Marble's Gun Sights, Glass Top, Hinged Lid, 1 1/2 x 12 1/4 x 7 5/8 In. 110.00
Handbook, Western Ammunition, Illustrations, Charts, c.1940, 5 1/2 x 7 3/4 In., 76 Pages 11.00
Label, Hazard Powder Co., Shotshell Box, Red & Black Ink, 2 x 3 5/8 .... 35.00
Label, Laflin & Rand Powder Co., Orange Extra Sporting, 4 x 1 7/8 In. 17.00
Postcard, A.F. Stoger Inc., Guns, New Catalog, Handbook, No. 29, 1937, 3 1/2 x 5 1/2 In. 30.00
Postcard, Austin Cartridge Co. Works, Factory Picture, 5 1/2 x 3 1/2 In. 88.00
Postcard, Parker Gun, Game Bird, Unused, 5 1/2 x 3 1/2 In. 440.00
Poster, Black Shells, Flying Birds, United States Cartridge Co., Frame, 30 x 20 In. 10175.00
Poster, Colt Fire Arms, Patches, Cowboy, Horse, No. 2, 19 5/8 x 32 3/4 In. 2750.00
Poster, Colt Revolvers, Tex & Patches, Cowboy, Horse, No. 4, 1925, 33 x 20 In. 3025.00
Poster, Dead Shot, American Powder Mills, Duck, Frame, 30 x 24 In. 3025.00
Poster, Federal Monark Shells, For Sale Here, Die Cut, Cardboard, c.1929, 21 1/2 x 9 In. . 606.00
Poster, Harrington & Richardson Arms, Guns, Revolvers, Hunter, Dogs, 1909, 27 x 14 In. 3870.00
Poster, Hercules Powder Co., Don't You Fool Me Dog, 1920s, 24 1/2 x 15 1/2 In. 798.00
Poster, Hopkins & Allen Arms Co., Cowgirl, Holding Pistol, Frame, 23 1/2 x 10 In. 2149.00
Poster, Infallible Smokeless, Dense Powder For Shotguns, Mallards, Frame, 20 x 25 1/2 In. 7779.00
Poster, Ithaca Guns, Cross Fox, Fox Chasing Bird In Snow, 1909, 30 x 16 In. 2520.00
Poster, Ithaca Guns, Extinct Passenger Pigeon, 1910, 16 1/2 x 27 3/4 In. 1540.00
Poster, Marlin Firearms Co., Gun For Man Who Knows, 1905, 24 x 13 1/2 In. ..2275.00 to 7642.00
Poster, Marlin Rifles & Shotguns, Falling Ducks, G. Muss Arnolt, 1908, 15 x 24 In. 1430.00
Poster, Smith & Wesson, Last Stand, Frank Presberry Co., Frame, 1902, 14 3/4 x 14 In. ... 495.00
Poster, US Shot Shells, Climax, Ajax, Romax, Load For Game, String Hanger, 17 x 10 In. . 385.00
Poster, Vos Munitions COL, Duck Hunters & Dogs, French Words, 27 x 21 In. 110.00
Poster, Western Ammunition, The Warning, Moose, 1921, 30 x 16 3/4 In. 1359.00

Poster, Western Super-X, Long Range, Wildfowl Load, Bullet, Geese, 8 x 15 In. 55.00
Poster, Western Super-X, Silvertip Bullet, See Them Here, 8 x 15 In. 88.00
Price List, Chamberlin Cartridge Co., Fixed Ammunition, 1887, 8 1/2 x 5 1/2 In., 24 Pages 191.00
Price List, J. Stevens & Company, Shotguns, Bifold, 1877, 8 7/8 x 5 3/4 In., 4 Pages ... 55.00
Program, Chamberlin Cartridge Co., Third Annual Tournament, 1887, 4 x 6 In., 8 Pages . 152.00
Sign, Austin Powder Co., Dog Holding Dead Duck, Paper, Cleveland, Ohio, 23 x 18 In. ... 5500.00
Sign, Browning Pistols, Renaissance Engraved, Laminated, Stand-Up, 8 x 11 In. 125.00
Sign, Colt Patent Firearms, Hartford, Ct., Cowboy, Horse, Print, Frame, Signed, 28 x 38 In. 935.00
Sign, Cowboy Bar Guns, Cowboys Leave Guns At Bar, Enameled, Porcelain, 12 x 9 In. ... 25.00
Sign, Daisy Air Rifles, Boy With Rifle, Metal Strips At Top & Bottom, 1913, 21 x 14 In. . 6050.00
Sign, Dead Shot Gunpowder, Duck Falling, Paper, Frame, c.1910, 25 x 31 In. ...1200.00 to 1800.00
Sign, Dead Shot Powder, Falling Mallard Duck, Tin, Self-Framed, 15 1/2 x 19 1/2 In. 1739.00
Sign, Federal Cartridge Corp., Dogs, Wood Print, Frame, 1937, 16 1/2 x 18 1/2 In. .110.00 to 127.00
Sign, Iver Johnson Revolver, Hammer The Hammer, Cutout, Tin, 2-Sided, 16 x 12 In. ... 4043.00
Sign, North American Ducks, Federal Ammunition, Tin, Cardboard, 1950s, 23 x 16 In. 110.00
Sign, Savage Rifles, Indian Chief, Holding Gun, Die Cut, Hanger, 1905, 8 x 15 1/2 In. 660.00
Sign, Savage Stevens & Fox Sporting Arms, Hunting Time, Cardboard, 53 3/4 x 19 1/4 In. 121.00
Sign, Savage Stevens & Fox, Buck, Cardboard, Easel Back, Self-Framed, 16 x 12 In. 143.00
Sign, Savage Stevens & Fox, Duck Hunters, Cardboard, 20 x 22 In. 66.00
Sign, Savage Stevens & Fox, Rabbit, Cardboard, Easel Back, 16 x 12 In. 143.00
Sign, Savage Stevens & Fox, Squirrel, Cardboard, Countertop, 18 x 13 1/2 In. 62.00
Sign, Stevens, Single Shot Rifles, Boy Showing Off New Rifle, 3-D, Die Cut, 12 x 9 In. ... 1805.00
Sign, U.S. Ammunition Co., Man, Pulling Horse, Bear, Cardboard, 16 x 12 1/2 In. 440.00
Sign, UMC, Shooting Gallery, Hit Bull's-Eye, Bull's Head Shape, Tin, 18 x 26 3/4 In. ... 2888.00
Sign, UMC, They Hit The Mark, 22s, Man Target Shooting, Box, Die Cut, 12 x 5 In. 866.00
Sign, US Cartridge Co., Romax, Climax, Ajax, Fox, Cardboard, Easel Back, 11 3/4 x 20 In. 1328.00
Sign, US Shot Shells, Dog, Duck, Puppies, Cardboard, Easel Back, 1926, 30 x 19 In. 1018.00
Sign, Western Lubaloy Cartridges, Cardboard, Easel Back, Countertop, 12 x 20 1/2 In. ... 495.00
Split Shot Container, Abercrombie & Fitch, Finest Fishing Tackle, Celluloid, 1 1/2 In. .. 154.00
Tag, Daisy Air Rifle, No. 25 Pump Gun, Price $5.00, Oval, 3 3/4 x 2 1/4 In. 182.00
Tie Clip, Smith & Wesson, Gun, Figural, Marked 18.00
Tin, American Powder Mills, Dead Shot, Paper Label, 1900, 1 Lb., 4 x 6 x 1 In. 275.00
Tin, Austin Powder Co., Rifle Powder, Paper Label, 1/2 Lb., 4 x 3 1/4 In. 495.00
Tin, Benjamin Air Rifle Pellets, Contents, 3 1/4 x 1 1/6 In. 12.50
Tin, Dominion Shot Shells, For Speed, Pattern & Penetration, 6 1/2 x 3 1/2 In. 176.00
Tin, Duck Shooting Gunpowder, Hazard Powder Co., 1860-1880, 5 1/2 x 4 x 1 3/4 In. ... 374.00
Tin, Fiendoil, Cleans & Protects Firearms, 1931, 2 Oz., 2 3/4 x 2 x 1 In. 44.00
Tin, Gold Dust Smokeless Shotgun Powder, Paper Label, 1/2 Lb., 3 x 4 x 1 1/2 In. 176.00
Tin, Golden Pheasant Gun Powder, Tin, c.1880, 4 x 6 x 1 1/2 In. 1540.00
Tin, Hazard Powder Co. Mining Powder, Sample, Keg Shape, Sand Filled, 2 1/4 x 2 In. .. 468.00
Tin, Imperial Gun Powder, Paper Label, Eureka Powder Works, 1 Lb., 4 x 4 1/2 x 2 In. .. 303.00
Tin, Kentucky Rifle Gunpowder, Hazard Powder Co., 1850s, 4 1/2 x 4 x 2 In. 978.00
Tin, Kentucky Rifle Gunpowder, Hazard Powder Co., 1870, 5 x 4 x 1 1/2 In. .....134.00 to 173.00
Tin, Kentucky Rifle Gunpowder, Hazard Powder Co., Woman Shooting Rifle, 4 1/4 x 3 In. 132.00
Tin, Laflin & Rand Orange Extra, Label, Hercules Powder Co., 1 Lb., 4 x 6 x 1 1/2 In. ... 105.00
Tin, Laflin & Rand Powder, Orange FFF Powder, Paper Label, 1/4 Lb., 2 3/4 x 3 x 1 In. .. 495.00
Tin, Marble's Gun Oil, Plastic Spout, Cap, Black, Orange, White, Bear, Moose, 3 Oz. 59.00
Tin, Marble's Nitro Solvent Gun Oil, Lead Spout, Cap, 3 Oz. ....117.00 to 163.00
Tin, Marble's Nitro Solvent Oil, Lead Spout, Cap, Black, Orange, Camping Scene, 3 Oz. .. 214.00
Tin, Marble's Nitro Solvent Oil, Lead Spout, Stenciled Labels, Black, Orange, 3 Oz. 58.00
Tin, Marble's Solvent Gun Oil, Round, Gold Ground, Black Print, 5 1/2 In. 117.00
Tin, Mathewson Gun Powder, Paper Label On Tin, 1 Lb., 3 1/2 x 7 x 1 In. 88.00
Tin, Orange Ducking Powder, Laflin & Rand, Paper Label, 4 x 5 1/2 x 1 1/2 In. 180.00
Tin, Orange Rifle Powder, Laflin & Rand Co., Paper Label, 4 x 6 x 1 1/2 In. 178.00
Tin, Orange Rifle Powder, Laflin & Rand, c.1890, 4 x 3 3/4 x 1 1/4 In. 489.00
Tin, Orange Sporting Gun Powder, 6 x 4 x 1 1/4 In. 149.00
Tin, Robin Hood Shotgun Powder, Smokeless, Swanton, Vt., 1 Lb., 4 x 6 x 1 1/4 In. 330.00
Tin, Schultze Gunpowder, Fist, Lightning Bolts, Paper Label, 4 x 5 x 1 1/2 In. 324.00
Tin, Selby, B.B. Split Shot, Gold, Brown, White, Partial Contents, 1 1/2 In. 83.00
Tin, Selby, Buck Split Shot, Celluloid Lid, American Art Works, 1 1/2 In. Diam. 44.00
Tin, Sharps Rifle Co., Powder, Bridgeport, Conn., 1/2 Lb., 4 1/4 x 3 x 1 1/4 In. 518.00
Tin, Superior Rifle Gun Powder, Paper Label, 2 1/2 x 3 1/2 In. 225.00
Tin, Union Gunpowder, Mills, Santa Cruz, Paper Label, Lead Cap, 1 Lb., 4 x 5 x 1 1/2 In. 225.00

Tin, Universal Buck Powder, A.V. Shotwell Co., Early 1900s, 4 1/2 In. 51.00
Tin, Wing Shooting Shot Gun Sights, Leader Co., American Can., 1909, 3 5/8 x 2 In. 1925.00
Token, Robin Hood Ammunition, Game Laws Token, Maine, c.1914, 1 1/2 In. 267.00
Trade Card, Ithaca Gun Co., Man Looking Through Barrel, 3 7/8 x 5 3/4 In. 55.00
Wristwatch, Colt Firearms, Water Resistant, Stainless Steel, Swiss, Box 66.00

HAMM'S   Theodore Hamm founded his brewery in 1865 in St. Paul, Minnesota. The Hamm's spokesbear, who advertised the beer "From the Land of Sky Blue Waters," debuted on television in 1953. In 2000 the bear was voted one of the 150 most influential Minnesotans of the past 150 years. The Hamm family sold the brewery in the 1970s and it closed in 1997. Hamm's beer is now brewed by Miller.

Ashtray, 6 1/2 In. 9.00
Beer Cooler, From The Land Of Sky Blue Waters, Sky Blue Vinyl Cover, 1960s 45.00
Bottle, Hamm's Bear Shape, Ceramic, 1972, 11 In. 61.00
Calendar, 1901, Hamm's Brewery, Chromolithograph, Mat, Frame, 36 x 30 In. 1430.00
Can, Keg Style, Aluminum, Pull Tab, 12 Oz. 2.50
Display, Motion, Bottle In Snow Drift, Sky Blue Waters, Plastic, Light-Up, 19 x 12 In. . . .   374.00
Figure, Bear, Holds Calendar, Big Beer/Bear Drinking Brotherhood, Plastic 83.00
Figure, Bear, Styrofoam, Black, White, Red Base, 62 In. 176.00
Sign, Beer, Water Fall, Plastic, Metal, Light-Up, 24 x 19 In. 248.00
Sign, Refreshing As The Land Of Sky Blue Waters, Bottle Light-Up, 15 x 14 In. 527.00
Sign, Water Fall, Plastic, Metal, Light-Up, Motion, Lakeside Plastics, 34 x 19 In. 385.00
Tumbler, New Patio, Aluminum, Box, Set Of 6 . . . .   72.00

HEINZ   Henry Heinz made, bottled, and sold his own horseradish in Sharpsburg, Pennsylvania. In 1869 he joined L.C. Noble to form Anchor Brand Food Company. It later became Heinz, Noble, and Company. The company went bankrupt during the depression of 1875, but was reestablished later that same year as the F. and J. Heinz Company. It became the H.J. Heinz Company in 1888. The term "57 Varieties" was chosen for its advertising effect, not because there were fifty-seven products. The Heinz pickle pin, which is still being given away, was introduced at the Chicago World's Fair in 1893. Thousands of cans, bottles, signs, advertising cards, and other materials can be found. To celebrate 120 years in business, the company offered a limited edition replica of the turn-of-the-century 14-ounce ketchup bottle in 1989. Heinz crocks, cans, and signs have also been reproduced. In recent years, the company has offered green, purple, and flavored ketchups. The company also makes food under the brand names Classico, Ore-ida, Bagel Bites, and Wyler's. Heinz is headquartered in Pittsburgh.

Bean Cup, 57 In Circle, 1950s, 3 In. 20.00
Bottle, Celery Sauce, Pour Spout, Embossed, Screw Top, 10 1/2 In. 55.00
Bottle, Ketchup, Paper Labels, Tin Lithograph Cap, 14 Oz., 9 1/2 x 2 5/8 In. 122.00
Bottle, Sweet Midget Gherkins, Paper Label, 7 1/2 x 2 1/2 In. 55.00
Bowl, Chili, Light Tan, McCoy, 1948, 4 Piece 60.00
Box, 57 Varieties, Pine, 21 x 17 x 15 In. 58.00
Box, Wood, Handle, Printing On 4 Sides, Pittsburgh, Pa., 22 x 10 In. 28.00
Cookie Jar, Ketchup Bottle, Napkin Holder, Sugar, Ceramic, Box, 10 1/2 x 8 x 8 1/2 In. . .   40.00
Crock, Apple Butter, Stoneware, Stone Lithograph Label, 8 x 4 In. . . . . .316.00 to 743.00
Crock, Damson Plum Preserves, Handle, 8 In. 165.00
Cup & Saucer, Pickle Images, Fine China, Reizenstein, Demitasse, 1 3/4 In. 285.00
Figure, Mr. Aristocrat, Tomato Head, Latex Rubber, Painted, 1940s, 2 1/2 x 5 1/2 In. 90.00 to 125.00
Jar, Dill Pickles, Paper Label, 13 x 8 1/2 In. 264.00
Jar, Fresh Cucumber Pickle, Paper Label, Embossed, 8 x 3 In., Pt. 44.00
Jar, Red Raspberry Preserves, Labels, 8 x 4 In. 550.00
Jug, Pure Cider Vinegar, Labels, Cork, Handle, Qt., 6 1/2 x 4 1/2 In. 1155.00
Jug, White Pickling & Table Vinegar, Cork, Labels, Qt., 7 1/2 x 4 1/4 In. 578.00
Label, Preserved Sweet Mixed Pickles, Frame, 14 In. 248.00
Pin, Pickle & Ketchup Bottle, Plastic, 1 1/2 In. 16.00
Sign, Breakfast Wheat, New Treat In Wheat, Lithograph, Trolley Card, 1930s, 11 x 21 In. .   125.00
Sign, Heinz's Keystone Brand, Mixed Pickles, Embossed Cardboard, 11 x 4 In. 99.00

Tin signs and cans will fade from the ultraviolet rays coming in a window or from a fluorescent light. Plexiglass UF-1 or UF-3 will cover the window and keep the rays away from your collection. There are also plastic sleeves to cover fluorescent tubes.

Heinz, Sign, Stringholder, Pure Foods,
Suspended Die Cut Pickle, Tin, 16 In.

Sign, Indian Relish, 1 Of The 57 Varieties, Cardboard, Frame, 14 x 23 In.	330.00
Sign, Pure Cider Vinegar, Has The Flavor, Cardboard, Mat, Frame, 15 3/4 x 26 In.	303.00
Sign, Stringholder, Pure Foods, Suspended Die Cut Pickle, Tin, 16 In. . . . . *Illus*	5225.00
Sign, Vinegars, 4 Kinds, Cardboard Lithograph, Trolley Card, 11 x 21 In.	275.00
Soup, Dish, Handle, Aqua, McCoy, 1950s, 2 x 7 In.	15.00
Spoon, Silver Plated, Home Of The 57 Main Entrance, In Bowl, 4 3/8 In.	22.00
Tin, H.J. Heinz Co., Allover Middle Eastern Design, Factory On Lid, 11 x 8 In.	86.00
Toy, Truck, Electric Lights, Pressed Steel, Decals, Metalcraft, Box, 12 In.	880.00
Toy, Truck, White, Goodrich Silvertown, Metalcraft, St. Louis, 1936, 5 x 12 In.	380.00
Trade Card, Pickle Shape, Chef Holding Tomato Soup Can, Die Cut, London, c.1885, 5 In.	38.00
Trade Card, Pickle Shape, Girl Holding Can Of Baked Beans, 5 1/4 x 2 In.	55.00
Watch Fob, 57, Hammered Ground, Pickle Logo, Leather Strap, 1 1/2 x 1 5/8 x 5 3/8 In. .	75.00

HERSHEY Milton Hershey worked for Joseph Royer, a confectioner in Lancaster, Pennsylvania. His aunt gave him $150 to start his own candy store in Philadelphia in 1876. He advertised with cards featuring buildings from that year's Centennial Exposition. He tried selling several types of candy and cough drops. In 1882 he closed his business and took off for Colorado. But he moved back East to New York City in 1883 and got a job with Huyler's, a well-known candy maker. Eventually he started the Lancaster Caramel Company in Lancaster, Pennsylvania, and managed to progress from pushcart to export to successful expansion. In 1893 he went to the World's Columbian Exposition in Chicago and bought some German chocolate-making machines. At first he made chocolate-covered caramels. In 1894 the Hershey Chocolate Company was founded as a subsidiary of the caramel business. Its products included breakfast cocoa, sweet chocolate, and baking chocolate. In 1900 Hershey sold the caramel company but kept the chocolate business. In 1903 he built a factory in Derry Church, which was renamed Hershey in 1906. Hershey's Kisses were introduced in 1907. The first Hershey chocolate products were wrapped in a variety of packaging labeled with the words "Sterilized Milk Chocolate." About 1905 a maroon and silver label was introduced. The early trademark was a cherub seated on a cocoa bean holding a cup of cocoa. Hershey's now makes several candy brands, including Reese's Peanut Butter Cup (acquired in 1963), Twizzlers (1977), and 5th Avenue (1986). Almond Joy, Mounds, and York Peppermint Pattie were acquired with the purchase of Peter Paul/Cadbury's U.S. operations in 1988. In 1996 Heath, Good & Plenty, Jolly Rancher, Milk Duds, and even more brands became part of Hershey when it acquired Leaf North America's confectionery operations. Hershey Chocolate World in Hershey, Pennsylvania, is a chocolate theme park. Milton Hershey did not believe in conventional advertising, so old Hershey items are almost all packages. Newspaper, radio, and television ads weren't used until 1970.

Bank, Truck, Die Cast Metal, Buff, Maroon, Gold Trim, Gearbox Toy, Box	34.00

Box, Honeybird Candy Bars, 2 For 5 Cents, Cardboard Lithograph, 2 Pieces, 9 x 5 In. ... 139.00
Camera, 110 Pocket, Brown, Silver, China, Box, Unopened, 1980s, 1 1/4 x 2 2/12 x 5 In. . 10.00
Club Kit, Chocolate Lover, Envelope, Contents, Certificate, Pin, 1989, 9 1/2 x 12 1/2 In. . 15.00
Coin-Operated Machine, Hershey-Ets, 5 Cents, Metal, Glass Globe, Key, 22 In. 121.00
Cookie Jar, Cow 32.00
Dispenser, 1 Cent, Metal, 18 In. 413.00
Gum Pack, 6 Sticks For 5 Cents, Mint Flavor, Contents, 7/8 x 3 x 5/8 In. 770.00
Mold, Metal, Bite Size Bars, 10 1/2 x 19 1/4 x 2 1/2 In. 66.00
Ornament, Trolley, Ivory, Brown, Holly & Bow, Box, 1987, 2 1/4 x 3 1/2 In. ....7.95 to 10.00
Paperweight, Hershey Bar, Gold Plate, Felt Back, 4 1/2 x 1 1/3 In. 13.00
Sign, Ice Cream, Light-Up, Metal Frame, Plastic Lens, 15 x 29 In. 44.00
Tin, Building A Legacy, Milton Hershey, Early Hershey Scenes, No. 1, 1996 .... 10.00
Tin, Kisses With Almonds, Hometown Series, No. 6, 1990, 7 x 4 In. 10.00
Tin, Milk Chocolate Fudge, Paper Label, 2 3/4 x 2 1/8 In. 85.00
Tin, Reese's Holiday Classic, Christmas Window, Train Pulling Candy, No. 9, 1996 ..... 10.00
Tin, Vintage Edition No. 3, 1995, 4 1/2 x 4 In. 12.00
Tin, Vintage Edition No. 5, 1999, 3 x 6 In. 10.00
Tin, Vintage Edition, Pure Milk Chocolate, No. 2, 1992 .... 10.00
Tray, Girl Stands On Syrup Can, Boy Stands On Milk Crate, 7 3/4 x 6 In. 8.00
Vending Machine, 5 Cents, Metal, Unit-E, 33 x 7 1/4 x 4 1/2 In. 475.00

HILLS BROS. COFFEE Austin H. and Reuben W. Hills opened a retail grocery store in a stall at San Francisco's Bay City Market in 1873. Within four years, they had established a store called Arabian Coffee and Spice Mills and were soon selling roasted coffee beans. They also sold tea, spices, extracts, butter, and eggs. In 1903 Edwin Norton patented a machine to can foods using a vacuum. The Hills brothers realized that this would keep coffee fresh, and in 1903 their company became the first to sell coffee in vacuum-packed cans. They applied for a trademark for the Hills Bros. name. The store and all company documents were destroyed in the 1906 San Francisco earthquake, but the trademark letter from Washington arrived just after the business burned. The company was rebuilt and its product name changed to Hills Bros. Highest Grade Coffee. In 1914 Hills Bros. introduced Red Can Brand coffee. Hills Bros. introduced a key-opening can in 1926. The keyless can was used in 1963. The company trademark from the earliest days pictured an Arab sipping coffee from a cup. The logo has been redesigned a few times, but it's still the official company symbol. In 1984 Hills Bros. Coffee, Inc., purchased Chase & Sanborn. Hills Bros. was purchased by Nestlé in 1985 and in 1999 it became part of Sara Lee.

Sign, Flavoring Extracts, Arab Man Drinking Coffee, Cardboard, 11 x 14 1/2 In. 66.00
Sign, Red Can, Flavor Determines Its Value, Cardboard, c.1930, 19 x 10 In. 176.00
Thermometer, Robed Man, Porcelain Enamel, c.1918, 20 3/4 x 8 3/4 In. ....303.00 to 715.00
Thermometer, Woman In Nightgown, Porcelain, 1915, 20 x 8 In. 275.00
Tin, Hills Private Stock, Key Wind, Contents, 1 Lb., 3 1/2 x 5 In. 413.00
Tin, Red, Yellow, 1939, 12 x 10 In., 15 Lb. 66.00
Tin, Regular Ground Embossed Lid, 2 Lb. 30.00

HIRES ROOT BEER Charles E. Hires owned a drugstore in Philadelphia, Pennsylvania, in the 1870s. He was served some special temperance tea while on vacation in New Jersey. The cook gave him the recipe and even took him into the woods to identify the sixteen plants she used to make the tea. Hires experimented with similar drinks using roots and herbs until he came up with his own product. He named it root beer rather than herb tea so it would appeal to the working man. He sold the drink at his drugstore and the syrup at grocery stores and soda fountains. At the Philadelphia Centennial in 1876, free samples of the drink were offered. Many types of promotional pieces were made, including signs, bottles, trays, mirrors, lamps, and some Mettlach mugs and dispensers. The use of the apostrophe in the name (Hires, Hires', or Hire's) does not follow a pattern or help date the advertising, but the clothing of the Hires boy in the ad can help. He wore a dress from 1891 to 1906, a bathrobe from 1907 to 1914, and a dinner jacket from 1915 to 1926.

After 1961 the ownership of Hires changed several times. It is now part of Cadbury-Schweppes' Dr Pepper/Seven-Up subsidiary. It is the oldest continuously marketed soft drink in the United States.

Advertisement, Drink Hires In Bottles, Woman, Paper, Frame, Early 1900s, 24 x 16 In. . . . 1650.00
Barrel, Cover, R-J Root Beer, Oak, Tin Signs, Steel Liner, 30 x 26 In. 316.00
Booklet, Owl, Parrot, Big Round Moon, Malvern, Pa., c.1900, 2 1/2 x 5 1/2 In., 8 Pages . 35.00
Bottle, Amber, Stopper, 7 1/2 In. 28.00
Bottle, Hires Household Extract, Glass, Aqua, Square, Embossed, 4 1/2 In. 20.00
Bottle, Hires Root Beer Extract, Metal Cap, Molded Letters, 1950s 9.00
Bottle, Orange, White Logo, Ingredient List On Back, 9 1/2 In. 27.00
Bottle, Syrup, Backbar, Hires Kid Holding Foamy Mug, Drink Hires Root Beer 15588.00
Bottle, Syrup, Reverse Glass Label, Metal Cover, 12 In. 220.00
Box, Improved Root Beer Liquid, Wood, Dovetailed, 5 1/2 x 5 1/4 x 7 1/4 In. 88.00
Checkerboard, Happy Blond Boy, Paper Lithograph, 12 x 12 In. 110.00
Checkerboard, Happy Boy, Cardboard, Folding, Color, 12 In. 125.00
Dispenser, Drink Hires, 5 Cents, Gold Barrel Bands, Pump, Ceramic, 16 x 9 In. 11550.00
Dispenser, Drink Hires, It Is Pure, Metal, Hour Glass Shape, 15 x 7 1/2 In. 660.00
Dispenser, Drink Hires, It Is Pure, Painted Porcelain, 14 In. 357.00
Dispenser, Hires Root Beer Syrup, Hourglass Shape, c.1920, 14 3/4 x 8 In. 1185.00
Dispenser, Hourglass, c.1918 . . . . 660.00
Dispenser, Hourglass, Spigot, c.1910 . . . . 825.00
Dispenser, Munimaker, Marble Base, Clear Glass Globe, 38 x 18 In. . . . . .5500.00 to 5720.00
Dispenser, White, Red, Hour Glass Shape, Ceramic, c.1920 . . . . 468.00
Display, Hires R-J Root Beer, Woman, Symbol Delicious Taste, Easel, Die Cut, 18 x 13 In. 345.00
Festoon, Woman In Red Dress, Sandwiches, Glasses, Cardboard, 5 Piece, 1940s 440.00
Mixer, Hires Milk Drink, Milk Glass Ceramic Base, Metal Lid, Cup, Embossed, 13 1/2 In. 770.00
Mixer, Malt, Porcelained Cast Iron, Hand Crank, c.1897 . . . . 770.00
Mug, Drink Hires Root Beer, Boy, Pink Bib, c.1885, 4 1/4 In. 475.00
Mug, Drink Hires Root Beer, Pointing Boy, Bib, Rounded, 4 1/4 x 4 1/2 In. . . . . . .121.00 to 154.00
Mug, Hourglass Shape, China, 4 x 4 1/4 In. 57.00
Mug, Join Health & Cheer, Pointing Boy, Bowtie, Rose, Straight Sides, 5 x 4 In. . .176.00 to 248.00
Mug, Ugly Boy, Villeroy & Boch, 4 1/4 In. 120.00
Mug, Use As Container Except For Hires Is Illegal, Stoneware, Early 1900s, 7 x 4 1/4 In. . 42.00
Pitcher, Boy, Dinner Jacket, Bowtie, Ceramic, Mettlach, 1915-1926, 8 1/2 x 4 In. 18700.00
Punch Bowl, Boy, Dinner Jacket, Bowtie, Porcelain, 1915-1926, 12 x 18 In. 57200.00
Sign, Barrel, Tin, Embossed, 64 x 47 In. 187.00
Sign, Bottle, Tin, Die Cut, Embossed, 56 In. 330.00
Sign, Bottle, Tin, Embossed, Presi Co., Self-Framed, 17 1/2 x 55 In. 413.00
Sign, Boy & Mug, Say Hires, Oval, Self-Framed, 1907, 20 x 24 In. . . . . *Illus* 935.00
Sign, Drink Hires, It Hits The Spot, Man, Bottle, Tin Lithograph, 9 x 18 In. . . . . *Illus* 1430.00
Sign, Enjoy Hires, Always Pure, Girl, Hat, Tin Lithograph, Embossed, 9 3/4 x 27 3/4 In. . . . 523.00
Sign, Enjoy Hires, Healthful, Delicious, Tin, 9 1/2 x 27 1/2 In. . . . . .385.00 to 770.00
Sign, Hires Coney Island Lunch, Tin, Self-Framed, 32 x 56 In. 275.00
Sign, Hires To Your Health, Boy, Blue Dress, Tin Lithograph, Frame, 27 x 19 In. 735.00
Sign, Hires To Your Health, Pointing Boy, Bib, Robe, Tin, 28 1/2 x 20 1/2 In. 3080.00
Sign, Hurrah For Hires Root Beer, Boy, Embossed, Tin Lithograph, 27 3/4 x 19 1/2 In. . . . 5060.00

Hires, Sign, Drink Hires, It Hits The Spot, Man, Bottle, Tin Lithograph, 9 x 18 In.

Hires, Sign, Boy & Mug, Say Hires, Oval, Self-Framed, 1907, 20 x 24 In.

Hires, Thermometer, Bottle Shape, Tin, Die Cut, 28 In.

Sign, Its Always Pure, Hires In Bottles, Redheaded Woman With Glass, Tin, 20 In. 385.00
Sign, Made With Roots, Barks, Herbs, So Refreshing, Logo, Flange, 2-Sided, 14 In. 236.00
Sign, Made With Roots, Barks, Herbs, So Refreshing, Tin, Embossed, 24 x 28 In. 193.00
Sign, Make A Real Oldtime Delicious Root Beer Float, Cardboard, 12 x 18 In. 55.00
Sign, R-J Root Beer, Real Root Juices, Die Cut Metal, 6 1/4 x 7 3/4 In. 66.00
Sign, R-J Root Beer, With Real Root Juices, Tin, Blue, Black, Red, White, 7 x 12 In. 66.00
Sign, So Refreshing, Made With Roots, Barks, Herbs, Tin, 28 x 24 In. 209.00
Sign, Take Home A Carton, Lady, Holding Glass, Cardboard, 9 x 11 In. 33.00
Sign, Triple AAA Root Beer, 5 Cents, Frame, 11 x 17 In. 17.00
Sign, With Real Root Juice, Tin, Embossed, 12 In. Diam. 187.00
Sign, Woman, Holding Glass, Hires R-J Root Beer, 1940-1950, 34 x 58 In. 250.00
Strawholder, Drink Hires, Cast Metal, Cutout Lettering, 10 In. 565.00
Thermometer, Bottle Shape, Tin, Die Cut, 28 In. . . . . *Illus* 154.00
Thermometer, Bottle, Drink Hires, Metal, c.1950, 27 x 8 In. 187.00
Trade Card, An Uninvited Guest, Unhappy Baby, Dog Drinking Root Beer, 5 x 3 In. 15.00
Trade Card, Offer For Ruth & Naomi Lithograph, c.1890s, 5 x 5 7/8 In. 13.00
Trade Card, Woman In Black Dress, Girl Holds Root Beer Box, 3 3/4 x 5 3/4 In. 22.00
Tray, Made With Roots, Barks, Herbs, c.1930s, 17 1/2 x 11 1/2 x 1 3/4 In. 150.00
Tray, Parrot, Orange, Blue, c.1950, 9 x 14 1/4 x 1 In. 28.00
Tray, Things Is Getting Higher, Hires Are Still A Nickel A Trickle, c.1915, 13 1/4 In. 440.00

HOOD'S   Charles I. Hood worked in his father's drugstore in Chelsea,
Vermont, until 1861, when he moved to Lowell, Massachusetts. He
apprenticed to a druggist and five years later went to work for Theodore
Metcalf & Company of Boston, Massachusetts. By 1870 he had opened
his own drugstore with a friend in Lowell, and six years later he owned
the entire store. Hood liked to compound his own medicines. He advertised the bottled medicines and soon was selling Hood's Sarsaparilla,
Hood's Pills, and other products nationally. Many types of advertising
pieces and bottles made by C.I. Hood & Co. can be found.

Calendar, 1887, 7 x 5 3/4 In. 66.00
Calendar, 1888, Serious Girl, Curly Hair, Blue Bonnet, Die Cut, Frame, 5 x 8 In. 138.00
Calendar, 1891, 3 Children, Playing Instruments, Frame, 11 x 15 In. 176.00
Calendar, 1892, Children, Round, Frame, 7 In. 110.00
Calendar, 1893, Boy & Girl, Globe, 8 1/2 x 6 In. 110.00
Calendar, 1894, Sarsaparilla, 5 1/2 x 9 In. 83.00
Calendar, 1894, Woman, Flowers In Hat, Frame, 9 x 12 In. 132.00
Calendar, 1896, Woman, Gray Hat, Frame, 10 x 13 In. 132.00
Calendar, 1897, Girl, Die Cut, 7 x 4 1/2 In. 132.00
Calendar, 1899, American Girl, 9 3/4 x 6 3/4 In. 132.00
Calendar, 1900, Cutout Of 2 Girls, Paper, Easel Back, 6 1/4 x 5 1/4 In. . . . . .55.00 to 110.00
Calendar, 1902, 4 Women, Frame, 8 x 21 In. 308.00
Calendar, 1907, Sarsaparilla, Frame, 14 x 21 In. 88.00
Calendar, 1910, Girl, Pink Bow In Hair, Frame, 13 x 12 In. 121.00
Calendar, 1911, 25th Anniversary, Birthday Roses, Wood Frame, 11 x 5 In. 385.00
Calendar, 1911, Woman, Red Flowers, Frame, 10 x 14 In. 154.00
Calendar, 1913, Children Playing With Kittens, 7 x 7 3/4 In. 154.00
Calendar, 1915, Smiling Girl, Red Hat, Book, Frame, 4 1/2 x 12 In. 110.00
Calendar, 1916, Woman, Red Bow In Hair, Frame, 9 x 17 In. 83.00
Calendar, 1921, Poppies, 11 x 4 1/2 In. 385.00
Curb Sign, Old Fashioned Ice Cream, Metal, 2-Sided, 33 x 21 In. . . . . *Illus* 1121.00
Postcard, Sarsaparilla Factory, Lowell, Mass. 15.00
Puzzle, 4 In 1, Box, 32-Page Booklet, c.1896, 18 1/4 x 11 1/4 In. 88.00
Trade Card, Parthenon, Athens, Greece, Black & White, c.1930, 4 1/4 x 6 1/4 In. 9.00
Trade Card, Patent Medicine, Purifies Blood, Creates Appetite, Cherub Blowing Horn . . . 12.00
Trade Card, Sarsaparilla, Little Girl In Big Hat, 4 3/4 x 3 In. 12.00
Trade Card, Sewing Circle, Children's Faces, 1892 Hood's Household Calendar, 4 In. . . . 17.00
Trade Card, Tooth Powder, Woman's Smiling Face, 4 3/4 x 3 1/8 In. 7.00

HORLICKS   James and William Horlick formed a company in 1873 to
produce Horlick's Food, an infant food made from bran and malt. Ten
years later, the product was reformulated and patented as Horlick's
Malted Milk. Since refrigeration was rare and milk was difficult to store,

malted milk was a nutritious, easily digested alternative for infants and invalids. Malted milk products were used in ration kits by American and British troops in both world wars. In 1890 James Horlick returned to his native England and began importing Horlick's Malted Milk. He opened a factory in Great Britain in 1908. The company advertised with the slogan "The Original Food Drink," and often pictured a girl with a small cow and a package of Horlick's. Horlick's sponsored the Lum and Abner radio programs during the 1930s. At about the same time, "malted milk" was removed from the product description. In 1926 the American and British Horlick's companies split; in 1945 they rejoined as UK Horlicks (without an apostrophe). The company was acquired by Beecham Products in 1969. Today, the major markets for Horlicks are Great Britain and India. In the United States, the drink and Horlicks Malties tablets are available from Internet retailers.

Jar, Apothecary, Malted Milk, Ground-In Glass Stopper, 9 1/2 In.	159.00
Jar, Original Malted Milk, Blue Embossed Enameled Letters, Metal Lid, 6 x 5 In.	330.00
Milk Bottle, Malted Milk, Racine, Wis., 11 In.	34.00
Milk Bottle, Malted Milk, Racine, Wis., Embossed, 7 In.	22.00
Milk Bottle, Malted Milk, Racine, Wis., Embossed, Screw-On Lid, 7 In.	50.00
Milk Bottle, Malted Milk, Racine, Wis., Embossed, Screw-On Tin Lid, 5 In.	39.00
Mirror, Malted Milk, Genuine, Nutritious, Maiden, Jersey Cow, Celluloid, 2 In.	106.00
Mirror, Malted Milk, Round, 2 1/8 In.	225.00
Mirror, Malted Milk, Woman, Cow, Stream, 2 1/8 In.	145.00
Mirror, Original Malted Milk, Woman & Cow, Round, 2 1/8 In.	44.00
Mug, H Chocolate, Restaurant Ware, Inca Ware, Shenango China, 1927-1954, 3 1/2 In.	20.00
Tin, Malted Milk, Fountain Brand, Graphics On 3 Sides, 8 1/2 x 6 1/4 In.	275.00
Tin, Malted Milk, Lithograph, Lid, Handle, 1920-1930, 10 In.	330.00

HOWARD JOHNSON   Howard Dearing Johnson was running a patent medicine store in Wollaston, Massachusetts, in 1925. He started making and selling his own ice cream, then added hot dogs. Johnson opened his first restaurant in Quincy, Massachusetts, in 1929. In 1935, in the depths of the Depression, Johnson came up with a clever idea— to sell franchises. In 1934 the company's first Red Coach Grill, a luxury restaurant, opened; in 1940, its first turnpike restaurant; and in 1954, its first motor lodge. The first famous orange roof was installed in 1931 and it topped every Howard Johnson building through the 1940s. It is one of the best-known identification tags in America. One of the company's first trademarks, stylized figures of Simple Simon and the pie man, was discontinued in the 1970s but has now reappeared. In 1966 the company's logo became a stylized picture of a Howard Johnson's building with a spire. In the 1980s, Howard Johnson Company changed ownership twice and the hotel system and restaurant chain were separated. In 1986 the restaurant licensees formed Franchise Associates Inc. (FAI). They own the original recipes and have exclusive rights to use and sublicense the Howard Johnson's name in connection with food products. In 1990 the name and lodging system were sold to HJ Acquisition Corp., later known as Howard Johnson International, Inc., a subsidiary of Hospitality Franchise Systems (HFS, now Cendant). At one time there were over a thousand restaurants and over five hundred motor lodges throughout North America. Currently there are nearly five hundred Howard Johnson hotels in fourteen countries and eighteen franchised restaurants. Today the restaurant franchise's logo includes the name in blue block letters and an orange triangle representing the famous roof. The hotel logo now features a hotel with sunrays behind it.

Advertisement, Ice Cream & Restaurants, 10 1/2 x 13 1/2 In.	5.00
Ashtray, Howard Johnson Motor Lodges, Aqua Silhouette, 3 3/4 In.	10.00
Ashtray, Motor Lodge, Clear Glass, Orange Roof Label, Octagonal, 4 1/2 In.	14.00
Ashtray, Motor Lodge, Restaurant, Glass, Orange Roof Label, Round, 4 1/2 In.	12.00 to 14.00
Ashtray, Restaurant, Lamppost, Boy, Man, Lantern, Square, 4 1/2 In.	14.00
Bank, Restaurant Shape, Orange Roof, Embossed, Plastic, 3 1/2 x 5 In.	29.00
Cup, Wax Paper, Dixie Cup, American Can Company, Sample, 1 1/2 x 1 2/3 In.	15.00

Hood's, Curb Sign, Old
Fashioned Ice Cream,
Metal, 2-Sided, 33 x 21 In.

Huntley & Palmers,
Tin, Chinese Vase,
Candleholder,
10 1/4 In., Pair

Directory, Host Of The Highways, Motor Lodges, Restaurants, 1960 .... 10.00
Matchbook, Enjoy Ho Jo's Famous Ice Cream, 28 Flavors, 20 Matches, Diamond 5.00
Matchbook, Landmark For Sleepy Americans, 20 Matches, Lion Match 5.00
Menu, Mask, Hat, Die Cut, Circular Slits, Child's, c.1960, 8 x 11 5/8 In. 18.00
Place Mat, Simple Simon, Ice Cream Shops, Restaurants, Early 1960s 10.00
Postcard, Midway, Pennsylvania Turnpike, 2 Scenes, Bedford, Pa., c.1950 .... 2.50
Postcard, Restaurant, Host Of The Highways, Lusterchrome, 3 1/2 x 5 1/2 In. 6.00

HUNTLEY & PALMERS   The word "biscuit" in England refers to what
is called a "cookie" in America. The first biscuit tins were made in
England during the 1830s. Thomas Huntley, a baker, asked his brother
Joseph, a tinsmith, to make some boxes so that he could ship his biscuits by stagecoach. George Palmer became a partner of Thomas Huntley in 1841, and by the end of the 1850s the other Palmer brothers were
involved in the biscuit-making business. The company was renamed
Huntley & Palmers. A method of doing transfer printing directly on
tinplate was patented by Benjamin George about 1860. Huntley &
Palmers biscuits were packed in tins with paper labels until 1868,
when the company began using printed tins. The first tin with a printed
scene was "Landscape," made in 1883. The words "by appointment"
appear on Huntley & Palmers tins made after 1885. The company
made hundreds of styles of colorful, imaginative tins, including figurals in the shape of teapots, books, baskets, clocks, and trucks. Huntley & Palmers formed Associated Biscuits Manufacturers Ltd. with
Peek Frean in 1921. Nabisco purchased Huntley & Palmers in 1982.
The company was renamed Jacob's Bakery Ltd. in 1989. Huntley
Bourne and Stevens, the primary manufacturer of Huntley & Palmers
tins, ceased production in 1985.

Postcard, Reading Factory, Divided Back, Postmark, c.1915 .... 22.00
Tin, 7 Books Between 2 Inlaid Sheraton Style Bookends, 8 3/4 In. 132.00
Tin, Biscuits, 8-Book Bundle, c.1900, 6 1/4 x 6 1/4 x 4 1/4 In. 61.00
Tin, Chinese Vase, Candleholder, 10 1/4 In., Pair ....*Illus* 176.00
Tin, Farmhouse, c.1931, 4 1/4 x 6 1/4 x 3 3/4 In. 832.00
Tin, Gold Instruments, Oranges, Faux Wood, Hinged Lid, Square, c.1910, 6 3/8 In. 85.00
Tin, Handbag, 7 x 6 x 2 1/4 In. 95.00
Tin, Lantern, 9 In. 42.00
Tin, Literature, 8 Classic Books, 1900-1940, 6 1/4 x 6 1/4 x 4 1/2 In. 319.00
Tin, Painter's Pallet Shape, Horse & Buggy, Lithograph, 7 3/4 x 9 1/4 In. 198.00
Tin, Purse Shape, Safari Scene, Elephant Handle, 6 1/4 x 7 3/4 x 3 In. 187.00
Tin, Roses, Pink, Yellow, Garden, 3 1/2 x 10 In. 36.00
Tin, Scottish Tartan, John O'Groats Shortbread, 4 1/2 x 5 In. 49.00
Tin, Square, 1 3/4 In. 70.00

I.W. HARPER   If you are looking for information on Mr. I.W. Harper,
you will have problems. I.W. Bernheim was a German immigrant who
arrived in the United States in 1867. He worked as a peddler, first with

a backpack, later with a horse and wagon. After his horse died, he worked in a grocery store and then for a wholesale liquor firm in Paducah, Kentucky. He and his brother Bernard started their own liquor business in 1872. They took in a partner, Nathan M. Uri, I.W.'s brother-in-law, and changed the company name to Bernheim Bros. & Uri in 1875. The company name reverted to Bernheim Bros. in 1889. I.W. wrote longhand letters to people listed in directories urging them to buy some of the company's specialty cordials. The family claims this effort was the origin of direct-mail advertising. One of the company's best salesmen was named Harper, so many orders asked for "Mr. Harper's whiskey." Bernheim decided to label his best-selling liquor brand "I.W. Harper," joining two of his own initials with his salesman's last name. Bernheim Distilling Company was incorporated in 1902. The family's interests were sold in 1933 and the company was sold to Schenley in 1937. The brand is now owned by United Distillers and Vintners, a division of Diageo; and unless you're in Japan, I.W. Harper is difficult to find. The Bernheim Distillery in Louisville, Kentucky, is now owned by Heaven Hill Distilleries.

Figure, Man, Top Hat, Cane, Ceramic, 16 In. 28.00
Sign, Grandfather, 3 Children, Glass, Reverse Paint, Frame, 32 x 44 In. 688.00
Sign, Hunting Dog, Cabin, Vitrolite Glass, Frame, 1909, 23 1/2 x 26 1/2 In. 3740.00
Sign, Hunting Dog, Camp, Bearskin, Vitrolite, Frame, 1906, 24 x 18 In. . . . . .750.00 to 1925.00
Sign, Hunting Lodge Scene, Milk Glass, Shadowbox Frame, 28 1/2 x 22 1/2 In. 715.00
Tray, Old Kentucky's Best, Oriental Woman, Wood, Glass, Handles, 18 x 13 1/2 In. 30.00

INK Ink was first used about 2500 B.C. in ancient Egypt and China. It was made of carbon mixed with oil. The first patented ink was made in England in 1792. Ink in bottles was available in the United States by 1819. Master inks contained about a quart of ink that could be poured into smaller dipping bottles. Bottles came in shapes known as cathedrals, teakettles, cones, igloos (or turtles), and umbrellas. Figural ink bottles can also be found. The bottle color affects its value. See related items in the Carter's Ink and Pencil categories of this book.

Bottle, Davids Electro Chemical Writing Fluid, Cobalt Blue, Original Cap, 32 Oz., 9 In. . 198.00
Bottle, Farley's Ink, 8-Sided, Amber, Pontil, 1840-1860, 1 3/4 In. 2090.00
Bottle, Harrison's Columbian Ink, Patent, Iron Pontil, Aqua, 1845-1860, 7 3/8 In. 358.00
Bottle, P & J. Arnold's, Combined Fluid, Contents, Embossed, Paper Label, 5 In. 121.00
Bottle, P & J. Arnold's, Ledger Red, Embossed, Paper Label, Top, 4 1/2 In. 143.00
Bottle, P & J. Arnold's, Writing Fluid, Embossed, Paper Label, Original Top, 4 In. 99.00
Bottle, P & J. Arnold's, Writing Fluid, Embossed, Paper Label, Original Top, 5 1/2 In. . . . 1322.00
Bottle, P & J. Arnold's, Writing Fluid, Embossed, Paper Label, Original Top, 9 In. 209.00
Bottle, Sanford's Fountain Pen, Clear, Embossed, Pamphlet, Box, 2 Oz., 2 3/4 In. 198.00
Bottle, Sanford's Penit Violet Fountain Pen Ink, Cap, 2 In. 5.00
Bottle, Stafford's Ink, Teal Green, Qt. 75.00
Bottle, Stovink, The Only Black That Stays Black, Unused, Box, 1908, 5 In. 77.00
Bottle, Underwood's Ink, Cobalt Blue, Qt. 125.00
Bottle, Warrens Congress Ink, 8-Sided, Aqua, Pontil, 1845-1860, 4 1/4 In. 1045.00

Ink, Sign, Sanford's, Faultless, Inks & Mucilage, Tin, Embossed, 14 x 20 In.

Jar, Ice Cream Cone, Glass, Metal Lid & Holder, Display, 14 x 7 In.

Bottle, Water's Ink, Umbrella, Blue Green, 6-Sided, Troy, N.Y., 1845-1860, 2 3/4 In. 2640.00
Bottle, Wood's, Black Ink, Cone Shape, Olive Amber, Portland, 1845-1860, 2 3/8 In. 5225.00
Box, Stovink, The Only Black That Stays Black, Cardboard, 1908, 6 1/2 In. 80.00
Calendar, Stafford's American Inks Do Not Thicken, Tin, Desk Top, 1890-1920, 4 3/8 In. . . 209.00
Jar, Sanford's Ink, Lid, Closure, Stoneware 187.00
Sign, Sanford's, Faultless, Inks & Mucilage, Tin, Embossed, 14 x 20 In. . . . . *Illus* 8250.00
Sign, Stephens Inks, 3 Ink Bottles, Blue, White, England, 23 1/2 x 15 1/2 In. 322.00

IVORY SOAP, see Procter & Gamble

JANTZEN In 1910 John A. Zehntbauer and Carl C. Jantzen founded the Portland Knitting Co. in Portland, Oregon, to produce sweaters, woolen hosiery, and other clothing. A member of a rowing club asked the company to make him a pair of rowing trunks, which led to the company's specialization in swimwear. In 1918 the company was renamed Jantzen Knitting Mills. Jantzen received a patent for the elastic rib-stitch swimsuit in 1921. Early suits were reported to weigh nine pounds when wet. In about 1923 the company's logo, the diving girl, was introduced. She wears a red Jantzen suit and knitted cap. Known as Jantzen, Inc., since 1954, the company is still headquartered in Portland.

Ashtray, Jantzen Swim Suit Co., Figural, Woman Diving, Plaster, Glass, c.1950, 6 x 5 In. . 578.00
Brochure, Jantzen Style Revue, Fold-Out, Die Cut, Paper, 1932, 5 x 10 In. 154.00
Logo, Lady Diver, Red Hat, Suit, Socks, Embroidered, 9 1/2 In. 44.00
Paperweight, Figural, Girl Diver, Enamel Painted, Metal, Wood Stand, 10 In. 963.00
Radiator Cap, Figural, Girl Diver, Boyce Moto Meter, Metal, Marble Base, 9 In. 1210.00
Sign, Girl Diver, Red Hat, Suit, Socks, Embossed, Metal, 12 1/2 x 18 In. 770.00
Swimsuit, Green, Striped Leg, Knit, 1923 . . . . 88.00

JAR Jars are glass and usually have a screw-on metal lid or a glass top. They may have held homemade jelly or canned foods or may have been placed on store countertops to encourage impulse purchases. Both types are listed in this category.

'76 Boot Polish, Metal Lid, Paper Label, Gadi, Memphis, 2 1/2 In. 8.00
Adams Pure Chewing Gum, 13 In. 198.00
Adams Pure Chewing Gum, Glass, Acid Etched, 5 x 5 x 11 In. 83.00
Adams Tutti-Frutti Gum, 100 Packages, Pepsin, Paper Label, 11 In. 413.00
Apothecary, Cer. Plumbi Subac, Recessed Gold Glass Label, Milk Glass, 6 1/2 In. 242.00
Banner Oxblood Shoe Stain Polish, Black Shoeshine Boy, 1 1/4 x 2 3/4 In. 55.00
Biscuit, Peek, Frean & Co., Ceramic, S.F. & Co., England, 6 1/2 In. 225.00
Bromo-Kola, For All Headaches, Cover, Detroit, Mich., 1885-1920, 7 1/2 In. 134.00
Bucklen's Arnica Salve, Only Genuine Article, Ground Glass Stopper, Square, 10 x 5 In. . 110.00
Buffalo Brand Salted Peanuts, Painted Label, F.M. Hoyt, 10 x 7 In. 440.00
Chamberlain's Tablets, Biliousness, Headache, Indigestion, Transfer Labels, 12 In. 265.00
Chamberlain's Tablets, They Help Nature, Ground Glass Stopper, 12 x 6 1/2 x 5 In. 385.00
Chicos Spanish Peanuts, 5 Cents, Glass, Metal Base & Cover, 1900, 11 x 8 In. . . .303.00 to 495.00
Compressed Tablets Soda-Mint & Pepsin, John Wyeth & Bro, Amber, c.1885, 2 In. 39.00
Cover, Eat Tom's Toasted Peanuts, 10 x 7 In. 55.00
Cover, Lay's Salted Peanuts, 5 Cents, Glass, Red Letters, 10 In. 50.00
Crispo, Ice Cream Cones, Round, Cake Cone Co., St. Louis, 11 x 9 In. 138.00
Curtiss Chicos Spanish Peanuts, 5 Cents, Embossed Tin Base, Tin Lid, 12 In. 413.00
Diaprex, Milk Glass, Metal Lid, Bell & Moss, Detroit, Mich., Sample, 1 3/4 x 1 3/8 In. . . 45.00
Dr. King's New Life Pills, Always Satisfy, Label Under Glass, 1890-1920, 13 In. 448.00
Dr. Samuel H.P. Lee's Lithotriptic, Cork, Wraparound Label, Contents, c.1931, 2 1/2 x 2 In. 33.00
Fox's Hot Chocolate, Genuine, Glass, Indented, 8 x 4 In. 50.00
Gibson Mixed Fruit Tablets, Paper Label, 2-Piece Mold, 13 In. 121.00
Gordon's Peanut, Red Car, 10 In. 110.00
Grand Union Toilet Cream, Milk Glass, 6-Sided, Embossed Lid, Label, 2 1/2 x 2 In. 45.00
Guth Fruit Tablets, Aqua, Baltimore, 1885-1900, 8 7/8 In. 112.00
Hall Ice Cream Soda, Lime Syrup, Porcelain, 1920s, 10 x 4 In. 85.00
Ice Cream Cone, Glass, Metal Lid & Holder, Display, 14 x 7 In. . . . . *Illus* 605.00
Johnson & Johnson, Linton Moist Gauze, Amber, Contents, Label, Metal Clamp, 4 1/2 In. 44.00
Kennedy's Salt Rheum Ointment, Contents, Wraparound Label, Wrapper, 3 1/4 In. 11.00
Kis-Me Gum, Glass, Square, Cover, Louisville, Ky., 10 1/2 x 4 5/8 In. 100.00

Knighthood Apple Butter, Stoneware, Paper Label, 7 In.	165.00
Lance Peanut, Crossed Swords, 12 1/2 In.	66.00
Lance Peanut, Lance Lid, 13 In.	77.00
Lance Peanut, Metal Lid, 14 In.	116.00
Lilly Tablet, Amber, 1000 Solvets, No. 23 Boric Acid, 5 Grains, Cork, 9 3/4 In.	132.00
Meredith & Drew, Meredith & Drew Biscuits On Metal Lid, England, 9 1/4 In.	265.00
Nut House, Embossed House & Letters, 10 In.	133.00
Nut House, Embossed House & Letters, 12 In.	286.00
Pacific Cherry & Fruit Co., Maraschino Cherries In Heavy Syrup, 1 1/2 x 3 In.	16.00
Pond's Extract Ointment, Amber, Labels, Tin Cap, Metal Pull Ring, c.1892, 2 3/4 In.	55.00
Ramon's Little Doctor, Counter Top, 12 Sample Products, 7 In.	165.00
Ramon's Medicine Store, Metal Cover, 7 3/4 x 7 In.	110.00
Red Tips Cigars, Glass, Label, Horse Head In Horseshoe, 50 Cigars, Glass Lid, 7 In.	148.00
Rowntrees Gums, Metal Art Nouveau Style Lid, England, 9 1/4 In.	104.00
Royal Marshmallow Container, Bulbous, Embossed Letters, 12 x 10 In.	275.00
Shac For Headache, Glass Stopper, Label Under Glass, 6 1/2 In.	880.00
Squirrel Brand Salted Peanuts, Paper Label, Tin Lithograph Lid, 9 x 6 In.	77.00
Su Su Salted Nuts, Hinged Aluminum Hatch Door, 12 In.	121.00
Teck Chocolate Billets, Embossed, 16 1/2 In.	565.00
Tip Top Nipples, Painted Label, Whitall Tatum Company, Round, 9 x 5 1/2 In.	1265.00
Tom's Roasted Peanuts, 5 Cents, Glass Lid, 10 In.	61.00 to 77.00
Tom's Toasted Peanuts, Delicious, Red Knob, 10 In.	33.00
Universal Vanishing Cream, Milk Glass, Paper Label, Screw Lid, 2 1/4 x 2 1/4 x 2 3/4 In.	5.50
Wise Old Owl, Glass, Owl Shape, Embossed, Metal Lid, Owl Drug Stores, 21 In.	325.00
Zubes, Breath In Comfort, Defy Cold, Cover, Paper Label, Contents, 17 3/4 In.	378.00
Zubes, Cover, Paper Label, Contents, England, 21 In.	378.00

JELL-O   Peter Cooper, the inventor of the Tom Thumb locomotive and the Peter Cooper rocker, patented a gelatin dessert about 1845. It seems to have been ignored until 1895, when Mr. Pearl Wait, a cough-syrup maker in LeRoy, New York, rediscovered the product, adapted it, and started selling it in 1897. His wife named it "Jell-O." It did not sell well. In 1899 the patent was sold to Francis Woodward for $450. The product's first trademark was a picture of Elizabeth King, the daughter of the trademark's designer. She was pictured stacking packages of Jell-O. Woodward's company, Genesee Pure Food Company, became the Jell-O Company in 1923. Two years later, it was purchased by the Postum Company, which became General Foods Corp. in 1929. After many changes in ownership, the Jell-O brand name and trademark are used today by Altria's Kraft Foods Company. In 1902 there were four flavors of Jell-O: strawberry, raspberry, orange, and lemon. From 1934 to 1944, Jell-O radio advertisements on the *Jack Benny Show* listed six flavors: strawberry, raspberry, cherry, orange, lemon, and lime. Other Jell-O products are Jell-O pudding and pie filling (1932), Jell-O instant pudding (1953), and sugar-free Jell-O gelatin (1984). The Jell-O brand is now found on more than 158 products, including gelatin, pudding, ready-to-eat snacks, and no-bake desserts.

Advertisement, Animals Series, Squirrel, Climbing Tree, Verse, Full Color, 10 x 13 In.	35.00
Advertisement, Humpty Dumpty, Rhyming Verse, 1956, 10 1/4 x 13 1/2 In.	13.00
Advertisement, Instant Pudding, 2 Boys Mixing Jell-O Instant Pudding, 10 1/4 x 14 In.	12.00
Box, Orange Flavor, 9 Cents	5.00
Cookbook, Ice Cream Powder, 1908, 16 Pages	16.50
Cookbook, Jack & Mary's Recipes, Jack Benny, Mary Livingstone, 1937, 23 Pages	35.00 to 50.00
Cookbook, Recipes, Want Something Different?, 1931, 23 Pages	10.00
Cookbook, What You Can Do With Jell-O, 1936	10.00
Figure, Giraffe, Eating Jell-O, Everyone Reaches For Jell-O, Baston, c.1955, 5 In.	135.00
Folder, Girl Eating Jell-O	8.00
Sign, Jack Benny Invites You To Try Jell-O, Cardboard, 30 x 20 In.	44.00

JEWELRY   Many types of pins, charms, bracelets, and other jewelry have been made with advertising trademarks or names as part of the design. Stickpins and watch fobs were popular advertising items in the early 1900s. Watch fobs have their own category in this book; additional advertising jewelry may be listed by brand name.

Ring, American Airlines, Junior Pilots 42.00
Ring, Mr. Softee, I Like Mister Softee, Vari-Vue, Flasher, Flicker 25.00
Ring, Sky King Electronic TV, Magnifier Lens, Metal Band, 1940s 125.00
Stickpin, D & M Sporting Goods, Dog, Gold Wash, 2 1/4 x 5/8 In. 132.00
Tie Bar, Evinrude Motors, Children In Boat, Gold Plated, Enamel, 1950s, 3 x 3 In. 58.00
Tie Clip, Packard Bell, 3 x 1/2 In. 85.00
Tie Tack, Peppy Flame, Diamond In Hand, 3/4 In. 38.00

JOHN DEERE   John Deere was a blacksmith in Grand Detour, Illinois, in 1836. He invented a new, more efficient plow blade. By 1848 he had sold hundreds of plows outfitted with his new steel blades. That same year, Deere moved his company to Moline, Illinois, where it is still in business. The leaping deer trademark, first registered in 1876, has been updated seven times, most recently in 2000.

Can, Heavy Duty Steering Gear Lubricant, Metal, Deer, Pt. 7.50
Sign, Farm Implements, Porcelain, 108 x 36 In. 3300.00
Sign, Farm Implements, Red, Yellow, Black, Tin, 30 x 12 In. 468.00
Sign, General Purpose Farm Tractor, Enameled, Porcelain, 10 x 10 In. 25.00

JOSEPH SCHLITZ BREWING COMPANY, see Schlitz

KELLOGG   Cold breakfast cereal was an innovation of the late nineteenth century. The Battle Creek Sanitarium in Battle Creek, Michigan, was established by the Seventh-Day Adventists as a health spa in 1866. Dr. John Kellogg became its manager in 1876. He experimented with new breakfast foods and, with his brother Will Keith Kellogg, made and patented the first dried wheat flakes in 1894. They developed cornflakes in 1898. About that time, the doctor started the Sanitas Nut Food Company, a mail-order health-food business. W.K. Kellogg eventually became the firm's general manager. In 1906 the Battle Creek Toasted Corn Flake Company was formed. W.K. Kellogg's signature was on the first packages, along with the slogan "The Original Bears This Signature." In 1907 an attractive girl holding corn was used with the slogan "Sweetheart of the Corn." The Kellogg's rooster, Cornelius, made his debut in 1953 with the slogan "The Best to You Each Morning." The company name was changed to Toasted Corn Flake Company in 1907, Kellogg Toasted Corn Flake Company in 1909, and Kellogg Company in 1922. Kellogg made many products, including Krumbles (1912), Pep (1912), 40% Bran Flakes (1915), All-Bran (1916), Rice Krispies (1928), Raisin Bran (1942), Corn Soya (1943), Frosted Flakes (1952), Special K (1955), Froot Loops (1963), Pop Tarts (1964), and Product 19 (1966). Snap, Crackle, and Pop, the Rice Krispies characters, were introduced in 1933. Many advertising collectibles picturing the three can be found. Tony the Tiger became the sole promoter of Frosted Flakes in 1958. The Froot Loops character, Toucan Sam, was introduced in 1963. The first Kellogg cereal premium, *The Funny Jungleland Moving Pictures Book,* was offered in 1910. The company's first advertising dolls were Goldilocks and the Three Bears, made in 1925. Kellogg's bought television advertising on *Tom Corbett, Space Cadet* (1950s), *Jimmy Durante's All Star Review* (1950s), and *Howdy Doody* (1947–1960).

Alarm Clock, Dig 'Em, Red Enamel Case, Chimes, 1979, 4 x 5 1/2 In. 30.00
Baseball, Tony The Tiger, Portrait, Paw Print Signature, 1980s, 2 1/2 In. 12.00
Booklet, Funny Jungleland Moving Pictures, Die Cut, 1932, 6 x 8 1/4 In. . . . . .20.00 to 38.00
Booklet, Nursery Rhymes, 1931, 8 1/4 x 3 3/4 In., 16 Pages 20.00
Booklet, Swimming & Diving Sports Library, 1934, 46 Pages 12.00
Bowl Set, Tony, Toucan Sam, Corny Jr., Snap, Crackle & Pop, 1995, 4 Piece 14.00
Box, Bran Flakes, Individual Serving, Unopened, Battle Creek, 3 5/8 x 2 1/2 x 1 3/8 In. . .   60.00
Button, Pep Cereal, 29th Bombardment Squadron, Rabbit, Boxing Gloves, Rocket, 1943 .   19.00
Canister, New Oata, Free Sample, 4 x 2 1/4 In. 55.00
Cookie Jar, Tony The Tiger, Ceramic, 1977, 10 1/2 In. 220.00

Kellogg, Sign, Corn Flakes, Scouts Today,
Leaders Tomorrow, 1951, 23 x 30 In.

Any lithographed can with a picture is of more value than a lithographed can with just names. Any paper-labeled can that can be dated before 1875 is rare. Any ad that pictures an American flag or a black person has added value.

Doll, Crackle, Early 1970s, 8 In.	20.00
Doll, Daddy Bear, Cloth, Early 1900s, 12 In.	80.00
Doll, Goldilocks & 3 Bears, Printed Cloth, 12 In., 4 Piece	242.00
Doll, Kelly The Dog, Cloth Dog, Kit, Uncut, Instructions, Envelope, 1948	80.00
Doll, Mama Bear, Cloth, 12 In.	46.00
Figure Set, Snap, Crackle, Pop, Plastic, Movable Head, Arms, 22 1/2 In.	2800.00
Flicker Disc, William Holden, Submarine Command, Plastic, Blue, 1951, 1 1/4 In.	29.00
Measuring Cup, 3 Spouts, Green, 1 Cup, 3 1/2 x 3 In.	30.00
Paper Doll, Cowboy & Indian Cutouts, No. 3, Premium, 1930s	8.00
Pin, Fire Chief, Pep Cereal Premium, Famous Artists Syn., c.1946, 3/4 In.	10.00
Pin, Superman, Pep Cereal Premium, Copyright D.C. Inc.	10.00
Puppet Set, Snap, Crackle, Pop, Push Button, Dancing, 1984, 4 1/2 In.	100.00
Ring, Tom Corbett Space Cadet Rocket, No. 1, Space Cadet Girl Uniform, Plastic, 1952	25.00
Ring, Tom Corbett Space Cadet Rocket, No. 2, Parallo-Ray Gun, Plastic, 1952	25.00
Ring, Tom Corbett Space Cadet Rocket, No. 8, Space Cruiser, Plastic, 1952	25.00
Sign, Corn Flakes, Deliciously Flavored, W.K. Kellogg, Cardboard, Hanger, 8 x 6 In.	138.00
Sign, Corn Flakes, Ear Of Corn, 1910 World's Best Ear, Die Cut, Paperboard, 11 x 5 In.	77.00
Sign, Corn Flakes, Scouts Today, Leaders Tomorrow, 1951, 23 x 30 In. *Illus*	688.00
Sign, Scouts Today, Leaders Tomorrow, Frame, 30 x 23 In.	413.00
Stencil, Rice Krispies, Snap, Crackle & Pop, 1970, 5 1/2 x 3 In.	13.00

KENTUCKY FRIED CHICKEN Harland Sanders started cooking chicken in a room behind a gas station in Corbin, Kentucky, in the 1930s. His restaurant grew until 1956, when he was forced to sell. Sanders, by then called "Colonel," decided to start a franchise business. He offered restaurant owners his secret blend of herbs and spices and showed them how to prepare his pressure-cooked chicken. He charged the restaurants a nickel for each chicken they cooked his way. In 1964 Sanders sold his Kentucky Fried Chicken franchise business with the stipulation that his recipe and standards not be changed, and he traveled the country as a spokesman for the product. His image soon became a trademark, reproduced on boxes, signs, toys, and other promotional materials. The company was acquired by Heublein, Inc., in 1971, then was sold several times. It is now part of Yum! Brands, Inc. Kentucky Fried Chicken became known as KFC in 1991. The Colonel died in 1980 at age ninety.

Cup, Tweety Bird, Looney Tunes, Plastic, c.1992, 3 x 3 1/2 x 5 In.	12.00
Figure, Colonel Sanders, Plastic, 6 In.	25.00
Light Globe, Chicken Bucket, Red, White, Black, 1969, 10 x 8 In.	43.00
Matchbook, Colonel On One Side, Building On Other	10.00
Model, Building, Life Like Buildems, Box, 1950s-1960s, HO Scale	6.25 to 21.00
Salt & Pepper, Colonel Sanders, Starling Plastics, Canada, 4 3/8 In.	65.00
Saltshaker, Colonel Sanders Bust, Plastic, Margardt Corp., 1972, 3 3/4 In.	45.00
Tumbler, Colonel Sanders, Recipe, North America Hospitality Dish, 3 3/4 In.	9.00

KOOL In 1933 Brown & Williamson introduced Kool, the first nationally distributed menthol cigarette. The cigarette was sold in tins until 1940. The brand's mascot, a penguin, appeared in print and radio advertisements for more than ten years before he was given the name Willie in 1947. Willie had become much more cartoonish than the original by the time he made his television debut in 1954. He appeared in ads until about 1960. In 2004 Brown & Williamson merged with fellow tobacco giant R.J. Reynolds to form Reynolds American Inc. The company still sells Kool cigarettes. Kool collectibles include Willie and Millie salt and pepper shakers, penguin figurines, magazine advertisements, posters, and signs.

Cigarette Case, Penguin, Metal, Pop Open, Pocket, 3 1/4 x 2 5/8 In.	151.00
Figure, Penguin, Dr. Kool, Chalkware, 4 1/2 x 2 3/8 In.	261.00
Lighter, Mr. Kool Penguin, Cast Metal, 1940s, 4 1/8 x 1 3/4 In.	410.00
Salt & Pepper, Kool Cigarettes, Penguin, Millie & Willie, 3 1/2 In.	38.00
Sign, Kool Cigarettes, Has The Union Bug On It, 15 Cents, Cardboard, 1940s, 18 x 12 In.	200.00
Sign, Kool Cigarettes, Snow Fresh Filter, Penguin, Tin, 30 x 12 In.	28.00

KRAFT James L. Kraft moved to the United States from Canada in 1903 with $65. He started what has become the largest packaged-food company in the United States and Canada by selling cheese to grocers from his horse-drawn wagons. Kraft and his brothers incorporated J.L. Kraft & Bros. Co. in 1909. In 1916 Kraft was granted a patent for making processed cheese. By 1917 Kraft cheese was being packed in tins for shipment to soldiers overseas. The first foil-wrapped five-pound loaf was marketed in 1921, and by 1923 wooden Kraft cheese boxes were being saved and reused by thrifty housewives. In 1937 Kraft Macaroni & Cheese dinner was introduced. Meanwhile, in 1930 the company, then known as Kraft-Phenix Cheese Corp., had been acquired by National Dairy Products Corp. That company changed its name to Kraftco Corp. in 1969 and then to Kraft Inc. in 1976. Philip Morris Companies acquired Kraft in 1988 and a year later Philip Morris's two food divisions, Kraft and General Foods, were combined to form Kraft General Foods. The division was renamed Kraft Foods, Inc., in 1995. Philip Morris Companies was renamed Altria Group in 2003. Kraft Foods, Inc., headquartered in Northfield, Illinois, is a division of Altria. Swankyswigs, decorated reusable glasses that held five ounces of cheese spread, were introduced in 1933. At first, the glasses were hand-painted, but by 1937 a silk-screening process was used. These are popular collector's items. The swankyswig was discontinued in 1958, although a few special glasses have been offered since then.

Sign, Mayonnaise, Hand Holds Jar, Cardboard, 2-Sided, Die Cut, 1930s, 11 x 10 In.	55.00
Sign, Pex, Milk-Bank Boost, Chicken Shape, Die Cut, Embossed, Metal, 19 x 13 1/2 In.	121.00
Swankyswig, Salmon & White Flowers & Leaves, 5 1/2 In.	8.00
Swankyswig, Yellow, White & Black Designs, 5 In.	8.00
Toy, Truck, Variety Of Cheese, Diecast Cab, Pressed Steel Body, Smith Miller, 14 In.	248.00

LABEL Paper labels on boxes, bottles, and packages are collected today. Labels were first used on packaged food at the end of the eighteenth century. Early labels were simple inked pieces of paper attached to a package. Since then, paper labels have been produced using whatever technology was available at the time. Labels went from stencil or woodblock print to color lithograph to photomechanical offset print. But the golden age of collectible labels came during the nineteenth century, when the process of stone lithography was perfected. Elaborate raised, embossed labels were being printed by the late nineteenth century. Wooden cigar boxes with paper labels were first made during the early 1800s. By 1870 there were nearly twenty thousand different brands of American cigars, and a unique label was needed for each brand. Early broom labels were woodblock prints; some companies have used the same broom label for over eighty years, so appearance is not always an accurate way to date a broom label. The first fruit crate labels were used by orange growers in California about 1880. The labels soon identified all types of oranges, lemons, apples, pears, grapes, and other produce. Today many mail-order catalogs sell fruit crate and tobacco labels.

Barrel, Dr. Hess Stock Tonic, Black Diamond, Paper, 21 In. 14.00
Cigar, A Huis Clos, 2 Women Smoking, Men Watching, 4 1/2 x 4 1/2 In. 125.00
Cigar, Ace, Champion Canadian Race Horse, 2 1/2 x 5 1/4 In. 45.00
Cigar, Ace, Champion Canadian Race Horse, 6 x 9 In. 150.00
Cigar, Acme, Cigar Over Valley, Sunburst, 1909, 4 1/2 x 4 1/2 In. 30.00
Cigar, Acropolis, Athens Citadel, Parthenon, 6 x 9 In. 40.00
Cigar, Actividad, Smoke Actividad Cigars, Mercury, Globe, Coins, Sample, 6 x 9 In. 100.00
Cigar, Adam & Eve, Apple Tree, Azaleas, 6 x 9 In. 7.00
Cigar, Affecionada, Woman, White Lace Mantilla, Factory, Coins, 4 1/2 x 4 1/2 In. 12.00
Cigar, Airedale, Dog, Yellow Ground, 6 x 9 In. 40.00
Cigar, Alameda, Woman Smoking, Heppenheimer & Maurer, 6 x 9 In. 175.00
Cigar, All Strikes, Men Bowling, Sample, 6 x 9 In. 750.00
Cigar, Allright, Man On Bicycle, Handlebar Mustache, 4 1/2 x 4 1/2 In. 15.00
Cigar, America's Pride, George Washington, Crossing Delaware, 4 1/2 x 4 1/2 In. 10.00
Cigar, American Belle, Woman, Flowers, Harbor, Schwencke, 1900s, 6 x 9 In. 30.00
Cigar, American Citizen, Hand Made, 5 Cents, George Washington, Eagle, 6 x 9 In. 3.00
Cigar, American Derby, Horse Race, Horseshoe, Sample, 6 x 9 In. 250.00
Cigar, Archimedes, 4 1/2 x 4 1/2 In. 60.00
Cigar, Aristocrat, Flor De Tabacos, 2 Men, Cuban Street, 6 x 9 In. 8.00
Cigar, Artola, Greek Woman, Olympian Statue, 6 x 9 In. 5.00
Cigar, Attaka, Art Nouveau Woman, Gold Feather, Cherubs, 4 1/2 x 4 1/2 In. 75.00
Cigar, Automobilist, Man, Woman & Butler In Early Car, Sample, 6 x 9 In. 1250.00
Cigar, Baby Pearls, J. Bruce Payne, 3 Little Girls, 6 x 9 In. 300.00
Cigar, Bantam, Worth Fighting For, 2 Fighting Cocks, Cigar, 6 x 9 In. 200.00
Cigar, Baronnet, Pigeon, Gold Leaves, 4 1/2 x 4 1/2 In. 10.00
Cigar, Bella De Cuba, Girl Playing Guitar, Fan Border, Flowers, 6 x 9 In. 85.00
Cigar, Ben Franklin, 4 1/2 x 4 1/2 In. 36.00
Cigar, Ben Hur, Chariot, 4 White Horses, 2 1/2 x 5 1/4 In. 15.00
Cigar, Bering, Man, White Beard, Red Hat, Havana, 2 1/2 x 5 1/4 In. 5.00
Cigar, Black Hawk, Chief Of The Broadleafs, 10 Cents, 6 x 9 In. 150.00
Cigar, Blitz, Thunder, Lightning, Water, 6 x 9 In. 650.00
Cigar, Blue Ribbon, Lithograph, Blue Sunburst, c.1900, 8 Piece 5.00
Cigar, Bombay, 3 Uniformed Men Smoking, 4 1/2 x 4 1/2 In. 150.00
Cigar, Bulldog, Dog, Gold Medals, Villazon & Company, 6 x 9 In. 25.00
Cigar, Calvano, Cavalier, Ruffled Collar, 6 x 9 In. 6.00
Cigar, Canvas Back, Cigar In Floating Shoe, Ducks, 4 1/2 x 4 1/2 In. 225.00
Cigar, Carl The Great, Knight On Horse, 4 1/2 x 4 1/2 In. 50.00
Cigar, Catador, Man, Red Turban, 4 1/2 x 4 1/2 In. 15.00
Cigar, Charles The Great, Charlemagne, Frankish King, 4 1/2 x 4 1/2 In. 35.00
Cigar, Chesterfield, Bust, Gloves, Letters, 4 1/2 x 4 1/2 In. 35.00
Cigar, Cicero, 6 x 9 In. 250.00
Cigar, Club Friends, Sample, 6 x 9 In. 1850.00
Cigar, Colonist, 4 1/2 x 4 1/2 In. 250.00
Cigar, Conrad Weiser, 4 1/2 x 4 1/2 In. 8.00
Cigar, Cornucopia, 6 x 9 In. 250.00
Cigar, Courier, Man On Running Horse, 4 1/2 x 4 1/2 In. 100.00
Cigar, Cuban Cousin, Smiling Woman Holding Cuban Flag, 6 x 9 In. 350.00
Cigar, Cuban Girl, Woman Hitting Tambourine, 4 1/2 x 4 1/2 In. 30.00
Cigar, Daily Habit, Cigar Of Merit, Parrot, 6 x 9 In. 85.00
Cigar, Diamond Habit, Good, Hygienic Smoke, 6 x 9 In. 30.00
Cigar, Double Eagle, Rough Havanas, 4 1/2 x 4 1/2 In. 7.00
Cigar, Dyke Cigars, Cigar Of The Select, 4 1/2 x 4 1/2 In. 9.00
Cigar, El Bubble, Bubble Gum Cigars, 6 x 9 In. 200.00
Cigar, El Corsicano, Napoleon On Horse, 4 1/2 x 4 1/2 In. 145.00
Cigar, Elk Social, 4 1/2 x 4 1/2 In. 125.00
Cigar, Even Steven, 2 1/2 x 5 1/4 In. 5.00
Cigar, Face Value, Large Cigar, Gold Medals, 4 1/2 x 4 1/2 In. 250.00
Cigar, Fleetwood, Harness Racer, Heppenheimer's Sons, 4 1/2 x 4 1/2 In. 250.00
Cigar, Flor De Bouquet, Lithograph, Woman, Garden, Birds, c.1874, 4 1/4 x 4 1/4 In. 5.00

Cigar, Flore De Scotia, Mary Queen Of Scots, 4 1/2 x 4 1/2 In. 35.00
Cigar, Florinda, Woman, White Lace Head Cover, Nail Tag, 4 1/2 In. 7.00
Cigar, Frazzle, Beats 'Em All To A Frazzle, 6 x 9 In. 150.00
Cigar, G. Washington, 3 1/2 x 2 In. 30.00
Cigar, Golden Buck, 4 1/2 x 4 1/2 In. 150.00
Cigar, Gouden Leeuw, Lion, 4 1/2 x 4 1/2 In. 20.00
Cigar, Grain Exchange Special, Sheaf Of Wheat, 4 1/2 x 4 1/2 In. 150.00
Cigar, Grand Prix, 6 x 9 In. 50.00
Cigar, Grandmother, 4 1/2 x 4 1/2 In. 300.00
Cigar, Happy Felix, Always Good, Smiling Man, 6 x 9 In. 15.00
Cigar, Henry G, Baseball Game, Horserace, 6 x 9 In. 125.00
Cigar, Honest Yankee, Uncle Sam, U.S. Map, 6 x 9 In. 125.00
Cigar, Infanta Eulalia, Queen, Jeweled Crown, 4 1/2 x 4 1/2 In. 8.00
Cigar, John Hancock, 4 1/2 x 4 1/2 In. 20.00
Cigar, Katy Barry, 6 x 9 In. 45.00
Cigar, Key West, c.1900, 8 x 6 In. 11.00
Cigar, King Coal, Top Wrap, 5 x 8 In. 35.00
Cigar, Kohler's Hand Made, 5 Cents, Big Value, 6 x 9 In. 2.00
Cigar, La Carita, Woman, Hat, Purple Flowers, 4 1/2 x 4 1/2 In. 4.00
Cigar, La Coronita, Seleccion Especiales, Queen On Throne, 4 1/2 x 4 1/2 In. 25.00
Cigar, La Festa, Roman Emperor, 1911, 4 1/2 x 4 1/2 In. 6.00
Cigar, La Flor De Lincoln, 4 1/2 x 4 1/2 In. 25.00
Cigar, Lagman's Havana, 6 x 9 In. 150.00
Cigar, Las Toscana, Reliance Cigar Factory, Esquisitos Tabacos, 6 x 9 In. 60.00
Cigar, Leatherstocking, Soldier Sitting On Log, Dog, Rifle, 6 x 9 In. 650.00
Cigar, Lipton, Lipton's Picture, Flower Border, H. Simon & Sons, Seal 25.00
Cigar, Lipton, Lipton's Flowers, Clover, Sailboat, 4 1/2 x 4 1/2 In. 85.00
Cigar, Little Cousins, 5 Cents, Straight, Clear Havana Filler, 6 x 9 In. 5.00
Cigar, Los Inmortales, Lincoln, Washington, Grant, Flags, Eagle, Medals, 6 x 9 In. 95.00
Cigar, Lumberman's Friend, 4 1/2 x 4 1/2 In. 150.00
Cigar, Marigold, 3 Flowers, Blue Ground, 4 1/2 x 4 1/2 In. 40.00
Cigar, Martellus, Red Robe, Griffins, Torches, Wood Grain, Top Wrap, 5 x 8 In. 25.00
Cigar, Monkey Brand, Blue On Vellum, Top Sheet, 5 x 8 In. 25.00
Cigar, Monroe Doctrine, Havana Cigars, Capital Building, W.F. Mc. Co., Nail Tag 6.00
Cigar, New Cuba, Los Heroes, Cuban Flag, 4 1/2 x 4 1/2 In. 75.00
Cigar, Nip & Tuck, 2 Collie Dogs, Yellow Ground, 6 x 9 In. 150.00
Cigar, Old Abe, End Flap, 2 1/2 x 5 1/4 In. 6.00
Cigar, Orakel, Green Man, Lizard On Helmet, Purple Ground, 6 x 9 In. 45.00
Cigar, Ornstein's ABC Cigar, 4 1/2 x 4 1/2 In. 5.00
Cigar, Papillion, Butterfly, Flower Garland, Purple Ground, 4 1/2 x 4 1/2 In. 50.00
Cigar, Percal Sari, Middle Eastern Dancer, 6 x 9 In. 150.00
Cigar, Pig Tail, 4 1/2 x 4 1/2 In. 15.00
Cigar, Porto Habana, Gold Eagle, Lighthouse, Blue Ground, 4 1/2 x 4 1/2 In. 4.00
Cigar, Quaker Quality, Quaker Man In Red Chair, 6 x 9 In. 15.00
Cigar, Race King, Harness Race, Sample, 6 x 9 In. 450.00
Cigar, Red Cloud, Indian Warrior On Horse, 4 1/2 x 4 1/2 In. 20.00
Cigar, Reina Bella, Woman, Red Roses, 6 x 9 In. 6.00
Cigar, Rose, C.C. Bickel, Louisville, Ky., 2 1/2 x 5 1/4 In. 25.00
Cigar, Royal Tigerettes, 6 x 9 In. 250.00
Cigar, Rubis, Man In The Moon Smoking Cigar, 4 1/2 x 4 1/2 In. 100.00
Cigar, Sailors Hope Cigars, Woman, Standing On Dock, Frame, 10 x 6 1/2 In. 39.00
Cigar, Seal Of Minnesota, World's Greatest Value Cigar, Now 5 Cents, 6 x 9 In. 300.00
Cigar, Silver Prince, Moses, Quill, Bible, Heywood, Strasser & Voight, 4 1/2 x 4 1/2 In. . . 2.00
Cigar, Spider, Gold Spider & Web, Black Ground, 4 1/2 x 4 1/2 In. 100.00
Cigar, Sporting Club, Hunter, Gun, Dog, 4 1/2 x 4 1/2 In. 200.00
Cigar, Standard Quality, High Grade, Awarded For Purity, 4 1/2 x 4 1/2 In. 5.00
Cigar, Susquehanna, 3 Indian Women, 6 x 9 In. 85.00
Cigar, Swan Smokers, Central Tobacco Co., Lexington, Kentucky, 6 x 9 In. 30.00
Cigar, Three Twins, A Howling Success, 3 Children In Basket, 4 1/2 x 4 1/2 In. 4.00
Cigar, Two Friends, Golden's Cigars, Woman, Large Dog, 6 x 9 In. 50.00
Cigar, Uncle Jake's Nickel Seegar, 5 Cents Wurth O' Dern Good Smokin', 6 x 9 In. 8.00
Cigar, Union Bird, Gold Eagle, A Smoke For All Lovers Of Our Union, 6 x 9 In. 75.00
Cigar, USY Co., Quality, Our Motto, Cow, Pig, Sheep, 4 1/2 x 4 1/2 In. 25.00

Cigar, Valrona, Cuban Man, Indian, Tobacco Field, 4 1/2 x 4 1/2 In.	12.00
Cigar, Victorex, Knight, 6 x 9 In.	150.00
Cigar, Walt Whitman, Man, Long White Beard, Hat, 4 1/2 x 4 1/2 In.	35.00
Cigar, Webster, Daniel Webster's Picture, Front Flap, 3 1/2 x 2 In.	20.00
Cigar, White Thief, White Pig Trying To Steal Milk From Cow, 6 x 9 In.	375.00
Cigar, William Tell, Man, Crossbow, Boy With Apple On Head, 4 1/2 x 4 1/2 In.	65.00
Cigar, Winner Plug Tobacco Cigar, Frame, c.1900, 10 1/2 In.	28.00
Cigar, Yankee Queen, Woman, Red Dress, Holding Eagle Picture, 4 1/2 x 4 1/2 In.	35.00
Cigar, Yellow Cab, Man, Hailing Cab, End Flap, 2 1/2 x 5 1/4 In.	10.00
Cigar, Yeoman Of The Guard, British Guard, Castle, Red & Gold Border, Nail Tag	3.00
Cigar, Zev, Horse Head, Horse Race, Columns, 4 1/2 x 4 1/2 In.	8.00
Cigar, Zomilla, Woman Warrior, Helmet, 4 Gold Coins, 6 x 9 In.	165.00
Crate, Don't Cry Brand Sweet Potatoes, Black Boy Shooting Craps, c.1950, 9 x 9 In.	18.00
Crate, Far West Brand Pears, Man's Silhouette, Gun, Trees, Sunset, Wash., 6 3/4 x 10 In.	12.00
Crate, Indian Belle, Boydson Bros. Citrus Fruits, Frame, 1920-1930, 10 x 9 1/2 In.	33.00
Crate, King's Cadets Brand California Green Asparagus, Soldiers, 9 1/2 x 10 1/2 In.	13.00
Crate, Nosegay Tobacco, Lady Holding Basket, Frame, 17 x 10 In.	232.00
Crate, Rose Brand Apples, 2 Red Roses, Navy Ground, Washington	15.00
Crate, Ryan & Newton Co., Chief Joseph, Frame, 9 x 9 In.	143.00
Crate, Splendid Spears To Please Milady, Oliver Farms, 10 x 9 1/2 In.	20.00
Crate, Watson McGill Tobacco, Eagle, Ships, Draped Flags, Stone Lithograph, 14 x 7 In.	99.00
Foodland Evaporated Milk, Holstein Cow, Blue, Yellow, Brown, Red, 1973, 10 x 3 1/2 In.	5.00
Gim-Me-Mor Onions, Bob Allen Vegetable Co., 50 Lbs. Net, c.1930, 16 In.	94.00
Hopalong Cassidy, Butter-Nut Bread	25.00
Ola Soda, Family At Seashore, Brooklyn, N.Y., 1935, 3 x 4 In.	12.00
Orange, Mammy Brand, Mammy Holding Orange, 1950s, 3 1/2 x 8 1/2 In.	14.00
Silver Spring Brewery, Life Saver, Victoria, B.C., 6 Doz. Quarts, Paper, 16 1/2 In. Diam.	55.00
Tobacco, Duke's Mixture, Paper Lithograph, Mat, Frame, Label 10 1/4 x 7 1/4 In.	121.00
Tobacco, Gold Mining, Boss Lump, Gold Prospectors, Nugget, 10 1/2 x 9 7/8 In.	2860.00
Tobacco, Royal Delight, Frame, c.1900, 13 x 16 1/2 In.	28.00
Tobacco, Stonewall Jackson, 1873, 12 x 12 In.	220.00

LAMP   Restaurants often use lamps decorated with their names; companies place lamps advertising their products in stores. Collectors can also purchase lamps that advertise the brand names of their favorite products. See brand-specific categories such as Coca-Cola and Kentucky Fried Chicken for other advertising lamps.

Cadbury, Figural, Smash Character, Metal, England, c.1970s, 8 In.	227.00
National Cigar, Hanging, Bent Glass, White Dome, Stars & Stripes Letters, 23 x 22 In.	3740.00
Nonesuch Condensed Soup, Pumpkin Pie, Tin, Glass, Lantern, c.1875, 16 x 7 In.	3360.00
Nonesuch Soup, Woman, Pumpkin, Tin, Hanging, 14 x 7 In.	605.00
Wilson's Extra Toast Bisquit, Phila., Brass, Glass Prisms, 15 In.	181.00

LARKIN   John Durant Larkin started working in Justus Weller's soap factory in Buffalo, New York, in 1865. Larkin moved with the company to Chicago in 1870 and became a partner. But in 1875 he sold his share of the Chicago company, moved back to Buffalo, and started the John D. Larkin Company. His first product was Sweet Home, a yellow laundry soap that was sold by many merchants. Larkin initiated the idea of selling a private-label brand by putting the merchant's name on the wrapper. He hired his brother-in-law, Elbert Hubbard, as his first salesman. Hubbard, a world-renowned author, wrote advertising and sales promotions for the Larkin Company. The company continually added products, including Sweet Home Washing Fluid (1879), Boraxine Soap Powder (1881), Pure White Soap (1883), Ocean Bath Soap (1883), Creme Oatmeal Soap (1880s), Modjeska Complexion Soap, toothpaste, and perfume (1880s), Elite Toilet Soap (1880s), and Ideal Toilet Soap (1880s). Premiums were given in each box of soap powder. By 1886 Larkin decided to sell directly to the consumer and offered a Combination Box. If a customer purchased $6 worth of soap, eleven silver-plated spoons, plates, and napkin rings were sent as a free gift. In 1889 a $10 box of soap was offered with a premium of a Chautauqua desk or lamp. They also sold by direct mail, housewives clubs, and a catalog first issued in 1893. About 1902, Larkin opened the Buffalo Pottery Company to make dinnerware and premiums for the soap company. By 1941 the dinnerware was selling better than the soap. So the soap company was closed, but Buffalo Pottery remained open. The business became Buffalo China in 1956 and was purchased by Oneida Ltd. in the 1980s.

A footnote for trivia experts: Elbert Hubbard was the author of *A Message to Garcia*, which sold over 40 million copies. He died at sea when the *Lusitania* was torpedoed by a German submarine in 1915.

Box, Soap, Buffalo, N.Y., 9 x 19 1/2 In.	95.00
Sign, Laundry Soap, Cat, Red Bow, Cardboard, Easel Back, Die Cut, 12 x 9 In.	242.00
Sign, Ocean Bath Soap, Cat, Die Cut, Cardboard, 12 x 9 In.	231.00
Sign, Ocean Bath Soap, Dog, Die Cut, Cardboard, 13 1/2 x 3 3/8 In.	209.00
Tin, Larkin Coffee, 3 Lb.	25.00
Tin, Larkin Talcum Powder, 6 x 2 1/4 x 1 1/4 In.	121.00
Trade Card, Boraxine Soap, Bride, Groom, Lithograph, 4 1/4 x 3 1/4 In.	10.00

LETTER OPENER Letter openers have been popular as advertising giveaways since the nineteenth century. Bronze, brass, lithographed tin, pot metal, silver plate, wood, plastic, and other types were made. Collectors prefer brass or celluloid openers.

Dutch Boy, Holding Paint Brush, Pure White Lead, Figural, 7 1/4 In.	50.00
Fuller Brush, Salesman On Handle, Red, Plastic	5.00
Fuller Brush Man, Plastic, Pink, 7 1/4 In.	8.00 to 20.00
Toledo Trust Corp., First Buckeye Bank, Metal, 7 1/4 In.	10.00
Welsbach Lights, 10 1/2 x 2 3/4 In.	85.00
Welsbach Mantle, Tin Lithograph, 10 1/2 In. …………… *Illus*	45.00

LIFE SAVERS Cleveland, Ohio, was the birthplace of Life Savers candy. Clarence Crane, a chocolate-candy maker, needed a product he could make in hot weather. He asked a pill-maker to press out a circular mint with a hole in the center. The shape inspired the name "Life Savers." His advertising proclaimed, "Crane's Peppermint Life Savers … 5 cents … For that Stormy Breath." Edward Noble, an advertising salesman, saw Life Savers in a store in New York City in 1913. He went to Cleveland to persuade Crane to advertise his candy nationally. Instead, Crane sold the rights to Life Savers to Noble for $2,900. Noble borrowed $1,500 from a friend, Roy Allen, who sold his interest back to Noble in 1926 for $3.3 million. Noble redesigned the Life Saver package, adding a foil liner to maintain the candy's flavor. The company name was changed to Life Savers Inc. in 1919, when a plant was built in Port Chester, New York. It merged with Beech-Nut Products in 1956, forming Beech-Nut Life Savers, Inc., which merged with E.R. Squibb & Sons in 1968. Life Savers then became a subsidiary of Squibb, Beech-Nut, Inc., until 1981, when Nabisco Brands acquired Life Savers, Inc. Wrigley purchased the brand in 2004. Life Savers are available in a number of mint, fruit, sugar-free, and gummy varieties. The original Pep-O-Mint flavor is still made.

Display Box, Life Savers 5 Cents, Mints & Candy Drops, Tin, 11 1/4 x 11 1/2 x 10 In.	462.00
Display Rack, Candy Mints, Blue, Brown, White, Tin Lithograph, 11 x 12 x 9 1/2 In.	935.00
Display Rack, Metal, 3 Tiers, Bakelite Ends, 10 x 38 In.	374.00
Display Rack, Metal, Blue, 3 Shelves	165.00
Display Rack, Tin Lithograph, 3 Tiers, Countertop, 1920s, 15 x 15 1/4 x 10 In. …… *Illus*	1100.00
Toy, Truck, Cast Iron, Blue, White Letters, 4 1/4 In.	880.00

LIGHTER Cigar and cigarette lighters are collected today, and not usually by the same group of collectors. Cigar lighters are either shelf models, used in stores beginning in the 1880s, or small pocket lighters with a long flame. The cigarette lighter as we know it was made popular by soldiers during World War I. Lighters as giveaway premiums became plentiful in the 1950s. Today collectors also hunt for cases of disposable lighters.

Atlantic, Imperial Gasoline, Penquin, No. 18250, Enameled, 2 1/2 x 1 7/8 x 3/8 In.	17.50

Letter Opener, Welsbach Mantle, Tin Lithograph, 10 1/2 In.	Life Savers, Display Rack, Tin Lithograph, 3 Tiers, Countertop, 1920s, 15 x 15 1/4 x 10 In.	Lighter, Plymouth, Chrysler, Fargo Trucks, Emblems, White, Red Letters, Penguin, Canada

Camel, Modern Superior Quality By Madder, Box 36.00
Camel Cigarette Pack Shape, Press Extended Cigarette To Light 14.95
Cinco Cigars, Black Smith Figure, Anvil, Cast Aluminum, 19 x 6 In. 1650.00
Cinco Cigars, Horse, 3 Lighter Wicks, Metal, c.1900, 17 In. 385.00
Consolidated Amusement Co. 14.00
Dodge Trucks, Flyer, 1937, 3 In. 85.00
El Praco, Cigar, Electric, Cardboard, Box, Countertop, c.1940 . . . . 77.00
Gargoyle, Oil, 4 x 2 3/4 x 3 In. 165.00
Graves Molasses Co., Black Man, Cow, Engraved, Enameled, Ft. Worth, 1950s, 2 1/4 In. . . 119.00
John Senior, Cigar, Countertop, 10 In. 413.00
Midland Jump Spark, Cigar, Davenport Manf., Countertop, 15 x 7 x 7 In. . . . . . . .275.00 to 413.00
Paul Jones, Cigar, Cast Iron, 9 x 7 1/2 In. 2640.00
Plymouth, Chrysler, Fargo Trucks, Emblems, White, Red Letters, Penguin, Canada . *Illus* 20.00
LIGHTER & CIGAR CUTTER, Aleppo Higrade Cigars, Nickel Pot, Ruby Globe, c.1880, 15 In. 1045.00
CCA Cigars, 2 Wicks, Oil, Ruby Globe, c.1880, 14 In. 1265.00
John Anderson & Co., Extra, Paperboy, By Streetlight, 1890, 23 In. 2640.00
McNeil & Higgins Guarantee Cigar, 2 Wicks, Oil, Ruby Globe, 13 In. 935.00
Piedmont, Metal, Glass, Wood, Ruby Globe, 13 x 8 1/2 In. 1100.00
Read Tobacco, Flottilla Superior Quality, Iron Base, White Globe, Oil, 1880, 12 In. 1045.00
Rosina Vokes Cigars, Restored, A. Davis Sons & Co., c.1900 . . . . 2070.00
Sen-Sen Chewing Gum, 5 Cents, Girl, Watermelon, Countertop, 23 In. 8800.00
Uncle Remus 5 Cent Cigar, 2 Wicks, Ruby Globe, Oil, 14 In. 1045.00

LION COFFEE C.C. Warren and L.B. Shattuck started roasting Lion Coffee in Toledo, Ohio, in 1864. Their company sold coffee, baking powder, yeast, mustard, spices, and other flavorings. In 1875 Alvin Mansfield Woolson started his own coffee and spice business in Toledo. In 1882 the C.C. Warren Company ran into financial problems, so Woolson and some other Toledo grocers bought the remnants of the company and renamed it the Woolson Spice Company. Woolson was probably the first company to sell roasted coffee beans in small packages instead of from open bins. It became the second largest coffee company in the United States. Just before retiring in 1897, Alvin Woolson sold a major part of the company to the Havemeyers, a family of sugar refiners, who competed in the coffee and sugar business with Arbuckle's. About 1979 James Delano resurrected the Lion Coffee brand and moved its production to Hawaii. Since then, Lion Coffee merged with Royal Kona Coffee to form the Hawaii Coffee Company. The company sells coffee with the historic Lion logo. There is a Lion memorabilia collection at the company's headquarters in Honolulu. Old trade cards, paper dolls, and many other promotional items can still be found.

Bin, Bulk, Red Paint, 30 In. 523.00
Box, Woolson Spice Co., Toledo, Ohio, 100 Lbs, Wood, 29 x 19 x 16 In. 55.00
Sack & Stringholder, Lion Is The King Of Coffees, Original Paint 1100.00

Sign, Easter Cards, Woolson Spice Co., Girl, Easter Lily, Frame, c.1893, 40 x 30 In. 2310.00
Sign, Premiums Given Free, Metal Bands, Frame, 14 1/2 x 11 In. 83.00
Sign, Santa Claus Holding Sign, Paper Lithograph, Frame, 27 x 16 1/2 In. 950.00
Tin, Golden Sun Ginger, Woolson Spice Co., 1912, 3 x 2 1/4 In. 44.00
Tin, Woolson's Fresh Roasted, Yellow, Black, Woolson Spice Co., Toledo, Ohio, 21 In. 177.00
Tin, Woolson's Vienna Coffee, Lithograph, Sample, Yellow Body, Black Lid, 2 3/4 x 3 In. 66.00
Trade Card, Mocha Java & Rio, 3 Cats Balancing On Ball, 5 1/4 x 3 1/2 In. 35.00

LIPTON TEA Thomas Johnstone Lipton moved from Scotland to New
York City in 1865, when he was fourteen years old. He worked as an
assistant in the grocery section of a New York department store, then
returned to Glasgow in 1869 and two years later opened his own grocery store. After he had opened twenty stores in Great Britain, he went
back to the United States and opened a meatpacking plant in Chicago
to supply his British stores. At age forty, Lipton owned hundreds of
shops selling groceries and he went on a trip to Australia by way of
Ceylon. While in Ceylon, he purchased tea plantations at bargain
prices because of a depression. He reorganized their system of picking
and packing tea and developed a special blend of tea. The tea was sent
from the mountains to the factories by aerial wires instead of on the
backs of human carriers. Tea was a relatively unknown drink in America, but soon Lipton opened U.S. sales offices and a packaging plant.
The company became Thomas J. Lipton, Inc., and was headquartered
in Englewood Cliffs, New Jersey. Lipton advertised his products. Slogans found in ads include "Direct from the Tea Gardens to the Teapot"
(1892), "Largest Sale in World" (1894), "The Finest Tea the World Can
Produce" (1894), "Buy Your Tea in Airtight Packages" (1914), "If You
Want the Best Tea, Buy from the Firm That Grows It" (1924), "Lipton
Tea Refreshes" (1939), "Lipton—America's Largest Selling Tea"
(1942), "Better Because It's Brisk" (1953), "Nothing Refreshes Like
Icy Lipton Tea" (1967), "Lipton's Gets into More Hot Water Than
Anything" (c.1986), and "100% Natural and 100% Real Tea" (c.2001).
Since 1938 the company has been part of Unilever, but it retained the
name Thomas J. Lipton, Inc. Unilever acquired Bestfoods in 2000, and
Lipton and Bestfoods were merged into Unilever Bestfoods.

Box, Multiple Images, Tin Lithograph, 4 x 9 x 6 In. 22.00
Sign, Indian Woman, Parasol, Belle, Cardboard, Frame, 13 x 19 In. 110.00
Sign, Lipton's Instant Cocoa, Woman, Cup, Tin Over Cardboard, 1920-1930, 13 x 9 In. ... 578.00
Sign, Lipton's Teas, Will You Have Some, Stone Lithograph, Frame, 14 x 20 In. 2200.00
Tin, Ladies Talking Over A Cup Of Tea, No. 401, 6 1/2 x 8 1/2 x 3 In. 10.00

LOG CABIN Log Cabin syrup, a blend of corn syrup and flavorings
that imitate maple syrup, was first made in 1887 by P.J. Towle in St.
Paul, Minnesota. At first, Towle syrup was packaged in rectangular
tins with printed paper labels. By 1897 the first cabin-shaped tin was
patented. The tin had a wire handle with paper labels on the front,
back, and front of the roof. The label included an offer of a $500
reward to anyone proving that the syrup was adulterated. From 1909
to 1914 the log cabin tins had paper labels showing the back door covered with a stretched animal skin. From 1914 to about 1918 the paper
label on the back showed a child standing at the cabin door. The tins
used from 1919 to 1927 were lithographed tin without paper labels,
and were in color. From 1928 to 1932 the tins showed the child at the
door, but the child is in black and white, not color. General Foods
bought Towle Maple Syrup Company in 1927, but tins were not
marked with the name General Foods until later. Cabin-shaped tins
with four lithographed sides were used from 1933 to 1939. From 1940
to 1942, the same tin was used, but the end panels were blank. Tins
were not used again until after World War II. By 1948 brown log cab-
ins with red and white labels were being made. These were used until
1949, when the syrup was bottled. A special series of Frontier Village
tins was offered in the 1950s, and a few other special tins made as
banks have also been offered. Syrup tins came in sizes ranging from

miniature to one gallon. In 1987 a special tin was issued to celebrate the 100th anniversary of Log Cabin Syrup. Other Log Cabin syrup advertising items include pictorial flasks, small cabin-shaped jugs, trade cards, blotters, and spoons. Wheels were available that would change some of the cabin tins into pull toys. Philip Morris acquired General Foods and the Log Cabin brand in 1985. From 1997 to 2004, the brand was owned by Aurora Foods, which merged with Pinnacle Foods in 2004. (H.H. Warner, listed in this book under Warner, had a brand of patent medicine called "Log Cabin" from 1887 to 1909. The bottle's label pictured a cabin.)

Decanter, Log Cabin Logo, Gold Eagles, Screw Top, 9 In. 12.00
Sign, Please Close Door, Girl Holding Log Cabin Tin 717.00
Tin, 100 Years Of Log Cabin Syrup, Log Cabin Shape, 1987, 5 x 5 x 3 In. 45.00
Tin, Blacksmith Shop, Express Office, Towle's Log Cabin Syrup, Screw Cap, 4 3/4 In. 88.00
Tin, Syrup, Cabin Shape, c.1950, 2 Lb., 4 1/2 x 5 x 2 3/4 In. 55.00

LORILLARD Pierre Lorillard founded the first American tobacco company in 1760. He was working in New York City packaging snuff in dried animal bladders. Soon he and his two sons were marketing many tobacco products, including vanilla-flavored snuff. The Lorillards advertised through newspapers and may also have conducted the first direct-mail advertising campaign. They sent a broadside describing their products to every postmaster in the United States. Many post offices were in stores or taverns, so the postmasters asked permission to sell Lorillard products. Lorillard is credited with introducing small metal-pronged tin tobacco tags in the 1870s, perhaps as a trademark for its "Tin Tag" brand of chewing tobacco. Other brands of plug tobacco were soon labeled with tin tags. Lorillard made navy-cut and fine-cut chewing tobacco and many brands of cigarettes. Murad was one of the first Lorillard cigarette brands. Today, Lorillard Tobacco Company, an indirect subsidiary of Loews Corp., makes Newport, Kent, True, Satin, Old Gold, Maverick, Triumph, and Max cigarettes.

Advertisement, Old Gold Lights Cigarettes, Woman, Bicycle, Be An OG, Full Page 4.50
Bin, Beech-Nut Chewing Tobacco, Tin Lithograph, 8 5/8 x 10 x 8 1/4 In. 605.00
Bin, Beech-Nut Chewing Tobacco, Yellow Ground, Hinged, 8 5/8 x 10 x 8 In. 495.00
Bin, Beech-Nut Tobacco, We Keep It Fresh, Tin Lithograph, Green, 8 5/8 x 9 3/4 x 8 In. ... 231.00
Box, Old Gold Cigarettes, Filter Kings, Cardboard, 3 7/16 x 1 7/8 x 3/8 In. 8.00
Box, Wood, Paper Label, 4 1/2 x 11 x 6 In. 132.00
Calendar, 1887, Climax, Man Cutting Tobacco, 12 1/2 x 12 1/2 In. 77.00
Display, Tobacco Samples, 100th Anniversary, 1882 .... 6875.00
Kickplate, Beech-Nut Chewing Tobacco, Porcelain, 1920-1930, 9 x 30 In. 440.00
Lunch Box, Redicut Tobacco, Break Off A Piece To Fit, Tin Lithograph, 7 1/2 x 8 In. 177.00
Pack, Wild Rose Chipped Plug Tobacco, Unopened, 4 1/2 x 2 3/4 x 1 In. 135.00
Playing Cards, Newport Cigarettes, 2 1/2 x 3 1/2 In. 5.00
Rolling Papers, 1760 Long Cut Tobacco, 5 Cent Size 6.60
Sign, Beech-Nut Chewing Tobacco, Porcelain, 12 x 9 In. 715.00
Sign, Beech-Nut Chewing Tobacco, Porcelain, 24 x 12 In. 990.00
Sign, Beech-Nut Chewing Tobacco, Porcelain, Embossed Letters, 10 1/2 x 22 In. 176.00
Sign, Beech-Nut Tobacco, 10 Cents, Porcelain, 9 x 5 7/8 In. 303.00
Sign, Climax Plug Tobacco, Blue, White, Porcelain, 11 x 13 In. 275.00
Sign, Climax Plug Tobacco, Seated Laughing Woman, 9 3/8 x 13 5/8 In. 304.00
Tin, Brig's Pipe Mixture, When A Feller Needs A Friend, Hinged, 3 x 4 1/2 x 3/4 In. 16.00
Tin, Lithograph, Swivel Handle, Early 1900s, 8 x 9 1/2 x 7 In. 28.00
Tin, Maccoboy Snuff, 5 Lb., 6 3/8 x 7 1/2 x 5 In. 110.00
Tin, Old Gold Cigarettes, Match Striker Bottom Strip, 3 x 2 5/16 x 1 1/16 In. 20.00
Tin, Possum Cigars, Am Good & Sweet, Red Ground, 5 1/4 In. ....*Illus* 403.00
Tin, Rose Leaf Chewing Tobacco, Nickel-Plated Brass, Compass, 2 x 3 1/2 In. ..... *Illus* 8.00
Tin, Sensations Cut Plug, 6 x 3 3/4 In. 24.00
Tin, Stag Tobacco, Jersey City, N.J., 6 1/2 In. 176.00
Tin, Union Leader Smoking Tobacco, Red, 14 Oz. 20.00
Tobacco Tin Tag, Cupid, Blue Ground, Oval 39.00
Tobacco Tin Tag, Cupid, Green Ground, Oval 55.00

Lorillard, Tin, Possum Cigars,
Am Good & Sweet, Red Ground,
5 1/4 In.

Lorillard, Tin, Rose Leaf
Chewing Tobacco, Nickel-
Plated Brass, Compass,
2 x 3 1/2 In.

Lucky Strike, Window Display,
Cream Of The Crop,
Cardboard, c.1915, 46 x 34 In.

Tobacco Tin Tag, Defiance Plug, Red, White, Blue, Rectangular 7.70
Tobacco Tin Tag, Liberty, Eagle, Spread Wings, Shield 212.00

LUCKY STRIKE   "Lucky Strike Green Has Gone to War" is one of the most famous slogans in American advertising. According to the company, bronze-based green ink was removed from the Lucky package in 1942 as a contribution to the war effort. Actually, the company may simply have wanted a new design—but the ad campaign increased sales dramatically. The Lucky Strike cigarette brand was introduced by the American Tobacco Company in 1917. The name referred to Gold Rush days, so the original trademark was a brawny arm with a hammer in his hand. The name had been used since 1871 for a sliced plug tobacco. The bull's-eye trademark of the plug was changed slightly into the bull's-eye for the cigarette brand. The first packages were sold with the slogan "It's Toasted." "Reach for a Lucky Instead of a Sweet" was the 1928 suggestion. "With Men Who Know Tobacco Best, It's Luckies Two to One" and "LSMFT" (Lucky Strike means fine tobacco) were later campaigns. Luckies sponsored many radio and TV shows, including musical programs featuring Eddie Duchin, Sophie Tucker, and a young Frank Sinatra on the *Lucky Strike Hit Parade.* Advertisements and the metal cigarette packages, especially the "flat fifties" tins, intrigue today's collectors. In 1994 the American Tobacco Company (ATCo) was acquired by British American Tobacco, the parent company of Brown & Williamson. The following year, ATCo operations were integrated into Brown & Williamson. In 2004 Brown & Williamson merged with R.J. Reynolds to form Reynolds American Inc.

Advertisement, Martin Johnson, African Explorer, American Tobacco, 1928, Full Page .. 8.00
Carton, 10 Sealed Cigarette Packs, Green, 1 7/8 x 10 7/8 In. ....296.00 to 413.00
Cigarette Case, Cigarette Pack Picture, Pearl, Box, 3 1/2 In. 22.00
Cigarette Machine, Soldier, War Bonds, Metal, Wall Mount, 1940s, 33 x 4 5/8 In. 303.00
Cigarette Pack, Green, 20 Cigarettes, No Cellophane, World War II Era 86.00
Cigarette Pack, White, 20 Cigarettes, World War II Era 29.00
Sign, Cardboard, Frame, 15 x 11 1/4 In. 75.00
Sign, Give A Christmas Carton Of Luckies, It's Toasted, Cardboard, 28 x 36 In. 220.00
Sign, Lucky Strike, Tuxedo Tobacco, Pipe Shape, Tin Lithograph, 2-Sided, 8 7/8 x 19 In. .. 2090.00
Sign, Tin, Die Cut Pipe, 2-Sided, 9 x 19 In. 2420.00
Tin, Flat, Cut Plug, R.A. Patterson Tobacco Co., Richmond, Va., 4 x 2 3/4 In. 25.00
Tin, Genuine Roll Cut, Cut Pipe, Red, Green, 2 3/4 x 2 In. 121.00
Tin, Genuine Roll Cut, Green, Black, Red, Gold, c.1915, 4 1/2 x 2 7/8 In. 79.00
Tin, Half & Half Tobacco, Collapsible, Pocket, Vertical, 4 1/2 x 3 x 1 In. 45.00
Tin, Half & Half, Roll Cut Tobacco, Genuine, Green, Black 171.00
Tin, It's Toasted, Flat Fifties, Green, 4 1/2 x 5 3/4 In. ....25.00 to 99.00
Tin, Lucky Strike Tobacco, R.A. Patterson Co., 4 1/2 x 2 5/8 x 7/8 In. ....25.00 to 55.00
Tin, Roll Cut Tobacco, Pocket, 4 1/2 x 3 In. 22.00
Window Display, Cream Of The Crop, Cardboard, c.1915, 46 x 34 In. .... *Illus* 1155.00

LUDEN'S William H. Luden was a candy maker in his mother's kitchen in Reading, Pennsylvania, in 1881. He made "moshie," a Pennsylvania German candy, from corn syrup and brown sugar and sold it to local stores. Because cough drops were made from almost the same ingredients as candy, he decided to make his own cough drop. He consulted a local pharmacist and together they developed a menthol cough drop. Luden colored his drops amber to distinguish them from the red drops made by other manufacturers. Luden's made many products, including 5th Avenue candy bars (1936), Mello mints, and several Luden's cough drop flavors. Hershey Foods Corp. purchased Luden's in 1986. In 2001 Hershey sold Luden's cough-drops business to Pharmacia, which combined with Pfizer two years later.

Sign, 5 Cents, For Quick Relief, Blue, Yellow, Tin, Embossed	358.00
Sign, Luden's Cough Drops, Poinsettias, Felt, 11 In. Diam.	88.00
Sign, Menthol Cough Drops, 5 Cents, Embossed, Donaldson, Covington, Ky., 19 x 35 In.	517.00
Sign, Menthol Cough Drops, For Quick Relief, 5 Cents, Die Cut Box, 18 x 35 In.	385.00
Tin, Cough Drops	575.00
Tip Tray, Cough Drops, Give Instant Relief, Tin, Red Rim, Round, Reading, Penna.	249.00
Tip Tray, Luden's Chewing Gum, Roses, Gum Packs, Felt, Round, 10 3/4 In.	110.00

LUNCH BOX, see Tobacco, Lunch Box

LUNCH PAIL, see Pail and Tobacco, Pail

LYDIA PINKHAM Lydia Estes Pinkham (1819–1883), a Quaker, was an advocate of women's rights and an opponent of slavery. She taught school in Lynn, Massachusetts, until 1843, when she married Isaac Pinkham. Legend says a machinist named Todd gave Isaac a medicinal formula to pay a $25 debt. Lydia, using this recipe or another from a medical handbook, mixed a batch of medicine on her kitchen stove. According to her records, she used unicorn root, life root, black cohosh, pleurisy root, and fenugreek seed. They were mixed with alcohol to create a concoction that was 18 percent alcohol (36 proof), a good pain reliever even if used alone! When Isaac lost his money in the 1873 panic, the four Pinkham children went to work selling "Lydia Pinkham's Vegetable Compound." The family advertised with circulars, pamphlets, and newspapers. The medicine, made by a woman, for women, treated ills that the male medical profession ignored: "falling womb," "flooding," "bearing down pains," "female complaints," menstrual pains, and even barrenness. In 1879 Lydia's face was pictured on the bottle and in ads, and sales doubled. It was unusual to see a woman's face in a newspaper at the time; in fact, it is claimed that when Queen Victoria died, some papers used Lydia's available picture instead of searching for a true picture of the queen. Mrs. Pinkham personally answered letters from customers until the letters amounted to 150 a day. She then hired a female staff to help answer mail to assure privacy for her customers. Lydia's son Charles and his wife continued the business after Lydia died. Lydia Pinkham's Compound was the most heavily advertised product in America by 1898. The company also made liver pills and a blood purifier. The Pinkham business was sold to Cooper Laboratories in 1968. Lydia Pinkham Herbal Compound, with a reduced alcohol content, is available from Numark Laboratories of Edison, New Jersey.

Bottle, Lydia E. Pinkham's Medicine, No. 4, 14 1/2 Oz., 8 1/2 x 3 1/4 In.	1.00
Bottle, Vegetable Compound, Aqua, Label, Contents, Box, 8 1/2 In.	358.00
Box, Liver Pills, 12 Sealed Packages, Cardboard, 3 3/4 x 4 1/2 In.	253.00
Cookbook, Vegetable Compound For Women Practical Cooking Recipes	15.50
Flask, Vegetable Compound Herb Medicine Pills, Silver Plated, Embossed, 1 1/2 x 2 In.	44.00
Pack, Sanative Wash, Advertising Paper, Envelope, Unopened, 4 x 4 In.	94.00
Sewing Kit, Engraved, Bullet Shape, 2-Spool Shaft, Metal Thimble	3.00
Sewing Kit, Lydia Pinkham's Vegetable Compound, Metal Tube, Bobbin, Thread, 2 1/4 In.	20.00
Sign, Vegetable Compound, Cardboard, Die Cut, Easel Back, 34 x 23 In.	767.00
Thermometer, 4 Pinkham Medicines, Better Health, Blue, Cardboard, 4 3/4 x 6 3/4 In.	187.00
Thimble, Porcelain, Information Booklet, Mark FP, 1980, 1 1/8 In.	9.50
Trade Card, Cabin In Snow, Vegetable Compound & Blood Purifier, 4 1/2 x 3 1/4 In.	7.00

M&M'S Frank and Ethel Mars started making candies in Tacoma, Washington, in 1911. In 1923 Frank introduced the Milky Way bar. It was followed by Snickers (1930) and 3 Musketeers (1932). Frank's son, Forrest, joined the family business, and on a trip to Spain during the Spanish Civil War he met soldiers who were eating chocolate pellets encased in a sugar coating. He brought the idea home and developed M&M's chocolate candies. They were first sold in 1941 to American GIs. By the late 1940s, they were popular with the American public. The packaging was changed from cardboard tubes to a brown pouch in 1948. In 1954 Peanut M&M'S were introduced along with the slogan, "The milk chocolate melts in your mouth—not in your hand." Other M&M products include M&M's Almond (1988), M&M's Peanut Butter Chocolate (1990), M&M's Chocolate Mini Baking Bits (1995), M&M's MINIS (1996), and M&M's Crispy (1999). The M&M characters first appeared in television commercials in 1954 and on packaging in 1972. Collectibles featuring the characters, including dispensers, pins, and toys, are popular with collectors.

Calculator, Yellow, Plastic, Package Includes Candy	21.00
Candy Dish, Acrylic, Yellow M&M Holding Red M&M, Removable Bowl, 7 x 7 x 2 In.	2.00
Candy Dish, M&M Characters Border, M&M's At The Bottom, 2 1/2 x 6 1/2 In.	34.00
Candy Dish, Santa Hat, Talks, Mouth & Eyebrows Move, Box, 7 3/4 x 7 3/4 In.	40.00
Candy Dispenser, Big Red M&M	9.00
Cookie Jar, M&M Bag, Ceramic, Box, 9 1/2 x 6 x 6 3/4 In.	40.00
Cookie Jar, M&M, Yellow, Ceramic, Box, 9 3/4 In.	44.00
Cookie Jar, Red & Green M&M's, Mixing Cookie Dough, Mars Inc., 1982	100.00
Costume, Red, White Gloves & Shoe Covers	20.00
Dispenser, Baseball Player, Green, Official M&M's Brand Collectible	43.00
Dispenser, Basketball Player, Peanut M&M, Green, Box	126.00
Dispenser, Football Player, Green	40.00
Dispenser, Green M&M, 1 Hand Up, 1 At Side, 1991, 3 x 2 1/2 In.	8.00
Dispenser, Soccer Player, Yellow, Painted Eyes, c.1991, 7 In.	20.00
Dispenser, Yellow Figure Holding Green M&M In Hand, Brown Base, China, 1993, 9 In.	28.76
Frisbee, M&Ms, M&M Mars Hackettstown Site 40th Anniversary, 1958-1998	22.00
Golf Ball, M&M Holding Flag For 18th Hole, Pinnacle	6.00
Keychain, Change Purse, Yellow M&M Bag, Zipper, 4 x 2 In.	6.00
Pin Set, Summer Olympics, Limited Edition, 1992	160.00 to 198.00
Store Display, Blue, Thumbs Up, Plastic, Metal Base, Casters, 54 x 24 In.	260.00 to 444.00
Tin, 1988, 5 x 2 3/4 In.	10.00 to 12.00
Tin, Holiday, Blue, M&M's In Sky, Stars, Trees, Dogs, Couples, 1988, 6 x 4 1/4 In.	6.00
Train, Yuletide Flyer Christmas Train, Cold-Cast Porcelain, Danbury Mint	61.00 to 103.00
Tube Topper, Pink Plain M&M Mailman, Holding 2 Letters, Heart Shaped Box	3.50 to 4.75
Wall Clock, Animated, Talking, Yellow M&M Pendulum, Red M&M Pop Out, Box	55.00

MAIL POUCH Samuel and Aaron Bloch went into the tobacco business in Wheeling, West Virginia, in 1879. Bloch Brothers made cigars and plug tobacco. Cuttings of tobacco that were left over, called "scrap," were mixed with water, molasses, licorice, salt, and sugar to form a new type of chewing tobacco. It was packed in paper bags marked "Chew Mail Pouch." The company advertised in many ways, including the famous painted barn signs. As the product grew in popularity, tobacco cuttings became scarce, so by 1932 the company used whole leaves even though the package continued to be labeled "scrap." Bloch Brothers merged with Helme Products in the 1960s; in 1975 Mail Pouch became a Helme Company brand. In 1971 Helme became a subsidiary of Culbro Corp. and in 1986 Helme and the Mail Pouch brand were acquired by Swisher International, Inc. Mail Pouch signs, tobacco tins, and thermometers are favored collectibles.

Bin, Gold Interior, Tin Lithograph, 14 x 10 x 11 1/2 In.	130.00
Charm, Mail Pouch Bag, Chew Mail Pouch, 1 1/4 x 11/16 In.	125.00
Display, Barn, Chew Mail Pouch Tobacco, Ohio, c.1954, 15 1/2 x 16 x 20 In.	295.00
Dominoes, Instructions, Paper Mail Pouch Label, 6 1/2 x 2 In., 28 Dominoes	1000.00
Sign, As Good As Gold, Gold Mining Scene, Cardboard Lithograph, 20 1/2 x 14 1/2 In.	15510.00
Sign, Chew Mail Pouch, Barn Shape, Tin On Wood, 56 In.	385.00

Sign, Chew, Smoke, Porcelain, 2 7/8 x 12 In. 275.00
Sign, Early Photographer, Cardboard, Easel Back, 1920s, 20 3/4 x 13 5/8 In. 70.00
Sign, Girl, Straw Hat, Cardboard, Frame, 15 x 19 1/2 In. 2250.00
Sign, Real Man's Choice, Indians, Stone Quarry, Cardboard, Easel Back, 1920s, 21 x 14 In. 132.00
Thermometer, Chew Mail Pouch Tobacco, Black, Yellow, Tin, Embossed, c.1950, 9 In. . . 413.00
Thermometer, Chew Mail Pouch Tobacco, Blue, Yellow, White, 9 1/2 In. 375.00
Thermometer, Chew Mail Pouch Tobacco, Sheet Steel, 39 In. 68.00
Thermometer, Chew Mail Pouch, Blue, Red, White, Steel Lithograph, 38 In. . . . . . . *Illus* 93.00
Thermometer, Chew Mail Pouch, Treat Yourself To The Best, Porcelain, 72 x 18 In. 605.00
Thermometer, Treat Yourself To The Best, Porcelain, 39 x 8 In. . . . . 132.00 to 248.00
Thimble, Porcelain, FP Mark, Pamphlet, 1980, 1 1/8 In. 9.50

MATCH The first friction matches were made in 1827 by John Walker
of Stockton-on-Tees, England. They were soon copied by many others.
Matches could spontaneously light in a pocket, so the invention of the
match safe was important. It was just a metal container with a flip-
open lid that held stick matches. They were especially popular in England. Many match safes had advertising messages on them. A match
holder was made to hang on the wall to hold large kitchen matches.
The holders were often given as premiums and were decorated with
product or store ads. Book matches were patented in the United States
in 1892 by Joshua Pusey. The first matchbook was issued by the Diamond Match Company as an advertisement for the Mendelssohn
Opera Company. Since then, millions of advertising matchbooks have
been made. A matchbox is a stiff box that holds any size stick matches.
It usually has a striking surface on one side. Collectors search for all
types of matchboxes, as well as the labels that can be found on them.
Matchbox labels came into use about 1827 with the invention of the
friction match. The first labels were merely black and white printed
instructions on how to use the new matches. By 1830 an English firm
was making green pictorial labels. The first printed matchbox labels in
the United States were made by P. Truesdell of Warsaw, New York,
from 1855 to 1857. Collectors began to search seriously for matchbox
labels in the 1880s. Many of the labels were made in Italy, Belgium,
Spain, Australia, and the Far East. Reproductions of old matchboxes
and their labels are available today.

MATCH HOLDER, A. Reynolds & Co, Hotel Bar Fitters, Leeds, Striker, 3 1/4 x 4 3/4 In. 20.00
Acorn Ranges, Cast Iron, 4 3/4 In. 69.00
Adriance Farm Machinery, Adriance Corn Binder, Tin, 5 x 3 1/4 In. 605.00
Allsopp's, Ask For, White Glaze, Black Print, Empire Works, 2 x 4 1/2 In. 31.00
American Brewing Co., Stoneware, Blue, Gray, 3 In. 150.00
American Steel Farm Fences, Tin Lithograph, 5 x 3 1/2 In. 88.00
Barker's South American Fever & Ague Cure, Striker, 3 x 4 3/8 In. 187.00
Barta Photo Studio, Tin Lithograph, New Prague, Minn., 4 7/8 x 3 3/8 In. 283.00
Bliss Native Herbs, 6 1/2 x 4 1/2 In. 39.00

Mail Pouch,
Thermometer,
Chew Mail Pouch,
Blue, Red, White,
Steel Lithograph,
38 In.

Match Holder,
Darling Mother's
Worm Syrup,
Grandma,
2 Children

**Never cut a matchbook or
paste the matchbook into a
scrapbook. It destroys the
value. Remove the staple
and the matches.**

Born Steel Range, c.1890, 5 In. 99.00
Boydell Brothers Paints, Calendar, 1908, 8 x 5 In. 121.00
Bruces Juniper Salve, For Family Use It Has No Equal, Striker, Shield Form, 4 7/8 x 3 In.   88.00
Bryant & Mays, Striker, White Glaze, Mintons, Round, 2 1/2 x 5 In. 20.00
Bull Dog Cut Plug, Won't Bite, Straight Leaf, Die Cut, 6 3/4 x 3 3/8 In. 550.00
C. Parker, Cast Iron, 1869, 6 In. 95.00
Cantrell & Cochrames Ginger Ales, Striker, Clear Glass, Enamel Letters, 2 3/4 x 3 1/4 In.   20.00
Captain Webb, Puck, Mintons, England, Striker, 3 1/4 In. 70.00
Celebrated Supremacy Cigar, Pyramid Shape, Striker, 3 1/2 x 5 1/2 In. 445.00
Club Matches, With Bryant & Mays Compliments, Striker, White Glaze, 2 3/4 x 4 In. . . . 20.00
Coates & Co., Original Plymouth Gin, Pyramid Shape, Striker, 2 x 5 In. 65.00
Columbia Flour, Miss Liberty, Embossed, Die Cut, Tin Lithograph, 5 1/2 x 2 1/4 In. 1870.00
Darling Mother's Worm Syrup, Grandma, 2 Children . . . . *Illus* 715.00
Dead Game, Shotgun, Cast Iron, 11 In. 220.00
Devenish's Weymouth Ales, Brewers By Appointment To King, Striker, 4 3/4 In. 189.00
Dewar's, Striker, Royal Doulton, 4 x 4 1/2 In. 111.00
Dockash Stove Factory, Scranton Pa., Tin Lithograph, 4 7/8 In. 25.00
Dockash Stove Factory, Tin Lithograph, 5 In. . . . . .34.00 to 69.00
Dr. Shoop's Health Coffee, Tin Lithograph, 4 7/8 x 3 3/8 In. . . . . .248.00 to 460.00
Dr. Shoop's Lax-Ets, Hanging, Tin Lithograph, 4 7/8 x 3 3/8 In. 165.00
Dunville's VR, Striker, J.A. Campbell, Belfast, 4 1/2 In. 32.00
Dunville's VR, Striker, White Glaze, Black Print, 2 x 4 1/2 In. 41.00
Dutch Boy, Embossed, Die Cut, c.1915, 6 1/2 In. 99.00
E.O. Webber Lumber, Metal, Hanging, Diamond Shape, Marysville, Kansas, 6 1/2 In. . . . 107.00
Eagle White Lead Co., Celluloid Over Metal, Box, 2 3/4 x 1 1/2 x 3/8 In. 495.00
Eclipse, Cast Iron, Match & Kindling Holder, On Board 385.00
Ellis's Ruthin Waters, Striker, Clear Glass, Etched, 2 1/2 x 3 1/2 In. 20.00
Ellwood Steel Fences, Tin Lithograph, 4 7/8 x 3 3/8 In. 140.00
Gargoyle Vacuum A Mobiloil, Woman Driver, 2 5/8 x 2 x 1 In. 66.00
Garland Stoves & Ranges, Somers Bros., c.1900, 7 x 4 x 1 In. 425.00
Green's August Flower, Cardboard, Die Cut, 7 1/2 x 4 1/2 In. 908.00
Hindle's Aerated Waters, Striker, White Glaze, 2 1/4 x 4 1/4 In. 101.00
Hunts Mineral Waters, Renwick High Class, Fred Payten, Striker, 2 1/4 x 4 3/4 In. 323.00
Ideal Family Flour, Wm. Tell Flour, 4 3/4 x 3 1/4 In. 22.00
Ind Coopes Burton Ales, Striker, Red Trademark, White, Round, England, 4 3/4 In. 123.00
J. E. Patzlsperger, Popular Shoe Man, Tin Lithograph, 4 7/8 x 3 3/8 In. 283.00
J.C. Stevens, Old Judson Whiskey, Tin Lithograph, 3 1/2 x 5 In. 176.00
John Clabrue Roofing, Tinning, Guttering, Blue Tin, 5 In. *Illus* 25.00
Lax-Ets, 5 Cents, Candy Bowel Laxative, Tin Lithograph, Dr. Shoops, 5 x 3 1/2 In. 176.00
Lax-Ets, Dr. Shoop's Laxative, Tin Lithograph, 4 7/8 x 3 3/8 In. 196.00
Lax-Ets Laxative, Only 5 Cents Per Box, Lotbiniere, Quebec 121.00
Michigan Stoves, Cast Iron, 7 In. 173.00
Milwaukee Binders & Mowers, Tin Lithograph, Hanging, 4 7/8 x 3 3/8 In. 248.00
Milwaukee Harvesting Machines, Always Reliable, Tin Lithograph, 5 1/2 In. 127.00
Monitor Ranges, Figural Range, c.1900, 5 x 3 1/2 x 2 In. 132.00
New Process Gas Range, Image Of Range, Metal Lithograph, 3 1/2 x 2 In. 165.00
New Process Gas Range, Saves Time & Gas, Tin Lithograph, 3 1/2 x 2 1/4 In. 495.00
Nicholson X.F. Files, Victorian Woman, Cardboard, Striker, 12 3/4 x 4 1/2 In. 413.00
Old Judson, J.C. Stephens, Kansas City, Mo., Tin Lithograph, 1910, 5 In. . . . . .144.00 to 193.00
Pioneers, Man Standing With Gun, Cast Iron, 4 x 4 1/2 In. 66.00
Richardson Butane Gas, Columbus, Miss. & Tuscaloosa, Ala., 5 x 3 In. 18.00
Rockford Watch, Tin Lithograph, 2-Sided, 4 3/4 x 2 3/4 In. . . . . *Illus* 275.00
San Felice Cigars, Metal, Oval Celluloid Image, 1/4 x 1 5/8 x 2 3/8 In. 425.00
Sharples, Tubular Cream Separators, Tin Lithograph, 7 In. . . . . .500.00 to 622.00
Sharples Cream Separators, 6 3/4 x 2 1/8 In. 110.00
Sharples Separator, Daughter, Mother, Cows, Tin Lithograph, 6 3/4 x 2 1/8 In. 468.00
Sharples Separator, Woman, Cows, Tin Lithograph, 6 3/4 x 2 1/8 In. 250.00
Shenango China, L. Barth & Son, New York, Sample, 1920s, 2 3/4 x 4 In. 115.00
Siegels, Reliable Department Store, Point Marion, Pa., 4 1/4 x 3 5/8 In. 149.00
Topsy Hosiery, Tin Lithograph, Green, Red, 5 x 3 3/8 x 1 1/4 In. 231.00
Topsy Hosiery, Woman On Beach, 3 x 3 3/8 x 1 1/4 In. 578.00
Universal Stoves & Ranges, Cribben & Sexton Co., 4 7/8 x 3 3/8 x 1 1/4 In. 154.00
Ushers Whisky, O.V.C., Ushers, WWI Soldier, Striker, England, Round, 2 3/4 In. 208.00

Match Holder, John Clabrue Roofing, Tinning, Guttering, Blue Tin, 5 In.	Match Holder, Rockford Watch, Tin Lithograph, 2-Sided, 4 3/4 x 2 3/4 In.	Match Holder, Wm. Miller Range & Furnace Co., Tin Lithograph, 4 3/4 In.

Vulcan Plows, Blacksmith, Tin, Die Cut, 8 In. . . . . .495.00 to 622.00
Wilson Bros Grinding Mills, Iron, Embossed, c.1900, 6 1/4 In. 81.00
Wm. Miller Range & Furnace Co., Tin Lithograph, 4 3/4 In. *Illus* 10.00
Wm. T. Burns, Woburn Mass., Tin, Painted, c.1900, 5 7/8 In. 20.00
Worthington, Striker, Fieldings, England, 2 3/4 x 4 In. 359.00
Zink Furniture, Salt & Pepper, 7 x 5 In. 45.00
MATCH SAFE, American Belting Co., Indian On Horse, Metal, Celluloid, 1 1/2 x 3 x 3/8 In. . 154.00
Buffalo Brewing Co., Sacramento, Cal., Cowboy, Wrangler, Nickel Plated, 2 3/4 x 1 In. . . 253.00
Everlasting Paint, Black Man Popping Out Of Barrel, U.S. Refining Co., 2 x 2 3/4 In. . . . 209.00
Fly, No Flies On Green, Joyce & Co. Hosiery, Simpson Iron Co., 4 1/4 x 2 In. 385.00
Gaint Powder Co., Nude Relief, Silver Plate, 3 x 1 1/2 x 1 In. 798.00
Gold Medal Flour, Celluloid Covered Metal, Striker 50.00
Home Insurance Company, New York, Sterling Silver, Firemen 575.00
Milwaukee Harvesting Machines, Tin Lithograph, 5 In. 192.00
Mother's Worm Syrup, Tin Lithograph, 7 In. 790.00
San Felice Cigars, Metal, Celluloid Image, 1/4 x 1 5/8 x 2 3/8 In. 425.00
Sharples Cream Separator, Tin Lithograph, 7 In. 678.00
Solarine, Metal Polish, Wise Wives Work Wonders, Tin Lithograph, 5 In. 77.00
Standard Oil Company, Celluloid Cover, 3/8 x 2 3/4 x 1 1/2 In. 495.00
MATCHBOOK, Atlantic Ale Beer, Full Of Good Cheer, Black Waiter 20.00
Bob's Seasoning Salt, 1960s, 1 x 3 3/4 In. 3.00
Brown Derby, Vine Street Derby Pictures, 1950s 8.50
Buick, Red Convertible, Spencer Buick, Taraval, San Francisco, 1958 . . . . 12.00
Chevrolet For 1936, Carlson Chevrolet, 121 No. Third St., 11 Matches, 4 1/4 x 3 1/4 In. . . 13.00
Gulistan Rugs, 11 Unused Matches, 4 1/4 x 3 1/4 In. 7.00
Happy Hollow Liquor Store, Liquor Bottles, c.1930 . . . . 11.50
Las Vegas Golden Nuggett, Roulette Wheel, Cards, Dice, Oversized Matches, 1950s 24.95
McCormack-Derring Farmall Tractor, Red Tractor 5.50
Shell Gasoline, Scallop Logo, Unused, 11 Matches, 1 Row, 1940s 45.00
Sunoco, List Of Services, Pump Shaped Matches, 21 Matches, Fort Wayne, Ind. 85.00
Tahiti Bar & Cocktail Lounge, Philadelphia, Hula Girls, 15 Matches, Lion Match Co. . . . 30.00
The Plantation, Denver Colorado, Smoked Dinners, 21 Matches 70.00
Victory U.S. War Bonds, V, Diamond Match Co., New York City 15.00
MATCHBOX, Ohio Blue Tip, Cardboard, Golfer 25.00

MAYO   Robert A. Mayo of Richmond, Virginia, contracted with the federal government to supply the U.S. Navy with plug tobacco about 1850. He called it—what else—"Navy Tobacco," a name that has often been copied. His son, Captain P.H. Mayo, continued the tobacco business under the name P.H. Mayo & Bro. Tobacco Company during the late 1800s, when the major tobacco manufacturers were having a plug tobacco war. Finally, in 1898, the American Tobacco Company acquired Mayo. It discontinued making Mayo tobacco brand in 1973.

Box, Tobacco, Cut Plug, Tin Lithograph, Handle, 6 1/2 x 8 In. 17.00
Lunch Box, Collapsible, Tin Lithograph, Wooden Handle, 7 3/4 x 5 1/2 x 5 In. 171.00
Lunch Box, Mayo's Cut Plug, Tin Lithograph, 8 In. 68.00
Sign, Mayo's Cut Plug, Men, In Car, Smoking Pipes, Paper, 11 x 18 In. 2530.00
Sign, Mayo's Plug Tobacco, Crowing Rooster, Lithograph, Frame, 20 x 33 In. 468.00
Sign, Mayo's Plug, Smoking Tobacco, Rooster, Lithograph On Linen, 23 x 60 In. 314.00
Sign, Mayo's Plug, Smoking, Cock O' The Walk, Porcelain, 13 x 6 1/2 In. .....1870.00 to 2475.00
Tin, Dutchman, Roly Poly, 6 1/2 x 6 In. 461.00

MCCORMICK McCormick and Company was founded in Baltimore, Maryland, in 1889, when Willoughby M. McCormick started making root beer-flavored extract and fruit syrups sold under the names Bee Brand and Silver Medal. He also made Iron Glue ("Sticks Everything but the Buyer"), and Uncle Sam's Nerve and Bone Liniment ("For Man or Beast"). Products were sold door to door. In 1896 McCormick purchased the F.G. Emmett Spice Company of Philadelphia. The business expanded and an export office was opened in New York City. Brands included McCormick's (1900), Reliable (1900), Banquet Brand spices and mustard (1902), and Tea House Tea (1937). As early as 1910, McCormick packaged tea in gauze pouches—the first teabags. The spoon or sift top was used on all ground spice tins after 1934. The large "MC" trademark was put on products in 1938. McCormick purchased many other spice companies and now sells seasonings, spices, flavorings, frozen foods, and other food products for retail and food service customers.

Bottle, Red Label, 3-Sided, Aqua, 4 1/2 In. 280.00
Calendar, 1910, Girl Kissing Boy, February Through December, 16 x 13 In. 518.00
Tin, Nutmeg, Pure Ground, Schilling Since 1881 .... 10.00
Tin, Pepper Flakes, 3 1/2 In. 8.00
Tin, Tea Bags, Tin Lithograph, Glass Top, Round, 10 In. 187.00
Tin, Thyme, 3 1/2 In. 8.00

MCDONALD'S Dick and Mac McDonald opened a food stand in San Bernardino, California, in 1948. They decided to feature a 15-cent hamburger. Ray Kroc, a Chicago milkshake-machine salesman, visited their restaurant in 1954 to learn why they wanted eight of his machines for such a small restaurant. He thought their concept was good and that other stands like it should be opened. When the McDonald brothers said they didn't want more restaurants, Kroc arranged to start his own McDonald's in Des Plaines, Illinois, in 1955. The building had golden arches and the symbol of a hamburger man called "Speedee." The McDonald's chain of restaurants grew; by 1958 the chain had sold 100 million hamburgers. Kroc bought out the McDonald brothers' name for $2.7 million in 1961. The logo was changed to the M-shaped arches in 1962. Another trademark, the character Ronald McDonald, was introduced in Washington, D.C., in 1963. The first Ronald was the famous weatherman, Willard Scott. McDonald's is currently headquartered in Oak Brook, Illinois. It is the world's leading food service retailer, with over 30,000 restaurants in 119 countries. Advertising materials of all sorts are collected. The premiums given or sold at the counter, such as glasses and Happy Meal toys, and advertising materials, such as signs or cups, are wanted. So are the toys sold in retail stores. Ronald McDonald and other characters from television ads, including Hamburglar, Big Mac, Grimace, Mayor McCheese, Captain Crook, and the Professor, have all been made as dolls.

Action Figure, Big Mac, Unopened, Card 18.00
Action Figure, Big Mac, Vinyl, Unopened, Card, Remco, 1976, 6 1/2 In. 20.00
Action Figure, Mayor McCheese, Unopened, Card 18.00
Action Figure, Ronald McDonald, Unopened, Card 18.00
Activity Book, Ronald Goes To Zoo, No. 2, 1968, 9 1/4 x 12 1/4 In., 12 Pages 24.00
Booklet, Travel Fun, 1970s, 8 1/4 x 10 3/4 In., 12 Pages 15.00
Bowling Ball, Ebonite, Child-Size Finger Holes, 1970s, 9 Lb., 9 In. 40.00
Cap, Manager's Service, Cellucap Mfg. Co., Philadelphia, 1954, 5 1/2 x 11 In. 25.00

If you collect the decorated glasses from fast food restaurants, never wash them in the dishwasher. The heat and detergent will change the coloring and lower the value.

McDonald's, Mug, Flinstones
Movie, Glass, 1993, 3 1/2 In.

Comic Book, Ronald McDonald, No. 4, Charlton Comics, March, 1971	80.00
Cookie Jar, Grimace, Box, 1997	42.00
Cup, Your Kind Of Place, Waxed Cardboard, Sweetheart, c.1970s, 4 3/4 In.	5.00
Display, Food Foolers, Happy Meals, 17 x 18 3/4 In.	100.00
Display, Furby, Happy Meals, 2000, 18 x 19 3/4 In.	90.00
Display, Looney Tunes, Bugs Bunny, Tazmanian Devil, Others, Plastic Case, 1991	125.00
Flag, Red, Golden Arches, 96 x 120 In.	129.00
Flying Disc, Ronald McDonald, Red, 1980, 5 3/4 In.	11.00
Game Sheet, 17 1/2 x 24 In.	45.00
Hat, Captain Crook Costume, Glossy Cardboard, 1978, 8 1/2 x 15 In.	8.00
Iron-On, Ronald & Porpoise, Early 1970s, 5 x 9 1/2 In.	14.00
Mask, Hamburglar, Prototype, Collegeville Costumes, 1990s, 9 x 15 x 4 In.	40.00
Mug, Fire-King, Good Morning, White, Orange Smiling Sun	8.00
Mug, Flinstones Movie, Glass, 1993, 3 1/2 In. . . . . *Illus*	10.00
Mug, Ronald McDonald Throwing Football, Smoked Glass, 1977, 4 3/8 In.	15.00
Patch, Good Gobblin, Cloth, Yellow Border, Arches, Round, 1972, 3 In.	14.00
Puppet, Hand, Ronald In Astronaut Globe Helmet, Vinyl, 1970s, 9 1/2 x 13 1/4 In.	12.00
Record, Night Before Christmas, Vinyl, Gee Gee Distributing, c.1960, 45 RPM, 7 In.	8.00
Toy, Parachute, Made In Taiwan, Late 1960s, 7 1/2 In.	8.00
Tray, Multi-Language, Yellow Plastic, 4 1/2 x 6 1/2 x 1/2 In.	15.00
Tumbler, Big Mac On Both Sides, Collector Series, 1970s	5.00
Tumbler, Great Muppet Caper, 1981	6.00
Tumbler, Ronald McDonald Jumping Into Fillet O' Fish Lake, 1977, 5 5/8 In.	10.00
Watch, Ronald McDonald, 1984	16.00
Wrapper, Roast Beef Sandwich, Silver Foil, 1965, 10 1/2 x 14 In.	15.00
Wristwatch, Metal, Leather Band, Plastic Case, CMI Corp., 1980s, 1 3/4 x 9 1/2 In.	40.00

MENNEN   Gerhard Mennen, a pharmacist with a drugstore in Newark, New Jersey, started experimenting with his own products in 1875. His first product, made in 1878, was called Mennen's Sure Corn Killer. The product was sold in his and other drugstores. He advertised using all of the standard methods of the day, including newspaper ads, circulars, salesmen, and lecturers urging listeners to buy the products at local drugstores. He made Mennen's Borated Talcum Infant Powder in 1889. The powder was also advertised by the Mennen's Talcum Show, a minstrel act. The cardboard powder containers leaked, so he ordered tin shaker-top cans from Somers Brothers of Brooklyn, New York. The shoulder of the can had a small picture of Gerhard Mennen's head as a trademark. The front of the tin pictured Mennen as a chubby baby. When Mennen died in 1902, his wife, Elma Christina, became president of the company. She turned it over to her son, William G. Mennen, in 1916. He was president until 1963, when his sons George S. and William G. Jr. took over. Colgate-Palmolive acquired Mennen in 1992. The brand appears on after-shave and deodorant products. Early Mennen tin containers are in great demand among collectors.

MENNEN

Bottle, Antiseptic Oil, Baby In Sailboat, Paper Label, Tin Top, 2 1/4 x 1 1/8 In.	48.00
Jar, Brushless Shave, Embossed, Glass, Green Metal Lid, 6 Oz., 3 1/4 In.	24.00
Tin, Borated Talcum Powder, Gerhard Mennen, Round	71.00

Tin, Shave Talc, 4 Oz., 5 In. 20.00
Tin, Toilet Talcum Powder, Gerhardt Mennen 88.00

MENU Menus that depict famous restaurants, historic figures, famous events, or well-known locales are prized by collectors. So are those with interesting graphics or that commemorate a special meal. Items listed here include hand-held restaurant menus and menu boards and special signs.

Crossroads Inn, Highway 50, Kansas City, Mo. 15.00
Filene's Salad Bowl, Boston, Mass., 1946, 9 x 6 In. 25.00
Grand Canyon Lodge, Utah Park Systems, Union Pacific, 1929, 4 3/8 x 5 5/8 In. 25.00
Plaza Hotel, USAAF Bombers, San Antonio, New Years, 1942 .... 25.00
MENU BOARD, Golden Drop Soda, Tin, Embossed, 19 x 27 In. 88.00
Hambone, 5 Cent Cigar, Mild & Mellow, Special For To-Day, 20 1/4 x 13 In. 39.00
Ice Cream, Enjoy Our Fountain, 11 Flavor Stripes, Chrome Frame, 26 x 14 1/2 In. 176.00
Kayo Chocolate Soda, Frame, 26 x 13 1/2 In. 138.00

MILK Milk bottles, caps, and other milk containers are listed here. The first milk bottle patent was issued in the 1880s to the Warren Glass Works Company. The most famous milk bottle was designed in 1884 by Dr. Harvey D. Thatcher, a physician and druggist from Potsdam, New York. His glass bottle had a *lightning* closure and an embossed picture on the side showing a cow being milked. In 1889 the Thatcher Company brought out a bottle with a cardboard cap that fit into a ledge inside the neck. Characteristic shapes and printed or embossed wording identify milk bottles for collectors. The name of the dairy is almost always on the bottle. The tall round bottle was the most popular until 1936, when the squat round bottle was invented. In 1940 a squat square bottle became the preferred shape. The paper carton was introduced in 1932. *Cop top, baby face, toothache,* and *cream top* are terms that refer to bottle-neck shapes popular in the 1930s that allowed the cream that separated from the milk to be poured off easily. The glass bottle was displaced by cartons by the 1960s. Plastic bottles have been used since 1964.

Bottle, 3 Cent, Embossed, 1/4 Pt. 17.00
Bottle, A Bottle Of Milk Is A Bottle Of Health, Embossed, Qt. 16.00
Bottle, Adams Pasteurized Milk, Rawlins, Wyo., Cowboy, Bucking Bronco, Red ACL, Qt. 100.00
Bottle, Annie Oakley, Gail Harris Rearing On Horse, Pt. 22.00
Bottle, Augusta Dairies, Staunton, Va., 3 Children Playing In Yard, ACL, Qt. 25.00
Bottle, Bartholomay Co. Inc., Rochester, N.Y., Raised Print, Cream Top, Qt., 1925 ...... 55.00
Bottle, Bireleys, Wavy, Qt. 6.50
Bottle, Blue Boy Sparkle Vitamin-Mineral Fortified Milk, Painted Label, Amber, Qt. 28.00
Bottle, Brookfield, Baby Face, Cream Top, Embossed, Hellertown, Pa., 1/2 Pt. 45.00
Bottle, Cannon's Dairy, Catlow, Nelson, Red ACL, International, 568 Ml, 5 7/8 In. 25.00
Bottle, Carnation, Amber, Qt. 25.00
Bottle, Central Dairy Co., Rockford, Ill., Embossed, Square, Qt. 16.00
Bottle, Chestnut Farms Sealtest Chevy Chase Dairy, Square, Cream Top, Qt. 30.00
Bottle, Coleman Dairy, Grade A Dairy Products, Belvidere & Merengo, Ill., Pt. 19.00
Bottle, Columbia, Qt., 8 3/4 In. 15.00
Bottle, Excelsior, Chas. F. Rothenhoefer, Frederick, Md., Embossed, Pt. 25.00
Bottle, F A Cobbs Dairy, Best Since 1910, Round, 1914, Pt. 35.00
Bottle, Fairfield Western Maryland Dairy, Frederick, Md., Embossed, 1/2 Pt. 25.00
Bottle, Farm Dairy, Edwardsville, Pa., Red ACL, Qt. 25.00
Bottle, Farmer's Dairy Products Co. Inc., Cumberland, Md., Embossed, Pt. 16.00
Bottle, Forest City Dairy, Rockford, Ill., Embossed, Qt. 20.00
Bottle, Freese & Rissler Dairy, Health & Wealth, Red Paint, 1914, Qt., 8 3/4 In. 23.00
Bottle, Funny Cow, Glass, 10 In. 30.00
Bottle, Gitt's Dairy, Stork Carrying Diapered Baby, Listen Pa!, Paper Cap, 9 1/2 In. 40.00
Bottle, Graham Bros. Dairy, Lincoln, Nebr., 1/2 Pt., 6 3/4 In. 14.00
Bottle, Green Spring Dairy, Belmont 4477, Square, Red Painted Label, Qt. 17.00
Bottle, H.R. & M.J. Eminson, Higham, Green Stripe, ACL, Embossed, Foreign, 5 In. 25.00
Bottle, Independent Dairies, Kansas City, Mo., Embossed, Top Ring, Round, 9 1/2 In. ... 25.00

Bottle, Independent Dairies, Kansas City, Mo., Embossed, Cursive, Round, Qt. 16.00
Bottle, International Milk Co. Inc., Hillside, N.J., Pyro, Pt. 25.00
Bottle, Johnson Farms Dairy, Waterloo, Iowa, Quality You Can Taste, Qt., 9 1/2 In. 28.00
Bottle, Kennedy's Dairy, Mt. Pleasant, New London, Winfield, Ia., Red Letters, 5 1/2 In. .   17.00
Bottle, Lawrence Dairy, Chocolate Milk, Smiling Black Children, Maine, Qt., 9 In. . .33.00 to 51.00
Bottle, Lawton Bros. Dairy, Dixon, Ill., For Mothers Who Care, Red Printing, 1/2 Pt. 22.00
Bottle, Liberty Dairy, Shillinton, Pa., Raised Letters, Pt., 7 1/2 In. 30.00
Bottle, Little's Dairy, Hanover, Pa., Red Painted Square Label, Pt. 22.00
Bottle, Manor View Dairy, Quality Dairy Products, Millersville, Pa., Cow Head, Qt. .22.00 to 25.00
Bottle, Maple Hurst Farms, Bound Brook, Red ACL, N.J., Qt.   25.00
Bottle, Mass O Seal, Sam Bookless, Pittsfield, Mass., Embossed, Qt. 20.00
Bottle, Mc Daniel's Dairy, Williamsport, Pa., Baseball Player, After Game, Cool Off, 1/2 Pt.   45.00
Bottle, Meadow Dairies, Leaksville, N.C., Blue Neck Swirl, Embossed, 1/2 Pt. 25.00
Bottle, Meyer, Phone 34-F-04, Red Paint, Round, Qt., 9 1/2 In.   18.00
Bottle, Meyer, Round, Red Paint, Qt., 9 1/2 In. 25.00
Bottle, Milk, Star, Cow, Canada, 1888, 9 1/2 In. 13.00
Bottle, Page Dairy Co., Toledo, Ohio, No. 5, Amber, 1920-1935, Qt. 123.00
Bottle, Perry's Creamery, Buy Defense Bonds, Tuscaloosa, Al., Qt. 45.00
Bottle, Pinehurst Farms Dairy, Rockford, Ill., Boy Drinking Milk, Girl Pouring Milk, 1/2 Pt.   31.00
Bottle, Queen City Dairy Company, Embossed, Pt. 25.00
Bottle, R.J. Smith Dairy, Red Silkscreen Letters, Square, Qt., 8 5/8 x 3 3/8 In. 15.00
Bottle, Rawleigh Farms, Good Health Milk, Freeport, Ill., Sealed BB-48, 1/2 Pt. 43.00
Bottle, Reik Dairy, Qt. 8.00
Bottle, Royale Dairy, Hanover, Pa., Fit For A King, 9 1/2 x 4 In. 16.00
Bottle, Scott Key Dairy, W.H. Moore Prop., Embossed, Qt. 25.00
Bottle, Sheffield, Qt., 8 3/4 In. 15.00
Bottle, Southern Dairies, Embossed, Pt. 25.00
Bottle, St. Lawrence Pasteurized Milk, St. Lawrence Dairy, Raised Letters, 1/2 Pt., 6 In. .   25.00
Bottle, St. Louis Dairy, St. Louis, Mo., Embossed, Qt. 25.00
Bottle, Stocker's Easton, Pa., Square, Red Painted Label, Have You Tried Our Other, Qt. .   22.00
Bottle, Store 5 Cent Bottle, Universal Store Bottle, Embossed, Qt. 17.00
Bottle, Tampa Stock Farm Dairy, Script Letters, Embossed, Duraglas Insignia, Qt. 25.00
Bottle, Thatcher's Dairy, Man Milking Cow, Absolutely Pure, Porcelain Top, Embossed, Qt.   25.00
Bottle, Unmarked Bottle, Young's Yankee Dairy On Cardboard Lid, 10 1/2 x 3 In. 15.00
Bottle, Uservo Inc., 1/2 Pt., 5 1/2 x 2 1/2 In. 7.00
Bottle, Valley Home Dairy, Ed Schlaepfer, John O'Leary, Embossed, Paper Lid, Qt. 325.00
Bottle, Vermont Country Milk, Burlington, Vt., Red Foil Cap, Late 1980s, Qt. 10.00
Bottle, Walander, Pt., 7 1/4 In. 10.00
Bottle, Westwood Farm, Aberdeen, Md., Embossed, Qt. 25.00
Bottle Cap, Hietpas Dairy Farm Grade A, Farm, Cows, Red Ink, Paper, 1 5/8 In. 5.00
Bottle Cap, How Would You Like To Be The Milk Man, Tin, 2 In. 22.00
Bottle Cap, Locust Lane Jersey Farms, Grade A, Howe, Indiana, Aluminum, 1 1/2 In. . . .   5.00
Bottle Top, Springbrook Dairy, Baby Drinking Milk, Aluminum, Dial 6721, 1 3/4 In. 4.00
Carton, Hancock Co. Creamery, Parafinned, Cone, Ellsworth, Me., 1/2 Pt., 4 1/2 In. 20.00
Container, Hancock Creamery, Waxed Cone, Cardboard, Ellsworth, Maine, 1937, 10 In. . .   30.00
Holder, Hy-Klas Milk, Pink, Plastic, 1/2 Gal. 18.00

MILLER Frederick Miller, a German brewmaster who moved to the
United States in 1854, bought a brewery in Milwaukee, Wisconsin, the
following year and sold beer in wooden barrels. Miller beer was first
bottled in 1879 by an independent contractor hired by the brewery.
Four years later, Miller was bottling his own beer. Ernst Miller became
president of the company when his father died in 1888. The company
labels have been changed through the years. In 1899, the eagle atop a
circle mark was used. This was dropped in the 1940s and reinstated in
1985. Slogans that have been used include "The Best Milwaukee
Beer" (1903), "Champagne of Bottle Beer" (1906), "Enjoy Life with
Miller High Life" (1938), "Champagne of Beers" (1969), "If You've
Got the Time, We've Got the Beer" (1971), "Tastes Great, Less Filling" (Miller Lite, c.1976), "Welcome to Miller Time" (1982), and
"Miller—Made the American Way" (1985). The Miller girl was first
used in ads in 1903. Miller High Life was introduced in 1903, Miller

Lite in 1975, and Miller Genuine Draft in 1986. Miller now owns Leinenkugel, Henry Weinhard, Hamm's, Milwaukee Best, and other brands. The company remained family-owned until 1966, when W.R. Grace and Company purchased 53 percent of the stock. Philip Morris Inc. bought the Grace shares in 1969. Miller is now part of SABMiller and is the second largest brewery in the world. The U.S. subsidiary, Miller Brewing Company, is the second largest brewing company in the country.

Button, Celluloid Hanger, Miller High Life, Girl On Moon & Girl Holding Tray, 1 x 3 In. ... 173.00
Display, Ice Bucket, Light-Up, Motion, Revolving, 19 In. ... 99.00
Figure, Miller Girl, Plastic, Gold Color, 1950s, 6 1/2 In. ... 65.00
Holder, Bic Lighter, Miller Lite, Beer Can Shape, 2 3/4 x 2 In. ... 8.00
Lighter, Miller Lite Beer Can, Miniature, 2 3/4 x 1 In. ... 10.00
Sign, Genuine Draft, Chicago Bulls Logo, Red, White & Yellow Neon, 28 In. ... 196.00
Sign, High Life Beer, Woman On Crescent Moon, Tin Over Cardboard, 17 x 11 In. 330.00 to 660.00
Sign, High Life, The Best Milwaukee Beer, Porcelain, 20 x 14 In. ... 415.00
Sign, Miller High Life, Champagne Of Bottle Beer, Blue Mirrored Heavy Glass, 8 x 4 In. . 56.00
Tray, Fred Miller Brewing Co., Milwaukee U.S.A., Eagle, Tin, Round ... 1280.00 to 3350.00
Tray, Moon Girl, High Life Beer, Round, 1907, 24 In. ... 1298.00
Tray, Moon Girl, High Life, Oval, 10 1/2 x 15 In. ... 413.00

MIRROR Pocket mirrors were made in a variety of shapes and sizes—roughly 1 1/2 to 5 inches in diameter for round mirrors, and 3 1/2 by 2 inches for rectangular mirrors. Most of them were made between 1900 and 1930 to be given away as advertising promotions. These mirrors usually had a picture and an ad on the celluloid or metal mirror backing. Other advertising mirrors were made in larger sizes to be displayed on a wall. Modern versions of the metal-backed pocket mirrors are made in many styles that might fool the novice collector into thinking a new design is an old one. The new designs are often copies of old advertisements. Examine the ad using a magnifying glass; modern halftones will appear as a field of tiny dots. Heavy, thick glass domes covering paper ads are another type of advertising mirror, called a paperweight mirror.

Admiration, Cigar That Wins, Tin Lithograph, 19 1/4 x 10 1/4 In. ... 660.00
Albers Cereals & Flours, Look For The Miner, Paperweight, Celluloid, 3 1/2 In. ... 1045.00
American Line, Philadelphia, Liverpool, Queenstown, Steamer, Round, 1 3/4 In. ... 200.00
Anderson's Concentrated Soups, Bald Man, Can, Celluloid, Round, Pocket, 1 3/4 In. ... 150.00
Angelus Marshmallow, Child Angel, Holding Package, Oval, Pocket, 2 3/4 In. ... 75.00 to 102.00
Armstrong-Turner Millinery Co., Celluloid Back, Oval, Colorado, c.1905-1915, 2 3/4 In. . 127.00
Barry's Tricopherous Hair Tonic, Grows Thick, Glossy Hair, Celluloid, 2 3/4 x 2 In. ... 2860.00
Bass In Bottle, Wood Frame, Red Triangle, Metal Stand-Up Bracket, 13 1/4 x 11 1/4 In. . 104.00
Battle Mountain Club Saloon, Topless Woman, 12 1/2 Cents In Trade, c.1908, 2 1/4 In. . 6038.00
Beautyskin For Health & Beauty, Celluloid, Oval, Chichester Chemical, 1 1/2 x 2 3/8 In. . 240.00
Beeman's Pepsin Gum, Celluloid, Round, 2 1/8 In. ... 198.00 to 275.00
Bell Roasted Coffee, America's Best, Buy No Other, Red, Green, 2 1/8 In. ... 110.00
Berry Brothers Varnishes, 4 Children, Wagon, Stairs, Multicolored, Round, 2 1/8 In. ... 209.00
Berry Brothers Varnishes, Boy Pulling Wagon, Dog, Oval, 1 3/4 x 2 3/4 In. ... 220.00
Big Boy Soda, Bottle, Sunrise Over City, Celluloid, Pocket, 2 3/4 x 1 1/4 In. ... 100.00
Big Jo Flour, Birthstones, Flour Sack, Riverside Mills Best, Minn., 2 1/4 In. ... 35.00 to 44.00
Biggs Company, Sterling Range, Thomasville, N.Y., 2 1/8 In. ... 130.00
Brotherhood Overalls, H.S. Peters, Topless Woman, Round, 2 1/8 In. ... 435.00
Buffalo Brewing Co., Reverse Image, Backbar, Frame, 1906, 10 x 14 In. ... 523.00
Buy Whitecat Union Suits, Cooper Underwear, Celluloid, Oval, Kenosha, 2 3/4 x 2 In. ... 250.00
Cantrell & Cochranes, Ginger Ale, Dry & Aromatic, Wood Frame, 18 1/2 x 12 1/2 In. ... 123.00
Capstan Navy Cut Cigarettes, Wood Frame, England, 22 1/4 x 18 1/4 In. ... 38.00
Carmen Complexion Powder, 1 3/4 In. ... 110.00
Carnation Bottling Co., Mirror Over Cardboard, 10 x 3 1/2 In. ... 11.00
Charles E. Lamb, Cigars For Banquets, Oval, Boston, 1 3/4 In. ... 380.00
Chew White's Yucatan Gum, Celluloid, Red Ground, Round, 2 1/8 In. ... 65.00
Cleaner's Choice, Woman, White Gown, Multicolored, 2 3/4 In. ... 38.00
Club Saloon, Good For 1 Drink, Woman, Celluloid, Round, 2 1/4 In. ... 578.00

Columbia Tool Steel, It Pays To Use Good Tool Steel, Celluloid, 2 1/8 In. 130.00
Commercial Hotel, Elko, Nev., Woman, Feather Hat, 12 1/2 Cents In Trade, c.1908, 2 In. .   1840.00
Congress Beer, Celluloid, Haberle Brewing Co., 2 3/4 x 1 3/4 In. 184.00
Continental Cubes Pipe Tobacco, Woman In Red Dress, 2 3/4 x 1 3/4 In. . . . . . .275.00 to 308.00
Corbett Tailor, Woman In Low Cut Dress, Hand Tinted Photograph, Chicago, Round, 2 In.   90.00
Cream Separator, Smith Mfg. Co., Chicago, Great Western, The World's Best, 2 3/4 In. . .   110.00
Dempster, Beveled Glass, Brass Frame, Oval, 14 x 13 In. 44.00
Dockash Stoves & Ranges Are The Best, Scranton Stove Works, Celluloid, 2 In. . . .44.00 to 135.00
Dr. Caldwell's Syrup Pepsin, Celluloid, Oval, 1 3/4 x 2 3/4 In. 121.00
Dry Goods Store, Syracuse, N.Y., Witherill's The Busy Corner, 2 5/8 In. 38.00
DuBelle Grape Juice, Happy Woman, Celluloid, Oval, 2 3/4 x 1 3/4 In. 220.00
DWD, Finest Whisky In The World, Pure Pot Still, Wood Frame, England, 28 x 23 In. 66.00
Emerson & Fisher Carriage Builders, For The Trade, Cincinnati, Ohio, 2 1/4 In. 75.00
Engman-Matthews Range Company, Sharpening Stone, South Bend, Ind., 2 1/4 In. 165.00
Erickson & McHugh, Pianos, Player Pianos, Talking Machines, Music Rolls, Records, 2 In.   20.00
Erika Typewriter, Multicolored, Round, 2 1/4 In. 87.00
Family Liquor Store, Los Angeles, 8 3/4 x 10 3/4 In. 35.00
Farm Implements, Harnesses & Wagons, Dutton, Mont., 9 1/2 x 9 1/2 In. 148.00
Flor De Baltimore Havana Cigars, Celluloid, Round, J.D. Oppenheimer, 2 1/4 In. 260.00
Fort Bedford P-Nut Butter, Largest 10 Cent Glass Sold, Celluloid, 1 3/4 In. 124.00
Frances Roberts Co. Guaranteed Hair Goods, Embossed, Celluloid, 2 1/2 In. 25.00
Fraternal Life Insurance, Omaha, Neb., Celluloid, 2 3/4 x 1 3/4 In. 95.00
Garland Flour, Best Made, Prize Winner, World's Columbian Exposition, Round, 1 3/4 In.   58.00
Gately's, Oval, Hand, 5 In. 68.00
Gates Hats, Celluloid, Pocket, Chicago, 1 3/4 In. 83.00
Geo. S. Schuyler, Piano, Watertown, N.Y., 2 1/8 In. 28.00
Globe A-1 Flour, Quality First Made In San Diego, 2 1/4 In. 49.00
Gold Flake Cigarettes, W.D. & H.O. Wills, Wood Frame, England, 22 x 18 In. 57.00
Goodyear's Rubber Glove Co., Celluloid, Round, Pincushion, 2 1/4 In. 65.00
Goodyear's Rubber Glove Co., L.P. Ross Co., Rochester, N.Y., Round, 2 3/4 In. 27.00
Gordon Hat, You Needn't Be Afraid To Look At Yourself, Celluloid, 1 3/4 In. 25.00
H. Bellmann, German Words, Round, Celluloid, 2 14 In. 80.00
Haines, Shoe Wizard, Man Who Makes Wonderful Prices Possible, 2 In. 75.00
Hamilton Medical Association, Cancer Or Tumor, Celluloid, Round, Pocket, 2 1/8 In. . . .   89.00
Hammond Dairy Feed, Feed Of Good Quality, Round, 2 1/4 In.   42.00
Hauger Suits, Hauger Overcoats, Your Lucky Change, Chas. C. Hauger Co., 1 3/4 In. . . .   46.00
Heald Chain Of Schools, Heald Business College & Engineering School, Oval, 2 3/4 In. .   58.00
Hess-Snyder Co., Boomer Furnaces For Coal & Gas, Massillon, Ohio, 1 3/4 In. 44.00
Highland Brand Canned Goods, Bagpipe Player, Oval, 2 3/8 x 1 1/2 In. 32.00
Hinton & Son, Ambulance Co., Safe, Dependable, Celluloid, Paperweight, 3 1/2 In. Diam.   385.00
Hobo Kidney & Bladder Remedy, Celluloid, Yellow, White, Black 125.00
Hofbrau Haus Restaurant, Famous Restaurant In New York, American Flag, 2 1/4 In. . . .   63.00
Holeproof Hosiery, Are Your Hose Insured?, 2 1/4 In. 25.00
Home Store, Millinery & Cloaks, McKeesport, Pa., Round, 2 In. 235.00
Horder's Stationary & Office Supplies, Chicago, Round, 3 1/2 In. 60.00
Hotel Raymond, Good For 10 Cents In Trade, 2 1/4 In. 264.00
Hudson Bay Fur Co., Exclusive Furriers, Celluloid Back, Oval, 2 3/4 In. 397.00
Humphrey's Witch Hazel Oil, Oak Frame, 11 1/2 x 10 In. 83.00
Insist On Mission Brand California Oranges & Grapefruit, Smiling Sun, c.1930, 2 1/8 In.   87.00
International Tailoring Co., Dexterity Game, Embossed, Tin Lithograph, Pocket, 1 5/8 In.   100.00
Irish Tea, F.M. Bill Co., Celluloid, 2 3/4 x 2 In. 413.00
Johnnie Doran Saloon, Girl, Dress, Dog, Ritzville, Wash., Round, 2 1/4 In. 184.00
Kendall Friday Co., Gas Power People, Woman Driving Car, Celluloid, 2 1/8 In. 514.00
Keth's Vaudeville, Lady, Holding Umbrellas, Celluloid, 2 3/4 x 1 3/4 In. 198.00
Killian Co., Department Store, Black On Cream, Celluloid, 2 In.   53.00
King Midas, Highest Price Flour In America & Worth All It Costs, Rectangular, 2 3/4 In. .   29.00
Klosed Krotch Union Suits, Heffner, Gilbert & Croll, Celluloid, Round, 2 1/8 In. 165.00
Knights Of Maccabees, Celluloid, Detroit, Michigan, Oval, 2 3/4 x 1 3/4 In. 100.00
L. Stroup Lumber & Roofing, Adjustable Handle, Black, Tin, 7 3/4 In. 65.00
La Mode Buttons, B. Bluementhal, Round, 1 3/4 In. 365.00
Lady Laurel, Laurel Stoves, Celluloid, Oval, 2 3/4 x 1 3/4 In. 365.00
Lifebuoy Royal Disinfectant Soap, Lifebuoy Man Tossing Buoy, England, 14 x 10 In. . . .   142.00
Litholin Waterproofed Linen, Celluloid, 2 3/4 In. 41.00

Littleton State Bank, Cream Colored Celluloid, Oval, Colorado, c.1910, 2 3/4 In. 138.00
Lucky Tiger, Cures Dandruff, Woman, Tiger, Red, Black, White, 2 1/8 In. 99.00
Ludlow Ambulance Service, Celluloid, Pocket, 3 1/2 In. 440.00
Matchless Cunningham Piano, Celluloid, Oval, 1 3/4 x 2 3/4 In. 165.00
McNish's Scotch Whisky, Doctor's Special, Wood Frame, Scotland, 9 1/4 x 11 1/4 In. 20.00
Minneapolis Hosiery, When Is Hose-Good Hose?, 2 1/8 In. 27.00
Minneapolis School Supply Company, Weighted, Round, 3 1/2 In. 65.00
Minnesota Linseed Oil Paint, 2 In. 130.00
Mission Brand Oranges, Smiling Sun, It's Real Juice, 1930s, 2 1/8 In. 40.00
Mohawk Club, German Beer On Draught, Angels, 12 1/2 Cents In Trade, c.1910, 2 In. ... 1725.00
Morrell's Pride Meats, Round, Celluloid, John Morrell & Co., 2 1/4 In. 75.00
Muskogee Taxi Co., Hotel Severs, Phone 23, Celluloid, Round, 3 1/2 In. 605.00
Nature's Remedy, Face, Pill On Tongue, Multicolored, 2 1/8 In. 24.00
Nature's Remedy Tablets, Blue Border, Celluloid, Round, 2 1/8 In. 145.00
Nebraska Clothing Retailer, Ladies & Misses Suits, Coats, Dresses, 2 3/4 In. 53.00
Nevada Club, Building's Doors, 12 1/2 Cents In Trade, Tonopah, Nev., Oval, 2 x 2 3/4 In. 1955.00
North Dakota, Farm Machinery In Field, Lithography, Celluloid, Pocket, 1 3/4 x 2 7/8 In. 303.00
Norton Mercantile Co., Girl, Holding Flower, Handle, 2 x 5 1/4 In. 209.00
Oak Motor Suit, Man In Suit, By Car, Celluloid, 2 3/4 x 1 3/4 In. 264.00
Old Reliable Coffee, Always Good, Man, Leaning On Box, Celluloid, 3 1/2 In. 66.00
Olympian Ice Cream, Westfield, N.J., 2 In. 295.00
Omar Pearls, Glamour Girl, Pearls, Gold Ground, Celluloid, Pocket, 2 3/4 x 1 3/4 In. 165.00
Owl Liquor Co., Girl, Roses, 12 1/2 Cents In Trade, c.1903, 2 1/4 In. 1840.00
Owl Liquor Co., Nude Woman, Green Scarf, 12 1/2 Cents In Trade, 2 1/4 In. 1438.00
Owl Tavern, Grass Valley, Ca., Good For 10 Cents In Trade, Blight Bros., Celluloid, 2 In. . 2965.00
Paperweight, New Human Interest Library, Midland Press, 3 In. 84.00
Paperweight, Yellow Taxicab Service, Rear Of Cab, Mt. Vernon, Celluloid, 3 x 1/4 In. 413.00
Patriot & Field Day, Runner, Eagle, Monday, May 31, Celluloid, Early 1900s, 1 3/4 In. .. 57.00
People's Store, Woman, Oval, Pocket, 2 1/2 In. 102.00
Phillips Invalid Coach, Celluloid, 3 1/2 In. 330.00
Players Please Everyone, Tobacco & Cigarettes, Wood Frame, England, 22 x 18 In. 38.00
Pyramid Soap Powder, Egyptian Scene, Celluloid, Round, 1 3/4 In. 330.00
Queen Quality Shoes, Woman, Oval, Pocket, 2 1/2 In. ....45.00 to 83.00
Queen Shoes, Miss Liberty, Celluloid, Pocket, 2 3/4 x 1 3/4 In. 90.00
Regans Carson City, Girl, Roses, 12 1/2 Cents In Trade, 2 1/4 In. 1380.00
Regans Carson City, Spread Winged Eagle, 12 1/2 Cents In Trade, Round, 2 1/4 In. 2185.00
Rosary Chocolates, Mueller-Keller Candy Co., Celluloid, St. Joseph, Mo., 2 1/4 In. 110.00
Rumford Baking Powder, Wreath, Celluloid, Early 1900s, 1 3/4 In. 127.00
Ryan's Beers, Indian Chief, Syracuse, Multicolored, Celluloid, 2 1/4 In. 285.00
S.F. Fatzinger Painting, Paperhanging, Decorating, Celluloid, c.1940, 4 In. 30.00
Salt & Co., Burton On Trent, Lettering On Frame, Oval Brass Frame, England, 17 x 15 In. 114.00
San-Tox, Nurse, Celluloid, Oval, Pocket, 2 3/4 x 1 3/4 In. 176.00
Sargent's Paint, Topless Woman, Celluloid, Pocket, 2 1/4 x 1 1/4 In. 495.00
Schaeffer Pianos, Tan Ground, Celluloid, Round, 2 In. 165.00
Security Life Insurance, Celluloid, Rectangular, 1 3/4 x 2 3/4 In. 125.00
Shell, Gold Letters, Red Oil Can, Wood Frame, England, 26 1/2 x 8 1/2 In. 114.00
Silverman Bros. Wool, Sheep, Celluloid, Round, 2 1/8 In. 303.00
Snow Drop Flour, Meek Milling Co., Marissa, Ill., Celluloid, 2 3/4 x 1 3/4 In. 44.00
Spalding, Bicycles & Sporting Goods, Celluloid, Pocket, 2 1/8 In. 330.00
Standard Brewing Co., Ale, Hand Holds Cards, Celluloid, Rochester, N.Y., 1 3/4 In. 222.00
Stylecraft Girl, Cohn-Goodman, Celluloid, Round, 2 1/8 In. 44.00
Sullivan's 7-20-4 Cigars, 10 Cent, Woman, Celluloid, Oval, Pocket, 2 3/4 x 1 3/4 In. 523.00
Thoroughbred Hats, 3 Wild Horse Heads, Round, 2 1/4 In. 316.00
Thwaites, Soda Water, Blue & Gold Letters, Beveled Edge, England, 16 x 12 In. 38.00
Tonopah Saloon, Girl, Roses, 10 Cents In Trade, c.1905, 2 1/4 In. 3565.00
Travelers Insurance Company, Hartford, Steam Train, Oval, Celluloid, 2 3/8 x 1 5/8 In. ... 195.00
Universal Theaters Concession Co., Handle, 3 1/4 In. 55.00
Van Camp's, Couple Holding Plate, 2 In. 45.00
Van Camp's, Pork & Beans, 2 1/8 In. 160.00
Ward Safety Razor, Natural Sliding Stroke, Man Shaving, Round, 2 1/4 In. 138.00
Wellington Conover Cable Kingsbury Inner Player Pianos, Celluloid, Round, 2 1/8 In. .. 155.00
Wellington Conover Cable Kingsbury Piano, Ottowa & Paolo, Kan., Celluloid, 2 1/8 In. . 40.00
White House Shoes, Brown Shoe Co., St. Louis, Celluloid, Round, 2 1/4 In. ......86.00 to 195.00

White Rolls Cigarettes, Woman Smoking Cigarette, Celluloid, Oval, 2 3/4 x 1 3/4 In. 443.00
Williams' Toilet Luxuries, Shaving Stick, Powder, Soap, Celluloid, Cream Color, 4 1/2 In. . . 127.00
Wills's Gold Flake Cigarettes, Wood Frame, 16 1/2 x 12 In. 20.00
Worcester Envelope Employees Picnic, Aug. 20, 1898, Celluloid, 1 3/4 In. 40.00
Yellow Taxi Company, Lowest Rates In Detroit, 3333 Cadillac, Celluloid, 3 1/2 In. 1265.00
You Can Do It If You Use Whiting-Adams Brushes, Celluloid, Round, Boston, 2 1/8 In. . 295.00
Youngs' Hotel, Nevada, Girl, Long Hair, Rose, 10 Cents In Trade, c.1905 . . . . 1840.00

MISCELLANEOUS   There are items that do not fit into the other categories in this book. Many are listed here.

Advertisement, American Gas, Kitchen Scene, 1936, 11 x 14 In. 10.00
Advertisement, Cannon Stockings, Woman, Black & White, Frame, 14 3/4 x 7 In. 15.00
Advertisement, Congoleum Floor, Kitchen Scene, 1939, 11 x 14 In. 10.00
Advertisement, Stanhome Products, 1954, 11 x 14 In. 8.00
Bag & Stringholder, Queen's Laundry Bar, Albert Toilet Soap, Tin 4675.00
Banknote, Dr. Mclean's Homeopathic Liver & Kidney Balm, 3 1/2 x 7 1/4 In. 44.00
Banknote, Dr. Seth Arnold's Cough Killer, Facsimile Confederate Note, 3 1/4 x 7 1/4 In. . 66.00
Beater Jar, Wilson's Variety Store, Clarion, Iowa, Stoneware, Blue, Gray, 5 In. 207.00
Bell, Encore Whisky, Is The Best, Raphael Tuck & Sons, London, 3 3/4 x 4 1/2 In. 323.00
Bench, Shoe, Peter's Shoes, Wood, Twisted Wire Frame, 14 In. 138.00
Bench, Wear Peter's Shoes, Wood, 36 x 70 In. 275.00
Bill Clip, Southern Grocery Co., Bulldog, Lithograph, Metal, San Marcos, Tex., 2 3/4 x 2 In. 132.00
Bill Spike, National Cash Register, Nickeled Bronze, 6 1/4 In. 23.00
Billhead, Humphrey's Homeopathic Medicine, Graphic Of Cabinet, 4 1/8 x 8 1/2 In. 55.00
Billhook, Famous Biscuit Co., Cardboard, Round, 5 3/4 x 3 1/2 In. 78.00
Billhook, Luxury Macaroni, Celluloid, Metal, 1920s, 6 1/2 x 3 1/2 In. 89.00
Bookends, Hartford Fire Insurance Co., Brass, 1810-1935, 5 1/2 In. 92.00
Bottle Holder, Whistle Soda, Figural Hand, Bottle, Iron, Wall Mount, 3 x 10 x 2 1/2 In. . . 1650.00
Broom Holder, Campbell's Varnish Stain, Tin Lithograph, Wire Handle, 3 3/8 x 2 1/2 In. . 167.00
Broom Holder, Lee Broom, Tin Lithograph, Red Ground, 6 1/4 x 2 1/2 In. 256.00
Broom Rack, Schmidt's Blue Ribbon Bread, 2-Sided, 31 In. . . . . .83.00 to 154.00
Brush, Wisdom Clothing, Celluloid, Tapp Co., 1 1/8 In. 205.00
Bucket, Dutch Boy, White Lead Paint, Metal, Yellow Letters, Black Ground, No. 50 . . . . . 77.00
Bucket, Washington Mills Pepper, Wood, Paper Label, Washington's Portrait, 12 In. 143.00
Bumper Tag, Tydol, Fat Man Running, Embossed, Tin Lithograph, 6 5/8 x 4 1/2 In. 95.00
Cake Mold, Swans Down Cake Flour Makes Better Cakes, E. Katzinger, Chicago, 1923 . . 85.00
Cake Pan, Tube, Swans Down Cake Flour, 3 1/2 x 8 1/2 In. 28.00
Can Opener, PET Irradiate Sunshine Vitamin D Milk, Wooden Handle, Metal Point, 4 In. . 56.00
Can Opener, Western Maryland Dairy, Balto., Metal, Triangle Point, Rounded Handle, 5 In. 22.00
Canister, Carmel Sea Salt, Perfumed, Langley & Michaels, Cardboard, 6 1/2 x 3 1/2 In. . . 71.00
Canister, Dr. Hess Instant Louse Killer, Girl, Sheep, 50 Cents, Cardboard, 2 1/2 Lb., 8 In. 413.00
Canister, Hi-Tone, Waiter, 5 Lb., 10 1/2 x 7 x 5 In. 750.00
Canister, Johnston's Hot Fudge, Aluminum, Electric, 8 1/2 In. 45.00
Canteen, Bardwell's Root Beer, Elk, Stoneware, Gray, Embossed, Bail Handle, 12 In. . . . 480.00
Chair, Garver's Furniture & Stoves, Hagerstown, Painted, Stenciled, Child's, 18 In. 385.00
Chair, Hides Franklin Mineral Water, Mahogany, Red Patent Leather Seat, 12 1/2 In. 83.00
Chair, Jewsbury & Brown Dispensing Chemists, Calvex Ointment, Wood, Arms 832.00
Chair, P. Nicklas's & Sons, Carpet Store, Painted, Stenciled, Wood, Maryland, 18 In. 165.00
Chalkboard, Abbott's Dairy Products, Tin, Cardboard Back, Painted, 16 x 24 In. 143.00
Change Receiver, Baby Ruth Peppermint Gum, Glass, Tin Lithograph, Countertop, 8 In. . . 247.00
Change Receiver, O'San, Desert Scene, Camel, Reverse On Glass, 7 1/2 In. 27.00
Charm, Ideal Dog Food & Good Luck, Verdi Gris, Metal, 1 In. 85.00
Churn, Dazey, Glass, Metal, 2 Qt. 220.00
Coal Scoop, Treasure Line, Stoves & Ranges, Tin, Canada, 9 x 4 In. 770.00
Coaster, Flower & Sons, As Supplied To HRH, Prince Of Wales, Round, 5 1/2 In. 486.00
Coaster, Rex's Steak House, Moorhead, Minn., Blue, Plastic, 1960s 8.00
Coaster, Sea View Awnings, Ruffled Edge, 3 In., 3 Piece 6.00
Coatrack, Garden Farm Milk, Hoppy's Bunkhouse Clothes Corral, Wood, 24 x 4 3/4 In. . . 110.00
Coatrack, Whistle, Thirsty?, Just Whistle, Wood, 8 x 35 1/2 In. 121.00
Comb, Sunbeam Bread, Reach For Sunbeam, It's Batter Whipped, Blue, Plastic, 5 In. 5.00
Cooler, Grapette Soda, Double Top, Open, Under Racks, 31 x 34 In. 625.00
Cooler, Grapette, White, Blue, Metal, Retro Products, 12 x 11 1/2 x 9 In. 66.00

Miscellaneous,
Pressing Board,
For Wool Hose,
Penobscot
Spinning Co.,
24 3/4 In.

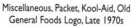

Miscellaneous, Packet, Kool-Aid, Old
General Foods Logo, Late 1970s

Miscellaneous, Razor Bank,
Langlois Lavender Shaving
Cream, 2 1/4 In.

Cooler, Orange Crush, 2-Door Top, Casters, Orange, White Letters, 38 x 40 x 23 In.	403.00
Cooler, Orange Crush, Help Yourself, Green, Model A, S&S Products, 31 x 31 x 21 3/4 In.	690.00
Cooler, Orange Crush, Iron Legs, Menu Board Ends, Drop Front Ice Door	1700.00
Cooler, Thirsty?, Just Whistle, Glascock, Tin Lithograph, Wood Frame, 32 x 32 In.	480.00
Counter, Parke-Davis, Dispenser, Gold Leaf, Reverse Paint On Glass, c.1880	2645.00
Crate Opener, Cremo, Cast Iron, Embossed Letters, 5 1/2 x 5 1/2 In.	33.00
Crock, J.T. Doores & Co. Distillers, Bowling Green, Ky., 10 1/4 In.	200.00
Crumb Scraper Set, Drake Mercantile Co., Kittens, Tin Lithograph, 6 1/2 x 9 1/4 In.	578.00
Cuff Links, Mack Trucks, Bulldog, Red, Green, Gold Enamel, Silvertone Metal, 2 Piece	29.00
Cup, Cone, Daly's Drive-In Restaurant, Get The Daly Habit, Paper, 6 1/2 In.	7.00
Cup, Ice Cream, Dairy Queen, Waxed Paper, 1949, 1 3/4 In.	8.00
Desk, Lap, Corticelli Spool Silk, Wood, Cat Decal, 20 x 36 In.	55.00 to 66.00
Desk Set, Bearcat Oil, Thermometer, Calendar, Metal Base, 1930s, 6 1/2 In.	169.00
Doorstop, Victorian Woman, Compliments Toledo Stove & Range Co., 9 1/2 x 4 1/2 In.	1430.00
Dust Pan, Compliments Drake Mercantile, Kittens, Tin Lithograph, 2 Piece, 6 x 9 In.	231.00
Egg Crate, Buy Dry Goods, Notions, Lippincott's, Wilmington, Del., Yellow, Stencils	742.00
Egg Timer, AT&T General Markets, Logo, 3 3/4 In.	22.00
Flagpole Holder, Eagle On Globe, Case Tractor, Cast Iron, c.1900, 24 x 52 In.	6325.00
Frame, Brooklyn Daily Eagle Almanac, Lithograph On Board, 1900, 18 x 13 1/4 In.	550.00
Game, Hercules Powder Co., Infallible Indicator, Heavy Stock, 1923, 5 3/8 x 3 1/2 In.	194.00
Game Counter & Pin Holder, Zonweiss Tooth Cream, Wood's Plasters, Tin, 1 1/2 In.	242.00
Gum Wrapper, Pulvers Yellow Kid Chewing Gum, 5 Sticks, 1 x 3 x 1/2 In.	1100.00
Handy Oiler, Flying A Household Oil, Red, White, Silver, 4 Oz.	40.00
Horseshoe, West Virginia Malleable Iron Co., Silvered Iron, Miniature	10.00
Ice Bucket, Beefeater Bust, Rubberoid, Glass Liner, 10 1/2 In.	51.00
Ice Chest, Orange Crush, Wood, Zinc Lined, Orange Paint	1045.00
Inkwell, Apollinaris, Queen Of Table Water, Round, England, 1 3/4 x 4 1/2 In.	45.00
Inkwell, Blackwood & Co., Blue Black Inks, Sloping Sides, Ceramic, England, 2 3/4 In.	67.00
Insert, Dunlop Tires, More Safe Miles, Tire, Tin, 17 In.	33.00
Juicer, Harter's Wild Cherry Bitters, Hand Operated, Metal, 1890-1910, 8 1/2 In.	336.00
Juicer, Sunkist, Electric, Milk Glass Reamer, Chrome, Handyhot Company, 8 3/4 x 5 In.	65.00
Key Chain, Trojan Powder, Makers Of High Explosives, 2 Chains, 1 1/4 x 3/4 In.	165.00
Kit, TWA Airlines, Welcome Aboard Passenger, 6 1/2 x 9 In.	42.00
Knife, Flamingo Casino & Hotel, Restaurant Ware, Engraved	15.00
Lap Board, Beech-Nut Gum, Cardboard Lithograph, 2-Sided, 26 x 18 In.	28.00
Laundry Scrubber, Crystal White Soap, Tin, Soap Box Image, 6 3/4 x 4 3/4 In.	152.00
Ledger Marker, Western Assurance, Tin Lithograph, Toronto, Canada, 12 1/2 x 3 1/8 In.	249.00
Light, Insure With Glens Falls Before The Fire, Burning Building, 17 1/2 x 24 In.	633.00
Map, Pankey Oil Of Brookfield Missouri, Photo Map Of Company's Service Area, 1932	10.00
Mask, Good Humor, Ice Cream Vendor, Die Cut, Stiff Paper, 1930s, 9 1/4 x 11 In.	24.00
Meat Hook, Gloeker's Country Store, 12 Hooks, Curled Ends, Steer On Top, 72 In.	590.00
Mold, Popsicle, Copper Exterior, 18 In.	963.00
Napkin Holder, Imperial Ice Cream, Tin, Die Cut Dish Of Ice Cream, 2-Sided	99.00

Notebook, Put A Little Sunshine In Your Home, Celluloid, 3 x 2 In. 88.00
Package, Sloan's Sure Colic Cure, Sealed, 2 Bottles, Unopened, Boston, c.1905, 3 x 4 In. . 385.00
Package, Starin's Renovating Powder, Unopened, Contents, Tax Stamp, c.1862, 3 3/4 x 5 In. 242.00
Packet, Kool-Aid, Old General Foods Logo, Late 1970s .... *Illus* 3.00
Patch, Burger Chef, Employee, Fabric, Burger Chef's Head, Slogan, 1950s, 4 x 4 1/2 In. . 12.00
Pin, Charms Candy, Enamel, 2 1/2 x 3/4 In. 65.00
Pin, Holsum Bread, I'm Not A Breakfast Battler, Tin, June 56, 2 In. 14.00
Plaque, Monda Cuba, Indian, Paper Board, No. 1, Ebonized Frame, 10 1/2 x 12 1/2 In. .. 264.00
Pot, Hercules Aluminum Ware, Brooklyn, N.Y., Aluminum, 2 Handles, 9 1/2 x 12 3/4 In. . 50.00
Pot Scraper, American Maid Bread, Tin Lithograph, Die Cut, 1 3/4 x 3 In. 413.00
Pot Scraper, Junket Tablets, Tin Lithograph, 2 5/8 x 3 1/4 In. 231.00
Pot Scraper, Penn Stoves, Clover, Tin Lithograph, 3 x 3 1/4 In. 154.00
Pot Scraper, Sharples Cream Separator, 3 x 2 1/4 In. 61.00
Pot Scraper, Sharples Tubular Cream Separator, Metal, Curved Edge 99.00
Pressing Board, For Wool Hose, Penobscot Spinning Co., 24 3/4 In. .... *Illus* 20.00
Price Board, Lewis Ice Cream, Tin, 19 x 13 1/2 In. 66.00
Program, Buffalo Bill's Wild West, Buffalo Head Shape, 1898, 9 1/2 x 7 3/4 In., 30 Pages 468.00
Puppet, Kagran Wonder Bread Premium, Howdy Doody, Cardboard, Jointed, c.1950 .... 104.00
Radio, Tropicana, Orange Shape, Hard Plastic, 2 Straw Shaped Antenna, 1970s, 3 1/4 In. . 12.00
Razor, Will & Finck Co., Cutlery Barber Supplies, Box, 1 x 6 1/2 In. 121.00
Razor Bank, Langlois Lavender Shaving Cream, 2 1/4 In. .... *Illus* 50.00
Relish, Bailey Co., Pressed Glass, Scalloped Edge, Rays, Thumbprints, 7 1/2 In. ..... *Illus* 18.00
Rolling Pin, Royal Household Flour, China, Wooden Handles, Canada, 19 1/4 x 3 In. 253.00
Rolling Pin, Wilson's Variety Store, Trade With Us & Save Dough, Stoneware, 7 In. . *Illus* 604.00
Ruler, Ful-O-Pep Hog Feeds, Wood, Trifold, 36 In. 11.00
Ruler, Stevenson Printing Co., Wood, 15 In. 15.00
Safe Plate, S.C. Herring, Fire Proof Safe, Bronze, Gilt, Factory, Dolphins, 1852, 4 x 6 In. 173.00
Scale, Merchants Metal Spanish Tiles, Roofing Plates, Shingles, Die Cut, Tin Lithograph . 440.00
Scale, Richmond Scale Co., Red, White, Marble Platform, 16 x 19 x 22 1/2 In. 83.00
Server, Red Cross Brand Condensed Milk, Ironstone, 4 In. .... *Illus* 45.00
Sharpening Stone, Goodyear's Rubber Gloves, Oval, 2 3/4 x 1 3/4 In. 125.00
Sheet Music, Warner's Island, St. Lawrence, Thousand Island River, 9 x 11 1/2 In., 8 Pages 33.00
Shoe Stretcher, Dr. Scholl's, Iron, Wood, 19 x 7 In. 88.00
Shoehorn, Fuller Brush, Red, Plastic, 4 1/2 In. 6.00
Shoehorn, Phillip Martin Cigars, Spanish Words, 4 3/8 x 1 1/2 In. 95.00
Shoehorn, Schoenecker, Princess Comfort Shoe, Tin Lithograph, 4 x 1 5/8 In. 178.00
Shoehorn, Shinola Shoe Polish, Brush, Shoe Polish, 1 3/4 x 6 3/4 In. 121.00
Shoehorn, Weslows, Santa Claus, Anderson, Ind., 2-Sided, 6 3/4 In. 40.00
Shoeshine Box, Cherry Blossom Boot Polish, Porcelain 3300.00
Shoeshine Stand, Whittemore Polishes, Victorian 935.00
Soap, Fuller Brush, 3 Little Pigs, Cardboard Houses, Yellow, Pink, Green 95.00
Spoon, Toddle House, Restaurant Ware, Engraved, Marked, Internation S. Co. X2 ...... 154.00
Stencil, Joseph Peyton Distilling Co., Bourbon Whiskey, Brass, 19 In. 55.00
Straws, Sunshine Soda, Box, 1947, 8 1/2 x 3 3/4 In. 29.00
Swizzle Stick, Benihana Breweriana, Red, Plastic, 1960s, 5 7/8 In. 9.00
Swizzle Stick, Heathman Hotel, Hula Dancer, Aloha Bar, Portland, Plastic, 5 3/4 In. 34.00
Tablespoon, Walgreen's Restaurant Ware, Engraved Handle 14.00
Toilet Paper Holder, A.P.W. Paper Co., The Equity, Cast Iron, 2 3/8 x 6 1/4 In. 220.00

Miscellaneous, Rolling Pin, Wilson's Variety Store,
Trade With Us & Save Dough, Stoneware, 7 In.

Miscellaneous, Relish, Bailey Co.,
Pressed Glass, Scalloped Edge,
Rays, Thumbprints, 7 1/2 In.

Miscellaneous, Server, Red
Cross Brand Condensed Milk,
Ironstone, 4 In.

Miscellaneous, Toothpick, The
Bailey Company, Pressed Glass

Miscellaneous, Towel Holder,
Hubbard Milling Co., Tin,
Wooden Ball, 7 1/2 In.

Token, Sambo's Restaurant, Good For 10 Cent Cup Of Coffee, Wood, Salem, Ore. 5.00
Toothbrush Holder, Listerine Prophylactic Toothbrush, Skeezix, Tin, Die Cut, 6 x 3 In. ... 77.00
Toothpick, The Bailey Company, Pressed Glass .... *Illus* 18.00
Towel Holder, Hubbard Milling Co., Tin, Wooden Ball, 7 1/2 In. .... *Illus* 25.00
Tube, Darkie Tooth Paste, Contents, Box, Hawley & Hazel, 4 7/8 x 1 3/8 x 7/8 In. 85.00
Tube, First National Dental Cream, First National Laboratories, Box, 4 7/8 x 1 1/2 x 1 In. 32.00
Tube, Rexall Dentutex Adhesive Jelly, Box, 6 1/2 In. 48.00
Umbrella, Sweet-Orr Overalls & Pants, Yellow, White, 5-Footed Base, 62 In. Diam. 201.00
Wallet, Chas. Odence Bacchante 10 Cent Cigar, Trifold, Leather, 3 In. Folded 45.00
Whiskbroom, Empire State Towel Co., Syracuse, N.Y., 3 3/4 x 2 In. 121.00
Window, Transom, Rexall, Thank You, 40 x 17 In. 198.00
Wrapper, Taylors Cough Syrup, Paper, 11 x 11 In. 22.00
Yardstick, Cannon Mills Textile Factory, Lufkin Rule Company, 36 In. 39.00

MONARCH The Monarch brand and its famous lion logo belonged to Reid, Murdoch & Co., which was established in Chicago in 1853. Monarch containers and advertisements featured William Donahey's Teenie Weenie cartoon characters from 1925 to 1929. In the early 1940s Canadian entrepreneur Nathan Cummings purchased Monarch and merged it with his other companies to form Consolidated Grocers Corp., which is now Sara Lee Corp. Monarch pails and tins featuring either the lion logo or Teenie Weenies are popular with collectors.

Box, Monarch Black Pepper, Cardboard, Tin Top & Bottom, 1 Lb., 6 x 3 3/4 In. 80.00
Box, Monarch Turmeric, Cardboard, 1 1/2 x 2 3/8 x 3 1/4 In. 35.00
Box, Monarch Turmeric, Cardboard, Tin Top & Bottom, Paper Label, 2 Oz. 8.00
Can, Monarch Coffee, Lithograph, Key Wind, Contents, Unopened, 1 Lb., 5 x 3 1/2 In. ... 121.00
Canister, Monarch Finer Foods, Glass, Screw-On Lid 50.00
Clock, Monarch Fine Foods, Pam, Telechron, 1940s 380.00
Jar, Monarch Extracted Honey, Embossed, Lid, 3 3/4 x 2 3/4 In. 95.00
Pail, Monarch Teenie Weenie Peanut Butter, Tin, 1920s, 1 Lb., 3 3/4 x 3 3/8 In. ...253.00 to 330.00
Pail, Monarch Teenie Weenie Peanut Butter, Tin, 1920s, 2 Lb., 4 3/4 x 4 1/4 In. 303.00
Table, Display, Monarch Foods, Metal, Letters On 4 Sides, c.1920, 31 x 25 In. 661.00
Tin, Cocoa, Free Sample, Square, 3 x 1 3/4 In. 160.00
Tin, Cocoa, Stamped Tin, Lithograph, Hinged Lid, 1920s, 6 x 3 1/8 x 3 1/8 In. 36.00
Tin, Coffee, Fine Or Drip Grind, Key Wind, Contents, Unopened, 1 Lb., 3 1/2 x 5 In. 149.00
Tin, Coffee, Lion, Key Wind, 1 Lb. 35.00
Tin, Coffee, Lion, Reid Murdoch Chicago, 1 Lb. 35.00
Tin, Coffee, Regular Grind, Unopened, Key Wind, Lithograph, 1 Lb., 3 1/2 x 5 In. 66.00
Tin, Monarch Allspice, 1 1/2 Oz. 12.00
Tin, Peanut Butter, Lion, Lithograph, 1 Lb., 3 3/4 x 3 1/2 In. 110.00
Tin, Popcorn, Reed, Murdoch & Co., Chicago, Ill., 3 3/4 x 3 3/8 In. 395.00
Tin, Saffron, Sample, 1 5/8 x 1 3/4 x 1 1/4 In. 85.00

MORTON SALT Joy Morton reorganized a salt company under the name Morton Salt Company in 1910. A free-running salt in a round package with a patented spout was one of its first products. In 1911 the famous Umbrella Girl with the pouring salt box and the slogan, "When It Rains It Pours," were developed for the company's first advertising campaign. The round blue box with the girl was first sold in 1914. The Umbrella Girl logo was updated with new clothes for the girl in 1921, 1933, 1941, 1956, and 1968. The company changed its name in advertisements and on packages from "Morton's Salt" to "Morton Salt" in 1948. A set of four reproduction packages showing the four oldest versions of the Morton girl and a set of four coffee mugs with the same pictures were made in the 1970s. In 1969 Morton International, Inc., and the Norwich Pharmacal Company combined to become Morton-Norwich Products, Inc. Since 2002 Morton has been a division of the Philadelphia-based Rohm and Haas Company.

Advertisement, More People Use Morton's, Paper, Life Magazine, Feb. 1954, 14 x 10 In.	5.00
Advertisement, Oranges, When It Rains It Pours, Life Magazine, 1954, 14 x 10 In.	15.00
Blotter, Cost A Family About 2 Cents A Week, Blue Paper	7.00
Blotter, When It Rains It Pours, Vegetables Sliding Down Salt Mound	9.00
Display, Never Cakes Or Hardens, It Pours, Girl On Back, Cardboard, 20 x 13 In.	236.00
Hot Pad, Girl, When It Rains It Pours, Round, 5 3/4 In.	8.00
Mug, Girl With Umbrella, Box, 3 3/4 x 2 3/4 In., 4 Piece	25.00
Notepad, Sheets Have 3 Different Slogans, 5 1/2 x 3 1/4 In.	15.00
Pencil Clip, It Pours, c.1925, 1 1/2 x 3/4 In.	16.00
Sugar & Creamer, Blue Band, Girl With Umbrella, When It Rains It Pours, 4 1/2 In.	25.00
Thermometer, Free Running, When It Rains It Pours, Umbrella Girl, Tin, 16 x 6 In.	176.00
Toy, Gun, Rubber Band, Paper, Lone Ranger, Frame, c.1938, 4 3/4 x 8 1/2 In.	55.00

MOVIE Movie memorabilia include posters, lobby cards, films, toys, press kits, stills, and miscellaneous items like Joan Crawford's false eyelashes. Major collector interest is in the "great" films, Disney-related materials, or science fiction movies. The memorabilia from the 1930s to 1950, when the star system still ruled Hollywood, are most expensive. There was some speculation in movie materials in the 1970s, and prices rose quickly only to fall in the 1980s. Today the market has returned to the true collector, and the investor has become a less-interested participant.

Lobby Card, Bluebeard, Richard Burton Kissing Raquel Welch In Coffin, 1972, 10 x 8 In.	11.00
Lobby Card, Gunfight At Comanche Creek, Audie Murphy, 1963, 11 x 14 In.	28.00
Lobby Card, King Of The Underworld, Humphrey Bogart, 1939, 11 x 13 In.	329.00
Lobby Card, Leather Burners, Hopalong Cassidy, No. 43, 1943, 11 x 14 In.	42.00
Lobby Card, Man Who Would Be King, Connery, Caine, Landau, Allied Artists, 1975	11.00
Lobby Card, Ten Nights In A Barroom, W. Farnum, Tom Santchi, Early 1930s, 14 x 22 In.	88.00
Lobby Card, Train Robbers, John Wayne, Ann Margret, Rod Taylor, 1973, 11 x 14 In.	121.00
Lobby Card, True Grit, John Wayne, Eye Patch, 1969, 11 x 14 In.	19.00
Lobby Card, Twilight On Rio Grande, Gene Autry, No. 7, 11 x 14 In.	25.00
Poster, Babe Ruth Story, Bendix, Trevor, Bickford, 1948, 81 x 81 In.	3450.00
Poster, Cahill United States Marshall, John Wayne, 36 x 14 In.	41.00
Poster, Dangerous Years & Invisible Wall, Marilyn Monroe, 1948, 28 x 22 In.	2875.00
Poster, Gene Autry & Mounties, 41 x 27 In.	111.00
Poster, Going Spanish, Bob Hope, Paper Lithograph, 41 x 28 In.	34.00
Poster, Let's Fall In Love, Ann Sothern, Columbia Pictures, 1933, 41 x 61 In.	44.00
Poster, Manhattan Merry-Go-Round, Joe DiMaggio, Gene Autry, 1937, 41 x 27 In.	690.00
Poster, Mummy's Boys, RKO Radio Pictures, 1936, 39 x 78 In.	88.00
Poster, Old Monterey, Gene Autry, 27 x 41 In.	163.00
Poster, Prince & The Showgirl, Marilyn Monroe, Laurence Olivier, 1957, 47 x 33 In.	690.00
Poster, Safe At Home, Mickey Mantle, Roger Maris, 1962, 81 x 41 In.	920.00
Poster, She Loves Me Not, Bing Crosby, Ames, Iowa, 22 x 28 In.	77.00
Poster, Story Of Seabiscuit, Shirley Temple, Warner Bros., 1949, 36 x 14 In.	120.00
Poster, Texas Trail, Hopalong Cassidy, Paper Lithograph, 41 x 27 In.	147.00
Poster, Triple Threat, Football Stars, Columbia Pictures, 1948, 41 x 27 In.	518.00
Poster, War Of Wildcats, John Wayne, Martha Scott, 41 x 27 In.	46.00
Program, Gone With The Wind, 1939	95.00

Moxie, Sign, Drink Moxie,
Flange, Tin Lithograph, 18 In.

MOXIE Dr. Augustin Thompson established a medical practice in Lowell, Massachusetts, in 1867 and began developing cures and remedies. In 1885 he began selling Moxie Nerve Food as a healthy beverage. Collectible trays, bottles, tin signs, and other items advertised the drink. The most famous sign shows an automobile driven by a man on horseback. A few Moxie items, including glasses, have been reproduced. Many items feature the Moxie Boy, said to be a likeness of Frank Archer. Archer started as a clerk at the Moxie Nerve Food Company in 1896, was soon in charge of the company's sales campaigns, and eventually became the company's vice president. The company continued in business under several changes of management. Moxie is now a brand of the Monarch Beverage Company. There is an annual Moxie Festival in Lisbon, Maine.

Case, 12 Unused Bottles, Wood, Dovetailed, 11 x 15 x 11 1/2 In.	176.00
Dispenser, Drink Moxie, Milk Glass, Clear Glass, Red Label, 1940s, 9 1/2 In.	102.00 to 158.00
Fan, 1925, 8 x 7 In.	95.00
Fan, Blond Woman Looks In Mirror, Man On Reverse, 1925	60.00
Fan, Muriel Ostriche, 9 x 8 1/4 In.	54.00
Fan, Woman & Compact, Man Pointing On Reverse, Cardboard, 2-Sided, 8 x 7 In.	17.00
Globe, Drink Moxie, Light-Up, Hanging, 10 In.	550.00
Match Holder, Nerve Food, Die Cut, Tin Lithograph, 7 1/8 x 2 5/8 In.	660.00
Mug, Embossed Moxie, Glass, Hourglass Shape, Handle, 4 Oz., 5 In.	99.00
Photograph, Nerve Food, Horse Drawn Wagon, Frame, 17 x 21 In.	935.00
Sign, Drink Made Name Famous, Horse In Car, Tin, Self-Framed, 12 1/2 x 36 In.	2200.00
Sign, Drink Made Name Famous, Tin Lithograph, Embossed, 42 x 15 In.	1074.00
Sign, Drink Moxie, Distinctively Different, Tin Lithograph, Embossed, 18 1/2 x 27 1/4 In.	231.00
Sign, Drink Moxie, Flange, Tin Lithograph, 18 In. .... *Illus*	357.00
Sign, Drink Moxie, Old Moxie, New Moxie, Tin, Embossed, 27 x 19 In.	143.00
Sign, Drink Moxie, Tin Lithograph, Embossed, Red Ground, 6 1/4 x 19 In.	242.00
Sign, Frank Archer Points, Learn To Drink Moxie, Tin, Die Cut, 5 5/8 x 2 7/8 In.	111.00
Sign, Frank Archer, Cardboard, Die Cut, Easel Back, 10 3/8 x 8 In.	185.00
Sign, Reverse Glass, Hanger, Original Chain, 5 x 7 In.	990.00
Sign, Yes!, We Sell Moxie, Very Healthful, Convex, Tin, 19 1/2 x 27 In.	880.00
Stereo Viewer, A Trip Through Moxie Land, Bakelite, Tru-Vue, Rock Island, Illinois	36.00
Thermometer, Drink Moxie, Frank Archer, Tin, Die Cut, Wood Crate, 38 x 12 In.	1898.00
Thermometer, Frank Archer, Girl With Bottle, Glass, 9 1/2 x 12 In.	1430.00
Tip Tray, Blond Woman, Moxie Glass, Tin Lithograph, Round, 6 In. .... *Illus*	303.00

Moxie, Tip Tray, Blond
Woman, Moxie Glass, Tin
Lithograph, Round, 6 In.

Moxie, Tip Tray, Woman,
Glass Of Moxie, Tin
Lithograph, 6 In.

Moxie, Toy, Moxiemobile,
Tin, Die Cut, Blue Variation,
6 1/2 x 9 x 2 3/8 In.

Moxie, Toy, Top, Moxiemobile,
Frank Archer, Tin Lithograph, Wood
Knob, 2 1/2 In.

Mug, Trader Vic's, Tiki
Man, 6 1/4 In.

Tip Tray, I Just Love Moxie, Don't You, Woman, Leaf Border, Tin, Round, 6 In. . . .330.00 to 550.00	
Tip Tray, Moxie, 5 Cents, Delicious, Feeds The Nerves, Tin Lithograph, Round, 6 In.	1760.00
Tip Tray, Woman, Glass Of Moxie, Tin Lithograph, 6 In. . . . . *Illus*	55.00
Toy, Moxiemobile, Tin, Die Cut, Blue Variation, 6 1/2 x 9 x 2 3/8 In. . . . . *Illus*	2860.00
Toy, Top, Man On Horse, Car, Spins, Celluloid, 1915, 1 1/2 In. Diam.	182.00
Toy, Top, Moxiemobile, Frank Archer, Tin Lithograph, Wood Knob, 2 1/2 In. . . . . . . *Illus*	176.00
Tumbler, Embossed Moxie, Flared Rim, Fluted Bottom, 6 Oz., 4 In. . . . . .35.00 to 89.00	
Tumbler, Etched, Drink Moxie, Fill Line, 6 Oz., 4 x 2 1/2 In.	99.00
Tumbler, Red Band, Drink Moxie In 3 Places, Flared Rim, 4 1/4 In.	79.00

MUG Mugs of all types are collected, often to be used. Giveaway mugs with advertising have been popular since the 1920s. Some were meant for children's drinks like Ovaltine, some for beer, and many recent ones for coffee.

Araban H Chocolate, Restaurant Ware, Iroquois China, 1940s-1960s, 3 1/2 In.	36.00
Carnation Hot Cocoa Mix, Ceramic, 3 3/4 In.	7.50
Dick Bros. Q.B. Co., Painted Under Glaze, Quincy, Ill., 6 In.	261.00
Entex, Prescription Drug	10.50
Esso, Tiger Eating Ice Cream, 3 1/2 In.	8.00
Keebler, Elf Shape, Plastic, Raised Features, Shipping Box, 1972, 3 In.	8.00
Lion Gas & Oil, Bill Armstrong Oil Co., Applied Label, 4 In.	25.00
Raid, Raid's Gone, Pass It On, 1980s, 3 1/4 x 4 In.	10.00
Rochester Root Beer, Ceramic, 9 1/2 x 6 In.	935.00
Ted's, Delicious Creamy Root Beer, Picture Of Ted Williams, Boston	58.00
Trader Vic's, Tiki Man, 6 1/4 In. . . . . *Illus*	20.00

NABISCO National Biscuit Company was founded in 1898. A company founder, Adolphus W. Green, was one of the first to package crackers and sell them under a brand name. A shaped red seal with "Inner" or "NBC Uneeda" printed on it was used starting in 1900. The logo was redesigned in 1918, 1923, 1935, 1941, and again for the current triangular-shaped seal. Through the years, the National Biscuit Company introduced or acquired such brands as Fig Newtons (1891), Shredded Wheat (1893; acquired 1928), Cream of Wheat (1895, listed in its own category in this book), Uneeda Biscuit (1898, with the boy in the yellow slicker trademark), Zu Zu Ginger Snaps (1900), Barnum's Animal Crackers (1902, shaped crackers in a box cage), Oysterettes (1900), Oreos (1912), Lorna Doones (1912), Ritz Crackers (1934), Premium Crackers, Wheatsworth Crackers, and Triscuits. Old cans and boxes for some of these brands have been reproduced. The company also acquired or started such brands as Chase & Sanborn's Coffee, Cracker Jack, Fleischmann's Yeast, Life Savers, Planters Peanuts (all listed in their own categories in this book), Baby Ruth (1920), Butterfingers (1928), Sun Maid Raisins, Campfire Marshmallows, Milk-Bone

FROM BOXES AND BINS TO SIGNS AND TINS

If it's a package or an advertisement for a product, there's a collector who wants to own it. Signs used either inside or outside a store, and display bins, cabinets, and racks that held packages on a countertop or on the floor are the largest and showiest of advertising collectibles. We have seen billboard signs used as wallpaper in a rec room and store cabinets converted into household medicine cabinets. Clocks, especially those with neon lights, are often used to decorate home bars. Cans of all kinds are emptied of their contents (full cans can eventually burst) and are saved by collectors who either build rows of custom shelves to hold single-size cans or admire the old graphics on the cans and like to display them as nostalgic decorations. Other collectors like banks or calendars or pens or toys of all types, and the advertising examples are one part of a larger collection. There are advertising antiques and collectibles of all types, all ages, and all prices that entice collectors—and others who like to remember the "good old days."

The American Lady Coffee tin is a desirable collectible for a couple of reasons: the picture of an attractive woman with a 1930s hairstyle and the appealing slogan, "Puts the Smile in 'Good Morning.'" The 1-pound tin, 6 by 4 1/4 inches, auctioned for $1,815.

This 1961 Coca-Cola enameled sign is die cut and painted to look like a six-pack of Coke. It is large, 3 feet high, and expensive, $1,100.

Any sign, bottle, box, tray, mug, or toy that says Coca-Cola is wanted by collectors. Marx made this plastic and cardboard truck in the 1950s. It sold with its original box for $413.

A printed piece of tin was bent over a cardboard backing to make this 1920s sign for Lipton's Instant Cocoa. Although it's a small sign, just 13 by 9 inches, it's worth $578—perhaps because of the picture of the attractive woman drinking cocoa.

The style of the cartoon cops, Pepsi and Pete, help date this Pepsi-Cola bag-rack. The two-sided tin and metal rack was made in the 1940s. It is 19 by 24 by 6 inches and worth $1,870.

Only an actress as famous as Evelyn Nesbitt could look less than ridiculous in a ruffled pink hat. The Seattle Brewing & Malting Company advertised its Rainier Beer on this 13-inch metal tray made by Bachrach Lithography of San Francisco. The tray sold for $1,280.

A Marigold Coach Lines sign would, of course, be yellow. The die-cut porcelain sign from the 1920s, 10 by 42 inches, sold for $5,170.

This Delco Freedom V Battery flasher-badge shows a car battery and brand name from one angle and a camel wearing sunglasses and the phrase "Never Needs a Drink" from another. The 2 1/2-inch pin from the 1960s auctioned for $23.

This Moxie thermometer pictures the Moxie Boy and Girl. The Moxie Boy is said to resemble Frank Archer, the brains behind Moxie's early advertising campaigns. The 12-by-9 1/2-inch thermometer, made about 1910, sold for $1,430.

Uncle Sam is cranking in jewelry and gold and cranking out dollar bills on this motor-operated pawnshop sign. Wooden gears and leather pulleys make this 29-by-19-inch sign work. It was made about 1915 and sold last year for $1,210.

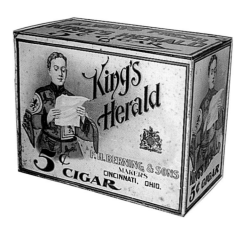

A store bin like this King's Herald cigar bin held packages of cigars. The lithographed tin humidor, 15 by 20 by 11 inches, was used about 1910. It is worth $770.

Diamond Dyes cabinets are well known and popular with collectors. This Diamond Dyes sign, "A Busy Day in Dollville," drawn by Besse Pease Gutmann, is less common than the cabinets. It sold at auction for $798. Wells & Richardson made the 11 1/2-by-17-inch sign in 1911.

These embossed copper ice cream cones were used as displays that hung in an ice cream parlor. The two cones, one 5 inches and the other 4 inches high, sold for $176.

Burt's seed packets from the early 1900s are often seen at shows and sales. A warehouse full of the packets was discovered a number of years ago at the site of a building owned by the William D. Burt Seed Co. in upstate New York. This assortment of color lithographed seed packets sold for $150.

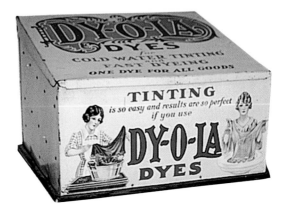

Clothing stains were hard to remove with the products available early in the twentieth century, so many dresses were dyed a darker color to cover stains. Small packages of Dy-O-La Dyes were sold from a lithographed tin and oak cabinet like this about 1910. It is 9 inches high and 14 inches wide and sold for $248.

Sets of glasses were popular promotion pieces. Sunoco gasoline distributed these American Wildlife glasses as a premium. The set of four includes an eagle, buffalo, moose, and humpback whale. This set came with a brochure about "clean-burning Ultra 94 high octane gasoline." All four 3 1/2-inch-high glasses sold as a set for only $15.

The picture of a boy pushing a huge bottle of orange Whistle soda added to the value of this lithographed tin sign. It brought $303 at auction.

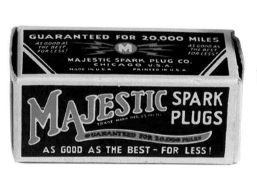

There are many collectors of old spark plugs, but few collectors own old spark plugs in mint condition in the original box. This mint set of Majestic Spark Plugs also comes with an original wartime paper insert that says: "To conserve brass during the emergency, the terminal connection has been left off these plugs. Please use terminal connections from old plugs." The insert dates the set to the years of World War II. Price, $25.

Cast-iron toys are always good advertising collectibles, but prices are high because toy collectors want them, too. This rare cast-iron Dutch Girl Cleanser pull toy was made by Hubley. It sold for more than most toys, $11,550.

The little Dutch Girl was such a popular trademark that the public demanded it be kept after the product's advertising agency tried to drop it. This tin Old Dutch Cleanser sign was made by the Niagara Litho. Company. The $358 sign measures 9 by 18 inches.

Cracker Jack toys are popular collectibles. Because they're so small, they're often overlooked in drawers full of odds and ends. The toys were included in every box of Cracker Jack starting in 1912. They were packaged in a separate section of the box at first, then wrapped in paper beginning in 1948. Collectors consider the toys of the 1930s the best. This group of lithographed tin prizes, including a Streamliner and passenger cars (1940s), delivery truck (1930s), ambulance (1930s), and no parking sign (1930s), auctioned for $220.

Names for cigar brands were often "borrowed" from other products, because then the cigar's name would be familiar. "Yellow Cab" cigars were offered for sale in this wooden box with a paper label. The box still holds five of the original cigars with cigar bands intact. It sold for only $358.

What barbershop would be complete without a Gem Damaskeene Razor pendulum clock? The 1910 wooden clock, 28 by 23 inches, is so rare it sold for $4,070.

This ashtray shaped like an art nouveau lady wearing a full skirt is embossed "Compliments of Kenton Hardware Co." on the left and "Iron Toys" on the right. Always check the bottom of ashtrays like this one. Similar ashtrays by other companies show more of the "lady" on the bottom—sometimes even her bare backside. This fully dressed example sold for $66.

Gun collectors and advertising collectors want this Golden Pheasant Gun Powder tin. The 6-by-4-by-1/2-inch tin was made by A.F. & Co. in the 1880s. It is worth $1,540.

A calendar is a good ad—it hangs in plain sight the entire year. The Harrisburg Taxicab and Baggage Company gave this calendar to customers in 1945. Notice the four-digit phone number, more proof that the calendar is old. The 19-by-14-inch calendar sold for $66.

Every kitchen once had a storage place for wooden matches to light the stove. This Ceresota Flour match holder pictures the company's trademark boy in red pants. The 5-inch-high die-cut embossed tin holder auctioned for $303.

Paperweights of all kinds have been popular advertising giveaways. This Tiger Bronze Cast Bearings paperweight is shaped like a machinery part and topped with a tiger. It is an ad for the American Brake Shoe Company. The 5-inch-long, gold-painted, cast-iron weight sold for $66.

Most people aren't familiar with the name for a pen and pencil set like this one. The pen and pencil are called "floaters," because the body of each one includes an object moving inside a tube of liquid. Bell Telephone once gave these sets to employees with perfect attendance. This 5-inch-long 1950s set is engraved with an employee's name. It cost $72.

National Maxipress gave out paperweights that were working models of a side pulley. The painted, die-cast model is 5 inches high and sold for $55.

This blue and red Whistle soda electric clock has a domed glass cover over a painted tin face. The clock, 15 inches in diameter, sold at auction for only $55.

This A&W Root Beer clock, known as a "double bubble" because the face is covered with two layers of glass, looks like a gas pump globe. The lighted electric clock sold for $1,210.

Collectors like clever Soaky bottles. This red and yellow plastic bottle represents the cartoon character Bullwinkle. It has the original cardboard neck tag and base and still contains the original Colgate bubble bath. Soakies date back only to the 1960s, so they're not very old, but this one sold for $103.

Little Orphan Annie is pictured on many items advertising Ovaltine because Ovaltine was a sponsor of her radio program. This shake-up mug for mixing milk and Ovaltine powder is probably the Annie-Ovaltine item most easily found. The green Beetleware cup with an orange lid has a 1933 decal, but the colors are more typical of the 1940s. Because the colors are unusual, possibly test colors, the cup is worth $827.

Dog Biscuits (1908; acquired 1931), Royal Baking Powder (1863), Royal Gelatin (1925), Blue Bonnet Margarine (1942), Droste's Chocolate, and hundreds more. The company merged with Standard Brands to become Nabisco Brands in 1981. Nabisco brands became part of Reynolds Industries Inc. in 1985. Philip Morris Companies (Altria Group since 2003) acquired Nabisco in 2000 and integrated the Nabisco brands into Kraft Foods.

Award, Youngster In Slicker, Plaster, Kroger Sav-On, 1982, 9 1/2 In. . . . . .60.00 to 100.00
Blotter, Shredded Wheat Biscuit, For Your Health & Strength, Easy To Digest 9.00
Box, Shredded Wheat, Factory, Niagara Falls, Bowl, Cardboard, 1920s, 5 3/4 x 7 1/2 In. . . 106.00
Box, Shredded Whole Wheat, Sample, Cardboard, Niagara Falls, N.Y., 4 x 5 In. 85.00
Cookie Jar, Cover, Barnum's Animals, Clown Head Finial, Pottery, c.1972 . . . . 300.00
Cookie Jar, Oreo Truck, China, Box, 6 1/4 In. 55.00
Cookie Jar, Stack Of Oreos, Pottery, 11 x 7 1/2 In. 23.00
Display, National Biscuit Company, Cast Iron Base, 2 Wood Poles, 57 In. 115.00
Display Rack, National Biscuit Co., 6 Boxes, Marquee, 39 In. 165.00
Display Rack, National Biscuit Co., Oak, 58 x 47 x 20 In. 1300.00
Letter Opener, National Biscuit Special Products, Gold Tone, Metal, 6 3/4 In. 14.00
Letter Opener, Uneeda Biscuits, Slicker Boy, Tin, Die Cut, 8 x 1 5/8 In. . . . . .66.00 to 96.00
Poster, Shredded Wheat Biscuit, An All Day Food For Everybody, c.1910, 16 x 12 In. . . . 1485.00
Premium, Winnie The Pooh Breakfast Buddies Set, Rice Honeys, 1965, 2 In., 7 Piece . . . 87.00
Puzzle, Shredded Wheat, Sgt, Biff O' Hara, Round, Metal, 3 Balls 15.00
Sign, National Biscuit, Slicker Boy, Lithograph, 1902, 9 1/2 x 6 In. 28.00
Sign, No Smoking, Use Of Tobacco In Any Form Forbidden, Porcelain, 8 x 15 In. 330.00
Sign, Uneeda Biscuit, 7 Boys In Yellow Slickers, 11 x 20 1/2 In. 495.00
Sign, Uneeda Biscuit, Give The Children, National Biscuit Co., Trolley Card, 11 x 21 In. . . 83.00
Tin, Barnum's Animals, Animal Crackers, 1914 Replica, 1979 . . . . .5.00 to 14.00
Tin, Famous Chocolate Wafers, Screw-On Lid, 10 Oz., 8 1/2 In. 15.00
Tin, Premium Saltine Crackers, 1969, 9 1/2 In. . . . . .18.00 to 20.00
Tin, Saltina Biscuit, Uneeda Bakers, National Biscuit Company, Cover, 7 x 6 In. 28.00
Tin, Uneeda Crackers, Victorian Flower Spray On Lid, 8 x 11 1/4 In. 14.00
Toy, Truck, Sit-N-Ride, Yellow Ground, Pressed Steel, Roberts, 1940s, 22 In. 154.00

NIPPER, see Victor

OATMEAL   For over a hundred years, national food distributors and local grocers have sold oatmeal, usually in cylindrical boxes. The boxes' colorful images of flowers, birds, animals, children, and women are popular with collectors. See also Quaker Oats.

Box, Betty Ann Rolled Oats, Quick Cooking, Girl, Rope, Cushing Co., 3 Lb., 9 5/8 x 5 In. 121.00
Box, Blue Ribbon Brand Rolled Oats, Cardboard, Oakford & Fahnestock, 7 3/8 x 4 1/4 In. 130.00
Box, Friends' Rolled Oats, Woman, Bonnet, Wood, Hinged Lid, 27 x 20 x 12 In. . . . . *Illus* 201.00
Box, Harvest Queen Rolled Oats, Quick Cooking, Contents, Unopened, 7 3/8 x 4 1/4 In. . . 198.00
Box, Hawkeye Oats, Muscatine Oatmeal Co., Wood, Rope Handles, 27 x 20 In. 115.00
Box, Hermitage Oat, Cardboard Lithograph, Robert Orr, 9 1/2 x 5 1/2 In. 223.00
Box, High Line Oats, Train, High Line Bridge, Cardboard Lithograph, 3 1b., 9 x 5 3/8 In. . . 358.00
Box, Home, Brand Oats, Cylindrical, 3 Lb. 7 Oz. 83.00

Oatmeal, Box, Friends' Rolled Oats,
Woman, Bonnet, Wood, Hinged Lid,
27 x 20 x 12 In.

Oatmeal, Box, Lee
Quick Cooking Rolled
Oats, 9 3/4 In.

Ovaltine, Mug,
Orphan Annie
Beetleware, Ivory,
Color Decal, 1933, 3 In.

Ovaltine, Mug, Shake-Up,
Leapin' Lizards,
Beetleware, White, Orange
Lid, 1931, 3 3/4 In.

Box, Jewett's Indian Girl Rolled Oats, Cardboard Lithograph, 3 Lb., 9 5/8 x 5 3/8 In. 1265.00
Box, Lakeland Rolled Oats, Red Owl, Cardboard, Minneapolis, 9 5/8 x 5 1/2 In. 135.00
Box, Lee Quick Cooking Rolled Oats, 9 3/4 In. .... *Illus* 25.00
Box, Lush'us Rolled Oats, Cardboard, 3 Lb., 9 1/2 x 5 3/8 In. 154.00
Box, Tiger Rolled White Oats, Snarling Tiger, Cardboard, Cylindrical, c.1930, 10 x 5 In. . 50.00
Box, University Oats, Cylindrical, 3 Lb. 7 Oz. 165.00
Box, Weideman Oat Flakes, Cardboard, 14 Oz., 6 1/4 x 4 1/4 In. 132.00
Tin, Pabena Precooked Oatmeal, Partial Contents, Mead Johnson, Ind., 2 1/2 x 2 In. 55.00

OVALTINE   In the late 1800s, Swiss chemist Georg Wander developed
a process to harvest malt extract, which he planned to fortify with vit-
amins and minerals and use to alleviate malnutrition. In 1904 his son,
Albert, added sugar, whey, and beet extract to the syrup, creating
Ovomaltine. The beverage became a hit on Switzerland's ski slopes. In
1909 the beverage was exported as Ovaltine. Cocoa was added a few
years later. Ovaltine sponsored radio favorites *Little Orphan Annie* and
Captain Midnight, and Ovaltine premiums from those shows are popular with collectors. Associated British Foods purchased Ovaltine from
Novartis in 2002.

Charm, 1950s, 1/2 In. 6.00
Mug, Captain Midnight, Heart Of Hearty Breakfast, Plastic, Red, U.S.A., 3 In. ......38.00 to 95.00
Mug, Howdy Doody, Plastic, 4 In. ....25.00 to 28.00
Mug, Little Orphan Annie Holding Mug, Sandy, Pottery, Wander Co., c.1932, 3 In. . .65.00 to 115.00
Mug, Orphan Annie Beetleware, Ivory, Color Decal, 1933, 3 In. .... *Illus* 38.00
Mug, Shake-Up, Leapin' Lizards, Beetleware, White, Orange Lid, 1931, 3 3/4 In. . . . *Illus* 50.00
Mug, Shake-Up, Little Orphan Annie & Sandy, Lid, Beetleware, Late 1930s, 5 In. . .52.00 to 110.00
Mug, Uncle Wiggily, Grandpa Goosey Gander, Sebring, c.1924, 3 x 2 3/4 In. .....145.00 to 165.00
Sheet Music, Little Orphan Annie, Wander Company, 1931 .... 24.00
Sign, Black Boy With Chocolate Biscuits, Lithograph, 1950s, 22 In. 182.00
Tumbler, Captain Midnight, Plastic, Red, Wander Co., 3 3/4 x 2 3/4 In. 20.00

OYSTER   Saddle-Rock, Blue Point, Wellfleets, Absecan Salts, and
Perth Amboys are just a few of the over four hundred edible varieties
that oyster connoisseurs could name during the oyster-crazed 1800s.
Oysters were first packed in New York in 1819; packing them in tins
became big business in Maryland in the 1840s. By the turn of the century, oyster beds along the coasts of New England, New York, and the
Chesapeake were being depleted. Today, oyster cans, which vary in
size from 8 ounces to 5 gallons and usually have pry-top lids, are the
most popular oyster collectibles. Other memorabilia include signs,
trade cards, shipping crates, and even sheet music.

Can, Adams Chincoteague & Metompkin Bay Salt Water Oysters, Accomac, Va., Gal. ... 95.00
Can, Bevans Oyster Co., Delicious Oysters, Sailboat, Gal., 7 1/2 x 6 1/2 In. 11.00
Can, H & B Brand Oysters, Sea Foods, Salt Water Oysters, Pt., 3 3/4 x 3 1/4 In. 126.00
Can, Maryland House Oysters 22.00
Can, McCready Brand Chincoteague Oysters, Chincoteague, Va., 7 3/8 x 6 5/8 In. 250.00
Can, McNaney's Superior Raw Oysters, Baltimore, Md. 85.00

Can, Metompkin Oysters 66.00
Can, Miles' Famous Oysters, Norfolk, Va., Gal., 7 1/4 x 6 3/4 In. 135.00
Can, Old Dominion Oysters 198.00
Can, Original Pac, Chesapeake Bay's Famous Oyster Beds, Qt. 456.00
Can, Quality Oysters, Freshly Shucked, Standard Stewing Size, See-Through Lid, 2 3/4 In. 20.00
Can, Ray's Seafood Fresh Oysters, See-Through Top, 2 3/4 x 3 1/2 In. 20.00
Can, Sailor Boy Oysters, Gal.. 75.00
Can, Sailor Girl Oysters 22.00
Can, Schneier's Seafoods, Fresh Oysters, Pry Lid, Akron, Ohio, 1 Pt., 3 3/4 x 3 3/8 In. 60.00
Can, Sea Hawk Oysters 275.00
Can, Stork Oysters 88.00
Can, T.A. Treakle & Son, Fresh Oyster, Palmer, Virginia, Pt., 3 3/4 x 3 1/2 In........... 32.00
Can, Woodfield's Oyster, Tin Lithograph, Galesville, Md., Gal., 7 1/2 In. ....34.00 to 59.00
Pail, Heyser's Oyster, Red, Black, Gold, Unopened, Baltimore, Md., 7 3/8 x 6 5/8 In. 70.00
Shipper, Oysters Sealshipticase, Metal Rack, Porcelain Sign, 35 In................... 413.00

PABST Philip Best and his sons started a brewery they named for
themselves in Milwaukee, Wisconsin, in 1844. By 1866, however,
Frederick Pabst and Emil Schandein, the husbands of Philip Best's
daughters, were managing the company. The brewery's name was
changed to Pabst in 1889, but the trademark of a B for "Best" in a circle has remained. About 1882 the company tied pieces of blue ribbon
around the necks of Best "Select" beer bottles. The words "Blue Ribbon" were used on the label in 1895. Slogans have included "Thirty-
three fine brews blended into one great beer" (1940), "Pabst Blue
Ribbon Time" (1956), "Pabst Makes It Perfect" (1957), "The Premium
Beer at a Popular Price" (1960s), "Give that man a Blue Ribbon"
(c.1979), and "PBR me ASAP!" (c.1991 to present). The company,
based in San Antonio, Texas, since 1996, owns many brands, including Blatz, Falstaff, Carling Black Label, and Schlitz (listed in their
own categories in this book), but no breweries. Its brands are made
under contract by other brewers, including Miller.

Advertisement, Good Taste For 94 Years, Liberty Magazine, July, 1938, 11 1/2 x 8 1/2 In. 8.00
Banner, Wilburs Stock Food, Pabst 6-Horse Team, Cloth, 36 x 60 In. 577.00
Bottle, Label, Blue Ribbon, 4 3/8 In... 11.00
Bottle Opener, Pabst Blue Ribbon, Flat Type 5.00
Calendar, 1914, Extract, Victorian Woman, Orange Dress, 10 x 37 In. 220.00
Calendar, 1914, Victorian Woman Front, Lithograph, Frame 176.00
Calendar, 1916, Pabst Extract, American Girl, Yard Long, 36 x 7 1/2 In. 335.00
Calendar, 1917, Pabst Extra, Woman, Yellow Dress, Black Stole, Frame, 13 x 40 In. 253.00
Can, Big Cat Malt Liquor, Pull Tab, 12 Oz. 13.00
Can, Pabst Blue Ribbon, Aluminum, Pull Tab, 12 Oz. 3.00
Can, Pabst Extra Light, Pull Tab, 12 Oz. 3.00
Clock, Bartender, Bottle, Pot Metal, Light-Up 110.00
Door Push, Blended Splendid, Tin Lithograph, Embossed, 4 x 9 In. 66.00
Door Push, Blue Ribbon, Finest Beer Served Anywhere!, Tin, 7 3/4 x 4 1/4 In. 193.00
Lighter, Blue Ribbon, Beer Can Shape, 12 Oz. 22.00
Picture, Drinking Scene, Paper, Lithograph, Frame, 35 x 27 In.................... 1500.00
Sign, 2 Bottles, Glass, Oysters, Original Signed Frame, 26 x 22 In. 176.00
Sign, Beer Bottles Next To Oysters, Cardboard, Frame, 20 1/2 x 24 1/2 In. 143.00
Sign, Blue Ribbon Winners, Wagon, 8 Horses, Wilbur Stock Food Co., 1904, 30 x 16 In. . 143.00
Sign, Blue Ribbon, Beer Of Quality, Gentleman Pouring Beer, Lithograph, 28 x 23 In. ... 220.00
Sign, Bottle Of Pabst, Tin, Cardboard, Bevel Edge, Prohibition Era, 7 1/4 x 11 In. 138.00
Sign, Cereal Beverage, Less Than 1/2 Of One Per Cent Alcohol, Porcelain, 4 x 7 In. 55.00
Sign, Factory Scene, Paper Lithograph, Mat, Frame, 42 x 52 In. 1540.00
Sign, Genuine Bock Beer, Black Ram, Ribbon, Cardboard, Easel Back, 29 x 22 In. 72.00
Sign, Genuine Bock Beer, Ram's Head, Paper, Mat, Frame, 17 1/2 x 14 In. 132.00
Sign, Pablo, Non-Alcoholic, Tin Lithograph, Cardboard, 6 x 13 1/4 In. 248.00
Sign, Pabst Blue Ribbon, Popular Prices, Tin Lithograph, 59 1/2 x 25 3/4 In. 52.00
Sign, Pabst Extract, Lady, Pink Dress, Gold Ground, 1916, 7 x 35 In. 314.00
Sign, Pabst Extract, Victorian Woman, Frame, 1916, 8 x 34 In. 176.00
Sign, Pabst Malt Extract, Best Tonic, Knight Riding Swan, 14 x 22 In. 375.00
Sign, Quality Yes Suh-h, Black Waiter, Beer, Cardboard, c.1938, 24 x 34 In. ......300.00 to 375.00

Sign, Smiling Man Pouring Beer Into Glass, Cardboard, c.1933, 20 x 25 1/2 In. 300.00
Sign, Spanish-American War Heros, Chromolithograph, Tin, Frame, c.1900, 33 x 27 In. . . 2300.00
Sign, U.S. Map, Blue Ribbon, This Is Blue Ribbon Country, 1940, 13 1/2 x 10 1/2 In. 12.00
Sign, Woman, Man, Parasol, Waterwheel, Cardboard, Light-Up, Motion, 28 x 22 In. 198.00
Spoon, Capt. Fred Pabst, President, Sterling Silver, Gold Washed 255.00
Tapster, Copper, Revere, 5 1/2 In. 94.00
Tray, Factory, Tin Lithograph, 12 1/4 x 17 1/4 In. 605.00
Tray, Pabst Blue Ribbon, Man Pours A Beer, 13 1/2 x 10 3/4 In. 88.00
Tray, Pabst Is The Name, Make Mine The Same, Blue, Silver, Round, 1950s, 13 In. 25.00
Tray, What'll You Have?, Pabst Blue Ribbon, Tin, Round, 11 3/4 In. 27.00

PAIL Lithographed tin pails decorated with advertising were popular
commercial containers during the late nineteenth and early twentieth
centuries. Many tobacco companies packed their products in pails
because they knew the pail would be used as a child's lunch bucket
(these can be found in the Tobacco category). Peanut butter and candy
makers liked pails because the containers would be used as toys in a
sandbox. Small pails continue to be made as toys, but few are decorated with advertising.

Buffalo Brand Peanut Butter, F.M. Hoyt & Co., Amesbury, Mass., 3 1/4 x 3 3/4 In. 27.00
Clark's Peanut Butter, Tin Lithograph, Canoe, Moose, Dog Sled, 1 Lb., 3 3/8 x 3 3/4 In. . 963.00
Climax Peanut Butter, J.W. Beardsley's Sons, Newark, N.J., 1 Lb., 3 1/2 x 3 1/2 In. 40.00
Cream Nut Peanut Butter, Tin, Bel-Mo-Butter Co., Michigan, 3 3/8 x 3 3/4 In. 385.00
Crown Jewel Peanut Butter, Gold, Tin Lithograph, Bail Handle, 14 Oz., 3 1/4 x 3 3/4 In. 66.00
Derby's Peter Pan Peanut Butter, Free Sample, 2 1/4 x 1 5/8 In. 205.00
Dixie Peanut Butter, Kelly Peanut Co., Boston, 3 1/2 In. 44.00
Eatagood Peanut Butter, Smith & Sons, White River Junction, Vt., Tin, Handle, 3 1/2 In. 176.00
Fi-Na-St Peanut Butter, Cover, First National Stores, 1 Lb., 3 3/4 x 3 1/2 In. . . . . .40.00 to 90.00
Gold Flake Peanut Butter, Bail Handle, Red Lid, Kelly Peanut Corp., 5 Lb., 6 x 6 In. . . . 25.00
Happy Home Peanut Butter, Tin Lithograph, 1 Lb., 3 3/4 x 3 1/4 In. 550.00
Hetzel's Roof Cement, Child Drums On Pail, Pail As Hat, Tin Lithograph, 4 1/2 x 5 In. . . 215.00
Hoody's Famous Peanut Butter, Tin, 1 Lb., 3 3/4 x 3 1/4 In. 743.00
Horne's Good Luck Peanut Butter, 3 1/2 Lb., 5 x 6 In. 32.00
Independence Hall Candy, Historical Images, Tin Lithograph, 3 Oz., 2 7/8 x 2 7/8 In. . . . 253.00
Jack & Jill Peanut Butter, Loblaw Groceterias, Toronto, Canada, 5 3/4 x 5 1/2 In. 28.00
Jackie Coogan Peanut Butter, Tin, Kelly Co., Cleveland, 12 Oz., 3 1/2 x 3 In. . . .350.00 to 375.00
Jackie Coogan Salted Peanuts, Yellow, School Silhouette, Tin Lithograph, 3 1/2 x 4 In. . . 440.00
John P. Squire & Co. Pure Leaf Lard, Bail Handle, 8 Lb. 10 Oz., 7 x 7 1/2 In. 26.00
Johnson Cakelets, Nursery Rhyme Characters, Tin Lithograph, Hinged Lid, 3 x 6 x 4 In. . 177.00
Jolly Time Popcorn, Hulless, Guaranteed To Pop, Red, 1 Lb. 99.00
Kid Candy, Jackie Coogan, Red Ground, Tin Lithograph, 3 3/8 x 3 3/4 In. 415.00
Kiddie's Delight Peanut Butter, Tin Lithograph, 12 Oz., 3 x 3 1/2 In. 358.00
Little Pig Peanut Butter, Tin, 2 7/8 x 3 1/8 In. 295.00
Lovell & Covel, Pure Hard Candies, Tin, Boston, 3 Oz., 2 7/8 x 2 7/8 In. 375.00
Lovell & Covel Candy, Historical Images, Tin Lithograph, Embossed Lid, 3 x 2 7/8 In. . . . 452.00
Meadow-Sweet Peanut Butter, Golden Sunset Over Pasture, Green, 3 5/8 x 2 7/8 In. 198.00
Morris Supreme Peanut Butter, Children At Seashore, Tin, Bail Handle, 3 3/4 x 3 1/2 In. 132.00
Mosemann's Peanut Butter, Wild Animals, Lancaster, Pa., 1 Lb., 3 3/4 x 3 3/8 In. 138.00
O! Boy Peanut Butter, Boy, Girl, Tin Lithograph, Stone Ordean Wells, 3 3/8 x 3 3/4 In. . . 715.00
Peter Pan Peanut Butter, Pry Lid, Tin, 2 3/4 x 3 1/2 In. 375.00
Peter Rabbit Peanut Butter, 1 Lb., 4 x 3 3/4 In. 660.00
Pride Of Ontario Honey, Foster & Holterman, Brantford, Canada, 4 7/8 x 5 1/4 In. 165.00
Queen Of Hearts Candy, Nursery Rhyme Scene, Tin, Bail Handle, 3 x 3 In. 77.00
Rival Peanut Butter, Gladiators, Tin, Bail Handle, 1 Lb., 3 1/2 x 3 3/4 In. . . . . . . .143.00 to 160.00
Robin Hood Peanut Butter, R.C. Williams & Co., 10 Lb. 28.00
Rosenberger & Currier Confections, Mankato, Wire Bail Handle, Cardboard, Early 1900s 250.00
Royal Mocha & Java, Edward D. Depew & Co., New York, Tin, Handle, 5 1/2 x 4 1/2 In. . 440.00
Sanders Satin Candies, Children Seated At Table, Handle, 2 1/2 Lb., 5 x 5 1/2 In. 143.00
Shedd's Peanut Butter, Red, Yellow, Elf, Handle, Lid, Shedd-Bartush Foods, 5 Lb., 6 In. 45.00
Staple Brand Peanut Butter, Syracuse Candy & Specialty Company, 3 3/4 x 3 3/8 In. 160.00
Sunny Boy Peanut Butter, White, Red, Tin Lithograph, 1 Lb., 3 1/2 x 3 7/8 In. 385.00
Sunshine Biscuits, Cardboard, Metal Bottom & Top, Bail, 5 5/8 In. 60.00
Sweet Home Pure Lard, c.1940, 4 Lb., 6 1/2 In. 75.00

Teddie Peanut Butter, Peanut, Plantation, Canada, 1 Lb., 3 1/2 x 3 3/4 In. . . . . . . .242.00 to 500.00
Thrift Brand Peanut Butter, Gold Label, Black Letters, 1 Lb., 3 1/4 x 3 3/4 In. 31.00
Toyland Peanut Butter, Circus Parade, Tin Lithograph, 1 Lb., 3 7/8 x 3 1/2 In. . . .143.00 to 361.00
Turnwright's Toffee De-Light, Red Ground, Handle, Tin, England, 8 In. 161.00
White Clover Peanut Butter, Amos-James Grocer Co., 1 Lb., 3 3/4 x 3 1/2 In. 495.00
Yankee Brand Peanut Butter, Paper Label, Red Lid, E.K. Pond Co., Chicago, 12 Oz. 110.00

PAMPHLET, see Booklet

PAPERWEIGHT   Many advertising paperweights are glass domes with
ads pasted to the backing and magnified by the glass. There are also
many metal and plastic forms of molded paperweights that advertise
products. Look for unusual or entertaining weights, like the turtle-
shaped ads with moving legs or the pile of "gold" coins that's actually
a single weight.

Aikens Tile & Fireplaces, 2 1/2 x 4 x 1 In. 71.00
Archies Lobster House, Clear Glass Globe, Roanoke, Va., 1950s, 1 1/4 x 3 x 3 In. 60.00
Boehringer & Soehne, Largest Makers In The World Of Quinine & Cocaine, 7 In. 330.00
C.F. Boehringer & Soehne, Factory, Manheim, Germany, 2 1/4 In x 4 In. 99.00
Carl Schaeffer Electric Co., Motor Shape, Bronze, 2 3/4 In. 58.00
Casket, Boyertown, N.Y., Famous Bronze, Antique Silver, No. 2400, 2 1/4 x 5 In. 110.00
Consolidated Ice Co., Glass, Bottle Shape, Raised Letters, Pittsburgh, Pa., 2 1/4 x 4 In. . . .   149.00
Danville Stove Co., Beaver, Oval Base, Nickel Plated Iron, 2 1/2 In. 46.00
Fairbanks Scales, 100 Years, Metal, Silver Plated, 100 Year Anniversary, 3 1/2 x 5 3/4 In.   75.00
Firemen's Insurance Co., Brass, Velvet & Leather Case, Newark, N.J. 23.00
Independent Stove Co., Elephant, Nickel Plated Iron, 3 1/2 In. 127.00
John A. Phoebus, Roll Top Desk, Painted Transfer, Glass, 4 x 2 1/2 In. 175.00
Lautz Bros. Soap, Who Is Taller, 4 x 2 1/2 In. 120.00
Owens Bottle Machine Co., Milk Bottle Shape, Toledo, 4 x 2 7/8 In. 358.00
Reeves Wood Burning Furnace, Cast Metal, Dover, Ohio 5.50
Richland Table Butter, Glass, White Bottom, 2 1/2 x 4 x 1 In. 195.00
Samuel Noyes Tailors & Trimmings, Boston, Cast Iron, Round, Knob Handle, 4 In. 81.00
Shackamaxon Worsted, Milk Glass Bottom, 3 1/2 x 2 In. 84.00
Southern Fruit Julep Co., 5 Year Calendar, Glass, c.1927, 1 3/8 x 4 x 2 7/8 In. 358.00
Stoakes' Aerate Waters, Clear Glass, Red Letters, 3 In. 41.00
Sun Gas Arc, Vapor Street Light, Milk Glass Bottom, Graeser, 2 1/2 x 4 x 3/4 In. 83.00
Taylors, Anchor, Dreadnought, Nickel Plate, Metal, 4 x 7 In. 94.00
Thatcher Furnaces, Figural, Chubby Man With Floppy Hat, Bronze, 3 1/2 In. 115.00
Tremble & Welcher Coal Company, Glass, Patterson, N.J., 1 x 4 x 2 1/2 In. 195.00
Tropical Street Marking Paint, Cast Iron, No-Parking Sign Shape, 4 3/4 In. 115.00
U.S. Steel Supply, Yellow Truck, Celluloid, Box, 1960s, 3 1/2 In. . . . . *Illus*   30.00
Victor Spring Beds, Noiseless, Will Never Sag, Glass, 4 x 2 1/2 x 1 In. 77.00
Westinghouse Tuff Guy Figure, Plaster, 1952, 5 In. 45.00

PENCIL   Pencils were invented in the mid-1500s. The eraser was not
added to the top until 1858. The automatic pencil was invented in
1863. Pens replaced hand-cut quills as writing instruments in 1780,
when the first steel pen was made in England. But it was a hundred
years before the commercial pen was a common item. The fountain
pen was invented in the 1830s, but it also was not made in quantity
until the 1880s. The ballpoint pen was invented in 1938. Advertising
pencils and pens, as well as display cases and other items related to
writing instruments, are listed here.

Display, John Holland Fountain Pen, Die Cut, Easel Back, Cardboard, 9 x 5 3/4 In. 176.00
Display Case, Eisenstadt's Fountain Pen, Floor Model, Etched Glass, c.1930 . . . .   220.00
Display Case, Esterbrook Fountain Pen, Pens, c.1950 . . . .   299.00
Display Case, Sheaffer's Pens, Pencils, Floor Model, Oak, Etched Glass, 40 x 58 x 25 In. . .   220.00
Display Case, Sheaffer's Sharp Point, Oak, Slanted Glass, Pens, Pencils, Countertop, 14 In.   467.00
Display Case, Spencerian Pen Point, Paper Lithograph Top Panel, c.1900, 15 x 11 In. 138.00
Display Case, Verithin Colored Pencils, Wood, Glass, Interior Slots, Angled, 14 In. 92.00
Pen, Old Hill Lines, Bullet, Phone 192 620 Brazos Portales, N.M., 3 5/8 In. 22.00
Pencil, Cadillac Bullet, Golfer, 3 1/4 In. 85.00
Pencil, Commonwealth Edison, Light Bulb 5.00

Paperweight, U.S. Steel Supply, Yellow
Truck, Celluloid, Box, 1960s, 3 1/2 In.

Pepsi-Cola, Sign, Listen To Counter-Spy, Radio
Thriller, c.1949, 8 x 19 1/4 In.

Pencil, Merle A. Frey General Hauling, 18 Wheeler, R.D. 3, Chamberburg, Pa., Mechanical	25.00
Pencil, Mountain Iron & Supply Co., Autopoint, Mechanical	9.00
Pencil, Philco, High Fidelity Television	15.00
Pencil Box, Dixon's Typhonite Eldorado, Master Drawing Pencil, Cardboard, 7 1/4 x 2 In.	10.00
Pencil Sharpener, Cincinnati Water Purifier, Water Pump	1293.00
Tin, Blue Jay Pencils, Blue Jay, Lithograph, 2 x 7 3/4 In.	50.00

PEPSI-COLA Pepsi-Cola was invented and named by Caleb Davis Bradham, a New Bern, North Carolina, druggist. He registered the trademark, the word "Pepsi-Cola" in calligraphy script, in 1903, but claimed that it had been used since 1898. A simpler version of the trademark was registered in 1906. The name in a hexagonal frame with the words "A Sparkling Beverage" was registered in 1937. In 1941, in support of the war effort, the bottle caps were changed from green to red, white, and blue. About 1950 a logo in an oval was introduced. A simulated bottle-cap logo was also used at the time. Until 1951, the words Pepsi and Cola were separated by two dashes, called the double dash. In 1951 it was replaced by a single hyphen. The shortened name "Pepsi" was first used in 1911, but it was not until 1966 that the block-letter Pepsi logo was registered. Both names are still used. The logo has been updated at least eight times and now consists of a red, white, and blue Pepsi Globe on a blue background. Pepsi-Cola merged with Frito-Lay in 1965, forming PepsiCo, Inc. In 2001 PepsiCo merged with Quaker Oats Company. Many reproductions of Pepsi advertising items have been made.

Blotter, Enjoy Pepsi-Cola, Hits The Spot, c.1930, 4 x 7 1/4 In.	65.00
Bottle, Escambia Bottling Co., Clear, Crown Top	110.00
Bottle, Green, Paper Label, Confair Bottling Co., c.1930, 12 Oz.	242.00
Bottle, Hutchinson, Clear, Escambia Bottling Co., Pensacola, Fl., 6 5/8 In.	220.00
Bottle, Ice Blue, Escambia Bottling Co., 8 1/4 In.	127.00
Bottle, Paper Label, 2 1/2 In.	18.00
Calendar, 1941, Paper On Cardboard, Girl Holding Bottle, Full Pad, 23 x 15 In.	193.00
Can, Syrup, Red, White, Blue, No Lid, 17 x 14 In.	33.00
Carrier, 6-Pack, Wood, 1940	125.00
Carrier, 6-Pack, Wood, Handle	55.00
Carrier, Wood, 6 Pepsi Bottles, c.1930	198.00
Chalkboard, Enjoy, Bigger, Better, Double Dash, Wood Frame, 30 x 19 1/2 In.	204.00
Chalkboard, Today's Specials, Tin, Embossed, Painted, 19 x 27 In.	61.00
Clock, Glass Face, Swihart, 14 In.	249.00
Clock, Light-Up, 15 In.	523.00
Clock, Light-Up, Plastic Front, Metal Frame, 30 x 41 In.	138.00
Clock, Plastic, Blue Numbers, Rectangular	83.00
Clock, Telechron, Light-Up, Round, 1940s	468.00
Cookie Jar, Mountain Dew, Can Shape, Limited Edition, Ceramic, Box, 11 In.	55.00
Cooler, Blue, White Letters, Double Dash	121.00
Cooler, Double Dash, Embossed, c.1940	990.00
Cooler, Ice Cold, Sold Here, 5 Cents, Metal Stand, 36 In.	716.00

Couch, Pepsi Cooler, Aqua, White, Embossed Lettering 1870.00
Crate, 4 Sections, 18 x 6 x 12 In. 48.00
Door Bar, Prenez Un Pepsi, France, 31 1/2 x 3 In. 110.00
Door Push, Have A Pepsi, Yellow, Red, White, Blue, Porcelain 165.00
Door Push, Worth Twice Its Price, Yellow, Tin, c.1930, 3 1/2 x 13 1/2 In. 825.00
Drum, Bulk Syrup, Tin, Red, White, 17 In. 66.00
Figure, Crossing Guard, Boy, Sheet Metal, Lithograph, Pepsi Cap Cast Iron Base, 64 In. . . 303.00
Figure, Crossing Guard, Boy, Slow, Tin, Cast Iron Base, Pepsi Cap Base, 62 In. 467.00
Hat, Soda Jerk, Say Pepsi Please, Cellucap Mfg. Co., Phila., Pa., 1950s 12.00
Rack, Bag, Drink Pepsi-Cola, Bigger, Better, 2-Sided, Tin, Metal, c.1940, 19 x 24 x 6 In. . 1870.00
Rack, Bottle, Take Home A Carton Sign, Wire, Folding Shelves 66.00
Radio, Figural, Bottle, Bakelite, Painted, Knob On Circular Base, 1951, 23 In. 805.00
Record, Voice Of Your Man In Service, Cardboard Envelope, 78 RPM, 1942, 7 x 7 In. . . . 25.00
Record Set, Cardboard Jacket, 1960s, 6 Records 100.00
Sign, 4 Young Women At Beach, Cardboard, Metal Frame, 1960s, 38 x 26 In. 72.00
Sign, 5 Cents, Bottle Shape, Die Cut, Tin Lithograph, 1930s, 29 1/2 x 8 1/8 In. 743.00
Sign, Be Sensible, Have A Pepsi, 2-Sided, Cardboard, Aluminum Frame, 38 x 26 1/2 In. . . 175.00
Sign, Be Sociable, Cardboard, Late 1950s, 11 x 28 In. 135.00
Sign, Big Shot, Boy & Girl, Cardboard, 11 x 28 In. 35.00
Sign, Bigger & Better Reputation, 5 Cents, Paper, Frame, 1920-1930, 12 x 30 In. 66.00
Sign, Bottle Cap, Die Cut, Metal Sign, 54 In. 143.00
Sign, Bottle Cap, Double Dash, Tin, 26 1/2 x 30 In. 138.00
Sign, Bottle Cap, Drink Pepsi-Cola, Celluloid Over Cardboard, 9 In. . . . . .132.00 to 193.00
Sign, Bottle Cap, Embossed, 19 In. 220.00
Sign, Bottle Cap, Enamel Painted, 1964, 60 x 42 In. 415.00
Sign, Bottle Cap, Porcelain, Round, 18 1/2 In. 330.00
Sign, Bottle Cap, Red, White, Blue, Round, 28 In. 154.00
Sign, Bottle Cap, Shoe Sign & Billiard Parlor, A.A. Ardinger's, Tin, 56 In. 220.00
Sign, Bottle Cap, Tin, Die Cut, Red, White, Blue, 13 1/4 x 13 7/8 In. 385.00
Sign, Bottle Cap, Tin, Diecut, Embossed, 1940s, 13 In. 1050.00
Sign, Bottle, 5 Cents, Sparkling Beverage, Tin, Die Cut, c.1940, 5 x 45 In. 575.00
Sign, Buy Pepsi-Cola Here, Tin, Flange, Round, c.1940, 16 In. 880.00
Sign, Cup, Celluloid, Metal Frame, Light-Up, 20 1/2 In. 303.00
Sign, Drink Pepsi-Cola, Tin, Yellow Ground, Red, White, Blue, Bottle Cap, 21 x 26 1/2 In. 242.00
Sign, Have A Pepsi, Light-Up, 17 x 22 In. 110.00
Sign, Listen To Counter-Spy, Radio Thriller, c.1949, 8 x 19 1/4 In. . . . . *Illus* 40.00
Sign, Man Carries Surfboard & 6 Packs, Beach, Cardboard, 24 1/2 x 36 In. 39.00
Sign, Mirror, Shadowbox, Light-Up, 1950s, 12 x 12 x 5 In. 660.00
Sign, More Bounce To The Ounce, Tin, 17 1/2 x 47 In. 275.00
Sign, Pepsi & Pete, Nickel Drink Worth A Dime, Frame, c.1940, 10 1/2 x 20 1/2 In. 990.00
Sign, Pepsi Pete Cop, 5 Cents, Cardboard, 17 In. 110.00
Sign, Refreshing & Healthful, Reverse Painted Glass, c.1940, 10 x 12 In. 6050.00
Sign, Refreshing, Enjoyable, 5 Cents, Tin, Die Cut Bottle, 44 1/2 x 12 In. 385.00
Sign, Say Pepsi Please, Bottle, Cap, Tin Over Cardboard, 9 x 11 In. 83.00
Sign, Say Pepsi Please, Bottle, Tin Lithograph, Embossed, Self-Framed, 46 1/2 x 17 In. . . 385.00
Sign, Say Pepsi Please, Bottle, White Ground, Celluloid Over Cardboard, 8 x 12 In. 113.75
Sign, Say Pepsi Please, Logo, Tin, 18 x 54 In. 138.00
Sign, Say Pepsi Please, Metal, 1966, 67 x 36 In. 385.00
Sign, Say Pepsi Please, Tin, Embossed, Frame, 1969, 47 x 17 In. 330.00
Sign, Shape Of 5 Cent Bottle, c.1940, 29 1/2 In. 1540.00
Sign, Sold Here, Tin, Die Cut, Flange, 2-Sided, 1940, 10 x 14 1/2 In. 715.00
Sign, Think Young, Say Pepsi Please, Cardboard Lithograph, Frame, 1960s, 29 In. 22.00
Sign, Why Take Less When Pepsi's Best, 6 Pack, Cardboard, Frame, 1940s, 11 x 25 In. . . 770.00
Sign, Woman In Green Dress, Man In Suit, Paper, 41 x 68 In. 55.00
Sign, Woman, White Dress, Flowers, Rolf Armstrong, Frame, c.1919, 30 1/2 x 24 1/2 In. . 770.00
Sign, Your Good Old Friend, Santa Holding Bottle, Cap, Cardboard, 11 x 28 In. 17.00
Stringholder, Join The Swing, Bigger & Better, 5 Cent, Tin Lithograph 413.00
Thermometer, Bigger, Better, Double Dash, c.1940, 16 x 6 1/2 In. 83.00
Thermometer, Bottle Double Dash, Bigger Better, 6 x 16 1/2 In. 165.00
Thermometer, Double Dash, Tin Lithograph, 27 In. 25.00
Thermometer, Folded Metal, 1970s, 28 1/4 x 7 1/8 In. 29.00
Thermometer, Have A Pepsi, Bottle Cap, Yellow Ground, 27 x 7 1/4 In. 55.00
Thermometer, Have A Pepsi, Light Refreshment, Folded Tin, 1950s, 27 x 7 1/4 In. 58.00

Peters, Calendar,
1910, Peters
Cartridge Co.,
2 Men In Canoe,
14 x 27 In.

Pepsi-Cola, Thermometer, Say Pepsi Please, Tin, 9 In.

Thermometer, More Bounce To The Ounce, Tin Lithograph, 1950s, 27 In.	203.00
Thermometer, Say Pepsi Please, Enamel Over Tin, Glass Cover, 9 x 9 In.	66.00
Thermometer, Say Pepsi Please, Tin Lithograph, Embossed Bottle Cap, 1960s, 27 In.	90.00
Thermometer, Say Pepsi Please, Tin, 9 In. ....*Illus*	176.00
Thermometer, Say Pepsi Please, Tin, Embossed, 1969, 28 x 7 1/4 In.	77.00
Tip Tray, Drink, Delicious, Healthful, Tin Lithograph, 1920-1940, 6 1/8 x 4 3/8 In.	672.00
Tip Tray, Woman, Hat, Holding Glass, Oval, c.1900, 6 In.	825.00
Tray, Bigger & Better, Tin Lithograph, 13 1/2 In.	283.00
Tray, Enjoy Pepsi-Cola, Hits The Spot, Tin Lithograph, 14 In.	90.00
Tray, Pepsi-Cola Bottle Cap, 13 1/8 In.	130.00
Tumbler, 1940s, 5 1/8 x 2 1/2 In.	25.00
Tumbler, Aquaman, Z50 Collectors Series, 6 5 1/6 In.	110.00
Vending Machine, Blue, Round Top, 60 In.	1760.00
Watch Fob, Eagle, Perched On 2 Crossed Arrows, 2 Pepsi Bottles, Sterling Silver	48.00

PETERS The Peters Cartridge Company was incorporated in 1887 by Gershon M. Peters, who was also the president of King's Great Western Powder Company. Both companies were located along Ohio's Little Miami River. The cartridge company became quite successful when it developed the first machine to load shotgun shells. Remington Arms took over the company in 1934 and closed the Little Miami plant in 1944. Ammunition boxes, buttons, posters, signs, and other Peters advertising items are popular with collectors. Related items may be found in Remington.

Banner, Come On In & Shoot, Safari Hunter, Lion, Canvas, 1940s, 55 x 29 In.	2200.00
Box, High Velocity Shotgun Shells, 20 Gauge, Extra Length, 3 1/2 x 3 1/2 x 2 3/4 In.	44.00
Box, High Velocity, 20 Gauge, Flying Mallard Drake, Contents, 4 x 4 x 2 1/2 In.	22.00
Box, High Velocity, 28 Gauge, New Peters Crimp, Flying Mallard, 4 x 4 x 2 1/2 In.	45.00
Box, Referee, 12 Gauge, Paper Shot Shells, No. 5, Contents, Unopened, 4 x 4 x 2 1/2 In.	404.00
Box, Referee, 16 Gauge, Semi-Smokeless Powder, 2 Piece, 3 3/4 x 3 3/4 x 2 1/4 In.	853.00
Box, Target Paper Shot Shells, Bulk Smokeless Powder, 4 x 4 x 2 1/2 In.	491.00
Box, Target Shells, 12 Gauge, Paper Shot, 4 x 4 x 2 1/2 In.	334.00
Box, Trap Load, 12 Gauge, Smokeless, Shotgun Shells, Rustless, 4 x 4 x 2 1/2 In.	393.00
Box, Victor, 12 Gauge, Rustless, Smokeless Shotgun Shells, 4 x 4 x 2 1/2 In.	66.00
Brochure, Big Game Cartridges, Grizzly Bear, 6 1/4 x 3 3/8 In.	220.00
Brochure, High Velocity, Shotgun Shells, Cartridges, Trifold, 6 1/4 x 3 3/8 In.	55.00
Brochure, Shotgun Shells, 1919, 3 1/2 x 6 1/4 In.	358.00
Button, Center P, Steel Where Steel Belongs, Multicolored, Bastian Bros., 7/8 In.	46.00
Button, Duck Theme, Multicolored, Celluloid, 7/8 In.	61.00
Button, Experts Use Peters Cartridges, Copper & Silver Colored Bullet, Bastian Brothers	59.00
Button, Large P, Flying Duck, Celluloid, 3/4 In.	36.00
Button, Peters Cartridge Co., Red, White, Blue, Stars & Stripes P, 7/8 In.	83.00
Button, Peters Cartridges, Experts Use, Bullet, Celluloid, Pinback, Round, 7/8 In.	66.00
Button, Peters Referee Shells, Multicolored, Bastian Bros., Round, 7/8 In.	91.00

Button, Peters Shells & Cartridge, Big P, Target, Multicolored Scene, Pinback, 7/8 In. . . . 110.00
Button, Peters Shells, Hunter, Duck, Multicolored, Celluloid, 7/8 In. 104.00
Button, Peters Superior Cartridges, Gold, Black, White, Red, Celluloid, 7/8 In. 39.00
Button, Shoot Peters Shells & Cartridges, Center P, Multicolored, Bastian Bros., 7/8 In. . . . 92.00
Button, Steel Where Steel Belongs, Green, Red, White, Celluloid, 7/8 In. 44.00
Button, Superior Cartridges, Celluloid, 3/4 In. 43.00
Calendar, 1908, 2 Hunters In Boat, Frame, 27 1/2 x 13 1/2 In. 8202.00
Calendar, 1910, Peters Cartridge Co., 2 Men In Canoe, 14 x 27 In. . . . . *Illus* 4400.00
Calendar, 1928, Peters Cartridge Co., Frame, 18 x 34 In. 413.00
Counter Felt, Peters Ammunition, Red, White, Black, 11 x 13 In. 523.00
Counter Felt, Peters Ideal, Smokeless Powder, Frame, c.1900, 12 3/4 x 11 1/2 In. 615.00
Counter Felt, Shells, Cartridges, Bull's-Eye, 1909, 11 3/8 x 10 3/8 In. 462.00
Letter Opener, Peters Cartridge Co., Brass, Silver, 7 3/4 In. 322.00
Postcard, Peters Cartridge Co., Canoeing For Ducks, Man, Dog In Canoe, 3 1/2 x 5 1/2 In. 110.00
Poster, High Velocity, Target, Victor, Duck Hunter, Easel Back, Die Cut, 3-D, 39 x 27 In. 2173.00
Poster, Peters Ammunition, Grizzly Bear On Mountain Ledge, c.1920, 20 1/8 x 14 In. 4352.00
Poster, Peters Ammunition, Hunting Scenes, Stand-Up, Trifold, c.1930, 58 x 32 In. 1146.00
Poster, Peters Loaded Shells, Steel Where Steel Belongs, Pheasant, Quails, 30 1/4 x 20 In. 990.00
Poster, We Sell Peters Shells, 3 Flying Ducks, Multicolored, c.1915, 9 x 12 In. 1155.00
Price List, Peters Cartridge Co., Cincinnati, 1887, 6 1/8 x 3 3/8 In. 223.00
Sign, Peters Ammunition, Bear, Branch, Cardboard, Die Cut, Easel Back, 19 1/2 x 12 In. . 523.00
Sign, Peters Ammunition, Hunting Scenes, Die Cut, 5 Panels, 35 x 42 In. 1544.00
Sign, Peters Big Game Ammunition, Elk, Philip R. Goodwin, 20 x 30 In. 3630.00
Sign, Peters Cartridge Co., Here's The Place, Easel, Die Cut, Stand-Up, Frame, 41 x 25 In. 1375.00
Sign, Peters Shells, Premier, Standard Smokeless Powder, Hanging, Case Insert, 8 x 13 In. 924.00

PILLSBURY   John Sargent Pillsbury arrived in what is now Minneapolis, Minnesota, in 1853. He opened a hardware business in 1855.
His nephew, Charles A. Pillsbury, joined him in the business, and in
1869 they decided to buy one-third of a nearby flour mill for $10,000.
Charles and the original mill owners, Wells Gardner and George
Crocker, controlled the mill. Charles bought the share owned by
Crocker in 1870. The next year, Gardner and Pillsbury bought another
mill and changed the name of the company to C.A. Pillsbury & Company. John Sargent Pillsbury and Charles's father, George Pillsbury,
joined the company in the 1870s. The famous XXXX trademark was
first used in 1872. In medieval times, XXX symbolized top-quality
flour. Charles decided if three Xs meant best, then Pillsbury's Best
needed four Xs to show it was even better. Through fires, rebuildings,
equipment purchases, speculation, receivership, changes in management, and deaths, the company grew and prospered. It became Pillsbury Flour Mills Company in 1908, Pillsbury Mills Inc. in 1914, and
The Pillsbury Company in 1958. For years, Pillsbury made only Best
Flour. Vitos, a wheat cereal, was introduced in 1898 and improved into
Farina in 1905. In 1915 wheat bran was added, in 1919 pancake flour,
in 1920 cake flour, in 1929 a refined cake flour called Sno Sheen, and
in 1932 buckwheat pancake flour. In 1944 the famous Ann Pillsbury
image was introduced. The Grand National Recipe and Baking Contest, also known as the Pillsbury Bake-Off, was started in 1949. The
Poppin' Fresh Doughboy trademark was created 1965. In 1989 Pillsbury was acquired by Grand Metropolitan, which merged with Guinness and became Diageo in 1997. In 2000 Pillsbury was sold to rival
General Mills. The baking mixes and frostings were sold to Multifoods
in 2001. Multifoods was acquired by Smuckers in 2004. General
Mills' Pillsbury Company manufactures refrigerated and frozen Pillsbury products and owns various Pillsbury logos, including the Pillsbury Barrelhead and the Pillsbury Doughboy.

Button, Pillsbury's Best, Flour Girl, Celluloid, Somme Badge Co., 1 3/4 In. 132.00
Cookbook, 5th Baking Contest, 100 Grand National Recipes, 1954, 5 x 8 1/4 In., 98 Pages 5.50
Cookbook, Family, Binder, 1960, 528 Pages 10.00
Cookie Jar, Doughboy, Ceramic, Lid, 5 x 5 1/2 x 10 1/2 In. 15.00
Figure, Doughboy, Poppin' Fresh, Stand, Embossed, Vinyl, Plastic, 1971, 7 1/2 In. . . .18.00 to 28.00

Figure Set, Granmommer, Granpopper, Polyvinyl, Box, 1974, 5 1/2 In. 150.00
Finger Puppet, Bun Bun, Vinyl, 1974, 3 In. 25.00
Finger Puppet, Flapjack, Popper, Poppin' Fresh, Box, 1974, 3 Piece 150.00
Mirror, Pillsbury's Best XXXX Minneapolis, Minn., Tin, 2 In. 36.00
Mug, Poppin' Fresh Doughboy Shape, Plastic, White, Made In U.S.A., 1979, 4 1/2 In. . . . 19.00
Sign, Ask For Pillsbury's Best Flour, Metal, Wood Frame, 13 5/8 x 59 1/2 In. 1100.00
Sign, Best Feeds, For Best Results, Tin, Embossed, Red, White, Blue, 10 x 20 In. 71.00
Sign, Chas. A. Pillsbury & Co., For Sale Here, Eagle On Barrel, Frame, 30 x 24 In. 9900.00
Telephone, Green Giant, Little Sprout, Touch Tone, 1984, 14 In. . . . . .85.00 to 100.00
Wagon Cover, Charles Zoller, Cash, Grocery, Minn., Painted Canvas, Wood 1208.00

PINBACK, see Button

PLANTERS PEANUTS Planters Nut and Chocolate Company was founded in 1906 in Wilkes-Barre, Pennsylvania, by Amedeo Obici and Mario Peruzzi. They made Planters Pennant Brand peanuts and sold them in blue tin cans. The Mr. Peanut figure with a monocle and top hat was introduced in 1916. In 1961 the company was acquired by Standard Brands, Inc., which merged with Nabisco to become Nabisco Brands, Inc., in 1981. Nabisco Brands became part of Reynolds Industries Inc. in 1985. Philip Morris Companies (Altria Group since 2003) acquired Nabisco in 2000 and integrated the Nabisco brands into Kraft Foods. Many old and new Mr. Peanut and Planters Peanut items are available. Glass jars with Mr. Peanut molded in the glass were reproduced in the 1970s and 1980s. In 1983 several of the old cans were reproduced, but they are clearly marked as new.

Ashtray, Mr. Peanut, Figural, Ceramic, 1930s, 4 1/4 In. 110.00
Ashtray, Mr. Peanut, Gold Tone, 50th Anniversary, 1906-1956, 5 1/2 x 5 In. 100.00
Blotter, Delivery Truck, Cardboard, c.1930s, 3 1/2 x 6 1/4 In. 15.00
Book, Happy Time Paint, Story Of Planters Peanuts, Photographs 20.00
Bracelet, 5 Charms, Metal, Plastic, 1960s 30.00
Charm, Mr. Peanut, Plastic, 1950s, 2 1/8 In. 15.00
Coloring Book, Mr. Peanut's 12 Months, c.1970, 8 1/2 x 5 In. 12.00
Container, Peanut Shape, Papier-Mache, c.1930, 12 x 6 x 5 In. 44.00
Container, Peanut, Embossed, Papier-Mache, 5 1/2 x 11 1/2 In. 35.00
Cup, Mr. Peanut Face, Top Hat, Pink, 1950s 30.00
Decals, Mr. Peanut, Nylon, Stick-On, 2 1/2 In., 40 Piece 25.00
Display, Stand-Up, c.1970, 4 Ft. 39.00
Doll, Mr. Peanut, Wood, Jointed, Schoenhut, c.1920, 8 1/4 In. 99.00
Fan, Mr. Peanut Driving Peanut Car, 1940s, 5 1/4 x 8 In. 253.00
Figure, Mr. Peanut, On Circular Base, Plastic, Box, 1990, 8 1/2 In. . . . . *Illus* 45.00
Figure, Mr. Peanut, Papier-Mache, 12 x 4 1/2 In. 165.00

Planters Peanuts,
Figure, Mr. Peanut,
On Circular Base,
Plastic, Box, 1990,
8 1/2 In.

Planters Peanuts, Figure,
Mr. Peanut, Top Hat & Cane,
Jointed, 1930s,
9 In.

Planters Peanuts, Jar,
4 Embossed Peanuts,
Peanut Finial, 14 In.

Planters Peanuts, Jar, Barrel
Shape, Embossed Mr. Peanut,
Peanut Finial, 12 In.

Planters Peanuts, Tin, High Grade
Peanut Butter, Bail Handle, Tin
Lithograph, 25 Lb., 10 In.

Planters Peanuts, Toy,
Mr. Peanut Walker, Plastic,
Windup, 9 In.

Figure, Mr. Peanut, Top Hat & Cane, Wood, Jointed, 1930s, 9 In. . . . . *Illus*   298.00
Flashlight, Mr. Peanut, Flippo Flashlight, Tipping Hat, Bantamlite 898.00
Jar, 1940 Leap Year Commemorative, Rectangular, 9 In. 52.00
Jar, 4 Embossed Peanuts, Peanut Shaped Finial, 14 x 9 In. *Illus*   187.00
Jar, 5 Cents, Embossed Images & Letters, Peanut Finial, 8-Sided, 12 In. 242.00
Jar, 8-Sided, 12 In. 154.00
Jar, Barrel Shape, Embossed Mr. Peanut & Letters, Peanut Finial, 12 In. 440.00
Jar, Barrel Shape, 4 Embossed Peanuts, Peanut Finial, 14 In. 165.00
Jar, Barrel Shape, Embossed Mr. Peanut, Peanut Finial, 12 In. . . . . *Illus*   385.00
Jar, Embossed Letters, Peanut Finial, Square, 10 In. 60.00
Jar, Embossed Peanut Corners, 13 In. 181.00
Jar, Embossed, Disc Sides, Side Opening, Metal Lid, 8 x 9 x 5 In. 66.00
Jar, Fired-On Logo, Embossed Back, Red Tin Lid, c.1940, 9 x 5 x 7 1/4 In. 88.00
Jar, Fishbowl, Cover, Paper Label, c.1929 . . . .   242.00
Jar, Football Shape, Cover, Glass, 8 In. 132.00
Jar, Peanut Butter, Tin Lid, Paper Label, 8 Oz., 4 1/4 x 2 1/2 In. 231.00
Jar, Planter's Salted Peanuts, Decal, Peanut Finial, 12 In. 143.00
Jar, Tin Lithograph Lid, Cellophane Labels, 1938, 8 1/2 x 10 In. 468.00
Jar, Yellow Letters & Mr. Peanut Figures, 6-Sided, 10 In. 77.00
Knife, Mr. Peanut, Red, Plastic, 1950-1960, 6 3/4 In. 9.00
Letterhead Block, Factory, Mr. Peanut, Metal, Wood, 2 1/2 x 7 3/4 In. 633.00
Patch, Mr. Peanut, Cloth, 1970s, 2 1/2 In. 8.00
Peanut Butter Maker, Mr. Peanut Shape, Plastic, 12 In. 33.00
Pen, Mr. Peanut On Barrel, Blue, Bic, 1970-1980, 6 In. 10.00
Pen, Mr. Peanut, Planters Snacks, Metal, Retractable, Ballpoint, 1970-1980, 5 In. 20.00
Pin, Mr. Peanut, 75th Anniversary, 1906-1981, Gold Tone, 1 In.   22.00
Pin, Mr. Peanut, Red, Plastic, Stickpin, 1 In. 14.00
Printer's Block, Miss Peanut, Metal, Wood, 5/8 x 1 1/4 x 1 In. 220.00
Printer's Block, Mr. Peanut, Metal On Wood, 5 1/2 x 2 5/8 In. 110.00
Printer's Block, Mr. Peanut, Metal, Wood, 9 x 3 3/4 In. 578.00
Punchboard, Cocktail Peanuts, 5 Cents, Red & Green Punched Squares, 7 x 8 In. 22.00
Punchboard, Laminated Cardboard, 1940s, 6 1/2 x 25 In. 45.00
Puppet, Hand, Rubber, Figural, 6 1/4 x 6 x 1 1/2 In. 688.00
Razor, Mr. Peanut On Handle, Bic, 1970s 8.00
Salt & Pepper, Mr. Peanut Leaning On Cane, Foil Label, 4 1/2 In. 60.00
Salt & Pepper, Mr. Peanut, Pink, Plastic, 3 In. 28.00
Salt & Pepper, Plastic, 4 In. 22.00
Salt & Pepper, Red, Box, Mailing Label From Planters Nut & Chocolate Co. 20.00
Salt & Pepper, Tan, Black, Plastic, 4 In. 25.00
Serving Set, Serving Bowl, 6 Bowls, 6 & 3 In., 7 Piece 45.00
Sign, 5 Cents A Bag, Red, White, Reverse Painted Glass, Frame, 22 1/2 x 20 1/2 In. 170.00
Snack Set, Mr. Peanut Center, Tin, 5 Bowls 29.00
Spoon, Mr. Peanut, Green, Plastic, 1950s 8.00
Stand, Chocolate Peanuts, Jumbo Block, Peanuts, Tin Lithograph, Display, 14 x 8 x 4 In. .   880.00
Tennis Ball, Mr. Peanut, Dunlop, 1970-1980 . . . .   10.00

Tin, Egyptian Designs, c.1919, 6 1/4 x 2 In. 1155.00
Tin, Hi-Hat Peanut Oil, Unopened, Tin Lithograph, Qt., 7 1/4 x 3 3/4 In. 51.00
Tin, High Grade Peanut Butter, Bail Handle, Tin Lithograph, 25 Lb., 10 In. .... *Illus* 209.00
Tin, Mixed Salted Nuts, Key Wind, 4 1/4 x 4 In. 105.00
Tin, Mr. Peanut Center, 3 1/2 In. Diam. 7.00
Tin, Pennant, Salted Peanuts, Lid, 10 Lb., 9 1/2 In. ....33.00 to 82.00
Tin, Planters Cocktail Peanuts, Vacuum Pack, c.1938, 8 Oz., 3 x 3 3/8 In. 165.00
Tin, Redskin Spanish Peanuts, Suffolk, Va., 4 1/4 x 4 In. 68.00
Tin, Salted Almonds, 2 3/4 x 2 5/8 In. 60.00
Tin, Salted Cashew Nuts, Key Wind, 3 x 3 3/8 In. 75.00
Tin, Salted Cashew Nuts, Key, Unopened, 7 1/2 Oz., 3 1/8 x 3 3/8 In. 122.00
Tin, Salted Peanuts, 11 In. 125.00
Tin, Spanish Peanuts, Tin Lithograph, Vacuum Pack, 1949, 3 1/8 x 3 3/8 In. 85.00
Toy, Mr. Peanut Walker, Plastic, Windup, 9 In. ....*Illus* 231.00
Transfer, Mr. Peanut, Iron-On, 1970s, 9 In. 12.00
Tray, Mr. Peanut, Fresh Roasted Peanuts, 15 5/8 x 11 1/8 In. 12.00
Whistle, Mr. Peanut, Blue, Plastic, Figural, 1970s 6.00

PLATE Advertising plates of many kinds have been made. Lithographed tin plates were popular in the late 1800s. They often had an attractive picture on the front and the advertisement only on the back. Glass and ceramic advertising plates have also been made. Collectors want plates given to customers as ads or restaurant plates imprinted with the restaurant's name.

Abbottmaid Ice Cream, 6th Anniversary, China, c.1920, 6 1/2 In. 250.00
Ballard, Amethyst, Carnival Glass, 6 In. 1300.00
Birmingham Age Herald, Amethyst, Carnival Glass, 9 In. 2600.00
Braziers Candies, Carnival Glass, Amethyst, Hand Grip, 6 In. ....900.00 to 1100.00
Broeker's Flour, Amethyst, Carnival Glasst, 6 In. 200.00
Central Shoe Store, Carnival Glass, Amethyst, 6 In. 1300.00
Coons Corner, Oxford, Jct., Watt, Apple, No. 29, Dinner 600.00
Davidson Society Chocolates, Amethyst, Double Hand Grip, Carnival Glass 1000.00
Dorsey & Funkenstein, Carnival Glass, Amethyst, 6 In. 2600.00
Dreibus Parfait, Carnival Glass, Amethyst, Hand Grip 1100.00
Eagle Furniture Co., Amethyst, Carnival Glass, 6 In. 1500.00
Exchange Bank, Carnival Glass, Amethyst, 6 In. 1700.00
Fern Brand, Carnival Glass, Amethyst, Double Hand Grip 950.00
Fireman's Fund Insurance, Fireman Carrying Little Girl, Syracuse China, 1963, 9 In. 38.00
Greengard Furniture Co., Carnival Glass, Amethyst, Hand Grip 7000.00
Hartford Fire & Accident Insurance Co., Green, Scammell's Lamberton, c.1930, 7 In. 16.00
J.N. Ledford Company, Carnival Glass, Cooleemee, N.C., Heart & Vine, Marigold, 9 In. . 9000.00
Jockey Club, Amethyst, Carnival Glass, 6 In. 1600.00
Lone Star Gas Company, Blue Flame, Syracuse China, 8 1/4 In. 20.00
Mobil Oil, Pegasus, White, Scalloped Edge, Restaurant China, 10 In. 70.00
Norris N. Smith, Carnival Glass, Amethyst, 6 In. 1400.00
Ogden Furniture, Carnival Glass, Amethyst, Hand Grip 1100.00
Old Barbee Whiskey, Tin Lithograph, Old Barbee Art, Vienna Art, 10 In. 440.00
Old Rose Distilling Co., Carnival Glass, Grape & Cable, Green, 8 3/4 In. ....300.00 to 375.00
Pan-Andy Bread, Woman With Flowing Hair, c.1900, 9 1/2 In. 110.00
Parkersburg Elks, Carnival Glass, Blue, 1914, 7 In. 2200.00
Rood's Chocolates, Carnival Glass, Amethyst, 6 In. 3600.00
Sterling Furniture Co., Carnival Glass, Amethyst, Hand Grip 1800.00
Telephone Pioneers Of America, AT&T Bell, N.E. T&T, No. 1, 1982, 8 3/4 In. 199.00
University Of Missouri, Columbian, C.B. Miller Shoe Co., Wheelock, England, 7 1/2 In. . 125.00
Utah Liquor Co., Carnival Glass, Amethyst, Double Hand Grip 1750.00

PLAYING CARDS, see Card

POLL PARROT Poll Parrot was a brand of the Roberts, Johnson & Rand Division of the International Shoe Company. It was named for Paul Parrott, who owned and operated Parrott Shoes of Knoxville, Tennessee. He kept a pet parrot in his store; and when a new brand name for juvenile shoes was needed, a salesman suggested the name Poll

Parrot. The name was copyrighted on July 25, 1922. The shoes and the trademark are well known because of advertising in all media, including the sponsorship of the Howdy Doody television show. Many Buffalo Bob and Howdy Doody Poll Parrot premiums can be found. The International Shoe Company became Interco Inc. in 1966. A division of the company retained the International Shoe Company name. The division ceased operations in 1987. In 1996, Interco, by then out of the shoe business, became Furniture Brands International. Red Goose and Weatherbird shoes, listed in their own categories in this book, were also made by the International Shoe Company.

Display, Composition Nodder, In Bent Wire Cage, Animated, Voice, c.1962, 41 In. 1380.00
Display, Parrot, Figural, Holds Pair Of Children's Shoes 245.00
Game, Target, Battery Operated, Lithographed Masonite, Box, c.1960, 24 In. 144.00
Shoe Bench, 5 Sections, Animal Dividers, Wood, 96 In. 7370.00
Sign, Parrot In Shoes, Shoes For Boys, For Girls, 2-Sided, Wood, Sidewalk, 46 In. 330.00
Sign, Steel, Multicolored Enamel, Outlined In Green Neon, c.1950, 24 In. .... *Illus* 2875.00
Toy, Spinner, Green Accent .... .50.00 to 60.00

POSTCARD There are postcard collectors for all sorts of cards— comic, scenic, historic, and advertising. One of the rarest postcards known is an advertising card nicknamed the "garbage" card. It advertised Booth, Dailey, and Irvins of New York City, a garbage-dumping service. The card has a rare printed stamp picturing President McKinley. Collectors want any card with a message or design that advertises a product. The easiest way to date a card is from the canceled postage stamp, if there is one. Rates were 1 cent (1872), 2 cents (1917), 1 cent (1919), 2 cents (1925), 1 cent (1928), 2 cents (1952), 3 cents (1959), 4 cents (1963), 5 cents (1968), 6 cents (1971), 8 cents (1973), 7 cents (1975), 9 cents (1976), 10 cents (1978), 12 cents (1981), 13 cents (1981), 14 cents (1985), 15 cents (1988), 19 cents (1991), 20 cents (1995), 21 cents (2001), and 23 cents (2002).

American Bus Lines, Linen, Curteich Publishing, c.1940 .... 15.00
Baby's Own Soap, Best For Baby, Best For You, Embossed, Unused, Canada 20.00
Bond Bread, Lone Ranger Safety Club, 1939, 3 1/2 x 5 1/2 In. .... *Illus* 75.00
Dame, Stoddard & Co., 1906, 3 1/2 x 5 1/2 In. 16.50
Dame, Stoddard & Kendall, Fishing Tackle, Dog Collars, c.1889, 3 x 5 1/8 In. 28.00
Darn-Saver Guaranteed Hose, 2 Pair, 25 Cents, Metropolitan Museum, 1915 .... 5.00
Fall Winter Millinery, Howard Barnes, Harrisburg, Huntington, Vermont, 1910 .... 28.00
Fleetwood Cover Service, Eisenhower, Queen Elizabeth II, 1952 .... 28.00
Gold Red Cross Shoes, Woman On Phone, 1947 .... 30.00
Hall Furniture & Upholstery, The Library, September Calendar, Vermont, 1913 .... 30.00
Hayes Hosiery, A.C. Webber, Albert Line Of 100 Hose, c.1898, 3 x 5 1/2 In. 10.00
Horrocks Ibbotson Co., Fisherwoman, 1921, 5 1/2 x 3 3/8 In. 44.00
J. Stevens Arms & Tools, Chicopee Falls, Mass., 1906, 6 1/2 x 3 3/4 In. 1650.00
Keen Kutter, Simmons Hardware, Ax Head, 1902, 3 1/4 x 5 1/2 In. 115.00
Keen Kutter, Workers, Multicolored Front, Black & White Back, 1909, 3 1/2 x 5 1/2 In. . 55.00

Poll Parrot, Sign, Steel, Multicolored Enamel, Outlined In Green Neon, c.1950, 24 In.

Postcard, Bond Bread, Lone Ranger Safety Club, 1939, 3 1/2 x 5 1/2 In.

Malvern's World's High Class Shooting Star, 6 1/4 x 3 5/16 In. 84.00
Old Town Canoe, Maine, Couple Paddling Canoe, 1908, 3 1/2 x 5 1/2 In. 44.00
Our Farmer's Fence Company, Bellefontaine, Ohio, Sepia Photograph, 5 1/2 x 3 1/4 In. . . 25.00
Post Cereal Club House, Battle Creek, Michigan, 3 1/2 x 5 1/2 In. 9.00
Radio City, Hollywood, NBC & CBS Studios, 1951 .... 15.00
Rice Rupture Cure Factory, Adams, N.Y. 25.00
United Art Publishing, Glossy View Portrait, Lover's Lane, Mayville, Wisc., 1908 ...... 15.00

POSTER   Sometimes it is difficult to differentiate between a poster and a sign. For the purposes of this book, a poster is a lithographed or printed piece of paper at least 10 inches by 12 inches, but more likely 20 inches by 30 inches. Included are posters advertising circuses, transportation and travel, and war propaganda. Movie posters can be found in the Movie category. Other posterlike materials are listed under Sign or by brand name.

2nd Liberty Loan, Uncle Sam, Paper Lithograph, Frame, 20 x 30 In. 770.00
2nd Liberty Loan Of 1917, Boy, Girl, 29 1/4 x 19 1/2 In. 127.00
American Airlines, Cubistic Tourist, E.M. Kauffer, 1948, 30 x 40 In. 1000.00
Arizona, America's Greatest Play, 1908, 49 x 28 In. 715.00
Auburn Wagon Co., Race Track Scene, c.1880, 16 x 24 In. 358.00
Babbitt's Best Soap, Girl With Kitten, Lithograph, 1896, 36 x 22 In. 440.00
Bachelor's Baby, Etienne Girardot, Strobridge Litho Co., 1909, 20 In. 77.00
Ben-Hur, Strobridge Co., 1910, 30 x 20 In. 143.00
Bill Lynch Shows Greater Exposition, Circus Scenes, Erie Lithograph, 1930s, 27 x 41 In. 110.00
Bond Bread, Jackie Robinson, At Home, Mat, Frame, 1947, 21 1/2 x 17 3/4 In. 1495.00
Bruni-Plage, French Perfume, Cardboard, Art Deco Style, France, c.1934, 10 x 14 In. 125.00
Buck & Bubbles Laff Jamboree, Red, White, Blue, 41 x 27 In. 220.00
Buffalo Pitts Co., Quality Machinery, Indian, Buffalo, Stone Litho., Frame, 26 x 20 In. . . 8800.00
Bunco In Arizona, Billy Craver & Bucking Pony, Early 1900s, 28 x 42 In. 1485.00
Bunco In Arizona, Richard Henderson, American Show Print Co., Early 1900, 42 x 28 In. 688.00
C&J Clark's Dainty Shoes, Woman Admiring Shoes In Mirror, Frame, 24 x 16 1/2 In. 38.00
C.F. Orvis Fine Fishing Tackle, Mill, Angler & Sweetheart, Frame, 14 1/2 x 21 In. 3080.00
Carson & Barnes Circus, Paper, 44 x 22 In. 66.00
Carter The Great, Beats The Devil, Ottis Lithograph, Cardboard, 22 x 14 In. 77.00
CIL Munitions, Bull Moose, Easel Back, French Words, 27 x 21 In. 116.00
Clear The Way, Buy Bonds Fourth Liberty Loan, Niagara, N.Y., 29 1/2 x 19 1/2 In. 136.00
Columbia Batteries, Paper, National Carbon Co., Cleveland, 29 x 19 In. 5775.00
Coopers Dipping Powder, To The Rescue, Sheep Dog, Lamb, Ram, England, 21 x 16 In. . 180.00
Cremo, Sports Flash, Sparkling Ale, Jackie Robinson, 1946, 17 x 14 In. 575.00
Custer's Last Fight, Otis Litho. Co., Cleveland, Ohio, Early 1900s, 41 x 27 In. 853.00
Dailey Bros. Circus, Animals & Trainer, Paper Lithograph, Frame, 12 3/4 x 15 3/4 In. ... 176.00
Delaware Rubber Co., Washington Crossing Delaware, Embossed, c.1900, 20 x 26 In. ... 259.00
Dewar's White Label Whisky, Stag, Monarch Of Glen, England, Frame, 24 x 21 1/2 In. . . 151.00
Donald Duck Bread, Donald, His Nephews, Loaf Of Bread, Black, White, 22 x 17 In. ... 165.00
Dr. Horne's Electric Belt, $20 Belt For $6.66, 2-Sided, Broadside, c.1901, 9 x 12 In. 93.00
Fly TWA, Rome, Stylized Vatican Guard, David Klein, c.1960, 25 x 40 In. 225.00
Fly TWA Jets, Los Angeles, Sun, Mission, Doves, David Klein, c.1959, 25 x 40 In. 425.00
Franklin Automobile, Charles Lindbergh, Frame, Broadside, 27 1/4 x 40 1/2 In. 201.00
Girl Of The Golden West, David Belasco's Great Play, 1906, 29 1/2 x 20 In. 963.00
Gradon & Koehler Druggists, Portland, Oregon, 19 1/2 x 15 In. 358.00
Ham Tree, McIntyre & Heath, World's Greatest Dancing Chorus, 1913, 30 x 20 In. 66.00
Heaney The Famous Magician, In Person, Paper, 22 x 13 1/2 In. 83.00
Heddon Lone Eagle, Fishing Reel, No. 206, Die Cut, c.1930, 15 x 8 In. 1264.00
Hey Kids!, Bardahl, 5 T-Shirts, 4 Oil Filter Villians, c.1955, 11 x 22 In. 45.00
Hindenburg, Zeppelin Airship, Heavy Paper, 1930s, 31 x 45 3/4 In. 4070.00
Homenta For Headaches, Coughs & Cararrh, Black Man, Articulated, 20 x 15 In. 14300.00
Inter-Tribal Indian Ceremonial, Gallup, New Mexico, 1936, 22 x 14 In. 345.00
International Colic Remedy, Horses, Cures Colic In 10 Minutes, Paper, 16 x 22 In. 1375.00
International Hoof Ointment, Horse, Hoof Graphics, Paper, 16 x 22 In. 880.00
International Worm Powder, Horse, Paper, 16 x 22 In. 1100.00
Jacob Hoffman Brewing Co., Oriental Brewery, Flowers, Wine, Cigar, 31 x 21 In. 88.00
JE Ranch Rodeo, Lakeside Park, Rodeo Scenes, 1929, 41 x 14 In. 605.00
Kellar, Man, Devils, Dragon, Bats, Strobridge Litho Co., 1897, 29 x 38 In. 3795.00

Little Shop Of Horrors, Mounted On Cardboard, Broadway, 72 x 42 In. 275.00
Marshall-Burr & Co., Girl, Blond Curls, Bonnet, Omaha, Neb., Frame, 14 x 21 In. 209.00
McCormick Harvesting Machine, Chromolithograph, Frame, 25 x 32 In. 690.00
Money In Bank Takes No Vacation, Where A Man's A Man, Goodwin, 1924, 15 x 22 In. . 154.00
New Hampshire, Land Of Scenic Splendor, Parrish, Frame, c.1936, 32 1/4 x 23 1/4 In. . . . 578.00
Parker Watts Circus, Kit Carson, Oak Frame, 26 x 41 1/2 In. 121.00
Phantom Of The West, Stairway Of Doom, 1910, 41 x 27 In. 1100.00
Prince Albert, The National Joy Smoke, Indian Chief Holding Pipe, 27 x 22 In. 1100.00
R. & G.A. Wright Perfumery, Mat, Frame, 15 x 17 1/2 In. 66.00
Red Belt Cigar, Lady, Red Dress, c.1920, 20 x 16 In. 770.00
Regina Music Boxes, 19 Different Models, Broadside, Late 1800s, 17 x 22 In. 250.00
Scribner's Magazine, Linen Backed, Parrish, Frame, April 1899, 27 1/2 x 19 3/4 In. 990.00
Seagram, Spirit Behind Grand National, 4 Winning Horses, England, Frame, 16 x 16 In. . 38.00
Seils & Sterling Circus, 3 Men, Tigers, Paper Lithograph, 41 x 28 In. 55.00
Snag-Proof, Lambertville Rubber Co., Paper, 25 x 17 In. 2090.00
Stanley Tool Chest, Christmas Morning, Pasteboard, c.1925, 18 1/2 In. 418.00
Stetson, The Last Drop From His Stetson, Horse Drinking, Cowboy's Hat, 31 x 24 In. . . . 908.00
Strouse & Brothers, Baltimore, Md., High Art Styles Spring, Summer, 1913, 16 x 20 In. . 150.00
Sun Valley Idaho, Gretchen Fraser, Skiers, Mountains, Shepler, 1948, 25 x 39 In. 1350.00
Swiss Air To Europe, Airplane, Mountain, Fisherman, Fritz Buhler, c.1955, 25 x 40 In. . . . 375.00
Thurston, World's Famous Magician, Baltimore, Cardboard, 1920s, 14 x 22 In. 500.00
Topps Baseball Cards, 1975, 17 x 24 In. 345.00
Topps Baseball Picture Cards, Bob Feller, Thin Stock, 1953, 11 x 6 3/4 In. 1610.00
Travelers Insurance, America's Top Newspaper Editors, Mat, Frame, 1882, 27 x 30 In. . . 55.00
Uncle Tom's Cabin, Elizas Escape From The Tavern, 42 x 28 In. 209.00
World's Champion Rodeo, Real Indian War Dance, Wood Frame, 1910, 56 x 21 In. 773.00

POTLID Potlids are just that—lids for pots. Transfer-printed potlids
had their heyday from the 1840s to the early 1900s. The English
Staffordshire potteries made ceramic containers with decorated lids for
bear's grease, shrimp or meat paste, cold cream, and toothpaste.
Printed advertising and pictures of historical events, portraits of
famous people, or scenic views were designed in black and white or
color. Reproductions have been made.

Almond Shaving Cream, Henry Bell, Waterford, Round, England, 3 In. 112.00
Anchovy Paste, Blue Transfer, Round, London, 3 1/2 In. 65.00
Areca Nut Tooth Paste, Saunders, Trees, Mosque, Round, Liverpool, England, 2 3/4 In. . 153.00
Atkinson's Rose Cold Cream, Round, London, 2 1/4 In. 20.00
Bale's Mushroom Savoury, 3 Mushrooms, Brown Transfer, Round, England, 3 1/2 In. . . . 225.00
Base, Cherry Tooth Paste, Beautifying & Preserving, Pottery, Round, England, 3 1/4 In. . . 368.00
Base, Golden Eye Ointment, Contents, Round, England, 1 3/4 In. 41.00
Base, Oriental Toothpaste, J&E Atkinson, Pyramids, Camels, Round, London, 3 1/4 In. . . 102.00
Cherry Tooth Paste, Crown Perfumery, Round, London, 2 3/4 In. 61.00
Cherry Tooth Paste, John Gosnell & Co., Round, England, 3 1/4 In. 35.00
Cherry Tooth Paste, Paris, Londres, Round, 2 3/4 In. 164.00
Cherry Tooth Paste, Thompson Millard & Co., Round, London, 2 3/4 In. 266.00
Fortnum & Mason's Mushroom Savory, Round, England, 3 1/2 In. 184.00
Pansalia Shaving Cream, Delicately Scented, Round, London, 3 In. 266.00
Thornton's Anthracoline, Pink Ground, Pottery, Leamington, Round, England, 3 1/2 In. . 245.00
Trouchet's Corn Cure, Safe, Reliable, Lighthouse, Round, Red Print, England, 2 In. 102.00
W.R. Roberts, Cold Cream Of Roses, Rusholme, Round, England, 2 1/2 In. 55.00
White Cherry Tooth Paste, S. Maw Son & Thompson, Round, London, 2 1/2 In. 61.00
White Rose Tooth Paste, England, Square, 2 1/2 In. 55.00

POTTERY & PORCELAIN Almost any type of pottery, porcelain, and
glass could have been made with an advertisement as part of the
design. Listed here are items such as bowls, jugs, pitchers, etc. More
ceramic and glass items are listed under Plate or by brand name.

Beaker, Mitchell & Butlers, Deer Leaping, Good Honest Beer, Ceramic, 4 In. 162.00
Bowl, Adams Feed & Hatchery, Storm Lake Iowa, Watt, Apple, No. 600 . . . . 70.00
Bowl, Farmers Lumber Company, Watt, Clutier, Iowa . . . . .50.00 to 55.00
Bowl, Hotel Clavendon, J.D. Moskowitz Co., Daytona, Shenango China, 7 x 5 1/2 In. 12.00
Bowl, Renville Co-Op Creamery, Renville, Minn., Watt, Starflower, No. 7 . . . . 55.00

Bowl, Salad, Olson Grain Co., Wilmont, Minn., Watt, Apple, No. 73 .... 85.00
Bowl, Salad, Pelican Rapids, Minn., Watt, Apple, No. 73 .... 65.00
Bowl, Willie Wirehand, Raised Image, Indian Electric Co-Op, Frankhoma, 7 1/2 In. 80.00
Calendar Plate, Julius M. Finck Co., Rabbits, San Francisco, Goodwin, 1911, 8 In. 232.00
Calendar Plate, Oriental Drug, Chanute, Kansas, Children Swimming, Verse, 1910, 6 In. . 59.00
Calendar Plate, W.H. Rowe Coal & Wood, Black Man Eating Melon, 1915, 7 3/4 In. 138.00
Creamer, Farmers Co-Op Creamery Milaca, 1907-1955, Watt, Starflower, No. 62 .... 145.00
Creamer, Fitz's Hatchery & Produce Ivanhoe, Minn., Watt, Apple, No. 62 .... 85.00
Creamer, Kiel Hardware 1957 Pease, Minn., Watt, Apple, No. 62 .... 185.00
Creamer, Lake Benton Hatchery Dutch & Chuck Phone 245, Watt, Apple, No. 62 .... 95.00
Creamer, Manannah Store Grove City, Minn., Watt, Rooster, No. 62 .... 185.00
Creamer, Onida Electric Paul-Bob-Ethel-Gladys, Watt, Apple, No. 62 .... 65.00
Creamer, Penhans Garage Shell Sales-Service, Avon, Minn., Watt, Rooster, No. 62 ..... 65.00
Creamer, Ryan Grain & Feed Bird Island, Watt, Apple, No. 62 .... 85.00
Creamer, Schori & Kuster Lbr. Co. Elgin, Iowa, Watt, Apple, No. 62 .... 85.00
Creamer, Winnebago Co-Op Creamery, Just A Little Thank You, Watt, Apple, No. 62 .... 95.00
Crock, Grover Farms Butter, Stoneware, 2 Lb., 6 x 3 1/2 In. 35.00
Crock, Poison, Swift's Arsenate Of Lead, Merrimac Chemical, Boston, 1/2 Gal. 59.00
Cup, Alcoa, Demitasse, Warwick China, 1946, 2 1/2 In. 14.00
Cup, Continental Coffee, Coffeepot Graphic, Mayer China, Beaver Falls, Pa., 1940-1960 . 32.00
Cup & Saucer, Robinhood Caterers, Arrow, Restaurant Ware, Tepco China, 1940s-1950s . 28.00
Cuspidor, Monogram Cigar, 10 Cents, Porcelain On Tin, 5 x 11 In. 880.00
Cuspidor, Plumbers Supplies, Shuster Foundry Co., Philadelphia, Porcelain, 5 x 8 In. 303.00
Dish, Eagle Furniture & Co., 2 Sides Up, Carnival Glass, Amethyst 1100.00
Dish, Golliwog, Air Canada, Royal Doulton, England, 4 x 4 In. 49.00
Dish, Gum, C.T. Heisel Chewing Gum, Embossed, Glass, Cleveland, Ohio, 5 1/2 x 4 In. .. 85.00
Dog Dish, Hudson's Soap, Cast Iron, Nickel Plated, Drink Puppy Drink, 8 1/4 x 16 x 7 In. 689.00
Eggcup, Chicken, Fanny Farmer, Porcelain, Yellow, 1940s, 2 1/2 x 3 1/2 In. 28.00
Eggcup, Eat Michigan Eggs, Japan, 2 1/2 In. 35.00
Eggcup, Fanny Farmer, Chicken Shape, Yellow, 1940s, 2 1/2 x 3 1/2 In. 28.00
Jug, 1996 Commemorative Iowa Society, Brown & White, 4 1/2 In. .... *Illus* 34.50
Jug, Bottlers' Supplies, Brown Top, Stoneware, Red Wing, 1/2 Gal. 116.00
Jug, Colfax Mineral Water Co., Stoneware, Blue Shield, 5 Gal., 17 In. 834.00
Jug, Compliments Of John Keller & Co., Fashion Saloon, Jerome, Ariz., 1/2 Pt. 2200.00
Jug, Compliments Of Reichert & Austgen, Denver, Colorado, 1890-1915, 3 1/8 In. 448.00
Jug, Cream Of Old Scotch Whiskey, Bonnie Castle, England, 1890-1915, 8 1/2 In. 202.00
Jug, Delmonico Rye & L & A Scharff Distillers, Gray, Stoneware, Cobalt Stamp, 3 In. ... 115.00
Jug, Fort Dodge Stoneware Co., Beehive Shape, 4 Gal., 15 1/2 In. 460.00
Jug, Hochstadter's Eachter Alter Nordhauser Kornbranntwein, Stoneware, c.1900, Qt. 59.00
Jug, Jas. Gioga, Goldfield, Nevada, Blue Ink, Glazed Clay, c.1910 .... 6038.00
Jug, Johnnie Walker, Seated, Limited Edition, Percy Metcalf, 14 3/4 In. 1619.00
Jug, Mackinlay's Whisky, Ceramic, Mottled Green, Brown, Presentation Box, England ... 89.00
Jug, McCormick Distilling Co., 100 Proof Straight Corn Whiskey, Stoneware, 1/2 Pt. 10.00
Jug, New England Tomato Relish, Pilrim Couple, Skilton, Foote & Co., 7 x 4 1/2 In. 110.00
Jug, O.L. Gregory Vinegar Co., Elko County, Pure Apple Juice Vinegar, 3 1/4 x 2 In. 85.00
Jug, Wm. Radam's Microbe Killer, 111 Oxford St., Man Beating Skeleton, 1889, 11 In. .. 99.00
Jug, Worthington, Lord Mayor, Behind Every Great Man, Handle, Green Label, 9 In. 180.00
Jug, Worthington, Lord Mayor, Behind Every Great Man, Handle, Red Label, England, 9 In. 132.00
Mixing Bowl, Tri-County Chickery Cedar Mills, Minn., Watt, Rooster, No. 8 .... 65.00
Pie Plate, Buffalo Lake, Minn., Watt, Apple, No. 33 .... 60.00
Pie Plate, Compliments Of Murdock Farmers Elev., Watt, Apple, No. 33 .... 80.00
Pie Plate, Elroy Co-Op Dairy, Elroy, Wisc., Watt, Apple, No. 33 .... 100.00
Pie Plate, Haugen-Johnson Impl. Allis Chalmers Benson, Minn., Watt, Apple, No. 33 .... 125.00
Pie Plate, Kingston Co-Op Dairy Ass'n & Feed Mill, Watt, Apple, No. 33 .... 105.00
Pie Plate, Plaza Park State Bank Established 1910, St. Cloud, Minn., Watt, Apple, No. 33 95.00
Pie Plate, Seasons Greetings Edinburg Farmers Elev. Co., Watt, Apple, No. 33 .... 145.00
Pie Plate, Seasons Greetings Howard Lake, Minn., Watt, Apple, No. 33 .... 70.00
Pitcher, Baker Equip., Monticello, Minn., Watt, Apple, No. 15 .... 85.00
Pitcher, Beemer Lumber Co., Beemer, Nebraska, Watt, No. 15 .... 94.00
Pitcher, Christmas 1955 Figge-Nelson Annandale, Minn., Watt, Starflower, No. 15 ...... 115.00
Pitcher, Cokato Co-Op Creamery, Watt, Apple, No. 15 .... 75.00
Pitcher, Compliments Of Gibson Farm Supply, Watt, Starflower, No. 15 .... 75.00

Pitcher, Compliments Of Rahs Produce, Waldorf, Minn., Watt, Rooster, No. 15 ....   105.00
Pitcher, Cornfield Auto Chevrolet, Dysart, Iowa, Watt, Cherries, No. 15 ....   165.00
Pitcher, Dollys Garage, New Auburn, Minn., Watt, Apple, No. 15 ....   85.00
Pitcher, Farmers Co-Operative Creamery Ass'n, Fair Haven, Minn., Watt, Apple . . .95.00 to 125.00
Pitcher, Fred Sorenson Lory Brunberg, Watt, Apple, No. 15 ....   55.00
Pitcher, Goodman Plumbing Heating & Wiring Jamestown, N.D., Watt, Apple, No. 15 ...   50.00
Pitcher, Kiel Hardware, Pease, Minn., Watt, Apple, No. 15, 1954 ....   125.00
Pitcher, Krebsbach Phillip 66 Petroleum Products St. Joseph, Minn., Watt, Apple, No. 15 .   135.00
Pitcher, Langes Grade A Dairy Producs, Watt, Rooster, No. 15 ....   65.00
Pitcher, Let Us Serve You, Cockato Co-Op Creamery, Cokato, Minn., Watt, Apple 125.00
Pitcher, McKleveen Lumber Co., Building Material & Coal, Rumells, Iowa, Watt, No. 15   77.00
Pitcher, Pink Roses, Louisville, Gold Lettering, Kentucky, Germany 10.00
Pitcher, Tang, Crisscross Pattern, Lid, 1960-1970 ....   11.00
Platter, Black Entertainment Television, Soundstage, Oval, Homer Laughlin, 15 1/2 x 11 In.   15.00
Platter, Central Creamery, 25 Years, Iroquois China, Syracuse, 1945, 13 In. 48.00
Platter, Sparks' Kidney & Liver, Mrs. Grover Cleveland, Porcelain, 16 1/2 x 11 1/4 In. ..   88.00
Poultry Feeder, Ko-Rec Feeder, Red Wing Stoneware 110.00
Pub Jug, Allsopps, Red Hand, 2 Men, Royal Cauldon, 5 In. 81.00
Pub Jug, Anchor Blend, Scotch Whisky, Wade Regicor, 4 1/4 In....................   81.00
Pub Jug, Cognac Martell Brandy, Man, Monocle, Figural, Lancaster & Sandland, 6 1/2 In.   85.00
Pub Jug, Cutty Sark, Scotch Whisky, Sailing Ship, Yellow Ground, H.C.W., 5 In. 55.00
Pub Jug, Dewar's, White Label Scotch Whisky, John Maddock & Sons, 3 1/2 In. . . . .44.00 to 65.00
Pub Jug, Gladstone, For The Million, Clear Glass, Embossed, 3 3/4 In. 31.00
Pub Jug, Grant's Stand Fast Whisky, H.C.W., 3 1/2 In. 65.00
Pub Jug, Haig, Fine Old Scotch Whisky, Beige Ground, Carltonware, 6 1/4 In. 20.00
Pub Jug, Jamie Stuart, Liqueur, Scotch, 5 1/2 In. 364.00
Pub Jug, Jim Beam, Mr. Pickwick, Royal Doulton, 3 3/4 In. 44.00
Pub Jug, Johnnie Walker, Born 1820, Still Going Strong, Square, 5 3/4 In. 34.00
Pub Jug, Johnnie Walker, Born 1820, Still Going Strong, Scotch Whisky, 6 1/4 In. 20.00
Pub Jug, King George IV, Old Scotch Whisky, Orange Ground, Shelley, 4 1/2 In. 81.00
Pub Jug, King George IV, Old Scotch Whisky, Wage Regicor, 4 1/4 In. 70.00
Pub Jug, King's Legend, Ainslie's Scotch Whisky, White Ground, 4 1/4 In. 91.00
Pub Jug, Mitchells & Butlers, Good Honest Beer, Yellow, Orange, 4 1/4 In. 105.00
Pub Jug, O.V.H., Greers 10 Years Old Whisky, Man's Head, 6 In. 132.00
Pub Jug, Ross's, Belfast, Ginger Ale, Mustard Glaze, 3 1/4 In. 61.00
Pub Jug, Sandy MacDonald, Special Scotch Whisky, Wade Regicor, 4 1/2 In. 102.00
Pub Jug, Simonds Reading, Pale Ales & Stout, 6 In. 152.00
Pub Jug, Take A Peg Of John Begg, Blue Ground, 6 In. 101.00
Pub Jug, Threlfall's Blue Label Ale, Adams Titian Ware, 4 1/2 In. 193.00
Pub Jug, Watney's Ales, Brown Ground, Royal Doulton, 4 1/4 In. 152.00
Pub Jug, White Horse Whisky, Coat Of Arms, Shelley, 5 In. 202.00
Pub Jug, William Younger's, Get Younger Every Day, Royal Doulton, 4 1/2 In. 111.00
Pub Jug, William Younger's, Scotch, Ale, Oi Be 101, Royal Doulton, 4 1/2 In. 132.00
Pub Jug, Wills's Gold Flake Cigarettes, Yellow Ground, 4 1/2 In. 61.00
Pub Jug, Worthington, Figural, Mayor, Behind Every Great Man, Green Label, 9 In. 264.00
Pub Jug, Worthington, Figural, Mayor, Behind Every Great Man, Red Label, 9 In. 222.00
Punch Bowl & Cups, Old Crow Punch, Porcelain, Verse, 8 x 13 In., 9 Piece 358.00
Saltshaker, Ivory Salt, Cardboard, Worcester Salt Company, New York City, 2 1/4 x 1 In. .   95.00
Saltshaker, White Villa Garlic Salt, Glass, Paper Label, 4 x 1 1/2 In. 58.00
Sugar Bowl, Joe Miller Land O'Lakes Janesville, Minn., Watt, Apple, No. 98 ....   175.00
Sugar Bowl, Kiel Hardware 1959 Pease, Minn., Watt, Apple, No. 98 ....   205.00
Tankard, O.V.H. Whiskey, Man's Head, Pink Cheeks & Nose, Assoc. Potteries Co., 6 In. .   28.00
Toby Jug, Charrington, Toby Ale, Green Jacket, Maroon Pants, 7 1/4 In. 91.00
Toothpick Holder, Norma's Cafe, Galva, Illinois, Stoneware, 2 x 2 3/4 In. 45.00
Toothpick Holder, Millersburg Glass Co. Founded 1909, Marigold, Carnival Glass 45.00

PREMIUM   Many radio shows, such as *Captain Marvel, Captain Mid-*
night, Davy Crockett, and *Orphan Annie,* gave premiums for box tops
and small amounts of cash. Today, all of these premiums are collected.

Button, Renfrew Of The Mounted, Pinback, Wonder Bread, 1936, 1 1/4 In. 13.65
Cake Decorating Kit, Swans Down Cake Mix, Football, 1950s 16.00
Decoder Badge, Little Orphan Annie, Brass Crossed Keys, 1935 ....   26.00

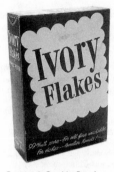

| Pottery, Jug, 1996 Commemorative Iowa Society, Brown & White, 4 1/2 In. | Procter & Gamble, Box, Ivory Flakes, Moon Logo, 12 3/4 Oz., 30 Cents | Putnam Dyes, Cabinet, General Putnam On Horse, Redcoats, Tin, Countertop, 15 x 19 x 8 In. |

Decoder Badge, Little Orphan Annie, Sunburst, 1937 . . . . .15.00 to 26.00
Decoder Badge, Tom Mix, 6-Gun, 9 Code Words, Brass, 1941 . . . . 22.00
Measuring Cup, Swans Down Cake Flour, Aluminum, 1 Cup 18.00
Ring, Lone Ranger, Saddle, Cheerio's 53.00
Ring, Lone Ranger, Silver Bullet 36.00
Ring, Secret Agent, Lookaround, Slits in Crown, Mirror Inside, 1940s 521.00
Telescope, Jack Armstrong, Explorer, Metal, Black Paper, 6 3/4 In. Closed 20.00
Train, Cocoa Puffs, Tin, Windup, General Mills, Mail Away, 1959, 12 In. 116.00

PROCTER & GAMBLE   Procter & Gamble was founded by brothers-in-law William Procter and James Gamble in 1837. They made soap and candles in Cincinnati, Ohio. James N. Gamble, the founder's son, developed a white bar soap in 1879. While sitting in church, Harley Procter, James N. Gamble's cousin, was inspired by a verse in the 45th Psalm: "All thy garments smell of myrrh and aloes and cassia out of the ivory palaces whereby they have made thee glad." He named the white soap "Ivory." Ivory was distinctive not just for its color, but also because it floated. Proctor & Gamble realized the sales potential of a floating soap and began advertising it as "99 44/100% Pure, It Floats." Ivory was advertised with outdoor posters (claimed to be the first use of this type of ad for a product), magazine and newspaper ads, bar labels, and door-to-door samples. The Procter & Gamble trademark was inspired by a cross mark used by wharf hands to label boxes of P&G's Star candles in 1851. This evolved into the man-in-the-moon and stars trademark found on most Procter and Gamble products until 1985. The trademark has been updated many times, most recently in 1991. Procter & Gamble has sold many other products through the years—Crisco (1911), Oxydol (1927), Duz (1929), Dreft detergent (1933), Drene shampoo (1933), Tide (1946), Joy liquid detergent (1949), Cheer (1950), Gleem (1952), Crest (1955), Comet (1956), Zest (1952), Jif (1956), Duncan Hines (acquired in 1956), Mr. Clean (1958), White Cloud (1958), Charmin (acquired in 1957), Fluffo (1953), Puffs (1960), Downy (1960), Pampers (1961), Head & Shoulders (1961), Folgers (acquired in 1963), Bounty (1965), Scope (1965), Gain (1966), Pringle's Potato Chips (1968), Sure antiperspirant (1972), Pert Plus (1986), Febreze (1998), and more. P&G acquired Gillette in 2005.

Box, Dreft Detergent, Unopened, 1940s-1950s, 15 Oz., 8 1/2 x 6 x 2 1/8 In. 15.00
Box, Ivory Flakes, Moon Logo, 12 3/4 Oz., 30 Cents . . . . *Illus* 5.00
Box, Ivory Soap, Box, 18 x 5 In. 66.00
Cookbook, Crisco, New Recipes For Good Eating, 1948 . . . . 8.00
Figure, Mr. Clean, Vinyl, White Outfit, 1961, 8 In. 48.00
Hand Puppet, Dopey, Rubber Head, Cotton Body, Polka Dots, Ivory Snow, 1960s 38.00

PRUDENTIAL INSURANCE The Prudential Insurance Company of America was founded by John F. Dryden in 1875. The famous service mark, the Rock of Gibraltar emblazoned with the legend "The Prudential Has the Strength of Gibraltar," was first used in 1896. The legend was removed and the rock modernized in 1970. The slogan "Get a Piece of the Rock" was introduced at the same time and was used until 1995. Prudential Insurance Company is now part of Prudential Financial, Inc. The Rock continues as the company's logo.

Bank, George Washington Bust, White Metal Cast, 6 In. 143.00
Calendar, 1902, Victorian Lady, Black Hat, Frame, 15 x 17 In. 138.00
Needle Holder, Woman Holding Baby, Foam, Cardboard, Oval, 2 1/2 x 1 1/2 x 1/4 In. .9.00 to 10.00
Needle Threader, Prudential Has Strength Of Gibraltar, 5 Needles, 2 3/4 In. 6.50
Needle Threader, Prudential Has Strength Of Gibraltar, Rock Sketch, Tin 9.00
Sign, Branch Office, Porcelain, 14 x 20 In. 385.00
Thimble, Aluminum 15.00
Thimble, Silver, Raised Letters 5.00

PUTNAM DYES Edward N. Monroe bought a drugstore in Unionville, Putnam County, Missouri, in 1876. He and Earl Cummins began making dyes they sold in the drugstore as Putnam Fadeless Dye. Monroe married and had three children. His son Neal and his daughter Octavia's husband later worked for the company. The dye was popular during World War I because of the shortage of imported dyes from Europe. By the end of the war, the company was also making Putnam Dry Cleaner and Putnam Oil. In 1966 the company's name, Monroe Chemical Company, was changed to Putnam Dyes, Inc. The family sold the business in 1974 and it went bankrupt in 1976. Collectors search for the Putnam Dye cabinets, fans, and trade cards.

Cabinet, Fadeless, Each Package Colors Wool, Silk, Cotton, 11 x 15 x 8 In. 220.00
Cabinet, Fadeless, Monroe Drug Co., Metal Front, 21 x 10 x 8 In. 66.00
Cabinet, General Putnam On Horse, Redcoats, Tin, Countertop, 15 x 19 x 8 In. . . . . . . *Illus* 143.00
Cabinet, Man, On Horse, White, Metal, 28 x 11 In. 248.00
Cabinet, Secret Of Charm Is Color, For Tinting, Dyeing, 11 x 16 x 8 In. 165.00
Cabinet, Tin Lithograph Front, Display, 10 x 21 In. 248.00
Cabinet, Tints, Tin Lithograph, 19 x 15 In. . . . . .59.00 to 104.00
Fan, 4 Generations Of Putnam Good Will, Founder, Great Granddaughter, 8 x 6 3/8 In. . . . 65.00
Fan, General Putnam Escapes From British Dragoons, Lithograph, 8 1/2 x 6 1/2 In. . .29.00 to 60.00
Fan, Proud Peacock, Lithograph, 7 1/4 x 6 1/4 In. 55.00
Trade Card, Little Miss Muffet, Sides Fold Back, 3 3/4 x 5 3/4 In. 8.00
Trade Card, Rabbit With Wheel Barrow, Filled With Eggs, 3 3/8 x 5 7/8 In. 7.00

PUZZLE In the late 1800s, companies began to use all types of puzzles, including jigsaw, dexterity, disentanglement, and sequential movement, to advertise their products. The jigsaw (also called dissected) puzzle was a popular eighteenth-century toy. Early jigsaw puzzles were made of soft wood or of paper backed with thin mahogany. They were much less expensive after 1880 because a die was invented that could cut the entire puzzle from a sheet of cardboard. Many companies used two-sided jigsaw puzzles as premiums. One side was an ad, and the other side an entertaining picture. Early mechanical puzzle premiums were made of cardboard and string, wood, and metal. More recently, advertising puzzles have been made of plastic.

American Airline, A Greeting From The Air, Jigsaw, c.1940, 13 x 9 1/2 In. 35.00
American Store Co., Woman & Horse, Jigsaw, Frame, 15 x 12 In. . . . . *Illus* 55.00
Borax, Hauling 20 Mule Team Borax Out Of Death Valley, Jigsaw, 1933, 10 1/2 x 8 In. . . 35.00
BP Energol, Race Car, Cardboard, Jigsaw, Wrapper, 4 1/4 x 5 3/4 In. 73.00
Carnival, Walrus, 2 Metal Balls, 1 1/2 In. Diam. 14.00
Columbian Metal Garage, Drive In-Do It Now, Black, Tin, Metal Balls, 2 In. 45.00
Dr. Jayne's Expectorant, Bottle Shape, Attached Malady, Remedy Paddles, Jigsaw, 5 1/2 In. 44.00
Dr. Jayne's Expectorant, Die Cut, Tin Lithograph, Bottle Shape, Jigsaw, 5 3/8 x 1 3/4 In. . 55.00
Keen Kutter, E.C. Simmons, St. Louis, Jigsaw, Box, 12 x 9 1/2 In. 682.00
Mr. Softee, Shakes-Sundaes, 3 Metal Balls, Plastic, 1 1/2 In. Diam. 12.00

Puzzle, American
Store Co., Woman
& Horse, Jigsaw,
Frame, 15 x 12 In.

Quaker Oats, Doll,
Puffed Rice, Puffy, Soldier,
Cloth, Uncut, c.1930,
17 1/2 x 16 1/2 In.

Rexall Milk Of Magnesia Tooth Paste, Tom Mix, Paper, Jigsaw, Frame, 125 Piece	83.00
Sohio Standard Oil, In Dutch, No. 2, Jigsaw, Box, 1933, 11 x 14 1/2 In.	30.00
Sunshine Biscuits, Birds, Nest, Hand Held, Dexterity, Round, 1 3/4 In.	161.00
White Sewing Machine, Between Glass, Jigsaw, Frame, 1883, 16 x 18 In.	165.00

QUAKER OATS   Henry Seymour and William Heston started an oatmeal milling company in Ravenna, Ohio, in the 1870s. In 1877 this
firm, named Quaker Mill Company, registered the Quaker man trademark, the first registered trademark for a breakfast cereal. The oats
were first sold in bulk, then in 1885 they were packaged in smaller
square boxes. The trademark continued after Quaker Mill Company
was sold and merged with at least two other mills to form the Quaker
Oats Company in 1901. The famous round Quaker Oats box was introduced in 1915. The Quaker man logo has been redesigned three times;
in 1946, 1957, and 1972. Since 2001 Quaker has been a division of
PepsiCo, Inc. Other Quaker brands include Aunt Jemima (listed under
its own heading in this book), Rice-a-Roni, Life cereal, and Mother's
Natural Foods (formerly Mother's Oats).

Bowl, Instant Oatmeal, It's Hot, Plastic, 1992	4.00
Box, Quick Mother's Oats, Lithograph Paper, 1930s-1940s, 1 Lb. 4 Oz.	14.00
Button, Box, Try Me, 30 Days, Celluloid, Pinback, 1 1/4 In.	28.00
Canister, Snausages, Smiling Dog, Orange, Plastic, 1991, 9 1/4 In.	25.00
Container, Scotch Brand Oats, Cardboard, Paper Label, Chicago, 9 1/2 x 5 1/2 In.	165.00
Cookie Jar, Regal China, 9 1/2 x 5 1/2 In.	125.00
Display, Babe Ruth, Puffed Rice, Puffed Wheat, Cardboard, 1930s, 15 1/2 x 19 3/4 In. ...	4313.00
Doll, Puffed Rice, Puffy, Soldier, Cloth, Uncut, c.1930, 17 1/2 x 16 1/2 In. .... *Illus*	50.00
Flip Book, Quaker Rolled White Oats, 1903	85.00
Notebook, Mother's Crushed Oats, Pan-American Exposition, Celluloid, 2 1/2 x 1 1/2 In. ..	66.00
Sign, Today The Dionne Quints Had Quaker Oats, Paper On Linen, 1935, 15 x 32 In.	83.00
Tin, 1896 Oatmeal Box Design, Limited Edition, 1984, 8 1/4 In.	15.00
Tin, Limited Edition, 1983, 4 1/4 x 7 1/4 In.	10.00
Transistor Radio, Miniature Quick Quaker Oats Container, Paper Cover, 5 In.	30.00
Whistle, Bosun's, Captain Crunch, Dog, Red, White, Hard Plastic, 1960s, 1 x 3 In.	33.00

RADIO PREMIUM, see Premium

RAILROAD   Railroadiana of all sorts is collected. Items include advertising signs and premiums as well as actual items used by the railroads.
Emblem-marked dishes, oilcans, uniforms, and similar pieces are
included.

Ashtray, Chesapeake & Ohio, Porcelain, Divided, Silhouette, Syracuse China, 7 3/8 In. ..	125.00
Ashtray, Pullman Company, Bakelite, 2 Cigar & 2 Cigarette Holders, 5 1/2 In.	65.00
Ashtray, Pullman Company, Bakelite, Brown, Orange & Black Specks, 5 1/2 In.	65.00
Calendar, Great Northern, Indian Man, Roll Down, Partial Pad, 1943, 33 1/2 x 16 In.	143.00
Calendar, Great Northern, Indian Woman, Roll Down, Partial Pad, 1943, 33 1/2 x 16 In. ..	143.00
Calendar, Missouri Pacific Railroad, Perpetual, 19 x 12 5/8 In.	325.00
Celery Dish, Milwaukee Road Traveler, Syracuse China, c.1947, 9 3/4 x 4 5/8 In.	165.00

Gravy Boat, Seaboard Air Line, Green Stripes, China, 10 1/2 x 3 3/4 x 4 3/4 In. 30.00
Hand Towel, Pullman Train Car, Linen, Property Of Pullman Company, 24 x 16 1/4 In. . . 17.50
Plate, Milwaukee Road Traveler, Geese, Syracuse China, 10 1/2 In. 150.00
Plate, Missouri Pacific Lines, Flower Border, 10 1/2 In. 220.00
Postcard, Florida East Coast Railway, Train, Key West Extension, Harris, c.1912 . . . . 45.00
Postcard, Hotel De China, Central Pacific, Worker's Hut, Master Photographers, No. 28 . 2.00
Postcard, West End Of Great Northern Railway Yards, Breckenridge, Minn., 1908 . . . . . . 33.00
Poster, Brotherhood Of Railroad Union, Paper, Frame, 32 1/2 x 25 1/2 In. 358.00
Poster, Orient Express, Victoria Station, London, Linen Back, 1985, 12 x 19 In. 260.00
Poster, Societe Nationale Des Chemins De Fer Francais, France, 1938, 40 x 25 In. 1160.00
Sign, Chicago & Alton Railroad, Cardboard, Frame, c.1910, 15 x 39 In. . . . . .635.00 to 775.00
Sign, D.L. & W. Railway, Do Not Deposit Cloths, Cigars, Matches, Porcelain, 2 x 5 In. . . 330.00
Sign, Lackawanna Railroad, Danger High Voltage, Red, White, Blue, Porcelain, 9 x 12 In. . 303.00
Sign, Not To Trespass, Philadelphia & Reading Railway Co., Porcelain, 7 x 10 In. 330.00
Sign, Railway Express Agency, 3 Strips, Porcelain, Early 1900s, 28 In., 3 Piece 385.00
Sign, Railway Express Agency, Porcelain, Black, Yellow, 72 x 11 1/2 In. 115.00
Sign, Railway Express Agency, Red, White, Porcelain, Diamond, 11 x 11 In. 152.00
Sign, Railway Express Agency, Tin, Cardboard, 13 x 19 In. 2530.00
Sign, Railway Express, Porcelain, 6 x 20 In., 2 Piece 110.00
Sign, Seaboard Coast Line Railroad Equipment Trust, Steel, 5 1/2 x 36 In. 19.00
Sign, Southern Railroad, Green & White, Premium, Tin, 3 In. 18.00
Sign, Southern Railway, Smoking Strictly Prohibited, Enamel, England, 16 1/2 x 12 In. . . 132.00
Stock Certificate, 10 Shares, Fort Street & Elmwood Railway Co., Michigan, 1866 . . . . . 125.00
Thermometer, Canadian-Pacific, Porcelain, 36 In. 7425.00
Timetable, Chicago To Milwaukee, 1962, 4 x 2 1/2 In. 1.50
Timetable, Nickel Plate Road Of New York, Chicago, St. Louis, Oct. 30, 1955, 9 x 4 In. . . 6.00

RALSTON William H. Danforth joined George Robinson and William Andrews in 1893 to start a business making horse and mule feed. The Robinson-Danforth Commission Company was formed in 1894 and used the slogan, "Cheaper Than Oats and Safer Than Corn." In May 1896, one day after Danforth purchased Andrews' share, a tornado destroyed the mill. Danforth borrowed enough money to rebuild. In 1898, after meeting a miller who had developed a process to keep wheat germ from turning rancid, Danforth began making a cracked wheat product he marketed as Purina Whole Wheat Cereal. A Dr. Ralston, who had gained fame from a book he wrote about health, agreed to endorse Purina cereal if the cereal were renamed Ralston Wheat Cereal. The cereal's name was changed, and by 1902 the names Ralston and Purina were so well known that the company was renamed Ralston Purina. The red and white Checkerboard trademark has been used since 1902. Many Checkerboard items, including Ralston Breakfast Food, Purina Whole Wheat Flour, and Purina Pancake Flour, were sold and given away at the 1904 St. Louis World's Fair. The word "Chow," taken from military slang, was used as the company's trademark for animal feed after 1914. In 1921 a new form of feed in cubes was named Checkers. Wheat Chex was introduced in 1937. Purina Dog Chow brand dog food was sold starting in 1957. The company purchased and sold many companies, including Bremner Biscuit (1978, spun off 1994), Continental Baking (1984, sold 1995), Eveready Battery (1986, spun off 2000), Beech-Nut (1989, spun off 1994), and Golden Cat Corp. (1995). It spun off its cereal business in 1994. In 2001 the company merged with a Nestlé subsidiary to become Nestlé Purina PetCare Company.

Advertisement, Tom Mix Radio Program, Paper, Child Life Magazine, March, 1935 . . . . 21.00
Bandanna, Tom Mix, On Horseback, Red Border, Premium, 16 1/2 x 16 1/2 In. . . . . *Illus* 85.00
Book, Mother's Manual, Health-Growth & Happiness For Boys & Girls, 1926 . . . . 25.00
Bowl, Cereal, Checkerboard Pattern On Outside, 1930s 225.00
Box, Instant Ralston, It's Daddy's Favorite Too, Premium Offer On Back . . . . *Illus* 375.00
Coloring Book, Pictures In TV Frames, 1950s 12.00
Gun, Tom Mix, Straight Shooter, Wood, Break Open Top, Revolving Cylinder, 9 In. 140.00
Illustration, Boys Flexing Muscles, Difference Appetite, F.T. Hunter, 1932, 13 x 10 In. . . 15.00
Insert, Paper, Tom Mix & 2 Friends On Horses, NRA Symbol, 1933 . . . . 59.00

Ralston, Bandanna,
Tom Mix, On Horseback,
Red Border, Premium,
16 1/2 x 16 1/2 In.

Ralston, Toy, Lario, Tom Mix,
Purple Crepe Paper, Thrower
String, Weight, Premium

Ralston, Box, Instant Ralston,
It's Daddy's Favorite Too,
Premium Offer On Back

Mug, Milk Glass, Checkerboard Pattern 22.00
Photograph, Tom Mix, Straight Shooters, Signed, Checkerboard Frame, 5 x 3 In. 91.00
Sack, Flour, Ralston's Best, Milled & Guaranteed, 19 x 10 1/2 In. 12.00
Sign, Purina Dog Chow, Cardboard, Die Cut, Folding, Countertop, 15 3/4 x 26 In. 605.00
Tin, Make-Up, Tom Mix, Straight Shooters, TM Logo, Checkerboard Border 22.28
Toy, Lario, Tom Mix, Purple Crepe Paper, Thrower String, Weight, Premium . . . . *Illus* 50.00

RCA, see Victor

RED GOOSE SHOES Herman Gieseke and two partners founded the
Gieseke-D'Oench-Hayes Shoe Company in St. Louis, Missouri, in
1869. Mr. Gieseke needed a trademark for his shoes and used Goose
Key, a play on his name. The original goose was white with a large key
in its mouth. In 1907 the goose became red, the key was removed, and
the name and symbol were registered. Red Goose shoes have been
advertised in all media since 1907. Television was being used by 1948.
A popular premium was the Red Goose Golden Egg dispensed at the
store by the Red Goose Egg Machine. The brand was later made by the
International Shoe Company, a division of Interco, Inc. The division
ceased operations in 1987. In 1996 Interco, by then out of the shoe
business, became Furniture Brands International.

Bank, Turnpin, Cast Iron, Arcade, 3 3/8 In. 193.00
Calendar, 1924, Getting His Goat, H.C. Edwards, 8 x 19 In. 77.00
Clicker, Duck Bill Large, 1 3/4 x 5/8 In. 145.00
Clicker, Duck Bill Small, 1 7/8 x 5/8 In. 165.00
Display, Figural, Composition, Nodding Head, Countertop 770.00
Figure, Goose, Chalk, Painted, 11 1/2 x 5 1/4 x 8 In. 290.00
Pencil, Mechanical, Unused, Instructions, L.C. Porter, Autopoint Better Pencils 24.00
Shoes, Baby's, Leather, White, Box, Vintage, Marked Lid, Rita's Second Pair Of Shoes . . 25.00
Sign, Children Running, Embossed Celluloid, c.1910, 11 x 13 1/2 In. . . . . .900.00 to 1300.00
Sign, For Boys & Girls, Mullins Hardware, Salt Lick, Ky., Tin, Embossed, 10 x 20 In. . . . 148.00
Sign, Goose Shape, Neon, 23 In. 523.00
Sign, It's Always Go, Die Cut, Cardboard, 40 x 30 In. 303.00
Sign, Neon, 40 In. 875.00
Sign, Porcelain, 2-Color Neon, c.1950, 36 In. 880.00
Sign, Red, Yellow, 2-Sided, Enameled, Metal, Flange, 16 x 10 In. 493.00
Sign, Red, Yellow, Porcelain, Neon, 36 x 22 In. . . . . .1430.00 to 2500.00
Stringholder, Goose, Die Cut, Tin Lithograph, 2-Sided, 27 1/2 x 17 In. . . . . .1760.00 to 2640.00
Thermometer, Finest & Best, Porcelain, Friedman & Shelby, 27 In. . . . . *Illus* 467.00
Whistle 54.00

REDDY KILOWATT It was 1926 and Ashton B. Collins Sr., a general
commercial manager for the Alabama Power Co., needed to market
electricity to people who were not yet comfortable with the mysterious

Reddy Kilowatt, Bowl & Cup, White, Red Figure, Red Border, 1950s, Bowl 4 3/4 In.

Red Goose Shoes, Thermometer, Finest & Best, Porcelain, Friedman & Shelby, 27 In.

Reddy Kilowatt, Fan, Keep Cool, Cook Electrically, Cardboard, Die Cut, Balsa Handle, 9 In.

power. So Collins created Reddy Kilowatt, a character with lightning-bolt limbs, a light-bulb nose, and a very big smile. In 1933 Reddy Corporation International (RCI) was formed and the character was licensed to the Philadelphia Electric Company, the first of over two hundred local power companies to use it. In 1998 Reddy Kilowatt was purchased by Northern States Power Company (now Xcel Energy). Reddy now has a brother, Reddy Flame, a character that represents natural gas.

Ashtray, Glass, Applied Portrait, 1950s, 3 1/2 x 5 In.	10.00
Ashtray, Round	19.00
Ashtray, West Penn Power	18.00
Bib, Little Bo Peep, Little Boy Blue, Cloth, 9 1/2 x 7 1/2 In.	65.00
Bowl & Cup, White, Red Figure, Red Border, 1950s, Bowl 4 3/4 In. .... *Illus*	25.00
Button, Ohio Edison, Celluloid, Parisian Novelty, 3 1/4 In.	60.00
Button, Pinback, Round, 7/8 In.	55.00
Cup & Saucer, Syracuse China, 3 x 4 1/2-In. Cup, 6-In. Saucer	95.00
Display, 3-D, Talking, Microphone, Speakers, Transportation Crate	2600.00
Fan, Keep Cool, Cook Electrically, Cardboard, Die Cut, Balsa Handle, 9 In. ...... *Illus*	20.00
Fan, Slogans, Die Cut Cardboard, Balsa Handle, 8 1/4 x 9 In.	20.00
Figure, Glow, Plastic, 1940s, 5 x 1 1/2 x 3 In.	90.00
First Aid Kit, Plastic, Red Bottom, White Lid, Contents, c.1960, 2 3/4 x 3 1/2 In.	30.00
Golf Ball Set, Titlist, Box, 1980s, 3 Piece	40.00
Key Chain Flashlight, Plastic, Brass, Unopened, c.1960, 3 In.	24.00
Mail Promotion, Boston Edison, Unopened, 1965, 3 x 3 x 6 1/2 In.	10.00
Memo Case, Plastic, Metal Reddy Figure, Autopoint, c.1950s, 4 x 6 1/2 In.	15.00
Sign, Die Cut Vinyl Outline, Neon, White Enamel Metal, 1970s, 36 In.	6500.00
Sign, Flameless Electric Kitchen, Star Shape, 33 x 31 In.	180.00
Soup, Dish, Ceramic, Maroon Image, Syracuse China, 1960s, 6 1/2 x 1 3/4 In.	24.00
Stove Pad, Table Of Weights & Measures, Tin Lithograph, c.1950s, 7 x 7 In.	8.00
Switch Plate, Hand Painted, On Blister Card, Made In USA, c.1960, 4 1/2 x 5 In.	30.00
Thimble, Runs Out Of Electric Socket, Plastic, Yellow, U.S.A., 7/8 In. ....6.00 to 10.00	
Toy, Spinner, Jones, Peterson & Newhall Children's Play Shoes	55.00

REMINGTON Eliphalet Remington made a flintlock rifle in Ilion, New York, in 1816. His gunsmith business grew, and in 1845 he signed a contract with the U.S. government for five thousand rifles. His sons, Philo, Samuel, and Eliphalet Jr., joined him in a new company, E. Remington & Sons, in 1865. Remington developed many improved guns. In 1888 Marcellus Harley and partners acquired and reorganized the company as the Remington Arms Company. In 1912 the company combined with the Union Metallic Cartridge Company, becoming Remington U.M.C. Peters Cartridge Company was purchased in 1934. Remington was a wholly owned subsidiary of E.I. Du Pont from 1980 until 1993, when it was sold to RACI Acquisitions.

Booklet, Remington Firearms, Geese Flying, 1930s, 32 Pages, 4 x 7 In. 44.00

Booklet, UMC, Red Leather, Price Lists, 1909, 5 3/4 x 3 In. 66.00
Bottle, Rem-Oil, UMC, Embossed, 5 x 1 3/4 In. 110.00
Bottle, Remington UMC Powder Solvent Oil, Embossed, 1 1/2 x 5 x 1 1/4 In. 31.00
Box, Express, Long Range, 12 Gauge, Contents 24.00
Box, Remington UMC, Nitro Club, Loaded Paper Shells, 24 Gauge, Unopened 702.00
Box, Typewriter Ribbon, Lady, Sitting At Vanity, 1934 .... 10.00
Box, UMC, .22 Automatic Rifle, Model 1903, Contents, 1 1/2 x 2 3/4 In. 127.00
Box, UMC, Central Fire Cartridges, .40 Caliber, 50 Grain, Creedmoor, 1 Cartridge 157.00
Box, UMC, Nitro Express Shot Gun Cartridges, 1915, 2 1/2 x 2 1/2 x 2 In. 55.00
Brochure, Model 30 Express Rifle, Hunter With Moose Call, 6 x 3 1/2 In. 44.00
Brochure, Rider Revolver, Self-Cocking, Frame, Bifold, 1860s 275.00
Button, Remington Autoloading, Rifle, Oval, Whitehead & Hoag, 1 In. 221.00
Button, Shoot .22 Lesmok Cartridges, Remington UMC, 7/8 In. 61.00
Button, Shoot Remington UMC Arrow Or Nitro Club Shells, Phelps & Sons, 7/8 In. 140.00
Calendar, 1912, Going In, Goodwin, 20 1/2 x 14 3/4 In. 2697.00
Calendar, 1925, Let'er Rain, Hunter In Boat, 15 x 28 1/2 In. .... *Illus* 358.00
Calendar, 1928, Hunter, In Cabin, Dog, Fireplace, 27 1/2 x 15 In. 403.00
Calendar, 1928, Old Man, Guns, Dog, Fireplace, March Sheet, 27 1/2 x 15 In. 575.00
Case, Remington Arms & Shells, Curved Glass, Chicago Made 523.00
Counter Felt, Remington UMC, Big Game Cartridges, Ram, 4 Colors, 14 x 12 In. 194.00
Display, Electric Shaver, Flip-Up Mirror, Light-Up, 19 x 16 In. 5.50
Display, Floor, UMC, Wetproof Shells, Die Cut, 3 Panels, Lynn Bogue Hunt 2021.00
Display, Nitro Club Game Load, Quail, Die Cut, Easel, Countertop, 10 1/2 x 10 1/2 In. 446.00
Display Case, Cutlery, 36 Sections, Wood, Velvet, c.1922, 11 x 16 x 15 In. 311.00
Display Case, Hi-Speed .22's, Wood, Glass, 16 1/4 x 10 x 6 1/4 In. 180.00
Knife, Trademark, Office Knife, Bone Handle, 2 Blades 65.00
Oiler, Rem-Oil, Tin, Lead Screw Cap, Oz., 3 1/2 In. 52.00
Oiler, Work Men Wrap Around, Red, Yellow, Black, 5 x 2 1/4 In. 34.00
Poster, Guns, Flying Mallard, Shotguns, Shells, Frame, Mat, c.1928, 22 x 17 In. 4851.00
Poster, Insist Upon UMC. Shells, Hands Reaching For Shell Boxes, 27 1/2 x 7 In. 889.00
Poster, Kleanbore .22 Ammunition, Boy Aiming Gun, Easel, Die Cut, 32 x 25 1/2 In. ... 550.00
Poster, Metallic Cartridges, Animals, Bullets, Die Cut, Easel Back, 14 1/4 x 12 1/4 In. 440.00
Poster, Redhead Ducks, Solid Breech Hammerless, 1908, 18 3/4 x 29 7/8 In. 6353.00
Poster, This Jap Crashed, Doughboy Got Him, Perfect Ammunition, c.1942, 17 x 22 In. .. 350.00
Poster, UMC Cartridges, Man Shooting Cougar, Everett Johnson, 1906, 16 x 24 1/2 In. .. 633.00
Poster, UMC Cartridges, Rifle, Wolf, Die Cut, Hanging, c.1910, 13 x 9 1/4 In. 840.00
Poster, UMC, 2 Men Examine Gun, Hunting Dog, 18 x 26 1/2 In. 726.00
Poster, UMC, 2 Men, Canoe, Bear, N.C. Wyeth, c.1930, 17 1/4 x 26 1/4 In. 3960.00
Poster, UMC, Bear At Campsite, American Lithograph Co., 1919, 23 1/2 x 14 1/2 In. 748.00
Poster, UMC, Black Powder, Bear, Cardboard, Easel Back, Countertop, 12 x 12 In. 578.00
Poster, UMC, Shot Shells, Flying Quail, 1908, 15 x 29 1/4 In. 1790.00
Poster, UMC, Smokeless Powder Shot Shells, Puppies In Pockets, 1904, 24 3/4 x 15 In. . 3137.00
Sign, Game Loads, 4 Game Birds, Die Cut, Stand-Up, Frame, 10 7/8 x 28 1/4 In. 919.00
Sign, Kleanbore Shells, Puppy, Die Cut, Cardboard, J. Clinton Sheperd Illustration, 35 In. .. 468.00
Sign, Kleanbore, .22 Cartridges, Smiling Boy Scout, Die Cut, 32 1/8 x 23 1/4 In. 495.00
Sign, Kleanbore, Sporting Rifles, 2 Guns, Buck, Cardboard, Easel Back, 13 x 31 In. 210.00

Remington, Calendar,
1925, Let'er Rain,
Hunter In Boat,
15 x 28 1/2 In.

Royal Crown Cola,
Thermometer, Tin
Lithograph,
Embossed, 13 In.

Don't store fabrics in plastic bags. Use a well-washed white pillow case. Plastic holds moisture, and the fabrics should "breathe."

Sign, Most Famous Name In Shooting, 12 x 24 x 4 In. 121.00
Sign, Pheasants, Die Cut, Cardboard, Lynn Bogue Hunt Illustrations, 34 In. 275.00
Sign, Sheath Knives, 2 Fishermen, DuPont, Easel Back, Die Cut, 15 1/2 x 16 1/2 In. 910.00
Sign, Sportsman's Equipment, Shell Box, Sault Sainte Marie, Mich., Tin, 10 x 28 In. 1000.00
Sign, UMC Cartridges, Hunter, Bear, Die Cut, Easel Back, c.1917, 15 x 10 1/4 In. 1733.00
Sign, UMC Shells, Nitro Club, Arrow, New Club, Die Cut, 12 x 12 In. 660.00
Sign, UMC, Big Horn Sheep, Cardboard, Easel Back, L.B. Hunt, 7 1/2 x 10 1/2 In. 347.00
Sign, UMC, Dog, Die Cut, Easel Back, 3-D Front, 13 x 16 3/4 In. 2334.00
Sign, UMC, Firearms, 2 Cowboys On Cliff, H.C. Edwards, 26 x 18 In. 6600.00
Sign, UMC, Rifle, Shooting Gallery Cartridges, Tin, Flanged, 23 1/8 x 17 3/4 In. 6602.00
Sign, UMC, Woman Hunter, Model 12 Rifle, .22 Cartridges, Die Cut, 14 1/2 x 18 3/4 In. . 495.00
Sign, Woman With Shotgun, Rifles & Shotguns, Die Cut, 1901, 10 1/2 x 16 In. 1272.00
Thermometer, Cutlery, Famous Razor Sharp Edges, Blue, Yellow, Porcelain, 39 x 8 In. .. 853.00
Thermometer, Cutlery, Remington DuPont, 39 x 8 In. 198.00
Trade Card, Got 'im, Boy Holding Rat, 3 1/4 x 8 1/2 In. 235.00
Trade Card, Hit The Mark, Boy, Barn Doors, Dead Rat, Mechanical, Unused 289.00

ROYAL CROWN COLA   Claud Hatcher of the Hatcher Grocery Company of Columbus, Georgia, started making Royal Crown Ginger Ale and other flavored drinks in the early 1900s to sell in his family's wholesale grocery business. Sales grew and Hatcher and his father founded the Union Bottling Works in 1905, adding Chero-Cola to their product line. The company was reorganized and renamed the Chero-Cola Company in 1912. It issued franchises to bottlers to produce Chero-Cola, Royal Crown Ginger Ale, and a fruit-flavored drink called Melo. Nehi, introduced in 1924, has a girl's leg as a trademark. The story behind the trademark is that in the early 1920s Hatcher sent one of his salesmen across the river to see what the competition was up to. The salesman returned to report that the competition was "only knee-high." The firm changed its name to the Nehi Corp. in 1928. Royal Crown Cola was first sold in 1934. Customers were soon calling it RC. The company's advertising during the 1940s often featured entertainment celebrities, such as Bing Crosby, Joan Crawford, and Hedy Lamarr. "Best by Taste Test" was adopted as the company's slogan in 1940. The firm became the Royal Crown Cola Company in 1959. Diet Rite Cola was introduced in 1961. The corporate name was changed to Royal Crown Companies, Inc., in 1978. Cadbury-Schweppes acquired the RC Cola brand in 2000 and made it part of its Dr Pepper/Seven-Up subsidiary.

Bottle Opener, Better Taste Calls For RC 5.00
Calendar, 1947, Joan Caulfield, December, 11 1/2 x 25 In. 204.00
Calendar, 1950, Woman, Bottle, Full Pad, Starts December 1949, 24 x 11 In. 77.00
Carrier, 6-Pack, Embossed, Aluminum, c.1940 .... 77.00
Door Push, Porcelain 303.00
Menu Board, Best By Taste Test, Tin, Embossed, Slate, 1948, 27 x 19 In. 138.00
Scale, Coin-Operated, Bottle Shape, Cast Iron Base, 45 In. 1045.00
Sign, Best By Taste Test, 2-Sided, Tin, Die Cut, 1940, 16 x 24 In. 255.00
Sign, Better Taste Calls For RC, Red & White, Tin, 28 x 20 In. 77.00
Sign, Bottle Shape, Tin Lithograph, Die Cut, Embossed, 30 x 7 3/4 In. ....124.00 to 385.00
Sign, Bottle Shape, Tin, Die Cut, 11 x 3 In. 138.00
Sign, Bottle Shape, Tin, Die Cut, 58 x 15 1/2 In. ....143.00 to 330.00
Sign, Bottle Shape, Tin, Self-Framed, 16 x 36 In. 99.00
Sign, Bottle, Metal Over Wood, Self-Framed, 36 x 16 In. 275.00
Sign, Diet Rite Cola, Sugar Free, Tin, 18 x 54 In. 143.00
Sign, Drink Royal Crown Cola, Tin, 18 x 54 In. 27.50
Sign, Drink Royal Crown Cola, Tin, Embossed, Frame, 11 x 18 1/2 In. 138.00
Sign, Drink Royal Crown Cola, White, Red, Blue, Tin, Embossed, 12 x 32 In. 110.00
Sign, Highballs, Smooth, Reverse Painted Glass, Foil Back, c.1935 .... 2750.00
Sign, Santa Singing, Merry Christmas, Paper, No. 213, 1960s, 24 x 13 1/4 In. 55.00
Sign, Tin, Die Cut, 2-Sided, 1941, 16 x 24 In. 770.00
Sign, Tin, Embossed, Self-Framed, 16 x 36 In. 220.00
Sign, Tin, Flange, 2-Sided, 10 1/2 x 18 In. 330.00
Thermometer, Bottle, Logo, Tin, 13 1/2 x 5 3/4 In. 66.00
Thermometer, Embossed Bottle, 13 1/2 x 6 In. 121.00

Thermometer, Red, Yellow Arrow, 1957, 26 x 10 In. . . . . .232.00 to 253.00
Thermometer, Sheet Metal, Painted, 25 In. 121.00
Thermometer, Tin Lithograph, Embossed, 13 In. . . . . *Illus*   220.00

SALT & PEPPER All types of salt and pepper shakers are collected. Of special interest to advertising collectors are sets that depict objects, such as the milk glass set shaped like General Electric dome-topped refrigerators or the Lenox porcelain set shaped like Nipper, the Victor dog. Other sets include the name of an advertised product as part of the design. Most salt and pepper sets date from after the 1920s. Because many are available, collectors want only perfect examples with no chips or paint flakes.

Anthracite Bit Co., Rotary Bits, Oil Centennial, Plastic, 1959, 3 In. 125.00
Ballantine Ale, Cardboard, Metal Lids, Box, 2 3/8 In. 19.00
Dairy Queen Girls, Authorized Set, Japan, 4 In. 195.00
Fort Pitt Beer, Glass, Label . . . . *Illus*   12.00
Green's Milk & Ice Cream, White Plastic, Green Logo, 4 In. 22.00
Handy Flame, Blue, 4 In., Pair 40.00
Ken-L-Ration, Dog & Cat, Plastic, F & F Mold & Die Works, c.1960, 3 1/2 In. 18.00
Koehler Beer, Bottle Shape, 4 In. 28.00
Monk, McWilliams Moselle Wine, Japan, 3 1/2 In. 95.00
Old Gunther Beer, Bottle Shape, Glass, Metal Lids, Foil Labels, Mini, 4 In. 28.00
Peerless Beer Men, LaCrosse Breweries, Hartland Plastic, 5 In.   95.00
Red & White Food Stores, Plastic, 1950s, 1 3/4 In. 12.00
Stein's Canadaigua Beer & Ale, Bottle Shape, Glass, Metal Lids, Buffalo, N.Y., 4 In. 25.00
Sunshine Bakers, Pottery, White, Black Shoe Tips & Eyes, 2 1/2 In. . . . . *Illus*   35.00
Tuborg & Carlsberg Beer, Bottle Shape, Glass, Wooden Stand, Metal Lid, 2 1/2 In. 29.00

SAMPLE For obvious reasons, salesmen could not carry full-size stoves, washing machines, lawnmowers, and other appliances to potential customers, so small, exact replicas of the machines were made. These were not toys. Less-detailed replicas of home appliances were sometimes made as toys. Salesman samples also exist for smaller items like pitchers and shovels. Also included in this category are displays that contain product samples, such as hosiery. Sample-size tins and boxes given away to encourage a customer to try a product can be found in the Box, Tin, Coffee, and Tobacco categories.

Hanes Absolutely Ultra Sheer Hosiery, 14 Samples, Cardboard Tags 28.00
Buck Saw, Henry Disston & Sons, Wooden Frame, 13 1/2 x 15 1/2 In. 220.00
Canoe, Otter Canoe Co., Wanakena, New York, 39 In. 2350.00
Manhole Cover, Cast Aluminum, Valve & Hydrant Co., 5 In. 358.00
Mannequin, Man, Suit, Red Tie, Traveling Case, 1921 Patent, 30 In. . . . . *Illus*   2530.00
Meilink Safe, Stencil, Handle, 9 1/2 x 14 In. 1320.00
Stove, Simmons Wilson 316, Cast Iron, 18 x 7 1/4 In. 6600.00

Salt & Pepper, Fort Pitt Beer, Glass, Label

Salt & Pepper, Sunshine Bakers, Pottery, White, Black Shoe Tips & Eyes, 2 1/2 In.

Sample, Salesman's, Mannequin, Man, Suit, Red Tie, Traveling Case, 1921 Patent, 30 In.

SAPOLIO Sapolio was the first commercial scouring powder made in the United States. It replaced sand and imported English Bath Brick. Sapolio was introduced in 1868 by Enoch Morgan Sons, a company that had made soap since 1809. Introducing the public to a totally new product involved elaborate and novel advertising. In 1892 Captain William Andrews was hired to sail alone from Atlantic City to Spain in a 14-foot sloop named Sapolio. He went to "repay Columbus's visit" and to promote the cleaning product. Spotless Town, one of the most famous trademarks of advertising, was introduced a few years later. Spotless Town pictures were accompanied by limericks that caught the public's fancy. One was: "In Spotless Town they got a bore/Who slyly spat upon the floor/They washed his mouth as white as snow/With water and SAPOLIO./If you don't expect his fate/You must not Expectorate." By World War I, the name Sapolio was so well known that it was close to becoming the generic name for scouring powders. It is no longer sold in the United States, but the Sapolio name is used on cleaning products made by the Peruvian company Intradevco.

Clicker, Clean Up, Celluloid, 1 1/4 In.	120.00
Sign, Because The Housewife Didn't Use Sapolio, Porcelain, Blue, White, 3 x 32 In.	990.00
Trade Card, Ange Dechu Statuette, Fallen Angel, Paris Exhibition Prize, 5 1/2 x 2 3/4 In. .	6.00
Trade Card, Cracked Open Watermelon Shape, Die Cut, c.1882, 4 x 2 3/4 In.	38.00
Trade Card Booklet, Modern Household Fairy, Metamorphic, 1880s, 12 Pages	95.00

SCHLITZ "The Beer That Made Milwaukee Famous" is Schlitz. The company that made the beer opened in 1849 when August Krug built a brewery and hired a bookkeeper named Joseph Schlitz. When Krug died in 1856, Schlitz became manager. He later married Krug's widow, and by 1874 the company name was changed to the Jos. Schlitz Brewing Company. A year later, Mr. and Mrs. Schlitz left on a trip to Germany and drowned when their ship sank. Krug's nephews, August, Henry, Alfred, and Edward Uihlein, took over management of the brewery. The "Famous" slogan dates from 1871, when Schlitz sent free beer to the waterless Chicago residents after that city's big fire. Schlitz was purchased in 1982 by Stroh's, which was purchased by Pabst (listed in its own category in this book) in 1999. Schlitz and Schlitz Malt Liquor brands are still marketed by Pabst.

Banner, Schlitz Famo, Thirst Quenching, Non-Intoxicating, Cloth, Frame, 22 x 57 In.	452.00
Bottle, Stand, Have A Bottle Now, Electric, Light-Up, Display, 1950, 19 3/8 In.	366.00
Paperweight, Jos. Schlitz Brewing Co., Factory Scene, c.1890-1905, 3 In.	300.00
Salt & Pepper, Bottle Shape, Amber Glass, Metal Lids, 4 In.	25.00
Sign, Beer That Made Milwaukee Famous, Soldier, Tin, Self-Framed, 19 x 8 3/4 In.	1045.00
Sign, Cone-Top Can, Opens Like A Bottle, Light-Up, 17 x 6 1/2 In.	468.00
Sign, Never A Bitter Note, Singing Bird, Tin Lithograph, Cardboard, Beveled, 16 x 11 In. .	112.00
Sign, No Bitterness, Just Kiss Of The Hops, Composition, Embossed, 1950s, 11 x 17 In. . .	33.00
Sign, Old Heidelberg, Girl On Keg, Altoplaster, Frame, c.1938, 36 1/2 x 22 In.	300.00
Sign, Schlitz Tonic, Beveled, Tin Lithograph Over Cardboard, 1920s, 9 1/4 x 13 1/4 In. . .	84.00
Tray, Ah Isn't Schlitz Always Good, Man, Beer, Woman, Tin Lithograph, Round, 24 In. . .	715.00
Tray, Serving, Beer That Made Milwaukee Famous, Tin, Round, 1954, 12 In.	36.00

SCHRAFFT'S W.F. Schrafft and Sons, The Boston Candy Company, was founded in 1861. In 1898, shortly after salesman Frank G. Shattuck began to work with the Schraffts, he created the first Schrafft's Candy and Ice Cream Shop on Broadway in New York City. Meals were added to the menu, and eventually Schrafft's Restaurants and Motels became a chain from Boston to Los Angeles. The chain also sold baked goods, candy, ice cream, and frozen foods. Though no longer owned by the Schrafft family, some Schrafft's brand products can still be found. The Schrafft's Ice Cream shop is a popular stop at the New York–New York Hotel & Casino in Las Vegas, Nevada.

Advertisement, Gay Bouquet, Paper, From Saturday Evening Post, 13 1/2 x 10 1/2 In. . . .	6.00
Box, Brass, Engraved, Woman In Sedan Chair, Carried By Servants, 7 1/2 x 5 x 2 In.	40.00
Box, Brass, Woman In Litter, Carried By 2 Men, Cardboard Insert, c.1935, 7 x 10 x 2 In. .	16.00

Box, Chocolate Covered Cherries, Cardboard, 6 1/2 x 4 x 2 1/2 In.	12.00
Box, Woman, Pink Victorian Dress, Hat, 1 Lb., 13 x 5 1/2 In.	121.00
Display Rack, 5 Cent, Slanted Compartments, Black Metal, Gold Letters, 12 x 9 In.	154.00
Tin, Cover, Round, Passaic Metal Ware Company, 4 x 7 1/2 In.	30.00
Tin, Schrafft's Chocolates, Hinged Top, 1 Lb., 8 x 2 1/4 x 5 In.	32.00

SEARS   Richard Sears was an agent of the Minneapolis and St. Louis railway station in North Redwood, Minnesota, in 1886. A load of watches without a buyer arrived at the station and Sears purchased it. He sold the watches to other station agents and made a profit. He ordered more watches, and in 1886 began the R.W. Sears Watch Company in Minneapolis. The next year he moved to Chicago and advertised for a watchmaker. Alvah C. Roebuck answered the ad and was hired. Sears advertised his watches in weekly rural papers and soon offered other jewelry. He sold guaranteed merchandise at a low price and convinced farmers to buy by mail. Sears sold out to Roebuck several times, but kept returning. In 1893 the company became Sears, Roebuck and Company. By then, it published a 196-page catalog. In 1895 Julius Rosenwald bought into the company and became vice president. Sears was president, and Roebuck, who was ill, resigned. The company sold stock in 1906 and has been publicly owned since. The mail-order business expanded. The catalog had a grocery section from 1896 to 1929, and the company sold many foods under its own brand name. Branch offices and plants were opened. Retail stores were opened in 1925. In 1931 the company founded the Allstate Insurance Company, which became a separate company in 1995. In 1985 the company introduced the Discover Card. Sears has over two thousand retail locations in the United States. The "big book" catalog was discontinued in 1993, but Sears still has specialty catalogs and offers online shopping. In 2004 Sears and Kmart announced plans to merge and form a new company, Sears Holdings Corporation.

Box, Mallard Sportload Shotgun Shells, 20 Gauge, 3 3/4 x 3 3/4 In.	44.00
Box, Sport Loads Mallard Shotgun Shells, Smokeless Powder, 12 Gauge, 4 x 4 x 2 1/2 In.	143.00
Bucket, Garland Blend Coffee, Tin, Bail Handle	550.00
Button, Sears Wishes You A Merry Christmas, Santa Claus, Celluloid, 1 3/4 In.	50.00
Canister Set, Cracked Chicken, Chick Emerging From Shell, Japan, 1976, 4 Piece	33.00
Catalog, Electric Belt, 1901, 7 3/8 x 5 1/4 In., 56 Pages	88.00
Honing Stone, World's Largest Store, Celluloid, 2 1/4 In.	145.00
Mirror, Our Merchandise Must Be Right To Bear This Guarantee, Black, Red, 1930s, 2 In.	35.00
Needle Book, A Gift To You From Kenmore, Japan	7.00
Needle Book, Kenmore, Fine Needle Work, Needle Packet, Japan	7.00
Rack, Catalog, Tin Lithograph, Wood Grain, 16 In.	110.00
Radio, Clock, Silvertone, Plastic, Pink, AM, 14 x 5 x 7 In.	85.00
Salt & Pepper, Snowdome, America's Largest Selling Washers, Dryers, 1960s, 2 3/4 x 4 In.	95.00
Tin, Berriman's Hand Made Havana Specials Cigars, 5 x 3 7/8 In.	62.00
Tin, My Baby's Talcum, Sears Roebuck & Co., 6 x 2 1/8 x 1 1/4 In.	176.00 to 350.00
Tin, Roasted Coffee, 11 x 16 In.	253.00
Tip Tray, Sears, Roebuck & Co., Chicago, Building, Tin, Oval, 4 1/2 x 6 In.	11.00
Tray, Sears, Roebuck & Co., Chicago, 6 x 4 3/8 In.	180.00

SEVEN-UP   Charles Grigg and coal merchant Edmund Ridgway started the Howdy Corp. in St. Louis, Missouri, in 1920. They sold an orange and lemon drink predictably called Howdy. At first it was sold in a plain 6 1/2-ounce bottle, but by 1928 it was marketed nationally in a unique bottle embossed with the name. Howdy Ginger Ale was introduced in 1925. When new laws required that an orange-flavored drink use real orange juice, Grigg developed a lemon-lime mixture. The slogan for the new drink was "Takes the Ouch Out of Grouch" because it was marketed as an antacid that promoted belching. Originally called Bib-Label Lithiated Lemon-Lime Soda, the name was changed to 7Up in October 1929, two weeks before the stock market crash. The story behind the name is that the "7" was for the 7-ounce bottles and the "Up" for the carbonation-derived belch. Or the "Up" may

have been used because the drink "picked one up." But medicinal drinks had only a limited market, so the carbonation was lowered and 7Up was marketed as simply a refreshing drink. The green 7Up bottle was in use by 1931, but some bottlers used clear or even amber bottles during the 1930s. The Seven-Up Company, successor to the Howdy Corp., was organized about 1936. It went public in 1967, the year 7Up became known as the "Uncola." Philip Morris Inc. purchased the company in 1978. In 1986 the Seven-Up Company was sold to an investment group and was then merged with Dr Pepper Company. Cadbury-Schweppes acquired the Dr Pepper/Seven-Up Companies in 1995. The following year, the company name became Dr Pepper/Seven-Up, Inc. The current advertising slogan, "Make 7Up Yours" was introduced in 1999.

Book Cover, Fresh Up With 7Up, Compliments Of 7Up Bottling Co., 1939 . . . . 15.00
Button, Zorro, Celluloid, Pinback, Walt Disney Productions, 1957, 1 1/4 In. . . . . . . .10.00 to 15.00
Calendar, 1940, Blond Woman, Bare Back, Seasons Greetings, 5 1/2 x 11 In. 99.00
Card, Happy Infant, Red Playsuit, Die Cut Cardboard, c.1950, 5 x 8 1/2 In. 5.00
Clock, Brass Trim, Round, 1960s 105.00
Clock, Light-Up, 16 x 16 In. 220.00
Clock, Light-Up, Plastic, 1970s 22.00
Clock, Plastic, Flower Shape, 16 x 17 In. 66.00
Cooler, c.1930s, 18 x 9 x 11 1/2 In. 125.00
Display Case, 4 Shelves, Wood, Glass, 7Up Decal, 24 x 18 In. 209.00
Fan, Woman, Bathing Suit, Large Towel, Beach, 1940s, 9 x 14 In. 66.00
Figure, Crossing Guard, Policeman, Lithograph Sheet Steel, 1955, 68 In. 743.00
Picnic Basket, Keep America Beautiful, Tin, 1970s, 8 x 9 1/4 x 14 In. . . . . *Illus* 90.00
Sign, 7Up Your Thirst Away, Tin, Embossed, c.1960, 19 x 13 In. 71.00
Sign, Bottle, Tin, 44 1/2 In. 265.00
Sign, Fresh Up Family, Father Reads Bedtime Story To Sons, 1948, 13 x 19 In. 25.00
Sign, Fresh Up With 7Up, It Likes You, Embossed, Oval, 1940s-1950s, 40 x 30 In. 2090.00
Sign, Fresh Up With, Porcelain, 1951, 12 x 30 1/4 In. 413.00
Sign, Fresh Up, Tin, Embossed, 47 x 18 In. 750.00
Sign, Go Steady, This Cool Clean Taste, Couple, Jukebox, Cardboard, Frame, 36 x 24 In. . 132.00
Sign, Horseracing Scene, Bottles, Mix With Chilled 7Up, Cardboard, c.1953, 21 x 30 In. . 44.00
Sign, Like, Lemon-Lime Flavour, White, Red, Green, Tin, 29 1/4 x 12 1/4 In. 99.00
Sign, Menu, Multicolored Light Bulbs Around Perimeter, 23 x 54 1/2 In. 165.00
Sign, The Best Stop Sign On The Road, Cardboard, Wood Frame, 13 x 22 In. 110.00
Sign, The Uncola, Tin, Die Cut Bottle, 70 x 29 In. 385.00
Sign, Tin, Wood Frame, 1971, 96 x 96 In., 2 Piece 110.00
Sign, Wet & Wild, Cardboard, Frame, 1966, 10 1/2 x 15 In. 50.00
Sign, You Like It, Bottle Shape, Tin, Embossed, 1962, 13 x 44 1/2 In. 413.00
Sign, Your Fresh Up, White, Red, Green, Bather On Bottle, Tin, 1947, 27 x 19 1/2 In. . . . 165.00
Sign, Your Stand-By, Man, Bottle, Die Cut, Easel Back, 1940-1950, 18 x 12 In. 66.00
Telephone, 7Up Spot Character, 8 3/4 x 5 x 11 1/2 In. 100.00
Thermometer, 7Up, Orange, Yellow, Round, 12 In. 99.00
Vending Machine, Vendo 81, 10 Cents, c.1957 . . . . 2250.00

SEWING Sewing utensils of all types have been used as advertising giveaways since the nineteenth century. Included here are buttonhooks, needle cases, tape measures, and others.

Buttonhook, Alexanders, Wheeling, Flat, Circular Handle, 5 In. 13.44

Seven-Up, Picnic Basket, Keep America Beautiful, Tin, 1970s, 8 x 9 1/4 x 14 In.

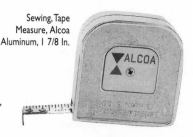

Sewing, Tape Measure, Alcoa Aluminum, 1 7/8 In.

Buttonhook, Bond Street Spats, Flat, Circular Handle, 3 1/4 In. 15.70
Buttonhook, Brown Bros. Shoes, Beloit, Wis., Flat, Circular Handle, 5 In. 15.70
Buttonhook, J.C. Penney Co., 475 Stores, Flat, Circular Handle, 5 In. 13.44
Buttonhook, Jebs Boot Shop, 503 Market Street, Flat, Circular Handle, 3 7/8 In. 11.20
Buttonhook, Johnson Bros. Duds For Men, Flat Handle, Full Loop End, 3 5/8 In. 16.80
Buttonhook, Kaufmann & Saer, Pittsburgh, Flat, Circular Handle, 3 3/4 In. 15.70
Buttonhook, M. & K. Shoe Shop, Cincinnati, Flat, Circular Handle, 5 1/8 In. 15.70
Buttonhook, R.E. Borst, Fine Shoes, Parish, N.Y., Flat, Circular Handle, 5 In. . . . . . .11.20 to 15.70
Buttonhook, R.K Stephens Shoe Company, Oswego, Flat, Circular Handle, 3 3/4 In. 15.70
Buttonhook, Rockford E. & E. Clothing House, Daisy, Full Loop End, 1916, 3 1/8 In. . . .   16.80
Buttonhook, Rosenbaum Co., Pittsburgh, Pa., Flat, Circular Handle, 3 7/8 In. 15.70
Buttonhook, Stretcher's Shoe Store, West Newton, Pa., Flat, Circular Handle, 5 In. 15.70
Buttonhook & Shoehorn, Petty's Enna Jettick Shoes, Jenkins Arcade, Folding, 5 In. 28.00
Buttonhook & Shoehorn, Petty's Shoe Repair Shop, Milady's Shoe Horn, Folding, 5 In. . .   28.00
Buttonhook & Shoehorn, Roberts Foot Friend Shop, Folding, 5 In. 28.00
Case, Crowleys Needles, Oak, Drawer, 8 x 14 x 4 In. 385.00
Kit, King Coal Trailways, Pack Up All Your Cares & Go, Needles, Buttons, 3 1/2 In. 4.48
Needle Book, First Savings & Loan Assoc., 1 Stockton St., San Francisco, Jan. 2, 1964 . .   15.00
Needle Book, Food Fair Grocery Store, 6 Needle Packets, Threader 8.00
Needle Book, Food Fair, America's Showplace Food Values, 6 Needle Packets, Threader .   8.00
Needle Book, Grand Union Supermarkets, Save Cash, Stamps, 6 Needle Packets, Threader   8.00
Needle Book, H.P. Hood, Milk Bottle Shape, Hood's, It's Fresh, It's Good, 6 x 2 1/2 In. . .   28.00
Needle Book, Liberty National Life Insurance Co., Statue Of Liberty, Birmingham, Ala. . .   5.00
Needle Book, National Life & Accident Insurance Company, Shield Shape, 3 x 3 In. 5.00
Needle Book, New York World's Fair, 1939, 7 x 3 3/4 In. 14.00
Needle Book, Rexall, Make A Point Of Saving At Our Store, Threader, 3 Needle Packets .   15.00
Needle Book, Virginia Slims, Men Would Needle Women, 1970s, 3 x 4 1/4 In. 10.00
Needle Book, Woolworth, Woolco/Woolworth Building, 6 Needle Packets, Dosco 14.00
Needle Case, Boye, Tin Lithograph, Revolving, 16 In. 121.00
Needle Case, Compliments Of Ratcliffe & Tanner, Richmond, Va., Brass, Enamel, 2 In. . .   25.00
Package, J. English & Co. Needles, Wistar's Balsam Of Wild Cherry, 4 1/2 x 3 1/2 In. . . .   55.00
Pin Holder, Ely's Cream Balm, Head Shape, Die Cut, Tin Lithograph, 1 3/4 In. 72.00
Pin Tray, Clover Brand Shoes, Always Just Correct, 2 Puppies, Tin Lithograph, 2 5/8 In. . .   44.00
Pin Tray, Clover Brand Shoes, Boy Eating Watermelon, Tin Lithograph, Oval, 3 3/8 x 2 In.   154.00
Pin Tray, Try Bee Candy Co. Chocolates, Dog, Tin Lithograph, 3 3/8 x 2 1/4 In. 77.00
Straight Pins, Warrior, Cardboard Box, 1 Lb., 4 1/4 x 2 3/4 In. 7.00
Tape Measure, Alcoa Aluminum, 1 7/8 In. . . . . *Illus*   30.00
Tape Measure, Figural, Rye Straw Hat, Paulson Bros., 75 Years On Wood Str., 2 3/4 In. . .   141.00
Tape Measure, Firestone Bank, Celluloid, Lisbon, Ohio, 1920, 1 3/4 x 1/2 In. 40.00
Tape Measure, H. Borenstein & Sons, Taneytown, Maryland, Cloth, Cardboard Tag, 60 In.   11.20
Tape Measure, H.D. Lee Company, Cloth, Cardboard End, 60 In.   35.00
Tape Measure, Newton Manufacturing, Newton, Iowa, Our 60th Year, 1 1/2 In. 15.00
Tape Measure, Red Kap Uniforms, Every Way You Measure, 60 In. 9.00
Tape Measure, Singing Tower, Florida, Metal, Celluloid, Cloth, Germany, 1930s, 1 1/2 In.   48.00
Tape Measure, Stouffer, Reduce & Keep Fit, Easy Stouffer Home Plan Way, Paper 8.00
Tape Measure, Stromberg Carburetor, Celluloid, J.H. McCullough & Son Co., 1 1/2 In. . .   77.00
Thimble, Absolom's Moss Bank Tea, Aluminum, Navy Enamel Ground, 15/16 x 3/4 In. . .   18.00
Thimble, McHutchinson's Better Bread, Gold Band, Metal, Canada 16.00
Thimble, Ride Bluebird Systems Buses, Red, White, Blue, Plastic 10.00
Thimble, Star Brand Shoes Are Better, Blue, Aluminum 10.00
Thread Box, Aunt Lydia's Carpet & Button Thread, 9 1/4 x 3 1/4 x 2 In. 39.00

SHAKER   The Shaker religious sect in the United States was an indus-
trious, inventive group. They earned money by selling many products
to those who were "worldly" (not of the Shakers). Medicines, seeds,
furniture, cloaks, and other products were sold and advertised. The
name "Shaker" was a guarantee of an honest, well-made product. It
was so trusted that it was used by others making medicines and food
products in conjunction with the Shaker communities. A few products,
like Shaker Salt (1894), made by Diamond Crystal Salt Company,
were marketed with the brand name Shaker although it was not made
by the Shakers. The pun of a Shaker with a shaker was compounded
on the box label, which pictured a Shaker woman pouring salt from a

saltshaker. Advertising materials available today include original labels from Shaker communities, as well as old signs, boxes, bottles, pamphlets, calendars, almanacs, seed packets, and dress labels. Today, those who collect Shaker furniture also like a few of the advertising items, especially the larger boxes or labels, so they are very expensive.

Flour Spiller, Flour Fred, England, 9 In.	38.00
Label, Apple Jelly, North Family, Society Of Shakers, Mt. Lebanon, N.Y., 2 1/2 x 1 In.	40.00
Label, Can, Pulverized Summer Savory, Bogle & Lyles, 7 1/2 x 2 1/8 In.	120.00
Label, Crabapple Jelly, North Family, Society Of Shakers, Mt. Lebanon, 2 1/2 x 1 In.	40.00
Label, Shaker Parlor Broom, Thomas Estes, New Lebanon, N.Y., 1 1/2 x 3 In.	65.00
Seed Bag, Beet Early Blood Turnip, D.M. From The Shakers Gardens, 8 3/4 x 5 1/2 In.	85.00
Seed Bag, Shaker Seeds, Blue Imperial Peas, West Pittsfield, Mass., 4 1/2 x 5 1/2 In.	150.00
Seed Bag, Shakers' Yellow Onion, N.F., New Lebanon, N.Y., 7 3/4 x 5 In.	150.00
Sign, Tamar Laxative, Paper, 10 3/4 x 8 3/4 In.	770.00

SHOT GLASS, see Decorated Tumbler

SIGN Advertising signs date back to the broadsides and notices posted on walls even before the seventeenth century. Collectors can choose from signs large enough to cover the side of a barn to signs small enough to hang from the end of a string light-pull in a store. The earliest signs were paper or wood, sometimes carved into the shape of a product. Tin, canvas, enameled metal, cardboard, metal mesh, neon, and plastic followed. Signs that are most in demand advertise well-known brands of medicine, soft drinks, tobacco, and alcoholic beverages, or depict bottles, sexy ladies, blacks, early automobiles, trains, or airplanes. Be sure any sign you buy has not been cut down from a large ad or made out of pages from old magazines. See also Banner and Poster.

2 For 1 Orange Drink, Ace Of Fruit Drinks, Red, Yellow, Tin, Embossed, 27 x 11 In.	220.00
66 Lithiated Lemon Soda, Double Eagle Bottling Co., Tin, Embossed, 11 1/2 x 29 1/2 In.	259.00
A.B. Haley, Sand Paint, Gold Letters, Maine, c.1880s, 10 1/2 In.	413.00
A.T. Wilson & Son's Milk, Cow Head, Porcelain, 11 In.	20.00
Acme Cowboy Boots, Cardboard, Self-Framed, 33 x 47 In.	99.00
Ada Brand Olive Oil, It's Pure, Imported From Italy, 13 x 19 In.	165.00
Adams' Pepsin Tutti Frutti, Sold Here, Reverse Glass, Mirror, Oak Frame, 11 x 18 1/2 In.	468.00
Adams' Pepsin Tutti Frutti Gum, Woman, Box, Tin Lithograph, Die Cut, 11 7/8 In.	1430.00
Admiral Whiskey, Reverse On Glass, Gold Letters, Waving Flag, Frame, 29 1/2 x 36 In.	440.00
Adriance Buckeye, Harvesting Machinery, Paper, Frame, c.1897, 30 x 24 In.	1210.00
Adriance Platt & Co., Lithograph, Frame, 29 x 34 In.	330.00
Aetna, Coast To Coast, Flange, 20 x 15 In.	176.00
Aetna, This Agency At Your Service, Composition, 3-Wood Frame, 21 x 15 In.	55.00
Agency For Evinrude Sporting Goods, Detachable Rowboat Motor, Come In, 14 x 19 In.	4500.00
Agency For Headlight Overalls, Red, White, Blue, 10 x 32 In.	2500.00
Akro Agates, Win The Game, Boys Playing Marbles, Die Cut, Cardboard, 15 x 13 In.	6325.00
Alaska Refrigerators, Life Preserver Form, Eskimos, Die Cut, Paperboard, 24 1/4 In.	325.00
Allerton Seed Supply, Super Q Seed, Thermometer, Chalkboard, Allerton, Ill., 24 x 18 In.	139.00
Alliance Insurance Company Of Philadelphia, Porcelain, 18 x 24 In.	44.00
Allied Mills, Die Cut, Porcelain, 32 x 25 In.	413.00
Alligator Steel Belt Lacing, Tin Over Cardboard, Green, Yellow, Black, 9 x 13 In.	110.00
Allis-Chambers, Tractor Manufacturing, Red, White, Blue, Porcelain, 16 x 16 In.	193.00
Alonzo Bliss, Our Native Herbs, Blood Purifier, Tin, Embossed, 6 3/4 x 9 3/4 In.	132.00
Alox Shoe Laces, Good Shoe Laces For A Nickel, Paper, Frame, 14 x 26 In.	33.00
Alpenkrauter Stomach Tonic, Feel Fine, Old Woman Holds Bottle, Masonite, 24 x 48 In.	121.00
Alta, Queen Of Mountain Mineral Waters, Woman, Tin Lithograph, 19 1/2 x 13 1/4 In.	1210.00
Alta Crest Farms, Ayrshire Cattle, Heavy Porcelain, 12 x 12 In.	358.00
Alta Crest Farms, Trespassing Forbidden, Steer, Porcelain, Flange, 18 x 12 In.	495.00
Amerada Hess, Private Road, Porcelain, 10 x 26 In.	55.00
American District Telegraph Co., Mounted Messengers, Embossed, Porcelain, 20 x 36 In.	6050.00
American Express Co., Porcelain, Flange, 2-Sided, 1914, 13 x 17 In.	440.00
American Fire & Casualty, Shield Shape, Wood, Orlando, Florida, 16 x 15 In.	35.00
American Gentleman Shoe, John A. Crescenzo, Tin, Embossed, 1915, 19 x 14 In.	143.00
American Insurance Co., Reverse Paint On Glass, Newark, 29 x 19 In.	248.00

American Lady Corsets, Voluptuous Woman In Corset, Paper, Frame, 20 x 14 In. 220.00
American Lady Shoe, Henry Kober & Co., Tin, Embossed, 9 x 19 In. 231.00
American Quality Coal, Orders Taken By Driver, Red, White, Porcelain, 9 x 12 In. 99.00
American Red Cross, Emergency First Aid, Porcelain, 1940-1950, 3 x 5 In. 232.00
American Stamps, We Give, Redeem, Red, Black, Yellow, Tin, Embossed, 27 3/4 x 10 In. 165.00
American Wall Paper Co., Red, Pittsburg, Chicago, Tin Lithograph, Embossed, 14 x 19 In. 110.00
American Wringer Co., Warranted For 5 Years, Tin, Embossed, c.1900, 13 x 10 In. . *Illus* 688.00
Anglo-Swiss, Condensed Milk, Milk Maid Brand, Paper, Hanger, 20 x 14 In. 88.00
Anker-Holth Cream Separator, Porcelain, 10 x 14 In. 61.00
Antons Tailor's, Ladies, Gents, Yellow, Red, Black, Curved Corners, 46 1/2 x 22 1/2 In. . . 115.00
Apco Oil Well, Edwards Field Grayburg Unit, Red, White, 10 x 26 In. 149.00
Apollo Chocolates Candy, Porcelain, 1930s, 12 x 32 In. 200.00
Arab U-Do-It, Termite & Pest Control, Light-Up, Plastic, 15 In. 22.00
Arden Fine Ice Cream, We Serve Delicious, Masonite, Beveled Edge, 7 1/4 x 12 In. 176.00
Arden Ice Cream, For Vital Energy, Porcelain, 28 x 32 In. 303.00
Argo Glass Starch, For Best Results, Girl, Doll, Laundry, 16 x 22 1/2 In. 468.00
Armots Rose Cream, Purity, Tin On Cardboard, c.1906, 19 x 13 1/4 In. 275.00
Armstrong's Quaker Rugs, Girl Holding Bunny, Die Cut Cardboard, Easel, 33 x 18 In. . . 77.00
Aspinall's Enamel, Cardboard, Hanger, 15 x 21 In. 1320.00
Atkins Silver Steel Saws, Tin Lithograph, Frame, 10 x 19 In. . . . . .523.00 to 935.00
Atlantic, Red, White, Black, Porcelain, 6 1/2 x 13 In. 39.00
Atlantic Ranges & Heaters, Porcelain, 11 x 20 In. 182.00
Atlantic White Flash, Red, White, Black, 13 x 17 In. 275.00
Atlas Assurance Co., Fire, Life, Accident, Burglary, England, Frame, 34 x 24 In. 57.00
Atlas Assurance Fire Agency, Enamel, Blue, England, 15 x 8 In. 984.00
Auburn Fish Market, Wood, 85 x 13 1/2 In. 176.00
B-1 Lemon Lime Soda, Metal, 2-Sided, Bracket, 1940-1950, 20 x 28 In. 550.00
B.E. Karshiner, Authorized Dealer, Porcelain, White, Blue, 72 x 9 In. 44.00
B.F. Goodrich, Tin, 1956, 18 x 42 1/2 In. 303.00
B.F. Goodrich Farm Tires, Tin, Trapezoidal Shape, 1947, 59 x 26 In. 660.00
Baby Ruth, Curtiss Candies, Rich In Dextrose, Tin, White, Red, 10 x 28 In. 176.00
Baggage Room, Porcelain, Shaped Ends, Blue Letters, White Ground, 3 1/2 x 23 In. 578.00
Bailey's Circus, Paper Lithograph, 20 x 30 In. 88.00
Baldwin Manualo Player Piano, Reliable, Reasonable Prices, Tin, 36 x 12 In. 116.00
Bamber Funeral Home, Black, Brass, 16 1/2 x 24 In. 17.00
Barber, Straight Razor, Carved, Painted, America, 19th Century, 20 In. 323.00
Barber Pole Chewing Gum, Woman, Die Cut, Cardboard, Easel Back, 10 1/2 x 4 1/2 In. . 523.00
Barber Shop Union, It Pays To Look Well, Tin, Embossed, Self-Framed, 6 x 15 In. 176.00
Bata Bullets Sneakers, Canvas Sneaker Shape, White Ground, Blue Letters, 24 In. 225.00
Batey's Lemonade, Porcelain, 20 x 30 In. 83.00
Bauer & Black, First Aid Supplies, Scout Mending Girl's Finger, Cardboard, 29 x 22 In. . . 489.00
Be Healthy Drink Milk, Milk Bottle Shape, Porcelain, 20 x 9 In. 798.00
Beatrice Ice Cream, Ice Cream Cone, Die Cut, Fiberboard, 46 x 26 In. 33.00
Beauty Parlor, Blue, White, Porcelain, Flange, 2-Sided, 12 x 24 In. 143.00
Beech Nut Beans, Cardboard, Beech-Nut Frame, 24 x 14 In. 242.00
Belmont Whiskey, Louisville, Ky., Glass, Reverse Painted, Chain Frame, 7 x 10 In. 110.00
Bendix, Sales & Service, Vacuum Power, Porcelain, 2-Sided, Round, 18 In. 154.00
Bendix Radio, Soldiers, Welcome Him Back, Die Cut, Cardboard, 1940-1950, 26 x 18 In. 88.00
Betsy Ross Bread, Boy With Football, Energy Wins, Cardboard, Embossed, 25 x 44 In. . . 66.00
Betsy Ross Bread, Hi Mama, Bring Some Home, Girl, Dog, Clock, Masonite, 31 x 28 In. 253.00
Biberon Robert Le Meilleur, Baby In Bird Nest, Tin, Embossed, France, 15 x 10 In. 546.00
Bickmore Easy Shave Cream, 35 Cent, Man, Cardboard, 31 x 21 In. 160.00
Bickmore Gall Salve, Die Cut, Horse Shape, Easel Back, Cardboard, 18 x 12 In. 165.00
Biddeford & Saco Coal Company, Our Coal Makes Warm Friends, Porcelain, 14 x 20 In. . 303.00
Bieres Fines Excelsior, Bottle, Orange, Gold, Green Ground, c.1930, 13 In. 45.00
Big Bang Toy Cannons, Tin Over Cardboard, 1915-1920, 9 x 16 In. . . . . *Illus* 1045.00
Big Boy Pale Dry, 5 Cent, In Green Bottles Only, Tin, 19 x 9 In. 330.00
Big Giant Cola, 16 Oz., Bigger, Better, Red, White, Tin, Embossed, 29 1/2 x 11 1/2 In. . . . 253.00
Big Jo Flour, Sack Of Flour, Tin Lithograph, 12 x 36 In. 80.00
Big Winston Overalls, Black, White, Red, Flange, Metal, 12 3/4 x 9 1/2 In. 880.00
Bireley's, Grape, So Drink Up & Smile, Motion Spinner, Light-Up, c.1950, 12 x 24 In. . . . 440.00
Bishop & Boyden Drug Store, Gilt, Polychrome, 2-Sided, c.1915, 59 x 29 1/2 x 2 In. 1495.00
BK Root Beer, Orange Letter, Cream Ground, Oval, 30 x 45 In. 173.00

Sign, American Wringer Co., Warranted For
5 Years, Tin, Embossed, c.1900, 13 x 10 In.

Sign, Big Bang Toy Cannons, Tin Over
Cardboard, 1915-1920, 9 x 16 In.

Black & White Fine Foods, Stringholder Panel, Tin, 16 x 15 In. 50.00
Black Bat Licorice, Metal, 11 1/4 x 11 1/4 In. 60.00
Black Bird Brand, Red Ground, Gold Border, Celluloid, Tin, Cardboard, 10 x 10 In. 119.00
Black Caps, Gonorrhoea, Gleet, Tin, Embossed, Yellow, Black Letters, 9 3/4 x 7 In. 220.00
Black Cat Hosiery, Your Dollar Goes Further, Tin, Yellow, Red, Black, 11 1/2 x 35 1/2 In. . . 330.00
Black Cat Silk Hosiery, Lithograph, Frame, Henry Hutt, 27 x 37 In. 3745.00
Blaul's Pancake Flour, Cardboard, Die Cut, Cloth Flour Sack, 11 x 14 In. . . . . .28.00 to 50.00
Blue Coal, America's Finest Anthracite, Porcelain, 13 x 10 In. 385.00
Blue Coal, Porcelain, White, Blue Letters, 3 x 9 In. 413.00
Blue Jay Brand Foot Powder, Woman, Cardboard Lithograph, Die Cut, 48 In. 200.00
Blue Mountain Chocolates, Pure As Nature, Embossed Tin Lithograph, 6 1/2 x 10 In. . . . 71.00
Blue Ribbon Bourbon, Farm Scene, Oil On Canvas, Frame, 29 x 39 In. 275.00
Blue Ribbon Bourbon, Mill, Mountains, Road, Canvas Lithograph, Frame, 46 x 36 In. . . . 187.00
Blue Wagon Staple Cotton, Enameled, Crystalline, Round, 6 In. 209.00
Boats For The Quarry, Pine, Beveled Edge, White, Black, 12 1/2 x 16 In. 550.00
Bond Bread, Better By Far, Red, Yellow, Black, Tin, 28 x 19 3/4 In. 77.00
Bond Bread, The Home-Like Loaf, Yellow, Black, Porcelain, 19 x 14 In. 66.00
Bondshire Shoes, Cavalier, Drawn Sword, Composition, K.C. & S. Co., 14 x 11 In. 25.00
Borax Dry Soap, For Washing Everything, Red, White, Tin, Embossed, 24 x 7 1/4 In. . . . 248.00
Boschee's Syrup, Laboratory, Canvas Lithograph, Frame, 27 x 35 In. 1100.00
Boston Celery Co., Kays Best 14 Long Wharf, Masonite, 30 1/4 x 36 In. 81.00
Bostonians Famous Shoes For Men, Tin Lithograph, Cardboard, 8 3/4 x 19 In. 193.00
Botl'o Grape, Call For Botl'o Grape, Other Flavors, Black, Green, White, Tin, 7 x 20 In. . . 44.00
Bovril, Woman At Kitchen Table, Girl Under Table, Frame, 24 1/2 x 20 1/2 In. 605.00
Boyd's Miniature Galvanic Battery, Broadsheet, 2-Sided, c.1880, 17 x 7 1/4 In. 209.00
Boyle & Murphy Co. Cut Meats, Black, Gilt, Tin, Frame, 22 1/4 x 53 In. 460.00
BPS Paint Flatlux, Porcelain, Die Cut, 24 x 34 In. 330.00
Braems Bitters, Bottle, Embossed Rope Edging, Tin Lithograph, c.1907, 13 1/2 x 7 In. . . 143.00
Breinig's Pure Linseed Oil Paints, Man, Hanging From Weather Vane, 20 x 12 In. 3300.00
Breyers Ice Cream, Tin Lithograph, Embossed, Oval, 51 In. 220.00
Brink's Express Company Only Can Open Safe, Porcelain, Oval, 8 x 12 1/2 In. 88.00
Broadies Drug Store, Reverse Painting, Copper Frame, c.1890, 18 x 26 In. . . . . .900.00 to 1300.00
Bromo-Mint With Caffeine, For Over Indulgence, 10 Cent, 8 3/4 x 8 In. 132.00
Brooke Bond Tea, Red, Black, Porcelain, 30 x 20 In. 110.00
Brookfield Rye, Girl Holding Bottle, Chromolithograph, 23 x 33 In. 2750.00
Brookfield Rye Whiskey, Seminude Woman, Tin Lithograph, Self-Framed, 33 x 23 In. . . . 5280.00
Brown's Jumbo Bread, Elephant, Die Cut, Frame, 17 x 19 In. 303.00
Brown's Jumbo Bread, Elephant, Die Cut, Tin Lithograph, c.1900, 13 x 15 In. . . . .468.00 to 605.00
Brown's Worm Lozenges Cardboard, c.1890, 14 x 11 In. 118.00
Brownie Root Beer, Tin, Embossed, 1940 . . . . 550.00
Brylcreem, For Smart Healthy Hair, Red Ground, Porcelain, 16 x 18 In. 248.00
Bubble Up, Just Pure Pleasure, Celluloid, 8 x 12 In. 39.00
Buchanan's Cafe, Glass, Reverse Paint, Frame, 19 x 42 In. 605.00
Buffalo Dental Mfg., Out, Will Return, Celluloid, 4 x 5 In. 50.00
Buffalo Nickel, Porcelain, Tin, 11 1/4 In. Diam. 25.00
Buffalo Rock Ginger Ale, Keep Healthy, Woman, Bottle, Tin, Easel Back, 14 x 10 In. . . . 495.00
Bulova, Give The Finest, Santa Claus, Roland Jewelers, 11 x 28 In. 11.00
Bunny Bread, Figural, Cutout, Tin, American Bakers Coop, Stout, c.1968, 56 x 32 In. . . . 295.00

Burkland Underwear, Infants, Children, Lace Trimmed Cloth Shirt, Embossed, 12 x 16 In.   468.00
Burrell's Paints, Enamels & Distempers, Girl Painting Arm, Beach, 17 1/2 x 12 In. 114.00
Bus Depot, National Trailways System, 2-Sided, Porcelain, 18 1/4 x 22 In. 688.00
Buthweg Clothing, Glass, Reverse Paint, Gold Leaf, Copper Flashed Frame, 20 x 25 In. .   578.00
Butlers, Local Favourite, Seated Man, Sideburns, England, Frame, 22 x 19 1/4 In. 104.00
Butter Color, Boy, Leaning On Cow, Paper, Frame, Wells, Richardson & Co., 21 x 42 In.   660.00
Button Engine Works, Paper Lithograph, Frame, 1868, Image 18 x 23 1/4 In. 4950.00
C.F. & I. Coals, For More Heat, 3 Devils Running With Buckets, Porcelain, 9 x 20 In. 1650.00
C.F. & I. Coals, For More Heat, Colorado Fuel & Iron Co., Porcelain, 22 x 11 In.........   275.00
C.F. & I. Coals, For More Heat, Red, Black, White, 9 x 20 In. 236.00
C.W. Parker Carousel, Stone Lithograph, Frame, 22 3/4 x 29 3/4 In. 1650.00
Cadbury's Chocolate, Red Ground, 11 1/4 x 9 In. 110.00
Camel Cigarettes, Arab Leading Camel, Tin, Die Cut, 3 Panel, 18 1/2 x 20 1/2 In. 330.00
Camillus Cutlery Co., Knife Opens & Closes, Electric, Animated, 14 x 24 In. 44.00
Campbell's Varnish Stain, Embossed, Tin Lithograph Over Cardboard, Frame, 11 x 17 In.   413.00
Campfire Marshmallows, Boy In Sailor Uniform, Stone Lithograph, 21 1/2 x 13 3/4 In. ..   330.00
Canada Paint, Quality In Every Drop, Paint Can, Porcelain, 2-Sided, 19 x 14 In. 689.00
Candee Rubbers, Cardboard, Hanger, New Haven, Conn., 12 1/2 x 10 1/2 In. 550.00
Canoe Club Beverage, Once You Try It, You'll Always Buy It, Metal, 14 x 30 In. 248.00
Caperns Bird Seed, Porcelain, Heavy Gauge Steel, England, c.1920s, 10 x 14 In. 255.00
Carborundum, Indian Chief, Niagara Falls, Die Cut, Cardboard, 39 x 30 In. 1210.00
Carborundum Scythe Stones, Indian In Headdress, Cardboard, Hanger, 3 1/2 x 12 In. ...   46.00
Carlisle Rye, 2 Images, Dogs Playing Poker, 11 1/4 x 30 In. 66.00
Carnation, Ice Cream, Porcelain, 22 x 22 In. 385.00
Carstairs Harmony Blended Whiskey, Tavern, Cardboard, Frame, 1940s, 16 1/2 x 21 In. .   25.00
Cascade Ginger Ale, A Toast In Every Glass, Cardboard, c.1920, 10 x 14 In. 340.00
Case, Eagle On Globe, Die Cut, Porcelain, 80 In., 2 Piece 8250.00
Case, Eagle On Globe, Neon, 18 x 40 In. 764.00
Case Farm Machinery, Eagle On Globe, Red, White, Black, Embossed, 72 x 30 In. 1150.00
Castile Cream Harness Soap Dressing, Tin Lithograph, Diamond Shape, 9 1/4 x 9 1/4 In.   96.00
Cat's Paw Rubber Heels For Shoes, Tin, 2-Sided, Original Stand, 29 x 20 In. 220.00
Catawissa Sparkling Beverages, Tin, White Ground, Red Letters, 18 x 12 In. 83.00
Cattle Raisers, Texas & Southwestern Association, Cobalt Blue, Porcelain, 20 In. 187.00
Celebrated Gibbs Imperial Plows, Harrows & Cultivators, Wood, Painted, 8 x 41 In. 880.00
Celluloid Starch, Sold On Its Merits, Girl, Holding Fan, Cardboard, Die Cut, 10 x 5 In. ..   198.00
Celluloid Starch, Sold Only In Packages, Die Cut, Cardboard, Easel Back, 1892, 10 x 4 In.   193.00
Centilivre Tonic, Builds Up The System, Red Cross Nurse, 12 x 22 In. 69.00
Cer-Ola, A Non-Intoxicating Cereal Beverage, Bay City, Mich., Poster, 11 x 17 1/2 In. ...   50.00
Cerva Soft Drink, Non-Intoxicating Beverage, Lemp, St. Louis, Bears, Tin, 4 3/4 x 6 1/2 In.   138.00
Cetacolor, Not A Soap, 10 Cent Package, Cloth On Wood, 23 1/2 x 36 In. 44.00
Cetacolor, Not A Soap, Victorian Lady, Red Hat, Lithograph On Linen, Frame, 25 x 37 In.   468.00
Champion, Agency For Binders & Mowers, Wood, Sand Paint, c.1880s, 12 In. 523.00
Chapin's Buchu-Paiba, Great Kidney Cure, E.S. Wells, Jersey City, N.J., 7 x 5 In. 39.00
Chapman Ice Cream, Good Ice Cream, Porcelain, 2-Sided, 28 x 20 In. 198.00
Charles Cuomo Cheese, Tin Over Cardboard, c.1920, 13 x 19 In. ....*Illus*   275.00
Cheer Up, Made Good For You, Metal, 9 x 3 In. 165.00
Chef Sauce, Shake & Be Friends For Life, England, Frame, 21 1/4 x 16 1/4 In. 57.00
Cherry Blossoms Drink, Girl, Boy, Tin, Die Cut, 2-Sided, c.1921, 11 x 7 In. 688.00
Cherry Blossoms Drink, In Bottles Only, 2 Men, Cardboard, Die Cut, 7 1/2 x 16 In. 220.00
Cherry Blush, Cherries Only Rival, Tin, Cardboard Back, c.1900, 6 1/4 x 9 In. ....650.00 to 800.00
Cherry Pepsin, Drink, A Delicious Beverage, At Fountains & In Bottles, Tin, 6 x 14 In. ..   66.00
Cherry Smash, Victorian Woman, Holds Glass, Die Cut, 15 x 12 1/2 In., 2 Piece 220.00
Cherry Sparkle, Taste Tells The Tale, Tin Over Cardboard, Self-Framed, 6 x 13 In. 303.00 to 550.00
Chico's Ice Cream, Porcelain, 36 In. 88.00
Chilean Soda, Natural, Yassuh, Uncle Natchel, Green Ground, Sheet Steel, 21 1/2 In. 330.00
Chivas Regal, Blended Scotch Whiskey, Stained Glass Window, 1959, 10 x 13 In. 21.00
Chums, Prize In Every Package, Cardboard, 2-Sided, 1905, 14 x 11 In. 2475.00
City Of New York, Insurance Company, Reverse Painted, Frame, c.1920, 22 x 30 In. 425.00
Clarke's Perfect Plug, Old Man, Stone Wall, England, Frame, 21 1/2 x 16 1/2 In. 142.00
Clear Quill Flour, Tin, Cardboard Back, Self-Framed, c.1890, 14 1/2 x 20 1/2 In. ..700.00 to 900.00
Cleo Cola, Drink, For Goodness Sake, Tin, Embossed, 27 x 28 In. 193.00
Clicquot Club, Eskimo Boy, Bottle, Red, Tin Lithograph, Embossed, c.1950, 9 x 20 In. ..   187.00
Clover Farm Stores, Green, Red Arrows, Store Front, Crate, Tin, Pre 1935, 30 x 240 In. ..   700.00

Clover Farm Stores, Green, Red Diamonds, Porcelain, Store Front, 30 x 240 In. . .500.00 to 875.00
Clover Farm Stores, Green, Wood Letter, 68 In. 132.00
Cloverdale Pale Dry Ginger Ale, 4-Leaf Clover, Metal, 12 1/2 x 9 3/4 In. 38.00
Cloverdale Soft Drinks, Tin Lithograph, Embossed, 11 x 29 In. . . . . *Illus*   77.00
Coach Stop, No Parking, Yellow, Black, Porcelain, 2-Sided, Holder, 12 x 17 1/2 In. 121.00
Coles Penetrating Liniment, Safe & Sure, Porcelain, Blue Ground, 5 x 16 In. 1210.00
Coles Peruvian Bark & Wild Cherry Bitters, Porcelain, c.1880, 8 x 18 In. . . . . . .700.00 to 1540.00
Coles Phillips Luxite Hosiery, Lady, Man In Wheelchair, Cardboard, Frame, 12 x 22 In. . . .   99.00
Colgan's Chips, Honus Wagner, Triangular, Frame, 1909, 20 x 26-In. Image 23000.00
Collins & Co., Axes Of The World Are Collins, Cardboard, Hanger, 20 x 10 In. 165.00
Collins Axes, Axes Of The World Are Collins, Cardboard, Frame, 12 x 22 In. 50.00
Collinson's 1/10 Tea, Agent For, Enamel, England, 12 x 8 In. 530.00
Colt Acetylene, Tin, Embossed, Hanger, 10 x 14 In. 660.00
Columbia Saloon, Embossed Die Cut, Lithograph, Early 1900, 11 1/2 x 15 In. 468.00
Columbian Rope, Old Fisherman Holds Rope, Cardboard, Frame, 34 x 54 In. 330.00
Commercial Union Assurance, Reverse On Glass, 13 1/2 x 19 1/2 In. 29.00
Community Silver, Celluloid, Oneida, New York, Whitehead & Hoag, 20 x 24 In. 83.00
Consolidated Tours, Blue, White, Die Cut, Porcelain, 2-Sided, 23 x 19 In. 1275.00
Converse Shoes, People, Car, Frame, c.1910, 30 x 34 In. 385.00
Corbin, Mendel & Co., Seminude Nymphs, Paper Lithograph, Frame, 1889, 33 x 21 3/4 In.   120.00
Cork Distilleries Co., Whisky Pure Pot Still, Tin, Bottle, Case, England, 16 x 12 1/2 In. . .   47.00
Cork Distilleries Co. Ltd., Whisky, Tin, Self-Framed, 12 1/2 x 16 1/2 In. 248.00
Cottolene, Frying & Shortening, Tin Lithograph, 19 1/2 x 13 3/4 In. 413.00
Cottolene Cottonseed Oil, Nature's Gift From The Sunny South, Tin, 20 x 14 In. 800.00
County Coal Co., Black Ground, Porcelain, 12 x 16 In. 187.00
Cowhide Brand Overalls & Pants, Metal, Flange, 2-Sided, 10 x 13 In. 531.00
Creagans Drug Store, Lilly Pharmaceuticals, Reverse On Glass, Frame, 15 x 22 In. 154.00
Creme Eclipse, Smiling & Crying Moon, c.1930, 9 1/2 x 13 1/2 In. 155.00
Crescent Chick Feed, Girl, Chickens, Tin Lithograph, Embossed, Hanger, 9 x 13 1/4 In. . .   963.00
Crescent Chicken Feed, Tin, Embossed, Die Cut, Mayer & Lavenson, N.Y., 13 x 9 In. . . .   209.00
Crosman Bro's. Seeds, Owl, Boys, Paper On Cardboard, Lithograph, 24 x 17 In. 891.00
Crow's Hybrid Corn, Chicken, Corncobs, White Ground, Masonite, 18 x 34 In. 44.00
Crown Wristwatches, Porcelain, Luster, Crownlit, Willstand, Dipak, 1940s, 15 x 28 In. . .   845.00
Crush, Ask For, Natural Flavor, Natural Color, Tin, Self-Framed, 2 x 16 In. 110.00
Crystal Cafe, Girl, Veil, Vallejo, California, Embossed, Cardboard, Die Cut, 20 x 13 In. . .   688.00
Crystal Club Beverages, Smart To Serve, Tin, Embossed, 10 x 28 In. 138.00
Crystal Club Ginger Ale, Tin, Embossed, Wooden Frame, 33 x 15 1/2 In. 88.00
Cudahy's Diamond C Hams, Bacon, Lard, Lady, Slicing Bacon, Tin, Embossed, 25 x 32 In.   550.00
Cudahy's Puritan Ham, Ripened Naturally, Tin Lithograph, 19 x 13 In. 124.00
Cunard Line Travel Agency, Berengaria Ocean Liner, Tin Lithograph, 34 x 44 In. 1430.00
Curlee Clothes, Cardboard, Easel Back, Artist Signed, 16 x 26 In. 44.00
Curtis Bros. & Co., Doors, Factories, Clinton, Iowa, Paper, Frame, 36 x 28 In. 385.00
D.M. Ferry & Co. Seeds, For Sale Here, 3 Women, Paper On Cardboard, 1898, 28 x 19 In.   1003.00
D.M. Ferry & Co. Seeds, Standard For Quality, Paper On Cardboard, c.1890, 33 x 23 In. . .   330.00
Dad's, Ask For, Old Fashioned Root Beer, Metal, 9 x 18 In. 110.00
Dad's, Have A Dad's, It's Delicious, Convex, Tin, Self-Framed, 9 x 12 In. 66.00
Dad's Diet Root Beer, Tin, Die Cut Bottle Cap, 29 In. 248.00
Dad's Old Fashioned Draft Root Beer, Tin, 10 x 28 In. 204.00

Sign, Charles Cuomo Cheese, Tin Over
Cardboard, c.1920, 13 x 19 In.

Sign, Cloverdale Soft Drinks,
Tin Lithograph,
Embossed, 11 x 29 In.

Dad's Old Fashioned Root Beer, It's Delicious, Tin, Embossed, c.1950s, 19 x 27 In. 300.00
Dairy Made Ice Cream, You're Sure It's Pure, Boy, Tin, Embossed, Frame, 30 x 22 In. *Illus* 935.00
Dairy Maid Ice Cream, Embossed Tin Lithograph, Frame, 27 x 19 In. 330.00
Daisy Hair Tonic, Tin, Hanger, 10 x 9 In. 248.00
Dakota Maid Flour, Tin Lithograph, Embossed, Yellow Ground, 9 x 19 1/2 In. 132.00
Dandro Solvent, Tin Over Cardboard, Self-Framed, 9 1/2 x 13 1/4 In. 88.00
Dandy Shandy, Down Goes The Thermometer, Cardboard, Frame, 19 x 11 In. 55.00
Davis Carriage, Tin Lithograph, Petersburg, Va., 20 In. 303.00
Davis Carriage M'f'g Co., Petersburg, Va., Headquarters, Everything To Ride In, 17 x 28 In. 330.00
Davis Carriage M'f'g Co., Petersburg, Va., Tin, Embossed, 7 x 20 In. 1540.00
Day & Nite Storage Garage, Steel, Hanger, 2-Sided, 42 In. 118.00
Day's Fruit Beverage, Tin, Painted, Green Ground, 9 1/2 x 19 1/2 In. 110.00
Dekalb Chix Hatcheries, Tin, 2-Sided, Metal Frame, 60 x 48 In. 440.00
Delmar's Restaurant, Steel, Reverse Painted Plexiglass, 2-Sided, 31 x 41 x 8 In. 58.00
Deming Pumps, World's Best Water Systems, Porcelain, Blue, White, 36 x 18 In. 1045.00
Dennis's Lincolnshire Pig Powders, Tin, Embossed, 10 x 13 1/2 In. 605.00
Dentyne, Hard Plastic, Countertop, 7 x 3 x 3 1/8 In. 265.00
Dentyne Chewing Gum, Helps Keep Teeth White, Mouth Healthy, 2 1/2 x 16 1/2 In. 99.00
Devoe Paint, Colors, 6 Houses, Tin Over Cardboard, 14 1/2 x 20 In. 33.00
Devoe Paint, Light-Up, Plastic Lenses, 31 x 31 In. 220.00
DeWitt's Pills, Cardboard, Die Cut, Stand-Up, 9 1/2 x 8 1/2 In. 303.00
Dexter Building, Curved Corners, Applied Lettering, Egg & Dart Molding, 21 x 22 In. 58.00
Diamond Crystal Salt, The Salt That's All Salt, Red, Yellow, Black, 1939, 15 x 23 In. ... 22.00
Diamond Edge Tools, Frank Lominack Hardware, Tin, Embossed, 9 1/2 x 27 1/2 In. 83.00
Diamond Horseshoe Calks, Horses Pulling Horseshoe Cart, Tin, Embossed, 36 x 24 In. .. 3500.00
Diamond Wine Co., Women, Bottles, Sandusky, Ohio, Frame, c.1896, 34 x 25 3/4 In. 935.00
Dickinson's Poultry Feeds, Porcelain, 27 1/2 x 14 In. 160.00
Diehl's Bread, It's Thoroughly Baked, Porcelain, 12 x 24 In. 132.00
Diet Rite Cola, Sugar Free, Green Ground, Tin, Embossed, 31 x 12 In. ....55.00 to 66.00
Diet Rite Cola, Sugar Free, Tin, 54 x 18 In. 220.00
Dingman's Soap, Girl Holding Package, Mat, Frame, 18 x 12 1/2 In. 330.00
Dingman's Soap, Kitty's Bath, Girl Bathing Cat, Paper, Mat, Frame, 35 x 29 In. 330.00
Dixon's Stove Polish, Girl & Kitten, Lithograph, Frame, 1898, 16 1/2 x 10 1/2 In. 110.00
DL & W, The Standard Anthracite, Scranton, White, Blue, Porcelain, 12 x 24 In. 160.00
Dodger Beverage, Tin, Die Cut Bottle, 66 x 15 1/2 In. 413.00
Doe-Wah-Jack Round Oak Stoves, Indian & Blanket, Embossed Cardboard, 23 x 8 1/2 In. 440.00
Dogs Need The Liver In Lassie, 2 Corgis, Woman, Stand-Up, c.1930s, 17 x 12 In. 151.00
Doluth Imperial Flour, Chef, Holding Bread Loaf, Tin Lithograph, 25 x 18 In. 935.00
Domaine Rolet Winery, Cotes Du Jura, France, c.1940, 38 x 26 In. 1035.00
Donald Duck Bread, Oven Fresh Flavor, Cardboard, 1950s, 25 x 11 In. 53.00
Donald Duck Cola, Tops For Flavour, Die Cut, Cardboard, Easel Back, 25 1/2 x 21 In. ... 110.00
Donald Duck Soft Drinks, Celluloid, Round, 9 In. 413.00
Double Cola, Enjoy, Green, White, Red, Tin, 31 3/4 x 11 3/4 In. 77.00
Double Cola, Tin, Die Cut, Flange, 1947, 15 x 18 In. 550.00
Double Cola, Woman, Holding Bottle, Frame, 27 x 22 In. 275.00
Douglas Battery, Sales & Service, Red, Black, Tin, 47 x 17 1/2 In. 72.00
Dr. A. Shull, Chiropractor, Interior Light, 36 x 18 In. 2200.00
Dr. Baker's, Pain, Panacea, For The Cure Of Pain, Paper, 16 x 12 In. 4400.00
Dr. Caldwell's Originator Of Syrup Pepsin, Man, Box, Cardboard, Easel Back, 15 x 6 In. 715.00
Dr. Caldwell's Syrup Pepsin, Cardboard, Die Cut Head, Easel Back, 42 x 32 In. 302.00
Dr. Caldwell's Syrup Pepsin, For Mother Or Child, Cardboard, Die Cut, Easel, 18 x 13 In. 295.00
Dr. Caldwell's Syrup Pepsin, Girl On Doctor's Lap, Cardboard, Frame, c.1892, 8 x 14 In. . 495.00
Dr. Cox's Barbed Wire Liniment, Cardboard, Frame, 29 x 25 In. 413.00
Dr. Fenner's Remedies, U.S. Battleship Iowa, Paper, Cures On Back, c.1898, 11 x 9 In. .. 242.00
Dr. Fenner's Remedies, U.S. Cruiser Olympia, Paper, Cures On Back, c.1898, 11 x 9 In. . 242.00
Dr. Fulton's Wild Cherry Cough Elixir, Girl, Well, Die Cut, Cardboard, Frame, 13 x 11 In. 1045.00
Dr. Grabow Pipes, 1 Pipe, Wood, 20 In. 45.00
Dr. Haile's Ole Injun System Tonic, Indian, For Sale Here, Cardboard, 13 1/2 x 20 1/2 In. 148.00
Dr. Harris' Cramp Cure, For Every Ache, Every Pain, Paper Lithograph, Frame, 11 x 46 In. 605.00
Dr. Harter's, Wild Cherry Bitters, Bottle, 1885-1887, Paper, Frame, 16 x 13 In. 209.00
Dr. Harter's The Only True Iron Tonic, Man, Woman, Paper, Frame, 14 x 10 1/2 In. 220.00
Dr. Jayne's Expectorant, Coughs, Colds, Consumption, Reverse Glass, 14 x 12 In. 165.00
Dr. Jayne's Family Medicine, Victorian Frame, 23 x 26 In. 468.00

Sign, Dairy Made Ice Cream, You're Sure It's
Pure, Boy, Tin, Embossed, Frame, 30 x 22 In.

Sign, Ebbert Wagons, Apple Tree, Tin Lithograph,
Self-Framed, c.1906, 26 x 38 In

Dr. LeGear's Screw Worm, Cow, Products, Easel Back, Die Cut, Cardboard, 17 x 11 3/4 In.   33.00
Dr. Meyer's Vet Medicines, Wenona, Illinois, 25 x 13 In. 55.00
Dr. Morse's Indian Root Pills, Cardboard, Countertop, 24 x 13 In. . . . . .77.00 to 110.00
Dr. Morse's Indian Root Pills, Indian, Canoe, Cardboard, 20 x 9 In. 198.00
Dr. Morse's Indian Root Pills, Indian, Landscape, Pills, Trifold, Cardboard, 27 x 42 In. . .   385.00
Dr. Murlless' Dental Purifico, To Sweeten & Cleanse, Frame, 13 x 11 1/4 In. 231.00
Dr. Odozone, Cleans Teeth Clean, It's A Fact, Cardboard, 20 x 11 In. 165.00
Dr. P. Hall's Cararrh Remedy, Only Genuine, Cardboard, 21 x 11 In. 132.00
Dr. P. Hall's Cararrh Remedy, Only Genuine, Paper, 42 x 28 In. 330.00
Dr. P. Hall's Cararrh Remedy, Paper, Frame, 45 x 31 In. 358.00
Dr. P. Hall's Celebrated Catarrh Remedy, Paper, Erie, Pa., Early 1900s, 30 x 45 In. 275.00
Dr. Pierce's Favorite Prescription For Women, 3 Women, Lithograph, Frame, 43 x 8 In. .   715.00
Dr. Pierce's Pleasant Pellets, Regulate Bowels, Soldiers, Lithograph, Frame, 43 x 8 In. . .   715.00
Dr. Price's Delicious Extract Of Vanilla, Paper, Frame, 27 1/2 x 17 1/2 In. 110.00
Dr. Ricord Celebrated Remedies, Sexual Diseases, Debility, Jorgensen, Frame, 10 x 8 In.   198.00
Dr. Rochester, Black, Gold Ground, Beveled, Reverse On Glass, 5 1/8 x 19 In. 385.00
Dr. Scholl's Zino Pads, Die Cut, Cardboard, 13 x 37 In. 44.00
Dr. Scholl's Zino Pads, For Corns, Callouses, Bunions, Yellow, Porcelain, 7 x 24 In. 1870.00
Dr. Walker's California Vinegar Bitters, Blood Purifier, Reverse Glass, Frame, 10 x 12 In.   495.00
Dr. Warner's Coraline Corsets, Cardboard, Frame, 1915, 18 x 26 In. 413.00
Dr. Wells, Delicious Carbonated Beverage, Tin, 24 x 2 3/4 In. 145.00
Drake's Cake, Marble Cake, Tin Over Cardboard, 13 1/2 x 9 1/4 In. 138.00
Drink Big Boy Beverages, Tin, Embossed, 34 x 18 In. 83.00
Drink Birchola In Bottles, 2 Bottles, Tin, 9 1/2 x 27 In. 149.00
Drink Braems Bitters For Appetitie, Aluminum Wrapped Cardboard, c.1900s, 13 x 7 In.   132.00
Drink Canoe Club Beverage, Once You Try It You'll Always Buy It, Tin, 14 x 30 In. 138.00
Drink Delaware Punch, Tin, Stout, 18 x 54 In. 440.00
Drink Double Cola, Flange, 2-Sided, Tin, 1947, 15 x 18 In. 1155.00
Drink Double Cola, Marquee, Tin, 20 x 30 In. 660.00
Drink Ginseng Liqueur, Tin, Embossed, Hanger, 11 3/4 x 8 1/2 In. 1100.00
Drink Grape Smash, You Will Like It, 5 Cent, Cardboard, Diamond Form, 12 x 8 1/2 In. .   55.00
Drink JC Cola, It's Delightful, Reverse Glass, Dura-Products, c.1940, 9 x 12 In. 844.00
Drink Mavis, It's Real Chocolate, Tin, Embossed, Baltimore, 10 x 28 In. 198.00
Drink Mavis, Woman By Pool, Cardboard, 29 1/2 x 18 1/2 In. 275.00
Drink Mt. Cabin, Washes Thirst Away, Bellhop, Tin Lithograph, Embossed, 18 x 12 In. . .   270.00
Drink Nehi, Ice Cold, Bottle, Tin, Self-Framed, 42 x 15 In. 495.00
Drink Nu Icy, Tin Lithograph, Embossed, 19 5/8 x 9 1/4 In. 413.00
Drink Orange Crush, Feel Fresh, Crushie, Embossed, Metal, 16 3/4 x 46 1/2 In. 291.00
Drink Pop Cola, America's Finest Cola, Mirror, Frame, c.1940, 9 x 13 In. 74.00
Drink Ski, Bottle, Tin, 11 1/2 x 32 In. 220.00
Drink Ski, Say Skee-E-E, Tin, Bottle Water Skiing, Self-Framed, 1950s, 12 x 31 3/4 In. . . .   413.00
Drink Sprite, Naturally Tart, Bottle, Tin, Embossed, 31 x 27 In. 220.00
Drink Sun Spot, Bottled Sunshine, Tin, Red, Yellow, Lithograph, Embossed, 12 x 10 In. .   264.00
Drink Tru Ade Not Carbonated, Red, Blue, Yellow, Orange, 2-Sided, 1940s, 14 x 20 In. .   81.00
Drugs, Reverse On Glass, Silver Background, Frame, 10 x 28 In. 468.00

Dub-L-Valu Soda, 5 Cents, Bottle, Embossed, Die Cut, Tin Lithograph, 30 x 7 1/2 In. 219.00
Dubec Waterloo, Victorian Woman, Red Hat, Dress, Lithograph, Frame, 24 x 29 In. 578.00
Duplate, For Your Safety, Shatterproof Plate Glass, Porcelain, 16 x 12 In. 220.00
Dura-Products, JC Soda, Reverse On Glass, c.1940, 9 x 12 In. 800.00
Duraline Floor Coverings, J. Frank Darling Co., New York, Tin, Embossed, 5 x 28 In. . . .   22.00
Dutch Boy, Anchor White Lead, Suspended Bucket Holder, Tin, Hanger, 19 x 13 In. 6160.00
Dutch Boy, Paint, Paper, Mat, Frame, 33 x 23 In. 198.00
Dutch Boy, Paint, Tin, Self-Framed, 23 x 35 In. 275.00
Dutch Boy, White Lead Paint, Passaic Metal Ware, Tin Lithograph, Embossed, 10 x 27 In.   440.00
Dutch Boy, White Lead, Boy, Man Putting On Coveralls, Mat, Frame, 55 3/4 x 32 In. 358.00
Dutchess Dress Trousers, Happy Man, Die Cut, Cardboard, Rockwell Art, 15 x 44 In. . . .   121.00
Dutchess Dress Trousers, Man, Fabric, Die Cut, Cardboard, Rockwell Art, 15 x 44 In. . . .   264.00
Duxbak, Hunter & Dog, Tin Lithograph, Easel Back, Hanger, Self-Framed, 13 x 17 In. . . .   137.00
Duxbak, Hunter, Dog, Flushing Quail, Tin, Hy S. Watson, Self-Framed, 15 x 19 1/2 In. . .   358.00
DuxBak & Kemp It, Man Fishing, Woman, Tin, American Artworks, 17 x 11 In. 550.00
Dyers Pork & Beans, Hand Holding Can, Tin Over Cardboard, 1920-1930, 11 x 8 In. 413.00
E.C. Simmons, Keen Kutter, Porcelain, Flange, 27 5/8 x 18 In. 1035.00
E.D. Pinaud's Eau De Quinine, Bottle, Tin, Wood Frame, c.1900, 17 1/2 x 23 In. 225.00
Eagle & Swan Flours, Flour Sack, Yellow, Black, Porcelain, England, 13 x 8 3/8 In. 1320.00
Eagle Angostura Bark Bitters, Nude Woman, Bottle, Frame, 1890-1910, 22 x 13 3/4 In. .   616.00
Eagle Patching Plaster, 2-Sided, Hanger, Die Cut, 11 x 7 In. 275.00
Eagle Star Insurance Co., Eagle Flying, Tin Lithograph, Over Cardboard, 9 x 12 In. 99.00
Early Times Distillery, Plaster, Frame, 28 x 23 In. 45.00
Eat Breyers Ice Cream, All-Ways, Porcelain, 2-Sided, 27 x 19 In.   127.00
Ebbert Wagons, Apple Tree, Tin Lithograph, Self-Framed, c.1906, 26 x 38 In . . . . . *Illus*   4675.00
Ed Price & Co. Tailors, Girl, Holding Chicks, Embossed, Die Cut, Easel, 9 1/2 x 6 1/2 In.   44.00
Ed Price Tailors, Girl In Hat, Die Cut, Embossed Cardboard, Easel, Germany, 9 x 6 In. . .   50.00
Eddie's Everlasting Black Dye, Hanger, Die Cut, Tin Lithograph, E-Jay-R, 6 1/2 x 8 In. . .   24.00
Eddie's Everlasting Dye, The Dye That Never Fades, Yellow, Red, Black, Tin, 6 1/2 x 9 In.   253.00
Eddy Good Bread, Red, Yellow, White, Tin, 12 x 27 In. 33.00
EFICO Equitable Fire Insurance, Charleston, Reverse On Glass, Frame, 16 x 22 In. 201.00
Egg-O-See Cereal, Dere Ain't Goiner Be No Leavins, Tin, Self-Framed, 10 1/2 x 16 1/2 In.   3960.00
Eggs, Write On Board, Black, Yellow, Tin, Embossed, 24 x 7 1/4 In. 44.00
Egyptian Regulator Tea, $500 Reward, Banknote, Nils Erickson, N. Dak., Paper, 8 x 12 In.   165.00
Eisemann's Klondike Head Rub, Embossed Cardboard, String Hung, 11 x 8 1/2 In. 132.00
Elephant Head Rubber Boot, Hunter, Canoe, Paper, Frame, 36 x 25 1/2 In. 1045.00
Elgin Watch, Made In America, Craftsman, Wood, Plastic, Light-Up, 18 x 22 In. 83.00
Elgin Watch, My Elgin's All Right, Boy Holding Watch, Wood Lithograph, 22 x 15 In. . .   650.00
Elgin Watch, My Elgin's All Right, Wood Lithograph, 18 x 26 In.   468.00
Elliott Ear Protector, Celluloid Over Cardboard, Easel Back, 7 1/2 x 9 1/2 In. 40.00
Emerson's Ginger-Mint Julep, Gives Pep, Quenches Thirst, Paper, c.1920, 4 1/2 x 20 In. .   22.00
Emerson's Ginger-Mint Julep, Gives Pep, Yellow Ground, Tin, Embossed, 28 x 10 In. . . .   55.00
Empire Cream Separator, M.D. Howard, Blue, Tin Lithograph, Embossed, 9 x 19 5/8 In.   220.00
Engles & Krudwig Grape Juice, Cherubs Dancing Around, Lithograph, 19 x 14 In. 259.00
Enna Jettick Health Shoe, Fashion Welt, Porcelain, 10 x 6 In. 330.00
Enterprise Stoves & Ranges, Flange, Sheet Steel, Lithograph, 18 1/2 In. 303.00
Entwistles Dog Biscuit, Porcelain, 24 x 18 In. 468.00
Erica Bicycle, Tin, Embossed, Painted, Germany, 12 x 6 1/2 In. 132.00
Escapernong, Garrett & Co., Uncle Sam, Liberty, Tin, Self-Framed, 18 x 26 1/4 In. 3960.00
Eshelman Red Rose Feed, Blue, Gold, Red, Porcelain, 11 x 17 In.   283.00
Eskay's Albumenized Food, Embossed Cardboard, c.1910, 26 x 23 In. 209.00
Esmond Ice Cream, Red Ground, Porcelain, 24 x 36 In. 176.00
Esso, Elephant, Kerosene, Porcelain, 2-Sided, 13 x 16 In. 605.00
Esso, Elephant, Kerosene, Porcelain, 24 x 12 In. 195.00
Eureka Harness Oil, Makes Old Harness Like New, Tin, Embossed, 4 1/2 x 19 1/2 In. . . .   605.00
Euthymol Tooth Paste, Woman, Kills Dental Decay Germs, Cardboard, Easel, 8 3/4 x 4 In.   138.00
Evangeline Maid Bread, Stays Fresh Longer, Loaf, Tin, 24 x 48 In. . . . . .193.00 to 330.00
Eveready, Extra Long Life Flashlight Batteries, 10 Cents, Tin, Countertop, 17 x 11 In. . . .   303.00
Eveready Columbia, Hot Shot Battery, Cardboard, Easel Back, Die Cut, 16 x 10 In. 605.00
Eveready Flashlights, 5 Flashlights, Tin Easel Back, Countertop, 19 x 5 1/2 In. 154.00
Eveready Flashlights & Batteries, Eveready Guy, Flashlight, Porcelain, 18 x 37 In. 1210.00
Eveready Flashlights & Batteries, Man Walking On Batteries, Porcelain, 18 x 41 In. 715.00
Eveready Flashlights & Batteries, Porcelain, Staircase, Middle Eastern, 12 x 18 In. 270.00

Everfast Department, Molded Composite, c.1940s, 10 x 28 In. 75.00
Eversharp Erasers, 10 Cents, Easel Back, 13 1/2 x 6 In. 44.00
Every Day Smoke, Foil Wrapped, Porcelain, Flange, 8 x 18 In. 605.00
Evian Cachat, Eau De Regime, En Vente Ici, Cardboard, France, 9 1/2 x 12 1/2 In. 110.00
Evinrude, Detachable Rowboat Motor, Tin, Flange, 2-Sided, 18 1/2 x 13 5/8 In. 1123.00
Evinrude Outboard Motors, Porcelain, 1 Neon Side, Milwaukee, 66 x 24 In. 4510.00
Excelsior Ice Cream, Celluloid Over Cardboard, Self-Framed, 6 x 8 3/4 In. 33.00
Eye-Gene, For Your Eyes, Porcelain Over Steel, Early 1900s, 3 3/4 x 5 In. 187.00
F.L. Grant Furniture-Undertaking, Salamanca, Yellow, Black, Tin, Embossed, 28 x 5 In. . 39.00
F.T. Dorney Bakery, Cardboard Lithograph, Embossed, Die Cut, Frame, 19 x 23 In. 220.00
Famous Reading Anthracite, No Smoke, More Heat, Porcelain, 11 x 21 In. 330.00
Fargo Way Wild West, Train, Across The Continent, Enameled, Porcelain, 8 3/4 x 14 In. . . 25.00
Farm Crest Bread, Elf With Loaf, Painted Wood, 24 In. . . . . *Illus* 150.00
Farmer's Pride, Everything Good To Eat, Tin Lithograph, Embossed, 5 3/4 x 11 3/4 In. . . 160.00
Farmers Fire Insurance Co., York, Penna., Reverse On Glass, Frame, 22 x 26 In. 220.00
Farnhams Reliable Shoes, Blue, White, Enamel On Metal, Flange, 2-Sided, 9 1/2 In. 248.00
Favorite Stoves & Ranges, Best In The World, Tin, Embossed, 6 1/2 x 28 In. 550.00
Fedtro, Wireless Intercoms, Mickey Mantle, Metal, Black, White, 1967, 13 1/2 x 32 In. . . 1610.00
Feen-A-Mint, The Chewing Gum Laxative, Porcelain, 7 x 29 1/2 In. 138.00
Fehrs Malt Tonic, Maiden, Cherubs, Tin, Oval, Self-Framed, 28 1/4 x 22 1/2 In. 420.00
Ferguson System, Porcelain, 34 x 60 In. 1650.00
Ferguson System, This Farm Uses, Metal, 10 7/8 x 22 In. 173.00
Ferguson-McKinney Make Shirts, Flange, Die Cut, 2-Sided, 14 In. 176.00
Fern Glen Rye Whiskey, I's In A Perdickermunt, Tin Lithograph, Frame, 33 x 23 In. 4181.00
Fidelity-Phenix Fire Insurance, Reverse On Glass, 13 1/2 x 29 1/2 In. 85.00
Field's Champion Whiskey, Tin, Frame, c.1890, 26 x 35 In. 1980.00
Finck's Detroit Special Overalls, Pig, Wear Like A Pig's Nose, Porcelain, 12 x 9 In. 110.00
Finck's Detroit Special Overalls, Pig, Wear Like A Pig's Nose, Porcelain, 17 1/4 x 12 In. . 303.00
Finck's Overalls, Steel, Enameled, Red, Blue, White, c.1925, 12 x 9 In. 201.00
Finck's Red Bar Overalls, Wears Like A Pig's Nose, Tin, 35 1/2 x 11 In. 440.00
Fireman's Fund Insurance, Fireman Carrying Girl, Tin, Self-Framed, 24 1/4 x 20 1/4 In. . 1430.00
Firemen's Insurance Co., Newark, N.J., Acid Etched, Aluminum, Frame, 11 x 14 In. 110.00
First-Aid, Thirsty?, Nature Is Calling For Help, Red, Black, Tin, Embossed, 27 x 10 In. . . 143.00
Fletcher's Castoria, Cardboard, Die Cut, Mother Feeding Baby, Easel Back, 22 In. 472.00
Foley's Honey & Tar Cures Coughs, Beehive, Tin, Embossed, 13 1/2 x 6 1/2 In. 523.00
Foley's Medicines, Columbian Exposition, Hold-To-Light, Cardboard, 15 1/2 x 8 1/2 In. . 715.00
Foremost Ice Cream, Tin, Die Cut, 24 x 34 In. 330.00
Foster Hose Supporters, Celluloid Over Cardboard, 17 x 9 In. . . . . .468.00 to 578.00
Foster Hose Supporters, Name On Buckles, Celluloid Over Cardboard, Frame, 22 x 14 In. 853.00
Foster Hose Supporters, Name On Buckles, Woman, Tin, 17 x 9 In. . . . . .253.00 to 440.00
Franklin Fire Insurance Company, Philadelphia, Porcelain, 12 x 18 In. 176.00
Franklin Sealtest Ice Cream, Porcelain, 2-Sided, 24 x 36 In. 215.00
Freihofer's Bread, Tin, Embossed, 23 3/4 x 17 3/4 In. 75.00
Frick Company, Waynesboro, Pa., Stone Lithograph, 1904, 34 1/2 x 22 1/2 In. 8250.00
Frick Machinery, Tin Lithograph, 24 1/2 In. 247.00
Fro-Joy Ice Cream, Light-Up, Electric, Glass, Metal Frame, 8 3/4 x 15 1/2 In. 176.00
Frog In Your Throat, 2 Girls, Die Cut, Cardboard, Frame, c.1894, 5 3/4 x 8 In. 254.00
Frog In Your Throat, Breaks Up A Cold, Frog Wearing Scarf, Paper, Frame, 14 x 42 In. . . 990.00
Frost's Tablets For Headache, 12 Boxes, Testimonials, Easel Back, 1913, 8 x 12 In. 143.00
Frostie Root Beer, Tin, 15 3/4 x 9 5/8 In. 165.00
Gardners Corn & Bunion Remedy, Ask The Druggist, Paper, Frame, 11 x 8 1/2 In. 88.00
Garland Stoves & Ranges, World's Best, Porcelain Tin, 24 x 24 In. . . . . .1300.00 to 1750.00
Gastobac Curing Systems, First & Best, Yellow, Green, Metal, 2-Sided, 20 x 28 In. 61.00
Gastobac Curing Systems, See Your Local Gas Company, Tin, 20 x 28 In. 44.00
Gavitt's Herb Tablets, W.W. Gavitt Medical, Paper, 12 x 7 3/8 In. 165.00
Gem Reversible Razors, 10 Full Boxes, Cardboard, Die Cut, Easel Back, 8 1/2 x 12 In. . . 55.00
Ghostley Pearls Poultry, Tin, 24 x 46 In. 55.00
Gilbert Rae's Aerated Waters, Tin Lithograph, Embossed, 3 Bottles, 28 1/4 x 20 In. 660.00
Glen Grant, Elk, Highland Malt Scotch Whisky, England, Frame, 23 x 19 In. 151.00
Glenmoore Distilling, Kentucky Whiskey, Man, Goatee, Newspaper, 27 1/2 x 21 1/2 In. . . 303.00
Glenmore Whiskey, Man, Bird Dog, Cardboard, Lithograph, Oval, Framee, 26 In. . .83.00 to 110.00
Glover's Mange Medicine, Dog Holding Box, Cardboard, Die Cut, 15 In. 1150.00
Glycerole, For Oiling & Dressing Shoes, Tin, Frame, 9 1/4 x 13 1/2 In. 193.00

Gobel's, Pure Meat Food Products, Quality First, Porcelain, Round, 19 In. 99.00
Gold Bond Ham, A Masterpiece, Woman, Green Ground, Masonite, 44 x 24 In. 44.00
Gold Bond Stamps, We Give, Yellow, Black, Red, Metal, Flange, 28 x 17 1/2 In. 143.00
Gold Seal Wine, Gentleman At Table, Holding Wine Glass, Tin, Frame, 16 x 12 In. 55.00
Golden Bear Cookies, Girl Scouts, Buy These Cookies, Cardboard, 21 x 14 1/2 In. 17.00
Golden Cola, Die Cut Bottle, 58 x 16 In. 413.00
Golden Shred Marmalade, Sunshiner Of Breakfast Table, Frame, 23 x 17 In. 123.00
Goldenson Furniture & Carpets, Saves You Money, Tin, Wood Frame, 29 x 10 1/2 In. 303.00
Goldthwaite's Golden Gum, Cardboard, Mat, Frame, Image 16 x 14 In. 220.00
Goldyrock Birch Beer, Clifton Bottling Works, Embossed Metal, Frame, 12 x 23 In. 230.00
Good Grape In Bottles, Embossed Tin Lithograph, 19 1/2 x 5 1/2 In. ....110.00 to 165.00
Goudy Gum, 1 Cent, It's Pure, Boy With Gum Packages, Tin, 15 1/2 x 7 1/4 In. 165.00
Grand Trunk Pacific Railway, Photograph, Frame, c.1900, 28 1/2 x 35 In. ......650.00 to 750.00
Grand Union Tea Company, 2 Children, Dog, Umbrella, Die Cut, Cardboard, 10 x 8 In. ... 66.00
Grapette Soda, Die Cut Bottle, 36 In. 325.00
Grapette Soda, Enjoy, Tin, Oval, 28 x 20 In. 468.00
Grapette Soda, Imitation Grape Flavor, Oval, Porcelain, 10 x 17 In. 248.00
Grapette Soda, Neon, Porcelain, 102 In. 1100.00
Grapette Soda, Porcelain, 10 x 14 In. 358.00
Grapette Soda, Real Fruit Juice Flavor, Tin, 11 1/2 x 31 In. 175.00
Grapette Soda, Woman In Swimming Pool, Cardboard, 1940-1950, 19 x 30 In. 132.00
Grapette Soda, Young Woman Holding Bottle, Paper Board, 18 x 11 1/4 In. 130.00
Great American Insurance, Cobalt Blue, White, Porcelain, New York, 12 x 18 In. 105.00
Greebe & Atwater-Kent, Radios & Electrical Fixtures, Painted, Wood, 84 x 14 1/2 In. ... 99.00
Green Mountain Boys, Balm Of Gilead & Cedar Plaster, Black, Paper, 20 x 15 1/2 In. ... 77.00
Greenfield Ice & Coal, Best Kentucky, Virginia Coal, Paper, Frame, 36 x 30 In. 176.00
Gridley's Milk Did It, Black Baby, Cardboard, Trolley Card, 11 x 21 In. 88.00
Gridley's Milk Did It, Blond Baby, Cardboard, Trolley Card, 11 x 21 In. 77.00
Gridley's Milk Did It, Brunette Girl, Cardboard, Trolley Card, 11 x 21 In. 83.00
Gridley's Milk Did It, Caroline, Girl's Face In Bottle, Trolley Card, 11 x 21 In.. .... 11.00
Gridley's Milk Did It, Dolly, Girl's Face In Bottle, Trolley Card, Cardboard, 11 x 21 In. .. 11.00
Gridley's Milk Did It, Walter, Boy's Face In Bottle, Trolley Card, 11 x 21 In. 11.00
Groceries, Copper, Over Wood, 7 x 57 In. 550.00
Gulf Marine Products Dealer, Arrow, Porcelain, 45 x 70 In. 1430.00
H & N, Kramer's Hatchery, Red Wing, Minn., Nick Chick, Leghorns, Tin, 17 x 17 In. 121.00
H.P. Miles Ice Co., Cardboard, 11 x 21 In. ....*Illus* 35.00
Haig & Haig Whiskies, Coat Of Arms, England, Frame, 32 1/2 x 24 1/2 In. 142.00
Hamilton Brown Shoe Co., Keep Quality Up, Porcelain, Flange, 2-Sided, 12 x 16 In. 385.00
Hamilton Brown Shoe Co., Lady, Blue Dress, Hat, Frame, 22 x 35 In. 468.00
Hamilton Clothes Dryer, Authorized Dealer, Composition, 14 In. 132.00
Hamilton Watch, Railroad Time Keeper, Tin Over Cardboard, Hanger, 24 x 14 In. 1650.00
Hanan Shoes, Etched & Filled Letters, Brass, 3 1/2 x 14 In. 210.00
Handy Package Dyes, Stahl & Jaeger Lithograph, New York, Paper, Frame, 21 x 17 In. .. 77.00
Hanover Pure Rye, Horse Head, Convex Glass, Reverse Painted, c.1890, 24 In. ..850.00 to 1100.00
Harrison's Town & Country Paints, Tin, c.1900, 13 3/4 x 19 1/2 In. 330.00
Harry's Lunchroom, Sheldon, Mo., Die Cut Cardboard, Embossed Lithograph, 7 x 12 In. .. 161.00
Hart Schaffner & Marx Clothes, A. J. DeMuth, Darlington, Tin, Wood Frame, 38 x 28 In. 121.00
Hartford, Fire Insurance, Tin Lithograph, Self-Framed, 20 x 24 In. 110.00
Harvard Pure Rye, Tin Lithograph, Frame, Klein Bros., Cincinnati, 23 x 29 In. 2200.00
Harvey's Pasteurized Milk, Taste The Difference, Glass, Frame, 10 1/2 x 13 1/2 In. 110.00
Hazel Club Birch Beer, Button, Metal Over Cardboard, Round, 9 In. 77.00
Headlight Union Made Overalls, Train, Porcelain, 15 x 45 In. 440.00
Hendler's Ice Cream, Picaninny Freeze, 5 Cent, Color, Cardboard, 1922, 14 x 11 In. 575.00
Henry H. Shufeldt Whiskeys, Man, Woman, Red Umbrella, Paper, Frame, 31 x 14 In. ... 165.00
HGC Patent Medicine, Yellow, Black, Embossed, 9 3/4 x 7 In. 253.00
Hickok Radio & TV Instruments, Choice Of The Experts, Reverse Glass, 15 x 13 In. 110.00
High Ball Ginger Ale, Sparkling Refreshing, Tin, Diamond Shape, 6 1/2 In. 220.00
Highland Tonic Water, Cures Brights, Diabetes, Cardboard, 11 x 14 In. 125.00
Hill, Evans & Co., Pure Malt Vinegar, Tin, Shield Shape, Embossed, c.1890s, 12 x 9 In. .. 118.00
Hill Top, Wood, Black, Painted, Frame, 9 1/2 x 24 1/4 x 1 1/2 In. 200.00
Hinkley & Garrett Country Store, Pumpkin Color Ground, 90 x 11 In. 225.00
Hoffman Sparkling Beverages, Pale Dry Ginger Ale Bottle, Tin, 1959, 42 x 16 In. 110.00
Holsum Bakes Real Bread, 2 Young Bakers, Tin, 37 x 10 1/2 In. 660.00

Holsum Bakes Real Bread, Tin, 15 1/2 x 60 In. 440.00
Holsum Bread, To My Valentine, Boy, Girl, Print, Frame, 18 x 41 In. 220.00
Holsum Enriched Bread, Enameled On Steel, 18 1/2 x 9 In. 77.00
Home Insurance Company, New York, Reverse Glass, Oak Frame, 24 1/2 x 34 1/2 In. ... 303.00
Home Of The Checker Smoker, R.O.G., Red, Black, Gold, Reverse Painted, 33 x 14 In. .. 29.00
Honey Razor Blade, 20 Packs, Cardboard, Easel Back, 12 1/2 x 9 1/2 In. 17.00
Hood Fishing Boots, Fish In Basket, Die Cut, Cardboard, c.1920s, 26 x 19 1/2 In. 413.00
Hoosier Water Pump, Cow Drinking Water, Lady, Paper, 35 x 23 In. 154.00
Horniman's Pure Tea, Enamel, 2-Sided, Yellow Ground, England, 16 1/2 x 10 1/2 In. 104.00
Horoscope Scale, Porcelain, Die Cut, 12 x 15 In. 187.00
Horse Drawn & Oliver Tractor Implements, Tin, Vance Hardware Co., 13 x 19 1/2 In. .. 715.00
Hose Of Luxite, Fulfilling Every Requirement, Cardboard, Easel Back, 13 x 17 In. 55.00
Hostetter's Stomach Bitters, Reverse On Glass, Frame, 1880-1895, 30 1/2 In. 2016.00
Hotpoint Appliances, Neon, Porcelain, 2-Sided, Top Hangers, 32 x 50 In. 1760.00
Houbigant Parfums, Paper On Cardboard, Frame, 1920s, 16 1/2 x 20 1/2 In. .....250.00 to 325.00
Hubbard Feeds, Metal, 18 x 36 In. 35.00
Hubbard's Bone Base Connecticut Fertilizers, Blue, Embossed, Porcelain, 10 x 20 In. .. 248.00
Hudson's Soap, Enamel, White Light Beam, Green Outline, England, 13 x 8 1/2 In. 322.00
Humble Restroom, Tin, 2-Sided, 30 x 30 In. 220.00
Hummingbird, Full Fashioned Hosiery, Woman, Lithograph, c.1925, 23 x 35 In. 92.00
Hummingbird Hosiery, Woman, Green Dress, Flowers, Lithograph, c.1925, 25 x 38 In. .. 104.00
Hummingbird Hosiery, Woman, Orange Dress, Hat, Lithograph, c.1925, 21 x 38 In. 138.00
Humphrey's Homeopathic Remedies, Cardboard, Self-Framed, 17 1/2 x 14 In. 523.00
Hunt's Ice Cream, Celluloid, Hanger, c.1940, 9 In. 585.00
Hunt's Ice Cream, Delicious Sundae, Celluloid Over Cardboard, Round, 9 In. 294.00
Husemans Soda, Clear & Sparkling, Red Bud, Ill., Tin, 20 x 13 In. 55.00
Hy-Line Chicks, Metal, 2-Sided, 16 x 24 In. 77.00
I.G.A., Shield Shape, Eagle, Spread Wings, Porcelain, 12 1/2 In. 77.00
Icey-Ike, The Ice-Illated Drink, Character Drinking On Snowy Hill, 32 x 24 In. 193.00
Ide & Willson's Boots & Shoes, Lithograph, Columbus, Oh., Frame, 23 x 17 3/4 In. 633.00
Ilco Independent Lock Co., Key Shape, Steel Lithograph, 2-Sided, 32 x 14 In. 225.00
Illinois Watch Company, Abraham Lincoln, Chromolithograph, 10 x 6 1/2 In. 136.00
Illinois Watches, Springfield, Metal, Wood Frame, 9 1/4 x 22 1/4 In. 350.00
Imperial Egg Food, Black Workers, Packing Eggs, Paper, Frame, 34 x 27 In. 550.00
Imperial Ice Cream, Flavor List, Mirrored Back, Chrome Frame, 13 x 28 In. 275.00
Indian Maid Coal, Pocahontas In Canoe, Porcelain, 24 In. 275.00
Indian Motorcycle, World's Record For Indian, 1600 Miles, 80 Hours, Paper, 30 In. 220.00
Indian Nickel, Porcelain, Tin, 11 1/4 In. Diam. 25.00
Ingersoll Dollar Watch, Embossed, Pocket Watch Shape, Metal, 34 x 25 In. .....990.00 to 1900.00
Ingersoll Watches, Blue Ground, White Letters, Porcelain, 7 x 16 In. 248.00
Ingersoll Watches, Boy With New Watch, Paper Lithograph, Frame, 23 x 14 In. ..209.00 to 220.00
Ingersoll Watches, Porcelain, Figural, Flange, 2-Sided, 16 1/2 x 9 In. 1018.00
Ingleside, Spring Ginger Ale, Roll Down, Woman On Man's Shoulders, 22 x 15 In. 154.00 to 230.00
Interloc, Section Repair Tire, Moulded To Fit, Tin, Embossed, 13 x 19 In. 220.00

Sign, Farm Crest Bread, Elf With
Loaf, Painted Wood, 24 In.

Sign, H.P. Miles Ice Co.,
Cardboard, 11 x 21 In.

Sign, Ivory Salt, Flavor's The
Thing, 17 3/4 x 11 1/2 In.

Interlux Marine Paints, Have Smartest Boat In The Fleet, Porcelain, c.1940, 14 x 24 In. . 4400.00
Interlux Marine Paints, Tin, Self-Framed, 28 1/2 x 46 1/2 In. 523.00
International Clothes, Perfect Fit, Popular Prices, 2-Sided, Porcelain, Flange, 17 x 21 In. 132.00
International Stock Food, Dan Patch, Paper, Frame, c.1910, 20 x 27 In. . . . . .225.00 to 325.00
International Stock Food, Do You Want More Milk, Paper, 21 1/2 x 15 In. 1100.00
International Tailoring, We Recommend, Die Cut, Triangle, Porcelain, 20 x 17 In. 121.00
Iron Clad Hosiery, Cardboard, Easel Back, 1920s, 10 1/2 x 13 In. 143.00
Iron Clad Hosiery, Copper Wells & Co., Metal, Stand-Up, St. Joseph, Michigan, 3 x 8 In. 50.00
Iron Fireman, Automatic Coal Burner, Red, White, Black, Porcelain, 11 7/8 In. Diam. . . . 605.00
Ironbrew, We Serve Ironbrew In Bottles Ice Cold, Blake Slee Bros., c.1940, 9 x 12 In. . . . 800.00
Iroquois Insurance, Metal, Die Cut, Danville, Illinois, 3 5/8 x 2 5/8 In. 85.00
It's Ashland, Highly Spoken Of Everywhere, 2 Men, Dog, Tin, Self-Framed, 24 x 20 In. . 575.00
Italian Swiss Colony, Tavern, Painted Plaster, Plasto Manufacturing, c.1950s, 5 x 9 In. . . . 30.00
Ithaca Guns, Every Gun Warranted, Tin, Embossed, c.1910, 6 1/2 x 13 7/8 In. 2548.00
Ivorene Cleanser, Elephant, People, Paper, Frame, 10 1/2 x 15 1/2 In. 231.00
Ivory Salt, Flavor's The Thing, 17 3/4 x 11 1/2 In. . . . . *Illus* 25.00
J. Carper, Buy Lumber & Millwork, Tin, Embossed, Frame, 21 1/4 x 29 1/4 In. 358.00
J.A. Lehane, Porcelain, 12 x 57 In. 22.00
J.B. Lewis Co., Footwear, For Sale Here, Porcelain, Blue Ground, 8 x 6 In. 715.00
J.I. Case Threshing Machine Co., Eagle On Globe, Glass, Hanger, Racine, Wis., 16 x 8 In. 935.00
J.I. Case Threshing Machine Co., Eagle On Globe, Tin, Embossed, Frame, 28 x 20 In. 1320.00
J.I. Case Threshing Machine Co., Traction Engine, Tin, Embossed, 14 x 20 In. . . . . . *Illus* 6875.00
J.N. Ward & Co. Shirts, Paper Lithograph, Cardboard, Frame, c.1880, 14 x 21 In. . .475.00 to 650.00
J.P. Primleys California Fruit Chewing Gum, Sweetens Breath, Bear, Die Cut, 4 x 6 In. . . 149.00
Jack Boeckmann's, Musical Instrument Hospital, Iron, 25 x 47 In. 2200.00
Jacob & Co., Cream Crackers, Woman Holds Tin, Frame, 25 x 20 1/2 In. 79.00
Jacob's Puff Cracknels, Girl Holding Tray, England, Frame, 29 x 20 1/2 In. 303.00
Japanese Oil & National Remedies, Boy, Bottle, Spoon, Cardboard, c.1892, 9 1/2 x 14 In. 385.00
Japp's Hair Rejuvenator, 7 Different Colors, Celluloid, Self-Framed, 9 x 13 In. . . .154.00 to 413.00
Japp's Hair Rejuvenator, Tin Over Cardboard, Easel Back, 9 x 13 In. 55.00
Jas. G. Johnson & Co., Beach Scene, Spring & Summer 1897, Paper, Frame, 55 x 36 In. . . . 3190.00
Jas. Johnson French Millinery, Mandolin Shape, Die Cut, 15 1/2 In. 60.00
Jay-An-Ay Ice Cream, Jessup & Antrim Ice Cream Co., 11 x 8 In. 55.00
JB Lewis, Shoe Maker, Working For You, Tin Lithograph, 22 x 16 In. 303.00
Jenkin's Dept. Store, Colonial Bread, Aluminum, Painted, c.1950, 42 x 60 In. . . . . . *Illus* 69.00
Jerome Wheel Lock, Steam Cylinder Packing Co., Paper, Frame, 29 x 36 1/2 In. 935.00
Jersey Creme, Perfect Drink, 5 Cents, Tin Lithograph, Flange, 2-Sided, 6 x 6 In. 798.00
Jevnes Bread, Red, Yellow, Tin, Embossed, 13 x 16 In. 99.00
Jic Jac, Pick A Pack, 6 Pack, Metal, 31 x 12 In. 83.00
John D. Parks Balsam, Wild Cherry & Tar, Tree Graphic, Paper Lithograph, 23 x 19 In. . . . 2530.00
John Peel, Port, Dye, Ken, Huntsman Holds Glass, England, Frame, 19 1/4 x 15 In. 47.00
John Player & Sons, Dublin Factory & Offices, Frame, 22 1/2 x 17 1/2 In. 66.00
Johnson Outboard Motors, Lukes Music Store, Ardmore, Ok., Tin, 14 x 20 In. 650.00
Johnsonian Shoes, That's A Fact, Round, Wood Frame, 36 In. 220.00
Jones Dairy Farm Sausage, Tin Lithograph Over Cardboard, Winter Scene, 8 1/8 x 12 In. 221.00
Jones Sewing Machines, Makers, Royal Warrant, Enamel, 2-Sided, England, 20 x 15 In. . . 284.00
Ju-See Beverages, Light-Up, Red Rim, Yellow Ground, Bakelite, 13 x 8 In. 99.00
Jung's Arch Braces, Light-Up, Reverse On Glass, Cast Iron Base, 1920s, 16 x 16 In. 116.00
Kaiser Frazer, Approved Service, Porcelain, 2-Sided, Round, 58 1/2 In. 1100.00
Kaufmann & Strauss, 2 Women, Chromolithograph, Frame, Early 1800s, 34 1/2 x 25 In. . 468.00
Kayo, In Bottles, It's Real Chocolate, Chalkboard, Embossed, Tin Lithograph, 29 In. 79.00
Kayo, Tops In Taste, Real Chocolate Flavor, Tin Lithograph, Embossed, 27 1/2 x 14 In. . . 330.00
Kayser Silk Gloves, Etched & Filled, Brass, Oval, 3 1/2 x 7 In. 264.00
Keds, Annual Wire Haired Terrier & Bicycle Contest, Paper, 1935, 13 x 9 In. 44.00
Keen Kutter, Cutlery, Tools, Razor & Case, Die Cut, Easel Back, 9 x 13 1/2 In. 376.00
Keen Kutter Hardware, Tin, Embossed, Self-Framed, 1950s, 29 1/2 x 29 1/2 In. 91.00
Keen Kutter Pocket Knives, Boy Whittling, Die Cut, Easel Back, 10 x 13 In. 590.00
Keen Kutter Tools, Stafford, Kans., Tin Lithograph, Embossed, 9 3/4 x 27 5/8 In. 143.00
Keen Kutter Tools, Tin, Embossed, Hillsboro, Kansas, 28 In. 77.00
Keiffer Bros. Shoes, Dixie Bell, Paper Lithograph, 18 5/8 x 12 3/8 In. 330.00
Keil, Key Shape, Cast Aluminum, Charlestown, N.H., 27 1/2 x 11 1/2 In. 77.00
Ken-L Biskit, Dog Food Of Champions, Tin, Embossed, 1950s, 29 x 18 In. 275.00
Ken-L Ration, Feed Your Dog The Best, Yellow Dog, Tin, Die Cut, 14 x 21 In. 330.00

Sign, J.I. Case Threshing Machine, Traction Engine, Tin, Embossed, 14 x 20 In.

Sign, Jenkin's Dept. Store, Colonial Bread, Aluminum, Painted, c.1950, 42 x 60 In.

Kerns Bacon & Sausage, Store Hours, Clocks, Tin Over Cardboard, Die Cut, 13 x 9 In. . . . 55.00
Kerns Bread, Take Home, Red, Yellow, Black, Tin, 54 x 14 In. . . . . .85.00 to 149.00
Key Denim Clothes, Yessiree, It's A Key, Boy, Overalls, Die Cut, Cardboard, 32 In. 77.00
Key Work Clothes, Light-Up, Countertop, 6 x 48 1/2 In. 55.00
Keystone Ice Cream, Smiling Blond Girl, Tin Lithograph, Embossed, 27 3/4 x 19 3/4 In. . 1980.00
King Aerator, King System Ventilation, Barn, Cows, Lithograph, Self-Framed, 19 x 13 In. 99.00
King Arthur Flour, King, Horse, Flag, Tin Lithograph, Minnesota, Round, Frame, 26 In. . 4140.00
King No-To-Bac, His Work In America, Paper, Mounted On Board, 18 x 11 In. 288.00
King Of Soaps, Girl, Puppy, Lithograph, Frame, 13 x 25 In. 242.00
King Quality Shoes For Men, Die Cut, Tin Lithograph, c.1920, 9 1/2 x 12 In. . . . . .24.00 to 35.00
Kingfisher Brand, Braided Silk Fishing Lines, E.J. Martin's Sons, 27 x 17 In. 6600.00
Kingston Roller Skates, Tin, Embossed, Rolled Edges, Kokomo, Ind., 15 x 6 In. 44.00
Kirk's Flake Soap, Cardboard, Frame, James S. Kirk Co., Chicago, 31 x 22 In. 990.00
Kirk's Flake Soap, Red Ground, White Letters, Porcelain, 3 x 21 In. 825.00
Kist Soda Pop, Bathing Beauty, Die Cut, Paper, c.1920, 7 1/4 x 5 In. 242.00
Knox Gelatin, Paper Lithograph, Mammy & Little Girl, Mat, Frame, 22 x 28 1/2 In. 330.00
Kolb Hardware, Trade Sign, Wood, Saw Shape, 104 In. 1100.00
Koldpruf Antifreeze, Penguin, Cities Service, Die Cut Cardboard, 2-Sided, 11 1/2 x 18 In. 231.00
Korbel Sec California Champagne, Woman Holding Grapes, Tin, Easel Back, 13 x 19 In. 193.00
Kotex, Woman Holding Box, Tin, Die Cut, Easel Back, 13 x 8 In. 248.00
Kreso Dip, No. 1, All Livestock, Sheep, Insect, Kills Scab, Lice, Ticks, Paper, 21 x 11 In. . 61.00
Kreso Dip, No. 1, Farm Sanitation, Prevent Disease, Paper, 41 x 17 In. 176.00
Kreso Dip, No. 1, Prevent Hog Cholera, Kills Hog Lice, Paper, 21 x 11 In. 198.00
Kreso Dip No. 1, Clark's Drug Store, Embossed, 12 x 23 In. 83.00
Kreso Disinfectant, Tin, Embossed, Yellow, American Artworks, Cosh., Ohio, 23 x 12 In. 121.00
L.N. Meadows & Co., Cameras & Supplies, Paint, Stencil, Tin, Frostburg, 36 In. 633.00
Lacrosse Hat Works, We Are Agents For, La Crosse, Wis., Metal, 6 x 10 In. 22.00
Lakeside Club Bouquet, Milk Glass Panel, Wood Frame, 18 1/2 x 21 1/2 In. 3300.00
LaPorta Fabrics, Factory Scene, Self-Framed, 1914, 27 1/2 x 9 1/2 In. 220.00
LaReine Rex Shoes, B. Rosenberg & Sons, Black, Yellow, Tin, 13 x 20 In. 61.00
Larro Sureraise & Surecalf, Metal, Flange, 2-Sided, 20 1/2 x 22 In. 260.00
Laverty's Family Liniment, Tin, Embossed, 6 1/2 x 9 In. 209.00
Lax-Ease, 10 & 25 Cents, Girl, Pink Dress, Die Cut, Cardboard, 2-Sided, 5 3/4 x 3 1/4 In. 330.00
Lax-Fos Way, 2 Seated, Happy Children, Die Cut, Cardboard, 6 1/8 x 9 1/2 In. 303.00
Le Figaro, Barber Shop, Shaving Brush, Wood Base, Natural Bristles, 9 1/2 x 3 1/4 In. . . . 578.00
Leaf Mint Chewing Gum, Tin Lithograph, 27 1/2 x 9 3/4 In. 92.00
Leaf Spearmint Chewing Gum, Flavor Lingers Longer, Tin, 25 x 9 In. 44.00
Lear & Oliver Ice Cream, Cardboard, Frame, 20 In. 55.00
Lee Overalls, Leg Kicking, Yellow, Tin Lithograph, Embossed, 1930s, 23 In. . . . . . . *Illus* 385.00
Lee Overalls, Union Made, Guaranteed, Tin, 23 x 3 1/2 In. 55.00
Lehigh Valley Antracite, Porcelain, 8 3/4 x 11 1/2 In. 165.00
Lenox Soap, Porcelain, 6 x 10 In. 275.00
Let Your Money Work For You, Light-Up, Celluloid, Metal Case, 24 In. 94.00
Levi Strauss, Neon, Plastic, 1980s, 16 In. 200.00
Levi's, Wood, Plastic Letters, 45 In. 55.00
Liberty Beef, 49 North St., Black, Gilt, Metal, Wood Frame, 28 1/4 x 81 In. 288.00
Lime Cola, Double Size, 5 Cent, White, Red, Parker Metal Co., 3 x 20 In. 44.00

Lincoln, Porcelain, Die Cut, 26 x 16 In. 1320.00
Lincoln Flour, Lincoln's Portrait, Paper, 17 x 25 In. 77.00
Lincoln Insurance, President Lincoln, Capital 200,000, 1865, 12 3/4 x 9 1/2 In. 440.00
Liner Brand, Pan Fried Green Tea, Wood, John Blaul, Cedar Rapids, Iowa, 58 x 83 In. 99.00
Liner Canned Fruits, Ocean Liner, Celluloid Over Tin Over Cardboard, Beveled, 6 x 8 In. 413.00
Lion Black, Lead, Red, White, Porcelain, 20 x 12 In. 132.00
Lion's Scotch, Woman Drinking, Celluloid, 15 1/2 x 11 1/2 In. 138.00
Liquer Hanappier, Lady, With Glass, Tin, Die Cut, Embossed, 19 1/4 x 19 1/2 In. 460.00
Lisk's Sanitary Enameled Roasters, Sackett & Wilhelms, Paper, Frame, 21 x 28 In. 798.00
Lithiated Lemon Soda, Embossed, 11 1/2 x 29 1/2 In. 198.00
Lotta Cola, Serves 3, 16 Oz. Soft Drink, Tin, Embossed, 1959, 11 3/4 x 21 1/2 In. 193.00
Louis B. Miele Wholesale Produce, 32, Painted, Tin On Wood, 26 x 15 In. 133.00
Louisville Slugger, Hillerich & Bradsby, Joe DiMaggio, Frame, 1940s, 43 1/2 x 24 1/2 In. 2875.00
Lov Me Perfume, Bottle Shape, Die Cut, Cardboard, Easel Back, 25 1/2 In. 88.00
Love's Fire Burns Forever, Pompeian Mfg., Frame, 9 x 33 In. 235.00
Lowney's Cocoa, Lithograph, Chalkboard, 2-Sided, Wood Frame, 33 x 14 1/2 In. 963.00
Lucky Tiger, For Hair & Scalp, Blond Woman, Tiger, Cardboard, 22 x 33 1/2 In. 550.00
Lyons Tea, Flange, Porcelain, 2-Sided, 11 x 15 In. 88.00
M. Hommel, Sandusky, Ohio, 22 x 28 In. 143.00
Ma's Root Beer, Woman, Smiling, White Hair, Embossed, Metal, c.1950, 19 x 27 1/2 In . 197.00
Maffits Gold Supply Co., Wilmington, N.C., Porcelain, 30 x 21 In. 44.00
Magcobar, Porcelain, 2-Sided, 18 x 30 In. 35.00
Magnolia, Porcelain, 1956, 16 x 26 In. 330.00
Majestic Ocean Liner, White Star Line, World's Largest Ship, Paper, c.1922, 20 x 26 In. . 95.00
Major's Cement, Is Good, Porcelain, 3/4 x 10 In. 193.00
Makepeace Evaporated Cranberries, Wareham, Mass, Cardboard, 12 x 7 1/2 In. 33.00
Malt Nutrine, Doctor, Bag, Umbrella, Tin, Cardboard, c.1915, 8 x 13 In. ....250.00 to 350.00
Malt Nutrine, Stork Carrying Baby, Tin, Cardboard Back, c.1915, 8 x 13 In. .....250.00 to 350.00
ManZan For Piles, Soothes & Cools, Die Cut, Cardboard, 10 1/2 x 9 In. 138.00
Mark Roger's Whiskey, Shadowbox Style, 4 Men Drinking, 11 1/2 x 13 1/2 In. 413.00
Marquette Club Ginger Ale, Embossed Cardboard, Stand-Up, Countertop, 11 3/8 x 7 3/4 In. 132.00
Marquette Life Insurance, Springfield, Ill., Frame, 13 1/2 x 17 In. 22.00
Marseilles Laundry Soap, 2 Children, Stone Lithograph Paper, Frame, 21 3/4 x 16 In. ... 2860.00
Martin-Senour Paint, 100% Pure, Porcelain, 4 x 32 In. 2035.00
Masurys Marin Swedish Marine Paints, Green, White, Red, Flange, 30 x 26 In. 39.00
Maurice's Printing Ink, Eagle, Oil On Paper, 19th Century, 37 x 49 In. 470.00
Maxine Shoes, For Women Who Know, Tin, Die Cut, Stand-Up, 19 1/2 x 13 3/4 In. . *Illus* 220.00
Mayer Honorbilt Shoes, Custom Made, Milwaukee, Tin, Flange, 13 1/2 x 18 1/4 In. 440.00
Mayer Shoes, For Sale By Q.B. Stout, Black, White, Tin, Embossed, 19 3/4 x 6 3/4 In. ... 55.00
Mayer Shoes, Q.B. Stout, Thick Paper, 30 In. 50.00
Mayflower, Great Stomach & Blood Remedy, Paper, 14 x 11 In. 44.00
Mazawattee Tea, Mother & Daughter, Tin Lithograph, 20 1/2 x 14 7/8 In. 440.00
Mazawattee Tea, Portrait Of Young Queen, England, Frame, 26 1/2 x 20 In. 114.00
McCloskey, Man O' War, Marine Varnish, Wood, 13 1/2 x 8 In. 88.00
McCormick, Reapers, Back From War, Horses, Reaper, Soldier, Print, Frame, 31 x 21 In. . 220.00
McCormick Dairy Equipment, Tin, Embossed, Self-Framed, 14 3/4 x 23 1/4 In. 77.00
McCormick Farm Machines, Twine, Tin, Embossed, Leonard Co., Warkarusa, 14 x 20 In. . 385.00
McCormick Harvesting Machinery, Horse, Equipment, Frame, c.1890, 33 x 43 In. 1100.00

Sign, Lee Overalls, Leg Kicking, Yellow,
Tin Lithograph, Embossed, 1930s, 23 In.

Sign, Maxine Shoes, For
Women Who Know,
Tin, Die Cut, Stand-Up,
19 1/2 x 13 3/4 In.

McCormick-Deering, Primrose Cream Separators, Wood, Trade, 70 x 20 In. 297.00
McCormick-Deering Line, Lady In Straw Hat, Print, Frame, 12 x 18 In. 198.00
McNally-Pittsburg Mfg. Corp., Designed & Built By, Porcelain, 30 x 10 In. 110.00
Meadow Gold Ice Cream, Metal, Flange, 2-Sided, 26 x 20 In. 176.00
Meals & Lodging Jitney Service, 2-Sided, 48 1/4 x 12 3/4 In. 759.00
Meckumfat, Ground Oats, Fowl, Cardboard, c.1920s, 14 1/2 x 18 1/2 In. . . . . *Illus*   358.00
Meckumfat, Sussex Ground Oats, Poultry, Multicolored, Cardboard, 20 x 23 3/4 In. 550.00
Mellin's Food, Child, On Chair, Die Cut, 12 x 7 1/2 In. 39.00
Mellin's Food, For Infants & Invalids, Tin Lithograph, Wells & Hope Co., 26 x 20 1/2 In. .   349.00
Mentholatum, For Sunburn, Lady In Water, Die Cut, Cardboard, Easel Back, 43 x 32 In. .   2400.00
Mentholatum, Till The Doctor Comes In Use, Aluminum, 2-Sided, 3 1/2 x 5 In. 98.00
Merchant Millers, Yahoo, Neb., Paper, Frame, 17 1/2 x 22 In. 715.00
Mercury, 2 Eagles, Embossed, Textured, Pressed Composition, 1942, 11 1/2 x 18 1/4 In. . .   161.00
Mercury, Outboard Motors, Sales & Service, Motorboat On Water, Neon, 11 x 24 1/2 In. .   1430.00
Mercury Outboards, Kiekhaefer, Sales & Service, Tin, Embossed, 24 x 30 In. 495.00
Merita Bread, Always Fresh, Tin, Embossed, 1940-1950, 55 x 18 In. 468.00
Merita Bread, Lone Ranger, Tin, 24 x 36 In. 495.00
Merry Wido Chewing Gum, Cardboard, 8 x 6 In. 413.00
Messer's Charcoal Gum, White Letters, Black Ground, Rectangular 504.00
Metallic Band Sleigh Bells, Horse, Cardboard, Frame, Donaldson Bros., 1877, 12 x 12 In.   5500.00
Mi-Grape, The Taste Lingers, Tin, Embossed, 23 1/2 x 12 In. 110.00
Midol, For Headache, Nervache, Cardboard, Easel Back, Stand-Up, 8 1/2 x 11 1/2 In. 358.00
Milwaukee Binders & Mowers, E.P. Armknecht, Cardboard, 7 x 25 1/2 In. 288.00
Miner's Friend Dynamite, Paper Lithograph, Woman, Miner, Frame, 9 x 14 1/4 In. 1668.00
Minnesota Paints, Blue Ground, White Letters, Porcelain, 3 x 32 In. 440.00
Mission Orange Of California, Naturally Good, Bottle, Tin, Yellow, Blue, 24 In. . . .95.00 to 232.00
Mit-Che, Ice Cold, New Refreshment, Tin Lithograph, Embossed, 15 1/2 x 23 1/2 In. 262.00
Modox, 5 Cents, Indian Chief, Tin Lithograph, Embossed, 27 1/2 x 19 1/2 In. 3960.00
Moehn Brewing Company, Maltodextrine Tonic, Tin, Round, 15 In. 495.00
Mohawk Tool Works, Arrowsharp Axes, Brass, Leather-Look Background, 10 x 16 In. . . .   853.00
Monarch Paint, Martin-Senour, Porcelain, Flange, 2-Sided, 14 x 19 In. 358.00
Montpelier Mineral Waters, Codd's Patent Stoppered Bottles, England, 19 x 14 In. 322.00
Morea Liquid Feeds, Yellow, Black, Tin, 20 x 42 In. . . . . .55.00 to 61.00
Morenci Roller Mills, Gold Lace Flour, 2 Kids, Barrel, Paper Lithograph, c.1890, 16 x 12 In.   121.00
Morning After Chaser Mixer, Heavy Cardboard, c.1920s, 8 x 10 In. 75.00
Morse's Duchess Filled Candies, Lithograph, Frame, 31 x 41 In.   1073.00
Mortar & Pestle, Rx, White, Red, Porcelain Over Steel, 2-Sided, 3 Piece, 23 x 12 In. 1050.00
Mother's Own Tea, Yellow Ground, Porcelain, 2 1/2 x 20 In. 275.00
Mott's Cider Vinegar, Pure Apple Juice, Canvas, Hanger, 15 x 12 In. 468.00
Mountain Dew, Do The Dew, Neon, 22 x 24 In. 127.00
Mountain Dew, It'll Tickle Yore Innards, Tin, Embossed, c.1960, 17 x 35 In. . . . . .468.00 to 770.00
Mountain Dew, Ya-Hooo!, It'll Tickle Yore Innards, Tin, Wood Frame, 34 x 58 In. 605.00
Mr. Cola, 16 Oz., Tin, Embossed, 12 x 12 In. 55.00
Mrs. Guntners Wart Remedy, No More Warts, Blue, Cardboard, 13 x 7 1/4 In. 88.00
Mumms Extra Dry Whiskey, Victorian Lady, Black Dress, Hat, Frame, 24 x 29 In. 578.00
Munsing Union Suits, Man, Woman, Child In Underwear, Cardboard, Easel, 16 x 12 In. . .   354.00
Munsingwear, Mother, Children, Tin Lithograph, 20 1/2 x 19 In.   605.00
Munsingwear, Perfection, Satisfaction, Twins, Tin Lithograph, Frame, 37 3/4 x 25 1/2 In. .   2640.00

Sign, Meckumfat, Ground Oats, Fowl,
Cardboard, c.1920s, 14 1/2 x 18 1/2 In.

Sign, Nelson's Ice Cream, Blue & Orange,
Porcelain, 25 x 30 In.

Sign, Niagara Fire Insurance
Company, Safety-Fund Policies,
New York, 11 x 21 In.

Murphy Paints, Porcelain, Die Cut, 7 Colors, 2-Sided, 24 x 36 In. 1100.00
Murphy's Concentrates, Livestock & Poultry, Embossed Metal, Lithograph, 35 x 23 In. ... 121.00
Mustang Liniment, For Man Or Beast, Tin Lithograph, Baltimore, Md., 20 In. 247.00
My Coca, Best Ever, Tin, Single-Sided, Embossed, Frame, 11 x 35 In. 4180.00
Narragansett Fire & Marine Insurance Co., Stone Lithograph, Tin, 19 1/2 x 14 In. 16500.00
National Refining Co., Boy, Check Knee Pants, Tin Lithograph, 2-Sided, c.1917, 28 x 45 In. 3500.00
National Security Fire Insurance Company, Metal, Frame, 27 x 15 In. 55.00
Natural Chilean Soda, Yassuh, Uncle Natchel, 2-Sided, Flange, 1950s, 2 In. 440.00
Nature's Remedy, Feel Like Million, Girl, Guitar, Cardboard, Easel Back, 13 x 17 In. ... 209.00
Nehi, Beverages, Green Ground, Woman's Legs, Cardboard, 20 x 11 In. 44.00
Nehi, Curb Service, Tin Lithograph, Embossed, 26 3/4 x 19 3/4 In. 231.00
Nehi, Drink Genuine Nehi, Woman's Legs, Cardboard, Frame, 15 1/2 x 22 7/8 In. 303.00
Nehi, Enjoy Nehi Orange, Cup, Light-Up, 14 x 18 x 5 In. 500.00
Nehi, Ice Cold, Bottle, Tin, Frame, 10 1/2 x 26 In. 248.00
Nehi, Quality Beverages, Bottle, Tin, 19 1/2 x 5 1/2 In. 94.00
Nehi, Red, Yellow, Tin, Die Cut, Flange, c.1940, 13 x 18 In. 413.00
Nehi, Soda, Bottle, Red, Yellow, Black, c.1930, 11 5/8 x 29 1/2 In. 275.00
Nehi, Take A Good Look At The Bottle, Woman's Legs, Metal, 34 x 58 In. 805.00
Nehi, Woman's Legs In Short Skirt, Cardboard, 16 x 23 In. 177.00
Nelson's Ice Cream, Blue & Orange, Porcelain, 25 x 30 In. .... Illus 708.00
Nelsons Dairies, 5 Cent, Chocolate Flavored Milk, Red, Black, Tin, 23 3/4 x 11 3/4 In. .. 303.00
Nelsons Ice Cream, Blue, Orange, White, Porcelain, 25 x 30 In. 708.00
Nesbitt's, All The Goodness Comes From Nesbitt's, Ottawa, Kansas, 1955, 31 x 7 In. ... 125.00
Nesbitt's, California Orange, 5 Cents, Tin, Die Cut Bottle, 12 In. 413.00
Nesbitt's, Orange Drink, Woman By Pool, Cardboard, Frame, c.1955, 28 x 39 In. .350.00 to 450.00
Nesbitt's, Soda, Distance From Waterloo, Iowa, Lithograph, Masonite, Frame, 7 x 29 In. . 55.00
Nesnah, Children Eating At Table, Trifold, Junket Co., Countertop, 7 x 19 In. 73.00
New York Garment Shop, Lead Glass, Cranberry, Milk Glass, 21 In. x 18 Ft. 6 In., 3 Piece 518.00
Niagara Fire Insurance Company, Niagara Falls, Porcelain, 11 x 21 In. 1035.00
Niagara Fire Insurance Company, Safety-Fund Policies, New York, 11 x 21 In. ..... Illus 2530.00
Nichol Kola, 5 Cents, America's Taste Sensation, Black, Red, White, Tin, 11 x 27 In. 39.00
Nichol Kola, 5 Cents, America's Taste Sensation, Tin, Embossed, 1940s, 10 x 14 In. 65.00
Nichol Kola, 5 Cents, America's Taste Sensation, Tin, Embossed, 12 x 36 In. 83.00
Nichol Kola, 5 Cents, Tin Lithograph, 8 x 24 In. 61.00
Nichol Kola, 5 Cents, Twice As Good, Tin, Embossed, Parker Metal, 12 x 35 1/2 In. 138.00
Nichol Kola, A Long Drink, America's Taste Sensation, Tin, 12 x 36 In. 110.00
Nichol Kola, Bottle Cap, Tin, Embossed, 1940s, 14 x 14 1/2 In. 79.00
Nichol Kola, Drum Major, Bottle Cap, Bottle, Yellow Ground, Metal, 12 x 29 1/2 In. 66.00
Nichol Kola, Toy Soldier, Bottle, Yellow, Red, White, Tin, 29 x 11 3/4 In. 72.00
Noll's Ice Cream, Light-Up, 2-Sided, 48 x 24 In. 55.00
None Such Mince Meat, Condensed, Indian, Tin, Syracuse, 24 x 20 In. .... Illus 9350.00
Norfolk, Food Of Strength, 3 Pictures Of Baby On Food Cans, England, 26 1/2 x 18 In. ... 85.00
Norka Orange, Tastes Better, Red, White, Black, Tin, 24 x 12 1/4 In. 138.00
North American Van Lines, Oneonta Transfer & Storage, Red, Tin, 2-Sided, 18 x 24 In. .. 39.00
Northrup King's Sterling Chick Mash, Paper, 18 x 22 In. 39.00
Northrup King's Sterling Turkey Starter, Paper, 18 x 22 In. 11.00
Northwestern Fire & Marine Insurance, Minneapolis, Wood, Red, Gold, 20 x 28 In. 88.00
NRA, National Rec. Act, Spread Winged Eagle, We Do Our Part, Cast Iron, 1930s, 4 In. .. 413.00
Nu Icy, Bottle, Flavors You Can't Forget, Embossed, 1930-1940, 20 x 9 In. 385.00
NuGrape Soda, Bottle Shape, Tin, Die Cut, 17 x 5 In. ....99.00 to 248.00
NuGrape Soda, Bottle, Yellow Ground, Tin Lithograph, c.1932, 12 x 4 1/2 In. 305.00
NuGrape Soda, Tin Lithograph, 36 In. 143.00
Nutex Condom, Baseball Players, Silkscreen Finish, Cardboard, Stand-Up, 11 x 14 In. ... 633.00
O-So Grape, Green, Tin, Embossed, Wood Frame, 30 In. 358.00

Occident Flour, Beveled, Tin Lithograph, Cardboard, Specimen Domes, 9 x 14 In. .245.00 to 275.00
Octagon Kirkman, Coupons Redeemed Here, Porcelain, Flange, 18 In. 275.00
Octagon Soap Premium Agency, Porcelain, Flange, Octagon Shape, 17 1/4 x 17 3/8 In. . . .   248.00
Ogden's St. Julien, Cool & Fragrant, Blue, Yellow, Tin, 29 x 10 In. 22.00
Oh Henry, Enjoy A 10 Cent Piece Of Dollar Candy, Tin, Embossed, 1925, 27 1/2 x 13 In.   413.00
OK Tires, Boy Saluting, OK On Chest, Masonite, Die Cut, 16 x 25 1/4 In. 121.00
Old Colony Insurance Company, Boston, Reverse On Glass, Frame, 18 x 24 In. 173.00
Old Company's Coal, Red Dot, Blue, White, Porcelain, 12 x 12 In. 99.00
Old Dutch, Cardboard Lithograph, Die Cut, 2-Sided, Fan Pull, 5 1/4 In. 66.00
Old Dutch, Cardboard, Curved, Corner, 20 In. 825.00
Old Dutch, We Sell, Large Sifter Can, 10 Cents, Porcelain, 20 x 14 In. . . . . *Illus*   770.00
Old English, Curve Cut, A Slice To A Pipeful, Tin, Slant Front, 9 x 13 x 11 In. 303.00
Old Harvest, Whiskey, Black Family, Rocking Chairs, Tin, Self-Framed, 16 x 22 In. 452.00
Old Hickory, Transfer On Glass, Hanger, Kentucky Wagon Manufacturing, 12 x 10 In. . . .   2640.00
Old Log Cabin Bourbon Whiskey, Die Cut Cabin, Woods, Composition, 8 x 10 In. 66.00
Old Overholt Rye, Fisherman, Canvas Lithograph, R. Bohunek, Frame, c.1913, 23 x 34 In.   495.00
Old Reading, Relax With, 2 Seated Men, Lighted, Half Moon Shape, Tabletop, 13 1/2 In. .   2200.00
Old Smuggler Scotch, Tin Over Cardboard, 11 x 15 In. 83.00
Old Stark Whiskey, Reverse On Glass, 4 x 14 In. 187.00
Oliver Chilled Plow, Steel, Walking & Riding, Wood, 5 1/2 x 48 In. 770.00
Oliver Chilled Plow, You Get Good Value, Ogden & Company, Tin, Embossed, 10 x 28 In.   660.00
Oliver Plows & Other Farm Equipment, Wood, 71 x 46 In. 112.00
Olixir, Unseen Power, Feel The Difference, Tin Lithograph, 20 x 22 In. 374.00
Olk Kirk, Enameled Brass, Saloon Cabinet Sign, Red Letters, 12 x 3 In. 149.00
Onyx Hosiery, Brass, Engraved, 6 x 7 1/2 In. 303.00
Orange Crush, Ask For, Natural Flavor, Natural Color, Tin, 3 1/4 x 26 1/2 In. 165.00
Orange Crush, Carbonated Beverage, Feel Fresh, Tin, Diamond Shape, 1939, 21 1/4 In. . .   385.00
Orange Crush, Fruit Flavored Drink, Orange, Celluloid Over Tin, Round, 9 In. 253.00
Orange Crush, Menu, Mirrored Glass, 1930s, 14 1/2 x 25 In. 2090.00
Orange Crush, Metal, Enamel Paint, 1968, 56 x 32 In. 295.00
Orange Crush, Mother Serves Children, Teddy Bear, Cardboard, 1920s, 19 x 10 3/4 In. . .   330.00
Orange Crush, Porcelain, 2-Sided, Hangers, Frame, 36 x 48 In.   3300.00
Orange Crush, Woman, Hat, Flowers, Cardboard, Self-Framed, c.1940s, 24 x 36 3/4 In. . .   495.00
Orange Julep, Couple, 2 Straws, Paper Lithograph, Frame, 7 1/2 x 12 In. 209.00
Orangeville, Tin, Reflective Paint, 4 x 16 In. 77.00
Orbit Gum, Good For The Kiddies, Paperboard, Frame, 15 x 11 3/4 In. 400.00
Ore-O-Dale Farms, Registered Guernseys, Cow, Porcelain, 30 x 30 In. 220.00
OshKosh, World's Best Overalls, 4 Men, Cardboard, c.1930, 13 1/2 x 14 In. . . . . . .175.00 to 250.00
OshKosh B'Gosh, Overalls, Red Ground, Porcelain, 10 x 30 In.   132.00
OshKosh B'Gosh, Work Clothes, Union Made, Tin, Embossed, c.1930s, 9 x 13 In. .100.00 to 150.00
OshKosh B'Gosh Overalls, Uncle Sam, Cardboard, c.1918, 14 x 30 In. 725.00
Ottekote Garment, Guaranteed Rainproof, Lithograph, Cardboard, Frame, 25 x 30 In. . . .   204.00
Overland Service, Tinkelpaugh Bros., Cobbleskill, Tin, Embossed, 10 x 28 In. 440.00

Sign, None Such Mince Meat,
Condensed, Indian, Tin, Syracuse,
24 x 20 In.

Sign, Old Dutch, We Sell,
Large Sifter Can, 10 Cents,
Porcelain, 20 x 14 In.

Sign, Page & Shaw Chocolates,
Santa, Cardboard Lithograph,
Stand-Up, 39 In.

P & G, White Naptha Soap, Time Saver, Cloth, Blue Letters, White Ground, 34 x 17 In. . .   95.00
P.H.C. Hall Dance, Pine, 2-Sided, Red Arrow, c.1930s, 48 1/4 x 28 1/4 x 1 3/4 In. 805.00
Pabst Chemical Co., Okay Specific, Paper, Frame, 7 1/2 x 10 1/2 In. 242.00
Page & Shaw Chocolates, Santa, Cardboard Lithograph, Stand-Up, 39 In. . . . . *Illus*   60.00
Paints By Armstrong, Since 1854, More Than 100 Years, Quality, Tin, Flange, 14 x 18 In.   165.00
Palethorpe's Sausage, Royal Cambridge, Enamel, England, 36 x 24 In. 908.00
Pan American World Airways, Winged Globe Logo, Porcelain, 17 3/4 x 24 In. 605.00
Panhandle, Porcelain, Die Cut, 2-Sided, 48 x 69 In. 5500.00
Par T Pak Beverages, 10 Cent, Full Quart, Serves 6, 33 x 12 In.   110.00
Park & Tilford's Chocolates, Porcelain, 15 x 48 In. 88.00
Parke, Davis & Co., Veterinarian, Protect Your Calves, Die Cut, Cardboard, 17 x 11 In. . . .   853.00
Parozone, Does More Than Bleach, Tin, Rolled Edge, 19 1/2 x 6 1/2 In. 72.00
Parry Mfg. Co., Indianapolis Factory Scene, Wood, Lithograph, 16 x 36 In. 413.00
Peacock Moreen, Celluloid, Cardboard, 17 x 14 In. 132.00
Pears' Soap, Henry Ward Beecher, Actresses, Lithograph On Cardboard, 10 x 14 In. 75.00
Pebeco Tooth Paste, Keeps Mouth Glands Active, Die Cut, Cardboard, Easel, 26 x 14 In.   99.00
Peninsular Furnaces Stoves & Ranges, Best, Porcelain, c.1890, 18 x 24 In. . . . .1300.00 to 1750.00
Pennsylvania Dutch Birch Beer, From Barrel Dispenser, Tin, 1955, 9 1/2 x 13 In. 150.00
Pennsylvania Dutch Birch Beer, Man In Black Hat, Metal, Celluloid, 1955, 9 x 14 1/2 In.   28.00
Pennsylvania Fire Insurance Co., Philadelphia, Brass, Etched, Raised Letters, 18 x 30 In.   148.00
Pennsylvania Vacuum Cup Tires, Porcelain, 2-Sided, 22 x 16 In. 3850.00
Pepsodent Toothpaste, Amos 'n' Andy, Cardboard, Easel Back, c.1930, 13 In. 330.00
Pepsodent Toothpaste, Amos 'n' Andy, Die Cut Cardboard, Easel Back, 1930, 54 x 62 In.   2185.00
Perks Are Best Here, Metal, 13 1/4 x 11 3/4 In. 60.00
Pet Milk, Tin, Bubble, 1959, 30 x 36 In. 523.00
Peter's Serum, Reverse Glass Insert, Wood Box, Backlit, Countertop, 6 x 12 In. 187.00
Peters Shoes, For All The Family, Glass, Reverse Painted, 5 x 15 In. 72.00
Petromax, Famous Petromax Sold Here, Green, Porcelain, 13 x 25 In. 220.00
Petromax, Genuine Petromax Sold Here, Blue, Yellow, Porcelain, 18 x 31 In. 220.00
Philips, Light Bulbs, Porcelain, Light Bulb, Logo, Middle Eastern, 12 x 15 1/2 In. 250.00
Phillips Rubbers, World Globe Ground, Circular, Glass, 2-Sided, England, 23 In. 208.00
Phillips' Milk Of Magnesia, Yellow, Red, Blue, Celluloid Over Cardboard, Easel, 6 x 9 In.   468.00
Phoenix Assurance Co., Wood, London, Established 1782, Frame, 18 x 22 In. 69.00
Picaninny Freeze Ice Cream, Black Boy Eating Watermelon, Cardboard, 1922, 9 x 12 In.   88.00
Pinkerton Detective Agency, Jewelers Security Alliance, Porcelain, Blue, 3 1/2 x 7 1/4 In.   187.00
Pizza Pie, Fresh Tomato, Tin, 14 x 12 In. 60.00
Popsicle, Everybody Likes, Easy To Eat, Tin, Embossed, 10 x 27 In. . . . . .110.00 to 358.00
Popsicles, 5 Cents, Tin Lithograph, Embossed, 2 1/2 x 18 In. 303.00
Post Toasties, Cardboard, Curved, Die Cut Child, 16 x 11 In. 660.00
Post Toasties, Couple On Swing, Die Cut, Cardboard, 29 x 18 1/2 In. 935.00
Post Toasties, Try New, Round, Cardboard, Light Hanger, Round, 10 In. 44.00
Postal Telegraph, International System Here, Blue, White, Porcelain, 16 x 30 In. 160.00
Postal Telegraph, Telephone Your Telegrams, Porcelain, Flange, 10 1/2 In. 154.00
Pratts & Vitality Pet Food, Dog, Embossed, Self-Framed, 27 x 19 In. 75.00
President Suspenders, Without A Rival, Lady, Poinsettias, Paper, Frame, 1907, 29 x 20 In.   354.00
Prest-O-Lite, Schenck Mfg. & Supply, Tin, 10 x 23 In. 330.00
Pretzel, Bakery, Brown, Figural, Urethane Foam, c.1960, 19 x 23 In. 60.00
Private Closet, 5 Cent, Directions, Blue, White, Porcelain, 3 1/2 x 12 In. 303.00
Profile Sign Co., Pine, Painted, Applied Cutout, Early 20th Century, 13 x 52 In. 1528.00
Pure Gold California Lemons, 17 Cents Per Doz., Cardboard, 5 Sides, Hanger, 10 x 5 In.   83.00
Purina Eggs, For Sale, Cardboard, 1954, 18 x 26 In. 28.00
Purity Butter Pretzels, Boy, Large Pretzel, Cardboard, Die Cut, Easel Back, 12 x 22 In. .   121.00
Purity Ice Cream, Boy, Die Cut, Stand-Up, 12 x 12 In. 45.00
Purity Ice Cream, Girl, Stand-Up, Die Cut, Wolf Adv. Co., N.Y., 12 x 12 In. 45.00
Quaker Bitters Maketh Life Sweet, Ben Franklin, Lady, Paper, Frame, 29 x 13 In. 330.00
Quaker Maid Milk, First In Quality, Red Ground, Porcelain, Die Cut, 24 x 41 In. 633.00
Quality Hardware, Deco Chrome, Faux Marble Wood Base, Countertop, 13 In. 165.00
Queen Cola, Ask For, It's Different & Better, Bottle, 19 1/2 x 7 In. 138.00
Queen Quality Shoe Dressing, Tin Over Cardboard, 13 x 9 In.   110.00
Quick Meal, Chick Breaking Out Of Egg, Porcelain, Oval, 33 x 45 In. 330.00
Quikrete, Tin, 18 x 28 In. 83.00
R&G Corsets, Woman Wearing Corset, Tin Lithograph, Frame, 18 x 13 1/4 In. 1210.00
R-Pep Beverage, Die Cut Bottle, Tin, Embossed, 48 In. 275.00

R.H. Thomson & Co.'s Scotch Whiskies, Leith, Scotland, Tin On Card, 11 x 15 In. 284.00
Railway Express Agency, Porcelain, 8 x 8 In. 110.00
Raleigh Whiskey, Sir Walter Raleigh, Indian Braves, Tin Lithograph, Frame, 19 x 27 In. ... 1500.00
Ramon's Laxative, Cardboard, Die Cut, 2-Sided, Samples, 19 x 8 In. 106.00
Ramsay's Paints, Agent, Porcelain, 2-Sided, Hollow Body, 28 x 36 x 3 In. 460.00
Rath's Black Hawk Sliced Bacon, Tin Lithograph, c.1910, 14 x 5 In. 132.00
Raymond Paint, Vilas Brothers, Chicago, Colors, Tin Over Cardboard, 11 x 16 In. 33.00
Raytheon Radio Tubes, Tube, Box, Flange, Tin, c.1934, 14 x 18 In. 270.00
Reach, Wright & Ditson, Softball, Lou Gehrig, Die Cut, Cardboard, Easel, 1940, 19 x 12 In. 1380.00
Red Cross, All May Help, Support Your 1950 Fund Campaign, Wax Board, 21 x 27 In. ... 22.00
Red Cross Brand, Condensed Milk, Tin, Embossed, 19 1/5 x 3 1/2 In. 330.00
Red Cross Notice, Zone Of Quiet, Porcelain, 18 x 24 In. 154.00
Red Rock Cola, Woman, Bathing Suit, Red Blanket, Cardboard, Frame, 28 x 23 In. 220.00
Red Rose Tea, Tin, 18 x 24 In. 143.00
Red Seal Battery, Guaranteed For All Circuit Work, Red, Porcelain, 33 x 14 1/2 In. 660.00
Red Seal Beverages, Red, Beige, Tin, 23 1/2 x 12 In. 110.00
Red Wing Shoes, Plymouth Shoe Store, Embossed, Metal, 18 x 24 In. 66.00
Redfern Rubber Heels & Shoes, Policeman Chasing Boy, Porcelain, 20 x 48 In. 303.00
Reed Manufacturing, Vice, Tin Over Cardboard, Self-Framed, 13 1/2 x 19 1/4 In. 165.00
Regina, Queen Of Toilet Soaps, Queen Victoria Medal, Red, Frame, 17 3/4 x 12 3/4 In. .. 98.00
Reints & DeBuhr, Aplington & Kesley, Iowa, Paper Lithograph, Frame, 15 x 19 In. 77.00
Rexall, Amos 'n' Andy, Fresh Air Taxi, Tin Lithograph, 2-Sided, 14 3/4 x 34 1/2 In. 242.00
Rexall, Porcelain, Self-Framed, 46 x 46 In. 248.00
Rexall Chemist, Enamel, Orange Ground, 2-Sided, Wood Frame, 17 1/2 x 11 1/2 In. 208.00
Reymonds Butter Crust Bread, Quality-Service, Yellow, Tin, 1939, 20 x 14 1/4 In. 33.00
Richard Hudnut Perfumer, Electric, 3 Panels, 1920-1930, 21 x 9 In. 2200.00
Richardson Root Beer, Rich In Flavor, Red, Tin Lithograph, Embossed, 9 3/4 x 14 In. ... 143.00
Richmond Stove Co., Stoves & Ranges, Porcelain, Richmond, Va., 17 x 14 3/4 In. 1783.00
Rinso, Soak The Clothes, That's All, Saves Coal, Enamel, Wood, England, 27 x 21 In. ... 170.00
Rising Sun Stove Polish, Woman, Long White Dress, Paper, Frame, 32 x 21 1/2 In. 1320.00
Rit Dye, Never Say Dye, Say Rit, Woman Holds Fabric, Metal, Lithograph, 14 x 17 In. .. 275.00
Rite-Way Milker, It Milks The Right Way, Red, Black, Tin, 9 3/4 x 13 3/4 In. 37.00
Robertson's Golden Shred, Golliwog, Lithograph Cardboard, Die Cut, 16 In. 410.00
Rochester Root Beer, Always Cold, Reverse On Glass, Frame, 10 1/2 x 12 1/2 In. 187.00
Rockford Watch, Woman, Holding Watch, Tin Lithograph, Embossed, 23 x 17 In. 1130.00
Roderick Dhu Highland Whisky, 8-Sided, On Glass, Wood Frame, 42 x 36 In. 492.00
Rogers Bros. Silverplate, Precious, Cardboard, Die Cut, Easel, J.M. Flagg, 10 x 14 In. ... 44.00
Rooster, Tin, 2-Sided, Black Side, White Other Side, 36 In. 2300.00
Rose Exterminator Co., Spraying Man, Die Cut Porcelain, 10 3/4 In. 358.00
Rose Lawn Milk Ice Cream, Porcelain, 15 x 40 In. 253.00
Rough On Rats, Clears It Out, 15 Cents Per Box, Chinese Man Eating Rat, 5 x 7 In. 825.00
Rough On Rats, Paper, Woman Chases Man Chases Boy Chases Dog, 8 1/8 x 5 1/8 In. .. 275.00
Rough On Rats, Well's Health Renewer, Buchu Paiba Ship, Paper, 8 1/4 x 5 1/4 In. 99.00
Rough On Rats, Well's Health Renewer, Man, Women Discuss Products, 7 7/8 x 5 1/8 In. 88.00
Round Oak Stove, Doe-Wah-Jack, Beckwith K16 Stove, Stecher, Die Cut, 62 In. 3575.00
Rowntree's Elect Cocoa, Makers To HM The King, Man, Black Coat, Enamel, 15 x 10 In. 643.00
Royal Mail, E II R, Crown, Metal, Red Ground, Yellow Letters, England, 14 x 7 1/4 In. .. 19.00
Royal Patent Flour, Satisfying, Nickel Plate Milling, Painesville, Ohio, 11 1/2 x 11 1/2 In. 61.00
Royal Stagg Bourbon & Rye, Tin Lithograph, Rolled Edge, 15 x 15 In. 490.00
Ruchti Bros. Baby Beef, Porcelain, 1951, 26 x 32 In. 550.00
Rutland Repair Products, Tin Lithograph, 15 x 9 In. 77.00
Ruud, Storage System, Automatic Hot Water, Tin On Cardboard, Self-Framed, 13 x 19 In. 66.00
S & H Green Stamps, We Give, Shield Shape, Tin, Embossed, 42 x 36 In. 55.00
S.H. Enke, Gold Letters, Sand Painted Finish, Beveled Edges, 1880s, 97 In. 176.00
Saddlery & Leather, Tin Lithograph, Frame, c.1890, 11 x 16 In. 275.00
Safewheels, Spring Spokes, Tin, Embossed, Resilient Safewheel Co., 17 x 23 In. 990.00
Sal Vet, Of Course We Sell, Tin Lithograph Over Cardboard, Embossed, 9 3/8 x 13 3/8 In. 715.00
Sal Vet, Worm Destroyer, Tin Over Cardboard, Embossed, Southern Can Co., 14 x 10 In. . 220.00
Salem Hill Anthracite, White, Red, Porcelain, Embossed, 10 x 20 In. 88.00
Samuel Clarke, Tea, Coffee, Fine Groceries, Woman, White Hat, Cardboard, 10 x 6 1/2 In. 28.00
San-Cura Hand Ointments, 5 Hands, Dunston Lith. Co., Cardboard, Frame, 38 x 7 In. ... 99.00
Sandersons Mountain Dew, Spirit Of The Mountain, Tin, England, 12 x 9 In. 151.00
Sands Plumbs & Levels, Always Tell The Truth, Aluminum, c.1930, 7 x 14 In. 185.00

Sanford's Ginger, Policeman Arrests Vegetables, Paper, Frame, c.1886, 14 x 18 In. 2860.00
Santa Fe Trail System, Bus Depot, Porcelain, 2-Sided, 1920-1930, 26 x 23 In. . . . . . *Illus* 7150.00
Santovin, Means Health For Sheep, Tin, Self-Framed, 27 x 21 In. 220.00
Sapolin, Stove Pipe, Iron Enamel, Lady At Stove, No. 66, Black, Tin, Embossed, 9 x 13 In. 3900.00
Sapolin Enamels, Elves, Frog, Reverse Stencil On Glass, Frame, 10 x 13 In. 605.00
Satin Skin, Cream & Powder, 25 Cents, Celluloid, Easel, Beveled Edge, 7 x 5 1/2 In. 1980.00
Satin Skin, Powder & Satin Skin Cream, Paper Lithograph, 28 1/2 x 42 In. 154.00
Satin Skin, Powder & Satin Skin Cream, Paper Lithograph, Frame, 31 x 46 In. 440.00
Saul Bros., Wines & Liquor, Paper Lithograph, Die Cut, Kutztown, Frame, 20 x 13 1/2 In. 170.00
Sawyers Crystal Blue, Man In Boat, Lady On Steps, Paper Lithograph, 31 x 15 In. 303.00
Say Mcvities, Mother, 2 Children, Parrot, Tin, 16 x 20 In. 220.00
Scandinavian American Line, Frederick VIII Ocean Liner, Tin, Self-Framed, 31 x 41 In. . 1540.00
Schenck's Pulmonic Syrup Sea Weed, Tin Lithograph, 27 3/4 x 22 In. 2035.00
Schenley Whiskey, Daniel Boone, Tin Lithograph, 28 x 20 In. 600.00
Schiffmann's Asthma Cure, Phthisic, Hay Fever, Cardboard, Frame, 9 x 15 In. 1485.00
Schlag's Pony Express Bread, Dainty Wrapped Loaf, Tin, Embossed, 14 x 19 In. 1210.00
Scotch Oil Liniment, Canvas, Roll Down, Wood Frame, c.1887, 17 x 30 1/2 In. 2420.00
Scotch Woolen Mills, Light-Up, Tin, Wood, Cardboard, 38 In. 110.00
Sealtest Ice Cream, Tin, Hanger, Mobile, Rotates In Wind, 12 x 17 In. 440.00
Sealtest Ice Cream, Velvet Brand, Porcelain, 54 x 40 In. 220.00
Sealy Mattresses, Black Figures Picking Cotton, Die Cut, Cardboard, c.1915, 4 Piece . . . 1155.00
Seiberling Rubber Heels, Cardboard Lithograph, 24 x 36 In. 150.00
Selz Shoes, Make Your Feet Glad, John Shoemaker, Tin, Zeeland, Mich., 13 x 20 In. 468.00
Selz Shoes, Porcelain, Frame, 120 x 20 In. 38.50
Sen-Sen Chewing Gum, 5 Cents, Tin, Embossed, Die Cut, Hanger, 3 1/4 x 6 In. 4070.00
Sewall's Paints, For Best Results, A. H. Lewellen, Wood, 60 x 28 In. 121.00
Shaler, 5 Minute Vulcanizer, A Friend In Need, Paper, 24 x 18 In. 2090.00
Sharples Cream Separator, Woman, Separator, Tin Lithograph, Self-Framed, 39 x 28 In. . 1187.00
Sharples Cream Separators, Smiling Woman, Die Cut, Cardboard, c.1910, 52 In. 633.00
Sharples Tubular Cream Separators, World's Best, Tin, Embossed, 10 x 14 In. 175.00
Shell, Marine Lubricants, Enamel, Circular, Ship's Wheel, Center Shell, Blue Edge, 36 In. 303.00
Sherwin-Williams, SWP Cover The Earth, Porcelain, Embossed, 36 x 20 In. 440.00
Sherwin-Williams Paints, Tin, Die Cut, 56 x 30 In. 825.00
Shoes For Men, Glass, Glass Rods, New Frame, 1920s-1930s, 4 1/2 x 17 In. 100.00
Shoes Rebottomed Entire Length, Wood, Shoe Sole Figural, 35 1/2 x 11 3/4 In. 863.00
Shredded Wheat Biscuit, Only Cereal In Biscuit Form, Frame, 12 x 22 In. 358.00
Silver Eagle, Die Cut Metal, Red, White, Blue, 72 x 17 1/2 In. 495.00
Silver Pine Healing Oil, Cure For Barb Wire Cuts, Paper, 21 x 28 In. 2090.00
Silverwoods Deluxe Ice Cream, Metal, 2-Sided, 35 1/2 x 23 1/2 In. 138.00
Ski Club Beverages, Downhill Skiers, Tin, 10 x 19 In. 330.00
Skinners Pasta, Hanger, Paper Lithograph, Tin Frame, 2-Sided, 28 1/2 In. 124.00
Slater's Boss Stogies, Metal, Painted, Chain Hung, 7 x 10 In. 244.00
Slenderize, Nonfat Milk, Overeating?, Tin, 2-Sided, 24 x 40 In. 165.00
Slidetite, Last Word In Door Hardware, Richards-Wilcox, Aurora, Ill., 13 x 19 In. 4180.00
Smith's Ice Cream, Tin, Embossed, Smith & Clark Co., 28 x 20 In. 2750.00
Smulekoff's Foremost Home Furnishers, Glass, Reverse Painted, 20 x 25 In. 110.00
Snider's Tomato Catsup, Tin, 6-Sided, 16 x 11 In. 450.00
Snow White Cream Soda, Snow, Trees, Red, Blue, Tin, Canada Barker, 14 x 29 In. 58.00
Snowflour, Quality Unsurpassed, Tin, Embossed, 10 x 18 In. 303.00
Sober Up, Woman On Ship's Deck, Cardboard, Easel Back, 14 1/2 x 19 1/2 In. 132.00
SOC Credit Card, Wood, Die Cut Boy, 1973, 48 x 26 In. 495.00
Solarine, World's Greatest Metal Polish, Cardboard, Die Cut, 3 Piece, 3-D, 8 x 12 In. 1320.00
Solarine Metal Polish, We Shine For All, Can, Moon, 2-Sided, Die Cut, Hanger, 6 x 6 In. 413.00
Solona White Port Wine, Couple Dining, Paper, Wood Frame, c.1900, 16 x 18 In. 175.00 to 225.00
Southern Dairies, Velvet Kind Of Ice Cream, Porcelain, Die Cut, 33 x 24 In. 495.00
Southern Girl Shoes, Lynchburg, Va., Woman's Head, Tin, Self-Framed, 19 1/2 x 16 In. . 440.00
Space Pops, 7 Flavors, 5 Cents, Tin, Blue, Orange, White, Diamond Shape, 16 x 16 In. . . 385.00
Sparkeeta Up, California's Favorite, Lady & Bottle, Cardboard, Easel Back, 30 x 24 In. . . 232.00
Spectacles & Eyeglasses Repaired, Reverse On Glass, Frame, 15 x 22 In. 385.00
Sports Argus, First For Sport, Porcelain, 17 x 24 In. 55.00
Spratt's Canary Mixture, Brown Letters, Cream Ground, Enamel, England, 24 x 12 In. . . 303.00
Squeeze, Scores Again, Boys Playing Baseball, Die Cut, Cardboard, 20 x 15 In. 468.00

Squeeze, That Distinctive Carbonated Beverage, Tin, 20 1/4 x 28 1/4 In. 165.00
Squeeze, That Distinctive Orange Drink, Tin, Embossed, Frame, 19 x 27 In. 247.00
Squeeze, That Distinctive Orange Drink, Tin, Embossed, Frame, c.1940, 18 x 26 In. 1375.00
Squires, Ham-Bacon-Sausage, Pig, Human Eyes, Tin, 20 x 24 In. 495.00
Squirrel Brand Salted Peanuts, Die Cut, Cardboard, 11 x 12 In. . . . . .121.00 to 297.00
St. Charles, Evaporated Cream, Cow, Tin Lithograph, Embossed, Frame, 21 1/2 x 27 In. .   358.00
Stabler's Cherry Expectorant, Embossed, Cardboard, Gold Leaf, Frame, Md., 10 x 13 In.   193.00
Stag Trousers, Elk Stag, Tin Lithograph, Self-Framed, 13 x 19 In. 440.00
Standard Fire Insurance Co., Iowa, Keokuk, Meyercord Co., Chicago, 13 x 19 In. 121.00
Standard Screw Fastened Boots, Shoes, Lilly Brackett, Boston, Paper, Linen, 16 x 32 In.   110.00
Stanley, Hardware, Metal On Pasteboard, c.1930s, 12 In. 132.00
Stanley, Quality Tools, Yankee, Tool Guy, Reverse Painted, Light-Up, 5 x 14 x 8 In. 275.00
Stanley, Square, Carpenter, Die Cut, Cardboard, 10 x 18 In. 28.00
Star, Milk Chocolates, Bloomer Candy, Zanesville, Oh., Tin Over Cardboard, 6 x 9 In. . . .   88.00
Star, Naphtha Washing Powder, For General Cleaning, Cloth, 17 x 34 1/2 In. 148.00
Star, Soap, Black, Red, White, Porcelain, 3 x 18 In. 770.00
Star, Soap, Extra Large, Extra Good, Porcelain, Curved, 28 1/2 x 19 In. 1100.00
Star, Soap, Paper Lithograph, Girl Holding 3 Puppies, Frame, 24 1/4 x 15 3/8 In. 2860.00
Star, Soap, Paper, Girl, 2 Dogs, Frame, Schultz & Co., Zanesville, Ohio, 27 1/2 x 19 In. . .   1045.00
Star, Steel Belt Lacing, A Better Lacing For Less Money, Only 8 Sizes, Tin, 14 x 19 In. . .   39.00
Star Brand Shoes, Are Better For All The Family, Cincinnatti, Tin, 13 1/2 x 19 1/2 In. . . .   275.00
Star Lumber Co., Diamond Edge Tools, Tin, Embossed, 9 1/2 x 28 In. 99.00
Stearns Electric Paste, Pests Leaving House, Cardboard, 3 Panels, Folding, 35 x 45 In. . .   3450.00
Sterling & Son Seafood, Woman, Boat, Paper Lithograph, Mat, Frame, 19 1/2 x 14 1/2 In.   367.00
Stetson Hats, Hunting Scene, Embossed, Paperboard, 20 x 11 1/2 In. 660.00
Stewart Clipper, Clip Your Horses, Tin, Embossed, Cardboard, Hanger, 9 1/2 x 12 In. . . .   1045.00
Stewart Clipping Machine, Horses, Courtroom, Lithograph Cardboard, 14 x 20 In. 523.00
Stoeker's Old Fashioned Lemon Soda, Got The Pep, Tin, Embossed, c.1920, 13 x 19 In. .   118.00
Stoneware, Best Food Container, Boy, Dog, Kitchen, Tin Lithograph, 19 x 13 In. 935.00
Stronger Than The Law Shoe, E.K. Elledge Co., Tin, Embossed, 10 x 26 In. 531.00
Stutts' Eas-It, For Toothache, Yellow, Black, Tin, 20 x 9 In. 413.00
Suddenly Everyone's Drinking Vodka, Cardboard, Lithograph, 1957, 10 1/2 x 9 3/4 In. . .   38.00
Sun Insurance, Office Agency, Sun Logo, Porcelain, 14 1/4 x 19 3/4 In. 176.00
Sun Spot, Bottled Sunshine, Tin, Embossed, 29 x 20 1/2 In. 110.00
Sun-Proof Paint, Can, Since 1855, Tin Lithograph, Self-Framed, Fluted Edge, 25 x 38 In.   440.00
Sunbeam Bakery, Come In, We Serve The Best, Red, Yellow, Tin Lithograph, 55 x 19 In.   990.00
Sunbeam Bread, Girl Eating Bread, Tin, 48 x 59 1/2 In. 330.00
Sunbeam Bread, Girl, Tin, Embossed, 1967, 12 x 29 1/2 In. 193.00
Sunbeam Bread, Girl, Tin, Embossed, 1972, 48 x 48 In. 385.00
Sunbeam Bread, Girl, Tin, Embossed, Self-Framed, 18 1/2 x 54 In. 935.00
Sunbeam Bread, Girl, Tin, Embossed, Self-Framed, 1956, 47 x 47 In. 990.00
Sunbeam Bread, Girl, Tin, Embossed, Self-Framed, Stout, 1973, 35 1/2 x 71 1/2 In. 385.00
Sunbeam Bread, Holiday Dinner, 1962, 25 x 35 In. 39.00
Sunbeam Bread, Loaf On Tray, Tin Lithograph, Self-Framed, 1950s, 11 3/4 x 29 3/4 In. .   413.00
Sunbeam Bread, Reach For Energy Packed Bread, Tin, 1950s, 55 x 19 In. . . . . . .715.00 to 1013.00
Sunbeam Bread, Stays Fresher Longer, Tin, Embossed, 18 x 54 In. 1400.00
Sunbeam Rolls, Sunbeam Girl, Hot Dog, Hamburger, 1952, 55 x 19 In. 3190.00
Sunkist Grower, Porcelain, 11 1/2 x 19 1/2 In. 303.00
Sunlight Soap, Lever Brothers, Enamel, White Letters, Blue & Green Ground, 30 x 20 In.   492.00
Sunlight Soap, Women & Girls In White Outfits, England, Frame, 33 x 22 1/2 In. 38.00
Sunsweet Prunes, Trolley Card, 11 x 21 In. 22.00
Superior Dairy Ice Cream, Flavor List, Painted Metal, Wood, 86 In. 165.00
Swan's Down Cake Flour, You Can Always Bake A Better Cake, Tin, 6 x 9 In. 165.00
Sweet Heart Products, Heart Shape, Enamel On Metal, Die Cut, Red Ground, c.1920, 5 In.   165.00
Sweet Orr Co., Pants, Overalls, Shirts, Porcelain, 10 x 24 In. 154.00
Sweet Orr Co., Pants, Shirts, Overalls, Tin, Frame, 23 x 29 In. 550.00
Take Thorns Genuine Sarsaparilla, Dog, Blue Bow, Cardboard, Die Cut, 10 x 7 1/2 In. . .   440.00
Tall One Soda, Wherever You're Thirsty, Flange, c.1930, 5 x 12 In. 625.00
Taylor, Tailor, Let Taylor Tailor You, Porcelain, Flange, 10 x 21 In. 440.00
Taylor Electric Coop, Porcelain, 13 x 16 In. 55.00
Taystee Bread, Best Loaf Of Bread In Town, Porcelain, 9 1/2 x 16 In. 17.00
Tekka Safety Match, Suits Of Cards, Porcelain, 12 x 18 In. 66.00

Tetley's Teas Please, Tin, Hanger, Self-Framed, 19 x 13 1/2 In. . . . . *Illus* 4400.00
Thompson Dairy Ice Cream, Porcelain, 21 x 13 In. 248.00
Tippecanoe, Fine As Silk, Try It, Reverse On Glass, 3 7/8 x 16 In. 358.00
Tippecanoe, The Best For Dyspepsia, Paper, Frame, 12 1/2 x 24 5/8 In. 275.00
Tippecanoe, The Best For Loss Of Energy & Appetite, Paper, Frame, 12 1/2 x 24 5/8 In. . . 330.00
Tippecanoe, The Best For Mal-Assimilation Of Food, Paper, Frame, 12 1/2 x 24 5/8 In. . . . 198.00
Tizer, Drink, Appetizer, Enamel, Red Ground, Letters, England, 36 x 10 In. 61.00
Toiletine, Man In Top Hat, Die Cut, Cardboard, 1913, 9 1/2 x 6 In. 94.00
Tongaline, Medicine Man, Indian Chief, Cardboard, 2-Sided, c.1903, 11 3/4 x 8 In. 132.00
Top Hat, Tin, Steel Band, Brass Buckle, Black Paint, 29 x 27 x 13 In. 1293.00
Tourist Golden Rule System, Yellow, Red, Black, Porcelain, 2-Sided, 18 In. 495.00
Town Talk Bread, Ask For, Rich In Pure Milk, Porcelain, 2 3/4 x 15 In. 715.00
Town Talk Flour, It Has No Equal, Cardboard, 15 x 12 In. 165.00
Tree Brand Shoes, For Sale Here, Tin, Flange, 13 1/2 x 18 In. 660.00
Triple Cola, 16 Oz. Bottle, It's Bigger, It's Better, Tin, Embossed, 31 1/2 x 11 1/2 In. 80.00
Tropical Heavy Duty Paints, Tin, Flange, 2-Sided, 15 x 12 In. 1430.00
Tru-Pak Aspirin, 12 Tablets, 10 Cents, Cardboard, Easel Back, 12 x 8 3/4 In. 44.00
True Fruit Soda, Statue, Fruit, Glass Of Soda, Table, Tin Lithograph, Frame, 24 x 38 In. . . 302.00
Tubbs Cordage Co., Rope Sizes, 31 x 9 In. 106.00
Tubular Cream Separator, Used On This Farm, Tin, Moscow, N.Y., 5 x 28 In. 440.00
Tums For The Tummy, Nature's Remedy, 3 Clips, Tin Lithograph, 5 1/2 x 19 In. 44.00
Turkish Dyes, Desert Scene, Wood, Tin Lithograph, c.1890, 23 x 33 In. 440.00
Turnbull's Scotch Whiskey, Tin, Embossed, Frame, 16 1/2 x 22 In. 154.00
Tuttle's Elixir, For Man & Beast, 100 Dollar Reward, Tin, 20 x 22 In. 413.00
Twin Gramophone Records, 2 Records, Green, Black, Porcelain, 2-Sided, 18 x 24 In. . . . 325.00
Twin Oaks, Couple On Swing, Die Cut, Cardboard, Hanger, 14 1/2 In. 2530.00
U.S. Army, Careers With A Future, Choose Yours Now, Porcelain, 2-Sided, 38 x 25 In. . . . 248.00
Ulypto Cough Drops, Stops Coughing Instantly, Black, White, Tin, 13 x 6 In. . . . . . .70.00 to 85.00
Union House, Hotel & Restaurant Employees, Bartenders, Cardboard, c.1900, 6 x 11 In. . 230.00
Union Mills Flour, Baby In Basket, Matted, 20 x 16 In. 231.00
Union Mills Flour, Best In The Market, Baby In Basket, Flowers, 14 x 18 1/2 In. 105.00
United Brand Night Shirts, Lithograph, Frame, 19 1/2 x 27 In. 193.00
United States Casualty Company Of New York, Reverse Paint On Glass, 35 x 24 In. 193.00
United States Express Co., White, Blue, Porcelain, 14 x 20 In. 1760.00
Universal Food Chopper, Landers, Frary & Clark, 19 1/2 x 14 1/2 In. 6050.00
Uptown, Bottle, Lemon, Lime, Stylized Crown, Tin, Embossed, 17 1/2 x 29 1/2 In. 182.00
Use Star Soap, It Fights Dirt, Cloth, 34 1/2 x 17 In. 71.00
Utah King Coal, Lasts Longer, Porcelain, 10 x 38 In. 330.00
Utah King Coal, Lasts Longer, Red, White, Black, Porcelain, 10 x 28 In. 770.00
Utica National Sportsman Fishing Tackle, For Sale Here, Lithograph Sheet Steel, 26 In. . 687.00
Utica Pliers & Nippers, Pliers Fit The Hand, Celluloid, Cardboard, Hanger, 8 x 12 In. . . . 1430.00
Utter Manufacturing Co., Horses, Farm Machinery, c.1880, 21 x 26 In. 413.00
Valentine's Valspar, It's The Coat That Makes The Boat, Tin Over Cardboard, 13 x 19 In. 1100.00
Valspar Varnish, Man Pours Water On Table, Woman, Cardboard, Easel Back, 33 x 50 In. 44.00
Valvoline, Marine Products, Tin, Bubble, 1960, 20 x 28 In. 633.00
Valvoline, Marine Products, Tin, Round, 1968, 29 In. 660.00
Van Camp Hardware & Iron Co., Die Cut, Metal, 2-Sided, NY Metal Signs, 18 x 14 In. . . . 143.00
Van Camp's Pork & Beans, 2 Children Carry Beans, Die Cut, Cardboard, 16 x 19 3/8 In. . 578.00
Van Houtens Cocoa, Best & Goes Farthest, Cardboard, Frame, c.1905, 25 x 34 In. 1265.00
Vanola Pure Mints, Winner For After Dinner, 2 Piece, Contents, 8 1/4 x 3 In. 225.00
Veedol Skater, Tin, Die Cut, Frame, 1956, 17 1/2 x 9 In. 523.00
Velvet Kind, DeLuxe Packaged Ice Cream, Reverse Decal, Under Glass, 10 In. 181.00
Vermont Mutual Fire, Tin, Self-Framed, 24 x 20 In. . . . . *Illus* 2090.00
Vernor's Ginger Ale, Man With Beard, Metal, 10 x 30 In. 220.00
Victory Liberty Loan, Man, Overalls, Lithograph, Gerrit A. Beneker, c.1918, 28 x 40 In. . 83.00
Vigorator Hair Tonic, Head Rub, Bellefontaine, Tin Lithograph, 9 x 5 In. . . . . .99.00 to 132.00
Vinolia Soap, For Sensitive Skin, Lady, Basket, Embossed, Cardboard, Frame, 24 x 18 In. 413.00
Vitalized Ginger Ale, Lady Surfer, Picks You Up, Tin Over Cardboard, 6 1/4 x 9 1/4 In. . . 204.00
W. D. Grover, Undertaker, Tin Lithograph, Embossed, 5 1/4 x 19 3/4 In. 154.00
W.L. Douglas, Manufacturer Of The Best $3.00 - $4.00 Shoes, Tin, Self-Framed, 31 x 23 In. 266.00
Walk-Over Shoes, Woman In White Dress, Tin, 11 x 7 In. 330.00
Walker's Kilmarnock Whisky, Bottle, Cigar, England, Frame, 22 1/2 x 17 1/2 In. 70.00

Sign, Santa Fe Trail System,
Bus Depot, Porcelain, 2-Sided,
1920-1930, 26 x 23 In.

Sign, Tetley's Teas Please,
Tin, Hanger, Self-Framed,
19 x 13 1/2 In.

Sign, Vermont Mutual
Fire, Tin, Self-Framed,
24 x 20 In.

Waterman's Ideal Fountain Pen, Santa Claus, Pen, Die Cut, Cardboard, 15 x 13 In. 385.00
Wayne Feed, Embossed, Die Cut, Tin Lithograph, 16 x 14 In. 55.00
We Give Eagle Stamps, Stamp, Porcelain, White, Black Letters, Red Border, 31 x 72 In. . . 220.00
We Install The Boyce Motometer Free, Tin On Cardboard, Hanger, 27 1/2 x 19 In. 5500.00
We Pay For Dead Stock, A.F. Frees, West Virginia, 10 x 14 In. 121.00
Wear-U-Well Quality Shoes, Porcelain, 2-Sided, Flange, 17 1/2 x 26 In. 110.00
Webaco, Credit Cards Honored, White, Red, Black, Tin, Flange, 14 x 20 In. 39.00
Welch's Grape Juice, Man, Woman, Child, Trifold, Cardboard, Easel Back, 20 5/8 x 33 In. 743.00
Welch's Juniors, 10 Cents, Drink A Bunch Of Grapes, Tin, Embossed, 13 1/2 x 19 1/2 In. . 105.00
Welcome Soap, 2 Women, Curtis & Davis, Frame, 31 1/2 x 16 1/4 In. 990.00
Welgar Shredded Wheat, Pyramid Of Welgar Boxes, Card, 24 1/2 x 32 In. 66.00
Wells Fargo & Co Express, Diamond Shape, Metal Ribbed Frame, 14 In. 1150.00
Wells Fargo & Co. Express, Porcelain, Flange, 21 x 23 In. 58.00
Westchester Fire Insurance, Established 1837, Blue, White, Porcelain, 20 x 14 In. 358.00
Western Flyer, America's Favorite, Boy, Girl, Yellow, Red, Green, Cardboard, 22 x 13 In. . 55.00
Western Land Roller Tubine Pump, Porcelain, 12 x 28 In. 27.50
Western New Chief, Running Rabbit, Hunter, Dog, Cardboard, Hanger, 14 1/4 x 5 7/8 In. 1061.00
Western North Carolina Tourist Association, Porcelain, 2-Sided, 24 x 18 In. 440.00
Western Union, Porcelain, 2-Sided, 17 1/2 x 30 In. 193.00
Western Union, Telegraph Here, Porcelain, Flange, 11 x 17 In. . . . . .193.00 to 248.00
Western Union, Telephone Your Telegrams From Here, Phone, Metal, Celluloid, 9 x 9 In. 165.00
Wetherill's Floor & Deck Enamel, Wood, Stencil, Hooks, Sample, 35 In. 44.00
Wheatlet Superior Oat Meal, Uncle Sam, Cardboard, Easel Back, 1899, 3 1/2 x 6 In. . . . 121.00
Wheeler's Nerve Vitalizer, Epileptic Fits, Black, Yellow, Tin, 13 1/2 x 10 In. 605.00
Whippet, Dollar For Dollar Value, Willy's Overland, Wood Frame, 1920s, 15 x 25 In. . . . 125.00
Whistle, 3 Brownies Carrying Sign, 1948, 18 x 54 In. 1980.00
Whistle, Brownie Pushing Bottle On Handcart, Tin, Embossed, 1948, 30 x 26 In. 1155.00
Whistle, Elves Enjoy Soda, Cardboard, Stand-Up, 14 x 17 1/4 In. 358.00
Whistle, Orange, Embossed, Metal, 30 x 26 In. 688.00
Whistle, Thirsty?, Just Whistle, Bottle Shape, Die Cut, Cardboard, 30 1/4 x 8 In. 99.00
Whistle, Thirsty?, Just Whistle, Bottle, Cardboard, Frame, 60 x 20 3/4 In. 198.00
Whistle, Thirsty?, Just Whistle, Tin Lithograph, Embossed, 14 x 20 In. . . . . .468.00 to 495.00
Whistle, Thirsty?, Just Whistle, Tin, Embossed, Self-Framed, 7 x 9 3/4 In. . . . . . . .413.00 to 715.00
Whistle, Thirsty?, Just Whistle, Tin, Flange, Square, 11 3/4 In. 385.00
Whistle, Thirsty?, Just Whistle, Woman, Bottle, Die Cut, Cardboard, Easel, 23 x 15 In. . . 132.00
Whistle Sparkling Orange Goodness, Blond Sips Straw, Cardboard, Die Cut, 6 1/2 x 17 In. 44.00
White Ace Shoe Cleaner, Will Not Rub Off, Die Cut, Cardboard, Easel, c.1940, 14 x 9 In. 176.00
White House Shoes, Lady, Red Dress, Paper, Frame, 11 x 26 In. 330.00
White House Tea, Lady Pouring Tea, Paperboard, 2-Sided, 15 x 10 In. 275.00
White Leghorns Chickens, C.A. Pitkin, Paper Lithograph, Hartford, Conn., 6 1/2 x 9 In. . 72.00
White Star Ship Lines, Imperator, Tin Lithograph, Frame, c.1911, 46 x 36 In. 468.00
Whitley Solid Steel Mower, Men, Horses, Paper, Frame, c.1890, 20 x 34 In. 660.00

Whitlock Waterflex Cordage, Tin, Embossed, Self-Framed, 13 1/4 x 9 1/4 In. 55.00
Wilbur's Stock Tonic, Paper Lithograph, Frame, 16 x 33 In. 330.00
Wildroot Hair Cream Oil, Fearless Fosdick, Die Cut, Cardboard, Easel, 30 x 30 1/4 In. . . 248.00
Wilkin Family Whiskey, Sweet Music, 2 Men, Dog, Desk, Frame, 21 x 18 1/2 In. 77.00
Willard Storage Batteries, Red Ground, White Letters, Porcelain, 2-Sided, 66 x 25 In. . . 99.00
Willard's Candy Bars, Boy, Hands In Pockets, Die Cut, Cardboard, 17 x 8 3/8 In. 440.00
Willard's Candy Bars, Girl, Hands In Pockets, Die Cut, Cardboard, 17 x 8 3/8 In. 743.00
Willis Benson Meats & Vegetables, Boy, Holding Vegetables, Die Cut, Paper Lithograph . 220.00
Wills's Champion Plug, Dog Handler, England, Frame, 21 1/2 x 15 3/4 In. 246.00
Wills's Handy Cut Flake, Deckled Sword, England, Frame, 20 x 14 1/2 In. 38.00
Wilsnap Garter Buckle, Pebbled Cardboard, Folding, Buckles, c.1920s, 3 3/4 x 6 In. 90.00
Wilson Whiskey, People, Around Carriage, Tin Lithograph, Frame, c.1890, 38 x 50 In. . . . 990.00
Witt Cornace Company, Cincinnati, Trash Can, Porcelain, c.1930, 4 1/4 In. 650.00
Wolf Co. Flouring Mill Machinery, Chambersburg, Pa., Paper, Frame, 13 x 21 In. 495.00
Wolverine Action Line Boots, Shoes, Grizzly, Fiberglass, 1970s, 19 x 10 In. 28.00
Wolverine Soap Chips, Not Kept In Stores, Lithograph, c.1900, 28 x 34 In. . . . . .750.00 to 1100.00
Women's Room, Lady, Powdering Face, Blue, Porcelain, 12 x 13 In. 99.00
Woolworth, Values Our Tradition Since 1879, 30 x 18 In. 83.00
Wooster Brushes, Tin, 2-Sided, Flange, Round, Ohio, 1907 Patent, 13 1/2 In. 3960.00
Wright's Coal Tar Soap, White, Green Shield Outline, Enamel, England, 32 x 20 In. 341.00
Wyandotte, Indian, Shooting Bow & Arrow, Tin, Self-Framed, 38 1/2 x 28 1/4 In. 2400.00
Wyeth Cutlery, Gold Name, Logo, Green Velvet Lining, Cardboard, 2 x 4 5/8 x 18 In. . . . 83.00
Yeast Foam, Makes Delicious Buckwheat Pancakes, Girl, At Table, Paper, 9 1/2 x 14 1/2 In. 88.00
Yellow Cab, Phone 600, Cardboard, 7 1/8 x 11 In. 99.00
Yerdons Ice Cream, Sealtest, Porcelain, 2-Sided, 17 1/4 x 16 3/4 In. 908.00
Yoo-Hoo Chocolate Drink, Baseball Players, Easel Back, 1964, 17 1/2 x 14 1/2 In. 1380.00
Your Doctor Says Weigh Yourself Daily, Peerless, Detroit, Porcelain, Shield, 9 x 5 In. . . . 523.00
Zulich's Vet Medicine, Blood, Alternative & Tonic Powder, Cardboard, 14 x 11 In. 59.00

SINGER Isaac Merritt Singer was born October 27, 1811, near Troy, New York. He worked as a mechanic and cabinetmaker in Oswego until the acting bug bit him and he moved to Rochester, where he used the stage name Isaac Merritt. He invented a mechanical excavator in 1839, sold the invention for $2,000, and used the money to organize a theatrical troupe called the Merritt Players. When the money ran out, Singer took a job in a plant that made wooden printer's type. He soon invented and patented an improved machine to carve type and tried to sell the machine in Boston. While there, he met Orson C. Phelps, who was making sewing machines. Singer designed an improved machine, then in 1851 founded I.M. Singer & Company, later renamed Singer Manufacturing Company. The first Singer sewing machines cost $100 and were sold all over the world. Singer moved to Paris, then England, where he died in 1875. The company became The Singer Company in 1963. It introduced the first electronic sewing machine in 1975 and the first computer-controlled model in 1978. The company now also sells vacuum cleaners, furniture, and appliances around the world.

Calendar, 1901, Sewing Machines, Cardboard, Technological Advances, 11 x 15 In. 225.00
Calendar, Perpetual, For Every Stitching Operation, 1905-1915, 19 x 13 In. . . . . *Illus* 523.00
Calendar, Perpetual, Tin Lithograph, 19 1/2 x 12 3/4 In. 81.00
Fan, 51st Season, 2 Parakeets, 3 Sewing Machines 30.00
Sign, Large Red S, Green Ground, Woman At Machine, Porcelain, Frame, 16 x 22 In. 275.00
Sign, Sewing Machines, Orders Taken Here, Enamel, 2-Sided, England, 22 x 11 In. 568.00
Sign, Sewing Machines, Red S, Green Ground, Woman, Enamel, England, 36 x 24 In. . . . 246.00
Sign, Sewing Machines, Woman Sewing, Red, Green, White, Porcelain, 16 x 20 In. 187.00
Sign, Troubador, Paper Lithograph, Frame, 1893, 16 x 20 1/2 In. 100.00
Tie Clip, Silvertone, Spring Clip, 1 3/4 In. 18.00
Tin, Sewing Machine Oil, 4 Oz., 5 1/4 x 2 1/4 x 1 1/8 In. 5.00
Toy, Sewing Machine, Cast Iron, Box, c.1914 . . . . 248.00
Toy, Sewing Machine, Sew Handy, Unopened, Box, c.1940 . . . . 105.00

SLEEPY EYE In 1883 the Sleepy Eye Roller Mill opened in Sleepy Eye, Minnesota. By 1889 it was producing many brands of flour, including Cyclone, Snow Flake, and Minnesota Chief. The proprietors were William Gieseke, F.H. Dyckman, and P. Benedixen. The name of the company became Sleepy Eye Milling Company in 1891. Old Sleepy Eye was a real Indian chief who had lived in the area. His Indian name was Ish-Tak-Ha-Ba, meaning "eyelids drooping," which his did. The mill decided to use a picture of the chief as its trademark in 1893. It later used a derby hat as a trademark for its Thrift brand, and hummingbirds for a brand named Hummer. Sleepy Eye also made Farina Cereal, Golden Harvest Breakfast Food, Koffeno (a beverage made from wheat), and Pankako (pancake flour). There is more than average interest in Sleepy Eye advertising collectibles. Of special interest is the pottery that was made and packed into bags of Sleepy Eye flour from 1903 to 1937. The company also gave away letter openers with an Indianhead handle (1900), sofa pillow tops (1901), caps (1904), postcards (1904), souvenir spoons, cookbooks, metal paperweights, and more. The company operated until 1921.

Cookbook, Bread Loaf Shape	99.00
Crock, Indian Chief, H On Bottom	400.00
Print, Paper Lithograph, Round, Frame, c.1900, 16 In.	468.00
Print, Sleepy Eye Mills, Sleepy Eye Cream, Indian, Minn., Frame, 30 x 24 In.	68.00
Sign, Chief, Paper, Round, Walnut Frame, c.1900, 25 In.	460.00
Sign, Indian, Old Sleepy Eye Joe, Tin, Frame, 25 x 33 In.	688.00

SMITH BROTHERS COUGH DROPS Trade and Mark are not the names of the Smith brothers. That was an old joke inspired by the bearded brothers' pictures on the cough-drop box. William (Trade) and Andrew (Mark) were real brothers who lived in Poughkeepsie, New York. Their father, James Smith, owned a restaurant, and in 1817 a customer mentioned a formula for a delicious cough candy. James Smith mixed up a batch on the kitchen stove and started selling it with the help of his two sons. The boys inherited the business when their father died in 1866, and the company became Smith Brothers. Many other companies tried to copy Smith cough drops, using names like Schmitt Brothers or Smythe Sisters, so the real Smith brothers decided to put their pictures on the package. At that time, the envelope-style packages were sold from glass bowls that sat on store counters. The Smith Brothers developed a factory-filled package in 1872 that also showed their pictures. Andrew died in 1895 and William in 1913. The family continued as owners and operators of the company until it was acquired first by Warner Lambert and then, in 1977, by F & F Laboratories Inc. (now F & F Foods) of Chicago. F & F Foods still manufactures Smith Brothers throat and cough drops, including Wild Cherry (1948), Black Licorice, Honey Lemon, and Menthol Eucalyptus flavors.

Blotter, Lithograph, c.1900, 8 1/2 x 3 1/4 In.	9.00
Display, Tin, 9 x 4 In.	748.00
Display Rack, Cough Drops, 5 Cents, 2 Boxes, 9 1/2 x 4 In.	303.00
Paperweight, Star Emblem On Bottom, Cast Iron, 2 1/4 x 3/4 In.	77.00
Tin, Cough Drops, Ginna Tin, 3 3/4 x 2 3/8 In.	385.00
Tin, S.B. Cough Drops, Brothers On Front, 3 7/8 x 2 3/4 x 7/8 In.	715.00

SODA BOTTLE The first soda was artificially carbonated in the 1830s by John Matthews. He used marble chips and acid to create carbonation. All forms of carbonated drink—naturally carbonated mineral water, artificially carbonated and flavored pops, and seltzer—are soda. Soda bottles held some form of soda pop or carbonated drink. Early soda bottles had a characteristic thick blob top and heavy glass sides to prevent breakage from the pressure of carbonation. Tops were cleverly secured; the Hutchinson stopper and Coddball stopper were used on many early bottles. The crown cap was not used until 1891. Some bottles have embossed lettering made with a slug plate, an extra piece inserted into the mold. Collectors search for heavy blob-top bottles, newer crown-top bottles with embossed lettering or applied color labels (also known as ACL, pyro, pyro glaze, and enamel), and newer commemorative bottles. Other soda bottles can be found in the Coca-Cola, Hires, Pepsi-Cola, and other brand-specific categories.

Allegheny Bottling Co., 48 Taggart St. N.S., Pittsburg, Pa., Hutch, Aqua	25.00
B.S.&M.W. Wks., Buffalo, N.Y., Hutch, Aqua	20.00
Big Hit, Baseball Player, Embossed, Brunswick, Ga., 8 Oz.	83.00
C.B. Casseoy, Warren, O., Hutch, Aqua	25.00
Cascade Ginger Ale, 6-Pack, Box, 8 x 10 x 5 1/2 In.	17.00
Cascade Sparkling Seltzer, Ashtabula, Ohio	176.00
E. Centsch, Buffalo, N.Y., Hutch, Aqua	25.00
Frostie Root Beer, Baltimore 28 Md., 12 Oz., 8 In.	9.00
Frostie Root Beer, Old Fashion Root Beer Baltimore, 12 Oz., 8 x 2 1/2 In.	9.00
G. Schmuck, Cleveland, O., Hutch, Aqua, Bubbles	20.00
Howell & Smith, Buffalo, Tapering, Cylindrical, Yellow Green, 1845-1860	1792.00
John Howell, Buffalo, N.Y., Hutch, Aqua	20.00
Mason's Root Beer Soda, Brown, 10 Oz.	7.50
P.H. Reasbeck, Braddock, Pa., Hutch, Aqua, P.R. On Base	25.00
Red Dragon Seltzer Co., Cylinder, Green, Wide Mouth, N.Y., 2 3/4 In.	30.00
Reno Brewing Co., Seltzer, Full Glass Stem, c.1915, 12 x 3 3/4 In.	207.00
Royal Palm Seltzer, Terre Haute, In.	220.00
San Francisco Seltzer Water, Etched	35.00
Sparkeeta Club Soda, 3 Horsemen, Black & Red Pyro Glaze, 35 Oz., 12 x 4 In.	98.00
Triple AAA Root Beer, You Will Like Root Beer, White Label, 6 1/2 Oz., 8 In.	11.96
Weiland Bottling Works, Seltzer, Washoe, Nevada, c.1908-1919	109.00

SPICE   It wasn't until just after the Civil War that spices were packed in tins. Stores also sold spices from large bulk bins. Early tins were japanned and stenciled; later, lithographed designs and paper labels were used. Early cans had full lift-off lids. The spoon-lift top first appeared in the 1930s. Besides tins, collectible spice memorabilia includes boxes, bulk store bins, cabinets, and signs. See Watkins, McCormick, and Durkee for related items.

Bin, Patapsco Mills, Pepper, Baltimore, Wood, Drum Shape, Paper Label & Lid, 20 In.	83.00
Box, Big Hit, Nutmeg, Cardboard, Metal Top & Bottom, 4 1/8 x 2 1/2 x 1 1/2 In.	55.00
Box, Forbes, Ground Sage, Cardboard, Metal Top & Bottom, 1 Oz.	12.00
Box, Forbes, Paprika, Cardboard, Metal Top & Bottom, 1 1/2 Oz.	8.00
Box, Forbes, Poultry Seasoning, Cardboard, Metal Lid & Bottom, 1 1/4 Oz.	12.00
Box, Jack Sprat, Spice Mixture, Contents, Jack Sprat Food Inc., Marshalltown, Iowa	35.00
Box, Millar's Spices, Poultry Seasoning, Cardboard, Metal Top, Bottom, 3 5/8 x 2 3/8 In.	55.00
Box, Old Foresco Brand, Turmeric, Cardboard, Tin Top & Bottom	8.00
Box, Slades Pure Spices, Wood, 19 x 2 1/2 x 12 In.	50.00
Cabinet, French's Pure Spices, Tin Lithograph, c.1880, 24 In.	2530.00
Cabinet, Monsoon Spices, Sprague, Warner & Co., Chicago	385.00

Singer, Calendar, Perpetual,
For Every Stitching Operation,
1905-1915, 19 x 13 In.

Spice, Tin, French's, Imported
Paprika, Red, Green Gold
Lithograph, 3 1/4 In.

Swift, Pail, Oz Peanut Butter,
Tin Lithograph, Wire Bail,
1960s, 5 Lb., 6 In.

Cabinet, Tone's Spices, Finest Quality, Des Moines, Iowa, 33 x 23 In. 176.00
Sign, Stickney & Poor Spice Co., Spice Containers, Wood, Frame, 32 1/2 x 24 1/2 In. 1980.00
Spoon, French's Mustard, Hot Dan, Plastic, 4 In. 28.00
Tin, Alabama Maid, Cinnamon, Tin Lithograph, 5/8 Oz., 2 1/2 x 1 7/8 x 1 In. 798.00
Tin, Ben-Hur, Paprika, Los Angeles, California, 1952 .... 8.00
Tin, Clover Farm, Cloves, Slide Lid, 1 1/2 Oz., Slide Lid, 2 1/2 x 2 1/4 In. 38.00
Tin, Clover Farm, Ground Sage, 2 1/2 x 2 3/8 x 1 1/4 In. 68.00
Tin, Clover Farm, Pumpkin Pie Spice, Slide Lid, Tin, Cleveland, O., 1 1/2 Oz., 2 1/2 x 2 In. 45.00
Tin, Clover Farm, Pure Spices, Mace, 3 x 2 3/8 x 1 1/4 In. 98.00
Tin, Colman's Mustard, 5 Scenic Panels, To The Queen, 7 x 10 In. 118.00
Tin, Colman's Mustard, Bull's Head, 4 Oz. 25.00
Tin, Colman's Mustard, Yellow, 4 x 1 1/2 x 2 1/2 In. 13.00
Tin, Colonial Brand, Cloves, 3 7/8 x 2 3/8 x 1 1/8 In. 135.00
Tin, Dean's, Ground Red Pepper, Witsell Bros., Dean Lilly Co., 2 1/2 x 2 1/4 x 1 1/8 In. ... 65.00
Tin, Dove Brand, Rubbed Sage, Turkey, Tin Lithograph, 2 Oz. 99.00
Tin, Ehlers, Allspice, Contents, 1 1/2 Oz., 2 1/4 x 1 1/4 x 2 3/4 In. 8.00
Tin, Farmers Pride, Cloves, Lithograph, Hulman & Co., 3 1/2 x 2 1/2 x 1 1/8 In. ..225.00 to 320.00
Tin, Frank's, Dove Spice, Marjoram, Rubbed, Slide Lid, 1 1/4 Oz. 20.00
Tin, French's, Curry Powder, Lift Off Style Top, 3 1/2 In. 8.50
Tin, French's, Imported Paprika, Red, Green Gold Lithograph, 3 1/4 In. .... *Illus*   30.00
Tin, Golden West Ginger Spice, Red, Black, 2 Oz., 3 x 2 x 1 In. 44.00
Tin, Hatchet Thyme, 2 Oz., 3 3/4 x 2 3/8 In. 99.00
Tin, Hitzelberger Bros., Allspice, Women, Children, Boat, Utica, Lithograph, 11 x 8 In. ... 300.00
Tin, J.P. Farley Company, Cinnamon, Dubuque, Iowa, 9 1/2 x 7 1/2 In. 177.00
Tin, Jewitts Indian Girl, Allspice, Paper Label, 2 Oz., 3 x 3 1/2 x 1 In. 88.00
Tin, Juno Brand, Ginger, Spokane, Wash., 3 1/4 x 2 3/8 x 1 3/8 In. 95.00
Tin, Juno Brand, Tumeric, Spokane, Wash., 3 1/4 x 2 3/8 x 1 1/8 In. 145.00
Tin, Keen's Mustard, Inner Lid, Butterflies, Keen Robinson & Co., London, 7 x 6 In. 189.00
Tin, Keen's Mustard, Multiple Scenes, Unusual Shape, Lithograph, 5 1/2 x 7 x 7 In. 99.00
Tin, Kroger's, Cloves, 1 Oz. 8.00
Tin, Leadway Spices, Ground Turmeric, Leadway Foods, Chicago, 2 3/4 x 2 x 1 1/4 In. ... 75.00
Tin, Lee, Red Pepper, 2 Oz. 17.50
Tin, Lion, Pepper, Cardboard, Metal, 1930s, 4 In. 12.00
Tin, Mexine, Chile Powder Seasoning, Paper Label, 4 1/4 x 1 5/8 In. 50.00
Tin, Mission Brand, Cayenne, Carmel Mission, Contents, Paper Label, 4 x 2 1/2 In. 165.00
Tin, Mohican, Allspice, Red, White, Black, 2 3/4 x 2 x 1 In. 66.00
Tin, Mohican, Cinnamon, Pure Spices, 2 Oz., 2 1/4 x 1 1/4 x 3 3/4 In. 55.00
Tin, Newmark's Highest Grade Ginger, 2 Oz., 2 x 3 x 1 In. 83.00
Tin, Oak Hill, Ginger, Tin Lithograph, Hall & Co., Brockton, Mass., 2 Oz., 3 x 2 1/4 In. ... 96.00
Tin, Old Judge, Nutmeg, Jesse C. Stewart Co., Pittsburg, Pa., 3 1/4 x 1 7/8 x 1 1/2 In. 165.00
Tin, Old Mansion, Ground Cloves, Shaker Top, 3 5/8 x 2 3/8 x 1 In. 85.00
Tin, Old Mansion, Paprika, Slide Lid, 1 Oz., 2 In. 20.00
Tin, Old Rawleigh's, Allspice, Paper Label, Oval, French, English Words, Canada, 3 1/2 In. 12.50
Tin, Pocono Brand, Cinnamon, Grand Union Co., 3 1/2 x 2 1/4 In. 110.00
Tin, Quaker, Curry Powder, Slide Lid, Lady, Red, White, Blue, 1 1/2 Oz., 2 5/8 x 2 1/4 In. 30.00
Tin, Quaker, Marjoram, Pry Lid, Lady, Red, White, Blue, 1 Oz., 2 5/8 x 2 1/4 In. 28.00
Tin, Rawleigh's, Pure Ground Allspice, Slide Lid, Freeport, Ill., 3 1/4 Oz., 3 3/4 In. 16.00
Tin, Richelieu, Whole Cinnamon, Slide Lid, 1 1/2 Oz., 3 3/4 In. 22.00
Tin, S.S. Pierce, Crystallized Canton Ginger, 1/2 Lb., 6 x 3 3/4 x 1 In. 25.00
Tin, Safe Owl, Pure Ground Sage, Tin Lithograph, Prudential National, 3 3/4 x 2 3/8 x 1 In. 182.00
Tin, Schilling, Allspice, 1950, 2 Oz. 10.00
Tin, Schilling, Allspice, Red Round, Oval Insert Top, 3 5/8 In. 8.50
Tin, Schilling, Cayenne Pepper, Turn Type Dial Top, 1940s, 3 1/2 In. 8.50
Tin, Scull's Ginger, Young Girl, Contents, 4 x 2 1/4 x 1 1/2 In. 187.00
Tin, Seal Of Kentucky, Mustard, Label, Cardboard, Studebacker & Cannon, c.1906, 4 x 2 In. 155.00
Tin, Silver Buckle, Red Pepper, Cayenne, Twist Lid, 1 1/2 Oz., 2 1/2 In. 25.00
Tin, Smart & Finial, Sage, 3 1/4 x 2 1/4 In., 1 1/2 Oz. 66.00
Tin, Stickney & Poor's, Cinnamon, Ship, Yellow, Red, Black, 3 3/4 x 2 1/4 x 1 In. 66.00
Tin, Stickney & Poor's, Tumeric, Shaker Top, Boston, 2 7/8 In. 38.00
Tin, Trupak Pure Quality, Pure Thyme, Haas Brothers, San Francisco, 3 1/4 x 2 3/8 x 1 In. 155.00
Tin, Valley Queen, Cloves, Wilson Mercantile, Paper Label, 1910, 1 Oz., 1 3/4 x 3 x 1 In. 77.00
Tin, Walker's, Mexene Chili Powder, Sample, 1 1/4 x 1 In. 125.00
Tin, White Villa, Curry Powder, 1 1/2 Oz., 3 x 2 x 1 In. 149.00

SQUIRT Squirt, a citrus-flavored carbonated beverage, was developed in 1938 by Herb Bishop of Phoenix, Arizona. Bishop and his partner, Ed Mehren, created the Little Squirt character in 1941. The brand was purchased by Brooks Products in 1977 and then A&W Beverages in 1986. Squirt has been part of Dr Pepper/Seven-Up, Inc. since 1993.

Chalkboard, Enjoy, Never An After-Thirst, Tin Sign, 28 x 19 1/2 In.	83.00
Clock, Drink With Happy Taste, White, Red, Yellow, Pam, Square	143.00
Cooler, Merry-Go-Round, Swing Handle, 14 In.	28.00
Sign, Drink Squirt, Bottle, Green, Yellow, Blue Ground, Embossed, Metal, 17 x 40 In.	243.00
Sign, Drink Squirt, It's Tart Sweet, Tin, Flange Type, 2-Sided, 1941	385.00
Sign, Soda, Never An After Thirst, Tin, 58 x 47 1/2 In.	231.00
Sign, Switch To Squirt, Never An After Thirst, Red, Embossed, Metal, 9 x 27 In.	165.00 to 207.00
Thermometer, Banner, Bottle, 5 3/4 x 13 5/8 In.	145.00

STRINGHOLDER In the pre-bag era, grocery store clerks tied goods together with paper and string. Stringholders allowed string to be stored and dispensed without tangling. Cast iron stringholders were first patented in the 1860s. Ceramic and chalkware versions became widely available in the 1930s. Companies supplied stores with stringholders that doubled as advertisements for their brands.

Crystal Syrup, Cast Iron, Hanging, 12 In.	424.00
Dutch Boy, Anchor White Lead, Boy On Scaffolding, Die Cut, Tin	3520.00
Dutch Boy, Red Seal Paint, Tin Lithograph, 2-Sided, 25 1/2 x 14 1/2 In.	1320.00
Dutch Boy, Southern White Lead, Tin Lithograph, Die Cut, 25 1/4 x 14 1/4 In.	3300.00
Lewis White Lead, Hanging Pail, Tin, Die Cut, 2-Sided, 27 In.	1062.00
Lowney's Cocoa, Tin, 2-Sided, 1908, 24 x 14 In.	3565.00
Post Toasties, Bully For Breakfast	770.00
Post Toasties, Improved Corn Flakes, Tin Lithograph, 1916	660.00
Postum, Health First, Tin Lithograph, Iron Frame, 11 In.	247.00
Shenandoah Valley Apple Candy, Figural Apple, 4 1/8 x 4 In.	66.00
Walker's King Of Soap, Beehive, Cast Iron, Embossed, 4 1/2 In.	83.00

SWIFT In 1855 Gustavus F. Swift borrowed $20 and bought a cow from a neighbor in Clinton, Massachusetts. After the cow matured, Swift slaughtered it and sold the meat and the hide. He made a profit and was in business as a meat dealer. Swift moved to Chicago in 1876 because he had figured out that slaughtering cattle there instead of shipping live cattle East would lower his costs. Swift bought refrigerator cars and expanded his plants. Swift & Company claims 1868 as its starting date, but it was incorporated in 1885, when it was already a $300,000 company. Advertised brands include Swift, Swift Premium, Brookfield, and Silverleaf. Swift sponsored the radio show *Don McNeill's Breakfast Club*. Many types of Swift recipe booklets have been offered. Swift has also made soaps, cleanser, and other products from animal by-products. About 1984 the company became part of Beatrice Meats, a subsidiary of Beatrice Company. ConAgra purchased Beatrice in 1990. In 2002 control of ConAgra's beef and pork processing business was sold to Hicks, Muse, Tate & Furst Inc. and Booth Creek Management Corp. Swift & Company reemerged in that transaction.

Swift

IOI ST YEAR

Advertisement, Cub Scout Swift Premium Meats, Scouts, Campfire, 1961, 8 x 11 In.	16.00
Booklet, Presidents Of The United States, Premium, Envelope, 1960s, 12 Pages	10.00
Brochure, 26 Ways To Fry Chicken, Martha Logan, Home Economist, Swift & Company	5.00
Button, Little Cook, Celluloid, Die Cut, 1915, 3 1/4 x 1 1/4 In.	44.00
Calendar, 1905, Swift's Premium Hams, Bacon, Celluloid, Pocket, 3 3/4 x 1 3/4 In.	45.00
Calendar, 1917, Premium Oleomargarine, Serves The Nation, Celluloid, 3 1/2 x 2 In.	55.00
Calendar, 1926, Brookfield Pork Sausages, Swift & Co., Ruler, Celluloid, 3 1/2 x 1 3/4 In.	55.00
Comic Book, March To Market, Story Of Meat, 1948, 10 x 7 In., 16 Pages	15.00
Figure, Easter Bunny, Holds 2 Premium Hams, Blow-Up, Sand Bottom Weights, 33 In.	20.00
Pail, Oz Peanut Butter, Tin Lithograph, Wire Bail, 1960s, 5 Lb., 6 In.	*Illus* 100.00
Pail, Peanut Butter, Wizard Of Oz, 5 Lbs.	60.00

Pail, Silverleaf Brand Lard, 4 Lb., 6 In. 16.00
Pencil, Mechanical, Compliments Of Swift & Company, 5 1/4 In.   15.00
Pencil, Premium Ham, Metal, Dark Maroon, 5 1/2 In. 7.50
Sign, Premium Cooked Ham, Girl, In Chefs Hat, Basket, Gilt Frame, 19 3/4 x 15 In. 316.00
Sign, Swift's Pride Cleanser, Die Cut, Cardboard, 2-Sided, Hanger, 1907, 9 x 10 1/2 In. . . .   66.00
Sign, Swift's Pride Soap, Curved, Corner, Porcelain, 14 x 8 In. 2750.00
Sign, Swift's Pride Soap, Winged Man, Washboard Feet, Cardboard Lithograph, 13 x 9 In.   146.00
Tin, Pork Tenderloins, 5 Lb., 6 In. 17.50
Tin, Silverleaf Brand Pure Lard, Handle, 8 1/2 In. 28.00
Tin, Silverleaf Lard, 4 Lb., 6 In. 14.50
Tin, Swift's Selected Sheep Brains, Lid, Red, White Logo, Gold Color, 10 Lb., 8 x 7 1/2 In.   75.00
Tumbler, Peanut Butter, Wizard Of Oz, Pink, White Letters, Wavy Bottom, 1930s, 5 In. . .   32.00

SYRUP DISPENSER, see Dispenser

TALCUM POWDER   Talcum powder is made by grinding mineral talc
and combining it with perfume. Originally stored in fancy wooden or
tortoiseshell boxes, refillable cardboard talcum powder boxes were
developed in the first half of the nineteenth century. Later in the century, talcum powder was available in tins. Today, collectors look for
talcum powder tins with sprinkle tops and interesting graphics. See
also Mennen.

Can, Dr. Sayman's Talc, Cardboard, Metal, Paper Label, St. Louis, 5 x 2 3/8 In. 107.00
Canister, Country Club Talcum Powder, Paper On Cardboard, Tin Lid, 5 1/2 In. 50.00
Tin, A.D.S. Baby Talc, Oval Base, American Druggists, N.Y., 5 1/8 x 3 x 1 1/2 In. 180.00
Tin, Air-Float Baby Powder, Borated, With Olive Oil, 9 3/4 x 7 In. 220.00
Tin, Amami Bouquet, Woman, Yellow, Sample, Prichard & Constance Co., 2 x 1 In. 176.00
Tin, As The Petals Talcum, Lazell Perfumer, 5 3/4 x 3 1/8 x 1 In.   340.00
Tin, Babcocks Corylopsis Of Japan, Lithograph, American Can, 6 x 2 In. 44.00
Tin, Barker's Nursery Talcum Powder, S.F. Baker, Keokuk, Iowa, 6 x 2 1/4 x 1 1/4 In. . . .   425.00
Tin, Cadette Baby Talc, Toy Soldier Form, Tin Lithograph, Contents, 7 x 2 In. . . . .154.00 to 255.00
Tin, California Perfume Co. Baby Powder, 2 Soldiers, Box, 4 x 3 x 1 1/2 In. 66.00
Tin, Cara Nome Talcum, Slide Lid, Holes, 3 1/2 x 2 1/2 x 1 1/2 In. 28.00
Tin, Cedar Brand Talcum Powder, Baby, Contents, c.1907 . . . .   358.00
Tin, Chamberlain's Talcum, Oval, Flat Finish, 6 x 2 3/8 x 1 In. 85.00
Tin, Comfort Talcum Powder, Unequalled In Nursery & Sick Room, Nurse, 4 x 2 1/4 In. .   385.00
Tin, Corylopsis Of Japan, Talcum Powder, 1906, 4 1/2 x 2 1/4 In.   66.00
Tin, Corylopsis Talc Powder, Page Prefumer New York, 5 1/8 x 3 x 1 5/8 In. 255.00
Tin, Cuticura Borated All Purpose Talcum Powder, Pottier Drug & Chemical, 4 Oz., 5 In. .   35.00
Tin, D.B. Brand Violet Talcum Powder, Contents, Diener Bros., Hamburg, Pa., 3 x 5 1/4 In.   35.00
Tin, Deliscent Talc, Woman, Hand Mirror, Contents, Foley & Co., Chicago, 6 In. 61.00
Tin, Desitin Medicinal Nursery Powder, Sample Not For Sale, 2 1/8 In. 30.00
Tin, Desitin Toilet, Nursery Powder, Oval, Desitin Chemical, Co., 4 5/8 x 2 x 1 1/4 In. . . .   45.00
Tin, Dr. Nebb's Baby Powder, Baby Playing With Blocks, 4 3/4 x 2 x 2 In. 88.00
Tin, Encharma Talcum Powder, 6 x 2 1/4 x 1 In. 295.00
Tin, Franco Talcum Powder, Franco American Hygenic Co., Chicago, 4 x 2 1/2 x 1 3/8 In.   175.00
Tin, Gardenia Talcum Powder, Flowers, Richard Hudnut, Sample, 2 1/4 x 1 1/4 x 3/4 In. .   176.00
Tin, Great Seal Talcum Powder, Contents 71.00
Tin, Health-O Bonded Products, Baby Talc, Milson Co., Cincinnati, 4 1/2 x 3 x 1 1/8 In. .   225.00
Tin, Hyacinth Talcum, Woman In Tennis Clothing, Jas. A Hetherington, Trapezoidal Shape   130.00
Tin, J&J Baby & Toilet Powder, Sample, 2 x 1 In. 245.00
Tin, Jap Rose Toilet Talcum Powder, Yellow, 6 x 2 1/4 x 1 1/4 In. 198.00
Tin, Jergens Miss Dainty Talcum Powder, Girls, Contents 187.00
Tin, Jergens Oriental, Geisha Doll, c.1930, 3 1/2 Oz. 59.00
Tin, Johnson & Johnson, Baby Powder, 1 1/2 Oz., 3 3/4 In. 15.00
Tin, Johnson's Baby Powder, 1940s, 5 3/4 In. 30.00
Tin, Kuco No Chafe Talc, Lithograph, Child, Man, Woman, 2 1/2 x 1 In. 330.00
Tin, Lilac & Roses Talc, Landers Blended Flower, New York, 1 Lb., 7 3/4 x 3 x 2 In. 45.00
Tin, Mason Perfumed Talcum Powder, Baby, Contents 303.00
Tin, Massatta Talc, Lazell Perfumer, Rectangular Base, Trial Size, 2 x 1 1/8 x 3/4 In. 95.00
Tin, McNess Humpty-Dumpty Baby Powder, Furst McKesson, Ill., 6 x 3 x 1 1/2 In. 225.00
Tin, McNess Humpty-Dumpty, Borated Talc, Baby Powder, Freeport, Ill., 7 x 3 In. 39.00
Tin, Mosquito Talcum Powder, Paper Label, Harmony, Boston, 4 x 2 1/2 x 1 3/8 In. . .61.00 to 85.00

Tin, Norwich Baby Powder, Norwich, N.Y., 2 1/4 x 5 7/8 In. 43.00
Tin, Nylotis Baby Powder, Nyal Company, Detroit, Mich., 4 3/4 x 2 1/4 x 1 1/4 In. 190.00
Tin, Nylotis Rose Talcum, Roses, Pyramid Shape, Contents, Nyal Company, Detroit, 5 In. 72.00
Tin, Nylotis Talcum, Oval Base, Nyal Company, Detroit, Mich., 6 x 2 x 1 1/4 In. 195.00
Tin, Oriole Talc, Foley & Co., Bird On Branch, Black, Orange, 5 7/8 x 2 1/4 x 1 1/4 In. ... 187.00
Tin, Peerless Talcum Powder, Tin Lithograph, 1 1/2 x 3 3/4 In. 99.00
Tin, Peter Rabbit Talc, Rabbit Characters, Lithograph, 3 5/8 x 4 1/8 In. 264.00
Tin, Pure Baby Borated Powder, Contents, Parfumerie Vovar, New York, 7 3/4 x 2 In. 565.00
Tin, Rawleigh's Talcum, Nursery Rhyme Images, 7 1/2 x 3 x 2 In. 413.00
Tin, Rawleigh's, Pan Jang Talcum Powder, Chinese Woman, Garden, 3 x 5 x 1 In. .121.00 to 325.00
Tin, Red Man After Shave Talc, Fly Fisherman, 3 1/2 Oz., 4 1/2 In. 61.00
Tin, Rexall Drugs Baby Talc, Pink, Blue, 16 Oz., 7 3/4 In. 36.00
Tin, Rexall Violet Talcum Powder, United Drug Co., Boston Mass., 4 1/2 In. 44.00
Tin, Select Lilac Talcum Powder, Contents, c.1907 .... 176.00
Tin, Sweetheart Talcum Powder, Manhattan Soap Co., N.Y., 4 5/8 x 2 1/2 x 1 3/8 In. 245.00
Tin, Taylor's Blue Bird Talcum Powder, Embossed, Tin Lithograph, 4 3/8 x 2 1/2 In. . 1018.00
Tin, Tetlow's Pussywillow Talc, Henry Tetlow Co., Philadelphia, 3 1/4 x 4 1/2 x 1 3/8 In. . 260.00
Tin, Vantines Kutch Sandalwood Talcum Powder, Mat Finish, Sample Size, 2 x 1 x 3/4 In. 225.00
Tin, Vantines Wisteria Talcum Powder, Oriental Woman 110.00
Tin, Violet Flesh Talcum Powder 38.00
Tin, Violet Sec Almond Talcum, Oval, Richard Hudnut, New York, 4 7/8 x 2 1/2 x 1 In. .. 225.00
Tin, White Lilac Talcum Powder, For The Good Of Your Skin, Contents, 5 x 1 3/4 In. ... 99.00
Tin, Williams' Baby Talc, Baby, Lithograph, 4 7/8 x 2 3/4 x 1 3/8 In. 633.00
Tin, Williams' Carnation Talcum Powder, Contents, 1906, 4 1/2 x 2 1/2 In. 110.00
Tin, Wrisley's Sam Toy Talcum, Tin Lithograph, 1906, 2 x 4 1/4 x 1 3/4 In. 55.00
Tin, Z.B.T. Baby Powder With Olive Oil, Square, National Brands, Cinco, 6 x 2 1/4 In. .. 38.00
Tin, Z.B.T. Baby Powder, Square, Gift From Manufacturer, 3 7/8 x 1 3/8 In. 35.00

TAPE MEASURE, see Sewing

TELEPHONE The telephone was invented in 1876. Collectors do
search for old telephones; but this book lists only advertising materials
used by the many phone companies. Signs indicating public phones or
offices, paperweights, and other memorabilia featuring the famous
Bell trademark are popular.

Bottle Opener & Paperweight, Bell Telephone Hard Hat, Box, Scott Products, Newark .. 50.00
Box, Western Electric Phone, Wood, Shipping, Stenciled, Impressed 55.00
Calendar, Bell Telephone, Illinois, Wallet, 1947 .... 5.00
Cigar Cutter, Wood, Cast Iron, Embossed Blue Telephone Bell, 3 1/2 x 3 In. 468.00
Mirror, Get A Bell Telephone, Celluloid, Oval, AT&T, 2 3/4 x 1 3/4 In. 245.00
Sign, Bell System Connections, Public Telephone, Porcelain, Flange, Canada 248.00
Sign, Bell System, Brass, Embossed, 4 x 20 In. 28.00
Sign, Bell System, Illinois Bell, Porcelain, Flange, 2-Sided, 12 x 11 In. 165.00
Sign, Bell System, Public Telephone, Porcelain, Flange, 18 In. 138.00
Sign, Bell System, Underground Cable, Do Not Disturb, Porcelain, 3 1/2 x 7 In. 54.00
Sign, Bell Telephone, Porcelain, 2 1/2 x 18 In. 110.00
Sign, Bell, Underground Cable, Do Not Disturb, Bell System, Porcelain 65.00
Sign, Employee Parking, Bell System, White, Black Trim, Porcelainized, 12 x 18 In. 65.00
Sign, Hudson River Telephone Co., Blue, White, Porcelain, Flange, 2-Sided, 18 x 17 In. .. 743.00
Sign, Local & Long Distance, Bethel, Mt. Aetna, Porcelain, Myerstown, Pa., Round, 6 In. 1018.00
Sign, Public Telephone Booth Inside, Chicago, Flange, Porcelain, 15 x 10 1/2 In. 358.00
Sign, Public Telephone, Bell System, 2-Sided, Porcelain, Flange, 11 x 11 x 1 1/2 In. 121.00
Sign, Public Telephone, Bell System, Flange, Porcelain, 11 x 12 In. 303.00
Sign, Public Telephone, Bell System, Porcelain, Flange, 2-Sided, 14 In. 99.00
Sign, Public Telephone, Bell System, White Ground, Porcelain, 7 In. 110.00
Sign, Public Telephone, Flange, 2-Sided, 18 1/4 x 20 In. 130.00
Sign, Public Telephone, Illinois Bell, Porcelain, 5 1/2 x 19 In. 77.00
Sign, Public Telephone, Sheet Metal, Flange, 13 In. 121.00
Sign, Telephone Office, Blue, White, Porcelain, 2-Sided, Pole Hanger, 25 x 72 In. 187.00
Sign, Telephone Pay Station, Blue, White, Porcelain, 2-Sided, Wood Frame, 11 x 21 In. .. 88.00
Telephone, Raid Bug Figural, Plastic, 1980s, 8 1/2 x 3 x 4 1/2 In. 45.00
Toy, Truck, Bell Telephone, Accessories, Hubley, 1932, 9 1/2 In. 1980.00

TEXACO   The Texas Fuel Company was started by Joseph S. "Buckskin Joe" Cullinan and Arnold Schalet in 1901. The following year the pair started the Texas Company and soon absorbed their smaller company. Nine years later, the Texas Company opened its first filling station in Brooklyn, New York. The firm acquired the Indian Refining Company and its Havoline brand in 1931 and introduced Fire Chief Gasoline in 1932. The company officially changed its name to Texaco Inc. in 1959. In 2001 Texaco and Chevron merged to form ChevronTexaco Corp.

Advertisement, Dalmation Puppies Water Skiing, Full Color, 1954, 10 x 13 In.	18.00
Badge, Name Badge, Cloisonne Enameling, 1 3/4 x 2 1/4 In.	468.00
Bank, 1925 Kenworth Stake Truck, Collector's Series, No. 9, Die Cast, Ertl, Box, 1992	55.00
Calendar, 1956, Texaco Service, Logo, Service Center, Dundalk, Md., 2 1/2 x 3 1/2 In.	30.00
Can, Home Lubricant, Red, Black, White, Metal, Black Plastic Cap, 4 Fl. Oz.	25.00
Can, Motor Oil, Heavy, Pour Spout, Green Ground, Port Arthur, Tex., 1/2 Gal., 7 In.	104.00
Can, Texaco Outboard, Qt.	20.00 to 35.00
Can, Texaco, Marfak, Bright Paint, 5 3/4 x 6 1/2 In.	25.00
Can, Texaco, Motor Cup Grease, 3 1/2 In.	132.00
Clock, Texaco Oil, Neon, Spinner, Steel, Pull Chain, 20 In.	400.00
Cookie Jar, Texaco Gas Pump, Ceramic, Box, 16 In.	55.00
Doll, Cheerleader, Made In Hong Kong, Box, 1960s-1970s, 11 1/2 In.	120.00
Doorstop, Texaco Oil Co., 2 Scotties, Listen, Cast Iron, 1930s, 6 x 9 In.	225.00
Figure, Gas Station Attendant, Angus, Uniform, Buttons, Patches, Life Size	605.00
Gas Pump Globe, Texaco Star, White On Glass, 13 1/2 In.	350.00
Hat, Fire Chief's, Bull Horn Speaker System, Battery Operated	135.00
Key Display, Texaco Restroom, Ladies & Men Key Holders, Metal, 2-Sided, 12 x 9 In.	244.00
Poster, Texaco, Bonds Buy Bombs, Buy Bonds, 1940s, 24 x 18 In.	523.00
Potholder, It Pays To Farm With Texaco Products, Red Border, Square, 1950s, 6 3/4 In.	20.00
Pump Plate, Texaco, Porcelain, Black T, Round, 1938, 8 In.	330.00
Pump Plate, Texaco, Sky Chief, Su-Preme Petrox, Porcelain, 1959, 18 x 12 In.	138.00
Salt & Pepper, Gas Pump, Logo, Sparky's Texaco Service, 215 Larimer Ave., 1950s	30.00
Sign, Gas Pump, Texaco Sea Chief, Logo, Tin, 6-Sided, 10 x 15 In.	275.00
Sign, Gas Pump, Texaco, Marine White Gasoline, Logo, Porcelain, 1939, 18 x 12 In.	1210.00
Sign, No Smoking, Logos On Ends, 6 x 24 In.	1320.00
Sign, No Smoking, White T, Single-Sided, Porcelain, 1941, 4 x 23 In.	248.00
Sign, Texaco, Diesel Chief, Tin, Single-Sided, Embossed, 10 x 15 In.	413.00
Sign, Texaco, Farm Lubricants, Sold Here, Porcelain, 1956, 30 x 42 In.	2090.00
Sign, Texaco, Fire-Chief Gasoline, Enameled, Porcelain, 16 x 10 5/8 In.	25.00
Sign, Texaco, Fire-Chief Gasoline, Porcelain, 1946, 12 x 18 In.	77.00
Sign, Texaco, Fire-Chief Gasoline, Porcelain, 1963, 18 x 12 In.	39.00
Sign, Texaco, Gasoline, Motor Oil, Porcelain, Round, 42 In.	1018.00
Sign, Texaco, Green T, Red Star, White Ground, Porcelain, Round, 15 In.	495.00
Sign, Texaco, Kerosene, Clear Burning, Red, White, Blue, Tin, 1957, 11 3/4 x 19 3/4 In.	165.00
Sign, Texaco, Keyhole, White T, Porcelain, Single-Sided, 1947, 18 x 12 In.	330.00
Sign, Texaco, Keyhole, White T, Porcelain, Single-Sided, 1954, 18 x 12 In.	385.00
Sign, Texaco, Marine White Gasoline, Porcelain, 1956, 12 x 8 In.	1540.00
Sign, Texaco, Marine White, Embossed, 10 x 15 In.	358.00
Sign, Texaco, Motor Oil For Ford Cars, Porcelain	500.00
Sign, Texaco, Motor Oil, Free Crankcase Service, Porcelain, 30 x 30 In.	50.00
Sign, Texaco, No Smoking, Logo At Each End, Porcelain, 4 x 23 In.	248.00 to 281.00
Sign, Texaco, Sea Chief, Tin, 6-Sided, 9 1/2 x 15 In.	303.00
Sign, Texaco, Sea Chief, Tin, Embossed, Single-Sided, 10 x 15 In.	303.00
Sign, Texaco, Sea Chief, White, Yellow, Black, Red, Tin, Embossed, 15 x 10 In.	468.00
Sign, Texaco, Sky Chief Su-Preme Gasoline, Porcelain, 1963, 18 x 12 In.	138.00
Sign, Texaco, Sky Chief Su-Preme, Petrox, Porcelain, 1962, 12 x 18 In.	110.00
Sign, Texaco, Sky Chief, Green, Red, White, Porcelain, 1947, 12 x 18 In.	105.00
Sign, Texaco, White, Red, Green, Black, Leaded Glass, Round, 22 In.	770.00
Sign, Texas Company, Petroleum Products, Metal, Round, 8 3/4 In.	109.00
Towel, Kitchen, It Pays To Farm With Texaco Products, Cellophane Package, 29 x 16 In.	35.00
Toy, Airplane, Texaco No. 2, 1932 Northrup Gamma, Box, 1994	85.00
Toy, Train Tank Car, Texaco Company, Gray, Black Letters, 7 1/4 x 16 1/2 In.	150.00
Toy, Truck, Tanker, Diecast Cab, Aluminum Tank, Smith Miller, 15 In.	253.00

Toy, Truck, Tanker, Pressed Steel, Buddy L, 1950s, 24 In. 99.00
Toy, Truck, Tanker, Texaco Oil, Republic Tool Co., Metal, Plastic, 1960s, 23 1/2 In. 65.00
Waste Bucket, Cast Iron, Steel, 1942, 18 In. 33.00

THERMOMETER The mercury-column thermometer was invented before the eighteenth century. In the days before easily available newspaper, telephone, television, or Internet weather reports, the outdoor thermometer was an important source of information. Advertisers gave stores many types of thermometers with messages for products. Enameled metal, tin, or wooden backs were used. The thermometers were often large so they could be read from a distance. Some were even shaped to represent a bottle holding a product. Advertising thermometers are still made; some are new designs and others are copies of older models. Other thermometers are listed throughout this book under brand names.

Abbott's Bitters, Best For Cocktails, Wood, Yellow Ground, 1890s-1910s, 21 x 5 In. 476.00
Abbott's Bitters, Round, 1899, 9 x 1 In. 187.00
Abbott's Bitters, Used To Flavor Grapefruit, Fruit Salads, Wood, 21 x 5 1/8 In. 220.00
AC Quality Spark Plug, Donkey In Tub, Embossed, Tin Lithograph, 21 x 7 1/2 In. 440.00
American Brakeblok, Dog, Yellow, Metal, 20 x 6 In. 259.00
American Fence, Stands The Test Of Time & Weather Changes, 27 x 7 In. 77.00
American Manufacturing Co., Metal, Glass Cover, 9 In. Diam. 154.00
August Flower & German Syrup, Brass, Glass Front, Round, Dial Type, 9 In. 121.00
Baltimore Tank & Tower Co., Celluloid, 6 1/4 x 2 In. 95.00
Barq's, Drink Barq's, It's Good, Bottle, Tin, 25 1/2 x 9 3/4 In. . . . . .143.00 to 220.00
Baugh's Fertilizers, Painted Wood, 12 In. 93.00
Berwick Savings & Trust, Stanwood Hillson, N.Y., 11 5/8 x 3 1/8 x 1/4 In. 40.00
Canadian Coal, British Coal Corp., Demander, Blue, Black, Porcelain, 30 x 8 In. 77.00
Case Implement Co., White, Red, Black, Metal, 13 In. 11.00
Castrol, Green Ground, Red Letters, White Trim, Round, 12 In. 55.00
Chaney Tru-Temp, Metal, Beige Ground, Black Letters, Made In USA, 7 x 3/4 In. 27.00
Cloverdale Soft Drink, Stay Lively Longer, Round, 12 In. 303.00
Country Fair Bourbon, Tin Lithograph, Paperboard Back, Round, 9 In. 33.00
Crystal Laundry, Wood, Cumberland, Md., 21 In. 99.00
Daily News, Want Ad Directory, Yellow Ground, Porcelain, Chicago, 39 x 8 In. 198.00
Diet Rite Cola, Sugar Free, Blue, Glass Cover, 12 In. Diam. 138.00
Doan's Pills, Die Cut Man With Backache, Is Your Back Bad Today?, Wood, 21 In. 489.00
Doan's Pills, Kidney Pills For Back Pain, Die Cut, Wood, 21 x 5 In. 160.00
Eagle Pencil, 75th Anniversary, Wood, Figural, 14 1/4 x 1 1/4 In. 577.00
Ex-Lax, Chocolated Laxative, Keep Regular, Porcelain, 1930s, 36 1/2 x 8 In. . . . . *Illus* 209.00
F.S. Farm Service, Plastic Pole Sign, 7 In. 50.00
Fidelity-Phenix, Fire Insurance, Blue, White, Porcelain, 27 1/8 x 7 In. 187.00
Franklin Fire Insurance, Philadelphia, Round, 9 1/4 In. 46.00
G.A. Hawver Jeweler & Optometrist, Eyeball At Top, 11 1/2 x 3 1/4 In. 99.00
Gardner's Purity Bread, Mirror, 11 x 17 In. 44.00
Hufeland Co., Sure Headache Cure, Price 10 Cents, Wood, 21 x 5 1/8 In. 220.00
Hy-Line Chicks, Neuhauser Hatcheries, Glass Dial, Round, Pam Clock Co., 12 In. 111.00
Icy Hot, Puts Pain To Sleep, Metal, 38 In. 58.00
International Stock Food, 3 Feeds For 1 Cent, Wood, 48 x 9 In. 6875.00
Ken-L-Ration, For Best Results Feed Your Dog, 26 3/4 x 7 1/4 In. 175.00
Kentucky Fuel Co., As Good As Gold, Union Central Bldg., 21 1/2 x 5 In. 61.00
King Midas Flour, Porcelain, c.1920, 27 x 7 In. . . . . *Illus* 1485.00
Mason's Root Beer, 14 1/4 x 4 1/2 In. 140.00
Mission Orange, 17 1/8 x 5 1/8 In. 135.00
Mitchell Radiator Co., Girl Reading Book, Metal, 10 1/2 x 8 1/2 In. 94.00
Mobil, Sanilac Cattle Spray, Cows, Pond, Tree, Wood, 18 3/4 x 8 5/8 In. 413.00
Modern Appliances, Washers, Refrigerators & Stoves, Wood, 13 In. 121.00
Nesbitt's, California Orange, Porcelain, 27 x 7 In. 413.00
Nesbitt's Orange Soda, Plein De Soleil, French Writing, Canada, 17 x 5 In. 165.00
NuGrape, Double Bottle, Green, Yellow, Red, c.1940, 17 x 6 In. 495.00
O.P. Elliston, Funeral Director, Ambulance Service, Reverse Painted, Frame, 36 x 12 In. . . 660.00
Occident Flour, Wood, Elongated Oval, 15 In. 132.00
Orange Crush, Round Dial Type, Cap On Face, 12 In. 193.00

Thermometer, Ex-Lax, Chocolated Laxative, Keep Regular, Porcelain, 1930s, 36 1/2 x 8 In.

Thermometer, King Midas Flour, Porcelain, c.1920, 27 x 7 In.

Thermometer, Ramon's Brownie Pills, Yellow Ground, c.1950, 21 x 8 In.

Orts Sof Spun Bread, Porcelain, 27 In.	132.00
Pale Reserve Beer, Ask For P.R. Junior, Reading, Pa., Round, 12 In.	110.00
Pennsy Supply Co., Metal, 13 x 4 In.	28.00
Perfection Mfg., Rock-A-Bye, Baby In Swing, Porcelain Enamel, 6 x 2 1/2 In.	314.00
Pierce College Of Business, Wood, 24 In.	118.00
Plantation Pipe Line Co., Plastic, White, Red & Blue Trim, U.S.A., 12 x 3 1/4 In.	8.50
Ramon's Brownie Pills, Dorfmass Bros., Corona, N.Y., Wood, 21 In.	220.00
Ramon's Brownie Pills, Pink Pills, Kidneys, Laxative, Metal, 21 x 8 3/4 In.	330.00 to 660.00
Ramon's Brownie Pills, The Little Doctor, Wood, 21 In.	99.00
Ramon's Brownie Pills, Yellow Ground, c.1950, 21 x 8 In. .... *Illus*	523.00
Ramon's Kidney Pills, Man In Suit, Hat, Wood, 21 x 9 In.	495.00
Red Rock Cola, Metal, c.1939, 27 x 7 In.	330.00
Red Seal, Dry Battery, Porcelain, 27 x 7 In.	143.00 to 165.00
Reliable Furniture Co., Largest In Northern New England, Tin, 39 In.	95.00
Roessner Brothers, Hagerstown, Md., Wood, 12 In.	136.00
Schmidt's Bread, Blue Ribbon, Round, Pam Clock Co., 1958, 12 In.	413.00
Stephenson Union Suits, For All Seasons, Red, Black, White, Porcelain, 40 x 9 In.	198.00
Suncrest, Bottle Shape, Die Cut, Embossed Tin, 17 x 5 1/4 In.	132.00 to 143.00
Tum's, For The Tummy, Quick Relief, Tin, 9 x 4 In.	138.00
Use Blue Coal, A.M. Graham Coal Co., Lockport, N.Y., Porcelain, 38 3/4 x 8 In.	743.00
USS American Fence & Posts, Porcelain, 19 In.	220.00
Veedol Tractor Motor Oil, Fiberboard, Black, Red, White, 5 x 20 In.	116.00
Walker's DeLuxe Bourbon, Round, Glass Lens, 12 1/2 In.	77.00
Whistle, 2 Brownies Carrying Bottle, 1940s, 21 In.	1100.00
Wool Soap, Dial Type, Metal Case, Glass Front, Round, c.1895, 6 In.	660.00
Yellow Cab & Baggage Co., Round, 6 In.	154.00
Zenith Long Distance Radio, Radio Tower, 1940s-1950s, 72 x 17 In.	825.00

TIN   Tin cans (or canisters, as they were first known) became important because Napoleon's army had to eat. Napoleon offered a reward to the person who could develop a safe way to preserve food for long periods of time. Nicolas Appert won the prize in 1809 for his method of preserving ("canning") food in glass jars. In England, Peter Durand patented an iron-coated tin can with a soldered cover in 1810. The British army was using his invention by 1813. The tin can did not come into commercial use in the United States until Ezra Daggett and Thomas Kensett patented their container in 1825. By the 1860s there were many American manufacturers of tin cans, including S.A. Ilsley and Company and Somers Bros., both of Brooklyn, New York. Somers was the first manufacturer of lithographed tin cans. Some early tins are marked with the name of the maker as well as the name of the product inside. Today commercially canned food is sold in tin-coated steel. The first metal containers for food or tobacco were used in England about 1780. Snuff was sold in lead drums marked with engraved paper labels. Thomas Huntley started packing biscuits in tins about 1830 (see Huntley & Palmers). Matches were packed in tins after 1845. People collect tins by type, such as roly poly or talcum powder tins; by brand name or type of industry, such as tobacco or food; or by the attractiveness of the tin's graphics. Items are listed in this book by brand name, if possible. Included are food, tea, biscuit boxes, and others. More tin containers can be found in the Baking Powder, Coffee, and Talcum Powder categories and in brand-specific categories. Related items are also in the Can category.

A-C Troches, Cough Drops, 2 1/4 x 3 1/4 x 1/4 In.	16.00
A-P-C Plaster, 1 3/8 x 1 In.	18.00
A.D.S. Fruit-Lax, Slip Top, Insert, 3/8 x 2 x 1 5/8 In.	45.00
Abercrombie & Fitch, Outfitters To Sportsmen, Split Shot, Tin, Celluloid, 1 1/2 In.	83.00
Acetidine Tablets, Sharp & Dohme, Baltimore, Md., 12 Tablet Size	17.00
Adams Pepsin Gum, Tin Lithograph, Hinged Lid, 5 3/4 x 6 5/8 x 4 3/4 In.	413.00
Advance Brand Wild Cherry Drops, For Coughs & Colds, 5 Lb., 8 3/4 x 5 1/8 In.	55.00
Airplane View Of Manhattan Island, 25 Scenes, 11 x 12 1/2 x 6 In.	156.00
Al. Foss Pork Rind Minnow, Cleveland, Ohio, 4 x 1 1/2 x 1 1/4 In.	18.70
Alkethrepta Chocolate, Red Ground, 4 1/4 x 3 1/4 x 2 1/8 In.	85.00
Allans Star Brand Pills, Allan-Pfeiffer Chemical Co., 3 x 1 5/8 In.	44.00
Allen's Sanitary Tooth Ease, Paper Label, Contents, 4 1/8 In.	72.00
Ambergloss, Removes Cuticle, Theo. Miller, N.Y., 1/4 x 1 1/2 x 5/8 In.	44.00
American Preserves Co. Vermont Maple Syrup, Butterfly, Handle, 7 3/4 x 5 x 3 1/2 In.	121.00
Ames, ABC Salve, 3 1/2 In. Diam.	22.00
Antikamnia, Hernia & Heroin Tablets, Nov. 13, 1902, 1 1/2 x 2 1/4 In.	330.00
Antikamnia Tablets, Free Physicians Sample, 1 3/4 x 1 1/4 In.	72.00
Aphro Compound, Square, 4 x 1 3/4 In.	90.00
Arabian Scratches & Gall Cure, Long Oval, Sample, 2 1/2 In.	143.00
Armand Cold Cream, Woman's Profile, Des Moines, Iowa, Purse Size, 1 3/4 In.	8.00
Aunt Nellie's Cream Of Tartar, Tin Lithograph, 2 Oz.	110.00
Austrian Style Filled Bonbons, Santa, Airplane, F.W. Woolworth, Oval, 3 3/4 x 2 1/4 In.	350.00
B. Paul's Henna Compound, Contents, B. Paul, New York, 4 Oz., 2 1/2 x 3 1/4 In.	16.50
Bacon, Stickneys & Co., Cream of Tartar, Albany, N.Y., 15 1b., 9 1/2 x 7 1/2 In.	50.00
Bagdad Short Cut, Pipe, Smoking, Multicolored, Lithograph, Pocket, 3 3/4 x 3 3/8 In.	228.00
Baker Castor Oil, Cold Pressed Castor Oil, 40 Lb., 14 x 9 1/2 In.	12.00
Bar Polish Cleanser, Cardboard, Paper Label, Tin Lid, 4 3/4 x 3 In.	30.00
Barbers Healing Ointment, Round, 2 1/4 In.	83.00
Barton's Candy Almond Kisses, 9 Oz., 4 x 3 1/2 In.	25.00
Bassett's Liquorice Allsorts, 7 In.	10.00
Bathasweet, Oval Bottom, Sample, C.S. Welch Company, New York, 2 7/8 x 1 x 3/4 In.	85.00
Bauer & Back First Aid Kit, Compact, 5 1/2 x 3 1/2 x 1/4 In.	12.00
Beechnut Packing Co. Christmas Chest, Mohawk Valley Scenes, c.1924, 6 x 12 x 11 In.	85.00
Beltel Massettes For Throat & Voice, 3/8 x 1 3/4 x 1 3/8 In.	28.00
Benzotol Tooth Powder, Cylinder, Contents, 3 3/4 In.	176.00
Betty Zane Popcorn, Marion, Ohio, 5 1/8 x 2 1/2 In.	85.00
Big Buster Popcorn, 4 5/8 x 2 5/8 In.	85.00
Big Sioux, Waldorf Soda, Manchester Biscuit Co., 9 x 7 x 8 In.	55.00
Bishop's Candies, Eagle Shield, Bear, Red Stripes, Screw Top, California, 5 x 7 x 5 In.	99.00
Black Cough Drops, Bone, Eagle & Co., Reading, Pa., 7 1/2 x 5 In.	173.00
Blackburn's Casca Royal Pills, Dayton, 1/2 x 2 1/2 x 1 5/8 In.	24.00
Blas Coconut, Monkeys In Jungle, Lithograph, Green, 5 1/4 x 2 5/8 x 2 5/8 In.	220.00
Blondie Paints, Box, 5/8 x 5 3/4 x 4 1/2 In.	42.00
Blue Ointment, Poison, Skull & Crossbones, Blue, Black, Round, 1 3/4 In.	17.00 to 33.00
Blue Spot, 5 Cents, Lithograph, Square, 5 1/2 x 5 In.	66.00
Bon Olive Oil, Unsurpassed For Culinary & Medical Purposes, 1950s, 6 x 3 3/4 x 1 1/2 In.	15.00
Boro-Salox Antiseptic Dusting Powder, Square, Boss & Seiffert, R.I., 4 5/8 x 1 3/4 In.	80.00
Bournville Cocoa, Cadbury, Sample, 1/2 x 2 1/2 x 1 5/8 In.	95.00
Brater's Asthma Powder, New York, 2 3/4 x 3 3/4 In.	39.00
Breethem, For The Breath, 2 1/8 x 1 5/8 In.	90.00
Brights Kidney Bean, Liver, Bowels, Blood, Statue Of Liberty, 50 Cents, 1 1/2 x 2 1/2 In.	1210.00
Brights Kidney Beans For Pain In The Back, Flat, Pocket, 2 1/2 x 1 1/2 In.	28.00
Brownie Brand, Salted Peanuts, Blue, Yellow, 10 Lb., 8 1/4 x 9 In.	132.00
Buffalo Brand, Fancy Salted Peanuts, Tin Lithograph, E.M. Hoyt, 25 Lb., 9 In.	242.00
Buffalo Brand, Peanut, 10 In.	154.00
Buffalo Brand, Salted Peanuts, 9 In.	143.00
Bull Dog Fire Extinguisher, Tin Lithograph, Contents, 22 x 2 1/8 In.	161.00

Bunte Fine Confections, Factory, Green, 14 In. 35.00
Bunte Fine Hard Candies, Bunte Brothers, Chicago, 5 Lb., 10 x 4 1/2 In. 25.00
Bunte Marshmallows, 2 x 4 1/4 In. 17.00
Bunte Marshmallows, Child, Factory, Tin Lithograph, 5 Lb., 5 x 12 3/4 In. 220.00
Butler Radiant Morsels, Square, 7 5/8 In. x 4 5/8 In. 185.00
C.P.C. Peanut Butter, California Peanut Co., 1 Lb., 3 3/8 x 3 3/4 In. 800.00
C.W.J. Dainty Bits, 12 Varieties, Delicious Toffees, Raised Letters, Display, 15 x 11 In. . . .   79.00
Cadette Tooth Powder, Toy Cadette, Tin Lithograph, Gray, 7 3/8 x 2 1/4 x 1 1/4 In. 176.00
Cadette Tooth Powder, Toy Cadette, Tin Lithograph, Red, 7 3/8 x 2 1/4 x 1 1/4 In. 688.00
Cadette Tooth Powder For Children, Toy Soldier Graphic, 3 1/8 Oz., 2 1/4 x 7 1/4 In. . . .   330.00
Calox Tooth Powder, Oval Base, Box, 4 3/8 x 2 1/2 x 1 3/4 In. 85.00
Calox Tooth Powder, Oval Base, Box, 5 1/4 x 2 1/2 x 1 3/4 In. 85.00
Camp Fire Cocoa, Pry Lid, Lotus Tea Concern, 1916, 4 3/4 x 3 1/4 x 2 1/8 In. 225.00
Campfire Marshmallows, Pry Lid, 12 Oz., 3 1/2 x 5 1/2 In. 210.00
Campfire Marshmallows, Scouts Toast Marshmallows, Lithograph, 1 Lb., 8 x 2 In. 110.00 to 139.00
Campho-Phenique Powder, Shaker Top, St. Louis, Mo., 2 x 1 1/4 In. 35.00
Canadian Explosives, Limited, Snap Shot, 1880-1900, 5 3/4 x 4 x 1 1/4 In. 104.00
Caparine For Headaches, Contents, 2 1/2 x 1 1/2 In. 33.00
Carbolic Toothpowder, Gold Ground, Paper Label, Round, 2 x 5/8 In. 18.00
Cardui Wash Antiseptic, 50 Cents, Chattanooga Medicine Co., 2 x 3 1/8 In. 770.00
Carnation Malted Milk, No. 10, Box, 10 x 7 x 7 In. 170.00
Carolina Brand, Hand Packed Tomatoes, German Hungarian Farm Colony, 5 In. . . . . *Illus*   50.00
Cascara Compound Hinkle Pill Compound, 1 3/4 x 1 In. 48.00
Certified Aspirin, Cream Color, Newark, N.J., 1939, 12 Tablet Size, 1 3/4 x 1 1/4 In. 10.00
Chamber Commerce Tobacco, 1 3/8 x 5 1/4 x 3 5/8 In. 95.00
Champion Dental Floss, 1 1/4 In. 35.00
Champion Insecticide & Bug Killer, Yellow, Black, Paper Label, 5 1/2 In. 495.00
Charles Chips, 1960s, 1 Lb., 9 1/2 In. 9.00
Charles Marvin Celebrated Electioneer Brand Food, Paper Label, Contents, 6 x 3 1/4 In.   94.00
Charms' Candy, Tin Lithograph, Glass Top, Round, 12 In. 44.00
Chas. F. Pusch's, Hand Made, High Grade Cigar, Paper Label, 5 1/2 x 3 1/2 In. 28.00
Chi-Namel, Prepared Wax For Stained Wood & Varnished Wood, Slip Top, 7/8 x 3 3/4 In. . .   45.00
Chinoiserie Biscuit Tin, Gray & Dunn, Scotland, 7 In. 25.00
Co-Re-Ga Dental Adhesive, Corega Chemical Co., Pocket Size, 3 3/8 x 1 5/8 x 7/8 In. . . .   20.00
Coach & Horses, Biscuit, 1960s, 9 In. 10.00
Colgan's Taffy Tolu Chewing Gum, Hinged Lid, 9 x 8 In. 177.00
Collins Street Bakery, Deluxe Fruitcake, Cowboy, Winter, Corisana, Texas, 7 x 2 1/2 In. . .   10.00
Condom, 3 Cadets, Carefully Tested, Round, Julius Schmid, 1 5/8 x 5/8 In. 391.00
Condom, 3 Cadets, Red, White, Blue, 1 3/4 x 2 1/8 x 1/4 In. 99.00
Condom, 3 Cadets, Tin Lithograph, Red Ground, Julius Schmid, 1 5/8 x 2 1/8 x 1/4 In. . . .   100.00
Condom, 3 Knights, Knights On Horses, Goodwear Rubber Co., 1 5/8 x 2 1/8 x 1/4 In. . .   166.00
Condom, 3 Pirates, 3 Women Pirates On Ship, Green, 1 5/8 x 2 1/8 In. 853.00
Condom, Altex Air Tested Prophylactics, Contents, Canada, 1 5/8 x 2 1/8 x 1/4 In. 523.00
Condom, Altex Liquid Latex, Tin Lithograph, Western Rubber Co., 1/4 Doz., 1 5/6 x 2 In.   358.00
Condom, Apris, Tin Lithograph, Killian, 1 5/8 x 2 1/8 x 1/4 In. 177.00
Condom, Blue Ribbon Brand Safety Tips, German Shepard, Lithograph, 1 7/8 x 2 In. 1018.00
Condom, Caravan Condom, Desert, Caravan, Lithograph, Tiger Skin Rubber Co., 2 x 2 In.   221.00
Condom, Carmen Brand Latex, Scantily Clad Woman, Lithograph, Round, 1 5/8 x 5/8 In.   605.00
Condom, Dominion Transparent, 3 For $1, Tin Lithograph, Canada, 1 5/8 x 2 1/8 x 1/4 In. 1073.00
Condom, Drug Pack Condoms, Blue, White, Tin Lithograph, Nutex Co., 1 5/8 x 2 1/8 In. .   187.00
Condom, Duro-Skins, Yellow, Red, Lithograph, 1 5/8 x 2 1/8 x 1/4 In. 440.00
Condom, Genuine Liquid Latex Condoms, Shunk Latex Co., 1 5/8 x 2 1/8 In. . . . .100.00 to 175.00
Condom, Golden Pheasant Condoms, Colorful Bird, Reed & Co., 1 5/8 x 2 1/8 In. 153.00
Condom, Hy Gee Prophylactic, Tin Lithograph, 3 Tubes, Partial Wrapper, 1 5/8 x 2 In. . . .   182.00
Condom, Improved Trojan Brand, Diamond, Black, Red, White, 1 3/4 x 2 1/8 x 1/4 In. . . .   550.00
Condom, Kamels Condoms, Tin Lithograph, Contents, 1 5/8 x 2 1/8 x 1/4 In. 142.00
Condom, Nu Tips By Nutex, Rolled, Tin Lithograph, Red, Blue, 1 5/8 x 2 1/8 x 1/4 In. . . .   440.00
Condom, Nunbetter Condoms, Arrow Rubber Co., White, Red, 1 5/8 x 2 1/8 x 1/4 In. 743.00
Condom, Nutex Prophylactic, Brand Of Purity, Blue, White, 1 7/8 x 2 7/8 x 3/8 In. 303.00
Condom, Optimus 3-Rolled Latex Prophylactic Sheaths, 1 3/4 x 2 x 1/4 In. 99.00
Condom, Patent Superior Latex Condoms, Yellow, Red, Lithograph, 1 1/2 x 2 In. 660.00
Condom, Patent Superior Liquid Latex Condom, Lithograph, Lift-Off Lid, 1 x 2 x 7/16 In.   468.00
Condom, Ramses Condoms, Egyptian Theme Graphics, Tin Lithograph, 1 7/8 x 2 7/8 In. .   190.00

Tin, Craftint Watercolors, New
York, Cleveland, Chicago, 8 1/2 In.

Tin, Carolina Brand, Hand
Packed Tomatoes, German
Hungarian Farm Colony, 5 In.

Tin, Dr. I.W. Lyon's
Tooth Powder,
New York, 3 1/2 In.

Condom, Romeos Prophylactics, Yellow, Killian Mfg., 1/4 Doz., 1 5/8 x 2 1/8 In.	139.00
Condom, Romeos Rubber Prophylactics, Reservoir Ends, Red, 1 5/8 x 2 1/8 x 1/4 In.	143.00
Condom, Romeos, Purple Letters, Tin Lithograph, Killian Co., 1 5/8 x 2 1/8 x 1/4 In.	413.00
Condom, Saf-T-Way Condoms, Gotham Rubber Co., Liquid Latex, 1 3/4 x 2 x 1/4 In. . . .	413.00
Condom, Sanitex Condoms, 1 5/8 x 2 1/8 x 1/4 In.	330.00
Condom, Sekurity Condoms, Red, Blue, Tin Lithograph, Dean Rubber Mfg., 1 5/8 x 2 In.	132.00
Condom, Shadows Condoms, Tin Lithograph, Youngs Rubber Co., 1 5/8 x 1 5/8 x 7/16 In.	150.00
Condom, Sheik Condoms, Horse, Tin Lithograph, Red, White, 1 3/4 x 2 1/8 x 1/4 In. .28.00 to 85.00
Condom, Sheik Condoms, Sheik On Horse, Tin Lithograph, 1 5/8 x 1 5/8 x 7/16 In.	167.00
Condom, Silk Skin, Contents, Blue Ground, 1 7/8 x 2 5/8 x 1/4 In.	715.00
Condom, Silver Latex Condoms, 3 For $1.00, 1 5/8 x 2 1/8 x 1/4 In.	385.00
Condom, Silver Tex Condoms, Contents, Shunk Latex Co., 1 5/8 x 2 1/8 In.	210.00
Condom, Silver Tex Deluxe Condoms, Askwell Corp., Akron, Ohio, 1 5/8 x 2 1/8 In.	210.00
Condom, Town & Country, Tin Lithograph, Nelson Products, 1 5/8 x 2 1/8 In.	1925.00
Condom, Velvetex Condoms, Protects Against Disease, 1 5/8 x 2 1/8 In.	578.00
Condom, White Nutex, Lithograph, Green, 1 5/8 x 2 1/8 In.	578.00
Condom, White Trojan Rubber Prophylactics, Young Rubber Corp., 2 1/4 x 2 x 1/2 In. . . .	38.00
Court Royal, 2 For 15 Cents, Lady, Crowns, 5 1/2 x 3 In.	128.00
CPC Tooth Powder, Contents, 2 1/4 x 1 In.	1980.00
Craftint Watercolors, New York, Cleveland, Chicago, 8 1/2 In. . . . . *Illus*	20.00
Crayola, Boy, Girl, Christmas Tree, 1992, 6 In.	12.00
Cream Nut Peanut Butter, Bel-Mo-Nut Butter Co., Grand Rapids, Mi., 3 3/8 x 3 3/4 In. .	385.00
Crescent Salted Peanuts, Children, Red, Yellow, Green, 10 Lb., 9 5/8 x 8 3/8 In.	798.00
Cresslers Antiseptic Tooth Powder, Round, Box, 4 1/8 x 1 5/8 In.	110.00
Crinoline Lady Cake, 1970s, 8 In.	10.00
Crisp-N-Good Potato Chips, IGA Big Big Can, 2 Handles, Pry Lid, 20 Oz., 9 3/4 x 11 In.	35.00
D&C Latex Diaphragms, Tin Lithograph, 1 x 3 3/8 In.	149.00
D.H. Wenger & Son, Lard, 9 Lb.	6.00
Daniel Boone Axle Grease, Heals Sores On Man Or Beast, 1 Lb., 4 x 3 1/4 In.	105.00
Decker's Iowana Brand Spiced Luncheon Meat, Soldered Seam, Key, 4 x 11 3/4 x 3 In. .	16.50
Deer Park Baking Co., Cookies, Buck, Doe, Fawn, Stream, Chicago, 8 3/8 x 3 3/4 In. . . .	10.00
Derby Peter Pan Peanut Butter, Key Wind, Derby Foods, Chicago, c.1960, 1 Lb. 12 Oz.	45.00
Derby Peter Pan Peanut Butter, Screw Top, Sample, 1930, 2 Oz., 1 3/4 x 2 In.	66.00
Dewitt's Witch Hazel, Veterinary & Gall Salve, Black Ground, Round, 2 1/2 x 2 1/2 In. . .	22.00
Diamond Brand, Lead Sinkers, Celluloid Top, Contents, St. Louis, Mo., 1 5/8 In.	110.00
Diamond Brand, Pennyroyal Pills, 7 1/8 x 3 x 3 1/4 In.	325.00
Dill's Best, Vertical, Pocket, 4 1/2 x 3 x 7/8 In.	170.00
Dill's Healing Salve, Dill Medicine Co., Norristown, Pa., 7/8 x 2 3/4 In.	30.00
Dimitrino & Co., Caire, Egypte, 1910, 5 x 6 x 1 1/2 In.	132.00
Dixie Jumbo Salted Peanuts, Kelly Co., Cleveland, 10 Lb., 10 In.	59.00
Dixie Mix, Man Walking Camel, Silver, 2 1/2 x 3 1/2 x 6 In.	10.00
Doan's Ointment, Round, Foster Milburn Co., Buffalo, N.Y., 3/4 x 1 7/8 In.	44.00
Donald Duck Chocolate Syrup, Walt Disney Productions, 4 1/2 x 2 5/8 In.	190.00
Dorothy Duncan Fine Chocolates, 1 1/2 Lb., 10 x 1 1/4 In.	16.00
Douglass & Sons Capscium Cough Drops, 7 x 6 x 4 1/2 In.	99.00
Dr. A.W. Chase Co., Herpes Ointment, Yellow, Round, 1 3/4 In.	50.00
Dr. Bells Anti-Septic Salve, 25 Cents, E.E. Sutherland Medicine Co., Flyer, Box, 2 1/2 In.	77.00
Dr. Charcot's Kola Nervine Tablets, Flat, Pocket, La Crosse, Wisconsin, 3 x 2 In.	633.00

Dr. Charles Foot Relief, 50 Cents, Dr. Charles Flesh Food Co., Brooklyn, 3 3/8 x 2 1/8 In. 75.00
Dr. E.L. Graves Unequaled Tooth Powder, Cylinder, Contents, 4 In. 94.00
Dr. Hand's Chafing Powder, Children's Faces, Lithograph, 1890s, 4 x 1 3/4 In. . . . .165.00 to 327.00
Dr. Hess Healing Powder, 25 Cent, Contents, 4 Oz., 5 x 2 1/2 In. 28.00
Dr. Hess Healing Powder, 50 Cent, 10 Oz., 5 1/2 x 3 3/4 In. 39.00
Dr. Hess Udder Ointment, Cow, Lithograph, 7 Oz., 4 1 1/2 In. 44.00
Dr. Hobbs Sparagus Kidney Pills, For Kidney, Blood Diseases, 50 Cents, 1 1/2 x 2 1/2 In. 165.00
Dr. Hobson's Arnica Salve, Round, Pfeiffer Chem. Co., New York, 3/4 x 2 3/4 In. 35.00
Dr. Hobson's Carbolic Salve, Round, Pfeiffer Chem. Co., New York, 3/4 x 2 3/4 In. 35.00
Dr. Hobson's Eye Salve, Round, Contents, Box, 1 1/8 In. 132.00
Dr. I.W. Lyon's Tooth Powder, New York, 3 1/2 In. . . . . *Illus* 85.00
Dr. J.A. Foster's Wonder Tooth Powder, Cylinder, 4 1/8 In. 143.00
Dr. Jayne's Expectorant Opium Tablets, 1 Grain To Ounce, 1 7/8 x 2 7/8 x 9/16 In. 550.00
Dr. King's Star Crown Pennyroyal Pills, Yellow Ground, 3 x 1 3/4 In. 83.00
Dr. Kinsman's Asthmatic Powder, Contents, Round, Augusta, Maine, 3 x 2 1/2 In. 28.00
Dr. LeGear's Cholera Remedy, Paper Label, 3 3/4 x 1 5/8 In. 110.00
Dr. LeGear's Lice Killer, Barnyard Scene, Paper Label, Contents, 6 1/2 x 3 3/8 In. 330.00
Dr. LeGear's Lice Killer, Woman, Barnyard, Animals, Paper Label, Unopened, 1 1/2 x 2 In. 71.00
Dr. M.A. Simmons' Liver Medicine, Square, 2 x 1 1/2 In. 66.00
Dr. M.A. Simmons' Vegetable Liver Medicine, 25 Cents, 2 1/8 x 1 3/4 x 1 3/4 In. 165.00
Dr. Morse's Indian Root Pills, Wrapper, Unopened, Oval, c.1881, 2 1/8 x 1 1/2 In. 50.00
Dr. Palmer's Almomeal Compound, For Rough, Oily, Dry Skin, Black, 3 1/4 x 3 x 2 In. . 34.00
Dr. Pierce's Lotion Tablets, Dr. Pierce's Proprietaries, Buffalo, N.Y., 3/4 x 2 1/2 In. 25.00
Dr. Roberts Dental Powder, Kissing Dutch Children, Paper Label, Aurora, Ill., 2 x 5 In. . 15.40
Dr. Roberts Dog Medicine, Roundworm Treatment, Paper Label, Flyer, 1 3/4 x 1 1/4 In. . . 143.00
Dr. Roberts Dog Medicine, Tonic Tablets, Paper Label, Flyer, 50 Cents, 1 3/4 x 1 1/4 In. . 154.00
Dr. Rubins, Vital Phosphor, Louisville Medicine Co., 2 1/2 x 1 1/2 In. 94.00
Dr. Seth Arnold's Continental Surgeons Adhesive Plaster, Green, Paper Label, 6 In. 99.00
Dr. Tuckers Cough Drops, No. 59, 2 1/4 x 3 1/2 In. 825.00
Dr. Von Breemberg's Homeopathic Bilious Powders, 4 1/4 x 1 7/8 In. 72.00
Dr. Weare's Gall Cure, Horse Head, Tin Lithograph, Ground, 5 1/2 x 3 1/2 In. 84.00
Dr. Welters Tooth Powder, Girl In Hat, Tin Lithograph, Blue Ground, 3 5/8 x 1 5/8 In. . . 413.00
Dr. Wernet's Powder For False Teeth, Trial Sample, 2 1/8 In. 20.00
Dr. White's Celebrated Cough Drops, E. Greenfield's Son, New York, 8 x 6 In. 236.00
Dri-Kleen Dog Bath, Hartz Mountain Products, 3 Oz., 2 1/2 x 5 1/2 In. 16.50
Droste Cocoa, Lithograph, Dutch Girl & Boy, Free Sample, 1 7/8 x 1 1/4 In. 55.00
Droste Holland Candy, Haarlem, Mid 20th Century, 4 1/2 x 7 1/4 x 3 In. 67.00
Droste Holland Milk Chocolates, 5 In. Diam. 15.00
Droste's Cocoa, Droste's Cacao & Chocoladefabrieken, Haarlem, Holland, 7 3/8 x 4 In. . . 210.00
Droste's Cocoa, Droste's Cacao & Chocoladefabrieken, Haarlem, Holland, Sample, 3 In. . 185.00
Droste's Cocoa, Holland, 4 Oz., 4 1/4 x 2 1/4 In. . . . . .30.00 to 32.00
Drucker's Revelation For Teeth & Gums, Cylinder, Contents, 4 In. 50.00
Drucker's Revelation Tooth Powder, Sample, 2 5/8 x 1 In. 35.00
Dubarry Perfume Golden Morn, Round, Needler's Ltd., 5/8 x 1 1/4 In. 45.00
Duble Tip, Woman Sitting By Water, Tin Lithograph, 1 5/8 x 2 1/8 x 1/4 In. 550.00
Durite Ribbon, Woman Typing, Chemical Process Co., Chicago, 2 1/2 x 2 1/2 In. 72.00
E&S C.W.S. Delicious Tea, Square Base, Sample, 1 3/8 x 1 1/2 In. 75.00
Eclectic Herbs, Barks, Roots & Gums, Lift Top, Tin Lithograph, 4 1/2 x 2 1/4 x 2 In. 187.00
Electric Pile Cure, Round, Lakeview, Michigan, 2 In. 523.00
Emerson Foot Powder, Foot Ease & Comfort, Young Boy Photo, 4 x 2 3/4 In. 110.00
Encharma Cold Cream Complexion Powder, Oval, 2 x 1 5/8 In. 45.00
Ex-Lax Figs, Brooklyn, N.Y., 1 x 5 1/2 x 3 1/2 In. 30.00
Eye-Lash-Ine, Eyelash Remedy, Woman, 1 1/2 In. Diam. 220.00
F.W. Cough Drops, Tin Lithograph, Geo. Miller & Son, Philadelphia, 8 x 5 1/8 In. 1540.00
F.W. Cough Tablets, Cured My Cough, 5 Cents, 18th Century Scene, 2 3/8 x 1 1/2 In. 578.00
F.W. Cough Tablets, Cured My Cough, 5 Cents, Lithograph, 7 1/2 x 6 x 4 1/8 In. 990.00
Fairy Foot Callus Remedy, Contents, Round, Box, 1 1/2 In. 22.00
FFV Orange Wafers, Southern Biscuit Company, Round, Lid, 14 Oz., 6 x 4 1/2 In. 35.00
Fig Newtons, 100th Anniversary, Limited Edition, 1991, 9 x 5 x 2 In. 10.00
First Prize Brand Pure Cocoa, Metal Top, Bottom, Paper Labels, 9 1/8 x 4 5/8 x 3 1/8 In. 125.00
Firstaid Readymade Bandage, Contents, United Dreu Co., Boston, 3/8 x 3 5/8 x 3 3/8 In. 28.00
Fishers's Peanuts, Tin Lithograph, 25 Lb., 20 1/2 In. 110.00
Flying Dutchman, Ship, Blue, Black, Theodorus Niemeyer Ltd., 4 1/4 x 1 1/4 In. 15.00

Tin, Forest City, Formosa
Blend Tea, Conant, Patrick,
Label, 4 In.

Tin, Heave Remedy,
International Stock
Company, Toronto, 6 1/4 In.

Tin, Jumbo Salted Peanuts,
Kelly Peanut Co.,
c.1910, 10 Lb., 9 In.

Forest City, Formosa Blend Tea, Conant, Patrick, Label, 4 In. . . . . *Illus* 45.00
Formic Iodide Compound, B.F.I., 2 1/2 x 1 1/4 In. 28.00
Fyr-Pruf Stove & Nickel Polish, Paper Label, 4 1/8 x 2 1/2 In. 20.00
Garwood's Peppermint Breath Gum, Green, 1 1/2 x 2 x 1/2 In. 33.00
Genuine Aspirin, Slip Top, 12 Tablet Size 18.00
Gilbert Bros. & Co., Cream Of Tartar, 9 x 6 In. 121.00
Gillies Tea, Stag In Woods, Small Top, New York, 6 x 4 1/4 In. 330.00
Gino Pills, Multi-Language Instructions, 7/8 x 1 3/4 In. 35.00
Glovers Imperial Liver Pills, For Dogs, Yellow, Black, Flat, Pocket, 3 1/8 x 2 In. . . .88.00 to 132.00
Golden Raven Salve, Skin Disorders, Blue, Yellow, Round, 2 In. 33.00
Golden Rule Tea, Lithographed, 9 1/2 x 6 In. 66.00
Gonocide Remedies, Charles L. Mitchell, M.D., Contents, Directions, 6 1/2 x 1 1/8 In. . . . 264.00
Goodrich Tires Repair Outfit, Best In Long Run, 1920s, 6 3/4 x 3 x 2 In. . . . . .44.00 to 60.00
Gray Dunn Biscuits, Grecian Scene, Scotland, 9 1/2 x 8 x 2 In. 16.00
Graziano Ointment, No. 2, Cuts, Eczema, Boils, Sores, 75 Cents, 2 1/2 In. 303.00
Gre-Solvent, Cleans Hands Clean, Utility Co., New York, 3 1/2 x 2 1/4 In. 22.00
Grimm & Tiepel, Katabak Die Beruhmte Deutsche, Germany, c.1849, 1 3/4 x 1 1/4 In. 35.00
H-Y Salmon Paste Trout Bait, Tin Lithograph, Pry Lid, 1920s, 2 1/2 x 2 3/8 In. 523.00
H. Anton Bock & Co., Box Shape, Lithograph, 2 x 6 1/2 x 5 1/2 In. 22.00
Hague's Pretzels, Case Manufacturing, England, 8 1/2 x 5 1/2 In. 16.00
Hall & Ruckel Druggists, Headquarters Building, 5 1/2 x 3 1/2 x 3 1/2 In. 303.00
Hall & Ruckel's Sozident Tooth Powder, Lithograph, Sample, 2 1/2 x 1 In. 330.00
Harley-Davidson 2-Cycle Motor Oil, Tin Lithograph, 12 Oz., 5 3/4 x 2 3/4 In. 57.00
Hartz Mountain, Canary, Song Food, 35 Cents, 3 1/2 x 2 1/2 In. 30.00
Health-O Carbolic Salve, Milson Co., 7/8 x 2 5/8 In. 42.00
Heather Rouge Daytime, Whitehall Laboratories, New York, 1 3/4 In. 35.00
Heave Remedy, International Stock Company, Toronto, 6 1/4 In. . . . . *Illus* 35.00
Heide's None Finer Marshmallows, Slip Top, Henry Heide, New York, 2 1/8 x 4 1/4 In. . . 245.00
Helen Harrison Home Made Candies, Wildflowers, Camco, Chicago, 1940s, 10 x 3 In. . . 30.00
Henalfa Hair Restorer, 4 Oz., 2 1/2 x 3 3/4 In. 99.00
Henri Bouillon Cubes, Cylindrical, Tin Lithograph, 1 x 3 1/2 In. 44.00
Hercules, No. 6, 10 Blasting Caps, 1 5/8 x 1 In. 265.00
Highlands Hi-Nutra, Swing Handle, 25 Lbs., 12 1/2 In. 11.00
Himrod's Asthma Powder, Contents, Box, c.1912, 2 x 3 1/2 In. 50.00
Hitt's Danger Lights, Red, Devil, Car, Tin Lithograph, Hitt Fireworks, 13 x 2 1/4 In. 132.00
Hollingshead Axle Oil, Easy Pour Spout, Man & Buggy, Pt., 5 1/2 In. 27.00
Holts Bowel-Manna Cures Constipation, Tablets, Everybody's Laxative, 2 7/8 In. Diam. . . 770.00
Horn Paste Wax, Wax Bucket Dumped Black Man's Head, 4 1/4 In. 131.00
Horner's Boy Blue Toffee, 3 Indian Chiefs, 4 x 5 1/2 In., 3 1/2 Oz. 55.00
Hostess, Fruit Cake, Lady Holding Cake, 11 1/4 x 3 1/2 x 3 In. 35.00
Howard's Perfection Oil, Screw Top, Bay City, Michigan, 2 3/4 x 3 1/4 x 1 1/2 In. 54.00
Huberd's Shoe Oil, Screw Lid, Cone Top, 4 1/4 In. 35.00
IGA Potato Chips, Big-Big Can, Red, Yellow, White, 20 Oz., 11 1/4 In. 35.00

Imperial Shaving Stick, Talcum Puff Co., Man Shaving, Stick Shape, 3 1/4 x 1 1/2 In. 55.00
Index Brand Breakfast Cocoa, Montgomery Ward, c.1930, 5 Lb., 6 x 10 In. 41.00
Indiola Gold, Silver & Nickel Polish, India Tea Co., Paper Label, 1911, 2 1/2 x 5 x 1 In. .   66.00
International Gall Cure, Yellow, Team Of Horses On Lid, Round, 3 x 2 1/2 In. 105.00
International Stock Food Tonic, 3 Feeds For 1 Cent, 2 Gal. 550.00
Italina Laxative Preparation, 5 x 3 3/4 In. 75.00
Ivins Cheese Flakes, Red Lid, Silhouettes, J.S. Ivins, Phila., Round, 12 Oz., 5 x 6 In. 45.00
Jack Sprat, Peanut Butter, Round, 25 Lb., 9 1/2 x 10 In. 1180.00
Jack Sprat, Tea, Square, 5 x 3 In. 175.00
Jackie Coogan's Brand Peanut Butter, Kelly Co., Cleveland, Ohio, 3 1/4 x 3 3/8 In. 625.00
Jaw Teasers, 1 Cent, Gum Balls, Handle, 7 3/4 x 6 In. 143.00
Jayne's Expectorant Tablets, Opium 1 Grain To Ounce, Pocket, Hinged, 3 x 2 In. .132.00 to 187.00
Jew David's Plaster, E. Taylor, Rochester, N. York, Embossed, Round, 2 In. 132.00
Jim Crow Corn Salve, Removes Corns & Bunions, 10 Cents, Yellow, Box, 1 In. 132.00
John Dickson & Son Fishing Tackle, Edinburgh, Glasgow, Aberdeen, 2 1/4 x 2 1/4 In. ...   24.00
Jolly Time Popcorn, 4 7/8 x 2 5/8 In. 395.00
Jubilee, Harem Of Topless Women, Hinged Lid, 3 1/2 x 4 1/2 x 3/4 In. 110.00
Jumbo Blanched Salted Peanuts, Chicago, Ill., 10 Lb., 9 In. ....55.00 to 66.00
Jumbo Salted Peanuts, Kelly Peanut Co., c.1910, 10 Lb., 9 In. ....*Illus*   440.00
Kampfe's Star Razor Strop, Man Shaving On Back, Yellow, 6 x 2 x 1 1/2 In. 121.00
Kan-Tartar Compound, For Baking, Bluegreen, Gold Letters, 8 x 5 1/2 In. 32.00
Kennedy's Asthma Remedy, Man Inhaling Product, Tin Lithograph, 5 x 2 1/2 x 1 3/4 In. .   107.00
Kennedy's Celebrated Fruit Cake, 1878, 4 x 6 x 2 In. 66.00
Kernel-Fresh, Salted Nuts, Key Wind, c.1950, 3 1/2 In. 75.00
Kitten Thornes Confectionary, 1960s, 6 In. 10.00
Klearoids For Voice & Throat, Slide Lid, Northrop & Lymon, Canada, 3/8 x 2 1/2 x 2 In. .   18.00
Kondon's Kidney & Back Tablets, 50 Cents, 2 1/2 x 1 5/8 In. 33.00
Kroger's, Grapefruit Juice, Paper Label, Patent Date 1938, 14 Oz. 10.00
Lady Orchid Hair Straight, Woman's Profile, New York, 3 In. 12.00
Lander Powder, Flower Bouquets, Man, Woman Sitting In Garden, Gold Trim, 4 1/4 In. .   28.00
Lanozol Ointment, J.E.T. Pharmacal Co., Allentown, Pa., 7/8 x 2 1/8 In. 28.00
Las Stik Cleaning & Polishing Cloth, No. PC-15, 3 1/2 x 1 1/2 x 5 1/4 In. 10.00
Lax-Ets, Bowel Laxative, Dr. Shoop's Laboratories, 5 Cents, 2 1/4 x 1 In. 44.00
Laxaco Capsules, Hinged Lid, Nyal Company, Detroit, 3/8 x 2 7/8 x 2 In. 24.00
Laxative Cold Tablets, Hinge Top, Miller, Druggist, Cadott, Wis., 1/2 x 2 1/2 x 1 5/8 In. .   17.00
Laxo-Koko, When Nature Fails, Paper Label, Unopened, 2 1/3 x 4 x 1 1/2 In. 66.00
Lederle Aspirin, Slide Lid, Dispense 1 Tablet At A Time, 2 1/2 x 1 1/2 In. 30.00
Lee's Pills, Contents, Unopened, Wrapper, 2 1/4 In. 33.00
Leichner Blending Powder, 1930s, 4 In. 17.00
Lindsay's Sure Cure Dyspepsia Remedy, Cleveland, 2 1/4 x 1 1/2 In. 94.00
Lindt Swiss Premium Chocolate Hazelnut Pieces, Lindt, Sprungli, Milk Can Shape, 6 In.   12.00
Listerine Tooth Powder, Round, 4 1/8 x 2 In. 110.00
Lloyd's Kidney & Rheumatism Tablets, Lloyd Preparation Co., 2 5/8 x 1 1/2 In. 61.00
Longs Covered Wagon Syrup, 1 Lb., 4 x 3 7/8 x 3 In. 1595.00
Lovell & Covel Candy, Peter Cottontail, 3 Oz., 2 7/8 x 2 7/8 In. 264.00
Loverin & Browne Co. Wholesale Grocers, Chicago, 8 1/2 In. ....*Illus*   40.00
Lowney's Breakfast Cocoa, Sample Size, 1 3/4 x 1 3/8 x 7/8 In. 132.00
Lucky Strike Weed Buster, 5 1/8 x 2 7/8 x 1 1/2 In. 35.00
Lyon's Sheep & Cattle Ointment, Yellow Ground, Norwalk, Conn., 3 1/4 x 2 1/2 In. 93.00
Lyons Standard Custard Powder, England, 2 3/4 In. 66.00
Mack's Foot Life, Dog Lying On Foot, 1 1/2 In. 72.00
Magic Foam Devil, Upholstery Cleaner, 16 Oz. 25.00
Magic Shaving Powder, Depilatory, Straight Razor, Pry Lid, Labels, 4 1/4 x 2 3/8 In. 330.00
Magnetic Nervine, Nerve Tonic & Restorer, 2 1/2 x 1 1/2 In. 143.00
Maiden Herbs Nature's Own Remedy, Hinged Lid, 3 1/4 x 2 1/4 In. 50.00
Marathon Foot Powder, Sample Size, 2 1/8 x 1 1/4 x 1 In. 45.00
Marshmallow Fluff, 3 1/2 In. 8.00
Marvel Mystery Oil, Gal., 6 1/2 x 9 1/2 In. 12.00
Max Factor Moist Rouge, Hollywood, Calif., 1 1/8 x 1/2 In. 85.00
Max-I-Mum Spice, Western States Grocery, 3 1/4 x 2 3/8 x 1 1/4 In. 110.00
Maxwell House Coffee, Red Ground, Key Wind, Lithograph, 1 Lb., 3 1/2 x 5 In. 249.00
Maynard's Toffee, Victorian, 5 x 1 1/2 In. 12.00
McVitie & Prices, Biscuits, Premier Biscuit Of Britain, 1 x 3 1/4 In. 95.00

Mellier's Ultra Bouquet Face Powder, Mueller, N.Y., St. Louis, Trial Size, 1/4 x 1 5/8 In. 44.00
Mellomints, Red Ground, c.1910, 8 x 10 In. 403.00
Mellos Popcorn, Red, White, Blue, c.1940, 4 Lb., 6 x 4 In. 44.00
Mentholatum Japanese Woman, Fan, 1 1/2 In. Diam. 209.00
Mentholatum Little Nurse, Pocket, 1 1/8 In. 25.00
Merck Zinc Stearate, Waterproof Toilet Powder, Sheds Water Like A Duck, 5 1/2 In. 36.00
Milky Way, Bear Soldiers Guarding Christmas Gifts, 1994, 6 x 16 In. 10.00
Milky Way, Snack Bars, 22 Oz., 6 x 5 1/2 In. 10.00
Millwoods Pulvola Foot Powder, Brewer & Co. Inc., 3 Sides, 4 1/4 In. 94.00
Mirelle Toilet Powder, Nude, Flowers, Lithograph, 2 1/4 x 1 1/4 x 3/4 In. 275.00
Mirro, Coffeepot & Perk Cleaner, Pressed Paper, 4 Oz. 5.00
Morrell's Pride Lard, Heart, Gold Ground, 14 1/2 x 13 In. 121.00
Morrell's Pride Lard, Kettle Rendered, Logo In Heart, 50 Lb., 14 x 12 In. 92.00
Mosemann's Peanut Butter, Animals, 3 3/4 x 3 3/8 In. 345.00
Mother Hubbard Energy, Energy Wheat Cereal, 5 Lb., 10 x 6 1/2 In. 50.00
Mother's B & B Salted Peanuts, Springfield, Mass., 10 Lb., 9 In. 39.00
Mother's Mustard Plasters, First Aid, Lithograph, June 30, 1906, 3 1/2 x 4 3/4 In. 88.00
Mother's Mustard Plasters, Hinged Lid, Contents, Bauer & Black, 4 3/4 x 3 3/4 In. 55.00
Mother's Pure Leaf Lard, Boston, Mass., 2 Lb. 11.00
Muco Salve, Muco Solvent Co., Memphis, Tenn., Sample Size, 3/8 x 7/8 In. 24.00
Mum, Tin Top, Plastic Bottom, Cardboard, Insert, Bristol-Myers, New York, 3/4 x 1 1/2 In. 10.00
National Cocoa, 2 Children At Table, Capital Dome, Lithograph, c.1920s, 4 7/8 x 2 5/8 In. 133.00
Nature's Cure, Celebrated Blood Purifier, Red, White, Flat, Pocket, 3 x 2 In. 61.00
Nature's Remedy Tablets, Acts On The Stomach, Liver, Kidneys, Bowels, 2 7/8 In. 12.00
Neal's Anti Gas Tablets, Hot Air Balloon Shape, 3 1/8 x 2 1/8 In. 121.00
Negrita Polish, Smiling Black Houseboy, German & French Titles, 3 1/2 In. 124.00
Nelsons Hair Dressing, Free Sample, Penalty For Sale, Lithograph, 1905, 2 x 1 In. 66.00
Nerve Berries, American Medical Co., Cincinnati, O., Flat, Pocket, 2 1/2 x 1 1/2 In. 687.00
Nerve Seeds, Great Nerve Restorer, Flat, Pocket, 2 1/2 x 1 1/2 In. 357.00
New Discovery Salve, Becker Chemical Co., Cincinnati, Ohio, 7/8 x 2 1/8 In. 35.00
Newton Horse Remedy Co., Heave, Cough, Distemper & Indigestion, 4 x 3 x 3 In. 99.00
Newton's Heave, Cough, Distemper & Indigestion Copound, Yellow Ground, 7 x 3 1/2 In. 187.00
None Finer Marshmallows, Slip Top, Heide's, N.Y., 2 1/8 x 4 1/4 In. 245.00
NR Jrs Laxative, Lewis Howe Co., 1 1/2 x 1 x 1/2 In. 42.00
Nuthouse Nuts, Butter Scotch Nuts, Lynn, Mass., Screw Top, 5 x 4 In., 1 Lb. 83.00
Nyal Cold Capsules, 2 7/8 x 2 In. 25.00
O-D Laxative Pills, Soldier, St. Louis, Mo., 1 3/4 x 1 1/4 In. 77.00
Oilzum Tar Remover, Tin Lithograph, Sample, 4 x 2 1/4 x 1 1/4 In. 182.00
Old Manse Syrup, 11 1/4 x 6 x 3 1/2 In. 88.00
Old Missouri Valley Peanut Butter, Paper Label, 25 Lb., 12 x 6 3/4 In. 45.00
One-Spot Flea Killer, Dog Silhouette, Use Before December 1942, 2 1/4 x 3 1/2 In. 14.00
Orange Wafers, Southern Biscuit Co., 4 1/2 In. 35.00
Oriental Polisher, 6 x 2 1/8 x 2 1/8 In. 45.00
Ovelmo Treatment, Lift Top, Fort Wayne, Ind., 6 x 2 3/4 In. 39.00
OXO Cubes, 1952, 7 In. 30.00
Painless Parker Tooth Powder, Oval, 3/4 Oz., 3 1/4 In. 143.00
Pansies Peanuts, Boy & Girl Picking Pansies, 10 Lb., 11 x 7 1/2 In. 190.00

Tin, Loverin &
Browne Co.
Wholesale Grocers,
Chicago, 8 1/2 In.

Tin, Porter's Liniment
Salve, Geo. H. Rundle,
Piqua, Oh., Box

Paramount Root Beer Syrup, San Francisco, 5 Gal., 14 In. 560.00
Parke Davis & Co., Choice Botanic Drugs, Poppy Leaves, Red Insert, 4 1/4 x 3 3/4 x 9 In.   143.00
Parto Glory Nerve Tonic, c.1913, 5 3/8 x 2 1/2 x 2 1/2 In. 209.00
Partola, Ideal Peppermint Laxative Candy, Square Corner, 1 1/2 x 3 5/8 x 2 1/4 In. 18.00
Partola, Mint Flavored Laxative, Hinged Lid, Contents, Chicago, 7/8 x 1 7/8 x 1 1/2 In. .   27.00
Partola, Original Mint Candy Laxative, 6 Tablets, Hinged Lid, 3/8 x 1 3/8 x 1 In. 38.00
Pasteurine Toothpaste, Woman Around Base & Lid, Celluloid, 6 x 6 1/2 In. 495.00
Peanut Kids Peanut Butter, Boy & Girl Riding Peanut, Yellow, Blue, Red, 5 Lb. 65.00
Peek Frean, Makers Of Famous Biscuits, 2 1/2 In. 42.00
Peek Frean, Pat-A-Cake Biscuits, Square, 3 1/2 In. 378.00
Pennsylvania Dutch Candy, Embossed, Mt. Holly Spring, Pa., 5 1/2 x 4 In. 15.00
Penslar Arnica Salve, Peninsular Chemical Co., Detroit, 7/8 x 2 5/8 In. 35.00
Pep-Pop Popcorn, Contents, Unopened, Peppard Seed Co., 5 1/8 x 2 5/8 In. 80.00
Perma Grip, Oval, 1 5/8 x 1 1/4 x 3/4 In. 48.00
Peter Pan Peanut Butter, Derby's, Free Sample, Lithograph, 2 Oz. 55.00
Peter Rabbit, Candy, Handle, 2 3/8 x 4 1/2 x 2 3/8 In. 225.00
Phonograph Needle, Beestone, Contents, 2 x 1 1/4 In. 49.00
Phonograph Needle, Gramophone Lux, Contents, Germany, 2 x 1 1/4 In. 49.00
Phonograph Needle, Gramophone Marschall, Contents, 2 x 1 1/4 In. 49.00
Phonograph Needle, Gramophone, His Master's Voice, Nipper Dog, England, 2 x 1 1/2 In.   49.00
Phonograph Needle, Gramophone, Parrot, Contents, 1 3/4 x 1 1/4 In. 49.00
Phonograph Needle, Leading Always Needles, 1/2 x 1 5/8 x 1 1/4 In. 36.00
Phonograph Needle, Light Gramophone Needles, 1/2 x 1 7/8 x 1 3/8 In. 36.00
Phonograph Needle, Lux Original, 3/8 x 1 7/8 x 1 3/8 In. 25.00
Phonograph Needle, Marschall, 1/2 x 1 5/8 x 1 5/8 In. 36.00
Phonograph Needle, Marschall, 1 5/8 x 1 1/2 In. 44.00
Phonograph Needle, Montgomery Ward, Contents, Slide Lid 35.00
Phonograph Needle, Mount Everest, Contents, Germany, 1 3/4 x 1 1/4 In. 49.00
Phonograph Needle, Pegasus Nadeln, 1 7/8 x 1 3/8 In. . . . . .38.00 to 48.00
Phonograph Needle, Rojar, 1 7/8 x 1 3/8 In. 40.00
Phonograph Needle, Solo, Contents, England, 1 3/4 x 1 1/4 In. 49.00
Phonograph Needle, Songster Needles, Blue, 1 7/8 x 1 1/4 In. 38.00
Phonograph Needle, Verona, Nude Woman, Tin, Square, 1 3/4 In. 80.00
Piccaninny Floor Polish, Rentokil, Twice The Shine In Half The Time, 4 In. Diam. 453.00
Piccaninny Shoe Polish, Reflects The Smile Of Satisfaction, Black Boy Grinning, 2 3/4 In.   246.00
Pineoleum Iron Tablets, Contents, Package Insert, 1/2 x 2 5/8 x 1 1/2 In. 95.00
Pinex Laxatives, Pinex Co., Fort Wayne, Ind., 1/2 x 3 3/8 x 2 3/4 In. 18.00
Pinko-Laxin, For Constipation, St. Louis, 2 3/4 x 2 In. 83.00
Pioneer Brand Golden Flake Cavendish, Man, On Stump, Hinged Lid, c.1930, 4 x 7 In. .   37.00
Pioneer Deluxe Cocoa, Pioneer Tea Co., Pry Lid, Square, 5 3/8 x 3 5/8 In. 325.00
Poehler King Jumbo Peanuts, Polar Bear, 10 Lb., 8 1/2 In. 1155.00
Polarine Oil, Imperial Oil Co., MacDonald Mfg. Co., Gal. 675.00
Pomeroy's Plaster, Extra Belladonna, 25 Cents, 8 1/2 x 5 7/8 In. 83.00
Popeye Popcorn, Pry Lid, King Features, Purity Mills, Contents, 1949, 4 3/4 x 3 x 2 In. . .   150.00
Porter's Liniment Salve, Geo. H. Rundle, Piqua, Oh., Box . . . . *Illus*   12.00
Poslam For Eczema, Other Skin Diseases, Emergency Laboratories, Sample, 5/8 x 1 5/8 In.   35.00
Poudre Dentifrice, Roussel, Cardboard, 3 1/4 x 1 5/8 In. 25.00
Poudre Dentifrice Antiseptique, Gold Ground, Paper Label, Round, 2 x 5/8 In. 18.00
Pounce Powder For Tracing Cloth, Contents, B.K. Elliott Co., Pittsburgh, Pa., 5 x 2 In. . .   35.00
Powdre Dentifrice Tandpoeder, Cardboard, 3 3/8 x 1 1/2 In. 25.00
Princess Salted Peanuts, Lummis & Co., Philadelphia, 10 Lb., 9 1/2 In. 143.00
Pruett Bait Can, Fish, Lift Lid, Belt Mount, Los Angeles, 3 x 2 1/2 In. 24.00
Public Benefit Boot Co., St. Paul's & St. Leeds, England, 7 x 5 1/2 x 3 1/2 In. . . . . .30.00 to 38.00
Pulvers Chewing Gum, Kola Pepsin, Wintergreen, Lithograph, 1 x 3 x 3/8 In. 743.00
Punch Polish Mop, Chicago, 3 1/2 x 7 1/2 In. 33.00
Quest, Positive Deodorant Powder, International Cellucotton Products Co., 1/2 Oz., 3 In. .   68.00
Quinine Sulfate, Animals Hauling Materials, 5 Oz., 6 x 3 3/8 In.   138.00
Rankine's Superior Sodas, Handle, 7 In. 115.00
Rawleigh's Aspirin Tablets, Hinged Top, Insert, 3/8 x 2 3/8 x 2 In. 48.00
Rawleigh's Laxative Tablets, 3/8 x 2 1/8 x 1 1/2 In. 28.00
Rawleigh's Medicated Ointment, W.T. Rawleigh Co., Freeport, Ill., 5 Oz., 3 1/2 In. 8.00
Rawleigh's Veterinary Ointment, Round, Partial Contents, 3 1/4 x 4 1/4 In. 44.00
Ray's Salve, Ray Products Co., Greenville, Ohio, 3/4 x 2 3/4 In.   30.00

Red Cough Drops, Reading, Pa., 5 Lb., 8 In. . . . . *Illus*   21.00
Reduco Fusion Mixture, Devil, Red Ground, Tin Lithograph, Hinged, 3 3/4 x 6 x 1 1/4 In.   187.00
Reed's Aspirin Tablets, Slide Lid, Red, 12 Tablet Size 18.00
Regal Loud Tone Needles, 1 3/4 x 1 3/8 In. 36.00
Regesan Lozenges, 4 x 1 In. 5.00
Repeater Ice Cream Cones, Square, Cheshire, Conn., 10 x 11 In. 220.00
Revivo, Nerve & Sexual Disease, Royal Medicine Co., 2 1/2 x 1 1/2 In. 232.00
Rexall, Antiseptic Tooth Powder, Green, Woman's Face, 2 x 1 1/8 x 7/8 In. 209.00
Rexall, Antiseptic Tooth Powder, Makes Pearly Teeth, 4 7/8 x 2 1/4 In. 132.00
Rexall, Briten Tooth Powder, Oval Base, 4 1/2 x 3 1/8 x 2 1/8 In. 80.00
Rexall, Denturex Adhesive, Oval, Rexall Drug Company, L.A., 4 3/8 x 2 1/2 x 1 3/8 In. . .   48.00
Rexall, First Aid Kit, Contents, 1 7/8 x 8 1/8 x 4 In. 25.00
Rexall, Foot Powder, Blue, 4 Oz., 3 7/8 In. 121.00
Rexall, Lesperine Vaginal Wash, Designed Especially For Women, Blue, Red, 4 In. 1980.00
Rexall, Quick Bands, Hinged Lid, 3 1/2 x 2 3/8 x 1 1/8 In. 38.00
Rigby, Rough Havanas, Rose, Paper Label, 5 x 3 1/2 In. 220.00
Riley's Toffee, Cinderella, Halifax, England, 5 3/4 x 3 3/4 x 1 1/8 In. 30.00
Robinson Crusoe, Salted Peanuts, Tin Lithograph, 10 Lb., 9 1/4 x 8 3/8 In. 798.00
Romac Puncture Kit, 1940s, 4 In. 10.00
Romeo Dates, Air Holes On Bottom, 3 1/4 x 7 3/4 In. 18.00
Rose Carbolic Tooth Powder, Prevents Decay, 2 3/4 In. 275.00
Rose Chemical Co., Corn Salve, Baltimore, Md., 1/2 x 1 In. 28.00
Rosebud Regulators, Rosebud Perfume Co., 1/2 x 1 5/8 x 1 5/8 In. 20.00
Rosekist Popcorn, Um-m-m-m Good, Heap Good, Unopened, Contents, 1950s, 10 Oz. . .   85.00
Rowntree's Chocolates, 1950s, 6 In. 10.00
Royal Tooth Powder, 25 Cents, 3 1/8 x 1 1/2 In. 77.00
Royal Tooth Powder, Warranted Strictly Pure, Woman, Round, 4 In. 1650.00
Runkel Brothers Cocoa, High Grade Breakfast, Embossed, Screw Lid, 1870, 1 1/2 x 1 In.   66.00
Runkel's Pure Cocoa, Sample, 1 5/8 x 1 1/8 x 3/4 In. . . . . .195.00 to 225.00
Runkel's Pure Cocoa, Screw Lid, Square, 1 3/4 x 1 1/4 In. 175.00
S&F Cream Of Tartar, Pry Lid, Smart & Final, So. California, 3 1/4 x 2 3/8 x 1 1/8 In. . . .   260.00
San Tox Foot Relief, Oval Base, DePree Chemical Co., Chicago, Ill., 4 1/2 x 2 x 1 3/4 In.   95.00
Sanders, Satin Candy Pail, Children, Swing Handle, 2 1/2 Lb., 5 x 5 In. 88.00
Santa Tindeco, Round, 1 3/4 x 3 7/8 In. 95.00
Satin Tooth Powder, Cylinder, Contents, 3 3/4 In. 154.00
Satin Tooth Powder, Pamphlet, Box, 3 3/4 In. 77.00
Satin Tooth Powder, Woman, Bird, Cylinder, Contents, Label, Pamphlet, Box, 3 3/4 In. . .   55.00
Savoy Quality Certified Cocoa, Hinged Lid, 6 x 3 1/4 In. 120.00
Sayman's Healing Salve, T.M. Sayman, St. Louis, 7/8 x 2 1/4 In. 48.00
Schratz's Oriental Bath Powder, Schratz Chemical Co., Detroit, 1904, 5 1/2 x 2 1/2 In. . . .   340.00
Scotch Gall Remedy, For Man & Beast, Man Sitting On Crate, Horse, 3 1/2 In. Diam. 55.00
Scotch Shortbread, Richmond Castle, Scotland, 6 1/4 x 9 In. 12.00
Scott's Blood Tablets, Woman, $1.00, Contents, Booklet, 2 x 3 1/8 In. 3630.00
Scott's Santal Pepsin Capsules, Partial Contents, Flat, Pocket, 3 x 2 In. 385.00
Seltzer Packing Co., Lard, Pottsville, Pa., 5 Lb. 17.00
Sentinel Handy Bandages, City Rubber, Cleveland, Ohio, 3 1/2 x 1 5/8 x 1 In. 25.00
Sentinel Utility First Aid Kit, Cleveland, Ohio, 6 1/8 x 3 1/4 x 1 In. 15.00
Severas Tooth Powder, Cylinder, Contents, 4 1/2 In. 319.00
Sharps Super Kreem Toffee, Parrot, Sir Kreemy Knut, Display, England, 13 x 11 In. 42.00
Shedd's Peanut Butter, Circus, 5 Lb., 6 1/2 In. 10.00
Sheridan Condition Powder, Horses, Sheep, Cattle, Hens, 5 In. . . . . *Illus*   30.00
Shores Family Salve, Partial Contents, Shores-Mueller, Cedar Rapids, Iowa, 3 x 3 1/8 In. .   28.00
Smith's Non-Irritant Adamantine Phosphate Cement, Leaf Design Edges, 3 1/2 x 2 In. .   198.00
Smith's Triple Cure Pills, 50 Cents, Boston, Mass., 2 7/8 x 1 5/8 In. 143.00
Snowdrift Shortening, Handle, Blue, White, Art Deco, 6 x 5 1/2 In. 12.50
Southern Star Pure Lard, Cover, 19 3/4 x 16 In. 200.00
Sozodont Powder, For Cleansing The Teeth, Man Brushing Teeth, 2 5/8 x 1 7/8 In. 485.00
Spartan, Cream Of Tartar, Slide Lid, 1 1/2 Oz. 22.00
Spartan Aspirin Tablets, 15 Cents, Petersburg, Va., 1 3/4 x 2 1/2 In. 8.80
Spartan Brand Pure Aspirin, 24 Tablet Size 20.00
Squirrel Peanut Butter, Squirrel Eating Nut, Tin Lithograph, Pry Lid, 3 Lb., 4 3/4 x 5 In.   467.00
St. Joseph Aspirin, 15 Cents, Plough, Inc., Memphis, Tenn., 12 Tablet Size 18.00
Staple Brand Peanut Butter, Syracuse Candy & Specialty Co., 3 3/4 x 3 3/8 In. 160.00

Tin, Red Cough Drops,
Reading, Pa., 5 Lb., 8 In.

Tin, Sheridan Condition
Powder, Horses, Sheep,
Cattle, Hens, 5 In.

Tin, Waltham Main
Springs, For Watches,
Louis C. Kreger, 3 x 5 In.

Startup's Buy-Roz Gum, Rose Fragrance, Tin Lithograph, 1 1/2 x 2 In. 200.00
Startup's Mountain Mint Gum, Keeps Your Teeth White, 1 1/2 x 2 In. 220.00
Stauffer's Animal Crackers, 6 x 4 1/4 In. 12.00
Steero Chicken Bouillon, Kitchen Products Co., New York City, 5/8 Oz., 3 x 1 x 3/4 In. ... 38.00
Stoherts Celery Pills, Red S, Atherton, Round, 3/8 x 1 1/2 In. 40.00
Stuart's Tablets, F.A. Stuart Co., Marshall, Mich., 1/2 x 3 1/4 x 2 In. 18.00
Sunshine, Chocolate Wafers, Loose Wiles Biscuit Company, 8 1/4 x 3 1/8 In. 95.00
Sunshine Biscuit, 20th Century American Folk Art, 14 1/2 x 12 x 4 In. 32.00
Sunshine Biscuit, Flagship Of Bicentennial, Frigate Ships, 1976, 14 1/2 x 12 x 4 In. 32.00
Sunshine Biscuit, Masters Series, Severin Roesen, Oval, 11 1/2 x 14 1/2 x 4 1/2 In. 32.00
Sunshine Biscuit, Mount Rushmore & Niagara Falls, 1986, 14 1/2 x 12 x 4 In. 32.00
Super Hickory Lighter Fire Starter, Key, Contents, Hickory Lighter Corp., 3 5/8 x 5 In. . 35.00
Superior Cycle Repair, 1940s, 3 In. 12.00
Superior Vanilla Marshmallow Drops, Green, 4 x 6 1/4 x 2 3/8 In. 143.00
Superior's Salted Mixed Nuts, Key Wind Lid, Canco, Superior Nut Co., Boston, 3 1/2 In. 16.00
Sur-Shot, Bot & Round Worm Remover, Yellow Ground, Canada, 3 1/2 x 2 1/2 x 2 1/2 In. 28.00
Sur-Shot Veterinary, Bot & Worm Remover, Indian, Farm Animals, 5 x 3 3/4 x 2 1/2 In. . 45.00
Sutherlands Pile Prescriptions, Green, Black, Cylindrical, 4 x 1 1/2 In. 209.00
Sweet Violet, Cube Cut, Vertical, Pocket, 4 1/2 x 3 x 7/8 In. ....1375.00 to 3410.00
Sykes Comfort Powder, 4 1/4 x 1 1/2 x 1 In. 335.00
Sykes Comfort Powder, Oval, Flat Top, Boston, 4 1/4 x 2 3/4 x 2 1/4 In. 485.00
Texel Tape, 5 1/8 In. Diam. 45.00
Thalax, Laxative, Palatable, Mild, Non-Injurious, Red, 2 1/2 x 1 1/2 In. 50.00
Tholene Salve, Rosebud Perfume Co., Woodsboro, Maryland, 7/8 x 2 1/8 In. 30.00
Thompson's Double Malted Malted Milk, Waukesha, Wisc., 8 1/2 x 6 1/4 In. 325.00
Thorne's, Candy, Thorne's Child, 1950s, 4 x 3 In. 12.00
Tod Co. Waxed Dental Floss, Round, Pocket Size, 1 1/4 In. 80.00
Tom Keene, Swordsman, Paper Label, 5 1/4 x 4 1/4 In. 50.00
Turpo Turpentine Ointment, Free Sample, Slip Top, 1 3/4 x 1 1/4 In. 28.00
Two In One Pasta Superior Shoe Polish, English, Spanish, F.F. Daley, 1 x 2 3/4 In. ... 12.00
Typewriter Ribbon, Allied Carbon & Ribbon Mfg., Corp., New York 34.00
Typewriter Ribbon, Allied Flagship Silk 6.00
Typewriter Ribbon, American Brand, Indian Chief, Lithograph, H.M. Storing Co., 3 In. ... 165.00
Typewriter Ribbon, Amneco, Square 75.00
Typewriter Ribbon, Flint Brand, Kee Lox, Rochester, N.Y., 2 1/4 x 3/4 In. 7.50
Typewriter Ribbon, Hallmark, Round, Cameron Manufacturing, Dallas 20.00
Typewriter Ribbon, Keelox 24.00
Typewriter Ribbon, Park Avenue, Unopened, 2 1/2 In. 12.00
Typewriter Ribbon, Thorobred, Underwood Corporation, Burlington, N.J. 25.00
Typewriter Ribbon, Type Bar Brand, LC Smith Corona 18.00
Typewriter Ribbon, Vertex Roytype, Unopened, 2 1/2 In. 12.00
Typewriter Ribbons, Webster Star Brand Non-Filling, F.S. Webster Co., Boston 18.00
Uncle Sam Shoe Polish, 7/8 x 2 1/4 In. 75.00
Urethral Bougies, Medicated, Grape Capsule Co., 1 1/4 x 6 5/8 In. 523.00
Valley Brand Malted Milk, Valley Dairy, New York, 20 Lb., 15 1/2 x 8 In. 135.00

Valleybrook Farms, Cashew Caramel Crunch, 1970s, 2 1/2 x 6 1/2 In. 8.00
Vander Derveer & Holmes Biscuit Co., N.Y., Woman, Cameo, House Shape, 8 x 10 x 7 In. 231.00
Vas-Oleum Petroleum Jelly, Peter Van Schaack, 7 1/8 x 5 x 5 In. 165.00
Veragreen Ointment, Genesee Pharmacal Company, Bergen, N.Y., 3/4 x 2 1/2 In. 35.00
Vicks Vaporub, Round, 3/8 Fl. Oz., 1 1/2 In. 10.00
Victory V Gums & Lozenges, Sailor, H.M.S. Victory, Shop Display, England, 9 1/2 In. ... 38.00
Viola V.N. Woodruff, Salted Nuts, Flushing, N.Y., 10 In. 77.00
Violet Sec Almond Meal Compound, Contents, Richard Hudnut, New York, 5 x 2 In. 225.00
W&R Jacob & Co. Biscuit Manufacturers, Coronation Coach, 5 1/4 x 9 In. 284.00
W.C. Enck & Co. Cough Drops, Price 5 Cents, 2 1/2 x 1 3/4 x 1 1/4 In. 303.00
Waltham Main Springs, For Watches, Louis C. Kreger, 3 x 5 In. .... *Illus* 15.00
Wampoles Grape Salt, Cleanses The System, Free Trial Size, Canada, 2 1/8 x 1 1/8 In. .. 180.00
Wampoles Grape Salt, Morning Refresher, Free Sample, Pry Lid, 2 1/8 x 1 1/4 In. 75.00
Well's Tablet, 5/8 x 3 1/8 x 2 In. 36.00
Wilbur's Breakfast Cocoa, Cupid, Paper Over Cardboard, Tin Top, Base, 8 Oz., 5 x 3 In. . 77.00
Wilbur's Cocoa, Paper Label, Contents, Unopened, Sample, 1 7/8 x 1 5/8 In. 660.00
Wilson's Co-Re-Ga, Perfect Adhesive For Dentures, Celluloid Brush, 1 1/2 x 3 3/8 In. ... 85.00
Wilson's Co-Re-Ga Dental Powder, Contents, Sample, 2 1/8 In. ....11.00 to 44.00
Witch Hazel Tooth Soap, Robinson & Halstead, Flat, Pocket, 3 1/8 x 2 In. 630.00
Witmors Marshmallows, 3 Oz., 2 x 4 In. 143.00
Wonder Heart Cure, Seroco Chemical Co., 3 x 1 3/4 In. 121.00
Wonder Salve, Harper & Sons, 7/8 x 2 In. 18.00
Wonderful Dream Salve, Hannah D. McDonald, Embossed, Wrapped, 2 3/4 x 2 3/4 In. .. 77.00
Wood's Corn Plasters, Johnson & Johnson, 2 3/4 x 1 3/4 In. 33.00
Wood's Improved Lollacapop For Mosquitoes, Black Flies, Gnats, 3 1/4 x 1 3/4 In. .28.00 to 68.00
Woolworth Superfine Marshmallows, Oval, New York, 2 5/8 x 4 1/4 x 2 3/4 In. 225.00
Y & S Licorice Wafers, 3/4 x 2 1/8 x 1 3/8 In. 20.00
Yankee Wax Polish, New York, 1930, 1 x 3 1/2 In. 95.00
York Minster Toffee, 1960s, 6 In. 12.00
Young & Smylie Licorice Lozenges, Tin Lithograph, 5 Lb., 7 x 6 In. 176.00
Zam Buk, Sooths-Heals, Great Skin Remedy, Free Sample, Round, 5/16 x 7/8 In. 28.00
Zanol Military Foot Powder, Soldier & Sailor, 4 1/2 x 2 1/2 x 1 3/8 In. ....128.00 to 225.00
Zara Imported Pure Spanish Licorice, Top, Tur Hermanos, N.Y., 1/2 x 2 1/2 x 1 5/8 In. . 48.00
Zit Automobile Dry Wash, Contents, 3 1/2 x 7 1/2 x 2 1/2 In. 33.00

TIP TRAY   The bill for food or drink used to be delivered to customers
at a bar or restaurant on a tip tray, a small, usually round, tin tray about
four inches in diameter. It was often a small version of a larger, match-
ing serving tray and was decorated with advertising pictures and slogans. Although tip trays are still made, they were most popular from
the 1890s to the 1940s. Collectors should beware of the many reproductions of old trays.

Aero, Jenney Gasoline, Tin Lithograph, Round, 4 1/4 In. 143.00
American Line, Ocean Liner, Philadelphia, Queenstown, Tin Lithograph, Round, 4 1/4 In. 248.00
American Perfect Beer, Man & Woman, Houston, Texas, Round, c.1914, 5 1/8 In. 550.00
American Wringer Co., Rubber Covered Rolls, Tin Lithograph, 4 1/2 x 6 1/2 In. 990.00
Angel Verdeau & Co., Barbezieux Cognac, Tin Lithograph, 3 1/2 x 8 7/8 In. 77.00
Angeles Brewing & Malting Co., Flag, Bottle, Seattle, 1909, 4 1/4 In. 96.00
Apollinaris, Queen Of Table Waters, Polly, Tin Lithograph, Rectangular, 6 x 4 In. ...33.00 to 88.00
Arnholt Schaefer Brewery, Woman, Flowers In Hair, Tin Lithograph, Round, 4 In. 225.00 to 248.00
Ask Your Grocer For Lindquist's Crackers, Bears, Tin Lithograph, 4 7/8 x 3 3/8 In. 264.00
Batholomay Brewing, Woman, Winged Disk, Tin Lithograph, Round ....176.00 to 650.00
Best Prepared Paint, Heath & Milligan Mfg. Co., Chicago, 4 1/8 In. 450.00
Beverwyck, Famous Lager, Factory Scene, Round 151.00
Bevo, All Year Round Soft Drink, Horse Drawn Wagon, Tin Lithograph, 4 5/8 x 6 5/8 In. . 220.00
Billman & Stegmeier, Milk & Cream, Woman Fishing, Tin Lithograph, 6 5/8 x 4 5/8 In. .. 154.00
Booth Bros. Bottlers, Dutch Girls, Tin Lithograph, Round, 4 1/4 In. 39.00
Bower & Davis, Real Estate & Insurance, Woman, Long Hair, Tin Lithograph, Round 45.00
Brading's Ale, Established 1865, Deer Head, Antlers, Red Ground, Round, 4 1/4 In. 44.00
Bradley Haberdasher, Gentleman's Shop, Woman, Rose, Tin Lithograph, Round 147.00
Broadway Brewing Co., Battleax, Round, Buffalo, N.Y., 4 1/4 In. 96.00
Bubier's Laxative Salz, Tin Lithograph, Round, 4 1/4 In. 110.00
Buffalo Brewing, San Francisco Exposition, Sacramento, Round, 1915, 4 1/4 In. ..316.00 to 500.00

Buffalo's Best, Becks Bottled Beer, Eagle, Tin Lithograph, Round, Magnus Beck, 4 In. .. 187.00
Bull Brand Feeds, Black Rim, Tin Lithograph, 4 5/8 x 6 5/8 In. 77.00
Bunola Bread, It Serves You Right, Woman, Goggles, Tin Lithograph, 4 1/2 x 6 1/2 In. . . 330.00
C. Worz Saloon & Restaurant, Phila., Pa., Liberty Bell, Tin Lithograph, 1907, 4 1/8 In. . . 110.00
Capital, Old Stock & Cream Ale, Tin Lithograph, Round, 4 3/8 In. 121.00
Cardinal Beer, Woman, Flowers In Hair, Tin Lithograph, Round, 4 1/4 In. . . . . . . .385.00 to 650.00
Carnation Milk, H.D. Beach, Pacific Coast Condensed Milk, 5 1/2 x 3 1/2 In. 75.00
Century Beer, Man & Woman Toasting, Tin Lithograph, Round, Trinidad, Co., 4 1/4 In. . . 385.00
Charles Denby Cigar, Factory, Tin Lithograph, Oval, 6 x 4 1/2 In. 121.00
Charles E. Lynch, Men's & Boy's Outfitters, Admiral Dewey, Aluminum, 4 1/4 x 3 3/8 In. 110.00
Christian Feigenspan, Woman, Red Ribbon, Tin Lithograph, Round, 4 1/4 In. . . . . .66.00 to 143.00
Cleveland & Buffalo, Ferry Route, Daily, 4 In. 204.00
Cleveland & Buffalo Oceanliner, Tin Lithograph, Oval, 6 1/4 x 4 1/2 In. 209.00
Clysmic King Of Table Waters, Woman, Elk, Tin Lithograph, Oval, 6 3/8 x 5 In. . .358.00 to 413.00
Columbia Brewing Co., Tin Lithograph, Tacoma, Wash., Round, 4 1/4 In. 303.00
Columbus Brewery, Select Pale Beer, Tin Lithograph, Round, 4 1/4 In. 88.00
Consult Sheldon, Optical Specialist, Bear On Giraffe, Tin Lithograph, 1906, 5 x 3 3/8 In. 358.00
Corby's Old Rye Whisky, Man Reading Paper, Sleeping Dog, Tin Lithograph, Round, 4 In. 55.00
Cottolene Shortening, Woman Picking Cotton, Tin Lithograph, Round, 4 1/4 In. . .102.00 to 110.00
Cunard Lines, RMS Aquitania Ocean Liner, Tin Lithograph, 4 5/8 x 6 5/8 In. . . . . .231.00 to 385.00
Dallas Brewery, Tin Lithograph, Round, Dallas, Texas, 4 1/2 In. 303.00
Davidson's Premier Leader Range, Codere & Fils, Limitee, Sherbrooke, Que., 5 3/8 In. . . 225.00
Denby Cigars, Factory, Evansville, Ind., 6 In. 25.00
Deppen Brewing Co., Muenchener, Elk Head, Reading, Pa., Round, 4 In. . . . . .550.00 to 605.00
Domestic, It Stands At The Head, Sewing Machine, Tin Lithograph, Round, 4 1/4 In. 99.00
Doniphan Vineyards, Wine Bottle, Grapes, Leaves, Atchison, Kansas, Round, 4 In. . .40.00 to 61.00
Dorne's Carnation Chewing Gum, Round, 4 1/2 In. 495.00
Dowagiac, Drills & Seeders, 4 1/4 In. 30.00
E. Robinson's Sons, Pilsener Bottled Beer, Tin Lithograph, Round, 4 1/4 In. 50.00
Eagle Run Beer, Pure & Aged, Nude Cherub On Eagle, 4 1/4 In. 550.00
Edelbrau, Roseneck Brewing, Richmond, Va., Round, 4 1/4 In. 300.00
El Roi-Tan Cigar, Man & Woman, Tin Lithograph, Oval, 4 1/4 x 6 In. 330.00
El Verso Havana Cigars, 6 1/2 x 4 1/2 In. 99.00
Emerson Hotel, Tin Lithograph, Baltimore, Md., Oval, 6 1/8 x 4 3/8 In. 77.00
Enterprise Meat & Food Choppers, Tin Lithograph, Round, Philadelphia, 4 In. . . .121.00 to 144.00
Evinrude Rowboat & Canoe Motors, Woman In Boat, Round, 4 In. 245.00
F-P Home Lighting & Cooking, Tin, Round, 4 In. 385.00
Fairy Soap, Have You A Little Fairy In Your Home, Girl On Soap, Tin, 4 1/4 In. . . .88.00 to 154.00
Feigenspan, P.O.N., Fine Brews, Tin Lithograph, Round, 4 1/2 In. 17.00
Fort Pitt Beer, Tin Lithograph, Round, 4 1/4 In. 39.00
Frank Jones Homestead Ale, Tin Lithograph, Round, 5 1/8 In. 165.00
Fraternal Life & Accident Insurance, 4 7/8 x 4 1/4 In. 135.00
Fraternal Life Insurance, 3 White Horses, Scalloped Edge, 4 1/4 In. 44.00
Fred. Halsteads Suburban Hotel, Baltimore, Md., 4 1/4 In. 225.00
Fredericksburg Bottled Beer, Girl, Hood, Flowers, Tin Lithograph, Round, 4 1/4 In. 440.00
Gallagher & Burton Beer, Gold Rim, 4 1/4 In. . . . . .33.00 to 66.00
Garland Stoves, Bake The Bread & Roast The Meats That Make The Man, 4 1/4 In. 231.00
General Arthur Cigars, Garfield's Vice President, c.1920, 4 In. 75.00
General Arthur Cigars, Man, Tin Lithograph, Kerb, Wetheim & Schiffer, 3 1/4 x 5 In. . . . 550.00
Geo. W. Schott, Bar Scene, Tin Lithograph, Round, 4 1/4 In. 132.00
Gerhard Lang Brewery, Lang Trademark, Buffalo, Tin Lithograph, Round, 4 1/4 In. 121.00
German American Brewing Co., Maltosia, Tin Lithograph, Round, 5 1/8 In. 132.00
Germania Brewing Co., Woman, Bonnet, Rose Bouquet, 4 1/4 In. 110.00
Globe, Phillips Nagel Furniture & Undertaking, 4 1/2 In. 187.00
Globe-Wernicke Sectional Bookcases, Kalamazoo, Mi., c.1910, 4 1/4 In. . . . . .105.00 to 122.00
Goebel Beer, Man, Holding Mug, Tin Lithograph, Detroit, Round, 4 5/8 In. 231.00
Gold Seal Urbana Wine, Champagne, 6 1/2 x 4 1/2 In. 79.00
Gottfried Krueger Brewing, High Grade Beer, Tin Lithograph, Round, 4 1/4 In. . .132.00 to 240.00
Gypsy Hosiery, Gypsy Woman, Campfire Scene, L.W. Berdolt, Round, 6 In. . . . . .176.00 to 200.00
Hampden On Tap, Tin Lithograph, Round, 4 1/8 In. 77.00
Hardy, Shoe Man, Woman, Tin Lithograph, Constantine, Mich., Round, 4 1/4 In. 523.00
Havana Cigars, Cavalier, 4 1/4 In. 77.00
Helvetia Milk Condensing, Cardstock Lithograph, Highland, Ill., 5 5/8 x 4 1/8 In. 358.00

High Grade, Beer That's Liquid Food, Tin Lithograph, Round, Galveston, 4 3/8 In. 303.00
Highland Evaporated Cream, Round, 3 1/2 In. 120.00
Home Of Stegmaier Beer, Tin Lithograph, Wilkes-Barre, Penn., Oval, 4 3/8 x 6 1/4 In. . . 88.00
Home Treasure Stoves & Ranges, Selling Agents, Adams Furniture Co., 6 x 4 In. 138.00
Hyroler Whiskey, Louis J. Adler & Co., Man In Tuxedo, Round, 4 1/4 In. . . . . .66.00 to 88.00
I.P. Thomas & Son, High Grade Fertilizers, Tin Lithograph, Round, 4 1/4 In. . . . . .358.00 to 385.00
Indianapolis, Lieber's Gold Medal Beer, Tin Lithograph, Round, 5 In. 66.00
Indianapolis Brewing Co., Tin, Round, 5 In. 358.00
International Harvester, Farm Machines, Tin Lithograph, Oval, 3 3/8 x 4 1/2 In. 121.00
Iroquois Beer, Indian Head, Round, Buffalo, N.Y., 4 In. 60.00
J. Chr. G. Hupfel Brewing, Beer, Ale, Tin Lithograph, Round, 4 1/4 In. 55.00
Jacob Schmidt Brewing Co., 4 1/4 In. 325.00
Jap Rose Soap, Lithograph, Round, 4 1/4 In. 160.00
John Hampden Havana Cigar, 4 1/4 In. 55.00
Kellmer Piano, Woman, Flowers, Tin Lithograph, Round, 4 1/4 In. 248.00
Kemp & Burpee, Success Manure Spreader, Tin, 3 1/2 x 5 1/2 In. 523.00
Kenny's, Che-On-Tea, Woman In Chair, Tin Lithograph, Round, c.1906, 4 1/2 In. 88.00
Kenny's, Teas, Coffees, Drink, Enjoy, Woman, Roses, Tin Lithograph, Round, 4 In. 165.00 to 253.00
King's Pure Malt, Panama & Pacific Medal Of Award, Tin Lithograph, Oval, 6 In. .110.00 to 176.00
King's Pure Malt, Strengthening, Good For Insomnia, Healthful, Oval, 4 1/2 x 6 In. 121.00
King's Pure Malt, Woman Holding Tray, Tin Lithograph, Oval, 6 1/8 x 4 1/2 In. 154.00
King's Pure Malt Liquor, Tin Lithograph, Oval, 4 1/4 x 6 In. 55.00
Kuntz Remmler Co. Restaurant, Tin Lithograph, 6 1/8 x 4 1/4 In. 44.00
Laxol, Castor Oil, Like Honey, Tin Lithograph, Round, 4 1/4 In. 143.00
Learn To Say Mi Lola, Quality Cigar, Red Ground, Tin Lithograph, 6 1/8 x 4 1/4 In. 176.00
Leisy Brewing Co., Scat Player's Dream, Hand Holding Playing Cards, Round, 5 In. 180.00
Lewis 66 Whiskey, Starus, Pritz & Co., Cincinnati, Tin Lithograph, Round, 4 1/4 In. 253.00
Liberty Beer, Bottles Only, Arrows, Tomahawk, Tin Lithograph, Round, 4 1/4 In. .140.00 to 154.00
Liberty Beer, Indian Maiden, Tin Lithograph, 4 1/2 In. 256.00
Lieber's Gold Medal Beer, Indianapolis Brewing Co., 5 In. 94.00
Little Red Riding Hood, Ohio Art, Tin Lithograph, Round, 4 1/4 In. 55.00
Los Angeles Brewing Co., Home Of East Side Beer, Tin Lithograph, Round, 5 1/8 In. 330.00
Maltosia, German American Brewing Co., Tin Lithograph, Round, 5 1/4 In. 88.00
Mokaine Is The Best Of All Liqueurs, Rectangular, 4 5/8 x 3 In. . . . . .195.00 to 245.00
Monticello Special Reserve, Whiskey, Fox Hunt, Tin Lithograph, Oval, 4 3/8 x 6 In. 209.00
Mount Vernon, Fresh Cream Flavor, Tin Lithograph, Oval, 4 5/8 x 3 3/8 In. 231.00
Muehlebach's Pilsener Beer, Purest & Best, Kansas City, Mo., Round, 5 In. . . . . . . .66.00 to 76.00
Narragansett Brewing Co., Tin Lithograph, Round, 5 1/2 In. 303.00
National Beer, Best In West, Cowboy On Running Horse, Round, 4 1/2 In. 770.00
National Beer, I Thank You, Baltimore, Md., Rectangular, 4 x 6 1/4 In. 28.00
National Beer, National Brewing, San Francisco, Round, 1907, 4 1/4 In. 380.00
Neuweiler's Beer, Tin Lithograph, Rectangular, 7 1/4 x 5 1/4 In. 110.00
New Home Sewing Machine, English & Spanish Text, Tin Lithograph, Round, 4 1/4 In. . . 253.00
Northampton Brewing, Hand Holds 3 Beer Bottles, Tin Lithograph, Round, 4 1/4 In. . . . 248.00
Oakville Co., Hand, Tin Lithograph, Oval, 6 x 4 1/2 In. 51.00
Oertelbrew, Louisville, Ky., Round, 4 1/4 In. 104.00
Old Fashion Beer, Billings Brewing Co., Round, 1911, 4 1/4 In. 468.00
Old Reliable Coffee, Woman, Drinking Coffee, Flowers, Tin Lithograph, Round, 4 1/4 In. 180.00
Oldburger, Perfect Beer, United Brewing, Tin Lithograph, Round, 4 In. 77.00
Olympia Beer, It's The Water, Gentleman, Holding Bottle, c.1920, 4 In. 45.00
Our Brands National Cigar Stands, Woman, Flowers, Tin Lithograph, Round, 6 1/8 In. . . 303.00
Owens & Johnson Hardware, Spirit River, Alberta, Tin Lithograph, Round, 7 x 4 5/8 In. . . 88.00
P. Ballantine & Sons, Ales, Beers, Tin Lithograph, Round, 5 1/2 In. 28.00
Parsley Brand Salmon, Round, 4 1/8 In. 170.00
Peter Doelger Bottled Beer, Eagle, Tin Lithograph, Rectangular, 6 x 4 1/4 In. 275.00
Pippins Cigar, 5 Cent, Apple, Lithograph, H. Traiser & Co., Boston, 5 3/8 x 5 In. 413.00
President Suspenders, Absolute Comfort, Tin Lithograph, Round, 4 1/4 In. 605.00
President Suspenders, Crook & Metz, Applied Glass, Round, 4 1/4 In. 88.00
Pulver's Cocoa, Package, Girl Drinking Cocoa, Round, 4 1/2 In. 468.00
Puritan Hams, First In Land, Puritan Boy, Tin Lithograph, Cudahy Packing, Round, 4 In. . 88.00
Quandt's Famous Beer & Ales, Mercury Figure Atop Globe, c.1900, 4 1/8 In. 80.00
Quick Meal Ranges, Ask Your Dealer, Chicks, Tin Lithograph, Oval, 3 3/8 x 5 In. . . .83.00 to 88.00
Quick Meal Ranges, Chicks, Lithograph, 4 1/2 x 3 1/4 In. 88.00

Rainier Beer, Mount Ranier, Seattle Brewing & Malting Co., Round, c.1909, 4 1/4 In. ...   270.00
Red Raven, Woman & Bird, Green Edge, Tin Lithograph, 4 5/8 x 6 5/8 In. 149.00
Red Raven Splits, Ask The Man, World's Fair, Tin Lithograph, Round, 1904, 4 In. 226.00
Resinol Soap & Ointment, Woman, Blue Dress, Roses, Round, 4 1/4 In. ....121.00 to 253.00
Rigby, La Toco Havana Cigars, Tin Lithograph, Round, Tampa, Fla., 4 1/4 In. 204.00
Rockford High Grade Watches, Woman, Blue Dress, Tin Lithograph, 5 x 3 3/8 In. 132.00 to 209.00
Roltair's House Upside Down, Pan-Am Expo, Tin Lithograph, 1901, 7 x 5 In. 220.00
Ruhstaller's, California Invites The World, Gilt Edge, Kaufmann & Strauss, 4 1/4 In. 469.00
Ruhstaller's, Gilt Edge Lager, San Francisco Exposition, Round, 1915, 4 1/4 In. 180.00
S.S. Pierce Co., Wine & Spirit Merchants, Tin Lithograph, Round, 4 1/4 In. 99.00
Schober's Export Brew, Tin Lithograph, San Antonio, Round, 5 1/8 In. 385.00
Seitz Beer, Spread Winged Eagle, Tin Lithograph, Round, 4 1/4 In. 99.00
Shawmut Furniture, Woman, Rose In Hair, Tin Lithograph, Round, 4 1/4 In. 198.00
Sign Of The Bulldog, Real Habana Segars, Tin Lithograph, 6 7/8 x 5 In. 138.00
Source Of Cottolene, Best For Shortening, Woman Picking Cotton, Tin Lithograph, 4 In. .   143.00
Stegmaier Beer, Factory Scene, Tin Lithograph, Oval, 6 x 4 1/2 In. 77.00
Stegmaier Brewing Co., Factory, Tin Lithograph, Wilkes-Barre, Pa., Round, 4 1/4 In. 264.00
Stegmaier Brewing Co., Hand Holding 4 Beer Bottles, Tin Lithograph, Round, 4 1/4 In. .   143.00
Stephen Gottwall, Blond Woman, Red Roses, Newark, N.J., 1908, 4 1/4 In. 275.00
Stollwerck, Red, Gold, Tin Lithograph, Round, 5 In. 66.00
Stroh's Malt Extract, For Weak People, Nursing Mothers, Tin Lithograph, Detroit, 4 In. .   154.00
Success Manure Spreader, Tin Lithograph, Syracuse, N.Y., 3 3/8 x 4 3/4 In. .....220.00 to 440.00
Sunshine Finishes, Heath & Milligan Paints, 4 1/4 In. 550.00
Taka-Kola, Every Hour, Clock & Woman Graphic, Tin Lithograph, Round, 4 1/4 In. 468.00
Texhoma Gasoline, Motor Oils, Tin Lithograph, 4 5/8 x 6 5/8 In. 231.00
The Fashion, Fashionable Dress For Women, Lehighton, Pa., Tin Lithograph, 4 1/4 In. ...   385.00
Tivoli, Select Lager, Woman Holding Glass, Tin Lithograph, Round, 4 1/4 In. 385.00
Treasure, Adams Furniture Co. Limited, Stove, Toronto, 4 1/4 In. 220.00
Universal Stove & Ranges, Round, 4 In. 275.00
Urbana Wine Co., Tin Lithograph, Rectangular, 4 1/4 x 6 1/4 In. 121.00
Welsbach Lamps, Shield, Spread Winged Eagle, Round, 4 1/4 In. ....35.00 to 71.00
West End Brewing Co., Franciskaner, Pilsener, Tin Lithograph, Round, 4 1/8 In. 550.00
Whann Lithia Water, Tin Lithograph, Green Ground, Round, 4 1/4 In. 99.00
White House Ginger Ale, Tin Lithograph, Round, Boston, 5 1/8 In. 138.00
White Top Champagne, Wood Grain Ground, 4 1/4 In. 25.00
Wolverine Supply Co., Sandy Andy Toys, Factory Graphic, Tin Lithograph, 4 1/2 x 6 In. .   253.00
Woodward's, Candy Man, Little Person, Mr. & Mrs. Gene Bregant, c.1920, 5 x 7 In. 63.00
Woodward's Candy, Council Bluff, Iowa, Man & Woman, 7 x 5 In. 165.00
Yaka-Cola Every Hour, Take No Other, 4 1/4 In. 425.00
Yeungling's, Beer, Porter, Ale, Eagle, Tin Lithograph, Round, 4 1/2 In. ....350.00 to 385.00

TOBACCO   When Columbus first received a gift of dried tobacco
leaves from the natives of the West Indies, he threw the leaves away.
About sixty years later, tobacco began to be used in Europe. Pipe,
chewing, and snuff were the earliest forms of tobacco. Cigars became
popular in the early 1800s and cigarettes after the Civil War. Collectors
hunt for all types of tobacco advertising and packaging, including tin
tags—small metal-pronged labels that identified brands of plug
tobacco from the 1870s until about 1930. Other brands of plug tobacco
were soon labeled with tin tags. See Ashtray and also brand categories,
such as Kool and Lorillard, for more tobacco collectibles.

Advertisement, Camel Cigarettes, DiMaggio, Popular Science, Frame, 1942, 9 x 11 In. ..   15.00
Advertisement, Chesterfield Cigarettes, Sailor, Love Letters, 1943, 8 1/2 x 11 1/2 In. 12.00
Advertisement, Laflin & Rand, Powders, Woman Hunter, 2-Sided, c.1903, 12 x 8 In. 138.00
Advertisement, Murad Cigarette, Pack, 2 Couples, 1 Ice Skates, 1917, 9 1/2 x 13 In. 9.00
Advertisement, Players Navy Cut Cigarettes, Sailor, England, Frame, 22 1/2 x 17 1/2 In. .   76.00
Advertisement, Players Please, Sailor, HMS Invincible, England, Frame, 25 x 19 In. 38.00
Advertisement, Wills's Capstan Navy Cut Cigarettes, England, Frame, 23 1/2 x 19 1/4 In.   19.00
Banner, American Navy Plug Tobacco, Canvas, 22 x 60 In. 1870.00
Banner, Camel, Woman Smoking, Pack Of Camels, Yellow Ground, Cloth, 95 x 43 In. 99.00
Banner, Plow Boy Tobacco, Canvas, 18 x 40 In. 1100.00
Banner, Star Tobacco, Man Holding Tobacco, Blue, White, Canvas, 36 x 88 In. 330.00
Bin, Game Fine Cut Tobacco, Tin, 2 Quails, Jno. J. Bagley & Co., Detroit, 18 In. 1100.00

Bin, Honest Scrap, Dog & Cat, Hand, Holding Hammer, 12 x 18 x 14 In. 6050.00
Bin, Polar Bear Tobacco, Always Fresh, Tin, Slanted Lift Lid, 12 x 18 x 14 In. 715.00
Bin, Sure Shot Chewing Tobacco, Indian, Tin Lithograph, 6 1/2 x 15 1/4 x 10 1/4 In. 1045.00
Bin, Sure Shot Chewing Tobacco, Tin Lithograph, Early 1920s, 8 x 15 x 10 In. . . . . . . *Illus* 743.00
Bin, Sweet Burley Tobacco, Yellow Ground, Red Letters, 10 3/4 x 8 1/4 In. 231.00
Bin, Sweet Cuba Chewing Tobacco, Fine Cut, Yellow Ground, 11 x 8 1/4 In. 1320.00
Bin, Sweet Mist Chewing Tobacco, Cardboard, Metal Top, Bottom, 11 x 8 In. . . . . .94.00 to 143.00
Bin, Tiger Chewing Tobacco, 5 Cent Packages, Cardboard, Tin, 1 x 8 1/8 x 6 3/8 In. 55.00
Bin, Tiger Chewing Tobacco, 5 Cent, Cardboard, Tin, Square, 6 x 8 x 11 In. 358.00
Bootjack, Use Musselman's Plug Tobacco, Cast Iron, Embossed, 9 1/2 In. . . . . *Illus* 69.00
Box, 5 Colors Cigar, Ethnic Children, Wood, 1878, 7 x 8 1/4 x 4 3/4 In. 154.00
Box, Ben Bey Cigars, Humidor, Tin, 9 x 3 In. . . . . .50.00 to 69.00
Box, Bensen & Hedges, Leather, Brass Hinges, Smith Crafted, 6 1/2 x 5 1/2 x 3 3/4 In. . . 50.00
Box, Bull Durham Tobacco, Bull, Cowboy Scene, Cardboard, 11 1/2 x 8 x 5 In. 440.00
Box, Bull Durham, Standard Of World, Cowboys, Bull, Tree, Horse, Cardboard, 11 In. . . . 825.00
Box, Chief Big Feather Cigars, Cedar, Lithograph, 1910, 5 x 4 In. 128.00
Box, Cremo Cigar, Humidor, Band Identifies It The World Over, Tin, 14 x 7 In. 69.00
Box, Fire King Cigar, Wood, 8 In. 17.00
Box, Flor De Franklin Cigar, 5 Cents, Ben Franklin, Kite, Wood, 7 3/4 x 8 1/2 x 5 1/2 In. . 66.00
Box, Gentlemen Cigars, Flor Fina, Black Man, Paper Label, Early 1900s, 8 3/4 In. 110.00
Box, Honest Long Cut Smoking & Chewing Tobacco, Paper Label, Contents, 5 x 3 x 1 In. . 165.00
Box, Honest Weight Tobacco, Weyman & Bro, Cardboard, 1887, 9 x 12 x 5 In. 248.00
Box, Key West Cigars, None Genuine Except, Fact 2076, Contents, 8 In. 295.00
Box, Little Abe Cigar, Black Child, Rooster, Wood, 1901, 6 3/4 x 8 x 1 3/8 In. 330.00
Box, Lucky-Lindy Cigars, Lindy's Plane, Wood, 8 3/8 x 9 x 5 3/4 In. 121.00
Box, Marbles Knuckles Cigars, Wood, Kid Shooting Marbles, 7 1/2 x 9 x 5 1/4 In. 605.00
Box, Montana Sport Cigar, Puritanos, 1941, 7 1/2 x 5 1/2 x 3 1/2 In. 55.00
Box, Original Orphan Boy Smoking Tobacco, Donkey, 7 1/2 x 4 1/2 x 2 1/2 In. 11.00
Box, Patterson's Tuxedo Tobacco, Humidor, Glass, Paper Label, 3-Sided, 1918, 7 x 6 In. . 303.00
Box, Patterson's Tuxedo Tobacco, Humidor, Glass, Paper Label, 3-Sided, 4 1/2 x 5 In. . . . 275.00
Box, Pittsburg's Finest Cigar, 2 For 5 Cents, Policeman, Wood, 10 7/8 x 7 5/8 x 7 In. 303.00
Box, Puritanos, Buffalo Bill Cody, 6 Cent, 5 1/2 x 9 In. 215.00
Box, Rocky Ford Cigar, 5 x 9 In. 11.00
Box, Silver Queen Cigar, Lady, Silver Dollars, Wood, 5 5/8 x 8 x 4 In. 66.00
Box, Sunset Trail Cigar, Metal & Glass Cover, 9 x 5 1/2 x 5 In. 385.00
Box, Sweet Cuba Fine Cut, 5 Cents, Lift Lid, Scalloped Edges, Knob Handle, 9 1/2 x 8 In. 345.00
Box, Tennyson, Cigars, Humidor, Glass Lift Lid, 13 x 9 1/2 In. 220.00
Box, Volunteer Cigars, Woman Firefighter, Wood, c.1901, 8 1/4 x 6 3/4 x 5 1/2 In. 308.00
Box, War Heroes Cigar, American Soldier, Sailor, 9 x 8 5/8 x 5 In. 77.00
Box, Yellow Cab Cigar, Takes The Right Of Way, 5 1/2 x 9 In. 119.00
Button, High Admiral Tobacco, It's Naughty But It's Nice, Celluloid, Pinback 35.00
Button, Tokio Cigarettes, Blind-I Can't See You, Blue, White, 3/4 In. 36.00
Cabinet, HMS Virginia, Sincola, Zulma, 6 Drawers, England, 25 3/4 x 19 x 5 1/2 In. 378.00
Cabinet, Mitchell's Tobacco, 8 Drawers, Glass Front, 8 Brands, England, 31 x 23 x 6 In. . 795.00
Can, Tiger Chewing Tobacco, Cardboard, Tin, 11 In. 55.00
Canister, Biggerhair Smoking Tobacco, Cardboard Lithograph, 7 In. 498.00
Canister, Sweet Burley Tobacco, 11 1/2 x 9 In. 160.00
Canister, Velvet Tobacco, Tin Lithograph, 8-Sided, 5 1/4 x 6 In. 60.00
Canister, Whip Tobacco, Tin Lithograph, Patterson Bros., 5 1/2 x 5 1/2 x 5 1/2 In. 275.00

Tobacco, Bin, Sure Shot Chewing Tobacco, Tin
Lithograph, Early 1920s, 8 x 15 x 10 In.

Tobacco, Bootjack, Use Musselman's Plug
Tobacco, Cast Iron, Embossed, 9 1/2 In.

Card, Playing, Virginia Slims, Women In Period Costumes, Male Joker, Gold Back 15.00
Chair, Piedmont Cigarettes, Wood, 2-Sided Porcelain Insert . . . . *Illus* 88.00
Chair, Piedmont Tobacco, Porcelain Back 248.00
Chair, Piedmont, Cigarette Of Quality, Wood, 2-Sided Porcelain Insert 220.00
Change Receiver, Parodi Cigars, Glass, Countertop, 7 1/2 x 5 1/2 In. 77.00
Change Receiver, Peachy Plug Tobacco, Glass, Scotten, Dillon Co., Countertop, 8 x 7 In. . 465.00
Change Receiver, Raleigh Cigars, Glass, Countertop, 7 1/2 x 7 1/2 In. 88.00
Change Receiver, Raleigh's Cigarette, Glass, Wood, Cigarette Pack, Brunhoff 88.00
Change Receiver, Red Dot Cigars, Glass, Slanted 1 1/2 To 2 1/4 In. 95.00
Change Receiver, Seminola 5 Cent Cigar, Indian Princess, Felt, 11 x 13 In. 230.00
Change Receiver, Swan Vestas, Smokers Match, Glass, 6 x 6 x 1 3/4 In. 143.00
Charger, Bull Durham Smoking Tobacco, Tin Lithograph, Shadowbox Frame, 38 x 36 In. 2310.00
Charger, Bull Durham Smoking Tobacco, Woman, Bull, Packages, Round, 24 In. 7150.00
Charger, Bull Durham, Woman, Bull, Tin Lithograph, Frame, 23 In. 2260.00
Charger, Lord Macaulay, 10 Cent Cigar, Tin Lithograph, 24 In. 237.00
Charm, Car, Shamrock On Door, Roi-Tan Cigars, Gold Tone Metal, 1 1/2 In. 10.00
Cigar Band, Hans Wagner, Proof 1840.00
Cigar Cutter, Betsy Ross 5 Cent Cigars, Cast Iron, Lever, c.1890, 9 In. . . . . .500.00 to 715.00
Cigar Cutter, Betsy Ross, Cast Iron, Embossed Letters, Patriotic Message, 8 x 6 In. 880.00
Cigar Cutter, Brooks & Co., Tebson, Metal, Embossed, Glass Plate, Lithograph, 5 In. . . . 593.00
Cigar Cutter, Brown's Mule Cigar, Cast Iron, Embossed Letters, 7 x 18 In. 50.00
Cigar Cutter, Chatfield's Roofing, Dachshund Shape, Cast Iron, 3 3/4 x 7 In. 550.00
Cigar Cutter, Col. J.J. Astor, 5 Cent Cigar, Cast Iron, Clock, Footed Base, 14 x 8 In. 3300.00
Cigar Cutter, El Sidelo Cigars, Reverse On Glass, Frame, 21 x 15 In. 220.00
Cigar Cutter, El Tino 5 Cent Cigar, Reverse Glass, Oak, Clockwork, c.1880, 9 x 5 In. . . . 578.00
Cigar Cutter, Flor Dey Melba, Cast Iron, 6 x 3 1/2 In. 303.00
Cigar Cutter, Havana Cigars, Cast Iron, c.1880 . . . . 715.00
Cigar Cutter, Hoffman House Bouquet Cigar, Iron, Wood Base, Erie Specialty, c.1890 . . . 440.00
Cigar Cutter, Krank Havana Cigars, Pig, Cast Iron, c.1900, 7 In. 431.00
Cigar Cutter, Las Amantes, Classical Couple, Glass Top, Wood Base, 7 x 8 1/2 x 5 In. . . . 468.00
Cigar Cutter, Lillian Russell, Cigar, 5 Cents, Cast Iron, Footed, 2 Handles, 8 x 4 x 6 In. . . 413.00
Cigar Cutter, Piper Heidsieck Cigars, Cast Iron, Bottle Shape, Lever Action, 12 x 4 In. . . . 748.00
Cigar Cutter, Rigby, Wm. Penn, 10 Cent, King Of Havana, Countertop, 9 In. 550.00
Cigar Cutter, Roi-Tan Cigars, Metal, Countertop, c.1900, 8 In. 825.00
Cigar Cutter, Roxboro Cigars, Blue, White, Nickel Plated, 8 x 6 In. 633.00
Cigar Cutter, Scup, Fish, Cutter & Match Dispenser Combination, Cast Iron, 14 x 6 In. . . 2090.00
Cigar Cutter, Spearhead Tobacco, Cast Iron, c.1890 . . . . 143.00
Cigar Cutter, Star Tobacco, Cast Iron, Embossed, 7 x 18 In. 99.00
Cigar Dicer, Sunshine Cigar, Crazy Dice, Brunhoff, c.1890 . . . . 3080.00
Clock, Josada, 10 Cent Cigars, Cast Metal, Footed, Cigar Cutter, 14 In. 990.00
Clock, Mexican Cigars, Matador, Bull, Iron, Hectermann, Louisville, 1880, 14 x 19 In. . . 1485.00
Clock, Xtra Mex 3D Cigars, T.W. Allen, The Toll Gate, Applied Letters, Walnut, 18 In. . . . 715.00
Container, Bigger Hair Tobacco, Cardboard Lithograph, 6 3/4 In. 136.00
Cutter, John F. Kelly Wholesale Grocer, Cast Iron, Davenport, Iowa, c.1914 . . . . 143.00
Cutter, Miller-DuBrul & Peters, Wood, Metal, 7 In. 95.00
Cutter, Smoke McApins Puff, Cast Iron, Chew Chocolate Cream Plug, 13 In. 173.00
Cutter, Star Tobacco 55.00

Tobacco, Chair,
Piedmont
Cigarettes, Wood,
2-Sided Porcelain
Insert

Tobacco, Door Push,
Chesterfield
Cigarettes, Blue
Ground, Porcelain,
9 1/8 x 4 In.

Tobacco, Door
Push, Duke's
Mixture, Roll Of
Fame, Porcelain,
8 5/8 x 4 1/4 In.

Dispenser, Duke's Mixture, Smoking Tobacco Packs, Contents, 23 In. 2200.00
Dispenser, Right Cut Chewing Tobacco, The Good Judge Recommends 248.00
Display Box, Stag Smoking Tobacco, Everlastingly Good, 17 x 14 x 4 In. 770.00
Display Box, Sweet Mist Chewing Tobacco, Children, Fountain, Cardboard, 10 x 8 x 6 In. 135.00
Display Box, Tiger Chewing Tobacco, 5 Cent Packages, Blue Ground, Tin, Square, 11 In. . 990.00
Display Box, Tiger Chewing Tobacco, 5 Cent Packages, Red, Tin, Cylindrical, 12 x 8 In. . 440.00
Display Box, Union Leader, Uncle Sam, Cut Plug, Smoke Or Chew, 12 x 9 1/2 x 7 In. . . . 880.00
Display Box, Union Workman Scrap Tobacco, Cardboard, Scotten-Dillon, Detroit, 16 In. . 110.00
Display Case, Tennyson Cigars, Humidor, Countertop, 13 x 9 1/2 In. 220.00
Display Case, Tennyson, Humidor, Tin Lithograph, Countertop, 16 In. 187.00
Display Rack, Bull Dog Cut Plug, Won't Bite, Straight Leaf, Bulldog, Green Holder 588.00
Display Rack, Chancellor, Mild Cigars, 5 Box Holders, Tin, Die Cut, 34 x 40 In. 5500.00
Display Rack, King Oscar Cigar, Broom Holder, Tin, 2-Sided, 3 Brooms, 62 In. 2655.00
Door Push, Bagley's Buckingham Cut Plug Tobacco, Aluminum, 5 x 3 In. 182.00
Door Push, Buttercup Snuff, Push, Pull, 8 1/2 x 3 1/2 In, Pair 358.00
Door Push, Chesterfield Cigarettes, Blue Ground, Porcelain, 9 1/8 x 4 In. . . . . *Illus* 413.00
Door Push, Copenhagen Snuff, Here, It's A Pleasure, Celluloid Over Metal, 8 1/4 x 3 In. . 121.00
Door Push, Copenhagen Tobacco, Best Chew Ever Made, Tin 220.00
Door Push, Domino Cigarette, America's Best Brand, Welcome, Package, 14 x 4 In. 138.00
Door Push, Duke's Mixture, Roll Of Fame, Porcelain, 8 5/8 x 4 1/4 In. . . . . *Illus* 770.00
Door Push, Edgeworth Ready Rubbed Pipe Tobacco, Tin Lithograph, 14 x 4 In. . . .187.00 to 330.00
Door Push, Stag Tobacco, Stag Tin Image, Porcelain Plate, 6 1/2 x 3 7/8 In. 1760.00
Figure, Exclusive Pipe Tobaccos, Scottish Guard Holding Flag, Rubberoid, 21 1/2 In. 79.00
Flag, Nebo Cigarettes, English Flag, Silk, c.1900, 9 x 7 In. 8.00
Holder & Ashtray, Hillbilly On Toilet, Cigarette Pack In Tank, Japan, c.1960, 5 1/2 In. . . . 10.75
Humidor, Garcia Grande Cigars, Tin Lithograph, Display, 9 x 13 In. 230.00
Jar, Aristocrat Cigar, 10 Cents, Amber, Screw Lid, 1885-1900, 5 1/4 In. 364.00
Jar, Crane's Imported Cigars, Crane Sign Graphic, Contents 275.00
Jar, Globe Tobacco Co., Screw Lid, Amber, Detroit & Windsor, 1882-1900, 6 7/8 In. 560.00
Jar, Hiawatha Tobacco Works, Screw Lid, Amber, Detroit, Mich., 1885-1900, 6 3/4 In. . . . 308.00
Jar, Stork Smoking Tobacco, Amber, American Eagle Tobacco, Detroit, c.1900, 6 5/8 In. . 560.00
Lunch Box, Central Union Cut Plug, Tin Lithograph, 7 In. 79.00
Lunch Box, Central Union Cut Plug, Tin, Wire Bail Handle, 7 1/2 In. 77.00
Lunch Box, Dan Patch Tobacco, Handles, 4 1/2 x 7 x 4 1/4 In. 88.00
Lunch Box, Dixie Kid Cut Plug, Nall & Williams, 5 1/4 x 8 x 4 3/4 In. 982.00
Lunch Box, Dixie Queen Cut Plug, Wire Handle, 5 x 7 3/4 x 3 1/2 In. 61.00
Lunch Box, Dixie Queen Tobacco, 3 7/8 x 7 3/4 x 5 1/4 In. 65.00
Lunch Box, Fashion Cut Plug Tobacco, Tin, Well Dressed Couple 275.00
Lunch Box, George Washington Cut Plug, Tin Lithograph, Wood Bail Handle, 7 1/2 In. *Illus* 23.00
Lunch Box, Green Turtle Cigars, Tin, 7 1/2 x 5 1/4 x 4 1/4 In. . . . . *Illus* 403.00
Lunch Box, Just Suits Cut Plug, Tin Lithograph, Wire Handle, 8 In. 77.00
Lunch Box, Laredo Burley Cut Plug Tobacco, Tin Lithograph, 4 3/8 x 7 1/4 In. 259.00
Lunch Box, Patterson Seal Tobacco 17.00
Lunch Box, Pedro Cut Plug Smoking Tobacco, Lithograph, 4 x 7 1/2 In. . . . . .55.00 to 118.00
Lunch Box, Redicut Tobacco, Tin, 7 1/2 x 8 x 3 3/4 In. 99.00
Lunch Box, Tiger Chewing Tobacco, Tin Lithograph, 2 Handles, 10 In. 44.00
Lunch Box, U.S. Marine Tobacco, Smoke Or Chew, Tin Lithograph, 4 3/4 x 7 x 4 1/2 In. . 415.00
Lunch Box, Union Leader Cut Plug, Tin Lithograph, 5 1/2 x 8 x 4 In. 22.00

Tobacco, Lunch Box, George Washington Cut Plug,
Tin Lithograph, Wood Bail Handle, 7 1/2 In.

Tobacco, Lunch Box, Green Turtle Cigars, Tin,
7 1/2 x 5 1/4 x 4 1/4 In.

Tobacco, Pail, Winner Cut Plug, Auto Race
On Both Sides, 4 x 8 In.

Tobacco, Sign, Bull
Durham, Smoking
Tobacco, Tin,
Die Cut, Flange,
28 1/2 x 19 In.

Pack, Bagpipe Chewing Tobacco, Unopened, 5 1/2 x 3 3/8 x 1 3/8 In.	140.00
Pack, Big Kick Plain Chewing Tobacco, Unopened, Scotten Dillon, 5 x 3 3/8 x 1 3/8 In.	110.00
Pack, Brownie Smoking, E.O. Eshelby Tobacco Co., 4 Oz., 4 x 5 x 1 1/2 In.	17.00 to 88.00
Pack, C & C Scrap Plain Tobacco, 4 7/8 x 3 1/4 x 1 1/2 In.	155.00
Pack, Good Bite Chewing Tobacco, Herman & Co., 4 1/2 x 3 1/4 x 1 5/8 In.	80.00
Pack, Helmar Cigarettes, Original Tax Stamp, Label, Empty, 1925-1930, 3 1/2 x 3 In.	37.00
Pack, Home Comfort Tobacco, Myers-Cox Co., Unopened, 4 1/2 x 3 x 1 In.	125.00
Pack, Landmark Cut Plug Smoking, Windmill, Paper, Tax Stamp, Unused	17.00
Pack, Master Workman Scrap Tobacco, 10 Cents, 5 1/4 x 3 1/2 x 1 3/8 In.	155.00
Pack, Northstate Cigarettes, B & W Frizo, Opened	12.00
Pack, Oceanic Cut Plug Tobacco, Scott, Dillon Co., Detroit, 4 1/2 x 2 3/4 x 1 In.	165.00
Pack, Players, Navy Cut, Magnum, 10 Cigarettes, John Player & Sons, England, 1940s	30.00
Pack, Raleigh Brand, 20 Cigarettes, Military Use Tax Stamp, World War II Era	35.00 to 40.00
Pack, Win Shag Tobacco, Folks Everywhere Like It, Unopened, 4 1/4 x 2 3/4 x 1 In.	120.00
Package, Reel Cut Plug Pipe Tobacco, Paper, Contents, Tax Stamp, 2 Oz.	5.50 to 11.00
Packing Case, Western Painted Leather, Cowboy Hat, Lariat, Cactus, 3 x 2 1/3 x 3/4 In.	18.99
Pail, Central Union Cut Plug, Tin, Red Ground, Rectangular	165.00
Pail, Cuban Star Tobacco, Spaulding & Merit, Chicago, 6 x 5 1/2 In.	28.00
Pail, La Turka, Plug Cut, Spaulding & Merrick, Liggett & Myers, 6 x 5 1/2 In.	22.00
Pail, Niggerhair Smoking Tobacco, Smoke Or Chew, Tax Stamp, 1939, 6 1/2 x 5 In.	440.00
Pail, Penn's Tobacco, Smoke & Chew, Always The Best, 1 Lb., 6 x 5 1/2 In.	28.00
Pail, Tiger Chewing Tobacco, Red, 2 Gold Handles, 8 x 10 x 5 1/2 In.	44.00
Pail, Union Leader Milk Pail Tobacco, Tin, Bail Handle, 8 1/2 In.	50.00
Pail, Winner Cut Plug, Auto Race On Both Sides, 4 x 8 In. *Illus*	374.00
Pail, Winner Cut Plug, Smoke & Chew, Tin	825.00
Paperweight, John W. Merriam & Co. Segars, Bulldog, Figural, Metal, 4 x 2 x 3 In.	137.00
Postcard, Bull Durham, Alaskan Miner Finds A Treat, 1913, 5 1/2 x 3 1/4 In.	121.00
Postcard, Spain, Bull Durham's Trip Around The World Series, Bullfighter, Bull	40.00
Poster, Allen & Ginter, Richmond Cigarettes, State Flags, Frame, 1888, 21 3/4 x 15 In.	460.00
Poster, Climax Tobacco, Representatives Of Pro Baseball, Mat, Frame, 1884, 26 x 32 In.	7475.00
Poster, Colonial Club 5 Cent Cigar, Lady, Yellow Hat, 23 x 17 In.	880.00
Poster, Sir Walter Raleigh Smoking Tobacco, New Frame, 19 x 13 In.	90.00
Poster, Tom Hood 5 Cents Cigar, Woman Leaning On Man, 1915, 20 x 15 In.	880.00
Pouch, Bride Rose Cut Plug Tobacco Mixture, Cloth, 4 x 2 1/2 x 1 1/2 In.	135.00
Pouch, George Washington Greatest American Cut Plug, Cloth, 4 1/4 x 4 x 1 1/8 In.	130.00
Pouch, None Such, Celebrated, Fine Cut Cavendish, Silver Foil, 3 1/2 x 2 In.	30.00
Pouch, Trout Line Smoking Tobacco, Cloth, Paper Label, Contents, 1902, 2 7/8 x 2 7/8 In.	363.00
Rolling Machine, Pocono Papers, Brown & Williamson, 6 3/8 x 3 x 2 1/2 In.	35.00
Rolling Papers, Army & Navy, 100 Leaves, Liggett & Myers., No. 500, Cardboard	5.50
Rolling Papers, Bull Durham, 100 Cigarette Papers, American Brands, New York	13.20
Rolling Papers, Model Smoking Tobacco, M-M-M! Model!, Cigar Store Figure	33.00
Rolling Papers, Tango Cigarette Paper, Couple Dancing Tango, Max Spiegal, New York	43.00
Rolling Papers, Top, 25 Gummed Cigarette Papers, Red, White & Blue Top	15.40
Rolling Papers, Velvet, Smoothest, Smoking Tobacco, Pipe, Red Ground	12.10
Rolling Papers, Wheat Straw Cigarette Paper, Only Genuine, Cardboard	6.60
Salt & Pepper, Cigarette Pack & Matches, Yenems Cigarettes, 1950s, 3 3/4 & 2 7/8 In.	24.00
Scoreboard, Piedmont Cigarettes, Tin Lithograph, Wood Frame, c.1920, 24 x 36 In.	309.00
Sign, 3 Cent Cigars, Ask For Fame & Fortune, Cardboard, Frame, 7 1/2 x 13 1/2 In.	62.00

Sign, 3 Feathers Tobacco, Hanger, Cardboard, Die Cut, 2-Sided, 15 In. 440.00
Sign, 7-20-4 Cigar, Porcelain, 12 x 30 In. 440.00
Sign, Abe Martin Cigars, Seasonal Scenes, Embossed, Celluloid Over Tin, 6 x 9 In. 121.00
Sign, Allen Tobacco Co., Elephant, Printer's Proof Lithograph, Frame, 25 x 30 In. 220.00
Sign, Anchor Automatic Tobacco Curer, Save Time & Money, Tin, 18 x 30 In. 50.00
Sign, Auto City, 5 Cent Cigar, Queen Bee Cigar Co., Reverse Glass, Oval, 9 x 13 In. . . . 7150.00
Sign, Bagdad Short Cut Smoking, Red, White, Porcelain, 7 x 18 In. 94.00
Sign, Bank Note Cigars, 5 Cent, 2 Men, Box, Easel Back, Cardboard, 21 x 14 In. 253.00
Sign, Bank Note Cigars, 5 Cent, 2 Men, Box, Frame, 22 x 30 In. 358.00
Sign, Bank Note Cigars, 5 Cent, Cardboard, Easel, Countertop, 13 1/2 x 21 1/2 In. 88.00
Sign, Baxter's Cigars, 5 Cents, Cigar Beats All, Metal, 13 1/2 x 9 1/2 In. 38.00
Sign, Bevering's Best 5 Cents Cigar, Lady Of Quality, Pregnant Woman, Tin, 19 x 13 In. . 330.00
Sign, Big 5 Cigars-Golden Veil, Frame, 16 1/2 x 21 In. 275.00
Sign, Bill Dugan 5 Cents Cigar, Gentleman, Tin, Clover Shape, 8 x 8 1/2 In. 468.00
Sign, Blackstone Cigar, Porcelain, Blue Ground, 3 x 24 In. 385.00
Sign, Blackstone Cigar, Waitt & Bond, Porcelain, 12 x 36 In. 99.00
Sign, Blue Ribbon, Ok'd By Millions, Mild Cigars, Cardboard Lithograph, 17 x 30 In. . . . 55.00
Sign, Booster Cigars, Black Man, Lady Pulling Stocking, Paperboard, c.1910, 24 x 16 In. . 605.00
Sign, Boston Club Cigars & Tobacco, Boston Base Ball Club, 1889, 20 x 24 In. 4500.00
Sign, Buck, Cigar 5 Cents, Yellow, Black, Metal, Wood Frame, 12 1/4 x 48 In. 1265.00
Sign, Buckingham Bros., Fine Cigars, Mirror, Concave Circles, Baltimore, Round, 12 In. . 715.00
Sign, Buckingham Swope, Fine Cigars, Round, Mirror Back, Concave Circles, 11 In. 220.00
Sign, Buffalo Cigars, Gentleman's Smoke, Cents, Die Cut, Cardboard, 5 x 6 In. 495.00
Sign, Bull Durham Smoking Tobacco, For 3 Generations, Paper, Frame, 24 x 29 In. 990.00
Sign, Bull Durham Smoking Tobacco, Matador, Bull, Lithograph, Frame, 23 x 35 In. 688.00
Sign, Bull Durham Tobacco, Bull, Sunset, Frame, 25 x 18 In. 500.00
Sign, Bull Durham Tobacco, Without A Match, Lithograph Paperboard, 1890s, 25 x 17 In. 950.00
Sign, Bull Durham, 1 Oz. Bag, 5 Cents, Bull, Tin Lithograph, Frame, 12 x 9 In. 715.00
Sign, Bull Durham, Smoking Tobacco, Tin, Die Cut, Flange, 28 1/2 x 19 In. . . . . *Illus* 16500.00
Sign, Bully Plug Chewing Tobacco, Soldier, Bulldog, Paper, Frame, 24 3/4 x 18 3/4 In. . . 990.00
Sign, Camel Cigarettes, Die Cut, Cardboard, 1920s, 48 x 60 In. 2640.00
Sign, Camel Cigarettes, Joe Camel, Neon, 24 x 22 In. 275.00
Sign, Camel Cigarettes, So Mild, So Good, Paper, 32 x 42 In. 28.00
Sign, Camels, Sold Here, Need Cigarettes, Yellow, Red Letters, Tin, Embossed, 14 x 22 In. 22.00
Sign, Canadian Club, 5 Cent Cigar, 3 Men, Cigar Box, Frame, 14 x 19 In. 308.00
Sign, Canadian Club, 5 Cent Cigar, Different From All Others, Frame 55.00
Sign, Castle Hall, Twin Cigars, New Arrivals, Stork, Paper Lithograph, 10 x 12 In. 121.00
Sign, Caswell Cigar Club, Wood, Fox Hunters, Hounds, Joxyl, 11 1/2 x 15 1/2 In. 275.00
Sign, Chancellor Cigar, King Of Quality, Paper, Lithograph, c.1910, 41 x 25 In. 354.00
Sign, Chesterfield Cigarettes, 21/20, They Satisfy, Red, Yellow, Tin, 17 3/4 x 23 3/4 In. . . 55.00
Sign, Chesterfield Cigarettes, Best For You, Black, Red, Yellow, Tin, 12 x 34 In. 39.00
Sign, Chesterfield Cigarettes, Big Clean Taste Of Top-Tobacco, Tin, 34 x 12 In. 55.00
Sign, Chesterfield Cigarettes, Big Clean Taste Of Top-Tobacco, Tin, Embossed, 19 x 29 In. 66.00
Sign, Chesterfield Cigarettes, Buy Chesterfield Here, Tin, 18 x 12 In. 44.00
Sign, Chesterfield Cigarettes, Tastes Great, Tin, Liggett & Myers Tob. Co., 19 1/2 x 24 In. 55.00
Sign, Chesterfield, Buy Here, Regular & King Size, Die Cut, Metal, 2-Sided, 16 x 11 In. . 55.00
Sign, Chew Old Honesty Plug Tobacco, Dog, Yellow, Cloth, 17 3/4 x 50 1/2 In. 495.00
Sign, Chew Polar Bear, Blue Ground, Porcelain, 5 x 8 In. 385.00
Sign, Cigars, Cigar Shape, Lighted, Metal, Glass Lights, Hanger, 60 In. 5775.00
Sign, Cinco Cigars, 5 Cent, Eisenlohr's, Frame, 33 x 47 In. 385.00
Sign, Cinco Cigars, Eisenlohr's, Acme Can Co., Philadelphia, Tin, Frame, 23 x 13 In. 66.00
Sign, Cinco Cigars, Eisenlohr's, Wood, Frame, 48 1/2 x 12 1/2 In. 825.00
Sign, Climax Plug Tobacco, Grand Old Chew, Porcelain, Square, 15 x 15 In. 143.00
Sign, Colonial Club 5 Cent Cigars, 2-Sided, Metal, Flange, 18 1/2 x 9 In. 220.00
Sign, Colonial Club 5 Cent Cigars, Victorian Lady, Lithograph, Frame, 27 x 32 In. 990.00
Sign, Copenhagen, Best Chew Ever Made, Tin, Wall Mount, 14 1/2 x 3 In. 99.00
Sign, Cranes Little Beveridge Cigars, 5 Cents, 14 x 6 In. 52.00
Sign, Cressmans Counsellor 5 Cent Cigar, Girl, Roses, Lithograph, Frame, 20 x 26 In. . . . 550.00
Sign, Cruwell-Tobak, Indian, Smoking Pipe, Tin, Germany, 9 3/8 x 14 1/4 In. 50.00
Sign, Days Work Chewing Tobacco, A Grand Chew, Paper, 1949, 13 3/4 x 19 In. 65.00
Sign, Deacon's Plug Tobacco, Horses, Wagons, C.H. Carruth, Boston, 17 x 23 In. 2090.00
Sign, Dental Sweet Snuff, Tin Lithograph, Embossed, 2-Sided, 6 1/8 x 27 In. 140.00
Sign, Derby Smoking Tobacco, Cardboard, Embossed, Felgner & Son, Frame, 27 x 22 In. 3080.00

Sign, Devilish Good Cigar, 5 Cents, Tin, Embossed, Hanger, 10 x 14 In. . . . . *Illus* 660.00
Sign, Dilbert Bros. & Co. Cigars, Hand Made, Paper Lithograph On Tin, 10 x 14 In. 495.00
Sign, Dolly Madison Cigar, Tin, Embossed, 5 1/2 x 20 In. 605.00
Sign, Drummond Tobacco, Victorian Woman, Paper Lithograph, 29 x 35 In. 275.00
Sign, Duke Of Parma Cigar, Central Label, Cardboard, Frame, 9 1/2 x 12 3/4 In. 30.00
Sign, Duke's Mixture Tobacco, Runaway Wagon, Black Men, Cardboard, 15 x 18 3/4 In. . . 468.00
Sign, Duke's Mixture, Quality Tobacco, Porcelain, Enamel, Flange, 11 x 14 1/8 In. 5060.00
Sign, Duke's Mixture, Roll Of Fame, Porcelain, Blue Ground, 8 1/2 x 5 1/2 In. . . . .825.00 to 990.00
Sign, Durham Smoking Tobacco, Man, Die Cut, Cardboard, c.1900, 13 x 6 1/2 In. 83.00
Sign, Durham Tobacco, 5 Cents, New Size, Bull's Head, Cardboard, 2-Sided, 12 x 11 In. . . 825.00
Sign, Durham Tobacco, Black Man Holds Package, Die Cut, Cardboard, Frame, 10 x 7 In. . 413.00
Sign, Durham Tobacco, Man Sitting, Cardboard, Die Cut, c.1910, 6 1/2 x 13 In. 575.00
Sign, Dutch Masters Cigars, 6 Men, Canvas Lithograph, Wood Frame, 22 x 30 In. 505.00
Sign, Edgeworth Smoking Tobacco, 2 Men, Tin, Embossed, 13 x 28 In. 440.00
Sign, Edgeworth Smoking Tobacco, Die Cut, Cardboard, Easel Back, 9 x 7 5/8 In. 195.00
Sign, Edgeworth Smoking Tobacco, Tin Lithograph, Embossed, 27 x 12 In. 382.00
Sign, Edgeworth Tobacco, Metal Over Cardboard, 9 1/4 x 13 1/4 In. 475.00
Sign, Egyptian Luxury Cigarettes, Convincingly Mild, Lady, Hat, Frame, 25 x 33 In. 330.00
Sign, El Paterno Cigar, 10 Cents, Flange, 2-Sided, Tin Lithograph, 13 1/2 x 18 1/2 In. 825.00
Sign, El Principal Cigars, The Taste Pleases, It Really Does, Cardboard, Easel, 17 x 30 In. . 92.00
Sign, El Principe De Gales, Havana Cigarettes, 13 1/2 x 9 3/4 In. 495.00
Sign, Elbeporo!, Cigars!, Die Cut, Cardboard, 13 x 21 In. 28.00
Sign, Emilia Garcia Cigars, Man Smoking, Die Cut, Cardboard, 3 Panels, 43 x 31 In. 242.00
Sign, Energos Cigars, Man, Oxen, Reverse On Glass, 17 x 24 In. 578.00
Sign, F. Lozano Cigars, Reverse Paint, Glass, Denzi & Philips, New York, 14 x 10 In. 1760.00
Sign, F.F. Adams & Co., Standard, Milwaukee, Yellow Pack, Cloth, Frame, 47 x 32 In. . . . 220.00
Sign, Fame & Fortune 3 Cent Cigars, Tin, A.K. Walch, Phila., Pa., Tin, 8 x 14 In. 275.00
Sign, Fatima Cigarettes, Lady With Cigarette, Die Cut, Cardboard, Easel, c.1940, 16 In. . . 47.00
Sign, First Cabinet Cigars, Washington's Cabinet, Embossed, Celluloid, Tin, 8 x 10 In. . . . 176.00
Sign, Frank Boskowitz Cigars, Lady, Flowers, Die Cut, Embossed, Cardboard, 16 x 12 In. . 232.00
Sign, Gail & Ax Navy Tobacco, Sailor, Cardboard, Frame, 40 1/2 x 31 1/2 In. 468.00
Sign, Gold Flake Cigarettes, Porcelain, 2-Sided, 18 x 14 In. 132.00
Sign, Golden Belle Cigars, Girl, Embossed, Beveled Celluloid Over Tin, 7 x 10 In. 176.00
Sign, Good Old B-L Tobacco, Porcelain, Heavy Gauge, c.1930, 18 x 18 In. 325.00
Sign, Granger Pipe Tobacco, Aviator, Smiling, Smoking Pipe, Cardboard, 11 x 15 In. 32.00
Sign, Granger Pipe Tobacco, Joe Hiestand, 1920, 14 x 20 In. 55.00
Sign, Grauley's Lord Caspar, 5 Cents Cigar, Tin Lithograph, Flange, 2-Sided, 18 In. 320.00
Sign, Grauley's Orange Flower, 5 Cents Cigar, Tin Lithograph, Flange, 2-Sided, 18 In. . . . 266.00
Sign, Habanas Cigar, Product Of Cuba, Tin, Die Cut Cigar, 29 In. 825.00
Sign, Harvester Cigar, Woman, Hat, Tin Lithograph, Convex, Oval, Self-Framed, 13 x 9 In. 220.00
Sign, Hav-A-Tampa Cigar, For Good Taste, 1955, 15 x 24 In. 85.00
Sign, Helmar Turkish Cigarettes, Porcelain, Round, 8 In. 160.00
Sign, Hi-Plane Tobacco, 10 Cent, For Pipe & Cigarettes, Tin, Embossed, 35 x 11 In. 138.00
Sign, Hi-Plane Tobacco, 10 Cent, Green Ground, Tin, Embossed, Self-Framed, 12 x 35 In. . 198.00
Sign, Hoffman House Bouquet, Cigar, Man, Top Hat, Lithograph, Frame, 9 1/2 x 9 In. 61.00
Sign, Hoffman House Cigars, Children, Naked Child, Cardboard, c.1900, 15 x 10 1/2 In. . 440.00
Sign, Hoffman House Cigars, Satyr, 4 Nymphs, Embossed, c.1896, 15 1/4 x 11 1/2 In. . . . 209.00
Sign, Hoffmanettes 5 Cent Cigar, Cardboard, Wood Frame, c.1900, 15 x 21 1/2 In. .350.00 to 425.00
Sign, Homestake 5 Cent Cigar, Americas Greatest, Reverse On Glass, Oval, 10 x 14 In. . . . 495.00
Sign, Honest Scrap Tobacco, Arm, Hammer, Red, White Letters, Porcelain, 12 x 9 In. 1540.00
Sign, Honest Scrap Tobacco, Cat, Dog, Paperboard, Frame, 32 x 24 In. 935.00
Sign, Honest Scrap, Arm, Holding Hammer, Red Ground, White, Porcelain, 12 x 9 In. . . . 578.00
Sign, Honest Scrap, Dog & Cat Fighting, Cardboard, Frame, 22 x 30 In. . . . . .770.00 to 880.00
Sign, Honest Weight Tobacco, Weyman & Bro. Mfg., Paper, Frame, 19 1/2 x 24 In. 660.00
Sign, Horse Shoe Tobacco, Finest Quality 10 Cent, Cardboard, 21 x 11 In. 77.00
Sign, Imperial Club 5 Cent Cigar, Tin Lithograph, Embossed, Hanger, 14 x 10 In. .149.00 to 330.00
Sign, Imperial Tobacco Co., Ringers Virginia Returns, Indian, Celluloid, 8 x 5 1/2 In. 55.00
Sign, Imperiales Cigarettes, Man In White Top Hat, Porcelain, Flange, c.1900, 14 x 21 In. 248.00
Sign, J.G. Dill's Tobacco, Die Cut, Cardboard, Richmond, Va., Frame, 11 1/2 x 7 In. 165.00
Sign, J.P. Alley's Hambone Cigar, 5 Cent, Cardboard Lithograph, 2-Sided, Hanger, 7 In. . . 192.00
Sign, Jim Hogg 5 Cent Cigars, James Stephen Hogg, Frame, 10 x 21 In. 193.00
Sign, John Ruskin Cigar, Best & Biggest, Tin, Embossed, 9 1/2 x 29 1/2 In. . . . . . . .99.00 to 248.00
Sign, Just Suits Cut Plug, Porcelain, 3 1/2 x 21 In. 605.00

Sign, JXA Cigars, Crossed Cigars, Hand Made, They Suit, Cardboard, Die Cut, 17 x 29 In. 58.00
Sign, Kick Plate, Sir Walter Raleigh, Smoking Tobacco, Ship, Porcelain, c.1930, 1 x 3 In. . 1450.00
Sign, Kildow's Old Stock Cigar, Paper, Cleveland, Ohio, 7 1/4 x 14 In. 25.00
Sign, King Edward Cigars, Man, Woman At Picnic, Cardboard, Rounded Top, 23 In. 154.00
Sign, Kyra Cigar, Chicago Herald Twentieth Year, 2-Sided, Cardboard, 5 3/8 Diam. 25.00
Sign, L & M Cigarettes, Filters, More Flavor, Less Nicotine, Tin, 22 x 18 In. 50.00
Sign, L & M Cigarettes, James Arness, Reach For Flavor, 25 x 8 1/2 In. .... *Illus* 250.00
Sign, L & M Cigarettes, Live Modern, Smoke Modern, Tin, 17 1/2 x 12 In. 33.00
Sign, La Fendrich Habana Cigars, Oval, Swivels, 10 x 10 In. 330.00
Sign, La Flor De Ampere, Broadleaf Cigars, Cardboard, 29 1/2 x 23 In. 358.00
Sign, La Flor De Carvalho Havana Cigars, Tin, Frame, 15 x 21 In. 176.00
Sign, La Flor De Erb Cigar, Bearded Man, Tin, Embossed, c.1900, 6 1/8 x 13 1/2 In. 56.00 to 132.00
Sign, La Flor De Erb, 10 Cents Cigar, D.S. Erb & Co. Makers, 6 1/4 x 13 1/2 In. 182.00
Sign, La Mia Cigars, Woman, Fan, Embossed, Beveled Celluloid Over Tin, 7 x 10 In. 176.00
Sign, La Preferencia Cigars, Man Smoking In Library, Frame, 12 1/2 x 9 In. 170.00
Sign, La Preferencia Cigars, Victorian Woman, Red Dress, Lithograph, Frame, 25 x 36 In. 1650.00
Sign, La Venga Cigars, Reverse On Glass, Frame, 27 x 21 In. 580.00
Sign, Lawrence Barrett Cigar, 10 & 15 Cents, Porcelain, 32 x 42 In. 303.00
Sign, Lawrence Barrett Cigar, Mild Havana, 10 Cents, Porcelain, 31 1/2 x 21 In. 220.00
Sign, Lawrence Barrett Cigar, Multicolored, Porcelain, Enameled, 34 1/4 x 20 In. 2750.00
Sign, Lord Digby 10 Cents Cigar, We Sell, Glass, 8 x 9 1/2 In. 39.00
Sign, Maestro, Man In Tuxedo Smoking, Cardboard, Die Cut, Easel, 17 x 14 1/2 In. . .61.00 to 66.00
Sign, Marvels Cigarettes, Cigarette Pack, Tin Lithograph, Beveled Edge, 19 x 14 In. 80.00
Sign, Matinee Cigars, Victorian Lady, In Hat, Frame, c.1880, 20 x 24 In. 418.00
Sign, Merry Prince 5 Cent Cigar, Reverse On Glass, 6 x 16 In. 242.00
Sign, Missing Miss Cigar, Woman, Rolled Edge, Tin Lithograph, 1908, 14 1/2 x 14 1/2 In. 1017.00
Sign, Model Smoking Tobacco, Sheet Steel Lithograph, 34 In. 143.00
Sign, Model Smoking Tobacco, Tin, 5 3/4 x 15 In. 235.00
Sign, Model Smoking Tobacco, Yes, I Said, Man Smoking, Mustache, Porcelain, 12 x 36 In. 88.00
Sign, Model Tobacco, Cigar Store Figure Holds Package, Tin, 15 x 5 3/4 In. 121.00
Sign, Murad, Turkish Cigarette, Man, On Horse, Print, Frame, 28 x 42 In. 358.00
Sign, Murad, Turkish Cigarette, Santa Carrying Large Package, 15 x 10 In. 165.00
Sign, Navy Scotch Snuff, Tin, Embossed, Blue, White, 18 x 12 In. 83.00
Sign, Nebo Cigarettes, Cork Tip, 1 Calls For 2, Tin Lithograph, Die Cut, 15 x 13 3/8 In. .. 523.00
Sign, Newsboy Plug Tobacco, Paper, Frame, c.1890, 32 x 41 In. 578.00
Sign, Nickel King Cigars, Fiberboard, Embossed, 6 x 18 In. 39.00
Sign, O'san Cigars, Cigar Of Smiles, Yellow, Black, Tin, Embossed, 28 x 10 In. 99.00
Sign, Ogden's Robin Cigarettes, Brick Wall Ground, Enamel, Square, England, 21 In. 151.00
Sign, Old English, Curve Cut Pipe Tobacco, Man Smoking Pipe, Paper, Frame, 23 x 27 In. 275.00
Sign, Old Gold Cigarettes, Cardboard, 3 Panels, Die Cut, 38 x 51 In. 132.00
Sign, Old Gold Cigarettes, Die Cut, Lithograph, 28 x 39 In. 358.00
Sign, Old Hundred Cigars, W.H.I. Hayes, Cardboard, 18 1/2 x 6 In. 99.00
Sign, Old Virginia Cheroots, Girl, Dress, Cardboard, Frame, c.1890s, 10 x 6 In. . . .110.00 to 121.00
Sign, Old Virginia Cheroots, Girl, Red Vest, Cardboard, Frame, c.1890s, 10 x 6 In. . .66.00 to 143.00
Sign, Old Virginia Cheroots, Girl, White Boa, Cardboard, Frame, c.1890s, 10 x 6 In. 181.00
Sign, Old Virginia Cheroots, Mildest & Best, Paper, Metal Strips, Frame, 21 In. 763.00

Tobacco, Sign, Devilish Good Cigar, 5 Cents, Tin,
Embossed, Hanger, 10 x 14 In.

Tobacco, Sign, L & M
Cigarettes, James
Arness, Reach For
Flavor, 25 x 8 1/2 In.

Sign, Old Virginia Tobacco, Girl, Holds Fan, Cardboard, Frame, 14 1/2 x 10 1/2 In. 468.00
Sign, Optimates Cigars, Tin, 9 1/2 x 13 3/4 In. 176.00
Sign, Optimo Cigars, All Havana Cigars, Man, In Hat, Paper, Frame, 22 x 28 In. 143.00
Sign, Orange Flower Cigar, Nickel Cigar, Cardboard, String Hanger, 6 1/2 x 11 In. 20.00
Sign, Park Drive, Plain & Cork Tipped, Enamel, 2-Sided, England, 16 x 12 In. 104.00
Sign, Passing Show, Cork Tipped Virginia Cigarettes, Man, Top Hat, Porcelain, 16 x 9 In. . 207.00
Sign, Pastime Plug, John Finzer & Bros., Hunter, Dog, Red, Black, Tin, 9 x 12 x 4 In. ... 1925.00
Sign, Pay Car Scrap, Tobacco, You'll Like, Cardboard, Trolley Card, 11 x 14 In. 100.00
Sign, Perfection Cigarettes, 5 Cigarette Packs, Embossed, Cardboard, Oval, 12 x 17 In. ... 44.00
Sign, Perfecto Cigar, Product Of Cuba, Tin, Die Cut Cigar, 29 In. 825.00
Sign, Peter Schuyler Cigar, Get Back Of, Back Of Man's Head, Porcelain, 12 x 36 In. 303.00
Sign, Peter Schuyler Cigars, Lithograph, Frame, 15 x 25 In. 165.00
Sign, Peter Schuyler, 10 Cent Cigar, Tin, Wood, Frame, Oval, 27 In. 495.00
Sign, Philip Morris, Call For Philip Morris, Do You Inhale?, Porcelain, 3 1/2 x 22 In. 358.00
Sign, Philip Morris, Call For Philip Morris, Red, Yellow, Black, Tin, 27 x 10 In. ...110.00 to 160.00
Sign, Philip Morris, Call For, America's Finest Cigarette, Tin, Embossed, 16 x 46 In. 330.00
Sign, Philip Morris, Johnny, Cigarette, Tin, Embossed, Wood Frame, 13 x 31 In. 55.00
Sign, Philip Morris, Johnny, Die Cut, Cardboard, Easel Back, 15 x 5 1/4 In. 198.00
Sign, Piedmont Cigarette, Victorian Woman, Frame, 19 x 29 In. 468.00
Sign, Piedmont Cigarette, Washington's Return To Mt. Vernon, Frame, c.1890, 24 x 30 In. 330.00
Sign, Piedmont, Virginia Cigarette, Paper Lithograph, 9 1/2 x 19 1/2 In. 55.00
Sign, Pippins Cigar, 5 Cents, Porcelain, c.1920, 10 x 38 In. .... *Illus* 770.00
Sign, Player's Country Life, Smoking Mixture, England, Frame, 23 1/4 x 20 In. 284.00
Sign, Player's Please, Glass, Metal Frame & Bracket, 2-Sided, England, 38 x 20 In. 151.00
Sign, Player's Please, Royal Navy Sailor, HMS Excellent, c.1910, 9 x 12 In. 225.00
Sign, Player's, Cigarettes, 9 Actor & Actress Cards, Cardboard, Frame, 7 x 14 In. 75.00
Sign, Player's, Navy Cut Tobacco & Cigarettes, HMS Sailor, Red, England, 62 x 42 In. .. 946.00
Sign, Pride Of Durham Smoking Tobacco, Lion, Tin Lithograph, Frame, 14 x 20 In. 424.00
Sign, Prince Albert Cigarettes Dubec, Victorian Woman, Print, Frame, 24 x 29 In. 198.00
Sign, Prince Albert, 10 Cents, Tin, Self-Framed, 13 x 38 In. 605.00
Sign, Quail Cigars, Die Cut, Paper, 8 x 12 In. 154.00
Sign, Quail Cigars, Made In Louisville, Hand Painted, Tin, Frame, 14 x 42 In. 61.00
Sign, R.G. Sullivan's 7-20-4 Cigar, Porcelain, Flange, 2-Sided, 12 x 18 In. 440.00
Sign, Raleigh Cigarettes, Well Dressed Couple, Cardboard, Frame, 14 x 20 In. 39.00
Sign, Randolph Macon Cigars, Man, Woman, Tin Lithograph, Self-Framed, 20 x 24 In. .. 653.00
Sign, Recruit Little Cigars, Pure Tobacco, Enamel, Metal, 11 3/4 x 29 3/4 In. 1430.00
Sign, Red Dot 5 Cents Cigar, Barnes Smith Co., Bingham, N.Y., Tin, 9 x 13 In. 275.00
Sign, Red Dot Cigar, Cigar Shape, Die Cut, Cardboard, Stand-Up, 36 In. 495.00
Sign, Red Indian, 5 Cents, Must Have It, Indian, Bow & Arrow, Frame, 25 3/4 x 31 1/2 In. 1540.00
Sign, Red Man Chew Tobacco, Porcelain, 2-Sided, 59 x 22 In. 440.00
Sign, Red Man Tobacco, Johnny Mizel, Free Baseball Cap, c.1953, 11 x 15 1/2 In. ...11.00 to 28.00
Sign, Redford's Navy Mixture, Heavy Cardboard, 1900, 8 x 12 In. 75.00
Sign, Redford's Tobaccos, Men, On Plantation, Print, Frame, 21 x 27 In. 138.00
Sign, Regal Cigar, Man With Cigar, Celluloid Over Cardboard, Easel, Oval, 13 x 9 In. ... 148.00
Sign, Richmond Cigarette, Woman In Victorian Dress, Paper, Frame, 17 x 14 In. 605.00
Sign, Richmond Straight Cut Cigarettes, Woman, Cardboard Lithograph, 15 x 12 In. 468.00
Sign, Robert Burns Cigars, Paper Printer's Proof, C.W. Shonk Lithograph, 17 x 12 In. 275.00
Sign, Robert Burns, 10 Cent Cigar, Curved Glass, Enamel, Frame, Backlit, 22 x 15 In. ... 880.00
Sign, Robert Emmet Cigar, 10 Cent, No After Taste, Printers' Proof, Paper, 19 1/2 x 13 In. 110.00
Sign, Robert Mantel Cigar, Paper Printer's Proof, C.W. Shonk Lithograph, 20 1/2 x 17 In. 220.00
Sign, Roi-Tan 5 Cent Cigar, Rabicoff Drug, Reverse Painted, Gold, Frame, 84 x 45 In. ... 2420.00
Sign, Roi-Tan Cigars, An Auto A Day Is Given Away, Tin, 1939 Chevrolet Car, 3 x 3 In. ... 193.00
Sign, Romance, Havana Cigars, Tin Over Cardboard, 9 1/2 x 12 In. 110.00
Sign, Rosa De Luzon Cigars, Battle Of Chattanooga, Mat, Frame, 27 1/2 x 34 1/2 In. 187.00
Sign, Rose-O-Cuba Domestic Cigar, Roses In Vase, Die Cut, 24 In. 143.00
Sign, Rose-O-Cuba, Boy Driving Car, 5 Cent Cigar, Die Cut, Cardboard, 16 3/4 x 11 In. ... 633.00

Tobacco, Sign, Pippins
Cigar, 5 Cents, Porcelain,
c.1920, 10 x 38 In.

Sign, Rough & Ready Tobacco, Look Out, Extra Mild, Felt, Jos. G. Dill Inc., 11 x 12 In. . 605.00
Sign, Royal Bengals Cigars, Paper Lithograph, Frame, c.1920, 21 x 12 In. 75.00
Sign, Rudolph Valentino Cigars, Embossed, Beveled Celluloid Over Tin, 7 7/8 x 9 7/8 In. . 132.00
Sign, San Felice Cigars, For Gentlemen Of Good Taste, Porcelain, 40 x 13 In. 385.00
Sign, Santa Fe Cigars, They Deserve The Best, Officers, Cardboard, c.1940, 26 x 19 In. . . 121.00
Sign, Seminola Cigars, Indian Princess, Embossed, Beveled Celluloid Over Tin, 6 x 9 In. . 176.00
Sign, Sir Walter Raleigh Smoking Tobacco, Ship & Pocket Tin, Porcelain, 12 x 36 In. 1430.00
Sign, Smoke Bo-Ko Cigars, Cardboard, Metal Frame, 42 x 15 In. 99.00
Sign, Smoke Hand Made Tobacco, Unique Letters, Paper, 21 1/2 x 13 1/2 In. 1760.00
Sign, Smoke Maritana 5 Cent Cigar, 2 Babies, Lithograph Cardboard, 17 x 12 In. 345.00
Sign, Spearhead Chewing Tobacco, Hits The Spot, Porcelain, 6 x 14 In. 413.00
Sign, Spearhead, Choice Chew, Plug, Save The Tags, Tin, Embossed, 9 1/4 x 13 1/2 In. . . 660.00
Sign, Stag Smoking Tobacco, Elk, Paper Lithograph, Frame, 28 x 42 In. 468.00
Sign, Star, Tobacco, Best For 70 Years, Tin, Embossed, Red, Yellow, Black, 12 x 24 In. . . 149.00
Sign, Star, Tobacco, Best For Over 3 Generations, 10 Cent, Tin, 12 x 23 1/2 In. 165.00
Sign, Star, Tobacco, Best For Over 60 Years, Cardboard, 21 x 11 In. 71.00
Sign, Star, Tobacco, Porcelain, 24 In. 303.00
Sign, Star, Tobacco, Slab Of Tobacco, Porcelain, Yellow Ground, 12 x 24 In. 431.00
Sign, Star, Tobacco, Sold Here, Yellow Ground, Porcelain, 12 x 24 In. 88.00
Sign, Star, Tobacco, Star Logo In Center, Tin, 6 1/2 x 13 3/4 In. 150.00
Sign, Strathmore Cigars, 2 Men, Sitting A Table, Tin Lithograph, 15 x 17 In. 110.00
Sign, Stud Smoking Tobacco, Bully For Makins, Cardboard, 2-Sided, 8 x 11 In. 127.00
Sign, Sunny South Cigarettes, Victorian Lady, Cardboard, Frame, 15 x 20 In. 302.00
Sign, Sunshine Cigarettes, 20 For 15 Cents, Tin Lithograph, Embossed, 18 x 14 In. . .80.00 to 95.00
Sign, Sweet Caporal Cigarettes & Smoking Tobacco, Lady In Hat, Cardboard, 12 x 9 In. . 236.00
Sign, Sweet Caporal Cigarettes, Majorette, Tin, Wood Frame, 61 x 19 In. 3000.00
Sign, Sweet Caporal Cigarettes, Woman, Black Hat, Easel Back, Self-Framed, 12 x 9 In. . 330.00
Sign, Sweet Violet, Boy On Case, Smoking Cigar, Paper, Frame, Image 12 x 9 1/2 In. 176.00
Sign, Thoroughbreds Cigarette, Horse, Frame, 25 x 32 In. 220.00
Sign, Tiger Chewing Tobacco, Tin Lithograph, Frame, 12 1/2 x 11 1/2 In. 248.00
Sign, Tobacco Shop, Telephones, Ceiling Mount, Illuminated, 12 x 25 1/2 In. 330.00
Sign, Tom Keene Cigar, 5 Cents, Blue, White, Porcelain, 18 x 40 In. 71.00
Sign, Tom Keene Cigar, Porcelain, Curved, 15 x 13 In. 633.00
Sign, Tom Moore Cigar, Lithograph, Frame, 24 x 30 In. 440.00
Sign, Tom Moore Cigar, Piecrust Edge, Self-Framed, 15 1/2 x 11 1/4 In. 160.00
Sign, Tops Mild Scotch Snuff, 12 x 18 In. 55.00
Sign, Torchlight Cigarettes, Asian Woman, Paper Lithograph, 15 x 21 In. 50.00
Sign, Tram Tabac Naturel, 5 Cent Le Paquet, Lithograph On Cardboard, 28 x 10 In. 288.00
Sign, Turf, Top Quality Cigarettes, Winged Horse, Enamel, England, 64 1/2 x 15 In. 136.00
Sign, Tuxedo Tobacco, Joy, Frame, 15 x 10 1/4 In. 99.00
Sign, Two Friends, Cigars 5 Cents, Woman, St. Bernard, Cardboard, 2-Sided, Ceiling, 7 In. 605.00
Sign, Uncle Sam, Big Chew For 10 Cents, Uncle Sam Shape Bag, Cardboard, 6 x 17 In. . . 99.00
Sign, Union Leader Cut Plug, Uncle Sam, Cardboard, Frame, c.1899, 28 3/4 x 20 1/2 In. . 1650.00
Sign, Union Leader Tobacco, For Pipe Or Cigarette, Tin, 10 x 22 In. 165.00
Sign, Van Dam Cigars, Trifold, Paperboard, 27 x 40 In. 120.00
Sign, Velvet Pipe Tobacco, Aged In Wood, Sold Here, Porcelain, 12 x 39 In. . . . . . .176.00 to 248.00
Sign, Velvet Tobacco, 2 Men, Boy, Dog, Tin, Frame, 26 x 32 In. 2200.00
Sign, Velvet Tobacco, 2 Men, Sitting, Boy, Dog, Tin Lithograph, 22 x 28 In. 550.00
Sign, Velvet Tobacco, Victorian Woman, Dress, Feathered Hat, Paper, Frame, 17 x 31 In. . 495.00
Sign, Vicente Portuonds Cigars, Green Ground, Tin, Embossed, Self-Framed, 13 1/2 In. . . 358.00
Sign, Washington Irving Havana Cigars, Tin Lithograph, Self-Framed, 18 x 26 In. 770.00
Sign, We Sell Horse Shoe Tobacco, Porcelain, Flange, 8 x 18 In. 605.00
Sign, We Sell Star Tobacco, Blue Ground, White Letters, Porcelain, Flange, 8 x 18 In. . . . 1100.00
Sign, Wills's Bulwark Cut Plug, Horse, Rider, Sea, England, Frame, 19 1/2 x 15 1/2 In. . . 38.00
Sign, Wills's Bulwark Cut Plug, Old Sailor Smoking Pipe, England, Frame, 21 x 16 In. . . 132.00
Sign, Wills's Flag Cigarettes, Blue Ground, Enamel, England, 36 x 24 In. 378.00
Sign, Wills's Gold Flake, Sir Francis Drake, Ships, Laminated, England, 20 x 15 In. 66.00
Sign, Wills's Rich Cut Virginia Tobacco, Enamel, White Ground, England, 36 x 18 In. . . . 454.00
Sign, Wills's Woodbine Cigarettes, Green & White, Enamel, England, 36 x 18 In. 142.00
Sign, Wills's Woodbines, Green Ground, White Letters, Enamel, England, 28 x 9 In. 42.00
Sign, Winchester Blended Cigarettes, Porcelain, 18 x 30 In. 165.00
Sign, Wings Cigarettes, Union Made, 10 Cents, Frame, 1934, 13 x 19 In. 68.00
Sign, Wm. Penn 10 Cent Cigar, Celluloid Over Cardboard, 10 1/2 x 13 1/2 In. 325.00

Sign, Wm. Penn, King Of Havana, 10 Cent Cigars, Tin, Self-Framed, 14 x 9 1/2 In. 248.00
Sign, Y-B Cigars, B-Y's & Buy Y-B's, Tin, 12 x 28 In. 77.00
Sign, Yankee Girl Chewing Tobacco, Red, White, 13 1/2 x 9 1/2 In. 38.00
Sign, Yankee Girl Cigarettes, Porcelain, 7 x 20 In. 220.00
Sign, Yankee Girl Tobacco, Tin, Embossed, 6 1/2 x 20 In. 605.00
Sign, Yellow Cab Cigar, 5 Cents, Takes The Right Of Way, Tin, Embossed, 6 1/2 x 20 In. . 2090.00
Silk, Chief Black Hawk, 2 x 3 In. 68.00
Silk, Clover, Early 1900s, 3 1/4 x 2 In. 14.00
Silk, Pansy, Early 1900s, 3 1/4 x 2 In. 15.00
Thermometer, Camels, Have A Real Cigarette, Embossed Pack, 13 1/2 x 5 3/4 In. 110.00
Thermometer, Chesterfield, Big Clean Taste, Embossed Cigarette Pack, 13 x 5 3/4 In. . 110.00
Thermometer, Copenhagen Tobacco, It's A Pleasure, Tin, Embossed, 12 x 3 3/4 In. 242.00
Thermometer, Fatima, Turkish Brand Cigarettes, Porcelain, 27 x 7 In. 204.00
Thermometer, Kentucky Club Pipe Tobacco, Painted Metal, 38 1/2 x 8 In. 220.00
Thermometer, Marvels Quality Cigarettes, Tin, 12 x 3 3/4 In. 105.00
Thermometer, Piedmont, The Virginia Cigarette, Porcelain, 72 In. 2530.00
Thermometer, Silver Cup Chewing Tobacco, Red, White, Blue, Gold Trim, 39 x 8 In. ... 95.00
Tin, 2 Orphans Cigars, 5 x 5 In. 303.00
Tin, 662 Minnesota Cigar, 5 x 3 3/4 In. 70.00
Tin, Admiral Tobacco, Rough Cut, Admiral, Battleship, 6 x 4 3/4 In. 165.00
Tin, Alcazar Cigars, Horse, Stable, Round, 5 1/2 x 5 In. 2200.00
Tin, American Beauty Tobacco, Fine Mixture, Popular Smoking, 3 x 4 1/2 x 1 1/2 In. 143.00
Tin, Anstie's Brown Beauty Tobacco, Mammy, Rectangular, Lithograph, 8 1/2 In. 60.00
Tin, Apache Trail Cigar, Indian Warrior, Hinged Lid, Tin Lithograph, 5 3/4 x 6 x 4 In. ... 1815.00
Tin, Army & Navy Special Blend Cigarettes, Paper Label, 5 1/2 x 4 x 1 1/2 In. 123.00
Tin, Autobacco Tobacco, Driver Smoking Pipe, Red, Hinged Lid, 4 3/4 x 6 x 4 In. 413.00
Tin, Bagley's Old Colony Mixture Smoking Tobacco, Woman, Bonnet, Sample, 3 x 2 In. . 853.00
Tin, Bagley's Old Colony, Girl, Pocket, 4 1/4 In. 82.00
Tin, Bagley's Sweet Tip, Jno. J. Bagley & Co., Pocket, Vertical, 4 1/2 x 3 x 7/8 In. 100.00
Tin, Bagley's Wild Fruit Tobacco, 6 x 3 1/8 x 3 7/8 In. 95.00
Tin, Banquet Hall Little Cigar, M. Foster & Co., N.Y., July 24, 1897, 3 1/2 x 3 1/4 In. ... 121.00
Tin, Belfast Cut Plug Tobacco, Smoke Or Chew, Cigars United Emblem, 6 x 4 x 3 In. ... 45.00
Tin, Between The Acts Little Cigars, 3 3/8 x 3 x 1/4 In. 25.00
Tin, Big Ben Tobacco, Horse, Brown & Williamson, Pocket, Vertical, 4 1/2 x 3 x 7/8 In. .. 155.00
Tin, Biggerhair Smoking Tobacco, Cardboard, Tin Bottom, 6 1/2 x 5 In. 450.00
Tin, Bishop's Move Tobacco, Unique Blend Of Rare Quality, 2 x 3 x 1 In. 154.00
Tin, Black & White, Tin, 5 3/8 x 5 1/4 In. 121.00
Tin, Black Cat Virginia Cigarette, Paper Seal, 5 3/4 x 4 1/4 In. 22.00
Tin, Blue Jay Cigar, 25 Count, 5 Cents, Tin Lithograph, 5 3/8 x 3 5/8 x 3 5/8 In. 330.00
Tin, Boldt's Specials Cigars, 1915, 3 x 5 1/2 x 1/2 In. 44.00
Tin, Bond Of Union Smoking Mixture, Irish, Scotch, English, England, 5 x 3 1/2 In. .66.00 to 79.00
Tin, Bond Street Pipe Tobacco, 100 Year, Pocket, Vertical, 4 1/2 x 3 x 3/4 In. 45.00
Tin, Bowl Of Roses Pipe Mixture, Fleming Hall Co., New York, Unopened, 4 x 2 x 1 In. . 145.00
Tin, Bowl Of Roses Pipe Mixture, Man, Fireplace, Roses, Lithograph, Pocket, 4 x 3 In. .. 221.00
Tin, Bruton Scotch Snuff, Paper Label, Unopened, 1 3/4 x 1 1/4 In. 42.00
Tin, Buckingham Cut Plug Smoking Tobacco, 1926, 4 x 3 x 3/4 In. 187.00
Tin, Buckingham Cut Plug Smoking Tobacco, Trial Package, 3 x 2 1/4 In. 143.00
Tin, Buckingham Half & Half Tobacco, 3 x 3 x 1 In. 19.00
Tin, Buckingham Smoking Tobacco, Bright Cut Plug, Trial Package, 2 3/4 x 2 In. 154.00
Tin, Buckingham Smoking Tobacco, Canister, John J. Bagley & Co.4 7/8 x 5 1/8 In. 185.00
Tin, Buckingham Smoking Tobacco, John J. Bagley Co., Pocket, Vertical, 4 x 3 x 7/8 In. . 175.00
Tin, Buckingham Smoking Tobacco, Trial Package, Pocket, 2 7/8 x 2 x 3/4 In. .....125.00 to 195.00
Tin, Bugle Cigar, Made By Hand, 5 3/8 x 4 1/4 In. 88.00
Tin, Bull Dog Smoking Tobacco, 4 1/2 x 3 x 7/8 In. 231.00
Tin, Cadena 8 Cigar, Black Man, Winking, Blue, Black, White, 7 In. 60.00
Tin, Cadena Fuminettes Tobacco, Black Man Holding Tobacco Leaf, Late 1920s, 4 1/4 In. . 460.00
Tin, Cadena Penaal Cigar, Black Man, Winking, Smoking Cigar, Green, 6 3/4 In. ..124.00 to 137.00
Tin, Camel Cigars, 5 Cents, Man Riding Camel, 5 x 4 1/2 x 2 1/2 In. 121.00
Tin, Cameron's Havelock Smoking Tobacco, Superior Mixture, 4 Oz., 2 x 3 1/2 In. 66.00
Tin, Caravellis Freres Egyptian Cigarettes, Turkish Tobacco, 3 x 5 1/2 x 1 In. 99.00
Tin, Carolina Gem Tobacco, Red, Lithograph, 3 x 4 x 2 In. 110.00
Tin, Central Union Cut Plug, 6 x 3 1/2 x 3 1/4 In. 45.00
Tin, Central Union Cut Plug, U.S. Tobacco Co., Richmond, Va., 4 1/4 x 7 x 4 5/8 In. 210.00

Tin, Charles The Great Cigars, Crusaders In Battle, Paper Label, 5 x 5 1/2 In. 77.00
Tin, Charm Of West Tobacco, Lithograph, Pocket, Spalding & Merrick, 2 3/8 x 3 3/4 In. . 216.00
Tin, Check Cigars, Good As Gold, 5 x 5 In. 264.00
Tin, Checkers Tobacco, Weisert Brothers, Tin Lithograph, Pocket, 4 1/2 x 3 x 7/8 In. 577.00
Tin, Chesterfield Tobacco, 5 3/4 x 4 1/2 In. 28.00
Tin, City Club Crushed Cubes Tobacco, Man, Wicker Chair, Pocket, 3 5/8 x 2 3/4 In. 550.00
Tin, Coach & Flour, English Pipe Blend, Vertical Pocket, 4 1/2 x 3 x 7/8 In. . . . . . .215.00 to 358.00
Tin, Columbia Cut Plug Smoking Tobacco, Free Sample, Lithograph, Pocket, 7/8 x 2 In. . 3190.00
Tin, Continental Cubes, George Washington, Tin Lithograph, 7 3/8 x 5 1/4 x 2 1/4 In. 4070.00
Tin, Continental Cubes, George Washington, Tin Lithograph, Pocket, 4 3/4 x 3 3/8 In. . . . 688.00
Tin, Counsellor Cigar, Lithograph, Man, White Beard, 5 x 3 1/2 In. 99.00
Tin, Culture Crush Cut Smoking Tobacco, Pocket, Vertical, 4 3/8 x 3 x 7/8 In. . . . .225.00 to 245.00
Tin, Culture Smoking Tobacco, Pocket, 4 1/4 In. 93.00
Tin, Custom House Club Perfectos Cigars, Tin Lithograph, 50 Count, 5 1/2 x 5 1/2 In. . . . 578.00
Tin, Cut Plug Tobacco, No. 10, White Cow's Head, Red Ground, 9 In. 173.00
Tin, Cyana Cigars, Mild, Mellow, Wrapped In Foil, 3 1/2 x 5 1/2 In. 44.00
Tin, Daily Double Cigars, Double Value, Double Satisfaction, Race Track, 5 x 4 In. 88.00
Tin, Daily Habit Cigars, Colorful Parrot, Tin Lithograph, 4 1/2 x 3 3/4 In. 963.00
Tin, Dan Patch Cut Plug, Horse & Driver, Hinged Lid, 6 x 4 In. . . . . *Illus* 80.00
Tin, Dan Patch Cut Plug, Tin Lithograph, Rectangular, 6 In. .77.00 to 102.00
Tin, Dark Sweet Burley Tobacco, Hinged Lid, Gold Letters, 11 1/4 x 8 1/4 In. 465.00
Tin, Desert Gold Tobacco, Horse Head, 6 In. 92.00
Tin, Detroit Club Plug Tobacco, Charles J. Holton, Detroit, Mi., 3 5/8 x 3 3/8 x 1 In. 4180.00
Tin, Dill's Best Cut Plug Tobacco, 1 3/8 x 4 3/8 x 3 3/8 In. 78.00
Tin, Dill's Best Smoking Tobacco, Concave, Pocket, Vertical, 4 3/8 x 3 x 7/8 In. . .166.00 to 255.00
Tin, Dixie Queen Canister, Woman In Hat, Tin Lithograph, 6 1/2 x 4 1/4 In. 660.00
Tin, Dixie Queen Plug Cut Smoking Tobacco, 5 x 8 x 4 1/4 In. 187.00
Tin, Dixie Queen Plug Cut, Girl In Hat, Tin Lithograph, 6 1/4 x 4 7/8 In. 303.00
Tin, Dixie Queen Plug Cut, Humidor, 6 1/2 In. 144.00
Tin, Dixie Queen Plug Cut, Singing Waiter, Roly Poly, Tin Lithograph, 6 x 6 1/2 In. 270.00
Tin, Donniford Blend Pipe Tobacco, Unopened, Christian Paper Co., Pocket, 4 x 4 In. . . 122.00
Tin, EB Pure Stock Cigars, 5 Cent, Tin Lithograph, Liberty Can Co., 5 1/2 In. 132.00
Tin, Eclipse Tobacco, Handle, 3 In. 69.00
Tin, Edgeworth Jr. Tobacco, Pocket, Vertical, 4 3/8 x 3 x 7/8 In. 55.00
Tin, Edgeworth Ready-Rubbed Pipe Tobacco, Striped, Lithograph, Canada, 4 x 3 In. 440.00
Tin, Edgeworth Ready-Rubbed, Larus & Bro. Co., Pocket, Vertical, 4 1/2 x 3 x 7/8 In. . . . 45.00
Tin, El Producto Cigars, 50 Corona Size, 5 1/2 x 5 1/4 In. 149.00
Tin, El Teano Cigars, 5 Cents Smoke, Satisfying, Lady On Box, 5 x 6 x 4 In. 176.00
Tin, El Verso Cigars, 10 Cents, The Sweet & Mellow Cigar, Lima, Ohio, 1 x 5 3/4 In. . . . 44.00
Tin, Emilia Garcia Cigar, Lithograph, Cylindrical, 5 x 5 1/2 In. 50.00
Tin, English Bird's Eye Tobacco, Yellow, Black, Hinged Lid, 4 1/2 x 3 1/2 In. 176.00
Tin, Epicure Shredded Plug Tobacco, Flowers, Embossed, 3 3/4 x 3 1/2 In. 94.00
Tin, Eve Cube Cut, Globe Tobacco Co., Nude, Leaf, Tree, Lithograph, 3 5/8 x 3 1/2 In. . . 361.00
Tin, Every Day Cut Plug, Nall & Williams Tobacco, Flat Pocket, 4 1/2 x 2 3/4 x 1/2 In. . . 275.00
Tin, Fast Mail Chewing Tobacco, Tin Lithograph, J.J. Bagley, 1878, 2 x 3 1/2 In. . .550.00 to 693.00

Tobacco, Tin, Dan Patch Cut
Plug, Horse & Driver, Hinged Lid,
6 x 4 In.

Tobacco, Tin, Forest & Stream Tobacco,
Fishermen In Canoe, Hinged Lid, 4 1/4 x 3 In.

Tobacco, Tin, Game Fine
Cut, 48 5-Cent Pkgs.,
Grouse, 11 1/2 x 7 1/2 In.

Tin, Field & Stream, Pipe Tobacco, Lake, Trees, Key Wind, Philip Morris, 4 x 4 In. . . .5.50 to 22.00
Tin, First Consul Cigars, Very Mild, Manhattans Unbanded, 10 Cents, 5 x 5 1/2 In. 468.00
Tin, Flick & Flock Cigar, Long Filler, 5 Cent, Barnesville, Ohio, 5 5/8 x 6 1/8 x 4 1/4 In. . . 4730.00
Tin, Flor De Franklin Cigars, 5 Cents, Paper Label, 5 x 3 In. 66.00
Tin, Flor De Girard Tobacco, Educators, 5 1/2 x 5 1/2 In. 66.00
Tin, Floral Gem Little Cigars, Moen Tobacco Co., 3 1/2 x 3 1/4 x 1/2 In. 109.00
Tin, Flycasters Smoking Tobacco, Fisherman In Stream, Contents, Paper Label, 3 3/4 In. . . 33.00
Tin, Forest & Stream Pipe Tobacco, Flying Duck, Pocket, 4 In. . . . . .43.00 to 91.00
Tin, Forest & Stream Tobacco, Fisherman, 2-Sided, 4 1/4 In. . . . . .140.00 to 154.00
Tin, Forest & Stream Tobacco, Fisherman, 6 x 3 x 1 In. 578.00
Tin, Forest & Stream Tobacco, Fishermen In Canoe, Hinged Lid, 4 1/4 x 3 In. . . . . . . *Illus* 440.00
Tin, Forest & Stream Tobacco, Fly Fisherman, Gun, Creel Top, 3 x 4 x 1 In. . . . . . .165.00 to 194.00
Tin, Forest & Stream Tobacco, Fly Fisherman, Striped Lid, Canister, 3 x 3 1/2 In. .194.00 to 212.00
Tin, Forest & Stream Tobacco, Fly Fisherman, Striped Lid, Canister, 4 1/4 x 5 1/2 In. 220.00
Tin, Four Roses, Flip Top, Pocket, Vertical, 4 x 3 3/8 x 1 1/4 In. 230.00
Tin, Gail & Ax Navy Tobacco, Sailor, Tobacco Pack, Lithograph, Hinged, 3 1/8 x 5 5/8 In. 72.00
Tin, Game Fine Cut, 48 5-Cent Pkgs., Grouse, 11 1/2 x 7 1/2 In. . . . . *Illus* 575.00
Tin, Girard Educators Cigars, Lithograph, Cylindrical, 5 1/2 x 5 1/2 In. 165.00
Tin, Gold Dust Tobacco, Gold Panning Scene, Tin Lithograph, Pocket, 4 1/2 x 3 In. 8360.00
Tin, Golden Leaf Navy Cut, Louis Dobblemanns, 2 x 3 x 3/4 In. 88.00
Tin, Good Cheer Cigar, Lithograph, Embossed, Stein Shape, Handle, Flip Lid, 5 x 4 In. . . 99.00
Tin, Granger Pipe Tobacco, Rough Cut, Leaf, Blue, Red, Cream, 5 3/4 x 4 3/4 In. 20.00
Tin, Granulated Sliced Plug 54, Pocket, Vertical, Free Sample, 3 x 2 1/4 x 3/4 In. 350.00
Tin, Gravely's Tobacco, Plug Cut, Flue Cured, 3 3/8 x 4 1/2 x 1 7/8 In. 77.00
Tin, Guide Pipe & Cigarette Tobacco, Hunting Guide, 4 1/4 x 3 x 7/8 In. 303.00
Tin, Guide Pipe & Cigarette Tobacco, Tin Lithograph, Pocket, 4 1/4 x 3 x 7/8 In. 253.00
Tin, H-O Cut Plug, R.A. Patterson Co., Richmond, Va., 2 3/8 x 6 x 3 3/4 In. 95.00
Tin, Half & Half Tobacco, 1/2 Size Pocket Tin, 3 x 3 In. 32.00
Tin, Half & Half Tobacco, Paper Stamp On Lid, 1 Lb. 42.00
Tin, Hand Bag Cut Plug, Hand Bag Shape, Larus & Bro., 7 x 6 1/4 x 4 1/4 In. 116.00
Tin, Handsome Dan Tobacco, L.L. Stoddard, 5 x 6 1/2 x 2 5/8 In. 66.00
Tin, Harmony Slice Cut Pipe Tobacco, Paper Label, Unopened, 3 1/4 x 2 3/4 In. 45.00
Tin, Havana Cadet Cigars, 5 Cents, Humidor, Standup, Tin On Side, Paper Label, 10 In. . . 177.00
Tin, Havana Cadet Cigars, 5 Cents, Lithograph, Liberty Can Co., 5 x 5 1/2 In. 275.00
Tin, Herald Dark Cut Flake Tobacco, 5 x 6 x 1 In. 413.00
Tin, Hi-Plane Smooth Cut Tobacco, Single Motor Plane, 4 3/8 x 3 x 7/8 In. . . . . . .150.00 to 165.00
Tin, Hiawatha Tobacco, Hinged Lid, Tin Lithograph, 4 Oz., 5 x 3 x 2 In. . . . . .110.00 to 187.00
Tin, Hickory Pipe Tobacco Mixture, Vertical, Pocket, 4 1/4 x 3 x 7/8 In. 65.00
Tin, Himyar Cigarette Tobacco, Man On Horse, 6 1/2 x 5 In. 44.00
Tin, Hoffman House Cigar, Man In Tuxedo, Embossed, Red Ground, 5 3/4 x 3 1/2 In. . . . 28.00
Tin, Honest Labor Cut Plug Tobacco, 1 1/4 x 4 1/2 x 2 3/4 In. 55.00
Tin, Honey Moon Rum Flavored Tobacco, Man On Moon, Pocket, 4 x 3 x 7/8 In. . .88.00 to 135.00
Tin, Honey Moon Tobacco, Penn Tobacco Co., Wilkes Barre, Pocket, 4 3/8 x 3 In. 265.00
Tin, Honeycomb Cigar, Class, Workmanship, Quality, Embossed Letters, 5 x 7 x 3 1/2 In. 22.00
Tin, Hunter Cigar, Man On Horse, Lithograph, 5 1/4 x 3 1/2 In. 300.00
Tin, Hurley Burley, Plug Cut, 5 Cents, P. Lorillord, Unopened, 4 1/8 x 2 1/2 x 7/8 In. 95.00
Tin, In-Be-Tween Cigaritos, 8 1/4 x 4 x 2 1/2 In. 32.00
Tin, Indian Tobacco, Manuel-Fernandez Habana, Tin Lithograph, 3 1/2 x 5 In. 220.00
Tin, J. Wright Co.'s All Nations Tobacco, Eagle, Flags, Hinged Lid, 3 x 4 5/8 In. 300.00
Tin, Just Suits, Tobacco, Cut Plug, Red, Gold, Black, Hinged Lid, 5 1/4 x 7 3/4 In. 90.00
Tin, Kadee Smoking Tobacco, Lithograph, 4 1/2 x 3 x 7/8 In. 3630.00
Tin, King Of All Tobacco, Long Cut, Hinged Lid, Red, 2 1/4 x 3 1/2 In. 99.00
Tin, La Corona Cigars, 10 Count, Man Surrounded By Treasure, 5 1/4 x 2 1/4 In. 66.00
Tin, La Fendrich Cigars, Contents, 3 1/2 x 5 x 1 In. 55.00
Tin, La Palina, Quality Cigar, Senators, Pocket Edition, 5 x 3 1/2 x 1 1/2 In. 39.00
Tin, La Resta Cigars, 2 For 15 Cents, Rothenberg & Schloss, 5 1/2 x 3 1/2 In. 105.00
Tin, Lafayette Mixture Tobacco, Marsburg Bros., 3 1/4 x 4 1/2 x 2 1/4 In. 50.00
Tin, Lifeboat Navy Cut Tobacco, Salmon & Gluckstein, 2 x 3 3/4 x 3/4 In. 72.00
Tin, Londres 5 Cent Havana Ribbon Tobacco, 5 1/4 x 3 1/2 x 3 1/4 In. 56.00
Tin, Lucky Star Cut Plug Smoking Tobacco, Toasted Mild, Red, Blue, 4 1/2 x 3 In. 770.00
Tin, Macanudo Ascot Tobacco, 5 x 4 1/4 x 1/2 In. 10.00
Tin, Mackintosh Tobacco, Brown Horse, 12-Sided, England, 1 1/4 x 5 x 3 12/16 In. 20.00
Tin, Mal-Kah Cigarettes, Finest Turkish Tobacco, Mal-Kah Company, 3 1/2 x 2 3/4 In. . . . 45.00

Tin, Mapacuba Blunt Cigars, Harbor Scene, Etched Glass Lid, Embossed, 5 x 5 x 5 1/2 In.   358.00
Tin, Maritana Chewing Tobacco, 2 3/4 x 6 1/2 x 3 1/4 In. 32.00
Tin, Marshall Field Distinctive Cigars, 3 1/4 x 5 1/4 x 1 In. 44.00
Tin, Maryland Club Mixture Tobacco, Lithograph, Flip Lid, Orange, 4 x 3 1/2 In. 495.00
Tin, Master Mason Smoking Tobacco, Brick Layer, Tin Lithograph, Pocket, 4 1/2 x 3 In. .   1760.00
Tin, Master Mason Smoking Tobacco, Ready Rubbed, 4 1/2 x 3 x 7/8 In. 1018.00
Tin, May Queen Tobacco, Pocket, 2 1/2 x 3 3/4 x 3/4 In. 275.00
Tin, Mi Wauki Cigars, Lady, 3 1/2 x 5 In. 55.00
Tin, Miners & Puddlers Smoking Tobacco, 3 Men Drilling, Bail Handle, 6 1/2 In. 230.00
Tin, Model Smoking Tobacco, Red, Silver, 4 1/4 x 3 x 7/8 In.   50.00
Tin, Model Tobacco, Paper Label, Nov. 1948, 4 1/2 x 5 3/4 In. 35.00
Tin, Murad, Turkish Cigarette, Paper Label, Pocket, Vertical, 2 7/8 x 3 x 7/8 In. . . . .95.00 to 150.00
Tin, Muratti's After Lunch Cigarettes, Man Drinking, Hinged Lid, 2 3/4 x 3 1/2 In. . .41.00 to 55.00
Tin, New Bachelor Cigars, Man Playing Cards, 5 x 4 In. 270.00
Tin, Nigger Hair Smoking Tobacco, Tan, Bail Handle, Punched Lid, Paper Liner, 6 1/2 In.   575.00
Tin, Nigger Hair Smoking Tobacco, Tin Lithograph, Wire Bail Handle, 7 In. 797.00
Tin, No-To-Bac, Tobacco Habit Cure, Makes Weak Men Strong, 2 1/4 x 3 3/4 In. 303.00
Tin, North Carolina Plug Cut Tobacco, 1900-1910, 6 1/2 In. 154.00
Tin, Oceangold-Blatt Tobacco, Hamburg, 3 x 5 x 1 In. 77.00
Tin, Oceanic Cut Plug, Ocean Liner, Fish, Hinged Lid, c.1900, 3 3/4 x 6 x 3 In. 75.00
Tin, Ogden's Redbreast Flake, Imperial Tobacco Co., 8 Oz., 2 1/2 x 6 1/4 x 1 In. 79.00
Tin, Old Gold Cigarettes, Bottom Match Striker Strip, 3 x 2 1/4 x 1 1/16 In. 20.00
Tin, Old Granger Tobacco, 5 x 6 In. 17.50
Tin, Old Rip Long Cut, Pipes & Cigarettes, Allen & Ginter, Tin Lithograph, 7 x 4 1/2 In. .   55.00
Tin, Old Squire Pipe Tobacco, Pocket, Vertical, 4 x 3 x 7/8 In.   315.00
Tin, Old Velvet Tobacco, 4 1/4 x 4 3/4 In. 25.00
Tin, Omar Cigarette, Turkish Woman, Lithograph, 1950s, 4 1/2 x 6 5/8 In. 52.00
Tin, On The Square Tobacco, Embossed, Tin Lithograph, Strat Bros., 3 1/4 x 1/2 In. 88.00
Tin, Orcico Cigars, 2 For 5 Cents, Indian, Tin Lithograph, 5 1/2 x 6 1/8 x 4 1/8 In. .325.00 to 605.00
Tin, Orcico, 2 For 5 Cents, Indian, Meekin Can Co., Cover, 1919, 5 1/2 In. 236.00
Tin, Osmundo Cigar, Pershing, Indian Princess, 3 1/2 x 5 1/2 In. 72.00
Tin, Owl Brand 5 Cents Cigars, Paper Label, 5 x 3 x 3 In. 132.00
Tin, Palmy Days Tobacco, Tin Lithograph, Penn Tobacco Co., Pocket, 4 3/8 x 3 In. 578.00
Tin, Pastime Plug Tobacco, Hunter & Dog, 12 1/2 x 9 1/2 In. 259.00
Tin, Pastime Plug Tobacco, Hunter Shooting Ducks, Dog, 4 x 1 1/2 In. 248.00
Tin, Pat Hand, Globe Tobacco Co., Yellow Hand, Detroit, 2 7/8 x 2 1/2 x 1 3/8 In. .143.00 to 155.00
Tin, Patterson's Tuxedo Tobacco, Gold, 4 1/4 x 3 x 7/8 In. 303.00
Tin, Patterson's Tuxedo Tobacco, Green, Gold, 4 1/2 x 4 1/2 x 2 1/2 In. 66.00
Tin, Patterson's Tuxedo Tobacco, Striped Lid, 1 Lb., 6 x 5 In. 165.00
Tin, Paul Jones Clean Cut Tobacco, Tin Lithograph, Pocket, 4 1/2 x 3 x 7/8 In. . .1870.00 to 1925.00
Tin, Peachey Double Cut Tobacco, Tin Lithograph, Vertical, 4 x 2 5/8 x 7/8 In. . . . .175.00 to 195.00
Tin, Penn's, Spells Quality Plug Tobacco, Hinged Top, 1 Dozen 20.00
Tin, Peregoy & Moore, Hand Made Cigars, Lithograph, 5 1/2 x 3 1/2 In. 33.00
Tin, Perfect Pipe Tobacco, S.S. Pierce Co., 4 1/4 x 3 3/8 x 1 In. 275.00
Tin, Picobac Tobacco, Flat, Pocket, 5/8 x 3 1/4 x 2 1/4 In. 36.00
Tin, Picobac, Pick Of Tobacco, Canada, Pocket, Vertical, 4 x 3 In. 45.00
Tin, Pipe Major English Smoking Mixture, Tin Lithograph, Pocket, 4 1/2 x 3 In. 358.00
Tin, Piper Heidsieck Tobacco, 4 1/4 x 3 3/4 In. 45.00
Tin, Pippins, 25 Cigars, Lithograph, Embossed Letters, 5 1/2 x 3 1/2 In. 66.00
Tin, Player's Navy Cut Cigarettes, Hinged Lid, Canada, 3 x 5 1/2 x 1 1/8 In. 33.00
Tin, Player's, Country Life Cigarettes, Cork Tipped, Virginia, 3 x 2 1/4 x 1/2 In. 66.00
Tin, Plow Boy, Chewing & Smoking, Farmer On Plow, Contents, 4 1/2 In. 46.00
Tin, Polar Bear Tobacco, Sloping Lift Lid, 18 x 14 In. 316.00
Tin, Popper's Ace Cigars, 10 Cents, Biplane, Hinged Lift Lid, 8 x 5 1/2 In. 719.00
Tin, Popper's Ace Cigars, 10 Cents, Biplane, Tin Lithograph, Pocket, 5 3/4 x 5 In. 413.00
Tin, Portuondo Cigars, Liberty Can Co., 1919, 5 x 5 In. 440.00
Tin, Pride Of Virginia, Sliced Plug, Blue, Hinged Lid, c.1910, 2 5/8 x 4 1/2 x 5 In. 59.00
Tin, Prince Albert Chop Cut, Pocket, Vertical, 1 3/4 x 3 x 7/8 In. 45.00
Tin, Prince Albert Now King Tobacco, Lithograph, Red Ground, Pocket, 4 1/2 x 3 In. 688.00
Tin, Prince Albert Tobacco, Lithograph, 5 1/2 In. 7.70
Tin, Prince Albert, Crimp Cut, Long Burning, Pipe & Cigarette Tobacco, 3 x 4 1/2 x 1 In.   16.00
Tin, Prince Hamlet Cigars, 10 Cents, Bon Ton Size, Embossed, 5 x 5 1/2 In. 160.00
Tin, Princeton Mixture Fine Tobacco, Paper Lid Label, Marburg, 4 1/2 x 3 In. 440.00

Tobacco, Tin, Sensation Smoking
Tobacco, 2 Swing Handles,
Tin Lithograph, 7 In.

Tobacco, Tin, Sunset Trail Cigar,
5 Cents, America's Finest, Cowboy,
Cowgirl, 6 x 5 1/2 x 4 In.

Tobacco, Tin, Yellow Cab
Cigar, Tin Lithograph,
6 x 5 In.

Tin, Pure Stock Cigar, Lithograph, 5 1/2 x 5 In. 66.00
Tin, Puritan Crushed Mixture Plug, Continental Co., 4 1/2 x 3 x 7/8 In. 330.00
Tin, Puritan Crushed Plug Mixture, Tin Lithograph, Pocket, 4 3/8 x 3 x 7/8 In. 330.00
Tin, Qboid Granulated Plug, Richmond, Oval, Vertical, Pocket, 4 x 3 x 1 1/4 In. 110.00
Tin, Quill Smoking Tobacco, American Eagle Tobacco Co., 2 x 4 1/2 x 3 1/2 In. 154.00
Tin, Red Dot Cigar, Federal Cigar Co., Truly Different, 5 x 5 1/2 In. 33.00
Tin, Red Dot Tobacco, 10 For 50 Cents, Barnes-Smith Co., 3 x 4 3/4 In. 65.00
Tin, Red Indian Cut Plug, Mammy, Roly Poly, Painted, American, 1800s, 7 In. 728.00
Tin, Red Jacket Smoking Tobacco, A Sure Winner, 4 1/4 x 3 x 3/4 In. 182.00
Tin, Red Man Tobacco, Indian Head, Contents, 5 In. 40.00
Tin, Red Turkey Brand Coffee, Screw-On Lid, J.B. Maltby, 1 Lb., 5 1/2 x 4 1/4 In. 98.00
Tin, Regimental Mixture, John Middleton Blend, Sample, 1920s, 1 3/4 x 2 1/4 x 1 1/2 In. . 182.00
Tin, Repeater Smoking Tobacco, Fine Cut, 1/2 Lb., 4 1/2 x 4 x 2 In. 176.00
Tin, Revelation, Philip Morris & Co., N.Y., Trial Size, 2 x 3 x 7/8 In. 45.00
Tin, Riverhead Gold Tobacco, Smiling Woman Wearing Hat, 6 In. 99.00
Tin, Riverhead Gold Tobacco, Smiling Woman Wearing Hat, 9 In. 143.00
Tin, Rockefellers Cigar, Estabrook & Eatons, Plantation Scene, 3 3/4 x 5 1/4 x 1 1/4 In. . . 94.00
Tin, Rose Leaf Chewing Tobacco, Compass, Nickel Plated, 5/8 x 3 1/2 x 2 1/4 In. 295.00
Tin, Rose-O-Cuba Cigar, Gleck Cigar Co., Lithograph, 5 1/2 x 5 1/2 In. 99.00
Tin, Rose-O-Cuba, Woman In Lace Veil, 5 x 5 In. 358.00
Tin, S.F. Hess Co. Premium Chewing Tobacco, Tin Lithograph, Hinged, Flat, 2 3/8 x 4 In. 825.00
Tin, Sail Pipe Tobacco, Dutch, 14 Oz., 5 1/2 x 5 In. 32.00
Tin, Scissors Cigarettes, Special Army Quality, W.D. & H.O. Wills, Bristol & London . . . 170.00
Tin, Scotch Snuff, Larkin & Morrill, Byfield, Mass., 2 1/4 x 1 1/2 In. 45.00
Tin, Seal Of North Carolina Plug Cut Tobacco, Tin Lithograph, 6 1/2 x 4 7/8 In. . . . 413.00 to 675.00
Tin, Sensation Smoking Tobacco, 2 Swing Handles, Tin Lithograph, 7 In. . . . . *Illus*   55.00
Tin, Silver Fern Smoking Tobacco, Mild, 8 In. 44.00
Tin, Sir Walter Raleigh Smoking Tobacco, 12 x 12 In. 55.00
Tin, Sir Walter Raleigh Smoking Tobacco, Christmas, 3 1/2 x 7 3/8 x 4 3/8 In. 155.00
Tin, Sir Walter Raleigh Tobacco, Key Wind, 7 Oz., 4 In. 55.00
Tin, Squadron Leader Mixture Tobacco, Plane Graphic, 4 1/4 x 3 1/4 x 1 In. . . . . . . 122.00 to 145.00
Tin, Stag Tobacco, 1910, 1 Oz., 3 1/2 x 2 1/2 In. 253.00
Tin, Sterling Fine Cut, 5 Cents Wax Bags, Always Good, 7 x 8 In. 47.00
Tin, Straiton & Storms Erminie Cigar, Somers Bros., Brooklyn, 1879, 4 1/2 x 3 3/4 In. . . . 132.00
Tin, Straiton & Storms Twenty-One Cigar, Lithograph, 1879, 4 1/2 x 4 In. 165.00
Tin, Sunset Trail Cigar, 5 Cents, America's Finest, Cowboy, Cowgirl, 6 x 5 1/2 x 4 In. *Illus* 575.00
Tin, Sure Shot Chewing, Indian Drawing Bow, Lithograph, Cover, 15 x 7 1/2 In. 1045.00
Tin, Sure Shot, It Touches The Spot, Indian Shooting Bow & Arrow, 8 x 30 x 10 In. 1350.00
Tin, Sweet Burley Tobacco, Light, Spaulding & Merrick, Yellow, Red, 11 x 8 In. . . 187.00 to 225.00
Tin, Sweet Cuba Chewing Tobacco, Red & Black, Yellow Ground, 18 x 14 In. 431.00
Tin, Sweet Cuba Fine Cut Tobacco, Light, 1 Lb., 8 1/4 x 2 In. 80.00
Tin, Sweet Cuba Tobacco, Canister, 11 x 8 1/4 In. 88.00
Tin, Sweet Cuba Tobacco, Light, 48 Packages, Square Hinged Lid, 11 1/2 In. 115.00
Tin, Sweet Mist Chewing Tobacco, 48 5-Cent Packages, Children, Hinged Lid, 11 1/2 In. . 288.00
Tin, Sweetser's Salt Scoth Snuff, 2 x 1 3/8 In. 48.00

Tin, Three Feathers Plug Cut, Pocket, Vertical, 4 1/8 x 3 1/4 x 1 1/8 In. 375.00
Tin, Tiger Stripe Medium Chewing Tobacco, Unopened, 5 x 3 1/4 x 1 1/4 In. 130.00
Tin, Toasted Navy Cut Tobacco, Bulldog In Sailor Cap, 6 In. 230.00
Tin, Tobacco Girl, Cigar, 50 Count, Girl, Leaf, Tin Lithograph, 5 1/2 x 6 1/4 x 4 1/4 In. . . . 3630.00
Tin, Tom Tough Tobacco, Rich Old Flake, 1 Lb., 4 3/4 x 6 1/2 In. 57.00
Tin, Totem Tobacco, Indian, Totem Pole, Tin Lithograph, 3 5/8 x 2 5/8 x 1 In. . .1375.00 to 1513.00
Tin, Traveler, Pry Lid, 3 1/2 x 4 1/4 In. 15.00
Tin, Trout-Line Smoking Tobacco, Fisherman, Tin Lithograph, 3 3/4 x 3 1/2 In. . .743.00 to 1045.00
Tin, Tuckett's Orinoco Smoking Tobacco, Fisherman Sitting By Tree, 6 1/4 x 2 1/4 x 4 In. 55.00
Tin, Turkish Mixture Tobacco, Square Corners, 3 3/8 x 4 1/2 x 2 1/4 In. 413.00
Tin, Tuxedo, Pipe, Green, Gold Letters, 4 1/4 x 3 x 1 In. 35.00
Tin, Tuxedo Tobacco, Recessed Lid, Pocket, Vertical, 4 1/4 x 3 x 7/8 In. 55.00
Tin, Twin Oaks Mixture, Silver Wash, Pocket, Vertical, 3 x 2 1/8 x 5/8 In. 350.00
Tin, Two Belles Perfectos Cigars, Heekin Can Co., 3 1/2 x 5 1/2 In. 127.00
Tin, U.S. Marine Flake Cut, 4 1/2 In. 302.00
Tin, Union Cut Plug Tobacco, Lithograph, 5 x 8 In. 72.00
Tin, Union Leader Redi Cut, Uncle Sam, Pocket, 4 3/8 x 3 In. . . . . .95.00 to 121.00
Tin, Union Leader Tobacco, Uncle Sam, Tin Lithograph, Sample, Pocket, 3 1/8 x 2 3/4 In. 2640.00
Tin, Union Leader, Eagle Trademark, Tin Lithograph, 4 x 4 x 5 1/4 In. 39.00
Tin, Vanko Cigars, 50 Count, Embossed, 5 1/2 x 6 x 4 In. 85.00
Tin, Vanko Cigars, Horse Racing Scene, Paper Label, 1917, 5 1/4 x 3 1/2 In. 121.00
Tin, Velvit Tobacco, Pipe Graphic, Pocket, Vertical, 3 3/4 x 3 3/8 x 1 1/8 In. 38.00
Tin, War Eagle Cigars, 10 Cents, Dark Green, 5 1/4 x 5 In. 385.00
Tin, Wascana Cigars, Indian Chief, Teepees, Kampen Holland, 5 x 9 x 2 1/2 In. 237.00
Tin, Webster 10 Cent Savoy Cigars, Lithograph, 3 1/4 x 4 3/4 x 1 In. 55.00
Tin, Webster Cigars, Belmont Size, Habana, 10 Cigars, 3 1/2 x 5 In. 66.00
Tin, Webster Cigars, Webster Picture, Book, Quill Pen, Hinged Cover, 5 1/4 x 3 1/2 In. . . 50.00
Tin, Weyman's Cutty Pipe, 5 Cents, Square, Store Tin, 13 x 10 In. 990.00
Tin, White Ash, 5 Cents, H.E. Snyder, Lithograph, Cylindrical, 5 1/2 x 5 1/2 In. . . . . .33.00 to 50.00
Tin, White Manor Pipe Mixture, Southern Plantation, Pocket, 3 x 3 1/2 x 1 In. 230.00
Tin, White Owl Brand Cigars, Owl On Cigar, Tin Lithograph, 50 Count, 5 3/4 x 5 1/2 In. . 743.00
Tin, White Owl Cigars, Invincibles, 5 1/4 x 5 In. 44.00
Tin, Winsome Little Cigars, H. Mandelbaum, New York, 3 1/2 x 3 1/4 x 1/4 In. 90.00
Tin, Yacht Cut Plug Tobacco, Sailing Ship, Hinged, 1 x 2 3/4 x 4 1/2 In. 300.00
Tin, Yale Mixture Smoking Tobacco, 1 3/4 x 3 3/8 x 2 5/8 In. 44.00
Tin, Yankee Boy Plug Cut Tobacco, Boy Batting, Tin Lithograph, 4 x 3 1/2 In. . . . .688.00 to 935.00
Tin, Yellow Cab Cigar, Taxi, 5 1/2 x 2 1/2 In. 550.00
Tin, Yellow Cab Cigar, Tin Lithograph, 6 x 5 In. . . . . *Illus* 1870.00
Tin, Yocum Brothers, Y-B Cigars, Tin Lithograph, 3 1/2 x 5 x 1 1/4 In. 55.00
Tin Tag, Alabama Coon, G. Penn Son's, Black Man, Suit, Top Hat, Yellow, Round 72.00
Tin Tag, Alamo, Round 55.00
Tin Tag, Alto, Horse Shape, Red 495.00
Tin Tag, American Navy Brand Tobacco, 1 3/4 x 1 In. 15.00
Tin Tag, B&D's Dark Cut, Ridgeway, Diamond Shape, Black Ground, Red Letters 20.00
Tin Tag, B&D's Dark Cut, Ridgeway, Diamond Shape, Red Ground, Black Letters 12.00
Tin Tag, Bachmannn's Fiddle, Red Fiddle Shape 43.00
Tin Tag, Bill Nye, Miner, Pick Ax, Ruffled Edge 72.00
Tin Tag, Black Mirah Tobacco, Late 1800s-Early 1900s 7.00
Tin Tag, Chinese Man, Ruffled Edge 55.00
Tin Tag, Crown Of Diamonds, Round 7.70
Tin Tag, Crown Shape 5.50
Tin Tag, Cup Greenville, Cup Shape 12.10
Tin Tag, Cures Hard Times, 5 Cents, Round 5.50
Tin Tag, D Shape, Red Ground, Letort 9.90
Tin Tag, D Shape, Red Ground, S.W. Venables Petersburg, Va. 5.50
Tin Tag, Daily Bread 7.70
Tin Tag, Daily Call, Oval 11.00
Tin Tag, Dalton, Farrow & Co., Wintson, N.C., 8-Sided 22.00
Tin Tag, Dandy Lion, Lion, Top Hat, Tails, Walking Stick, Casey & Wright, Winston, N.C. 61.00
Tin Tag, Daniel Boone's Navy, Pie Slice Shape, Red Ground 24.00
Tin Tag, Deer Lick, Deer Head, Antlers, Round 61.00
Tin Tag, Democrat, Red Script Letters 28.00

Tin Tag, Derby, D. Ritchie & Co. Trademark, Red, Derby Shape 28.00
Tin Tag, Derby, Red, White & Blue Derby, Yellow Ground, Oval 12.10
Tin Tag, Deshazo, Rough & Ready, Joe Deshazo, Spencer, Va., Red Letters 29.00
Tin Tag, Dew Drop, Leaf Shape, WWT Co. 43.00
Tin Tag, Dick's Pet, Running Horse, Yellow Ground, Oval 39.00
Tin Tag, Diem Navy, 10 Cents, White Ground, Round 12.10
Tin Tag, Dinner Horn, Horn Shape 55.00
Tin Tag, Dog's Head Smoking, Dog Head Picture, Round, Yellow Ground 165.00
Tin Tag, Double Six Chewing, 2 Stacked Die, Black Dots 55.00
Tin Tag, Doughboy, Soldier, Yellow Ground, Round 21.00
Tin Tag, Dried Peach, Peach Shape, Red Letters 19.80
Tin Tag, Drum, Eagle, Shield, Red, White, Blue, Large 83.00
Tin Tag, Drum, Eagle, Shield, Red, White, Blue, Small 50.00
Tin Tag, Dynamite, Leak Bros. & Hasten, Greensboro, N.C., Yellow Ground 24.00
Tin Tag, E.J. & A.G. Stafford, Greensboro, N.C., 2 Horses Pulling Steaming Wagon 152.00
Tin Tag, Easley's Best, Round, Yellow Ground 23.00
Tin Tag, Eden, Yellow Leaf, Red Ground, Black Dot Border, Rectangular 16.50
Tin Tag, Evans, Augusta, West Winfree Tob. Co., Girl's Picture, 1 In. . . . . .220.00 to 817.00
Tin Tag, Everson Wilson & Co., Louisville, KY, Round, Blue Ground 28.00
Tin Tag, Excelsior, Ruffled Edge 59.00
Tin Tag, Extra Navy, Red, Triangle 14.30
Tin Tag, F&R Double Team, Man In Horse Drawn Carriage, Yellow Ground 215.00
Tin Tag, Fair Rebel, Penn Bros. Co., Red Ground, Woman's Profile 147.00
Tin Tag, Fat Back, Liipfert Scales & Co., Winston, N.C., Hog In Field, Multicolored .42.00 to 55.00
Tin Tag, Fat Back, Red Pig, Yellow Ground, Oval 254.00
Tin Tag, Fat Boy, Baby Head, Mfd By Sherrill Tob. Co., Catawba, N.C. 152.00
Tin Tag, Fat Possum, Made By Bitting & Hay, Winston, N.C., Round 28.00
Tin Tag, First Call, Red Rooster Playing Bugle, Round 55.00
Tin Tag, Fly Rod, Fish, Fly, Red Ground, 8-Sided 182.00
Tin Tag, Fox Ridge Twist, Red Running Fox 39.00
Tin Tag, Gay Bird, Octagonal, Red Bird, Irvin & Poston, Statesville, N.C. 31.00
Tin Tag, Gay Bird, Rectangular, Irvin & Poston, Statesville, N.C. 28.00
Tin Tag, Girofla, Yellow Ground, Ruffled Edge 48.00
Tin Tag, Happy Nig, Smiling Black Man, Oval 165.00
Tin Tag, Hard A Port Plug, Sailor At Ship's Wheel, Blue, White, Round 855.00
Tin Tag, Hero, Robert E. Lee's Picture, Vertical Oval 770.00
Tin Tag, High Life, Man Lounging In Living Room, Multicolored, Round 402.00
Tin Tag, His Nobs, Frog, Smoking Pipe, Top Hat, 6-Sided, Yellow Ground 55.00
Tin Tag, John L., Boxer, Red Ground, Round 73.00
Tin Tag, Juliet, 6-Sided 55.00
Tin Tag, Mascada Americana, Spread Winged Eagle, Oval, Yellow Ground 23.00
Tin Tag, McAlpins, Woodcock 12.00
Tin Tag, Michigan Tob. Co., Detroit, Red Key, Yellow Ground, Square 28.00
Tin Tag, Nancy Hanks, Time 2:04, J. Wright Co., Harness Race Horse, Oval 484.00
Tin Tag, Nickel Jack, Black Man, Donkey, Rectangular 24.00
Tin Tag, Nigger Baby, Pegram & Penn. 55.00
Tin Tag, Old Hickory, Round, Red Ground 55.00
Tin Tag, Perry's Curly Pine, Log Shape 152.00
Tin Tag, Pigeon Wing, Pigeon Shape 76.00
Tin Tag, Rang Tang, Harvey, Yellow Ground, 3 Black People 537.00
Tin Tag, Sutter's Double Eagle, 2 Headed Eagle, Round 440.00
Tin Tag, Taylor Brothers, Rich & Ripe Tobacco, Late 1800s-Early 1900s 6.00
Tin Tag, The Governor, Man, Walking Stick, Top Hat, Round 48.00
Tin Tag, Tiger, Dog, Ruffled Edge 48.00
Tin Tag, Tom, Cat, Round 66.00

TOY   Toys are designed to entice children, and today they have attracted
new interest among adults who are still children at heart. Tin, iron, bat-
tery-operated, and other types of toys are collected. Those listed here
have some type of advertising as part of their design. Other toys may
be found under brand-specific categories.

Car, Ford Motor Co., Thunderbird, Friction, Free Gift, Box, 1957, 1 7/8 x 3 x 7 1/4 In. 295.00

Cribbage Board, Buffalo Brewing, Bohemian New Brew, Wood, 13 x 4 1/4 x 3/4 In. 121.00
Elephant, Today, Sunshine Animal Crackers At Your Grocer, 5 1/2 In. 143.00
Farm Wagon, Ford, White Ground, Blue Trim, Child's, 40 In. 1208.00
Game, Rex Kidney Bitters, Ring On Clown's Nose, Cardboard, 8 In. .... *Illus* 30.00
Pull Toy, Old Dutch Cleanser, Girl Chasing Dirt, Cast Iron, 8 3/4 In. 11550.00
Tanker Truck, Mobil Gas, Tin Lithograph, Japan, 11 In. 44.00
Tanker Truck, Mobiloil, Diecast Cab, Pressed Steel Trailer, Smith Miller, 22 In. 385.00
Tanker Truck, Mobiloil, Electric Headlights, Key, Citroen, France, Box, 23 In. 2310.00
Tanker Truck, Pure Oil Co., Pressed Steel, Streamlined, Metalcraft, 15 In. 523.00
Tanker Truck, Shell Oil, Cast Metal, Black Rubber Tires, Tootsietoy, 1940s, 6 In. 43.00
Tanker Truck, Sinclair Fuel Oil, Tin Lithograph, Marx, 18 In. 176.00
Tanker Truck, Texaco Oil, Pressed Steel, Plastic, Park Plastics, Box, 1960s, 24 In. 294.00
Tanker Truck, Texaco, GMC, Buddy L, 1959 .... 395.00
Train Car, Korff Cacao, Tin, Anno 1811, 14 1/2 x 23 x 10 In. 3300.00
Truck, Allied Van Lines, Moving Van, Pressed Steel, Pull Rod, Buddy L, 29 In. 1045.00
Truck, American Railway Express, Pressed Steel, Keystone, 26 In. 743.00
Truck, Decker's Iowana Ham, Taste Is Good, Pressed Steel, Streamliner, Metalcraft, 13 In. 2310.00
Truck, Esso, 7 Cans, Streamlined, Electric Headlights, Metalcraft, 13 In. 1045.00
Truck, Hess Gasoline, Training Van, Hong Kong 135.00
Truck, Sheffield Farms Dairy, Pressed Steel, Mack, Steelcraft, 21 In. 770.00
Truck, Shell Motor Oil, Pressed Steel, Electric Headlights, 8 Cans, Metalcraft, 13 In. 523.00
Truck, Shell, No. 938, Pressed Steel, Buddy L, Box, 21 In. 3080.00
Truck, Sunbeam Bread, 4 Figures, Punch Out, Stiff Paper, 1940s, 2 x 2 1/4 x 4 1/2 In. 24.00
Truck, Sunshine Biscuits, Pressed Steel, Electric Headlights, Metalcraft, 12 In. ...385.00 to 1430.00
Truck, Supplee Ice Cream, Pressed Steel, Steelcraft, 21 In. 8800.00
Truck, Wrecker, Goodrich Silvertown Tires, Pressed Steel, Streamlined, Metalcraft, 13 In. 770.00
Truck & Trailer, North American Van Lines, Tin Lithograph, Windup, Marx, 15 In. 132.00
Wagon, Berry Brothers Varnishes, Wood, 19 x 27 In. 303.00
Wagon, Berry Brothers Varnishes, Wooden Wheels, Child's 1815.00
Wagon, Good Will Soap, Wood, Metal Hardware, Child's, 15 1/2 x 32 1/2 In. 880.00
Wagon, Welcome Soap, Always Reliable, Wood, Jas. Hill, Exeter, N.H., 27 x 36 In. 7150.00
Wienermobile, Oscar Mayer, Pull Toy, 1950s, 4 1/4 x 9 1/2 In. 295.00

TRADE CARD Color pictures were once a luxury. Even early prints were colored by hand. But by the 1870s, the development of color lithography had led to the printing of millions of small multicolored picture cards promoting products. The cards were given away as advertisements by storekeepers or were put into packages of gum, cigarettes, or baking soda. Collectors search for cards by product, by company name, by artist's name, or by pictured subject. The advertising card lost its appeal in the 1920s, when color illustrations became commonplace in magazines. Some bubble gum brands have carried on the card tradition.

Allen's Lung Balsam, Grandmother, Child, Fireplace, Bottle Of Balsam 28.00
American Can Co., Tin Cans, Boxes, World's Fair, 2-Sided, Tin Lithograph, 3 x 5 In. 154.00
American Caramel, Eddie Plank, Baseball Player, No. E125, Die Cut, 1910 .... 8050.00
American Caramel, Joe Jackson, Baseball Player, No. E90-1, 1909-1911 .... 3738.00

Toy, Game, Rex Kidney Bitters, Ring On Clown's Nose, Cardboard, 8 In.

Don't repaint old metal toys. It lowers the value.

B.T. Babbit's 1776 Brand Soap Powder, Colonial Boy Holding Artist Pallet, c.1885 . . . . . 15.00
Babbitt's Soap, A Thing Of Worth Is A Joy Forever, Uncle Sam 10.00
Bailey, Farrell & Co., Hunting Dogs, Pittsburgh, Pa., 3 3/8 x 5 1/4 In. 255.00
Boston Garter, Christy Mathewson, Velvet Grip, 25 & 50 Cents, 1912, 8 1/4 x 4 In. 31625.00
Boston Garter, Tris Speaker, 25 Cents, 50 Cents, 1913, 8 1/4 x 4 In. 11500.00
Buffalo Bill Cody, 5 Cent Cigar, Punch Card, 11 3/4 x 10 1/2 In. 160.00
Burdock Blood Bitters, 2 Girls At Beach, 2 1/8 x 4 1/8 In. 12.00
Burdock Blood Bitters, Invalid Ladies, Boy Carrying Books To School, 4 1/4 x 3 3/8 In. . . 19.00
C.M. Henderson & Co. Warehouse, Child Drawing Schoolhouse, Bird, 2 3/4 x 4 1/8 In. . . 12.00
Caswell Hazard & Co., Coca Wine, 5 1/2 x 4 1/4 In. 105.00
Clay, Cossack Physician & Surgeon, Drs. Matchette & France, 4 x 2 5/8 In. 61.00
Clipper Ship Galatea, Polyphemus Crushing Acis, Greek Myth, 6 1/2 x 4 In. 748.00
Cudahy's Puritan Meat Products, Calendar, Celluloid, 1926, 2 1/4 x 3 3/4 In. 10.00
Daisy Air Rifle, 2 Boys Duck Hunting, Description On Back, 5 1/2 x 3 1/2 In. 416.00
Daisy Air Rifle, Fletcher Hardware, Latest Parlor Amusement, 2-Sided, 5 3/4 x 3 1/4 In. . . 405.00
Deering & Co., Folding, Farm Settings, Farm Equipment, 14 In. 115.00
Dr. Grove's Anodyne For Infants, Glove Shape, 6 3/8 x 2 1/8 In. 286.00
Dr. O. Fitzgerald, Office Hours, Locations, 8-Sided, 4 3/8 In. 110.00
Dr. Pierce's Golden Med Discovery, Our Artist At Niagara, 3 3/4 x 2 3/8 In. 176.00
Edwin C. Burt Fine Shoes, Black Children Carrying Shoe, 1880s, 4 3/4 x 2 3/4 In. 24.00
Faricum Cough Drops, Before & After Images, 4 7/8 x 3 In. 22.00
Flexible Flyer, Sled That Steers, Figural, Die Cut, 3 1/4 x 6 x 1/2 In. 44.00
Hallet & Davis Pianos, Baby In Scale, Accepted Boston Standard, 5 x 3 1/4 In. 28.00
Henry C. Blaires Sons, Apothecaries, Philadelphia, 5 Vignettes, 3 1/4 x 5 1/4 In. 523.00
Honest Abe Work Shirts-Overalls, Paper, c.1910, 2 1/2 x 4 1/2 In. 4.00
Hunt's Remedy, Kidney & Liver, Men Discussing The Remedy, 3 1/8 x 4 3/4 In. 231.00
J.W. Lincoln, Wood & Canvas Decoys, Accord, Mass., 5 1/4 x 3 1/4 In. 335.00
Jayne Jungle Folk Folder, No. 1, Lion, Hippo, Giraffe, Snake, Fold-Out, 6 x 13 7/8 In. . . . 990.00
Jewel Gasoline Stove, Black Man Wearing Sandwich Board, 2 5/8 x 4 1/8 In. 10.00
King & Chicago Air Rifle, Girl, Boy, Dog, 3 x 5 1/2 In. 231.00
Kress Fever Tonic, Ha, Famous Medicine That Kress Tonic, c.1871, 3 7/8 x 2 5/8 In. 88.00
Lows Magnetic Liniment, Man, Moustache, Left For The Year 1875, 4 1/8 x 2 1/2 In. . . . 468.00
Mexican Mustang Liniment, Jockey, Horse, Cow, Bottle, 2 5/8 x 4 In. 220.00
Murphy Rich Soap, Will Babe Ruth Make 60 Home Runs, c.1922, 3 1/2 x 9 In. 230.00
N.R. Davis & Co., Green, Black Print, 2-Sided, 5 1/4 x 2 7/8 In. 55.00
New Household Ranges, Black Man's Face, Winking, 1880s, 5 1/2 x 4 In. 35.00
Norton Brothers Signs, Cans, Boxes, Tin Lithograph, c.1870s, 2 3/4 x 4 In. 633.00
Packer's Cutaneous Charm, Scenes Of Product Curing Ailments, 5 1/4 x 3 1/4 In. 28.00
Parker Gun, Pigeon Shoot On Front, Price List On Back, 5 3/4 x 3 1/2 In. 193.00
Parker Gun, Shooting Meet, Live Birds, 5 3/4 x 3 1/2 In. 275.00
Pemberton's French Wine Coca, Boat On Lake, Mountains, 4 1/2 x 6 3/4 In. 2640.00
Pemberton's French Wine Coca, Cabin In Woods, 4 7/8 x 7 1/4 In. 2640.00
Pond's Extract, Seated Frog Gives Bottle To Frog With Arm In Sling, 3 1/2 x 5 1/2 In. . . 165.00
Post Toasties Corn Flakes, 1926, 3 1/2 x 5 In. 15.00
Redwood Portable Range, Black Woman, 1880s, 6 x 4 In. 32.00
Remers Tea Store, Girl In Egg, Larned Building, Syracuse, N.Y., 8 x 7 In. 25.00
Rumford Chemical Works, Horsford Bread Preparation, Girl, Curly Hair, 4 7/8 x 3 In. 20.00
Sage's Catarrh Remedy, Man & Huge Nose In Wheelbarrow, c.1871, 4 x 2 5/8 In. 385.00
Sage's Catarrh Remedy, Peter, Peter Pumpkin Eater, c.1872, 4 1/4 x 2 7/8 In. . . . . 121.00 to 154.00
Scotch Oats Essence, Woman Stirs Barrel Contents, c.1900, 4 x 6 In. 4.00
Snider's Catsup, Mechanical, 5 1/4 In. 86.00
Spencer Optical Mfg., Celluloid Eyeglasses, Butterfly Shape, 8 1/8 x 6 In. 50.00
Sterling Pianos, Man, Woman Walking, M. Sonnenberg Piano Co., 4 x 3 In. 5.00
Tatham & Brothers, c.1890, 3 x 4 7/8 In. 72.00
United States Cartridge Co., Man Treed By Bear, US Ammo, 3 1/4 x 6 In. 121.00
US Cartridge Co., Between 2 Fires, R. Farrington Elwell, 1912, 5 1/2 x 3 1/4 In. 77.00
US Cartridge Co., Pack Horses, Titled Elk, R. Farrington Elwell, 1912, 3 1/4 x 6 In. 88.00
Van Stan's Emulsion, 2-Sided, Metamorphic, 5 1/2 x 3 1/4 In. 72.00
White Mountain Ice Cream Freezer, Boy, Pouty Face, 5 x 3 1/4 In. 55.00
Willard & Lane's Eagle Stove Polish, Black Lady, 2 Children, 1880s, 5 3/4 x 3 In. 25.00
Williams Yankee Corn Killer, Black Man Uses Cure, Dances, 3 1/4 x 3 3/8 In. 44.00
Williams' Blood Purifier, Woman Sitting On Couch, Sweeping Floor, 3 x 4 5/8 In. 550.00

TRAY   In the 1880s, two firms in Coshocton, Ohio, were manufacturing advertising novelties, including printed school bags, aprons, fans, calendars, and chair backs. About 1890, one of the companies, owned by H.D. Beach, began printing ads on enameled metal. The other firm, owned by J.F. Meek, tried the same type of printing. Soon hundreds of thousands of printed metal advertising trays were being made by the two firms. The companies merged, but later separated. The H.D. Beach Company is still in business. Other companies in California, Illinois, New York, and Ohio made similar trays. Many trays are marked with the name of the maker in small printed letters on the rim or the back. But beware: Many reproductions and new trays with old-looking designs are made today; some are dated in small numbers on the tray rim.

A. Gettelman Beer, Glass Of Foaming Beer, Gettelman Brewing, Milwaukee, 13 In.	50.00
Abe Freeman, Liquor Dealer, Name Your Brand, I Have It, Tin, Oval, 12 3/4 x 16 In.	2200.00
Adam Scheidt Brewing, Valley Forge Special Beer, Tin Lithograph, 13 1/4 x 10 1/2 In.	66.00
Alabama Brewing Co., The 2 Ideals, Woman, Beer Bottle, Lithograph, 13 In. Diam.	495.00
Altes Lager, Man Pouring Beer Into Glass, Lithograph, Round, Detroit, 12 1/8 In.	358.00
American, Baltimore, Modern Beer, Tin Lithograph, Round, 13 In.	22.00
American Brewing Co., 20th Century Bottled Beer, 2 Kids, Puppy, Kitten, 13 x 13 In.	413.00
Arnholt Schaefer Beer, Woman, Roses, Tin Lithograph, Rectangular, 10 1/2 x 13 1/4 In.	209.00
B. Vedeler, Helping Hand, Waitress, Wood, Minneapolis, Minn., 1914, 13 x 10 1/2 In.	35.00
Baetzhold's Deer Run Whiskey, Buck, Lithograph, 12 In. Diam.	154.00
Bartels Beer, Ale, Porter, There Is None Better, Tin, Oval, 15 1/4 x 12 1/2 In.	39.00
Bartlett Spring Mineral Water, San Francisco, Lady Next To Bottle, 13 In. Diam.	1430.00
Bass & Co. Pale Ale, White Label, McMullen, Horse Heads, Tin Lithograph, 10 3/4 x 13 In.	88.00
Beer Drivers Union Local 132, Capt. Konig & The Deutschland, 1916, 13 In. Diam.	468.00
Beer Drivers Union Local 132, Submarine Scene, Tin Lithograph, Round, 13 In.	413.00
Beer Drivers Union Local 132, Union Beer Only, Tin Lithograph, 10 1/2 x 13 1/4 In.	66.00
Bellmore Whiskey, Man Holding Bottle, 12 In. Diam.	325.00
Bethlehem Liquor, Pure Family Liquors, Children, Rowboat, Tin, Square, 13 In.	825.00
Beverwyck Lager, Woman, Roses, Albany, New York, Round, c.1911, 13 In.	143.00
Bevo, Horse Drawn Wagon, Red Rim, Rectangular, Tin Lithograph, 13 In.	113.00
Buckeye Root Beer, 5 Cents, Large Mug, Boy, Girl, Tin Lithograph, Square, 12 1/2 In.	1300.00
Buffalo Brewing Co., Life Saver, Fireman Holds Beer Glass, Round, 1911, 13 In. .... *Illus*	1623.00
Bushkill Beer, Brewers Since 1849, Easton, Pa., Tin, Round, 12 In.	50.00
C.A. McCubbin, The Globe, Clothing, Shoes, 2 Women, Stove, 14 x 16 In.	195.00
Capudine, It's Liquid, Prompt Results, Tin Lithograph, Round, 10 In.	650.00
Carnation Evaporated Milk, 1990s, 13 3/4 x 10 1/4 In.	17.00
Carnation Milk, Cows, Pasture, Pacific Coast Condensed Milk Co., Oval, 5 1/2 x 3 1/2 In.	143.00
Cherry Sparkle Bottling Co., So. Milwaukee, 13 x 10 In.	175.00
Chippewa's Pride Beer, Indian, Round, Jacob Leinenkugel, Brewing, Wis., 13 In.	99.00
Christian Feigenspan, Woman, Red Ribbon In Hair, Tin Lithograph, Round, 13 1/4 In.	385.00
City Dairies Co., Ice Cream, Smiling Boy & Girl, Plates Of Ice Cream, Round, 12 In.	825.00
Clysmic King Of Table Waters, Woman, Stag, Tin Lithograph, Oval, 13 x 10 In. . .523.00 to	715.00
Cohens Low Price Store, Girl, Flowers, Tin Lithograph, Oval, Somerset, Pa., 16 In.	260.00
Cold Spring Brewery, Woman, Flower In Hair, Tin Lithograph, Oval, 13 3/4 x 16 3/4 In.	358.00
Consolidated, Metal, Pittsburg Ice Co., 11 3/4 In.	33.00
Cook's Beer, Ale, Tin Lithograph, Self-Framed, Oval, 13 1/2 In.	176.00
Crutch Rye, Chrysanthemum Girl, c.1910, 13 1/4 x 10 1/2 In.	132.00
Daeufer's, Beer Glass, Tin Lithograph, Round, 12 In.	66.00
Daeufer's Peerless Beer, Yellow, Black Rim, Tin Lithograph, Oval, 15 x 12 1/2 In.	44.00
Dawson's Ale & Lager, Couple Dining, Tin Lithograph, Round, 12 1/4 In.	303.00
Dear Old Red Raven, Woman Hugging Bird, Tin Lithograph, Round, 24 In.	550.00
Deer Brand Beer, Deer Head, A. Schell Brewing, Round, New Ulm, Minn., 14 In.	176.00
Derby Brand, Ham, Bacon, Tin Lithograph, Rectangular, 13 In.	90.00
Derby King Beer, Horse Race Scene, Southern Breweries, Tin Lithograph, Round, 13 In.	715.00
Dobler Brewing Co., Woman, Red Ribbon In Hair, Tin Lithograph, Round, 13 1/4 In.	55.00
Doebler Beer, Tin Lithograph, Oval, New York, Pre-Prohibition, 13 5/8 x 16 5/8 In.	2310.00
Drink Koch's Beer, Fred Kock Brewery, Tin, Round, 13 In.	154.00
Du Bois, Woman, Flower Vase, Kauffman & Strauss Lithograph, Tin, Round, 13 1/2 In.	143.00
Duesseldorfer Beer, Grand Prize Winners, Baby, Bottle, Robin, 12 In.	300.00
Dunville's Whisky, VR, Crown, Green Letters, Pale Blue, Enamel, England, 11 3/4 In.	38.00

E. Robinson & Sons, Boating Scene, Tin Lithograph, Round, 12 In. 330.00
Early Times Distillery Co., Tin Lithograph, Paducah, Ky., Round, 24 In. 1045.00
Edelweiss Beer, Girl, Short Red Hair, Tin Lithograph, 1913, 13 In. 176.00
Edelweiss Beer, Smiling Woman, Peter Schoenhofen, Chicago, Round, c.1913, 13 In. 116.00
El Gallo, Roy Lopez Ca. Key West Cigars, Rooster, Tin Lithograph, Round, 10 1/8 In. . . .   330.00
Enterprise Meat & Food Choppers, Red Rim, Tin Lithograph, Round, 4 1/4 In. 77.00
Falls City Brewing, Waitress, Tin Lithograph, Round, 12 In. 90.00
Fehr's, Beer, Tin Lithograph, Round, 16 In. 77.00
Frank A. Brunke, Table Luxuries, Woman In Window, Tin, Square, Chicago, 13 In. 198.00
Frank Jones, Monk, Drinking Beer, Round, Portsmouth, N.H., c.1905, 10 1/8 In. 468.00
Frank Jones Ales, Red Shield, Blue Edge, White, Tin Lithograph, Round, 13 1/2 In. 55.00
Frank's Pale Dry Ginger Ale, Red Border, Tin Lithograph, 10 1/2 x 13 1/4 In. 77.00
Franklin Cigar, 5 Cent, Glass, Round, 8 1/4 In. 303.00
Frontenac, Canada's Best, Factory Scene, Montreal, Round, 12 1/4 In. 143.00
Fruit Syrups, Tray Of Fruit, Tin, Logan Johnson, Boston, Rectangular, 10 1/2 x 13 3/4 In.   55.00
Fulgor Polish, Salvador Rull Of Barcelona, Spain, Tin, c.1920s, 3 x 5 In. 35.00
Gambrinus Brewery, King Holding Beer, V. Loewer's, Tin Lithograph, Round, 13 In. 176.00
Gambrinus Quality Pale Beer, August Wagner & Sons, Ohio, Oval, 12 1/2 x 15 1/2 In. . .   176.00
Geo. Ehret's Extra, Oval, Red, Black, Gold, Tin Lithograph, Oval, 13 3/4 x 16 3/4 In. . . .   275.00
German American Brewing, 2 Beer Bottles, Tin Lithograph, Square, 13 1/4 In. 121.00
Gibbon's Beer, Ale, Tin Lithograph, Round, 14 In. 66.00
Ginseng, Beverage Of Purity, Woman On Rickshaw, 10 x 13 1/2 In. 220.00
Goldenrod Beer, Porter, Ale, Factory Scene, Tin Lithograph, 13 1/4 In. 165.00
Goldenrod Beer, Porter, Ale, Hittelman Goldenrod, Tin Lithograph, 12 1/2 x 15 1/4 In. . .   83.00
Gretz Beer, Bottle & Glass, Tin Lithograph, Philadelphia, Round, 13 1/2 In. 193.00
Gypsy Hosiery, Tin Lithograph, Round, 6 In. 440.00
Haberle's, Congress Lager, Black River Ale, Light Ale, Round, Tin, Syracuse, 12 In. 66.00
Hagerstown, Tin Lithograph, Oval, 13 3/4 x 16 3/4 In. 1320.00
Hagerstown Brewing Co., Griselda, Tin Lithograph, Round, 13 In. . . . . .102.00 to 158.00
Hampden Brewing Co., Who Wants The Handsome Waiter?, Tin, Round, 1940s, 13 In. . .   88.00
Hanley's Peerless Ale, Man Gazing At Beer Glass, Tin Lithograph, 11 1/2 In. 121.00
Hanley's Peerless Ale, Porcelain, Baltimore Enamel & Novelty, 12 In. 254.00
Hanover Whiskey, Horse Head, Landscape, Tin Lithograph, c.1907, 28 x 38 In. 690.00
Harvard Brewery, Lady, Calendar On Rim, 1907, 10 In. Diam. 220.00
Harvard Brewing Co., Woman In Long White Dress, Tin Lithograph, Round, 12 In. 770.00
Hauenstein's Beer, New Ulm, Minn., 14 In. Diam. 95.00
Heidel-Brau Beer, Round, Sioux City Brewing, Iowa, 12 In. 66.00
Horlacher's Beer, Girl Smelling Flower, Tin Lithograph, Oval, 13 3/4 x 16 3/4 In. 2750.00
Horlacher's Beer, Woman In Garden, Blue Border, Tin Lithograph, 10 In. 99.00
Horlacher's Beer, Woman, Cupids, Garden, Red Border, Tin Lithograph, 10 In. 121.00
Huedepohl Beers, Decidedly The Best, Green Ground, Tin Lithograph, Round, 14 3/4 In.   39.00
Ideal Beer, Alabama Brewing Co., Beautiful Woman, 13 In. 450.00
Indianapolis Brewing Co., Lieber's Gold Medal Beer, 9 1/4 In. 125.00
Iroquois Indian Head Beer & Ale, Buffalo, N.Y., 12 In. 110.00
Isaac Weil & Son, Monk, Keg, Tin Lithograph, Oval, 13 1/2 x 16 1/2 In. 385.00
Jacob Ruppert, Beer, Ale, Hands Holding Beer Mugs, Tin, Oval, 14 1/2 x 10 3/4 In. 33.00
Jacob Ruppert, Beer, Ale, Hands Holding Mugs, Tin Lithograph, Oval, 16 3/4 x 13 3/4 In.   22.00
Jersey Creme, Perfect Drink, Smiling Woman, Tin Lithograph, Round, 12 1/8 In. 440.00
Jersey Creme, Woman, Bonnet, Charles W. Schaump Lithographing, Tin, Round, 12 In. 275.00
Jersey Creme, Woman, Hat, Tin Lithograph, Round, 12 In. 203.00
John Hauenstein Beer, Beer Bottle, Oval, New Ulm, Minnesota, 16 In. 154.00
Kaiser Wilhelm Bitters Co., For Appetite & Digestion, Tin Lithograph, 14 x 10 1/4 In. . .   440.00
Kansas City Brewery's Old Fashioned Lager, Lady, Tray, Tin Lithograph, 12 In. Diam. . .   550.00
Kauer's, Beer, Ale, Porter, Tin Lithograph, Rectangular, Mahonoy City, Pa., 13 x 10 1/2 In.   39.00
Keeley Brewing Co., Our Malt Tonic Should Be In Every Home, Round, 1915, 12 1/8 In. .   264.00
King Coin Cigar, Woman, Roses, Tin Lithograph, Round, Martter Cigar Co., 10 1/4 In. . . .   396.00
Kings Beer, Crown, Round, 12 In. 210.00
Kuebler Beer, Since 1852, Tin Lithograph, Round, Easton, Pa., 12 In. 187.00
Kueller's, Chinese Child Holding Lantern, Tin Lithograph, 10 1/2 x 13 1/4 In. 77.00
Labatt's, London, Canada, Established 1832, Round, 12 1/2 In. 50.00
Land O' Lakes Sweet Cream Butter, Indian Maiden, Lake, Trees, Cows, 13 x 10 3/4 In. .   28.00
Leisy Brewing Co., Factory, Tin Lithograph, Multicolored, 13 5/8 x 16 5/8 In. 853.00
Lemp St. Louis, Woman Pouring Beer Into Man's Tankard, Tin Lithograph, c.1930, 24 In.   414.00

Limbergs Ice Cream Co., Woman, Feeding Horse, Tin Lithograph, 13 In. 525.00
Los Angeles Brewing Co., East Side Beer, Factory, Tin Lithograph, Round, 13 1/8 In. 798.00
Maxwell House Coffee, Old Couple Drinking Coffee, Since 1892, Lithograph, Oval, 17 In. . 214.00
McDonald Patent Maple Syrup Spouts, Winter Scene, Tin Lithograph, Oval, 15 x 18 In. . 230.00
Melrose Distillers, Metal, N.Y.C., 11 3/4 In. 22.00
Menk's Bottle Beer, Try A Bottle, Man, Top Hat, Louisville, c.1912, 13 1/2 x 16 1/2 In. . . 523.00
Midwest Pure Cream Ice Cream, Ritzy Rich, 10 1/2 x 13 1/4 In. 65.00
Minnesota Club Bourbon, Bottle, Brown Ground, A. Hirschman, St. Paul, 10 x 13 In. . . . 99.00
Mistletoe Creameries, Ice Cream, Tin Lithograph, Square, c.1925, 13 1/4 In. 154.00
Moores & Ross, Cream Of All Creams, Vanilla Sundae, Spoon, Doily, Red, 13 3/8 In. 26.00
Narragansett Banquet Ale, Red Ground, Black Rim, Round, Tin Lithograph, 13 In. 28.00
National Brewery, Factory Scene, Lithography, Pre-Prohibition, 10 1/4 x 13 1/2 In. 495.00
National Cigar Stand, Woman, Flowers In Hair, 1 Bare Shoulder, Round, 6 In. 220.00
National Enameling & Stamping Co., Porcelain, 16 1/2 In. 1413.00
Neff's Ice Cream, Tin Lithograph, Round, 13 1/4 In. 99.00
Nehi Soda, Woman In Wave, Rectangular, Tin Lithograph, 10 1/2 x 15 1/4 In. 220.00
Neuweiler's Famous Brews, Tin Lithograph, Round, 13 In. 66.00
North Western National Bank, Portland, Tin Lithograph, Oval, 4 1/4 x 6 In. 132.00
NuGrape, Flavor You Can't Forget, Woman, Bottle, Tin Lithograph, 1920s, 13 x 10 1/2 In. 248.00
NuGrape, Girl Drinking Soda, Tin Lithograph, 11 x 13 In. 182.00
NuGrape, Hand Holding Bottle, Tin Lithograph, Rectangular, 1920s, 13 In. 90.00
NuGrape, Woman, Child, Fountain, American Art Works, 1920s, 10 1/4 x 13 1/4 In. 358.00
NuGrape Soda, Soda Bottle, Tin Lithograph, Rectangular, 10 1/2 x 13 1/4 In. 110.00
Old Barbee Distillery, No. 32, 7th District, Mountain Distillery, Round, Ky., 10 1/8 In. . . 330.00
Old Catasauqua Dutch Beer, Eagle Brewing, Tin Lithograph, Round, 13 In. 88.00
Old Crutch Rye, Monk Bottling Whisky, Oval, 16 1/2 x 13 1/2 In. 132.00
Old Dutch Breweries, Dutch Tavern, Lager Beer, Mug, Tin Lithograph, Round, 12 3/4 In. 187.00
Old Dutch Premium Beer, Eagle Brewing Company, Catasauqua, Pa., 11 7/8 In. 200.00
Old Reading Beer, Fat Man, Begging Dog, Round, 14 In. 99.00
Olympia Bottling Co., Golden Brew, Chrysanthemum Girl, 1910, 13 x 10 1/2 In. 468.00
Orange Julep, Girl Holding Drink, 13 1/4 x 10 1/2 In. 165.00
Orange Julep, Girl On Beach, Tin Lithograph, 1920s, 13 1/4 x 10 1/4 x 1 1/4 In. 231.00
Orange Julep, Woman, Bathing Suit, Parasol, Tin Lithograph, 1920s, 10 x 13 In. . . .275.00 to 358.00
Par-Ex, Woman, Tiger, Tin, Round, 1904, 12 3/8 In. 605.00
Perfect Brew, Bulldog, Tin Lithograph, Square, 13 In. 198.00
Peter Doelger, Bottled Beer, Eagle, Tin Lithograph, Oval, 16 3/4 x 13 3/4 In. 440.00
Peter Doelger, Bottled Beer, Expressly For The Home, Spread Winged Eagle, 6 1/4 x 4 In. 297.00
Pickwick Ale, Tin Lithograph, Horse Drawn Wagon, Round, 12 In. 28.00
Piels, Beer Enjoy, Tall Man, Short Man, Tin Lithograph, Round, 13 In. 17.00
Player's Cigarettes, Navy Cut, Yellow, Glass, 6 1/2 x 6 In. 88.00
Polar Ginger Ale, Polar Bear, Green, Yellow, Round, 13 In. 61.00
Progress Beer, Men, Table, Fire In Fireplace, Indianapolis Brewing, 13 x 10 In. 132.00
Prosit, Men Seated At Table, Chas. Lutz & Bro, Lithograph, Brooklyn, 1910, 10 x 13 In. . 303.00
Purity Ice Cream, Tin Lithograph, Rectangular, 13 In. 124.00
Rainier Beer, Cowgirl On Horse, 13 In. Diam. 1660.00
Rainier Beer, Evelyn Nesbitt, Chinese Honeymoon, Round, 1903, 13 In. 1210.00
Rainier Beer, There's New Vigor & Strength In Every Drop, 13 x 10 1/2 In. 770.00
Rainier Pale, Beer Bottle & Glass, Round, 13 In. 462.00
Ravenswood, Sparkling Table Water, Red Tree, Tin Lithograph, Round, 12 In. 99.00
Red Raven, Ask The Man, Child, Bottle, Papa Has A Headache, Round, 12 In. 220.00
Red Raven, Ask The Man, Dear Old Raven, Woman, Bird, Lithograph, Round, 12 In. 358.00
Red Raven, For Headache, For Indigestion, Bird, Bottle, Tin Lithograph, Square, 13 In. . . 468.00
Red Ribbon Beer, Bear Drinking From Bottle, Tin Lithograph, Square, 13 In. 330.00
Red Ribbon Beer, Old Dutch Lager, Mathie Brewing Co., Girl, Ukulele, 13 In. Diam. . . . 660.00
Renner Products, 2 Beer Bottles, Gold Color Rim, Rectangular, 13 1/4 x 10 1/2 In. 55.00
Rheingold, Beer, Scotch Ale, Soldiers Marching, Uniforms, Tin Lithograph, Round, 12 In. 11.00
Robin Hood Beer, A.B. Co. Brewers, Scranton, Pa., Oval, 11 x 8 In. 425.00
Royal Bohemian Beer, Duluth Brewing, 2 Lion Crest, Round, Duluth, Minn., 13 In. 50.00
Royal Purple Grape Juice, Nature's Best Tonic, Woman, Tin Lithograph, Round, 13 In. . . 385.00
Rubsam & Horrmann, Bottle Beers, Topless Woman, Tin Lithograph, Round, 12 1/2 In. . . 1650.00
Ruhstaller's Gilt Edge, Man, Standing, 2 Women In Car, Tin Lithograph, Square, 13 In. . . 715.00
Ruppert, Beer, Ale, 2 Hands Holding Beer Mugs, Tin Lithograph, Round, 13 1/2 In. 33.00
S. Killiam, Furnisher, Clothier, Angels, Tin Lithograph, Lewistown, Pa., Oval, 16 In. 452.00

Tray, Buffalo Brewing Co., Life Saver, Fireman Holds Beer Glass, Round, 1911, 13 In.

Tray, Utica Club, West End Brewing Co., Round, 12 In.

Say Reading Beer, Bartender, Begging Dog, Tin Lithograph, Round, 13 1/2 In. 176.00
Schaefer Fine Beer, Tin Lithograph, Red, Black, Gold, Round, 13 1/4 In. 17.00
Scheidt's, Valley Forge, Tin Lithograph, Round, 13 1/4 In. .39.00 to 66.00
Schmidt, Asian Woman, Umbrella, Tin Lithograph, 10 1/2 x 13 1/4 In. 28.00
Schmidt's, Beer & Ale, Pilgrim Scene, Tin Lithograph, Oval, 12 1/2 x 15 1/4 In. 55.00
Schnecksville State Bank, Woman In Wide Brim Hat, Musselman, 1920, 4 1/2 x 6 1/2 In. 187.00
Schoenfelds Clothing & Shoe, Tin Lithograph, Altoona, Pa., Oval, 16 1/2 In. 170.00
Seitz Beer, Spread Wing Eagle, Brewers Since 1821, Easton, Pa., Tin Lithograph, 12 In. . 176.00
Seitz Brewing Co., Bulldog, Tin Lithograph, Square, 13 1/4 x 13 1/2 In. 330.00
Soo Line Railroad, Michigan, Dakotas, Wisconsin, Minnesota, 15 x 10 In. 176.00
Souvenir Of San Francisco, United States Shape, Metal, Japan, 1940-1950, 4 x 2 1/2 In. . . 14.00
St. Pauli Brewery, Bremen, St. Pauli Girl, Tin, Round, 12 In. 6.00
Standard Brewing Company, Tin Lithograph, Execution Of Sioux, 12 In. 550.00
Standard Distilling & Distributing, Victor Cocktails, 2 Cocks, 1 Dead, Round, 12 1/4 In. 440.00
Standard Pale Beer, Woman, Roses, Fred Sehring Brewing, c.1911, 10 x 13 In. 121.00
Stanton Beer & Ale, Tin Lithograph, Red, Black, Gold, Troy, N.Y., Round, 12 In. 17.00
Stegmaier Brewing, Factory Scene, Wilkes-Barre, Pa., Round, 12 In. 303.00
Stegmaier Brewing, Woman, Long Brown Hair, Tin Lithograph, Round, 13 In. 303.00
Stegmaier's Gold Medal Beer, Factory, Round, 12 In. 330.00
Stokely's Finest Foods, Black Border, Rectangular, 10 1/2 x 13 1/4 In. 17.00
Stroh's, Bohemian Beer, Tin Lithograph, Round, 12 In. 550.00
Stroh's, Lager Beer, Detroit, Tin Lithograph, Round, 12 In. 2200.00
Stroh's, Square, Red Cloaked Person Carrying Beer Crate, 13 In. 34.00
Supreme Beer, South Bethlehem Brewery, Blue Ground, Tin Lithograph, Round, 13 In. . . 17.00
Taka-Kola, Take No Other, Woman, Roman Numerals, 13 In. Diam. 330.00
Tanglefoot, Sanitary Fly Destroyer, Non Poisonous, Metal, 1880-1900, 9 x 11 In. 48.00
Tip, see Tip Tray
Tom Moore Cigar, America's Favorite, Tin Lithograph, Round, 13 1/8 In. 1595.00
Trayders Ginger Ale, Belfast Mineral Water Co., Enamel, England, Round, 11 1/2 In. 38.00
Tru-Blue Beer & Ale, Tin Lithograph, Round, 13 In. 44.00
Utica Club, West End Brewing Co., Round, 12 In. . . . . *Illus* 50.00
Utica Club Brewing Co., Round, 13 In. 58.00
V.A. Oswald, Man In Green Jacket, Red Hat, Tin, Altoona, Pa., Oval, 16 1/2 In. 165.00
Velvet Champagne Radium, Terre Haute Brewing Co., Ind., Tin, Oval 121.00
Velvet Kind Ice Cream, Tin Lithograph, Round, 13 1/2 In. 367.00
W.M. Sehrt, Girl, Blue Ribbon In Hair, Tin Lithograph, Oval, 13 3/4 x 16 1/2 In. 55.00
Walter Brewing Co., Brewery, Eau Claire, Wis., 10 x 14 3/4 In. 330.00
Welz & Zerweck, Tin Lithograph, Oval, 16 1/2 x 13 3/4 In. 303.00
West End Brewing Co., Woman, Flag Dress, Tin Lithograph, Utica, N.Y., Round, 13 In. . . 825.00
West End Brewing Co., Wuerzburger Pilsener, Tin Lithograph, Utica, N.Y., Round, 13 In. 22.00
Whann Lithia Water, Woman In Center, Tin Lithograph, Round, 10 In. 34.00
Williams's Whisky, Lithograph, Porcelain, Metal, Aberdeen, Round, 12 In. 143.00
Wooden Shoe Lager Beer, 2 Dutch Girls, Star Beverage Co., Tin Lithograph, Round, 12 In. 154.00
Yeungling's, Fine Beer, Tin Lithograph, Round, 12 1/4 In. 358.00
Yosemite Lager, Lady Holding Flowers, 13 In. Diam. 523.00
Young's Ocean Pier, Atlantic City, New Jersey, 12 In. Diam. 468.00
Zipp's, Cherri-O, Bird, Drinking From Glass, c.1920, 12 In. . . . . .625.00 to 647.00

TV PREMIUM, see Premium

VICTOR   Eldridge Johnson formed the Victor Talking Machine Company in 1901 and introduced the Victor record brand the same year. In 1903 Victor launched another record brand, Red Seal. Meanwhile, the trademark now known as Nipper was owned by the Gramophone Company of Bristol, England. Nipper was based on a painting by Francis Barraud that pictured Barraud's dog listening to a recording. Barraud added a Gramophone horn to the picture and sold it as an ad to the Gramophone Company. He and the company titled the picture "His Master's Voice." In 1906 Victor acquired U.S. rights to use the popular trademark. RCA, the Radio Corporation of America (formed in 1919 by General Electric and AT&T), purchased the Victor Talking Machine Company, including the Nipper trademark, in 1929. RCA was acquired by General Electric in 1986. In 1988 GE sold the record business to Bertelsmann AG and the consumer electronics business to Thomson Grand Public (now named Thomson). Thomson introduced Nipper's puppy companion, Chipper, in 1990. GE retains rights to the RCA brand and trademarks. RCA and Nipper items are listed here.

Bank, RCA, Nipper, Fuzzy Flocking Over Metal, Radio Corp. Coin Trap, 6 1/4 In.	253.00
Bank, Truck, RCA Victor Talking Machines, Dog, Die Cast Metal, Gearbox Toy, Box	34.00
Brush, RCA Records, Celluloid, Soft Pile Fabric, c.1940, 3 1/5 In.	20.00
Display, RCA Radiotron, Shadowbox, Radio Shape, Cardboard, 19 x 14 1/2 x 3 3/4 In.	132.00
Figure, Nipper, Papier-Mache, 34 In.	880.00
Figure, RCA Radiotrons, Blue Shirt, Red Boots, Red Sash, Wood, Jointed, 16 In.	.633.00 to 825.00
Lighter, Chrome, Enameled, RCA Television, Box, 2 3/4 x 2 1/8 In.	55.00
Mirror, RCA, Dog Listening To Victor, Celluloid, Oval, 2 3/4 In.	413.00
Print, Talking Machine, His Master's Voice, Nipper, 7 x 9 3/4 In.	20.00
Sign, RCA Victor Radios, Porcelain, Self-Framed, 72 x 18 In.	660.00
Sign, RCA Victor Radios, Victrola & Nipper, Light-Up, 13 x 12 In.	165.00
Sign, RCA Victor, His Master's Voice, Plastic, Aluminum, Light-Up, Square, 37 In.	29.00
Sign, RCA, His Master's Voice, Dog, Phonograph, Porcelain, 24 x 18 In.	853.00
Sign, Victor Phonograph, His Master's Voice, Dog, Phonograph, Porcelain, 9 x 12 In.	358.00

WARNER'S SAFE   Hulbert H. Warner worked as a farmer before he was apprenticed to a tinsmith in Memphis, Tennessee. He set up a tin shop in Michigan, but went bankrupt in 1870. He set out as a traveling salesman of pots and pans, and eventually settled in Rochester, New York. He and a partner started to sell safes. In the late 1870s, now the sole owner of a large safe company, Warner sought to gain more prominence and money by opening another business. Patent medicine appeared to offer the best opportunity. Warner designed a trademark of a picture of an iron safe. Later, the trademark included the word "safe." Warner's first medicine was Warner's Safe Kidney & Liver Cure (1879), made of herbs, alcohol, and water. He advertised via newspapers, almanacs, booklets, posters, trade cards, calendars, cookbooks, puzzles, games, and pamphlets, using testimonials by presidents and famous authors. Within two years, his sales topped $5 million. Warner is credited with writing and paying for the first newspaper advertisement that looked like a local news story. His other medicines included Warner's Safe Diabetes Cure, Warner's Safe Rheumatic Cure, Warner's Safe Nervine, Benton's Hair Grower, Warner's Safe Yeast, Warner's Safe Bitters, Warner's Safe Tonic, H.H. Warner & Co. Tippecanoe (1883), Warner's Log Cabin Hops and Buchu Remedy (1887), Warner's Log Cabin Sarsaparilla (1887), Scalpine (1887), Warner's Log Cabin Cough & Consumption Remedy (1887), Log Cabin Extract (1887), and Log Cabin Rose Cream (1887). By 1890 Warner was rich—he had a yacht, a mansion, an observatory, and the respect of the scientific community because he donated money for research. He was also a patron of the arts. Warner sold his business in 1889 to a group of Englishmen for over $3 million, but he regained control in 1893. When the United States passed the Pure Food and Drug Act of 1906, advertising had to be more truthful. Warner replaced the word "Cure" with "Remedy," and could use the word "Safe" only as a trademark. Another group of English investors then bought the

company and moved its headquarters to London. Warner's moved back
to Rochester in 1910, when it was purchased by J.J. Demay and S.R.
Keaner. It remained in business until about 1934. Shortly after selling
his company, Warner moved to Minneapolis, Minnesota, where he
died in 1913.

Booklet, Remedies, Woman On Ship's Deck, 1909, 5 x 7 1/4 In., 16 Pages 83.00
Bottle, Bitters, Amber, Applied Mouth, Rochester, N.Y., 1880-1885, 7 1/2 In. 1008.00
Bottle, Cure, Amber, Embossed, London, 7 1/4 In. . . . . .35.00 to 51.00
Bottle, Cure, Green, Embossed, London, 7 1/4 In. 127.00
Bottle, Cure, Greenish Yellow, London, 1/2 Pt. 75.00
Bottle, Cure, London, England, Olive Green, 1885-1900, 9 1/4 In. 179.00
Bottle, Diabetes Cure, Australia, Amber, 1885-1900, 9 1/2 In. 308.00
Bottle, Diabetes Cure, England, Yellow, 1885-1900, 9 1/2 In. 224.00
Bottle, Diabetes Cure, Rochester, N.Y., Amber, 1880-1895, 9 5/8 In. 213.00
Bottle, Diabetes Remedy, Amber, Label, Contents, Flyers, Box, 16 Oz., 9 1/2 In. 468.00
Bottle, H.H. Warner & Co., Tippecanoe, Amber, Rochester, N.Y., c.1883, 9 In. . . .159.00 to 364.00
Bottle, Kidney & Liver Cure, Rochester, N.Y., Amber, 10 In. 41.00
Bottle, Kidney & Liver Remedy, Amber, Label, Contents, Flyers, Box, 16 Oz., 9 1/2 In. . . .   385.00
Bottle, Kidney & Liver, Contents, Label, 12 1/2 Oz., 9 1/4 In. 55.00
Bottle, Kidney, Liver & Brights Disease, Honey Amber, Embossed, Paper Label, 9 In. 176.00
Bottle, Nervine, Rochester, N.Y., Amber, 1880-1895, 7 1/2 In. 157.00
Bottle, Rheumatic Compound, Amber, ABM, Label, 12 1/2 Oz., 9 In. 176.00
Bottle, Rheumatic Cure, Rochester, N.Y., Amber, 1880-1895, 9 1/2 In. 112.00
Bottle, Rheumatic Remedy, Sciatica, Lumbago, Gout, Embossed, 12 1/2 Oz., 9 In. 132.00
Bottle, Safe Nervine, Non-Alcoholic, Embossed, Paper Label, Contents, 6 Oz., 7 1/8 In. .   187.00
Canister, Yeast, Cardboard, Paper Label, 5 x 2 1/4 In. 286.00
Crate, Wood, Rochester, N.Y., 10 1/2 x 10 1/2 x 14 In. 143.00
Sign, Log Cabin Remedies, Reverse On Glass, Frame, 13 x 11 In. 2200.00
Sign, Rheumatic Cure, Reverse On Glass, 3 7/8 x 16 In. 220.00
Sign, Yeast, Health Preserving, Indians, Canoe, Stream, Frame, 18 x 34 In. 3520.00
Tin, Asthma Remedy, Paper Label, 3 1/4 x 2 In. 253.00
Vial, Warner's Cathartic Pills, Glass, Cylinder, Unopened, 2 1/4 In. 88.00

WATCH FOB   Watch fobs are charms worn on a watch chain. They
were popular in Victorian times. Many styles, especially advertising
designs, are collected today.

Abraham Fur Co., Fox Head, Black Enamel Bezel, St. Louis, U.S.A. 46.00
Abraham Fur Co., Fox Head, Leather Strap, G.D. Childs Co., St. Louis, U.S.A., Chicago .   117.00
Abraham Fur Co., Fox Head, Red Enamel Bezel, St. Louis, U.S.A. 50.00
American Powder Mills, Dead Shot, Falling Duck, Brass, Celluloid, 1 3/8 In. 157.00
Clarke's Pure Rye, Man Holding Glass, Bottle, Sterling Silver, 1930s, 1 1/2 x 1 3/4 In. 38.00
Colt Mfg. Co., Rearing Horse, Brass, Scroll & Filigree Edge, 1 5/8 x 1 3/8 In. 85.00
Dead Shot Powder, Falling Duck, Brass, Celluloid Insert, Leather Strap, 1 1/2 In. .231.00 to 381.00
Funsten Fur Co., Pewter, 5 Discs, 4 Centuries Of Fur Trading, Bear, 7 x 1 3/8 In. 440.00
Hercules, Logo, Kenvil, Employee Photograph, c.1918, 1 1/4 In. 92.00
Hunter Trader Trapper, Brass, Bear In Shield, Columbus, Ohio, 2 1/4 x 1 1/2 In. 46.00
Indian, Linked Chain, Sterling Silver, Early 1900s, 4 x 1 1/4 In.   165.00
National Sportsman's Magazine, Embossed Buck, Gun, Gold Color, 1 5/8 x 1 1/2 In. . . .   58.00
National Sportsman's Magazine, Raised Deer, Fishing Rods, Leather Belt, 1 1/2 In. 28.00
Red Man Tobacco, Indian Chief, Good Cigar Leaf, Metal, Leather Strap, 1 x 1 1/2 In. 77.00
S. Silberman & Sons, Fur Shipper, Otter, S, Copper 70.00
Savage Arms Co., Indian In Headdress, Bronze, 1 1/4 In. 35.00
Savage Arms Co., Panama Pacific Exposition, Metal, Copper Flash, 1915, 1 1/2 In. Diam.   330.00
Savage Automatica Pistol 90.00
Schuetzen Rifles, Crossed, 25 Targets, Engraved, Nickel Plated, 2 x 1 1/4 In. 66.00
Shapleigh Hardware Co., DE, Diamond Edge, Diamond Shape, Copper, Silver Bezel 44.00
Smith & Wesson, Brass, S&W Logo, Revolver, Round, 1 1/8 In. 22.00
Trojan Powder Co., No. 141, Embossed, Brass, Stamped, c.1915, 1 1/2 x 1 1/2 In. 77.00

WATKINS   J.R. Watkins opened a business in Plainview, Minnesota, in
1868 after he purchased rights to Dr. Ward's liniment. Over the next
decade he added more products to his line. In 1884 he reorganized the
company as J.R. Watkins Medical Company and moved the business

to Winona, Minnesota, the following year. More locations were opened and more products, including gourmet foods, were offered. About 1920, the company dropped the word "medical" and became J.R. Watkins Company. In 1959 the name was changed to Watkins Products, Inc. The Watkins family transferred ownership of the company to Irwin Jacobs in 1978. Mark Jacobs became president in 1997. The company's U.S. headquarters remain in Winona, Minnesota.

Bottle, Watkins Cough Syrup, For Coughs From Colds, 6 1/4 In.	10.00
Bottle, Watkins Imitation Vanilla Extract, Embossed, Label, Screw Top, 8 x 3 x 1 3/4 In. .	75.00
Bottle, Watkins Trial, Hindu Pain Oil, Paper Label, Aqua, 8 1/2 In.	22.00
Tin, Baking Powder, Purity Guaranteed, Lithograph, 2 Oz., 2 1/2 x 1 3/4 In.	66.00
Tin, Cloves, Pry Lid, Square Base, J.R. Watkins Co., Winona, Minn., 3 1/2 x 1 3/4 In.	70.00
Tin, Deodorant Powder, W.R. Watkins Co., Free Trial Size, 2 3/4 x 1 1/2 x 7/8 In.	38.00
Tin, Laxative & Cold Grip Tablets, Early 1900s, 3 1/2 x 2 3/4 x 1/2 In.	10.00
Tin, Lemon Dessert, Free Trial Size, Cardboard, Metal, 3 x 2 1/2 In.	145.00
Tin, Petro-Carbo Salve, Round, 1 1/4 x 2 5/8 In.	28.00
Tin, Sweetened Malted Milk, Pry Lid, 5 3/4 x 3 3/8 In.	120.00
Tin, Tooth Powder, Embossed, 6 In.	187.00
Tin, Violet Talcum Powder, Oval Base, Winona, Minn., 6 1/4 x 3 x 1 1/2 In.	95.00

WEATHERBIRD   Claflin-Allen Shoe Company of St. Louis, Missouri, was manufacturing footware in the late 1830s for people heading west in wagon trains. Peters Shoe Company, successor to Claflin-Allen, copyrighted the name "Weather-Bird" for its children's shoes in 1907. Peters merged with Roberts, Johnson & Rand Shoe Company in 1911 to form the International Shoe Company. The company became Interco Inc. in 1966, but the International Shoe Company remained as one of its divisions until 1987. The Weatherbird brand was discontinued at about the same time.

Bank, Figural, Rooster, Parasol, Hard Plastic, c.1960, 2 x 3 x 4 In.	15.00
Bank, Rooster, Standing Atop Weathervane, Plastic, 1960s, 3 3/4 x 3 1/4 In.	15.00
Clicker, Peters Weatherbird Shoes, Tin, Blue Green, Kirchof, USA	22.00
Clicker, Rooster, All Leather, For All Weather, Tin, Red, Yellow	25.00
Sign, Boy Holding Sign, Embossed, Cardboard, 1940-1950, 9 1/4 x 6 In.	29.00
Sign, Peters Weatherbird Shoes, For Girls, For Boys, Glass, 8 x 4 1/2 In.	138.00
Stickpin, 2 1/2 In.	25.00
Whistle, All Leather Best For Boys & Girls, Rooster, Tin, Yellow, Peters, 2 In.	28.00
Whistle, Cylinder, Blue	.60.00 to 75.00
Whistle, Cylinder, Green	60.00
Whistle, Happy Days & Healthy Feet, Barrel Shape, Green, Solid Leather, Kirchhof	24.00
Whistle, Peters Weatherbird Shoes, Barrel Shape, Tin, Green, Kirchof, USA	24.00

WENDY'S   David Thomas had worked with several restaurant chains before he decided to open his own restaurant in Columbus, Ohio, in 1969. A pickup window and fresh, square hamburgers set it apart from the competition. The square burger was developed for two reasons: it took up less space on the grill and the corners protruded from the bun, making it appear larger. Wendy, the company trademark, was based on a photograph of Wendy Thomas, the owner's daughter. Wendy's first national TV campaign ran in 1977 with the slogan "Hot 'n Juicy." Then came "Wendy's, Ain't No Reason to Go Anyplace Else" (1981), and "Wendy's Kind of People" (1982). Its most memorable campaign was the 1984 "Where's the Beef?" series. Wendy's installed its first salad bar in 1979. Wendy's merged with Tim Hortons, a Canadian restaurant chain, in 1995. Dave Thomas, who appeared in numerous commercials for his company, died in 2002. Collectors want all types of advertising materials from Wendy's, including paper plates, store promotion signs, place mats, and giveaways. The original restaurant is still open at 257 East Broad Street in Columbus. The Wendy's name, logos, and slogans are owned by Oldemark and are licensed to Wendy's International.

Book, Wishbone Classic Tales Photo Book, Wishbone The Dog, Stickers, 1996	10.00

T-Shirt, Hot 'n Juicy, Yellow, Red Slogan, Kings Sportswear, Poly/Cotton, Medium, 1980s 28.00
Tumbler, New York Times, Columbia Returns, Shuttle Era Opens 9.00
Tumbler, New York Times, Nation & Millions In City Joyously Hail Bicentennial 9.00
Tumbler, World's Fair, Knoxville, Tennessee, 1982 .... 3.00

WHEATIES Wheaties cereal was introduced in 1924 by the Washburn Crosby Company of Minneapolis, Minnesota. The cereal's first advertising was aired on Washburn Crosby's Minneapolis radio station, WCCO, on Christmas Eve 1926. A male quartet made up of a municipal court bailiff, a businessman, an undertaker, and a printer sang "Have Ya Tried Wheaties?" It was the first singing commercial. Wheaties sponsored the radio shows *Skippy* (1931–1933) and *Jack Armstrong, All American Boy* (1933–1951). In 1933 Wheaties began to sponsor baseball broadcasts, and "Wheaties—Breakfast of Champions" became the product's trademarked slogan. In 1939 Wheaties was the first sponsor of a televised commercial sports broadcast. Wheaties advertising included many premiums. Skippy Secret Service Society pins, buttons, and certificates were exchanged for box tops. The Jack Armstrong shooting plane (1933) was so popular that grocery stores ran out of Wheaties for almost six months. The 1939 Jack Armstrong hike-o-meter was mailed to 1.2 million listeners; a torpedo flashlight offered the same year went to 6.6 million homes. Shirley Temple blue glass cereal bowls were offered in 1935 and 5 million were distributed. A Shirley Temple milk pitcher (1936), Jack Armstrong explorer telescope (1938), Jack Armstrong Sky Ranger model plane (1940), World War II model airplane kits (1944), and a set of miniature auto license plates (1953, 1954) were all premiums sent to millions of Wheaties buyers. Endorsements by sports figures were used starting in 1933 and are still popular. In 1984 gymnast Mary Lou Retton became the first female sports figure to be pictured on the front of a Wheaties box, although Patty Berg, Babe Didrikson, and other women athletes had endorsed the cereal. Washburn Crosby and several other milling concerns merged to form General Mills in 1928. The company is also known for Betty Crocker products, Gold Medal flour, Yoplait Yogurt, Old El Paso Mexican foods, Progresso soups, and Green Giant products. Since 2000 General Mills has also owned Pillsbury, which is listed in its own category in this book.

Advertisement, Boy Eating Wheaties, Dreaming, Babe Ruth, 1956, 13 x 10 In., 2 Pages .. 15.90
Box, Muhammad Ali, 1960s Photograph, 1998 .... 20.00
Charm, Cereal Box, 1/2 In. 6.00
Hike-O-Meter, Jack Armstrong, 1938, 2 5/8 In. 35.00
Pedometer, Jack Armstrong, Premium, Instructions, Mailer, 1940, 2 3/4 In. 61.00

WHISTLE Toy whistles have been made out of wood, tin, brass, ceramic, and plastic. Plastic is the most common material. A variety of plastics have been used: celluloid (1920–1930), Bakelite (1930–1940), variegated hard plastic (1940–1950), hard plastic (1940 to present), and vinyl (since 1970). The number of digits in the postal code on a whistle also help date it: no zip code (before 1943), one or two digits (1943–1963), five digits (1963–1984), and nine digits (after 1984). Look for other whistles in brand-specific categories.

Chicken Dinner Delicious Candy, Flat, 3/4 x 2 In. 80.00
First Federal Savings & Loan, Yellow, White, Plastic, Atlanta, Ga., 4 1/4 In. 5.00
Foremost Dairy, Bugle Boy, Horn Shape, Plastic, 1950s, 5 In. 32.00
Hurd Shoes For Boys & Girls, They're Tops, Metal, Red Lithograph 22.00
Robin Hood Shoes, Flat, 1 x 2 5/8 In. 95.00
Twinkie Shoes For Girls & Boys, Balloon Shape, 1 1/8 x 1 1/4 In. 125.00
Wienermobile, Plastic, 1970s, 1 x 2 1/2 x 1 1/2 In. 1.00

WHITE ROCK In 1871 H.W. Culver bought land in Waukesha, Wisconsin, where there was a spring he named White Rock for the white limestone nearby. He began to sell the spring water in brown bottles and operated a spa offering the water's healthful effects. Psyche kneeling on a rock looking at her reflection was the subject of an oil painting displayed at the 1893 World's Columbian Exposition in Chicago. Officials of the White Rock Mineral Springs Company saw the painting and decided it was the perfect trademark for their product. She had the measurements of a beauty of that day, 37-27-38. In 1924 the company modernized her hairstyle. In 1947 her hairstyle was updated again and she also lost weight, grew two inches, and was given new measurements, 35-25-35. In 1960 she donned a more revealing costume. In the 1970s she grew two more inches, lost more weight, and had new measurements, 35-24-34. One of the country's best-known trademarks, she has been featured in cartoons and has also walked off her rock in some ads. White Rock Products Corp. of Whitestone, New York, still sells many White Rock brand beverages.

Sign, Drink White Rock, The Leading Mineral Water, Tin, 4 x 10 In. 149.00
Sign, Psyche Leaning Over Rock, Tin, Round, 11 In. . . . . .990.00 to 1100.00
Tray, Atlantic City, Honest Water Which Ne'er Left, Tin Lithograph, Round, 4 1/2 In. 121.00
Tray, World's Best, Psyche On Rock, Tin Lithograph, Black Rim, 6 5/8 x 4 5/8 In. 110.00
Tray, World's Best, Psyche On Rock, Tin Lithograph, Green Rim, 6 5/8 x 4 5/8 In. 231.00
Tray, World's Best, Psyche On Rock, Tin Lithograph, Red Rim, 6 5/8 x 4 5/8 In. 88.00

WHITMAN Stephen F. Whitman opened a fruit and candy shop in Philadelphia in 1842. He made a variety of candies using rare fruits and nuts. He even kept notes on customers' preferences and would make a box of candy to order. His son, Horace, joined the business in 1869 and Stephen F. Whitman & Son was formed. The company won a bronze medal at the Philadelphia Centennial in 1876. Whitman candy was being distributed and promoted nationally by 1907 and was advertised nationally in a 1909 issue of *Saturday Evening Post*. The Whitman's Sampler was introduced in 1912. The cover design and the candy index inside the cover were ideas of the company president, Walter Sharp. The box design had only minor changes for twenty years, but in 1932 its paper cover was replaced with a linen-textured embossed paper. The Whitman's Messenger boy has been a registered trademark since 1915. From 1924 to 1926, the company used special gift boxes, including Salmagundi, an Art Nouveau metal box picturing a woman and a tile pattern. Other early boxes were Lebrun, which pictured a mother and child; Pleasure Island, with pirate scenes; Cloisonne; and Prestige, a domed-lid box with heraldic designs. Much of Whitman's advertising featured movie stars. In 1939 the company introduced the slogan, "A Woman Never Forgets a Man Who Remembers." Pet Inc. acquired Whitman's in 1963. It later became part of IC Industries Company. Since 1993 it has been part of Russell Stover.

Bank, Snoopy On Doghouse, 6 1/4 In. 12.00
Box, Pleasure Island Chocolates, Cloth Bags, Paper Lithograph, Doily, 1924 . . . . 145.00
Display Case, Sampler Chocolates, Man, Candy Box, Cardboard, Die Cut, 40 x 24 In. . . . 110.00
Sign, Chocolates, Calendar, Yellow, Red, Tin, Paper, 1962, 13 x 19 In. 248.00
Tin, 150th Anniversary, Limited Edition, 1992 . . . . 10.00
Tin, Salmagundi Chocolates, Tin Lithograph, c.1930, 2 x 4 x 7 1/2 In. 15.00
Tin, Whitman Sampler, Hinged Lid, 10 x 8 1/2 x 1 1/2 In. 10.00

WINCHESTER Oliver Winchester, a Baltimore, Maryland, carpenter, invested in a store in the 1840s, then decided to open a shirt factory in New Haven, Connecticut. During the Civil War, he started thinking about manufacturing firearms, and in 1867 he founded the Winchester Repeating Arms Company near his shirt factory. In 1931 Winchester was purchased by Western Cartridge Company, but it continued to operate under its original name and became a division of Western Cartridge Company in 1938. In 1944 it became a division of Olin Industries, which merged with Mathieson Chemical Corp. in 1954. In 1969 Winchester became Winchester Group of Olin Corp., based in East Alton, Illinois. In 1981 U.S. Repeating Arms Company purchased Winchester's rifle and shotgun manufacturing facility and began mak-

ing Winchester brand rifles and shotguns. Today Winchester is the
world's largest ammunition producer.

Bag, Winchester Store, Brown, Red Letters, Paper, 7 x 8 In. 44.00
Banner, 410 Repeating Shotgun, Model 42, Paper, c.1950, 21 3/4 x 5 5/8 In. 1213.00
Bolo Tie, Pewter Logo Medallion, Winchester Salutes Bicentennial, c.1976 .... 19.46
Booklet, How Many Birds Get Through, 5 1/2 x 3 1/4 In., 14 Pages 264.00
Booklet, Shot Guns & Loaded Shells, 12 Fold-Out Pages, 1918, 6 x 4 1/8 In. 94.00
Bottle, Crystal Cleaner, Stopper, Unopened, Box 235.00
Box, .50 Caliber, Primed Shells, 10 Cartridges, 2 Piece, 1910 Patent 289.00
Box, Fowler Plating Co., Brass Shell, Winchester Or Wesson No. 2 Primer, Contents 825.00
Box, Leader 16 Gauge, Loaded Shotshells, Smokeless, Contents 996.00
Box, Leader Smokeless, Staynless, Lacquered, 16 Gauge, 16 Shells, 2 Piece 110.00
Box, Lesmok Rifle Cartridges, 50, .22 Cal., Unopened, 1 1/4 x 2 1/2 In. 160.00
Box, No. 10-1511, Single Cell Batteries, c.1925, 6 3/4 x 2 3/4 x 2 3/4 In. 283.00
Box, Peters 22 Winchester Automatic, Lead Bullet No. 2337, Contents, 1 x 2 3/4 In. 66.00
Box, Repeater Speed Loads, 12 Gauge, 2 Piece, 4 x 4 x 2 1/2 In. 165.00
Box, Repeater, Shot Gun Shells, Cardboard, 25 Shells, 3 3/4 x 3 3/4 x 2 1/2 In. 143.00
Box, Star Paper Shot Shells, 100, Water Proofed, Christmas, c.1889, 2 3/4 x 8 1/4 In. 28175.00
Box, Staynless, 50, .22 Auto., 2 Pieces, 1 1/2 x 2 1/2 In. 99.00
Box, Super Speek Rifled Slugs, 410 Gauge, Contents, 2 1/2-In. Slugs 33.00
Brochure, Close Out Special, Order Blanks, 1932, 8 1/2 x 11 In. 55.00
Brochure, Model 12 Gauge Duck Gun, Folding, 3 1/2 x 6 In., 3 Pages 44.00
Bullet Board, Double W, Oak Frame, c.1897, 58 x 40 1/2 In. 15917.00
Bullet Board, Inverted V, Cartridges, New Frame, 1886, 45 1/4 x 33 1/2 In. 11666.00
Button, Always Shoot Winchester Cartridges, Bull's-Eye, Multicolored, Round, 7/8 In. .. 65.00
Button, Always Shoot Winchester Cartridges, Center W, Pinback, 3/4 In. 22.00
Button, Repeater, Celluloid, Pinback, 7/8 x 5/8 In. 440.00
Button, Shoot Winchester Shotgun Shells & Shotguns, Red W Logo, 1 In. 62.00
Button, Shoot Winchester Shotgun Shells, Red, Black, White, Celluloid, 7/8 In. 31.00
Button, Winchester Leader, Champion Shot Of World, W.R. Crosby, Celluloid, 1 1/4 In. . 164.00
Button, Wonderful Topperweins, Always Shoot Winchester, Celluloid, 1 1/4 In. 173.00
Calendar, 1897, A Chance Shot, An Interrupted Dinner, December Page, A.B. Frost 8624.00
Calendar, 1900, 2 Hunting Scenes, Full Pad, A.B. Frost, 14 3/8 x 27 5/8 In. 9818.00
Calendar, 1901, Fresh Meat, Winter Fun, A.B. Frost, December, 27 7/8 x 14 3/8 In. 3058.00
Calendar, 1912, Hunters, Bear, Rocks, 15 1/4 x 30 1/4 In. 3234.00
Calendar, 1913, Hunter, With Model 12, 29 1/2 x 15 1/4 In. 4125.00
Calendar, 1914, Hunter, Dogs, Corn, 15 1/4 x 30 1/4 In. 1819.00
Calendar, 1921, Man, Boy, Dog, Arthur Fuller, October On, Frame, 14 3/4 x 26 3/4 In. 1516.00
Calendar, 1921, Old Winchester Trader, Full Pad, 13 3/4 x 8 In. ....473.00 to 550.00
Calendar, 1923, Hunter, On Cliff, Goodwin, November, 19 1/2 x 10 In. 976.00
Calendar, 1927, Hunter, Snowshoes, Full Pad, Frank Stick, 10 x 21 In. 1097.00
Calendar, 1929, Clough & Pillsbury, Frame, December, 10 x 20 1/2 In. 825.00
Calendar, 1929, Game Birds, Dog, Frame, 14 3/4 x 26 In. 2079.00
Calendar, 1929, Game Birds, Full Pad, 26 x 15 In. 1650.00
Calendar, 1934, Boy, On Fence, Dog, 27 1/4 x 16 In. 2185.00
Calendar, 1934, I Wish I Had Dad's Winchester, Full Pad, Frame, 15 x 27 3/4 In. 4422.00
Can, Gun Oil, Green, Red, 3 Oz., 3 1/2 x 2 In. 248.00
Can, New Gun Oil, Red Ground, Yellow Target Circles, Red Cap, 3 Oz. ....31.00 to 88.00
Card, Playing, Sleeve, 1929, 52 Cards 275.00
Case Cover, Western Winchester, Come In, Shoot For Fun, Rider Logo, 55 x 50 In. 385.00
Case Insert, Shotgun, Puppies, Cardboard, Frame, 12 x 8 1/2 In. 826.00
Catalog, Black Moroccan Bound, Gold Letters On Spine, 1887, 80 Pages 748.00
Catalog, Guns & Ammunition, J.G. Widmann Hardware, 1920s, 6 x 3 In., 30 Pages 55.00
Catalog, No. 75, 1909, 182 Pages 142.00
Catalog, No. 77, 1911, 202 Pages 157.00
Catalog, No. 78, 1913, January, 8 1/2 x 5 1/2 In., 212 Pages 116.00
Catalog, No. 81, 1918, 212 Pages 79.00
Catalog, Repeating Rifles, Shotgun & Ammunition, No. 64, 1899, 158 Pages .....216.00 to 363.00
Catalog, World Standard Guns & Ammunition, 1930s, 3 1/4 x 6 In., 56 Pages 44.00
Catalog, World Standard Guns & Ammunition, 1932, 128 Pages 55.00
Clock, Wall, Battery Operated, Wood, Pendulum, 1970s, 21 1/2 x 15 1/2 In. 121.00
Clock, Wall, Century Of Leadership, Rider Logo, Electric, Square, 1966, 15 1/2 In. 243.00
Clock, Winchester Store, Wood, Gilbert Clock Co., c.1920, 12 x 18 In. ....*Illus* 3300.00

If your electric clock stops, turn it upside down for a day. The oil inside may flow into the gears and the clock may start working again.

Winchester, Clock, Winchester Store, Wood, Gilbert Clock Co., c.1920, 12 x 18 In.

Container, Split BB Shot, No. 9114, Metal, Celluloid Top, 1901, 1 1/2 x 1/4 In. 132.00
Counter Felt, .22 Cal. Rim Fire Cartridges, Frame, 13 1/8 x 11 In. 480.00
Counter Felt, Cartridges, Shotgun Shells, 13 x 11 In. 647.00
Counter Felt, Celebrated, Repeating Rifles, Green, Yellow, 12 7/8 x 11 In. 435.00
Counter Felt, New Revival, Paper Shot Shells, 3 Colors, 13 x 10 1/4 In. 809.00
Counter Felt, Repeating Rifles, Shotguns, Ammunition, Black, Red, 13 1/4 x 10 1/2 In. . . 289.00
Counter Felt, Repeating Rifles, Shotguns, Ammunition, Green, Yellow, 13 x 11 In. 318.00
Display, 2 Deer Hunters In Canoe, 4 Panel, c.1924, 56 x 38 In. 1100.00
Display, Bore Cleaning Solvent, 6 Bottles, Carton, 6 x 4 1/2 x 3/4 In. 200.00
Display, Emergency Safety Signal Kits, Olin, No. 1764, Shipping Box, 12 Pack 462.00
Display, For Quality, Reliability, Rodent Silhouette, Easel Back, 1952, 5 x 8 In. 117.00
Display, Man, Fringed Coat, Cardboard, Die Cut, 8 Page Booklet, 30 1/2 x 40 In. 660.00
Display, Roller Skate, Die Cut, 3 Colors, Heavy Cardboard, Shipping Carton 579.00
Display, Winchester Tools, 1866-1920, Easel Back, 8 1/2 x 10 1/2 In. 468.00
Display, Wrenches, W146, Wood, Easel Back, 58 1/4 x 18 In. 2211.00
Display Rack, .22 Rifles, Shotguns, 3 Attachments, Cardboard, c.1950, 18 x 12 In. 633.00
Display Rack, Fishing Rod, 28 Rod Holes, Oak, Folding, 18 x 48 In. 2059.00
Door Plate, Recommend & Sell, Brass, Mounted On Stand, 6 7/8 x 3 In. 231.00
Fan, Birch Trees, Order Form, Sample, 7 x 9 In. 468.00
Fan, Lithograph, Clark & Sons, Jamestown, Indiana, 9 x 15 In. 77.00
Gun Case, Oak, Glass, Hinged Door, Removable Top, c.1920s, 17 3/4 x 74 1/2 In. 6670.00
Gun Rack, Pronghorn, Wood, 1975, 24 1/2 x 9 In. 92.00
Knife Sharpener, Winchester Store, Schlichter & Oglestone Dealers, Mich., 12 1/2 In. . . . 267.00
Magazine, Herald Dealer, May 1923, 12 x 9 In., 50 Pages 358.00
Magazine, Winchester Herald, Hockey Players, Jan., 1923, 12 x 9 1/4 In., 50 Pages 133.00
Mirror, Repeating Firearms, Reverse Painted, Wood Frame, 17 1/4 x 24 1/4 In. 35.00
Nail Apron, Winchester Store, S.H. Ralph & Son, New York, 18 x 21 1/2 In. 715.00
Nail Bag, Paper, Buff Color, Red Print, 8 x 7 1/4 In. 115.00
Pencil, Carpenter's, Yellow, Made In U.S.A., 7 In. 43.00
Pencil, John J. Walter Hardware & Kitchen, Unused, 7 3/4 In. 176.00
Postcard, Shoot Them & Avoid Trouble, 1908, 5 1/2 x 3 1/2 In. 413.00
Poster, 2 Cowboys On Bluff, Goodwin, Frame, c.1906, 15 x 29 3/4 In. 2293.00
Poster, 2 Grouse Flying, 1909, 30 1/2 x 15 In. 3850.00
Poster, 20 Gauge Shotguns, 2 Dogs, c.1906, 15 7/8 x 29 1/4 In. 2697.00
Poster, 401 Caliber Self-Loading Rifle, Hunter, Bear, Cabin, 15 x 30 1/2 In. 3685.00
Poster, Bear Dogs, Frame, Signed, H.R. Poore, 1925, 31 1/2 x 41 In. 550.00
Poster, Canada Geese, Winning Combination, 1907 . . . . 7260.00
Poster, Factory Loaded Shells, They Are Hitters, 3 Flying Ducks, c.1905 . . . . 5335.00
Poster, Grizzly Bear Coming Out Of Cabin, 1909, 29 1/2 x 15 1/4 In. 3900.00
Poster, Guns, Ammunition, Die Cut, Hunters, Campsite, c.1920, 40 1/4 x 30 1/8 In. 2292.00
Poster, Herbert Parsons, Thrilling Exhibition Of Fancy Shooting, 10 x 18 In. 63.00
Poster, Meet Every Shooting Requirement, 1912, 30 x 16 1/2 In. 1210.00
Poster, New Rival Shells, Hunter's Choice, Die Cut, 16 3/4 x 10 1/4 In. 1671.00
Poster, Ranger Shot Shells, Dog, Bird In Mouth, 18 x 24 In. 198.00
Poster, Repeating & Single Shot, Hunter, Snowshoes, 1906, 15 3/8 x 29 In. 4274.00
Poster, Repeating Shotguns, Flying Game Bird, Frame, 1909, 15 x 29 1/2 In. 2390.00
Poster, Repeating Shotguns, Satisfactory, Hunting Dogs, 30 1/2 x 16 3/4 In. 1630.00

Poster, Rifles & Cartridges, Deer, Snow, Mountains, Goodwin, c.1912, 17 x 30 In. 1698.00
Poster, Rifles & Cartridges, Winter Hunter, Die Cut, Easel Back, 1906, 28 x 20 In. 1327.00
Poster, Self-Loading Shotguns, Dog Retrieving Duck, Frame, 15 1/2 x 26 1/4 In. 1272.00
Poster, Shells, Game Birds, Cardboard, 1937, 13 x 21 1/2 In. 204.00
Poster, Shoot Them, Avoid Trouble, Boys, Skunk, Dog, Frame, c.1908, 30 x 22 1/2 In. ... 751.00
Poster, The Unexpected, Black Man Burns Out Raccoon, Snake, 1900s, 28 In. 105.00
Poster, Winchester Western, Duck Camp, Hunters, Dogs, Decoys, 20 1/2 x 28 In. 58.00
Poster, World Standard Shot Shells, 2-Sided, Form No. 1448, 21 3/8 x 13 1/4 In. 110.00
Poster, World Standard Small Game & Gallery Rifles, Boy, Dog, Frame, 17 x 35 In. 5313.00
Poster, World Standard Small Game, Man Teaching Boy To Hunt, 36 x 18 In. 2241.00
Print, Poore Dogs, Rifles, Shotguns, Paper, 1907, 32 1/4 x 41 1/2 In. 1650.00
Razor, As Good As The Gun, c.1920, 1 1/2 x 4 x 1/2 In. 126.00
Roller Skates, No. 50, Full Girder, Double Ball Bearing, Box, 11 x 5 x 4 In. 303.00
Rule Book, Junior Rifle Corps, 5 1/2 x 3 1/4 In. 55.00
Ruler, Portola Hardware Store, Wood, c.1920, 12 In. 44.00
Scorecard, Shotguns & Shells, Excel At The Trap, 3 1/4 x 5 1/2 In. 330.00
Sign, 4 Deer Going Up Snowy Mountain, Goodwin, 1912, 16 1/2 x 30 In. 2365.00
Sign, Cutlery, Tools, Kitchen, Workshop, Die Cut, Easel, Frame, Counter, 20 x 15 1/4 In. . 289.00
Sign, En Vente Ici, Armes & Cartouches, Stag Head, W, Die Cut, 12 1/4 x 8 1/8 In. 232.00
Sign, Factory Blue Print, Gun, Bullets, Tin, Flanged, 18 1/4 x 13 3/4 In. 3300.00
Sign, Great Guns & Ammunition, Die Cut, Trifold, Stand-Up, A.D. Fuller, 38 x 31 In. ... 825.00
Sign, Grizzly To The Squirrel, Easel Back, Die Cut, Stand-Up, Counter, 22 x 13 In. 1141.00
Sign, Grouse, Shotgun Shells, Die Cut, 13 3/4 x 9 1/4 In. 2541.00
Sign, Gun Oil, Gun Cleaning Preparations, Stand Up, Die Cut, Easel Back, 10 x 7 In. 347.00
Sign, Guns & Cartridges, Pronghorn, Large W, Die Cut, 12 x 9 1/4 In. 1335.00
Sign, Guns & Ducks On Door, Tin, Alexander Pope, Frame, c.1912, 30 x 36 In. 3830.00
Sign, Guns & Shells, Duck Hunting Scene, Die Cut, Stand-Up, 2 Piece, 31 x 63 In. 3956.00
Sign, Have You Shot Your Nublack Shells, Cardboard, 2-Sided, 16 3/4 x 10 1/4 In. 1995.00
Sign, Hunter's Choice, Factory Loaded, Quails, Die Cut, Frame, 12 x 8 In. 1123.00
Sign, Hunter's Choice, Quails, Die Cut, Frame, 12 1/8 x 8 1/8 In. 1019.00
Sign, Hunter, Farmer, Dog, Shell Boxes, Die Cut, Easel Back, 3-D Type, 37 1/2 x 30 In. .. 1419.00
Sign, Jumping Ram, Revolver & Pistol Cartridges, Die Cut, 10 3/4 x 10 1/8 In. 1877.00
Sign, Junior Rifle Corp, Carving Set, 2-Sided, 5 1/2 x 7 In. 2035.00
Sign, Kind You Need, Factory Loaded, Woodcock, Dog, Die Cut, 12 1/2 x 8 3/8 In. 1283.00
Sign, Lawn Mowers, Cardboard, Easel Back, Envelope, No. W227, 13 x 19 In. 1540.00
Sign, Leader Paper Shot Shells, Grouse, Die Cut, 12 1/4 x 7 3/8 In. 2127.00
Sign, Leader Paper Shot Shells, Shell Box Design, String Hanger, c.1900, 8 3/8 In. 549.00
Sign, Loaded Shells, Shoot Them & Avoid Trouble, 1908, 32 5/8 x 24 5/8 In. 1265.00
Sign, Model 12 Gun, Bamboo Casting Rods, 2-Sided, 7 1/4 x 11 1/4 In. 1444.00
Sign, Model 50 & 12 Shotguns, Mallard, Die Cut, Trifold, Easel, 28 x 24 1/4 In. 450.00
Sign, Model 50 & 12 Shotguns, Pheasant, Die Cut, Trifold, Easel, 28 x 24 1/4 In. 641.00
Sign, Model 70 & 88, Man On Horse, Bear, Die Cut, Trifold, 28 x 24 1/2 In. 346.00
Sign, New Rival, Raised Bobwhite Quail, Easel Back, Hanging, Counter, 10 x 9 7/8 In. ... 1559.00
Sign, Nublack, Flying Grouse, Die Cut, Hanging, Standing, Easel, Counter, 10 x 10 In. ... 1733.00
Sign, Paint, Garden Tools, Cardboard, 2-Sided, 18 1/2 x 39 1/2 In. 579.00
Sign, Perfect Pattern Shells, Man, Boy, Die Cut, Easel, Frame, 1915-1925, 33 x 27 In. ... 6685.00
Sign, Plug Bait, Lure They Can't Seem To Resist, 2-Sided, Oak Frame, 1920s, 12 x 8 In. . 2750.00
Sign, Pointer & Setter, Repeating Shotguns, 16 1/2 x 30 1/2 In. 1430.00
Sign, Red W Brand, House Paint, 12 Brass Hooks, Wood, 18 1/4 x 6 1/2 In. 1502.00
Sign, Repeater Shells, Multiple Action Reels, 2-Sided, 7 1/4 x 11 1/4 In. 1697.00
Sign, Rider Logo, Lined Globe, Distribuidor, Spanish, Self-Framed, 17 3/4 x 21 5/8 In. .. 58.00
Sign, Shot Shells Sold Here, Quail, Die Cut, Counter, c.1920s, 10 3/4 x 12 3/4 In. 1975.00
Sign, This Year Give A Winchester, 22, 21 x 20 In. 357.00
Sign, Tools, Best Workmanship, Cardboard, Easel Back, c.1920, 10 x 4 1/2 In. 275.00
Sign, Western Super-X, Gee I Wish I Had Dad's Winchester, Die Cut, 31 x 42 In. 495.00
Sign, Western, Sporting Arms, Ammunition, Components, Target, Metal, 8 1/2 x 11 In. ... 21.00
Sign, Winchester, Devil's Tail W, 4 Shell Boxes, Die Cut, Frame, 1908, 18 x 4 3/4 In. 550.00
Sign, Winter Fuel, Nail Hammer Special, 2-Sided, 7 x 11 In. 1210.00
Stickpin, Shoot Winchester Repeater, Shotgun Shell, Yellow Enamel 114.00
Thermometer, AA, Clay Target Ammunition Sold Here, 26 1/2 x 7 1/4 In. 303.00
Thermometer, Western, AA, Shell Shape, Metal, 1960s-1970s, 26 1/2 x 7 1/4 In. 74.00
Thermometer, Winchester Repeating Arms, New Haven, Conn., 1920s, 9 1/8 x 2 3/8 In. . 1161.00
Tin, After Shave Talc, 4 1/2 x 3 In. 272.00

Tin, Gun Oil, Green, 3 Oz. 83.00
Tin, Heavy Machine Oil, Paper Label, Lead Spout, Cap, 3 Oz. 182.00
Tube, Split B.B., No. 9134, 1 5/8 In. 252.00
Window Decal, Cowboy Riding Horse, Phillip R. Goodwin, 8 In. Diam. 55.00

WRIGLEY   William Wrigley, Jr., was only eleven when he ran away
from his Philadelphia home. He sold newspapers all summer in New
York City, then returned home and to school. When he was expelled
for throwing a pie at a school sign, his exasperated father put him to
work in the family soap factory. After two years, young Wrigley persuaded his father to let him sell rather than stir the soap. At nineteen,
he headed west to find gold. He ended up in Kansas City, Kansas, after
his hat and ticket blew out of a train window. He earned money as a
waiter and returned home. In 1891 he moved to Chicago to open an
office for his father. He found that his father's 5-cent bar of soap
wasn't profitable for dealers, so he raised the price to 10 cents and gave
away an umbrella with every store box. Before long, he was selling
baking powder by giving a 150-page cookbook free with a 50-cent can.
The baking powder sold so well that he stopped selling soap but continued looking for premiums to give away. He offered silver-plated
perfume bottles, but they tarnished before delivery and he lost money.
Next he tried giving away two packs of chewing gum with every can
of baking powder. This program was so successful that he stopped selling baking powder and started selling gum. With the gum, he gave
away anything storekeepers could use, including desks, showcases,
ladders, and even trucks. He tried selling his nickel gum in New York
City in 1902, and was successful after he spent $200,000 on advertis-
ing. Next, he advertised with posters, streetcar cards, and newspapers
in Buffalo, Rochester, and Syracuse, and again was successful. About
1911 Wrigley's company merged with the company that made its gum,
Zeno Manufacturing. Wm. Wrigley Jr. Company became a public corporation in 1919 and was listed on the New York Stock Exchange in
1923. The Doublemint Twins advertising campaign debuted in 1939.
William Wrigley Jr.'s great-grandson, also named William Wrigley Jr.,
is now the company's CEO and president. Wrigley gum brands have
included Vassar (1892), Lotta (1892), Spearmint (1893), Juicy Fruit
(1893), Doublemint (1914), Blood Orange, Wrigley's Pineapple,
Wrigley's Lemon Cream, Zeno, and Orbit, a wartime brand. Today it
sells Spearmint, Doublemint, Juicy Fruit, Freedent (1975), Big Red
(1976), Extra sugar-free (1984), Winterfresh (1994), Eclipse (1999),
and a new Orbit brand (2001). In 2004 Wrigley purchased Life Savers
and Altoids brands from Kraft Foods. Wrigley offers novelty bubble-
gum products through its Amurol Confections Company.

Booklet, Mother Goose, Wrigley Adapted Nursery Rhymes, 1915, 4 x 6 In., 24 Pages   . . .   12.00
Box, Spearmint Tooth Paste, Red, White, Blue, Contents, 1 1/4 x 4 5/8 In. 1210.00
Calendar, 1911, Mrs. P.J. Murphy Groceries & Provisions, Children, Cat, 9 1/8 x 5 In.   . . .   121.00
Display, Juicy Fruit, Young Girl, Metal, Marquee 353.00
Display, Moon Faced Man, Holds 4 Boxes, Die Cut Metal, c.1920, 14 x 14 In. . . .688.00 to 1430.00
Display, Mother Giving Gum To Daughter, Cardboard, Die Cut, Stand-Up, 36 x 26 In. 1320.00
Display, Woman, Healthful, Refreshing, Delicious, Cardboard, 7 x 13 In. 472.00
Display, Wrigley's Double Mint Gum, Arrow Man, Metal, Celluloid, 14 In. . . . . *Illus*   150.00
Display Box, Corrugated Cardboard, Seven Sticks 10 Cents, 1960s, 8 x 10 x 36 In. . . *Illus*   84.00
Display Case, Wrigley Man, Early 1900s, 13 x 12 In. 825.00
Display Rack, Spearmint, Doublemint, Juicy Fruit, Metal, Glass, 3 Tiers, c.1930s, 9 x 7 In.   121.00
Display Rack, Spins, Mirrored, 1900-1930, 15 In. . . . . .165.00 to 495.00
Gum Pack, Sweet 16, Pineapple, Orange, Pepsin, 3 Piece 220.00
Match Holder, Man Juicy Fruit Made Famous, Tin Lithograph, 4 7/8 x 3 3/8 In. . . . .440.00 to 605.00
Sample Card, Doublemint, Spearmint, Juicy Fruit 28.00
Santa Claus Premium, Straw Filled Body, c.1930, 25 In. 220.00
Scale, Spearmint Gum, Brass, 8 1/2 In. 286.00
Sign, After Every Meal, Wrigley's Spearmint Gum, Frame, Trolley Card, 13 x 23 In. 176.00
Sign, Blonds Like Wrigley's Spearmint, Women, Boy, Cardboard Lithograph, Trolley Card   180.00

Wrigley, Display,
Wrigley's Double
Mint Gum, Arrow
Man, Metal,
Celluloid, 14 In.

Wrigley, Display Box, Corrugated Cardboard,
Seven Sticks 10 Cents, 1960s, 8 x 10 x 36 In.

Sign, Chew Juicy Fruit, Woman In Store, Paper Lithograph, Frame, 16 1/2 x 22 In. 1430.00
Sign, Delicious Lasting Flavors, 4 Gum Packs, Tin On Cardboard, Hanger, 7 x 11 In. 550.00
Sign, Delicious Lasting Flavors, Cardboard, Easel Back, c.1920s, 7 x 11 In. . . . . . .325.00 to 400.00
Sign, Doublemint Gum, Real Peppermint Flavor, Frame, 17 x 27 In. 88.00
Sign, Doublemint Is Spearmint's Popular Brother, Cardboard, Trolley Card, 11 x 21 In. . . .   121.00
Sign, For Flavor Wrigley's Gum, Yellow, Green, Red, Cardboard, 11 x 42 In. 17.00
Sign, Good & Good For You, Paper, Glass Cover, Frame, 21 1/4 x 11 1/2 In. 195.00
Sign, Juicy Fruit Gum, Lady, Red Feathers, Frame, 14 x 19 In.   55.00
Sign, Juicy Fruit, Man Sailing, Woman In Sunglasses, Paper, 28 x 11 In. 22.00
Sign, P.K. New, Handy, 3 Packs, 5 Cents, Cardboard, Frame, c.1928, 12 x 22 In. . .650.00 to 750.00
Sign, Pepsin Chewing Gum, 20 5 Cents Packages, Scale, Black, Ivory, Rectangular 195.00
Sign, Spearmint Gum, Football Stadium, Cardboard, 11 x 42 In. 22.00
Sign, Wrigley Boy, Spearmint Gum, Die Cut, Frame, 27 x 41 In. 523.00
Sign, Wrigley's P.K. Gum, Boy, Checkered Hat, Decal On Glass 330.00
Sign, Wrigley's P.K. Gum, In The Evening By The Moonlight, Paper, Frame, 15 x 25 In. . .   290.00
Stick Of Gum, Orbit, Waxy Paper, Green, Yellow, Orange, c.1940, 3/4 x 3 In. 26.00
Tip Tray, Mineral Scouring Soap, Black Cat, Tin Lithograph, Round, 3 5/8 In. 154.00
Toy, Squeaker, Spearmint Chewing Gum, Vinyl, A.J. Clarolyte, 1950s, 1 1/2 x 2 x 7 In. . .   45.00
Toy, Truck, Spearmint Gum, Green, Buddy L, 15 In. 358.00
Toy, Truck, Wrigley's Spearmint, Railway Express, Steel, No. 435, Buddy L, c.1935, 23 In.   715.00
Toy, Truck, Wrigley's Spearmint, Railway Express, Steel, No. 953, Buddy L, c.1940, 24 In.   1540.00
Tube, Spearmint Tooth Paste, Wrigley Pharmaceutical Co., Box, 5 3/8 x 1 1/4 x 1 1/8 In. .   45.00
Vending Machine, Chewing Gum 5 Cent 116.00

INDEX

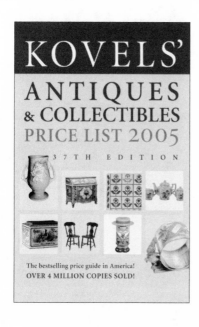

Kovels'
Antiques &
Collectibles
Price List
2005
37th Edition

The bestselling
price guide in
America!

- 50,000 actual retail prices gathered from shops, shows, sales, auctions, and the Internet—no estimated prices—and every price is reviewed for accuracy

- Hundreds of photographs of genuine antiques and vintage collectibles—from Empire furniture to Barbie dolls

- Great tips on restoring and preserving your antiques and collectibles

- Company histories and hundreds of identifying marks and logos of artists and manufacturers

- Special 16-page color section

- Comprehensive index, extensive cross-references

896 pages, paperback, $16.95 • ISBN 0-375-72068-5

KOVELS'
AMERICAN ANTIQUES
1750-1900

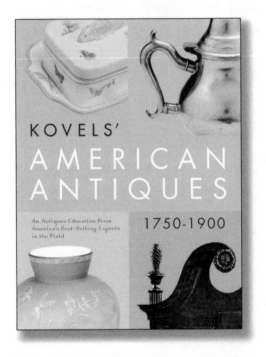

THE ULTIMATE GUIDE TO OUR
AMERICAN TREASURES!

A full-color reference complete with basic facts, fresh information, helpful historical details, and hundreds of photographs, all designed to make you a smarter, more discerning collector

- Furniture, pottery and porcelain, jewelry, silver, glass, and more

- Over 400 color photographs, plus hundreds of identifying marks

- Extensive lists of designers and manufacturers, with locations, dates, and marks

400 PAGES • PAPERBACK • $24.95 • ISBN: 0-609-80892-3

KOVELS' DEPRESSION GLASS & DINNERWARE

PRICE LIST · 8TH EDITION

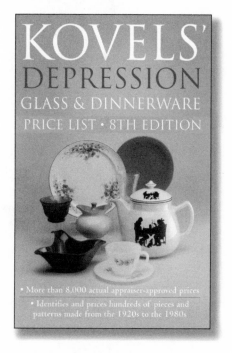

LEARN FROM AMERICA'S ANTIQUES EXPERTS!

- *More than 8,000 actual appraiser-approved prices*

- *More than 250 Depression glass patterns,*
  with photos and line drawings

- *Ceramic dinnerware patterns from the 1920s to the 1980s—*
  the patterns seen most often at shops and flea markets

- *Prices and histories of collectible plastic dinnerware*

- *Sixteen-page full-color report featuring "Decades of Design"*

- *Factory histories, makers, dates, and marks*

272 PAGES • PAPERBACK • $16.00 • ISBN: 1-4000-4663-7

Kovels'
Bottles
Price List
12th Edition

*The indispensable
bottles price list*

- More than 12,000 actual appraiser-approved prices

- Identifies bottles made from the 1700s to the 1990s

- Hundreds of bottles pictured in black-and-white and color

- 16-page full-color report, featuring collectible plain and fancy bottles

- Easy-to-use picture dictionary of bottle shapes, closures, and bottoms

- Clubs, publications, auction galleries, and museums

288 pages, paperback, $16.00 • ISBN 0-609-80623-8

Kovels' New Dictionary of Marks

Pottery and Porcelain 1850 to the Present

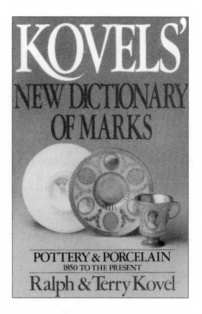

- Provides the quickest, easiest way to identify more than 3,500 American, European, and Oriental marks
- Arranged by symbol and alphabetically according to name
- Each mark is illustrated and accompanied by factory, city, and country of origin, material used, color mark, date mark was used, and name of current company
- Includes the vocabulary of marks, fakes and forgeries, and a cross-referenced index

304 pages, hardcover, $19.00 • ISBN 0-517-55914-5

Kovels' Library

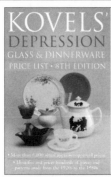

Kovels' Depression Glass,
8th Edition
1-4000-4663-7 • $16.00

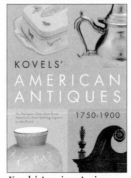

Kovels' American Antiques
1750-1900
0-609-80892-3 • $24.95

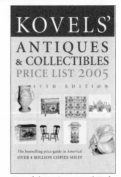

Kovels' Antiques and Collectibles, 37th Edition
0-375-72068-5 • $16.95

Kovels' Bottles Price
List, 12th Edition
0-609-80623-8 • $16.00

Kovels' Know Your Collectibles, Updated
0-517-58840-4 • $16.00

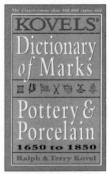

Kovels' Dictionary of
Marks: Pottery & Porcelain

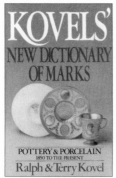

Kovels' New Dictionary
of Marks
0-517-55914-5 • $19.00

Kovels' Yellow Pages,
2nd Edition
0-609-80624-6 • $19.95

AVAILABLE AT
BOOKSELLERS
EVERYWHERE

We Want to Send You a Gift: More Prices from the Kovels

Because you love antiques and collectibles, you will be interested in our award-winning monthly newsletter, *Kovels on Antiques and Collectibles*, a nationally distributed color-illustrated publication now in its 30th year.

- Sales reports, color photos, current prices, and news about what's gaining in popularity
- Warnings about fakes and reproductions
- No advertising. Just news you can use in an easy-to-read, full-color, 12-page format. Published monthly. Free annual index.

For a *free* sample copy of the newsletter, just fill in your name and address on this order form and mail to:

Kovels on Antiques and Collectibles
P.O. Box 420349
Palm Coast, Florida 32142-9655

[ ] **YES!**   Please send me a FREE sample of *Kovels on Antiques and Collectibles.*

05KAB

Name _____

Address _____

E-mail (optional) _____

City _____ State _____ Zip _____

Kovels on Antiques and Collectibles can be previewed at www.kovels.com